How To Deal With And Care For Your Annoying Little Brother

Written by: **Nia Mia Reese**
Illustrations inspired by: **Faith Martin**

Copyright: ©2016 by Nia Mia Reese
All rights reserved.
ISBN: 978-1-942451-62-4

Published by
Yorkshire Publishing
www.yorkshirepublishing.com
Printed in the United States.

ACKNOWLEDGEMENTS

Thank you **Mom** and **Dad** for giving me the idea to write this book and being loving parents.

Thank you **Mrs. Beth Hankins** (Deer Valley Elementary) for teaching me about journal writing – thank you for ALL of your help.

Thank you to **Grandma Annie, Auntie Kisha** and to all of my teachers at The Learning Center at New Life (**Ms. Keyana, Ms. Franki, Mrs. Melinda, and Mrs. Cheryl Wright**), for helping me start reading, writing, and learning.

Thank you **Mrs. Freeman** (Deer Valley Elementary) for the "free writing, free reading, and free drawing" that you taught me.

A special thank you to my little brother, **Ronald** for helping me in taking care of you as a sibling.

And finally, thank you **Faith Chapel**, my church, for teaching me how to deal with my brother and people.

Love,

Nia Mya

INTRODUCTION

Hi, I'm **Nia Mya**.

Do you want to know how to take care of your annoying little brother?

Take it from me; I'm an expert at it...just follow all these steps.

CARING FOR HIM

About caring for him. Say for instance if your brother falls off his bike and a parent or grown-up is not right there to help.

You should get a band-aid or first aid kit and help him.

If you don't have a band-aid, ask your mom and dad or a grown-up that you can trust – not just any grown-up.

Now you have to get him to calm down. I get him to calm down by singing him a song.

HAVING FUN

If you want your brother to not be annoying, then try having fun with him.

It will be fun for you too.

Your brother will think, "Why is she playing with me when I'm annoying?"- Try asking him what does he want to play – he will like that.

SLEEPING-TIME

Your little brother will probably want to sleep in your bed ALL OF THE TIME – well get used to it because I did and you can too.

Just sing him a lullaby so that he is not wild.

You can then go to sleep or take him to his own bed.

TEACHING HIM

If you want to put some "sense" into your little brother, you need to teach him sometimes - it ends up that your brother thinks it is a game or you can make it a game -then it's easy to teach him...my brother likes that.

Here comes another "Why is she playing with me when I'm annoying?" thought from him.

SPENDING TIME

About spending time...even though you have to spend time with your brother, you should still remember that you should spend time with yourself, your friends, and your other family.

So, you just tell your brother "Bye, I'm going off to see the world."

He will ask "Can I go", but you have to say "No" and leave.

SAYING "NO"

Hmmm, saying "No". Well do you want to know how to say "no" and when to say "no"?

Because if you say it at the wrong time, it may make him feel sad.

Well if your brother says "could you play with me," and you are tired, this is a good time to say "no" and do not play – just rest.

Even if he keeps asking, just ignore him, and go tell him "I'm trying to rest, I will play with you when I get up."

HELPING HIM

Helping, helping what a time! Time to help with...
HOMEWORK!!

Your brother will need some help and you should
help him.

What if it was math that he got stuck on?

You discuss it out, and he will have the answer. He
will then learn because of you!

LAUGHING TIME

Laughing time is a funny time.

It's a happy time, and it's a way to make your brother giggle and laugh.

This might be a good time for your brother to stop being annoying because he likes to laugh.

MAKING HIM FEEL BETTER

Ok, making him feel better is my favorite time.

Say for instance, if you and your brother are at a water park and he wants to go to the playground, but he does not tell you and you take him to the pool instead and he starts crying. You should then ask him what is the matter, and if he says "I want to go to the playground"... then just take him.

Sometimes, you may not be able to do what he wants, like getting on a ride because he is too little and he starts crying about it.

You still have to say "no, you are too little, and I don't think you will like it, so let's go somewhere else".

BEING FIRM

Being firm can make your brother cry, but it helps.

So in times like when your brother asks if you can play with him, "Say no" (but in a friendly way).

It won't always be that easy.

If he asks you again, say "no" in a firm way (and in your "I really mean it voice")... like this "N-O – NO"!

SAYING SORRY

Saying "sorry" is just being nice.

So if you hit your brother accidentally, you HAVE to say "sorry" because you might get in trouble because he might cry.

You also have to say "sorry" because you love him.

COMPLIMENTING TIME

Complimenting is when somebody does something good or that you like and you say something like:

"Great Job"!

You have to do this for your brother, even though sometimes it might not look that good, you still should do it to make him feel good.

It's more important to think about other people and how they feel.

TICKLING TIME

It's tickle time – it's tickle time!

Tickle time is like laughing time, but you make him laugh by tickling him.

It's a fun thing to make him laugh.

There are many ways to tickle him, so you have to find those ways yourself.

I hope that I have helped you some in dealing with and caring for your little brother.

The moral of this story is that if you have a brother or sister – called a sibling, help your parents in taking care of them.

The End

CPSIA information can be obtained
at www.ICGtesting.com
Printed in the USA
LVOW02s1407131216

517082LV00005B/362/P

Managing Your Documentation Projects

WILEY TECHNICAL COMMUNICATION LIBRARY

DESIGN   EVALUATION   MANAGEMENT   RESEARCH   WRITING

SERIES ADVISERS:

JoAnn T. Hackos, Comtech Services, Inc., Denver, CO
William Horton, William Horton Consulting, Boulder, CO
Janice Redish, American Institutes for Research, Washington, DC

JoAnn T. Hackos — Managing Your Documentation Projects
Larry S. Bonura — The Art of Indexing
Jeffrey Rubin — Handbook of Usability Testing: How to Plan, Design, and Conduct
   Effective Tests
Karen A. Schriver — Dynamics in Document Design: Creating Texts for Readers

Other Titles of Interest

William Horton — The Icon Book: Visual Symbols for Computer Systems
   and Documentation
Deborah Hix and H. Rex Hartson — Developing User Interfaces: Ensuring Usability
   Through Product & Process
William Horton — Illustrating Computer Documentation: The Art of Presenting
   Information on Paper and Online
William Horton — Designing & Writing Online Documentation, Help Files
   to Hypertext
R. John Brockmann — Writing Better Computer User Documentation, From Paper
   to Hypertext, Second Edition
Tom Badgett and Corey Sandler — Creating Multimedia on Your PC
Robert Virkus — Quark PrePress: A Guide to Desktop Production
   for Graphics Professionals
Helena Rojas-Fernandez and John Jerney — FrameMaker for UNIX Solutions
Jim Mischel — The Developer's Guide to WINHELP.EXE: Harnessing the Windows
   Help Engine

Managing Your Documentation Projects

JoAnn T. Hackos

John Wiley & Sons, Inc.
New York / Chichester / Brisbane / Toronto / Singapore

To my mother,

Mary Josephine Burde,

who taught me always to plan my journeys
carefully and carry many maps.

Publisher: Katherine Schowalter
Editor: Theresa Hudson
Managing Editor: Elizabeth Austin
Composition: Science Typographers, Inc.

This text is printed on acid-free paper.

This publication is designed to provide accurate and authoritative
information in regard to the subject matter covered. It is sold
with the understanding that the publisher is not engaged in
rendering legal, accounting, or other professional services. If
legal advice or other expert assistance is required, the services
of a competent professional person should be sought.

Library of Congress Cataloging-in-Publication Data:
Hackos, JoAnn T.,
      Managing your documentation projects / JoAnn T. Hackos.
         p.   cm.—(Wiley technical communication library)
      Includes index.
      ISBN 0-471-59099-1 (pbk. : alk. paper)
      1. Communication of technical information.   2. Technology—
Documentation.   3. Technical manuals.   I. Title.   II. Series.
T10.5.H33 1994
806'.066'00068—dc20   93-41802
                                                             CIP

Printed in the United States of America

10 9 8

Contents

About the Author

Dr. JoAnn T. Hackos is president of two organizations that represent the two hats she wears in the publications project-management world. First is Comtech Services, Inc., of Denver, Colorado, and San Jose, California. Comtech designs, produces, and helps others to produce technical information in support of projects and processes. The company develops user interfaces, online information, paper documentation, and training systems and conducts usability testing of products and documentation. JoAnn founded the company in 1978 with partners Bill Mattingly and Bill Hackos to provide project-oriented technical communication services to the business community. As president, JoAnn manages Comtech's project managers and has tested the techniques and theory presented in this book.

The second company is JoAnn Hackos & Associates, JoAnn's management consulting and training organization. Through this organization, JoAnn teaches courses in project management and the design of usable products and information. She also conducts research on the information customers need to learn and use products and on the processes used by organizations to produce products and documentation. Using these research studies as a base, she helps organizations develop strategies to design more usable products and improve both the technical information accompanying them and the information used to train employees and communicate company procedures and policies.

JoAnn has published numerous articles on management and technical information that have appeared in technical journals such as *Technical Communication*, *IEEE Transactions on Professional Communications*, the Proceedings of the International Technical Communication Conference, the Proceedings of the STC Annual Conference, and *Franchise Update Magazine*. Her books and monographs include an article on total quality management in *The Franchise Handbook*, published by the American Management

Association; a book on typography entitled *About Type: IBM's Guide for Type Users*; and NBI's *Designing High-Impact Documents (Legend 2.0)*. She has, over the past 15 years, written many technical manuals and designed many training programs for products of all kinds. Her clients include Hewlett-Packard, Federal Express, Dupont, Cadence, Octel Communications, IBM, Storage Technology, Ungermann-Bass, Oracle, Compaq, Northern Telecom, Wells Fargo, the Veterans Administration, and many others.

Preface

I started this book many years ago—as I began looking for ways to keep my company's projects under control and profitable. We have always been dedicated to producing high-quality work. But as the organization grew and new people joined us, it became more difficult to ensure that everyone understood our original dedication to quality. We quickly discovered that without guidance and direction, individual contributors would naturally go off in very individual directions, sometimes producing excellent work and sometimes not.

We obviously needed a better way—a way to produce high-quality products consistently. Not only did we need a way to take advantage of the talents of our most creative people, but we also needed a way to help the moderately talented produce outstanding work. For our customers, we needed to ensure that they could count on us to meet their needs and requirements that did not depend solely on the individual skills of those assigned to their projects. Out of these very genuine concerns, as well as our desire to sustain a successful business, came the concepts and methodology of publications project management outlined in this book.

More than ten years ago, I gave my original presentation at a meeting of the Society of Technical Communication (STC) about achieving quality in technical publications. In that presentation, I announced my conviction that quality lies in a well-managed process. Standards and good people, although useful, are simply not enough to sustain quality through many years and many different people and projects. Only with a sound process in place and people trained in managing the process can quality be consistently produced.

This presentation took place before I had heard of Deming or Crosby—before the Total Quality Management (TQM) movement had gained momentum. No one I knew in technical publications was talking about process and project management very much or very loudly. But many of us in the STC recognized how badly our organizations needed better project management. Perhaps it was because technical communication always seemed in those days to be at the end of the life cycle. Publications were often forgotten until the last minute. Even when technical publications were better integrated into the product-development process, that process was so poorly managed that the publications had to be changed constantly to accommodate the frequent and late changes to the product design. Many of us were convinced that there had to be a better way—that it was indeed possible to put some common sense into the process by managing the development life cycle and planning for publications from the outset.

In the late seventies, many of us interested in the software-development life cycle were influenced by the work of Edward Yourdon. Much of my thinking about a managed process started with Yourdon's work on managing the software-development process and using structured techniques to build reproducible quality into software design. I became convinced that these techniques could be transferred into publications management. I learned even more about the management and control of software projects from Tom DeMarco's work, which demonstrated that you could indeed quantify the development process and develop reliable estimates of the work to be done. Many of the techniques for estimating and tracking projects owe much to DeMarco.

You will also find substantial influences from the field of instructional design in the emphasis I place on front-end analysis and project planning. My study of instructional-design techniques was influenced first by my former colleague at the University of Colorado at Denver, Martin Tessmer, whose work on front-end analysis finds a substantial place in my thinking. Marty also introduced me to his mentor, Robert Gagne, as well as contributors like Ronald Zemke. We found that many instructional-design techniques were directly transferable to technical communication.

In the end, it is difficult to account for all of the influences on one's ideas. I've often had the experience of rereading a significant article or book that I had first read many years earlier and discovering that I had made the ideas my own and fully incorporated them into my conceptualization of the subject. The Acknowledgments testify to how many people I know have influenced my thinking. There are many more. I hope you will learn from the ideas and participate in the dialogue. In fact, I hope to hear from people who have read the book and tried some of the techniques and concepts in their own organizations. Let me know what goes well and what goes badly. Your feedback will help to further our understanding of how to become better managers.

How should you read this book?

This book is divided into six parts. Part One is an introduction to publications project management. Parts Two through Six follow the five phases of the publications-development life cycle.

In Part One, you are introduced to aspects of project management, beginning with the issue of quality. In reading Chapter 1, I hope you will think seriously about the relationship of projects and project management to producing technical publications that provide value to your customers. In *Liberation Management* (1992), Tom Peters claims that projects and their management are crucial to success in the "nanosecond nineties." Chapter 1 is designed to inspire you and to encourage you to question your assumptions about how quality is achieved.

Chapter 2 encapsulates Parts Two through Six. In Chapter 2, I introduce the entire publications-development life cycle, identifying the basic components of each phase in terms of three types of activities: the development of the information content and form, the management of the development project, and the inclusion of usability testing as a new form of quality assurance. Note the large table in Chapter 2 that summarizes all the activities and deliverables of each of the five phases of the life cycle.

If Chapter 2 is the key to the rest of the book, Chapter 3 is the key to the future. If you are dedicated to improving the way publications are produced in your organization, then concentrate on Chapter 3. In this chapter, I introduce you to a new model of process maturity for publications organizations. Process-maturity models are a new element in the study of software development today; I extend these models to the publications arena. Use the belief statements in Chapter 3 to identify your organization's maturity level. Then, study the next level to establish process-improvement goals and a process for reaching them.

Tom Peters claims that project managers will be the star players of tomorrow. "Everyone will routinely fill project management/network management roles, directly or indirectly. Attention to these skills, and training in these skills, will be vital. Promotion will go to those who are particularly adept at exercising such skills" (Peters, 1992). Chapter 4 in Part One provides you with a "job description" for the future publications project manager. In this chapter, I outline the skills and the temperament that you need to succeed in the fast-moving development styles that are already emerging in our organizations.

As you can see, each chapter in Part One plays a distinct role in building a portrait of the future project manager. If you want to give careful thought to your career direction and how you intend to face the rapid pace of change in your organization, you need to consider these four chapters as a set.

Parts Two through Six parallel the five phases of the publications-development life cycle introduced in Chapter 2. The focus of each chapter is not, however, on the information-development process, although aspects of it are discussed, because we cannot really separate information development from the process of managing the development. The focus of Parts Two through Six is on the management of the publications-development process.

The five parts are organized chronologically, beginning with the earliest phases of information planning (Phase 1) through the development of the information products (Phases 2 and 3) and their final production and distribution (Phase 4). Phase 5 addresses the process of evaluating the project's success, as well as the success of all the team members, including the project manager.

If you are managing a project yourself, read each of the parts in preparation for the next phase of the project. If you are about to start a new project from scratch, start with Part Two and learn how to guide your team in investigating and writing a persuasive Information Plan.

If you are at the stage of outlining the content of a book, a training course, online documentation, or any other type of deliverable, start with Part Three and learn how your team can better specify the details of their design and communicate those details to others in your organization.

If you are tasked with estimating and tracking a project, start with Part Two to learn how to produce early estimates based on too little information. Then, move on to the details of project estimating in Part Three.

If you and your team members are getting ready to commit words to paper, start with Part Four and learn how to introduce a tracking process so that you can handle changes without falling apart. Learn in Part Four how to manage the change process so that you control it rather than it controlling you.

If you are entering the production phase, especially if you find yourself having to implement translation and localization, start with Part Five. In Part Five, you will learn how to manage the production cycle.

If you have just finished a project and would like to evaluate its success, consider starting at Part Six. Learn in Part Six how to evaluate the success of a project by measuring its impact on your customers.

No matter where you begin in the book or in the process of publications-project management, make a pact with yourself to read the previous parts that you may have skipped in your haste to get on with the task. It is by putting the entire process into place that you can best control the costs of a project. Remember that costs include more than budget and schedule: Costs include the wear on people that comes with poor management, as well as the cost of failing to listen to customers and understand their information needs.

Finally, once you have completed Parts Two through Six, go back to the beginning and read once again about process maturity in Chapter 3. Chapter 3 will help you evaluate your successes and your failures in terms of the culture of the larger organization in which you function. Then, reread Chapter 4 on becoming a more effective project manager. Tom Peters (1992) quotes Takahiro Fujimoto's research on project management, which revealed that "the 'heavyweight PM' is important, perhaps more so [than product quality], in coping with today's consuming time-to-market issue."

The chapters also contain many case studies in the form of dialogues to help you relate the conceptual and procedural information to your own experiences. I hope that you recognize yourself in some of the dialogues—some of you may actually have been models for the characters, although the resemblances will be quite distant, I hope. No real people are quoted in the dialogues—the characters are composites of many individuals I have worked with over the years.

You will also find summarizing guidelines at the end of most sections. Use the "Guidelines" as quick references.

Note also that the book contains five appendixes. Appendixes A, B, and E contain detailed, annotated templates of Information Plans, Content Specifications, and Wrap-Up Reports. Please feel free to use these templates in your own organization, either verbatim or modified to meet your own special requirements. Appendixes C and D provide samples of checklists you might use to conduct user studies so that you can better target your publications to meet your users' needs.

Who should read this book?

Few books or training programs exist that deal with the specific requirements of publications-project management. Few organizations provide more than the most generic training in project management and often do not include publications people in that training. Project management skills in the publications organization seem to be taken for granted.

If you are a publications-project manager, you will find much food for thought, as well as specific procedures, in this book. If you are responsible for managing your own projects as an independent contributor, you will find a great deal to get you started toward improving the quality of your management activities. If you are a publications manager who is either responsible for managing projects directly or for training and supervising those who manage projects, you will find new ideas about the "people" part of the publications project.

If you are a publications manager or a project manager, you may want individual writers, editors, graphic designers, and production specialists to read the detailed accounts of how the planning, implementation, and evaluation activities all add up to higher-quality work.

If you are a product manager, a marketing director, a development manager, or anyone else in the organization who is responsible for getting information into the hands of customers and other users, then this book is also for you. I find that many people responsible for the production of technical publications do not have much information about how they should be developed. If you would like to know more about managing the publications-development process, especially about estimating the costs of projects and designing schedules, begin with Chapter 2 for an overview and read Parts Two through Six for the details.

If you are an instructor of future technical communicators and publications project managers, I recommend using this book to teach the life-cycle phases and address the management issues in the publications process. In combination with a book that directly addresses the "what" of information development, this book will introduce students to the "how to." I recommend using the dialogues as mini-case studies that will encourage students to address the day-to-day problems that project managers face.

Acknowledgments

I have many people to thank for their help in developing not only this book but the practice and theory of project management that underlies it. My ideas about project management have been developing for more than 20 years, helped by the example, writing, and conversation of many people, many whose names I regretfully do not remember. The best I can do is to thank those I do remember and to whom I owe a great debt. All of you who also contributed silently, please accept my gratitude and excuse my faulty memory.

First of all, I would like to thank the small, hardworking, dedicated group who helped me prepare this manuscript. Dennise Brown, of Oracle, read every word, sometimes more than once, and provided me with hours of patient listening and feedback. Dennise has been a most valuable sounding board for all of my new ideas. I could not have found an equal to her for enthusiasm, criticism, and helpful nudges in the right direction. Donna Sakson, of Sakson and Taylor, reviewed the entire manuscript and pointed out places where I was unclear, incomplete, or just too hard on the readers. In sharing our experiences in managing complex projects with hard-headed clients, I also thank Donna for years of commiseration. Ray David did a wonderful job on the artwork for the book, turning my amateurish sketches into an interesting and professional art package. I appreciated his willingness to take my vague notions of what a drawing might contain and turn them into reality. Rodney Sauer took the sketches and turned them into camera-ready art.

Equally important have been the folks at Comtech. They have helped in many ways, recently by preparing the manuscript and over the long term in trying out my latest ideas for managing projects. Lori Maberry helped put the final manuscript together, pointing out inconsistencies and fixing typographical errors. Donna Shephard helped in standardizing the bibliography, keeping track of the files, sending out emergency shipments to the publisher and the reviewers, and generally keeping everyone else out of my hair while I was trying to write. I also want to thank the Comtech project managers, especially Tiffany Corgan and Dawn Stevens, for the feedback they provided about the effectiveness of all the new ideas in the crucible of day-to-day project management. It was invaluable to the development of the concepts in the book that they were tested at Comtech first and changed when they did not work as well as we had hoped. Finally, I must mention Bill Mattingly, Comtech vice president, who team taught the management courses with me for several years and now handles a significant number of the courses himself. He has provided feedback from the course participants on how newcomers respond to the publications-development life cycle and the management techniques we teach.

Many people over the years in many different companies have influenced my thinking about project management. I can mention only some of the most influential.

On top of my list is Ralph Jones of IBM, who taught me about tracking time and weighing the contributions of new and maintenance projects. Ralph's article on project data analysis that is listed in the bibliography has greatly influenced the sections on project estimating throughout the book. Others at IBM, like Robert Ward, Lori Fisher, and Joan Knapp, have also influenced how I think about task analysis, quality, and the role of the technical communicator in managing the process.

At the same level of importance have been all my friends in the Society for Technical Communication who have accounted for many wonderful conference presentations and long hours of discussion about managing projects. These have included Cheryl Herfurth of Novell, Wayne Wieseler of Ross Systems, Jay Winstead of Federal Express, Liz Babcock of the Naval Weapons Center, Jody Heiken of Los Alamos National Laboratories, Judy Glick-Smith of Integrated Documentation, Kay Goodier of Northern Telecom, Don Barnett of Hewlett-Packard, Kathy Sharpe, Celia Clark of Celia Clark Consulting, Diane Davis of Octel Communications, Van Diehl, Nancy Deakin of Hewlett-Packard, Judy Gordon of Software Publishing, Charlie Breuninger of Dupont, Bill Horton of William Horton Consulting, Don Singer of Cadence, Mary Kay Porter of Perkin-Elmer, Kathy Kitcho of ESL, Jonathan Price of the Communication Circle, Ruth Steinberg of Bellcore, Peter Daniels of Honeywell, Cassandra Rodgers of Norwest Information Systems, Donne Ruiz of Rocky Mountain Translators, Henry Kormann of Wordplay, Shirley Krestas of SK Writers, the members of the Bay Area Publications Managers' Forum, Linda Momsen of Ungermann-Bass, Steve Murphy of DEC, Janice Redish of American Institutes for Research, Susan Riedel of Wells Fargo, Kate Whittley of Synoptics, and Jill Nicholson of the University of Technology, Sydney, Australia. These are only a few of the people from STC that have had a significant influence on my work. I also owe a continuing debt of gratitude for their support and encouragement to David Armbruster, former STC president, and William Stolgitis, STC executive director.

At John Wiley and Sons, I could not have asked for a more enthusiastic and hardworking editor than Terri Hudson. She kept me watching the deadlines when I was getting bogged down in too many changes. Thanks also to Elizabeth Austin, who handled all the production details.

Finally, I would like to thank my family, who provided me with encouragement throughout the long hours of writing and rewriting. First among all is my husband, Bill Hackos, who listened to my discussions and provided examples (a few of which are disguised in the book) from his own extensive experience managing software development projects. As Comtech's chief financial officer, he also took over some of my responsibilities at the office so that I could gain time to write. He had to take on more of the responsibility of building our new house this past year, because of the time I needed (weekends and nights) to work. My sons, who are now off on their own careers, have for years provided me with the challenge of managing the family project. They will be delighted when this book is finally done. Finally, I would like to thank my sister, Marilyn Whitesell, for her many years of support and contribution to building a project-management theory. As a graphic designer, she manages an entirely different cast of characters in her work on multimedia, interactive computer systems, but has shown me that the problems are all the same.

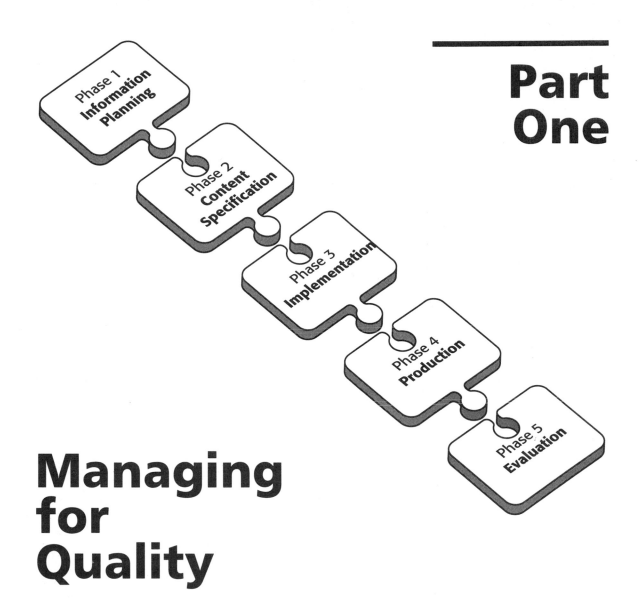

Phase 1
Information Planning

Phase 2
Content Specification

Phase 3
Implementation

Phase 4
Production

Phase 5
Evaluation

Part One

Managing for Quality

An Introduction to Publications Project Management

Quality is not someone else's responsibility. Quality is the responsibility of everyone in an organization. It cannot be legislated by standards. Standards are only as good as the care taken by the people responsible for following them. Quality is linked to having good people but is not dependent upon stars. Quality is not a matter of technologically sophisticated tools. Good tools help us get the job done efficiently, but quality can be produced anywhere, even with the worst tools. Quality cannot simply be measured at the end of the project. The end of the project is too late. Quality happens as the result of a well-managed, well-organized process.

Part One of this book explains the concept of project management and the relationship between good management and producing a high-quality publications product (or any other product, for that matter). Putting a sound project-management process in place takes work, commitment, and the ability to convince others of the importance of the process and their roles in the process. In Part One, I hope to convince you that instituting good project management is worth the effort. To do so, you need to understand the connections among management, quality, cost efficiency, team effort, and all the other aspects of the work of managing.

To become effective project managers, you need to

- Get closer to the customer and establish the connection between satisfying customer needs and providing them with the technical information they need to reach their goals.
- Collaborate with the customer in the development of publications.
- Communicate effectively with developers, technical experts, and others in the organization about the publications-development process.
- Reduce redundancy and inefficiency in publications projects.
- Improve the quality and usefulness of the information produced.
- Provide opportunities for innovation where they count.
- Reduce unnecessary costs associated with the development of publications.
- Respond effectively to changing project requirements and organizational needs.

In addition to the model of quality as management, Part One describes two significant models for publications managers and project managers to understand and implement.

The first model is a five-phase publications-development life cycle, introduced in Chapter 2 and expanded through the rest of the book. This life cycle is consistent with a number of models of the publications process that have been in use by large publications organizations for several years. However, the description of the life-cycle phases emphasizes the role of the project manager in guiding the process and ensuring its success in producing quality publications on schedule and within budget.

The second model defines the publications organization as a whole. In the last few years, software-development consultants have presented models of the software-development process. These models suggest that the process can be improved in significant ways. In the model I have developed for this book, I have looked at a wide variety of publications organizations. From this study, I suggest that publications organizations also fall within a reasonably predictable structure, as presented in Chapter 3. This structure contains five levels of process maturity. Process maturity refers to the type of development process used, its management, and its continual improvement. In studying the maturity levels, I recommend that you try a self-assessment of your organization. By determining where you are today in the sophistication of your process, you can decide how you want to improve in the future. The five-level process-maturity model suggests that you can improve your development process by setting your sights on the next level of process maturity and using it as a goal, along with the development life cycle, to form an improvement plan.

Finally, in Chapter 4, I discuss the attributes of a successful project manager. This discussion provides a job description and a way to assess your own progress.

Contents

Chapter 1: Managing for Quality — A Process Model

- Quality in technical publications—What value does it add?
- Quality in technical publications is relative
- All we need are standards
- All we need are better people
- All we need are better tools
- Process as quality
- Management as quality

Chapter 2: A Model of the Publications-Development Life Cycle

- Why have a life-cycle model?
- How is a model different from a prescription?
- A five-phase model
- Parallels to the product-development life cycle
- An implementation plan for a development life cycle

Chapter 3: A Process-Maturity Model for Publications Organizations

- Five-level publications-maturity model
- Analyzing your organization
- Level 0: Oblivious
- Level 1: Ad hoc
- Level 2: Rudimentary
- Level 3: Organized and repeatable
- Level 4: Managed and sustainable
- Level 5: Optimizing
- Managing in chaotic environments

Chapter 4: The Roles of the Project Manager

- The characteristics of a good project manager

Results

By reading Part One, you will understand the focus of the book and its primary concentration on the management of documentation projects. You will learn the major phases in the publications-development life cycle. You will also be able to assess the level of your publications organization using a five-level model of process maturity. Finally, you will understand the characteristics that you will need to become a successful project manager.

Managing for Quality — A Process Model

"Have you seen *RC Magazine*? We're in it—we're the best. Look at the review." Tom was so excited when he saw Eleanor that he could hardly speak. *RC Magazine* had finally published its review article on modem switches. The entire company had been anxious about the review of their MR10.

RC Magazine had rated their product the best modem switch on the market. They had explained what a great product it was.

"Look at this," said Eleanor, who was the project manager. "There's a major heading that says 'Great Documentation.' And an entire paragraph about how easy the installation instructions are to follow."

"I know," said Tom. "You guys did a great job. If it weren't for the new manual, we wouldn't be in business. This article is going to increase our sales unbelievably. John is even considering moving us to a bigger building when the new products come out in the fall. He thinks we'll need to double the staff."

"That's wonderful," said Eleanor. "I came over to tell you that we've just won an award from the Society for Technical Communication for the MR10 manual. The judges thought it was great."

"Fantastic," said Tom. "I can't thank you enough. I never thought the manuals were so important."

During the past year and a half, Danube Electronics (a fictional company) had had a rough time with the MR10. It was the company's first product. They had only a small staff—six people—when it was released. The marketing department, which consisted of Tom alone at the time, had worked very hard to set up distribution channels. He had gotten the MR10 into the biggest computer and business stores, and prospects were encouraging.

The product looked good and worked great. All the preliminary tests in the field were positive. Early beta customers were very happy with the product.

But as soon as retail sales started to climb, the problems started. It seemed to Tom that everyone who bought the MR10 was having problems getting it installed. He couldn't figure it out—installation was a breeze. He and Joe, the engineer, had worked on the manual. They had explained the whole process in great detail. Joe was a telephony expert. He knew exactly how a customer's phone system had to be set up to work with the switch. It was all in the manual. Right from the start, Tom was worried about the phone calls. He was answering them and enduring 10 minutes of angry screaming from the customers. They were really upset because they couldn't get the MR10 installed. Most of them had spent several hours working through the manual before they called. After he calmed them down, he could usually talk them through the installation. They even acknowledged that it was easy—they just couldn't understand the manual.

Tom really didn't mind helping the customers, but the calls were taking up all his time. He had even hired Iris full-time just to handle calls. He was thinking about installing a third 800 number. The calls were lasting between 12 and 15 minutes and getting really expensive.

Then Tom received a call from the purchasing agent at their biggest distributor, Business Marketplace. Customers were returning the MR10, complaining that they couldn't get it to work. Returns at Business Marketplace were running at 75 percent, and they threatened to remove the product from their shelves. Tom was desperate.

That's when he heard about CTS. They write technical manuals for all sorts of products. He called to explain the problem and ask for an estimate. Tom was impressed by Eleanor. She reviewed their manual and asked him a lot of detailed questions about their customers that he had never thought about before. She pointed out several problems with the manual that he had never noticed. She was sure CTS could help.

When Tom got Eleanor's estimate, however, he was shocked. It was three times more than he had thought it would cost. "The manual only has 24 pages," he said to Eleanor. "How long could it take to write 24 pages?"

Eleanor carefully explained the process CTS uses and how they estimated the project. Tom really wasn't sure they needed all that planning, editing, and testing, but she seemed to know what she was talking about. And he knew they needed help. Even though he and Iris answered the phone full time, they couldn't handle all the calls. The angry customers were wearing Tom down. Business Marketplace was threatening Danube with a lawsuit over the returns.

When the CTS team started the new manual, they interviewed Tom's people. They had Joe install the switch while they watched. Then they had him watch while they installed it. They asked about all the possible configurations that the customers might have. They even helped Tom with the customer calls. But what most impressed Tom was their scheduling. They kept to their schedule and gave him regular progress reports. The final cost, even though it still seemed like a lot of money to Tom, was exactly what they said it would be. There were no surprises. They were even able to include some of the new features in the manual before it was finished.

Two months later, as soon as the new manual hit the market, Tom immediately noticed the difference. The call volume went down precipitously, about a two-thirds drop. And the calls were easier on the staff. Instead of 12 to 15 minutes, they usually lasted only 3 or 4 minutes—the customers had stopped screaming. They even mentioned that the instructions were really easy to follow. Everyone in customer service was more relaxed. The purchasing agent called from Business Marketplace, telling Tom that returns were down to 30 percent and dropping. They were anxious to stock Tom's new products. The company added three new products to their line with CTS-prepared manuals, but Tom didn't have to add more people to customer service.

Tom calculated that he had recovered the cost of the new manual for the MR10 in less than three months. Sales were increasing steadily, even before the magazine review. They were adding staff, and profits were on target.

Quality in technical publications — What value does it add?

The story of Tom and the MR10 is a true one, although the names are changed. I believe that the restructuring of the installation and operation manual contributed substantially to the success of Tom's company. A disaster became a great success. The real rewards were the cost savings to Tom's company, the increased sales and decreased returns, and the continuing good relationship with their customers.

As a publications project manager or even as an individual contributor to a publications project, why should you be concerned about achieving quality in the publications you produce? Sometimes it seems as if customers, from external users of the information to internal subject-matter experts, do not care if the technical publications are effective and produced according to high standards. Product developers, software engineers, and technical professionals of all types argue that "nobody reads the manuals, anyway."

Any discussion of the quality of technical publications is closely associated with a discussion of the value added by technical publications to a product, a process, or an idea. When publications are carefully planned and well executed by trained professional communicators, they add value. They help customers understand and use a product or perform a process more effectively; they communicate ideas and help to transfer knowledge from those who originate it to those who need to use it.

This is a book about quality and the processes needed to produce quality in a reliable and repeatable way. Quality in technical publications is important to writers and their managers because producing quality work provides them with a sense of personal and professional satisfaction.

This is also a book about managing projects. You have probably already discovered the connection between your ability to do your job well and the quality of the work you produce. You know, for example, that if you have an opportunity to learn about your users and their goals, you will be better able to produce information that meets their needs. You know that if you have an opportunity to participate in the development of a new product, you may be able to influence its usability and make the job of writing effective instructional text easier. You know that if you are able to assemble a team of writers, editors, illustrators, graphic designers, and production specialists, you will be able to produce a more effective set of technical publications in less time than if you have to do everything yourself. You know that if you manage your team well and foster communication, the team will produce work they can be proud of.

Because you are aware of the connection between your ability to produce effective technical publications and how well you do your job, you have also learned that you cannot do your job well if you do not have the time or the resources you need. But to earn the resources you need, you must be able to manage the publications-development process. When you manage your projects effectively—accurately estimating the time and budget you need to produce the level of quality required by your users and your organization—you are more likely to gain the resources to do your job.

Quality in technical publications is relative

Quality in technical publications has never been simple to define because quality in technical publications is relative. What may be a high-quality publication to you may not be a high-quality publication to your customers, and vice versa. They may find an instruction difficult to follow because they are unfamiliar with the terminology used or they don't have enough experience with similar products. You may find the same publication very useful and easy to use because you know the terminology and have used similar products before. I may conclude that a technical publication is useless at the same time you decide that it is excellent. Quality in technical publications depends, at least in part, upon the perceptions of the users.

Because of this relative nature of quality, technical communicators have been reluctant to define narrowly what constitutes quality in technical publications. When forced into a quality corner by upper management, many communicators fall into the trap of focusing on aspects of quality in technical publications that are most easily measured. We might refer to these simple measurements as "manufacturing quality."

Manufacturing quality results from optimizing the details of the production part of publications development. It involves performing a series of quality-assurance steps at the end of the development process, such as checking the final text for spelling, grammar, and formatting errors. These "manufacturing problems" are often relatively simple to fix. Add a few quality inspectors (also known as copy editors and proofreaders) at the end of the development line, and you can come close to eliminating manufacturing problems and enhancing manufacturing quality.

On the other hand, after you have spent much of your publications-development resources and schedule on additional rounds of copyediting, you may discover that the content and style you have labored so hard to present perfectly are unusable by substantial portions of your customers. You have done an excellent job of ensuring manufacturing quality, but you have inadvertently been performing a less important task from the customer's point of view. You have focused your efforts on what is measured, rather than on what is important although difficult to measure.

Although manufacturing quality is important to the appearance and credibility of your publications and the professional reputation of your publications groups, it fails to account for most of the activities that take up your time in the process of developing technical publications. Manufacturing quality does not add enough value to the producer or benefit to the customers to warrant emphasizing it beyond all other measures of quality. Only a small portion of the publications-development process is concerned with manufacturing. Most of the process is devoted to the design and development of unique information.

The process of designing and developing technical publications is custom work. The most significant parts of the development effort focus on accommodating human learning processes. Whenever you deal with human behavior, as you always do in technical publications, you are treading on slippery quality ground as far as defining quality goes.

You are writing for people, and people are both varied and unpredictable. Sometimes they have habits of mind we find difficult to anticipate. Clusters of them have completely different ideas about what information they need. Some need less detail, while others need more. Some find information more easily using one design, while others are more productive with an entirely different one. Some work best with more graphics; others work better with more text. In this confusing world of relative quality, it is extremely difficult for the technical communicator to find the right path.

Even if you look to the experts on quality, you may find little assistance in resolving the quality dilemma. Philip Crosby, in *Quality Is Free* (Crosby, 1979), defines quality as

Conformance to requirements

How should you respond to this definition? Whose requirements do you follow in designing and developing technical publications? If you do even the briefest study of your customers, you will find that different customers have different requirements for technical information. Whose requirements should you use to define quality?

The quality dilemma

In some organizations, people in senior management positions decide that *their* requirements are the most important to the task of defining publication quality. And their requirements are simple: publications that ship with the product and don't cost too much. By this definition,

- Rapid development is quality.
- Low cost is quality.

Marketing managers argue that customers will not pay higher prices for better publications. And if the publications don't ship with the product or do not appear in a timely manner, customers will be justifiably unhappy.

Others in your organization, such as engineers and developers, define quality according to their own needs as internal customers:

- A complete technical description of the product is quality.
- An absence of technical errors is quality.

Completeness and the absence of errors represent quality even if it means that the writers spend 80 percent of their time writing about features and functions that 10 percent of the customers will use.

Still others, especially those in marketing and sales, equate attractiveness with quality. If the technical publications look good, it doesn't matter what's in them.

- An attractive publication is quality.

The publications manager may decide that quality is the absence of copyediting errors in the final publications.

- Zero copyediting errors (i.e., no typos) is quality.

Finally, some people in your organization may believe that quality in technical publications is measured in usability, that is, meeting the usability requirements of the most numerous, most inexperienced, most sophisticated, most frequent, most infrequent, or most valued customers.

As you can see, you have returned full circle to the original dilemma. Quality is meeting the needs of the customer. That makes quality a *political* issue in most organizations because the requirements of diverse customer communities must be balanced against one another. Unfortunately, the politics of quality may mean that the group in your company that has the most power gets to define quality for you.

The issue of quality is also *economic*. If you choose the wrong customer requirements to define quality in technical publications, you may experience an unprofitable increase in calls for assistance and general dissatisfaction among your customers. If you spend too much money on technical publications, you may price your product out of the market. If you spend too little, you may reduce the effectiveness of your product.

And the issue of quality is *emotional*. As a professional technical communicator, you may be frustrated and embarrassed at producing publications that you feel are inadequate to meet customer needs, are badly written for lack of time, are inadequately verified for accuracy and completeness, and contain many copyediting errors.

Technical publications add value

You may find a way out of the dilemma of conflicting and relative measures of quality by focusing once again on the primary customers for your publications, balancing their needs against the legitimate needs of your internal customers for timeliness and cost-effectiveness.

Here is a definition of quality in technical publications that includes the needs of your diverse customers:

- Technical publications that add value have quality.

If you argue that your publications should add value to a product by making it more useful and easier to maintain, to an idea by making it more accessible to its public, to technical information by making that information as clear and as useful as possible to its intended audience, you have a way of investigating the customers for your information and defining its quality.

Anything that you do that adds value to the product, however broadly defined, will help you achieve quality in your technical publications.

If you conduct studies of the customers of your publications, you will have an opportunity to discover what they value most and what would be nice to have but is less important, particularly if it is more expensive and takes longer to get.

Your customers may decide that

- High-quality publications make information more accessible.

Customers want to spend as little time as possible finding the information they need. This applies to technical reports, proposals, and policies and procedures, as well as technical manuals.

- High-quality publications make customers productive more quickly.

  If customers can quickly learn to use a product or perform a process with the help of technical information, they are more likely to experience the increase in productivity often promised during the sale.

- High-quality publications reduce training costs.

  Customers who have publications that answer their questions are less likely to require lengthy and repetitive training sessions and continued on-the-job training. Excellent technical publications make learning less expensive.

- High-quality publications lower the barriers for discretionary and infrequent users.

  Many customers for high-tech products can choose to use a product or not. If you work as a bank teller, you have to learn to use the bank's data-processing software or risk losing your job. But if you are the bank president, you can choose whatever spreadsheet software you prefer. If you work as a technical writer, you may have to use the word-processing software that your company has selected. If you write at home, the software choice is up to you. One of the criteria for these discretionary choices is ease of use. High-quality technical publications promote ease of use.

  Many customers, discretionary or not, find themselves to be infrequent users of many technical products and processes. I have a home accounting package I use once a month to balance my checkbook. As an infrequent user, I have neither the time nor the inclination to become an expert. I want to perform a specific task with as little learning time as possible. Well-designed technical publications can help infrequent users perform specific tasks quickly and with a minimum amount of confusion.

- High-quality publications foster use by diverse user communities.

  The better the design and implementation of technical publications, the more opportunity for those publications to be used by diverse, often unanticipated customers. Poor-quality publications, those that are difficult to use or difficult to read, usually support only a narrow band of customers. Often these customers most resemble the original product developers. They can use the publications to understand the product, but no one else can.

  In addition to the value by high-quality technical publications for the external customers, high-quality publications also add value to the product or process from the viewpoint of the internal customers.

- High-quality publications reduce the cost of customer support.

  If your customers can find the answers to their questions quickly and easily in the documentation, then they may make fewer and shorter calls to customer support.

  In addition, the customer support staff can use the documentation to quickly find the information they need to diagnose and correct problems.

- High-quality publications can reduce the cost of field maintenance.

Customers who are able to find and understand the information they need to perform preventive maintenance and solve problems are likely to require fewer field-maintenance visits.

- High-quality publications can increase sales of a product.

Customers who have the information they need to use a product effectively will not only become return customers themselves but will also recommend your product to their friends and colleagues.

If you define quality in technical publications as the value added to the product, process, or idea, then you should be able to find ways to measure when quality has been achieved. For the modem switch company, improved technical publications reduced the volume and cost of customer service calls, reduced the percentage of returned products, increased sales, and resulted in improved relations with both end-user and distributor customers.

Achieving quality in technical publications

If you want your technical publications to add value to the product, process, or ideas that you support, you need a reliable process in place with sound quality-assurance steps. The most commonly accepted practices to ensure quality in technical publications are to

- Set standards.
- Hire good people.
- Use good tools of the trade.

These accepted practices may assist you in achieving quality and adding value to your product. However, they do not *ensure* that quality will be achieved.

All we need are standards

Many people find it simplest to think about quality in terms of setting standards. Publications standards ordinarily establish rules for

- Format and typography
- Writing style
- Use of special terminology
- Spelling and abbreviations

Sometimes standards include requirements for the

- Organization of publications
- Organization of libraries
- Publications-development process

Standards such as these contribute to the quality in technical publications. They help ensure a consistent approach to the information being created, especially when that information is developed by many different individuals. They save individuals from having to make the same decisions again and again. They help bring your organization's practices closer to approved industry practices.

Setting standards is one of the first steps often taken by publications organizations when they decide to improve quality. Either formally through a style guide or informally through notes and checklists, publications developers define the standards they will use to write, edit, and format their publications.

Besides standards published by individual companies and government agencies, certain industries publish standards for technical publications within those industries. For example, the telephony industry uses publications standards to control the style and content of publications produced by and for the telephone companies in various countries. Their goal is to establish consistent style and organization of information for the technical workforce.

Unfortunately, despite the best efforts of the standards writers, publications prepared in conformance with standards can still fail to meet the usability requirements of customers. Publications may conform perfectly to inhouse standards. They may be formatted according to requirements, with the words all spelled correctly and the grammar correct. Yet they may be difficult to use because

- They are badly organized for their subject matter and audiences.
- They present information inconsistently.
- They fail to conform to the products they support.
- They are badly indexed, making it difficult for users to access information.

Nothing in the standards ensures good audience and task analysis, task-oriented organization of information, effective indexing, or accuracy. Standards alone are not sufficient to ensure quality.

Publications standards definitely provide useful guidelines for technical communicators, especially when the standards represent current best practices recommended by researchers and industry leaders. They are an excellent starting point for publications organizations that want to maintain a consistent look and feel in their publications libraries. But more is needed to ensure that high-quality publications are produced in a consistent and reliable manner.

We can follow all the best standards available for writing, editing, illustrating, and producing technical publications and yet produce publications that do not add value for the customer.

 Guideline: Set standards for your technical publications based upon the best practices currently available in your industry. However, remember that standards are not enough to ensure that your organization will consistently produce technical publications that add value for the customer.

All we need are better people

Many publications managers and technical communicators in general link the production of high-quality publications with the contributions of the most talented, experienced, well-trained people. They argue that if they just had better people, had more people with formal degrees in technical communication, or had people officially certified by professional organizations, they could produce higher-quality work. Certainly more education and training in the technical-communication field would produce better-prepared writers, editors, illustrators, production specialists, and others. But none of these solutions is likely to be reliably available soon nor will better people guarantee quality.

In the following scenario, Barbara expresses the opinion of many publications managers who have chosen hiring experienced people as their way to produce quality in their publications.

❝ We only hire people with five years experience in technical communication for our department. We prefer people with technical backgrounds who have already written reference manuals and programming guides for language compilers. It would be a waste of time for us to consider beginners," said Barbara, the publications manager for RTM Software.

"That would be nice," answered Joan, her colleague from M-Z, "but there don't seem to be enough experienced people to go around. I've interviewed a lot of people with long resumes and years of experience who seem to know little about technical writing."

"I know what you mean," said Barbara. "We've hired several people in the last year who haven't done well. They have a lot of experience on their resumes; however, when you ask them to participate in a design team or work with an editor, they have no idea what to do. I think they spent their entire careers cleaning up work written by engineers. We end up having to spend too much time getting them to fit into our organization."

"That's why I'd rather hire people with a good education but not much experience," said Joan. "I'd rather have people who are willing to learn. We depend a lot on teamwork. A lot of experienced writers have never worked on a team. Some learn quickly, but others insist on doing their own thing."

"Well, I don't really have time for training," answered Barbara. "I need people who can get started immediately and work entirely on their own. I don't have time to keep looking over their shoulders."

"But how do you know if their work is any good?" asked Joan. "Don't you worry that they may be doing a poor job?"

"Well, that's a problem," said Barbara. "The only feedback we get is from the engineers. If the engineers don't like what they've written, we have to change it."

"But the engineers don't know what makes a technical publication usable," said Joan. "Do you do any quality checks in the department?"

"Well, I've always felt the experienced writers can do their own editing," said Barbara. "We can't afford editors, and I don't have time for anything but spot checks. I have to assume that if there are no complaints from engineering, they're doing OK."

"What about customers?" asked Joan. "Do you get any feedback from them?"

"Sometimes customers complain about the manuals," answered Barbara. "And occasionally we get feedback from customer service and marketing. I just have to rely on my people to do a good job. I really don't have time to check."

"I don't know," replied Joan. "That really makes me uncomfortable. I think I have some great people on my staff, but I don't know if they would do as well if they never got any professional feedback from the others in the group. I'd be afraid that the real stars might produce good manuals, but everyone else would be struggling.

Good people are in great demand, especially those who

- Understand the technology they are writing about
- Know how to interview customers, technicians, and subject-matter experts, working well with all these diverse groups
- Are skilled in document design
- Consistently bring projects in on budget and on schedule
- Are talented writers who need no editing of their work
- Know how to proofread accurately and create clear and comprehensive indexes
- Are expert users of three or four major electronic publishing systems
- Understand the production and printing processes in detail
- Can effectively negotiate with developers and marketing specialists

If you think it is unlikely that you will find many technical communicators who have all these qualifications, you are probably correct. Such Renaissance communicators are rare. More often, people are good at some aspects of the job and could use experienced assistance with others.

In most technical publications organizations, you find a mix of experienced writers and those with fewer years, writers with a flawless command of the language and those who make mistakes and write awkwardly, good interviewers and researchers and those who are have difficulty with oral communication, innovators and those who prefer doing maintenance work. If you had to rely on hiring only highly skilled and experienced people, especially in a field in which formal education is rare and skills are difficult to assess during job interviews, you would find yourself sorely understaffed. Even if you hire people who look good on paper, you will still find yourself with a mix of skills and aptitudes.

But what if you had the best people available for the job? That does not ensure that you will always be able to produce high-quality publications. Talented people who have no standards to guide them will produce inconsistent publications. Talented people who do not keep up with the current research into the best publication practices may produce mediocre publications that no longer meet industry standards. Even the best people will be faced with inaccurate source information, uncooperative technical experts, changes late in the project life cycle, and too much work to do in too little time. Even the best people will not be able to solve all the problems that occur in developing publications.

Good people can only do their best work when well-designed standards and practices are in place and when the publications-development process is well managed.

Without good management, even the best people will have difficulty producing work of consistently high quality. With good management, even less experienced or skilled individuals will have the opportunity to do the best work they are capable of doing.

 Guideline: Highly skilled, well-trained, and experienced technical communicators are an asset to any publications organization. However, such people are in short supply. Good people alone will not ensure that you can produce high-quality technical publications consistently and reliably.

All we need are better tools

Some people define quality in terms of tools. If they just had better tools, such as the latest electronic publishing system, they could achieve quality in their publications. Especially in publications that are produced by people who lack technical-communication training, there is an undue reliance on tools. Many technical organizations believe that they can produce adequate technical publications from engineering source documents. All they need is a production specialist who can operate the desktop publishing system. As long as the final publication "looks good" and is printed on a laser printer, adequate quality has been achieved.

Fortunately, good tools are easier to find today than just a few years ago. Electronic publishing tools have become more sophisticated, in response to the requirements of professional technical communicators. But the best tools will not ensure that the information you write is appropriate for your customers and adds value to the product.

Some professional technical communicators appear to believe that the use of electronic publishing tools is a major part of producing quality in technical publications. They search out candidates for their writing positions among people who not only are fine writers and have technical experience but who can also use the required publishing tools. In fact, many organizations place a higher value on expertise in a publishing tool than on any other qualification.

Electronic publishing tools that are sophisticated in their functionality and produce high-quality output have contributed to the quality improvements in many technical publications in the past ten years. Before electronic publishing and laser printing technologies became commonplace, many technical publications were typed or handled with a word processor, and final copy was produced on impact or low-quality dot-matrix printers. In typed copy, changes to the text were difficult. In word-processed copy, there was often minimal graphic capability. As a result, the final copy looked as if it had been typed, with decreased readability of fonts and few graphics. Customers found the publications to be unattractive, difficult to use because of a lack of emphasis and graphic techniques, and difficult to read because of the poor quality of the text.

Current electronic publishing technology has made typeset-quality output available at low cost. The latest technology makes it possible for the operator to automate many of the processes that were once done entirely by hand or not at all. You can automate the process of generating an index, produce accurate tables of contents, and add cross-references that automatically reflect pagination changes. The tools allow you to add quality in terms of accuracy, accessibility, and ease of use to technical publications.

The penalty for the sophisticated functionality of current electronic publishing technology is a longer production process. To enhance the appearance of the final publication, more time is spent by technical communicators developing style templates, formatting text, and adding graphics to the electronic files. Although the quality of the output is increased, the processes to produce that quality often take longer than they once did. When text was sent to professional typesetters and graphics were added by the printers, less time was spent by technical communicators on production activities. The production tasks were also handled by experts who gained speed and efficiency by frequent performance. In many technical-publications organizations, in fact, the promised gains in productivity either have not been realized or have been disappointing in comparison with vending out production activities. The result in many organizations is usually a small increase in quality at a high cost unless internal production tasks are handled by production specialists.

For organizations that never were able to produce typeset-quality publications in the past because of budget limitations, electronic publishing systems and laser printers have substantially increased the quality of their output. However, the increase in quality has come at the cost of development time. Many technical communicators today spend more of their shrinking schedules on production activities than they did ten years ago.

Publication tools also permit technical communicators to produce information for electronic delivery. Online help compilers, CD-ROM development processes, and systems for adding hypertext capabilities to traditional text for electronic delivery are methods for enhancing the usability and quality of technical publications. Many of the tools, however, are difficult to learn and use, especially to produce more complex special effects. The tools are powerful, but they also require that technical communicators know as much about tools as they do about designing and developing usable text and graphics.

Better tools enhance but do not guarantee quality. A publication might be produced with the most sophisticated electronic publishing system but still be poorly written, poorly organized, inaccurate, and incomplete for the audience.

 Guideline: Select tools carefully to ensure that productivity is not sacrificed and that quality is genuinely enhanced. The best tools, however, will not ensure that you produce high-quality technical publications.

Process as quality

Producing quality in technical publications is aided by sound standards, productive tools, and good people, but standards, tools, and people do not ensure quality. To ensure that standards are followed, tools are used effectively, and people do the best work they are capable of, you must put into place an effective and sustainable publications-development process.

A sound process has the following characteristics:

- It allows you to produce high-quality technical publications consistently.
- It gives you the ability to estimate a budget and schedule and meet your commitments.
- It allows you to respond thoughtfully to changes in the product-development schedule.
- It allows you to meet the expectations of your customers in a predictable way.

The publications-development process is the set of procedures, standards, and management methods you use to produce consistently high-quality technical publications. The procedures provide you with a sequence of tasks to perform through the course of developing publications. The standards are the set of rules that you use to assess quality. The management methods are the ways that you, as project manager, keep the process under control. If you perform the process tasks properly, then you should produce the results you want.

You will find a detailed outline of the tasks that I and others who have implemented process improvement recommended for the publications-development process in Chapter 2. Parts Two through Six of this book expand the outline of tasks into a full exposition of development procedures. Forms and templates that support the procedures are included in the appendixes. As you work to improve the development process used in your organization, you can adopt all the practices and methods, use some of them, or adapt them to your special circumstances. But the more practices and methods you are able to put into place and perform well, the more likely you are to ensure the quality of the outcome.

 Guideline: By instituting a sound and comprehensive publications-development process, you will be on the right path to sustaining the quality of your publications.

Management as quality

Although a sound and comprehensive publications-development process is the most important part of your program to improve the quality of publications, an unmanaged process is unlikely to produce the results you want. You may require your staff to produce planning documents, such as an Information Plan and Content Specifications, but if they do not understand why they need to plan and learn the importance of planning, the planning documents will feel like empty exercises.

Every process must be managed to be successful. A managed process means

- Estimating project scope at the beginning of the process and at major milestones
- Estimating the time and resources needed to complete the project
- Carefully defining the objectives and milestones to be met by the end of the project
- Measuring progress toward completion
- Assessing the effect of change on budget and schedule

In short, a managed process is one that is under control. That implies, of course, that a managed process includes measurements. As Tom DeMarco explains in *Controlling Software Projects* (De Marco, 1982):

> *You cannot control what you cannot measure.*

Managing the publications-development process essentially means keeping track, knowing how much time you have expended on your project compared with what you have to spend, identifying what percentage of your project is complete at any point, and knowing if you have met your quality goals. Publications project management means measuring the progress of your team against your original estimates of schedule, budget, and resources. It means knowing exactly how far you have come and how far you need to go to reach your destination.

Project management is a lot like traveling. With a good map and a travel plan in place, you will know where you have been and where you are going. And you will know exactly where you are. You will be able to make continuous course corrections as changes occur. You will be able to redefine the project if a major directional change is required.

To put a publications-development process in place in your organization and to ensure that it is well managed will require considerable effort and commitment of time and energy. You will find that you will progress through various levels of growth as you struggle with process improvement. In Chapter 3, I outline five levels of process maturity for technical publications organizations. As your organization gains in process maturity, you will find yourself implementing more of the publications-development process tasks and managing the tasks more effectively.

Watts Humphrey outlines six steps that organizations must take to improve the processes they use to develop software in *Managing the Software Process* (Humphrey, 1989). I have rephrased the steps slightly to adapt them to the development of a managed publications-development process:

1. Understand where you and your organization are today in your implementation of process.
2. Construct a clear picture of your process and management goals.
3. Create a list of the process improvements you will need to make to reach your goals in order of priority.
4. Develop a plan of action to reach your goals.
5. Gather the resources you will need to implement the plan.
6. Start over with Step 1.

The benefits of publications project management

Publications managers are usually very familiar with the consequences of failing to manage development projects. In many cases, they find themselves in organizations, especially high-tech development organizations, that neither follow nor manage the process. Projects are inadequately planned and implemented. Poor planning results in unrealistic deadlines, inadequate resources, and one crisis after another. Projects are poorly implemented, resulting in frequent changes of direction and detail. Features and functions are added, deleted, and changed throughout the life cycle, which puts pressure on downstream tasks such as publication production.

On the other hand, the benefits of a sound development process and thorough project management are clear:

- Audience requirements are analyzed in advance and tested throughout the development life cycle.
- Publication solutions are carefully defined in scope and complexity.
- Risk factors are adequately assessed at the beginning of the life cycle and at every significant milestone, and steps are taken to mitigate the risks.
- Projects are staffed adequately from the start so that milestones can be met and quality maintained.
- Project changes are carefully assessed so that costs are balanced against benefits.
- Quality and usability goals are established well in advance of development and monitored continuously.
- The level of quality required by the customers is consistently achieved.

When you experience a well-planned and well-managed process, you are frequently amazed at the ease with which goals are achieved. In the following scenario, the project manager has succeeded in keeping a large project under control and achieved a remarkable degree of quality in the publications.

I really didn't think we could do it. We produced over 2,000 pages of technical information, in addition to the help screens and the computer-based training, the customers are very positive in their initial response, and the team members are still good friends," exclaimed Tom, the lead writer for the online documentation.

"It's amazing all right," said Jim, the project manager. "Once again, good planning pays off. We defined what we wanted to do in the Information Plan, and we did it."

"You told us we needed eight people for eight months," said Joan, the project editor. "At first I thought you were crazy, but that was exactly right. We all had to put in some extra time at the last to be sure that the final draft was ready for the translators, but it was a lot less than I had expected."

"Now that the documentation has been shipped," said Jim, "we need to sit down and assess the process. I'm sure there's lots we can improve. We need to be able to scope the translation requirements more effectively so that we don't run into schedule problems next time."

"I'm ready," said Joan. "I'm much more confident that developmental editing is the right thing to do. I thought I was wasting time editing so early in the process. The writers didn't even have first drafts done. But we were able to correct problems early. It made the final copyedit a breeze. I'd like to know how my level of effort varied during the project in comparison with the writers' time."

"No problem," said Jim, "I have all the numbers. Why don't you and I work together tomorrow and graph the relationship. That will give us a good idea of how to allocate editing time on the new project."

"I think we can decrease the editing percentages next time," said Tom. "The writers are comfortable with the new style standards. You won't have to work as hard, Joan, as you did this time around. We're ready."

"Do you know that, even with the late changes to all those screens, we were only 5 percent over our original estimate?" offered Jim. "I couldn't believe how well everything tracked."

"That's only because you kept reminding us of how much time we had for each interim milestone," said Tom. "You did a great job."

"Everyone did a great job," answered Jim. "This is the best project I've ever worked on.

Not every project goes this well, of course, especially when the rest of the organization has never heard of project management. But successes like this one are not as rare as you may believe. As you put the process into action and learn to manage effectively, you will find that the processes become natural.

The challenges of publications project management

No one ever said that managing complex development projects was easy. Project management is a learned skill, and managers become better with careful practice. To succeed in improving the development process so that you consistently produce quality requires hard and sustained work.

To succeed in establishing a sound process and managing it effectively, you will need

- Support from your upper management
- Support from other parts of the development organization
- The cooperation of everyone on your team
- Time invested in planning, an adequate budget, and time to manage

Without support from upper management, you can still accomplish some degree of planning and project management in your own organization. However, you may be stymied every time you have to request resources, negotiate changes of scope, and measure the quality of your production.

With the support of your upper management, you can move much more quickly toward a more mature process level. If you can count on your management to help you set priorities, provide the resources you need, and give you continuing support, you will have a greater likelihood of success. You will also have a better chance of convincing yourself that long-term changes are achievable even if progress seems slow.

If you have the support of the other parts of the development team (the technical and marketing experts in particular), you will have a much easier time of instituting change in your organization than if the management and parallel groups fight you every step of the way. In one case, a product-development manager tried to fire a technical communicator who produced an Information Plan. That manager thought that publications planning was a waste of time.

As a publications project manager, you will certainly encounter people who are unsupportive and block your path at every turn. If you have the support of upper management in these circumstances, you will have a court of appeal if you encounter obstacles. Without that support, progress will be slower but not impossible.

Look for opportunities among the most open and innovative development managers that you work with. Do not look for victory among the most recalcitrant. A cooperative developer who will work with you to ensure that milestones are met and resources are available will give you vital early success. A good success story will go a long way toward convincing other development managers of the value of a managed process in publications. It may even influence their own management of the product-development process.

In addition to support of your management and your peers, you need to cultivate the support of your own team members. Everyone is somewhat afraid of change, especially when they perceive high risks associated with the changes. In instituting new processes, you may find your own team members balking. They are more comfortable with their old ways of working, even if their methods are ineffective. You will need to show your team members that a publications-development process will eventually enhance their position in the larger organization, ensure that they have more adequate schedules and resources in the future, and help them avoid the continuing crises of the past.

Finally, you will need to make your own commitment to planning so that you can present a cogent argument to your management for the budget and resources you need to produce high-quality publications. You may have to institute quality measurements to show that the new processes make a difference to the bottom line.

Most important, you will need to make a personal commitment to finding time to manage. It is easy to become immersed in the everyday activities of writing, editing, and producing publications. It is easy to avoid management activities, especially if they are unfamiliar. Yet, if you are going to succeed in moving from chaos to an orderly, managed, and repeatable process, you are going to have to make time for managing. In fact, your managing time is the most important time you give to a project. If your project comes in on schedule, on budget, and without dreadful amounts of extra time, and you succeed in producing publications that please your customers and your staff and colleagues, you will experience the rewards of managing projects well.

CHAPTER
2

A Model of the Publications-Development Life Cycle

In this chapter, I provide a high-level summary of the five phases of the model publications-development life cycle. Parts Two through Six supply the details, taking you through the requirements for each phase. This summary helps you put the rest of the book in perspective.

The five-phase model of the publications-development life cycle is similar to several well-accepted models of the product-development life cycle. (See Humphrey, 1989.) You need to understand the parallels so that you can introduce your new life-cycle model to your development organization and senior management. If your organization already uses a phased development model for products, then a publications-development model will fit in easily. If your organization has only a rudimentary product-development model, then you need to be prepared for the potential conflicts that may occur if you try to introduce a more fully developed and managed development process. If your organization has no product-development process, then you need to plan a strategy for gaining acceptance of a simplified process.

If your organization has moved into user-centered design and Rapid-Application Development (RAD), you may need to modify the model to account for design iterations and innovative design concepts. No matter what challenges you face in introducing a publications-development life cycle to your organization, you need to anticipate them and plan a strategy that will succeed.

If you are new to the concept of a publications-development life cycle, you may find that the entire life-cycle process is more than your organization can handle in the beginning. To get started, consider a short list of some of the activities you might implement first. You can add to the short list as you gain experience and acceptance, eventually implementing the complete process. Or just start wherever you are today, which might mean starting with a wrap-up report. It would be better to take advantage of your enthusiasm for new ideas than to postpone them and lose momentum.

Why have a life-cycle model?

Models are significant tools for the management of complex development activities. Models of the life cycle of a development effort provide us with a means for planning and controlling our actions so that we can hope for some guarantee of success. A life-cycle model consists of descriptions and specifications of the activities that must be performed at different phases in the development and production process. The descriptions and specifications are designed to ensure that you perform the series of activities correctly and consistently across many projects and over a long period of time. By dividing the life cycle into phases, you schedule significant opportunities to review the specified activities and ensure that they have been performed well. In short, a well-defined life-cycle model helps you answer these questions:

- Where do I start?

- Am I on the right path?

- How do I know if I'm done?

A publications-development life cycle gives you a way of organizing the activities of your team, establishing common definitions of those activities, communicating about your activities to others in your organization, and planning your activities so that you can ensure that they are performed well and as scheduled.

Once you have a life-cycle model in place and defined, you can use it to plan and monitor the activities of the life cycle as a whole and within each phase. Planning is the key. Without a life-cycle model, you may find yourself following the old technical publications model—just keep writing until someone tells you to stop. No plans, no goals, no way to tell if you are doing the right thing, with lots of opportunities for doing the wrong thing.

You will find that in most technical organizations, the lack of a life-cycle model for publications has two results: The publications people do not plan and control their activities and the rest of the organization believes that publications people have no idea what they are doing. If publications people fail to plan or fail to communicate their planning and development processes to the rest of the organization, then it is easy for management to conclude that anyone can produce technical publications. They can be produced by the engineers and programmers in their spare time; they can be produced by the clerical staff with input from the technical experts; they can be produced by just about anyone who can type and use a desktop-publishing system.

If publications people plan well and communicate their planning and development processes to the rest of the organization, they increase their credibility as responsible professionals. Having a detailed development process signals that you perform activities that are not universally known and cannot be duplicated by others in the organization. It communicates that as the publications project manager, you lead a team of professionals who perform unique, complex, and valuable activities that lead time and again to successful publications. It lets developers know that their schedules have an impact on yours.

Having a detailed publications life-cycle model communicates that you know what you are doing and that you proceed with deliberation and caution through a pre-planned sequence of actions and reviews. You impress others by the thoroughness of your planning and by your management of the process. You are able to repeat the process again in a reliable and consistent way. You are able, with a well-managed life-cycle process, to produce consistently high-quality technical publications that meet the needs of your audiences. You are able to increase the quality of your writers' contributions, helping good writers produce exceptional publications.

Without a well-managed life cycle, you may produce high-quality publications occasionally, but more likely you will spend your time buffeted by ever-changing requirements and content, the opinions of opinionated but uninformed outsiders, and the decisions of people who do not know how to make good decisions about your area of expertise. You will spend your time reworking information that was complete, making major changes in publications at the last minute, producing publications that contain errors and are difficult to use, and becoming increasingly frustrated by the lack of quality and control over your work and the huge amounts of time you are asked to expend doing a poor job.

I suggest, because I have seen it happen many times in many organizations, that if you adopt a sound and thorough publications-development life cycle, you can exert control over your activities and gain credibility in your larger organization. However, you cannot simply introduce a life-cycle process and expect it to manage itself. You must be prepared to manage the process, to ensure that the activities happen the way they are planned. In the rest of the book, I discuss how to manage the life cycle and to keep the publications-development process under control.

How is a model different from a prescription?

I do not offer the five-phase model presented in this book as a prescription, although you will find no disadvantage in adopting all of the steps outlined. The five phases of publications development are a true model, one that you may modify to accommodate the special circumstances of your organization and product. Some of the phases may be combined, others expanded. But before you decide to change the model, I urge you to understand it thoroughly. The activities outlined in Parts Two through Six of this book are thoroughly tested and represent the wisdom and collective experience not only of myself and the organization I have led for 15 years, but the experience of many other individuals who have contributed to our understanding of the publications-development life cycle by leading their own publications organizations.

Most of the concepts and activities presented in the five-phase model are neither new nor unique, although they are combined here in a new way. They represent the accumulated experience of many years and many diverse organizations worldwide. They work for technical publications that range from proposals and scientific reports, to internal policies and procedures, to instructional and reference manuals of all sorts.

In each case, of course, some modifications to the specific activities included with the life-cycle model must be made.

A five-phase model

The model of the publications-development life cycle has five phases:

Phase 1: Information Planning (Part Two)
Phase 2: Content Specification (Part Three)
Phase 3: Implementation (Part Four)
Phase 4: Production (Part Five)
Phase 5: Evaluation (Part Six)

The five phases are discussed in detail in each of the subsequent sections of this book.

The five phases are roughly parallel to some of the more common models of the product-development life cycle. For many of you in the software and hardware industries, this parallelism will help you introduce the life-cycle model to your organization. The five phases will fit well with other models being used or considered for the product-development process.

Modifying the model for your own needs

As you work with the concept of a publications-development life cycle and begin to apply it to your special circumstances, you will most likely modify the phases so that they better conform to the needs of your organization. I do not, for the most part, recommend that you omit any of the phases, especially the planning phases. It is certainly tempting to forego planning when time and resources appear short, but that is often the worst possible decision.

Although you should never omit the planning phases, you may choose to combine them. I often recommend collapsing Phases 1 and 2 into a single planning phase for very short projects or projects that focus on maintaining existing publications that have already been well planned. Even if Phases 1 and 2 are both relevant to your projects, you may find it useful in some projects to combine the two deliverables—the Information Plan and the Content Specification(s)—into a single document.

It is very tempting on short projects to decide that there is "no time to plan." Short projects are just as difficult to manage as longer projects and perhaps more difficult because all required activities are compressed. The only way to keep short projects under control is with very, very good planning. If you are half prepared or completely unprepared on a project, you will more likely find yourself reworking substantial pieces of the text and graphics at the end—when you can least afford to do so.

Unplanned projects take longer, require more resources, produce less quality, and are harder on morale than planned projects. No matter how tempting it looks to omit the planning and "just start writing," never succumb. You will find a complete discussion of the pitfalls of omitting the planning phases, in the discussion of

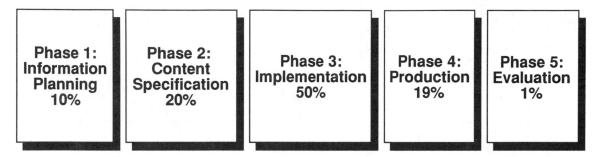

Figure 2.1 The five phases of the publications-development life cycle

information planning in Part Two. You will also find arguments that you can use to explain the value of the planning phases to senior management and your staff.

Figure 2.1 illustrates the five phases of the publications-development life cycle and the approximate percentages of the total project that each phase represents. The relationship of each phase to the total project depends on the requirements of a specific project.

The life-cycle phases are summarized in Figure 2.2 and briefly below. They are explained in detail in Parts Two through Six of the book.

Phase 1: Information Planning

This first phase of the publications-development life cycle has two major deliverables, often combined into a single document. The deliverables of Phase 1 are

- The Information Plan
- The Project Plan

The Information Plan is the document that results from your initial investigation into the requirements of the publications project. The Information Plan cannot be written until you have gathered significant information about

- The audience for the publications
- The goals of the audience and the major tasks they want to perform with the help of the publications
- The environment in which the publications will be used
- The nature of the product or subject matter to be discussed

Publications-Development Life Cycle

Phase	1	2	3	4	5
Phase name	Information Planning	Content Specification	Implementation	Production	Evaluation
Project management activities	Develop a Project Plan: • estimate of scope • estimate of hours • estimate of required resources • preliminary milestone schedule • plan for translation • plan for production Acquire resources: • Bring writers, editors, illustrators, production specialists, and others onto your team • Acquire the tools needed for the project Begin a project management notebook Plan and conduct the Phase 1 review Write progress reports	Revise the Project Plan: • re-estimate the project scope • re-estimate the hours • re-estimate the required resources • revise the milestone schedule as needed • acquire additional resources as needed • acquire additional tools as needed Add the Content Specifications and revised Project Plan to the project management notebook Plan and conduct the Phase 2 reviews Write progress reports	Monitor the project: • track hours expended • track %complete • track milestones • monitor changes Control the project: • coordinate draft reviews • estimate the effect of changes • revise schedules and budgets as needed • negotiate for additional resources and time as needed Plan and conduct the first and second draft reviews Obtain final signoff approval before production Add tracking spreadsheets, weekly reports, progress reports, meeting minutes, change request orders, and memos to the project management notebook Write progress reports	Manage the translation and localization process: • Work with the translators to facilitate the translation process Plan the production activities: • Locate and negotiate with vendors • Produce and implement a production checklist Monitor the production activities: • Conduct production process reviews Add the production activities and decisions to the project notebook: • list vendors • record publishing specifications	Evaluate the project: • Calculate project statistics • Write the project wrap-up report • Plan and conduct the project wrap-up meeting Evaluate the product: • Plan and implement customer surveys • Obtain customer feedback • Conduct customer site visits Evaluate the process: • Evaluate the success of the life cycle • Plan for process improvements Evaluate the team: • Conduct a team evaluation • Conduct individual evaluations • Do a self-evaluation Plan for revision: • Establish project archives • Create a revision plan • Plan for end-of-life Complete the project notebook

Figure 2.2 Publications-development life-cycle summary

Phase	1	2	3	4	5
Phase name	Information Planning	Content Specification	Implementation	Production	Evaluation
Publications development activities	Gather information: • develop a user profile • conduct a high-level task analysis • understand the plans for the product development • understand the plans for marketing the product • establish usability goals Write the Information Plan: • describe the users • describe the high-level tasks • describe the product • describe the marketing plan • state the usability goals • outline the design implications • create a user/task matrix • create a media plan Edit the Information Plan for content and persuasiveness Participate in the reviews of the Information Plan Revise the Information Plan as needed	Gather information: • expand the user profile • conduct a detailed task analysis • learn about the details of the product and the interface Write the Content Specifications: • revise the user description • describe the detailed tasks • explain the organization of the publication • create a detailed, annotated outline • estimate the number of pages and graphics required to meet the usability requirements Edit the Content Specifications for organization, thoroughness, and accuracy Participate in the reviews of the Content Specifications Revise the Content Specifications as needed	Design the format of the publications: • develop an electronic style template • begin a style guide for the project Create prototype sections: • implement the page design • establish a writing style • establish a graphics style Write, format, and illustrate: • create interim drafts of individual sections • compile interim drafts into a first draft • revise the first draft and add information for a second draft • revise the second draft and add information for the final signoff draft Edit the drafts: • developmental edit • literary edit • copyedit Create indexes Participate in the draft reviews	Translate and localize: • prepare the copy for the translators • translate and localize the copy and format the copy appropriately • edit the translated and localized copy Prepare the camera-ready copy: • perform a final copyedit • generate indexes and tables of contents Work with the production vendors: • create collating lists • create dummies • review bluelines • review color keys • perform press checks • perform final quality assurance checks • arrange for assembly, distribution, and delivery	Archive the project: • archive electronic files • archive hardcopy files Participate in the project evaluations

Figure 2.2 (Continued)

Phase	1	2	3	4	5
Phase name	Information Planning	Content Specification	Implementation	Production	Evaluation
Testing	Conduct early paper-and-pencil tests of library designs Conduct tests of previous and competitive products and publications Test index ideas	Conduct early paper-and-pencil tests of your ideas for organizational patterns in the publications, terminology, instructional text designs, graphic designs	Conduct tests of early prototype instructional and reference text Conduct tests of early and later publication drafts Test indexes		Conduct evaluative tests of completed publications Conduct user site studies

Figure 2.2 (Continued)

Armed with the fruits of your early investigations into the product and its customers, you are ready to construct an Information Plan that outlines the library of publications that you believe will best meet the needs of the audience, as well as the internal requirements of your own organization.

Put succinctly, the Information Plan is a proposal. Consequently, it should have all of the characteristics of a good proposal. It should be written to persuade the readers that you have

- Conducted your preliminary research thoroughly
- Thought through the alternatives carefully
- Presented a sound recommendation for addressing the needs you have identified
- Presented a cogent argument for the library of publications that you recommend

To produce a persuasive proposal, you must understand the decision-making process of the people who must approve the proposal and provide you with sufficient resources to implement it. The better you know how to persuade the decision makers in your organization, the more success you will have in winning approval for your publications plan.

The second half of Phase 1 is your Project Plan. The Project Plan contains an early estimate of the resources you will need to implement the Information Plan. In it, you estimate

- The hours needed to complete the project
- The milestone schedule you will follow
- The deliverables that you will produce at each milestone
- The number of people you will need to implement the plan
- An assessment of the risk factors that will help you to succeed in delivering your plan or impede your progress

The Project Plan is, in fact, your detailed proposal for controlling the project and ensuring success.

Without both the Phase 1 deliverables, you have an incomplete plan. It is not enough to outline a list of publications that you intend to create. You must also show how you intend to ensure that they will be created in a timely and cost-effective manner.

Phase 1 ends with a phase review. At this review, all interested parties, especially those who make decisions about resources, either approve the plan as presented or request modifications of the content, schedule, cost, or required resources.

Phase 1 ordinarily takes 10 percent of total project hours to complete. That means for a 6-month project of 1,000 hours, 100 hours or $2\frac{1}{2}$ weeks are devoted to information planning.

Phase 2: Content Specification

The second planning phase is called the Content Specification. In Phase 2 of the publications-development life cycle, you add the details to the publications that you outlined in Phase 1 and have been approved for implementation in the Phase 1 review.

Phase 2 has two deliverables, the Content Specification and a revised Project Plan. The Content Specification, while representing one type of deliverable, is produced for as many individual publications as you have planned for the project. If you have planned to develop two manuals and a videotape, you will need three Content Specifications. One Information Plan—many Content Specifications.

Each Content Specification contains the detailed results of considerable additional research into the audiences and the product. To prepare the Content Specification, technical communicators must learn as much as possible about the product and how it will be used. They will also develop a deeper understanding of the audience and their goals, as well as a much more extensive knowledge of the specific tasks that the audience will perform to use the product. They will also keep busy researching and writing the Content Specification, rather than trying to write the documents before you are ready to start Phase 3. Perhaps the most important part of the process of specifying detailed content is a detailed task analysis or, for non-task-oriented publications, a detailed analysis of the information needed by the audience.

Once the technical communicators have researched the content thoroughly and gained a substantial understanding of audience needs, then they are prepared to develop an organizational pattern for their planned publication. This organizational pattern is often communicated through a detailed annotated outline of the topics—a preliminary table of contents. If sufficiently thorough research occurs, and the content is not altered dramatically during the course of the project, there should be little deviation by the end of the project from the original table of contents.

In addition to the detailed Content Specifications, Phase 2 also requires a major revisiting of your original Project Plan. When the Content Specifications are complete, you will have much more detailed knowledge of the scope of the publications project. Thorough Content Specifications should produce sound estimates of the size of each of the planned publications, information that may have been largely unavailable during Phase 1. In Phase 1, you most likely produced a rough order-of-magnitude estimate of the scope of the publications project. In Phase 2, you revise that estimate with much firmer predictions about scope.

If the estimate of scope has changed substantially between Phase 1 and Phase 2, which it frequently does, you may need additional resources to complete the project on schedule.

Phase 2 also ends with a phase review. At this review, all interested parties, especially those who make decisions about resources, either approve the plan as presented or request modifications of the content, schedule, cost, or required resources. In many instances, the phase reviews for each of the specified publications are conducted separately with different groups of developers and other content experts.

Phase 2 ordinarily takes 20 percent of total project hours to complete. For the 6-month, 1,000-hour project, that means the Content Specification should take 200 hours or approximately 5 weeks to prepare.

Phase 3: Implementation

Phase 3: Implementation is the phase in which the actual design and development of the technical publications takes place. Many deliverables occur in Phase 3, because your team produces multiple drafts of text and graphics that are reviewed, modified, reviewed again, and frequently modified again.

Phase 3 deliverables might include

- Designs for the style of multiple publications
- Prototype sections that demonstrate how the style will be implemented
- Informal drafts for review by a limited number of experts
- Formal first drafts
- Formal second drafts
- Final approval drafts

Not every project has all of the pieces outlined above. If you have an established organizational style for your publications, you may not produce a new design for your project publications. You may choose not to produce informal drafts for interim review, but save all reviews for a formal first draft, although I do not recommend this policy. Your organization may require more than two formal drafts before the final draft is ready for sign-off. You have considerable flexibility to define what you need for Phase 3. However, always remember that the more deliverables you produce, the longer the project will take.

In addition to the content-related deliverables of Phase 3, as project manager you have project-related deliverables:

- Weekly time sheets and progress reports
- Weekly and monthly tracking spreadsheets
- Periodic reports of progress
- Change request memos

As the project proceeds through its development phases, you are responsible for tracking its progress. Your original Project Plan detailed the hours you needed and the milestones you would reach. During development, you track time against milestones to ensure that the project remains on schedule and within budget.

If you detect any deviations from the schedule and budget, your responsibility during Phase 3 is to evaluate the effect of those deviations on your team's ability to meet its future deliverable schedule. As soon as you believe that the schedule is likely to change, it is your responsibility to report on the change and negotiate changes to the project's scope, schedule, or budget.

Many reviews occur in Phase 3 of the publications-development life cycle. You may need to schedule reviews of new design concepts, prototype sections of publications, and interim early drafts. In most instances, you will have the major reviews on your milestone schedule from the first. Major reviews generally occur at

- First or alpha draft
- Second or beta draft
- Final approval draft

Phase 3: Implementation should take all project time between the planning phases (the first 30 percent of the project) and the production phase. The percentage of time available for Phase 3 will depend upon the amount of time needed for production activities in Phase 4. Production time depends upon the complications of the production cycle, the size and complexity of the production deliverables, and the requirements for translation and localization.

For the example 6-month, 1,000-hour project, you may expect to spend at least 50 percent of the total time (500 hours) or $12\frac{1}{2}$ weeks on implementation through second draft.

Phase 4: Production

In many cases, Phase 3 and Phase 4 will overlap enough to reduce the impact of Phase 4 on the final schedule. Phase 4 consists of all the activities required to deliver the final publications to the customer. Phase 4 may be very short—requiring nothing more than a few photocopies stapled together and handed out to the audience. More likely, Phase 4 will consist of

- Preparing the final camera-ready copy of text and graphics
- Translating and localizing into all required languages (not included in the overall estimate of the project hours)
- Printing, binding, and packaging hardcopy publications (not included in the overall estimate of the project hours)
- Preparing other forms of publication such as videotapes, audiotapes, CD-ROM, online help, and other electronic forms of delivery (not included in the overall estimate of the project hours)
- Assembling the publications for distribution to the customers (not included in the overall estimate of the project hours)

In most cases, Phase 4 requires considerable liaison with outside vendors.

Phase 4 is the manufacturing part of the development of technical publications. As a manufacturing process, it also needs to be estimated, planned, and controlled. In some organizations, the publications project manger is responsible for all of Phase 4. In others, Phase 4 is handled by a professional production staff with only oversight by the publications project manager. In either case, you would be well advised to understand how the process works, if only so that you can accurately estimate what percentage of your total project schedule must be devoted to production.

Production activities are often quite inflexible, especially to the extent that you must depend upon the services of outside vendors. You will find it difficult to substantially shorten the time required for printing, collating, binding, packaging, and assembling publications. Translations and localizations also add to the time required during the production cycle. That means that the more thoroughly you plan these activities, the more control you can exercise in reducing their impact on your development cycle.

Most publications project managers learn early in their careers that they must always plan the production cycle first and estimate all other activities in relationship to the needs of manufacturing.

Since Phase 5 represents a post-production evaluation, you should expect to spend the remaining 20 percent of your 1,000-hour, 6-month project on production.

Phase 5: Evaluation

Phase 5: Evaluation has two significant activities for the publications project manager:

- Evaluating the current project
- Planning for the next version of the project

In the evaluation process, the team and the project manager produce several deliverables:

- Project wrap-up report
- Team and individual project-specific evaluations
- Project manager self-evaluation

The project wrap-up report is delivered to the larger development organization and records the end-of-project statistics, as well as an evaluation of project successes, problems, and opportunities for improvement. The evaluations of the team performance as a whole and the performance of individual team members are for internal use only by the publications group. Individual performance evaluations become part of each team member's personnel file. An evaluation of the project manager can either be a self-evaluation or may include a team evaluation and management evaluation of the success of your efforts as project manager and your opportunities for improvement.

Phase 5 activities should take place as early as possible so that the details are not forgotten and the response to opportunities for improvement is rapid. The only exception to an early review is when people are upset at the end of the project. Phase 5 activities can often take place while Phase 4 activities are continuing, although certain parts of the project wrap-up statistics and evaluation will have to wait until the production cycle is completed.

The second part of Phase 5, the plan for the new version, often begins during Phase 3. Many times, decisions must be made during Phase 3 to stay on schedule. That means eliminating or reducing the effectiveness of publications plans. You often find yourself cutting out parts of the publications that you had planned to do simply because time is too short. You trade off the addition of new information against the better presentation of the information you had originally planned. You forego usability testing because information about the product is not ready in time. All of these tradeoffs and cuts provide you with opportunities for the second version of the technical publications, just as they do for the product itself.

During Phase 5, you begin to formalize the transition into a new project. You account for the missing pieces, plan for external evaluations of the success of the publications, design feedback mechanisms for the customers, and prepare for post-publication testing. In the interim between the end of one project and the beginning of the revision project, you may find time for the usability testing you had wanted to include from the first. The results of the testing and other information gathering from customers all help you prepare for the next edition.

Parallels to the product-development life cycle

A major advantage of the five-phase model of the publications-development life cycle is its parallelism with standard product-development life cycles. Figure 2.3 shows the

Publications-Development Life Cycle

Phase	1	2	3	4	5
Phase name	Information Planning	Content Specification	Implementation	Production	Evaluation

Product-Development Life Cycle

	1	2	3	4	5
Phase name	Feasibility study and Requirements Definition	Detailed Specifications	Implementation and Testing	Manufacturing	Evaluation
Marketing	Feasibility study • statement of objectives • requirement plan • requirements for documentation and training	Release schedule	System changes	Sales and Support	Customer Satisfaction
Development	System requirements	Detailed design • external • internal Interface design	Code development	Production	Bug reports Maintenance
Testing			Unit testing Integration testing	Quality assurance	

Figure 2.3 The relationship of publications- and product-development life cycles

relationship between each of the five phases and similar phases in the process of development products.

Fitting the publications process to the product-development life cycle

Because the life-cycle models are parallel, the publications-development process may occur at the same time as the product-development process is occurring. There is no need to wait until the product is nearly complete before the publications planning and development are started. In fact, the publications process can be managed more easily and effectively if it is not delayed. The later the publications life cycle begins in relationship to the product life cycle, the more difficult it will be to plan and produce high-quality publications.

Please note, however, that the activities that occur early in the development process emphasize planning rather than writing. Too often, publications people, invited to take part in early product-planning activities, assume that they are to begin creating documents rather than doing their own plan. That is clearly a mistake and leads to an enormous amount of rework. Early involvement in the parallel product-development process provides an opportunity for thorough user and task analysis and understanding of the organization's hopes and plans for the new product.

Great diligence must be exercised by the publications project manager to avoid creating text too soon. That may require beginning with a small, even part-time team rather than the full contingent you will need later during Phase 3 (Implementation). Limited time commitments early in the life-cycle process will ensure that you don't expend too much of your project resources before they are really needed. Keep the 30-percent planning goal firmly in mind when you begin early.

The usefulness of the parallel cycles continues throughout development. If your team can produce very detailed Content Specifications while the product-development team is specifying its design, then your team will be ready to fill in the blanks as soon as pieces of the product begin to take shape. As a result, you are more likely to have subsections of the publications ready for early prototype testing, alpha releases, and beta releases than if you waited until all the product details were final before you began your own planning.

Most of the difficulties inherent in parallel processes stem from the perceived need of many technical communicators for closure. Many writers are used to working quickly to make up for time lost during the early phases of product development. They view planning activities as keeping them away from their real work of producing pages. They want the sense of completion that comes from an increasing number of "finished" pages. Unfortunately, that feeling of satisfaction lasts only as long as the "finished" pages remain finished. When writing takes place too early, most of the "finished" pages will be rewritten, sometimes several times.

As they participate in the early phases of product development, writers on your team, especially if project planning is new to them, will need constant reminders that planning is real work. Writing plans is real writing and can be quite challenging and satisfying. Running review meetings and negotiating changes in scope and schedule are also challenging. You need to remind yourself that the planning activities will eventually pay off, even if tangible output is frustratingly absent.

Working with rapid-application development models

The basic product-development life cycle presented in this chapter is sometimes referred to as the "waterfall" model, because extensive planning precedes implementation (see Humphrey, 1989). However, the need for greater involvement of users in the development process, an interest in developing a usable product, as well as the need to shorten traditional development schedules, has increased the appeal of a different type of development model in recent years. The RAD model, especially when it is combined with the techniques of user-centered design, suggests that attempts to fully specify a product during the initial planning stages may be misguided (Andriole, 1992).

In a user-centered, rapid-prototyping model, some user requirements are gathered early, initial development ideas are prototyped and tested with users, at which time more requirements are identified, leading to iterations of prototyping, testing, and redevelopment. The purpose of this model is to get much closer to meeting user needs early in the development process, rather than spending time and money implementing requirements that may be seriously inadequate in identifying real user needs.

The publications-development life cycle has the flexibility of fit into the rapid-prototyping model. Technical communicators have historically been interested in producing more usable publications and are often very sensitive to the needs of their audiences. Consequently, they welcome the opportunity for early testing of prototype publications.

Under a rapid-prototyping model, the Phase 1 requirement to investigate the users, their goals, and their tasks remains the same. But unlike the more traditional model, no closure is reached on either the Information Plan, the Project Plan, or the Content Specifications until early design ideas are tried out on the user community. For example, in a traditional Information Plan, you may outline a library of publications to be part of the product. In using a rapid-prototyping life-cycle model, you would test your ideas for a library by presenting a storyboard of the library plan to actual users. As a result, the information-planning phase will often take longer than in the traditional model, as will the Content Specifications. The planning milestones may increase from 30 percent of the total project hours to 50 percent or more. Ideas for publication design will be tested, rejected, revised, and tested again.

A rapid-prototyping model of development can be both exciting and frustrating for technical communicators and a genuine challenge for project managers. The excitement comes from creating a design idea, testing it with real users, creating a better idea, testing it again, and so on. The iterations continue until you reach a design that fulfills your usability goals. For innovative people, that process is exhilarating.

For people who prefer to set a more steady course toward the development of a publication, the prototyping model may be frightening. Even your best design ideas are likely to be challenged in the crucible of usability testing. As a project manager, you may want to involve your most confident innovators in rapid prototyping, reserving your strongest developers for the steadier state of Phase 3. Once the design is final, then implementation activities often proceed normally through production and evaluation. The time allowed for implementation and production may be less than in the more traditional life-cycle model. As project manager, that will challenge your ingenuity for finding ways to avoid rework during implementation and production. As usual, careful and thorough planning is a significant part of the solution.

When there is no formal product-development life cycle

I have been proceeding under the assumption so far in this discussion that you are managing a publications project in an organization that has an established product-development process. For many of you, that is likely not to be the case. Some experts on the software-development life cycle believe that only about 20 percent of all software developers follow a consistent life-cycle model. The other 80 percent proceed in an ad hoc manner, designing whatever they like until someone decides it might be salable. Then there is a great rush to market. The other 80 percent may actually write down some requirements, an activity often handled by the product-marketing group. Unfortunately, the barriers between marketing and development guarantee that development will not produce a product that does exactly what marketing wrote about in the requirements. Development will do something *different*, something *better*, something more interesting and challenging for the developers.

If you work in an organization where specifications are either never written down or the written ones are considered a joke, you know that there *is* no product-development process, despite what might be officially on paper. What happens, then, when you try to introduce a publications-development life cycle into an organization that does not support a product-development life cycle? Frequently, you will have a battle on your hands. Sometimes, however, you will succeed in very dramatic ways.

Many publications project managers argue that they cannot introduce a publications-development process because no one in their organizations will support them. While that may be true, that is no reason not to institute planning activities within the publications groups. Jean-Paul Sartre put it very well:

There's only one sin, and that's failing to believe you have a choice.

You always have a choice, especially when your decision affects the way you manage your projects internally. You may not be able to get the support you would like for information planning and Content Specifications from the rest of your organization, but you should do the planning anyway. The planning activities will help you manage your own process and keep your sanity, even when everything around you is chaotic.

On a more optimistic note, you may discover, as some publications project managers have, that your efforts at developing a sound process will be contagious. In one software company, the information plans so impressed a product-development manager that he asked the publications manager to help his development staff develop their own planning tools. In a communications company, the estimating spreadsheets developed by the publications project manager became a model for estimating spreadsheets in the development group. In a worldwide software development company, the entire publications management process was adopted by the publications organization after it was modeled by a single project manager. My impression has been that people are anxious to find ways to create order out of chaos and handle the pressures of shorter deadlines and increased work loads. Introducing a publications-development life cycle, run in parallel to a product-development life cycle, represents a move in the right direction.

An implementation plan for a development life cycle

What if you would like to implement a publications-development life cycle but you don't know where to start? Your goal should be to put the entire process in place eventually. However, you'll discover many benefits in the process even if you decide to start small.

Getting started

To begin implementing a new life-cycle process, consider the following:

- Develop a detailed, annotated Content Specification for your next project.
- Include a user profile and a statement about user goals and tasks, even if these statements are based on untested assumptions (you can always test them later).
- Estimate as thoroughly as possible the size of the publication you are planning by doing a detailed accounting of pages for text and graphics.
- Use this estimate of size to determine the scope of the project and to estimate the number of hours you will need to perform the work (use 5 hours per page as a starting point).
- Track the number of hours it takes you to complete the project.
- Write a wrap-up report that compares the actual hours with the estimated hours and explain why they are different.

Each of these steps is described in detail in Part Three of the book. The first few times you try to create detailed Content Specifications, you may find that you wish you had been more thorough or spent more time understanding the product and its users before you finish the plan. Continue to put more time into the planning process; the complaints from those who don't support planning should gradually settle down to a dull roar.

Work on your estimating. The more practice you get in estimating and the more carefully you track actual hours and schedules, the better you will get at estimating. Be careful that you track the actual hours to compare to the estimates. Unless you know how well you did, you will never be able to improve your estimates. Many beginning project managers make an initial estimate, never track to the estimate, and simply declare at the end that the estimate was completely wrong as usual.

Estimating is a learned skill that profits from repeated practice. Don't neglect the practice. You'll find yourself becoming remarkably good at predicting the course of a project as you increase your understanding of project dynamics within your organization.

Gaining experience

Once you have established a policy of creating detailed Content Specifications and doing project estimates, move to the next stage:

- Add an Information Plan to the process (see Part Two).
- Construct a preliminary Project Plan to implement the Information Plan.

- Define your milestones and establish a milestone schedule.
- During the project, track your milestones until the end of the project and start trying to predict the effects of change on your schedule.
- Write a wrap-up report that accounts for how well you were able to anticipate the effects of change.

At this point, you will have introduced two planning phases and created a more sophisticated milestone-tracking process. The payoff will be that you will feel more in control of your projects, not so much a victim of constant change.

Becoming more sophisticated

With Phases 1 and 2 firmly in place, work on strengthening your management of the implementation process. Phase 3 is most critical for really exerting management control over a project. Lots of people are capable of creating plans, but far fewer are capable of implementing those plans under the pressure of changing circumstances. In many organizations, project managers will be very enthusiastic about planning but they will immediately abandon their plans at the first sign of trouble during implementation.

Lots of backsliding can occur at this point. Managers who optimistically put the first parts of a development process in place may lose heart when faced by the recalcitrance of the rest of the organization and the seemingly endless cycles of uncontrolled change. The tendency is to abandon the planning altogether. The critical message at this point is to

Hang in there.

If you have a good process and you are working hard to manage the process, you will succeed. If you believe that the publications-development process is a sound one and can contribute to building a more successful publications organization, you must stay with it, even in the face of obstacles and disappointments. Eventually, you will find that the project-management process gives you the tools to examine alternatives and make decisions in times of apparent chaos. The control mechanisms won't always work. Sometimes you are simply too inexperienced to invoke them quickly enough. Sometimes you will encounter the opposition of stubborn, egotistical managers who will not listen to reason. But the control mechanisms will work enough of the time, if you have confidence in them and yourself, that you will begin to see the successes and the rewards of consistently high-quality work.

In the next chapter, you will learn more about the relationship between the publications-development life cycle and the maturity level of your publications organization, as well as the maturity level of the rest of the development groups in your larger organization. An examination of your publications organization's maturity level will help you find the most appropriate ways to implement change and institute a fully managed life cycle.

A Process-Maturity Model for Publications Organizations

If we look at many publications organizations today, we find many examples of process gone awry. Deadlines are routinely missed, original schedules are considered impossible, little or no planning occurs, plans that are written are ignored, project management is virtually unknown, and writers madly write and rewrite until someone blows the whistle and insists that the whole mess be shipped to the unwitting customers. This scenario is so common that many technical communicators hardly believe any other is possible.

Yet some organizations do manage to do it better. Do they have extraordinary people? Mysterious influences working on their behalf? Just plain luck? No. They have a development model in place, they believe in planning, and they manage to their plans. We say that these organizations have a more mature process.

An effective and mature process produces results. With a mature process in place, projects are well planned and managed, original schedules and budgets are maintained, changes are made rationally and deliberately, and projects are diligently managed so that everyone knows what is expected of them. The products developed through mature processes are planned to meet the quality expectations of the customers.

If this all sounds like an impossible dream, beyond the reach of ordinary professionals, it is not. If your organization is in the early levels of process maturity, the promise of achieving stability and repeatable quality does sound like a dream. Yet, a more mature process is achievable.

The five-level process-maturity model I present here establishes the goals for a publications organization at each level of maturity.

As you review the maturity model, try to identify where your own organization is placed. If you realize that you are at Level 1 or Level 2, don't be surprised or shocked. The vast majority of technical publications organizations are at the same level. It's alright to be "immature"; it just means that you have a great opportunity to grow. The definitions of each maturity level will give you concrete goals to work on. If you are in a Level 1 organization, struggling with chaos, set your sights on Level 2. You just need to learn what maturity looks and feels like and try on pieces of a more mature model gradually to see how well they meet your organization's needs.

No change is easy, especially not fundamental changes in the way we do business in technical publications. Publications organizations don't work in a vacuum. You are affected by the level of process maturity in your development and marketing organizations. The lower on their own scale of process maturity your developers are, the harder your road will be. But don't be discouraged. The journey is possible and worth taking because the rewards are great.

Joe Duncan, Director of Oracle Forms Development, related a story to his new staff soon after joining the company. The story serves as a metaphor for managing projects as an organic, rather than a scientific, process.

"A gardener looks out at the land behind his house and decides to make a garden there. He could, of course, just go out and start tearing up sod. Maybe he'd tear up sod in a square or a circle or maybe a random sort of shape. Then, he could sprinkle some seeds around and wait to see what grows. That's one way to make a garden.

"But perhaps he's a bit more methodical. Perhaps he makes his decision in February, when it's too early to go out and start digging up sod. But this gardener is from Minnesota, where it once snowed in August, and he knows he has a limited growing season, even if he can't predict exactly when it will end. He also knows that because his time is limited, his hours in February are just as important as his hours in May. He doesn't want to waste them because he knows that hours lost in February can't be made up in May. So in February, he gets out the seed catalogs and begins to plan the garden. Perhaps he's the kind of guy who likes charts and pictures—he starts to sketch out his garden, its shape and size, and what he wants to plant there.

"In addition to being methodical, he is also scientific. He researches what plants grow well beside what other plants. He has the soil tested and decides what he needs to add to support the best growth for the kind of plants he wants. He studies annual rainfall and looks up long-range weather forecasts, deciding when he should plant his crop.

"Then, the spring comes, and he actually begins to work in the garden. Once he's out there, he may find that some of his plans won't work. Perhaps he starts to dig and finds a solid rock under the surface where he'd planned to put the carrots. He couldn't have known this in advance, and it seriously changes his plans. He goes back and redraws his pictures, placing a birdbath there and moving the carrots.

"Once his garden is planted, there are even more factors that affect his success. The rains come, and the winds blow, and some days the sun shines, and some days it doesn't. There is not much he can do about that. He can water if the ground gets dry, at least if there isn't a drought. He can add fertilizer or compost; he can be vigilant about weeding. But just because the garden's planted doesn't mean he can leave it alone to grow. Day by day, he continues to pay close attention to the garden. Maybe there's a bug on one of the plants—he needs to deal with that right away, or it will spread to the rest of the garden.

"And with all this effort, he still enjoys gardening. It takes a lot of work and a lot of attention to detail, but he finds it rewarding. In fact, there's nothing he'd rather do."

Note that the gardener started planning for his metaphorical garden in the snows and cold of February, long before he could even see the ground. He planned for the garden despite the knowledge that some catastrophe could destroy all the plans. A late frost, a hailstorm in July, or a drought is a normal occurrence that might destroy the best-planned garden. Yet, the fear of those challenges and potential failures was not enough to make him forsake the February planning.

When you look around your organization and see writers working long into the night and giving up their weekends to meet deadlines, you may think your February will never end. It can, and it will. Use the process-maturity model as a planning tool.

Take small steps, proceeding with care and deliberation. You will find, sometimes to your great surprise, that you can achieve a new level of maturity and confidence in your organizational strategies.

As you work on the process maturity of your organization, people will notice. The teenager starts acting like an adult, at lease some of the time, and everyone begins to notice. The chaos becomes a little less pervasive; planning becomes more ingrained. You may discover that others in the organization are being quietly influenced by the changes you are making.

Too many technical communicators keep hoping that someone else in the organization will take the lead in planning and implementing new processes. I often hear laments about how "they won't let us plan." It doesn't take permission to improve your own organization. Even though development organizations, especially in high-tech industries, have been and continue to be notoriously bad at planning, you can still make progress in the right direction. Don't worry about changing everyone else; change yourself or your team or your department first.

The maturity level of your publications process is your responsibility. No one else is going to help you improve. In fact, if you operate as if there are no requirements and you have no responsibility for quality, someone may come along and take the job away from you. Using the development and process models in this book as guidelines, set yourself in the right direction and start now.

Five-level publications-maturity model

This publications-maturity model is based on my work with many publications managers and studies of how their organizations operate. It reflects the work of real people in real organizations. It is informed by the work of Crosby (1979), Weinberg (1992), and Humphrey (1989) on the process maturity of organizations in general and software-development organizations in particular.

As I have studied publications organizations, I have found that most are at Level 1 or 2 of process maturity. Only a small number that I have worked with or discussed with senior managers are at Level 3. For the most part, Levels 4 and 5 are theoretical, based upon the most desirable extensions of the three earlier levels. This picture parallels the findings of others who write about process maturity.

The model is itself being refined by additional observations of publications organizations and commentary from their staff members and managers. The refinement will continue as more technical communicators work with the model and report their experiences.

Figure 3.1 summarizes the highlights of the five process-maturity levels. Brief descriptions of each level follow.

Level 1: Ad hoc

A Level 1 organization is best identified by its lack of process. Little planning takes place for publications projects. Most projects begin late in the product-development life cycle, so that little time is available to verify the accuracy or test the quality of the

Level	Description	Publications project management	Transition to the next level
Level 0: Oblivious	Unaware of the need for professionally produced publications. Publications are produced by anyone who is available and has time.	None	Staffing with professional technical communicators
Level 1: Ad hoc	Technical communicators act independently to produce publications with little or no coordination. They may be assigned to different technical managers.	None	Development of a style guide
Level 2: Rudimentary	The beginning pieces of a process are going into place. Some coordination occurs among the technical communicators to assure consistency, but enforcement is not strong.	None to very little	Introduction of some project planning
Level 3: Organized and repeatable	A sound development process is in place and being refined. People are being trained in the process. Project management is in the beginning stages, with senior technical communicators learning the rudiments of estimating and tracking.	Introduction of project management	Strong implementation of project planning
Level 4: Managed and sustainable	Strong project management is in place to ensure that the publications-development process works. Estimating and tracking of projects are thorough, and controls are in place to keep projects within budgets and schedules. Innovation gains importance within the strong existing structure.	Strong commitment to project management	Beginning of the implementation of more effective processes

Figure 3.1   The five levels of publications process maturity

Level	Description	Publications project management	Transition to the next level
Level 5: Optimizing	Everyone on the teams is engaged in monitoring and controlling projects. As a result, effective self-managed teams are becoming the norm. Innovations in the development process are regularly investigated, and the teams have a strong commitment to continuous process improvement.	Strong commitment to project management and institution of self-managed teams	Strong and sustainable commitment to continuous process improvement

Figure 3.1 (Continued)

information. Technical communicators in a Level 1 organization work as independent contributors, primarily directed by managers from a variety of development-related departments. There is little or no teamwork, no quality assurance (editing) except that done voluntarily by individuals, and no project management to maintain control of budgets and schedules.

Level 2: Rudimentary

A Level 2 organization has begun to put the rudiments of a process into place. The first activity is usually to develop style standards for all technical publications, although enforcement may be lax or impossible. Some copyediting may occur. The Level 2 organization moves forward by introducing Information Plans. The plans may be rudimentary, but they represent a major attempt to define the publications goals for a project. Project management is still largely absent, which means that projects are frequently overwhelmed by change. Most of the direction for projects is provided by technical or marketing specialists.

Level 3: Organized and repeatable

A Level 3 organization is clearly in transition toward a fully developed process. Information Plans are standard, and project-management plans are put into place as early as possible. Writers work as teams on complex projects, and all work is edited by specialists in editing. Project managers have a database of experience from previous projects to use as an estimating guide. Projects are estimated carefully, and change is controlled throughout the development process.

Level 3 technical communicators are beginning to recognize that all projects must be planned, especially when the technical content of the project changes frequently. Project managers believe in the management of process and product in Level 3 and begin to recognize that the product will not meet the required quality standards without a strong process in place to guide team members and help them work toward common goals.

Level 4: Managed and sustainable

A Level 4 organization has a well-defined process that is always followed. Yet, on special projects and under increasingly common rapid development, teams have the option of modifying the process so that they can respond to the need for innovation and experimentation. Technical communicators are regular members of the product-development teams from the very beginning of the development life cycle. They begin moving into wider areas of responsibility for the product and process. Project management techniques are well developed, with projects kept under control. Often, there is a division of responsibilities so that specialists handle production, translation, planning, editing, and usability assessment but remain integral members of the technical-communication team.

Level 5: Optimizing

The Level 5 organization is ahead of the curve. Not only are team members doing a good job of managing their projects and producing work of consistently high quality, but they also have the luxury of self-examination. All team members review their own process and institute changes to improve. They introduce quality measurements and promote innovative techniques.

Analyzing your organization

As you analyze your own organization in light of these brief descriptions and the more detailed descriptions that follow, you may notice that many publications organizations exhibit a mix of characteristics. Don't concentrate on the differences. An organization's maturity level is best characterized by its steady-state behavior. You may have had one project in which a technical communicator worked successfully as part of the development team early in the product-development life cycle. However, one instance does not define your organization as Level 4. Look at the publications organization as a whole and over a longer period of time. If you have more than one publications group in your organization, each of them may be at a different level of process maturity.

Figure 3.2 illustrates the journey from Level 1 to Level 5. In the subsequent sections, you will find a creed (general statement of belief), a detailed description of the level, the planning activities inherent in the level, a discussion of the transition events that will carry you to the next level, and a list of typical belief statements.

Note that the communicators climbing over the rocks of Level 1 have the most difficulty reaching the path to a more mature process. In fact, they may not recognize that a path exists or that a sound development process is even possible. At Level 2, an emerging organization at least recognizes that a path exists, although the climb will

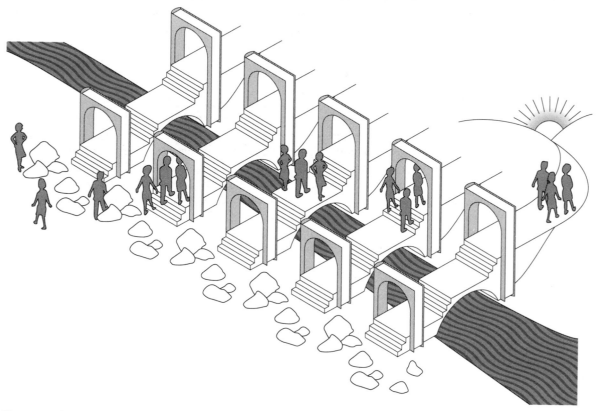

Figure 3.2 A picture of the journey to process maturity

continue to be difficult to reach each succeeding level. But at Level 2, the management and staff are prepared to continue.

Some organizations, however, are in a state of maturity that comes before Level 1. I call this Level 0: Oblivious. Organizations at Level 0 don't even know that the journey exists.

Level 0: Oblivious

> *Creed: We're writing down what we know about the product. We don't even know we're performing a process. We didn't know there was a process.*

Some organizations with a collection of technical writers may find themselves at a lower level of process maturity than Level 1: Ad hoc. I refer to this as Level 0 and label it Oblivious. At Level 0, organizations generally do not have a dedicated staff of technical writers. Rather, the technical documentation is written by product developers, marketing specialists, field engineers, customer-service agents, and others. In most cases, the people who write the documentation are those who consider themselves the product-development experts.

Some development experts are capable of producing readable, usable, and attractive documents for customers. More often, subject-matter experts have neither the time, skills, nor inclination to produce high-quality customer documentation. As a result, the customer documentation produced in Level 0 organizations is inconsistent, generally difficult to use, and of little value to the customers. Often, it contains a collection of information from diverse sources, much of it unchanged from the originals except for occasional formatting. In general, formatting is done either by the subject-matter expert directly or by production clerks.

People in organizations operating at Level 0 frequently feel confident that they are able to produce adequate technical documentation for their customers, especially when the customers have a high degree of technical experience and training. The subject-matter experts believe that they have no need for professional technical communicators. They argue that if they had to explain everything to technical communicators, they would spend just as much time as they currently spend on documentation with no added value. In fact, they are concerned that the accuracy of the documentation might decrease. They often believe that the sole function of technical communicators is to make the documentation look more attractive, an added value that is insufficient to counter their concerns about accuracy, completeness, and the drain on their time.

Problems occur, however, when customers complain that the technical information they receive is difficult to use. They claim that the information is written at too high a level or that it is difficult to find. They also claim that the information is not "task-oriented" enough. This complaint generally means that the customers are not able to navigate through the mass of technical information they have been given because it is badly organized for their needs. In most cases, the information is descriptive rather than instructional.

The transition events from Level 0 to Level 1

At this juncture, two decision points may occur. The Level 0 organization may decide to hire a few technical writers, either directly or by contract, to fix the usability problems and quiet the customer complaints. In most cases, these writers are assigned to work directly for a particular group of development experts. The experts generally hire either a writer who has a very technical background similar to their own or one who has no technical background or experience as a technical writer but who, they believe, may represent the customer's naiveté.

In either case, the results may be unfortunate. If the Level 0 organization is lucky, they succeed in hiring a skilled technical communicator who quickly moves them into

Level 2 or 3 by putting a sound development process into place. If they are unlucky, they hire someone with marginal skills who proceeds to take the experts' original material and reformat it. The information is more attractive but not more usable. If the individual hired is not experienced at learning technical information, the experts' prophecy is fulfilled. It takes considerable time for them to educate the writer in the technology and review the work. Out of frustration at the lack of either technical expertise or expertise in document design, they may even tell the writer exactly how to organize the information and how to write. Meanwhile, the customers continue to be unhappy, their requirements poorly met.

If a Level 0 organization happens to hire a skilled technical communicator, the difference is soon apparent. Not only are the technical publications more attractive, they are also more usable, with task-oriented instructions, supporting descriptive and conceptual information, and good access tools such as indexes, tables of contents, and meaningful headings. If the technical communicator knows something about process and has some project-management skills, the Level 0 organization may even bypass the uncertainties of Level 1 and move immediately into Level 2 or 3.

Of course, it is far easier for the technical communicator to bypass Level 1 if the development organization has its own process in place. If the development organization is itself at Level 1, where individual developers work without process or management, even a communicator with good management skills may find it difficult to overcome the corporate culture. This difficulty will be compounded by the absence of a publications group that is able to support the changes that need to be made to achieve a higher level of process maturity.

In many cases, an organization that moves from Level 0 by hiring a few writers usually emerges as a Level 1 publications organization. However, the more well-trained and skilled the writers hired, the greater the opportunity for the Level 1 writers to begin the task of growing into a Level 2 organization. Therefore, it would be worthwhile for managers in organizations that have no technical communicators to seek out job candidates or independent consultants who have a strong potential for publications management. That means they have the following types of knowledge and experience:

- They are thoroughly familiar with a publications-development life cycle (Phases 1 through 5 or some variation on the life cycle).
- They know how to prepare planning documents for publications projects and value planning activities.
- They can estimate resources needed for publications projects and justify their estimates.
- They want to serve on the development teams and know how to define their roles.
- They are interested in finding out as much as possible about the users of their technical information and the tasks those users perform.

With these skills, communicators entering a Level 0 organization will be able to make quick progress.

The belief statements of Level 0

Here is a list of statements that a Level 0 organization may make about itself.

Writer beliefs:

- Anyone can write.
- Nobody reads manuals anyway, so it doesn't matter how well they're written.
- Everyone writes his or her own documentation.
- Programmers and engineers write user manuals.
- Clerks format and copyedit what programmers and engineers write.
- We "don't know who writes [the manuals]... I suppose it's someone over in Korea" (Wurman, 1992).
- People writing the manuals have no special qualifications or training.

Planning and managing beliefs:

- There is no development process for creating manuals; they're just written.
- There are no standards for the manuals written.
- Everyone writes until they run out of time.

Quality beliefs:

- Everyone's manual is different; individual manuals exhibit different styles.
- Manuals are a conglomeration of disparate pieces of information.
- What we want to know should go into the manuals.

Level 1: Ad hoc

> *Creed: We do whatever we feel like at the moment.*

The simplest transition from Level 0: Oblivious is to Level 1: Ad hoc. While the Level 0 organization has few if any technical communicators, the Level 1 organization has a staff of individual contributors who largely work alone or under the control of the development teams. The individual communicators in a Level 1 organization may be talented and produce high-quality work, but they do not work together. Consequently, a Level 1 organization ordinarily has no standards that reach across project boundaries. Even individual projects may not display a standard approach if there is more than one

Figure 3.3 In the rocks of Level 1

writer involved. From their vantage point in the rocks, the writers at Level 1, shown in Figure 3.3, are often not aware the higher levels of process maturity are possible.

The individual communicators rarely have any degree of support to get their jobs done. Their need for specialized equipment or supplies is not recognized. Management assumes that they can function with the same type of support provided for people doing entirely different jobs.

Writers in a Level 1 organization are frequently responsible for all project activities. They are expected to handle their own editing, electronic publishing, illustration, and transference of information to electronic sources. Because Level 1 writers succeed by being strong individual contributors, they often take great pride in being able to handle all project activities on their own. They see no great need for specialization and often believe that having others handle some aspects of their project will simply slow them down and jeopardize quality. Level 1 writers often have strong convictions that the way they currently work is the correct way to work and that their standards of quality are the only standards.

The individual writers working independently in a Level 1 organization may themselves adhere to standards they have learned working in other organizations or from their industry networks. However, it is just as likely that the individual contributors will work toward personal standards, which may be uninformed by industry-wide practices. Publications produced by the individual contributors will often not be organized, written, or formatted in a uniform manner.

The place of the planning process in Level 1

If planning occurs in a Level 1 organization, it will again result from the work of individual contributors. In any collection of technical writers, a few will be interested in producing document plans or detailed outlines. Some development managers may even require that outlines be approved before documents are written. However, if the technical writers are not familiar with planning processes themselves, then little planning will occur.

Even with some rudimentary planning in place by individual contributors, Level 1 organizations will have a marked absence of project management. In fact, many people in a Level 1 organization will argue that project management is unnecessary or impossible to institute. Because their publications projects are generally chaotic, Level 1 writers often feel strongly that it is not possible to estimate the scope of projects or to set schedules in advance. They simply work hard to meet their immediate responsibilities. They have little idea in advance of whether a project can be completed at the quality level they have assumed for themselves.

In Level 1 organizations, quality levels are internally established by individual contributors. There is no external standard of quality nor any measurement of the quality of technical publications. All reviews that take place are conducted by development experts who focus on accuracy and completeness. Frequently, the development experts dictate the level of quality in technical publications based largely upon their own personal concepts of accuracy and completeness.

Although individual writers in a Level 1 organization may be personally concerned about the needs of the customers, they have little opportunity to understand customer requirements independently. Others in the larger organization believe they can explain enough about the audience from their perspectives to satisfy the requirements of the communicators.

Most Level 1 publications organizations exist within Level 1 product-development organizations. Consequently, little or no project planning occurs outside the publications group. Product development itself is often chaotic, with little scheduling or estimating. Most projects experience considerable cost and schedule overruns.

With publications under the direction and control of people who are not communication professionals, a Level 1 organization frequently continues to produce a set of technical manuals that were often defined in the Level 0 days. These publications are often large, although largely ineffective in meeting the needs of customers. Little thought is given to their usability or to the usability of the product. Testing, if it does occur, focuses strictly on technical accuracy.

The role of the publications manager in Level 1

Level 1 organizations may have a departmental manager, called a publications manager. The publications manager is responsible for the administration of the department but not for the management of projects. The manager hires new communicators, conducts performance reviews, handles vacations and sick leave, fires when necessary, and gives out assignments to individual writers but does not directly review the work of writers for compliance to standards or engage in any project planning or control activities. In many cases, the publications manager knows little about the individual projects to which the writers are assigned.

A publications manager in a Level 1 organization often has substantial responsibility for the coordination of the production phase of the publications activities. This means locating printing, translation, binding, and packaging vendors; contributing to contract negotiations; and overseeing the outside work in general. The manager may also contract for special services such as illustration, graphic art, or indexing, but the contractors doing the work are directed by the individual writers.

Because of personal interest in controlling projects, some individual contributors in the organization may take on project-management responsibilities for large projects. In many instances, these individuals are viewed as troublemakers who are trying to change things. Since they lack the resources to track and plan, get little (if any) positive response for planning activities from the development organizations, and are often not supported by their own management, individuals interested in a more managed process often leave the organization.

When they choose to remain, they work hard on the transition events and try to change the organization from the bottom, a difficult proposition in most cases and especially difficult in a Level 1 development organization.

The transition events from Level 1 to Level 2

The events that trigger the move from a Level 1 to a Level 2 organization often occur with the introduction of a catalyst from outside the organization. This catalyst may take on a variety of identities: a new publications manager, a writer from outside who has vastly different experiences, or even a new senior manager who decides that technical publications should be more organized. The greatest success in instituting the changes required to become a Level 2 organization is achieved when the change is inaugurated by management and wins the support of the staff members.

Sometimes, when a new manager takes over the organization, innovative team members are encouraged to attend outside conferences or seminars in which standards and documentation planning are discussed. They become convinced that planning will be worth the trouble, especially when it appears that they have the support of their management. In other cases, the new management brings in an outside consultant to educate team members in a new process.

When new processes are introduced from the outside, a division often occurs between those who were happy as Level 1 writers and value their independence from any standards or controls and those who are willing to sacrifice a little independence for some freedom from chaos. In many cases, the transition to Level 2 means that some members of the team leave the organization because they are unable to make the transition. Or the reluctant team members are allowed to work on their own special projects or are moved to maintenance writing.

One of the first transition activities taken on by a Level 1 organization is the development of publications standards. As standards are being developed, the need for someone to assume responsibility for the standards is often recognized. This recognition results in the hiring of an editor to educate the team members and enforce the standards. Often, however, this editing activity takes place late in the development cycle and only at the level of mechanical copyediting.

The belief statements of Level 1

Here is a list of statements that a Level 1 organization may make about itself.

Writer beliefs:

- We have appointed some people as official technical writers.
- We can't think of any training they need; they already know how to write.
- The technical writers only need to know word processing and desktop publishing.
- The technical writers only clean up what the engineers write, so they don't need to know anything about the product.
- The software or hardware already provides a perfectly good organization for the information. Just follow the screens.
- All writers need are the product specifications.
- Writers don't need to know the users.
- The writers don't need to have access to a working model of the system.

Engineering and marketing beliefs:

- The engineers and marketing will tell the writers what they need to know about the users.
- Nobody reads the manuals anyway, so it doesn't matter how well they're written.
- Nobody reviews the drafts carefully or at all until the last minute.
- The engineers are too busy to be interviewed.
- We can document the product directly from the code; we don't need writers (a fallback to Level 0).

Planning and managing beliefs:

- We don't write documentation plans; topic outlines are good enough, but we don't follow them. The final manuals never look like the outlines anyway.
- We don't estimate because each of our projects is unique. Our estimates are never correct anyway, so we don't need to try to make them more accurate.
- We just keep writing until we get it right, but we don't know what "right" is.
- We don't track our projects because we don't want to know what they really cost.
- We don't want to estimate because we really don't want to know that we can't do the project in the amount of time allotted.

- We'll do whatever it takes to get the job done, working late hours and weekends.
- Schedules are unpredictable because every project is unique and every writer is unique.

Quality beliefs:

- Our own quality standards are more important than the customers' (internal or external).
- It's important to have the grammar and formatting correct, even if the information is mostly wrong or unverified.
- The publications manager isn't supposed to monitor what the writers are writing.
- The writers don't need editing or reviewing by management; they're all stars.
- The only reviews needed are those done by the technical experts.
- The writers should perform all the tasks themselves; they don't need graphic artists or production specialists.

Level 2: Rudimentary

> *Creed: We follow our routines (except when we panic).*

A Level 2 organization often faces a difficult transition. Team members have begun to believe that something is better than the utter chaos of Level 1, but they are not sure what that improvement will look and feel like. In fact, the changes may be so difficult for some of the individual contributors of Level 1 that they either leave the organization or agitate against the change. If the rest of the organization is at Level 1, the reluctant team members may be successful in returning the publications organization to Level 1. They inform development members and managers that technical publications is wasting its time on lots of planning and that projects are taking longer as a result. If they are influential enough, they may persuade the developers to take action to eliminate the publications-management organization and reassign writers to individual projects.

Figure 3.4 illustrates the communicators on the first steps in their journey toward a higher level of process maturity.

If the managers who are trying to build a Level 2 organization are prepared and have established their own support in the larger organization, they may be successful in overcoming the forces resisting change. They may find that they will have to spend considerable time and effort convincing team members that the changes will be positive and will make their jobs simpler, not more difficult.

As the managers continue to put a publications process in place, they will find that the convincing becomes more difficult. When everyone is simply engaged in developing

Figure 3.4 On the first steps toward Level 2

standards, most of the staff will support the effort. Publications standards, especially if they agree with the personal standards of team members, may even be welcomed as a way to bring some control over other team members who are not as standards-oriented. Some Level 1 writers view standards as a means to enforce their own opinions about how publications should be written. When the forces for change move from editing and formatting standards to planning, the degree of resistance may increase.

The place of the planning process in Level 2

One of the first steps toward a publications process in an emerging Level 2 organization is the development of Information Plans or Content Specifications. This document is often a combination of some portions of the planning tools that I label Information Plan and Content Specification in Chapter 2. Usually, the documentation plan contains a description of the project and an outline of the document to be produced. Sometimes, the plan includes a brief description of the audience, as well as the production requirements and the engineering schedule that must be met. The plan ordinarily contains no business case for the publications, no independent assessment of the audience requirements, and no estimate of the size of the job.

Rudimentary plans of this sort are often written by the individual writers and briefly reviewed and filed by the publications manager. Since project management is not well understood in an emerging Level 2 organization, it is rarely put in place at the same time as the initiation of document plans. As a result, no one estimates the size of the project or the resources required to complete the project. No schedules are estimated independent of the product-development schedule, and no quality goals are set. In fact, much of the structure of Level 1 remains, although writers are now told to create a plan and their work is reviewed for conformance to departmental standards.

In general, documentation plans are created, but they have little impact on the course of the project, primarily because of the lack of project management. Since no estimates are made, there are no estimates to measure progress against. The only parts of the process that are in place are the rudimentary planning activities, but with no enforcement of the process, the plans may simply be written and ignored.

Nonetheless, the most enthusiastic team members are beginning to succeed in having planning taken seriously. Those who are not overwhelmed by change become advocates for the new system, introducing the plans to their product developers and using increasingly more detailed plans as guidelines. The most innovative team members may recognize the need to track time and level of activity on their projects as they begin to function as project managers.

Many of the team members, as they learn about the planning process from seminars, conferences, and consultants, begin to decry the fact that they have little opportunity to understand the needs of their audiences. They want to have time to conduct user studies and visit customer sites, but they are so overwhelmed by schedule demands and so busy handling everyday crises of completing the publications that they simply cannot find the time.

The most reluctant team members continue to believe that planning is a waste of time and work hard to avoid it. They are vehemently against more planning and insist that projects like theirs cannot be estimated and scheduled rationally. They would like to know more about their users but dismiss that as an impossible dream and really not part of their responsibilities. They are satisfied that the engineers and marketing specialists can tell them enough about the audiences for them to write the kinds of publications they have always written. They may insist that their audiences are technically astute and will easily understand the level of information in the current documentation.

The more enthusiastic team members still feel strongly controlled by the product developers although they are beginning to see some opportunities for influencing their own destinies. The Information Plans are a start. They want to begin their publications project earlier so that they can influence the quality of the product and make it easier to explain. They are beginning to recognize that the documentation they have been creating all these years is probably very difficult for the customers to use. However, they are much more convinced that the product is difficult to use and that their documentation is the one saving grace in a vast wasteland of disregard for the customer. They would like to include usability goals and actually measure usability, but they see little opportunity to do so in the immediate future.

Because the individual writers are still responsible for all aspects of the publications process, they still have a tendency to view concepts such as audience analysis, planning, and usability testing as too time-consuming and expensive. In this view, they are often supported by those in the larger organization who consider the technical publications to be a "necessary evil" that adds no real value to the product.

The role of the publications manager in Level 2

The publications manager in a Level 2 organization may, at first, greatly resemble the manager in a Level 1 organization. This manager performs primarily administrative tasks and oversees production. As the Level 2 organization matures, the publications manager takes on an increasingly important role in building and implementing a publications-development process.

In many cases, the publications manager leads the effort to institute changes and create a more reliable process. In fact, without some leadership from the publications manager, the institution of a new process is unlikely to succeed. But the manager need not do all the work. With the support of strong team members, the manager need only oversee the process and provide leadership. The team members can handle the details.

A publications manager can also derail efforts toward becoming a strong Level 2 organization by panicking when problems occur. If the manager is not personally convinced of the importance of a new process and its ultimate effectiveness, the manager may hesitate at the least sign of resistance from the larger organization. This hesitation may take the form of agreeing to implement the new processes only if the product-development manager does not complain. If the development managers complain, the publications manager may retreat from the process.

The publications manager also has to guard carefully against letting the process deteriorate when schedules change and activities become increasingly chaotic. Abandoning a process under crisis conditions is taking the worst course. The mark of an effective process is that you rely on it to guide decision making in a crisis. If the manager allows the team to abandon the process, the manager demonstrates little trust in the process in the first place. The most reluctant team members will be vindicated; the enthusiastic team members will be disappointed and begin to distrust the process and the manager.

The best work that a publications manager can do in moving a publications organization firmly into Level 2 and forward into Level 3 is to stay with the planning process. The manager must work hard to educate team members and reinforce their determination even in the face of a crisis. Certainly, the manager should be prepared to admit that the establishment of a sound process will take time. The team is likely to experience setbacks as well as successes. Leadership sometimes requires that you have to admit you don't always know what you're doing. But leadership also requires that you keep working on the process improvements.

The transition events from Level 2 to Level 3

To make the transition from Level 2 to Level 3, a publications organization requires strong leadership. Frequently, it is a new publications manager or a team of senior team members who encourage and facilitate the commitment to process and planning that strongly distinguishes the two levels. A Level 2 organization that decides to add project management, publish and enforce standards, and educate everyone in the use of planning documents has the most success in establishing a more mature process.

To be successful, team members at Level 2 need to develop the confidence that a sound process will result in consistently higher-quality publications and a more sustainable personal lifestyle. They must believe that order is possible even amid chaos and crisis. With practice, the planning process will grow more firm, and team members will grow more confident in their commitment to it.

In addition, as a Level 2 organization experiences more successes in its own planning processes, the staff will begin to educate others in the larger organization about the value of planning. I have seen publications organizations moving from Level 2 to Level 3 become catalysts for change in their larger organizations. Those product-development managers who are interested in changing their own processes may find that the processes initiated in publications can become a model for their change needs as well.

The belief statements of Level 2

Here is a list of statements that a Level 2 organization may make about itself.

Writer beliefs:

- All writers manage their own projects.
- All writers take full responsibility for their assigned publications, including doing their own editing and production.
- Many writers do their own illustrations.
- Writers are supposed to prepare Information Plans but can never get the developers or marketing to review them or take them seriously.
- Writers prepare Information Plans, but projects change so much that we cannot really follow the plans.
- Some writers believe it is a waste of time to prepare Information Plans.

Engineering and marketing beliefs:

- We put all the required information in the Information Plan, but the developers and marketing define who the audiences are and what to tell them about the products.
- We would like to know more about our audiences, but no one will give us time to study them.
- We can usually guess what our users need.
- Our users are just like us.

Planning and managing beliefs:

- We write outlines instead of Content Specifications, but we don't really follow them in the final documents.
- The Information Plans and Content Specifications are unnecessary busy work that keeps us from our real work of preparing drafts.

- We don't have to write down our Content Specifications or even our outlines because we do all our planning in our heads.
- We don't need management review of our plans because we know what we're supposed to do (a fallback to Level 1).
- We sometimes estimate projects, but the estimates often don't mean anything and are usually wrong.
- Our projects change too much to estimate.
- We sometimes track our projects, but tracking does not give us much information and can be a great waste of writing time.
- We keep to our milestone schedules, but we turn in whatever we have done when the milestone date arrives because we have never defined the milestone requirements.
- Planning is really not important; we have really good writers who are so experienced that they do not need to plan.

Quality beliefs:

- Our own quality standards are more important, but we'd like to know what the customers think.
- It's important to have the grammar and formatting correct, but we are trying to find time to verify what we write.
- The publications manager is beginning to monitor what the writers are planning and writing.
- The writers are beginning to get some editing and reviewing by management.
- The writers still perform all the tasks themselves, but we are interested in the possibility of using graphic artists or production specialists.

Level 3: Organized and repeatable

> *Creed: We always follow our routines because they work, and they get us through the crises.*

In a Level 3 organization, technical communicators consider themselves to be well organized. They have a sound publications-development process in place; they use it under all circumstances. They have moved from working as individual contributors to working in teams, with the support of a skilled project manager. If they work alone on smaller projects, they themselves have responsibility for project-management activities. They have achieved an important plateau of success in their journey toward higher levels of process maturity, as illustrated in Figure 3.5. Many publications organizations remain at Level 3.

Figure 3.5   On the plateau of Level 3

The development process is important to all team members because they are convinced that it guarantees the quality of their publication products. Their processes are sound and repeatable. Publication quality is no longer dependent upon the individual skills of superwriters; it is something that everyone in the organization has a role in achieving. Writers, editors, illustrators, and production specialists are beginning to recognize that teamwork counts heavily in an efficient organization. They no longer believe it is more efficient to do everything themselves.

In driving the development of the publications-development process in a Level 3 organization, the project manager often assumes a significant role. The manager advocates and supports the development of a strong publications-development process and begins to put into place a project-management system. The development process is considered reliable and is always relied upon, especially under crisis circumstances.

The place of the planning process in Level 3

If team members collected some project-tracking data in Level 2 activities, the project managers now have in place a rudimentary database of previous projects. As a result, they are able to estimate new projects more accurately and develop achievable milestone schedules. This ability to estimate and schedule has begun to convince the less cooperative team members of the effectiveness of "all this management stuff."

The project managers are given the responsibility of monitoring changes to their schedules and requirements carefully so that they can plan their responses. However, they still often feel victimized by the schedule chaos in the rest of the organization. They are working hard to communicate the importance of good scheduling and change-control procedures.

The project managers are most seriously committed to the front-end planning process at this stage in process maturity. They always produce Information Plans and Content Specifications to serve as development and project-management guides. They believe that planning activities are beginning to bear fruit by giving them more control over their team's activities.

In a Level 3 organization, project managers are still working hard at gaining credibility for the publications-development process with the developers and marketing people, as well as with their own team members. They are willing to spend time analyzing audiences and tasks so that they can design more targeted and useful publications, but they cannot always obtain the resources for the front-end analysis or the support of their own management.

At Level 3, some progress is being made to involve technical communicators on the product-development teams. Some teams that have more enlightened and innovative project managers are happy to include them. Other development teams still contact the publications group at the last minute, well after the product designs have been solidified.

To respond to the requirements of a sound publications-development process, Level 3 project managers are working with their publications managers to establish specialist positions for developmental editing and production. They are still faced, however, with senior management requirements that all team members perform all activities except for management. The project managers would prefer to use their most senior team members for design and planning activities, especially to gain a better understanding of the customers.

The technical publications group continues to have a credibility problem in the larger organization. There is still some talk of publications as a "necessary evil." However, some marketing and development managers are committed to including effective publications with their products, even though saving money is still viewed as more important than quality in meeting customer requirements.

The interest in usability testing is growing in a Level 3 organization, although often in an informal and sometimes ineffective way. Sometimes, Level 3 staff members believe that they are doing usability testing when they verify the publications against the products or invite colleagues to test their procedures. As a Level 3 organization gains experience with publications development, they may do some initial usability tests with actual representatives of the user community.

The role of the publications manager in Level 3

In a Level 3 organization, the publications manager has a strong role in maintaining the publications-development process. That maintenance means making education and training opportunities available for all staff members, working closely with the project managers to develop their skills, working with them to handle personnel problems, and generally overseeing the activities of others and helping them to handle crises. Many of the project managers in an emerging Level 3 organization are inexperienced and need regular coaching and peer review to become more effective.

The publications manager is involved in the day-to-day management of projects from the position of overseer. That means ensuring that the processes take place according to plan. Probably the most significant role is leadership in finding new ways to innovate and better meet the needs of the customers. The publications manager, as the primary liaison with upper management, has the task of acquiring additional opportunities for customer involvement and promoting the goals of the project managers and team members. Often the manager is responsible for advocating the following: adding communicators to the development teams, starting the publications project in tandem with product development, and finding the resources for usability testing.

An effective publications manager will assume a public relations role for the communication team, promoting their successes and helping to keep problems from becoming disasters.

Perhaps the greatest danger in Level 3 is for the publications manager to become complacent. The processes are working; customers are reasonably satisfied; everything seems to be working well. However, trouble may be brewing in other parts of the organization, especially when the larger organization is suspicious of planning activities (Level 1 or 2). In such situations, the publications manager may be attacked by forces that want to reduce the cost of publications or believe that publications take too much time.

In Level 3, the entire publications organization may itself become complacent. This complacency often results from success with the development process. Instead of using the development process as an opportunity to explore innovative responses to customer and business needs, the publications organization insists that its process be followed no matter what else is occurring around them. They become stuck in the process, using it as a weapon to stifle innovation rather than promote it. When the process becomes too overwhelming in a Level 3 organization, team members spend all their time with paperwork and too little time thinking about design and working with users and developers to better understand their needs.

For the publications manager to keep the process from dominating all innovative thinking requires discipline and continued leadership. The manager needs a vision, perhaps a vision of a Level 4 organization, to keep the publications-development process from becoming overly bureaucratic.

The transition events from Level 3 to Level 4

The transition from Level 3 to Level 4 often occurs when the value of project management continues to prove itself and team members begin to trust the processes. In many cases, a team of strong, well-trained project managers leads the way, with senior staff members following close behind.

A danger exists for an organization to get stuck in Level 3, however. This problem often occurs under the influence of continuous project crises, where poor management of the development process results in confusion and failures. If the process fails often enough under pressure, then team members may begin to believe that it is not worth following. This problem is especially serious for publications organizations that try to introduce process in larger organizations that fail to value planning and process in product development.

The transition to Level 4 comes through leadership and confidence. The publications-development process works so reliably that team members can begin to innovate, changing the process to respond to changing product-development models. The team is beginning to understand the nature of the business decisions that take place to keep a company profitable and customers satisfied. They begin to learn how to participate in these business decisions without sacrificing the quality of technical publications. By participating in development teams, they begin to take more responsibility for the usability of the publications and the product. They begin to look for ways to target publications more thoroughly and avoid giving customers more information than they need.

Note

Many independent publications developers and consulting organizations have learned to operate at Level 3, with a strong sense of process and the effective use of project management in their projects. The use of a sound publications-development process is essential for keeping projects on schedule and within budget. Without a sound process, a consulting organization is likely to lose money on most projects it conducts.

It is difficult, however, for a consulting organization to maintain Level 3 processes under all circumstances. Because consulting organizations frequently must work with clients who do not understand the process and involve them only late in the product-development cycle, they often have to function at Level 2, where they use as much of the process as possible to keep the project under control. Because they have little opportunity to start early, influence the product developers, or establish a sound process with their short-term clients, they often have to respond to the constantly changing demands of a project, not by abandoning their processes, but by keeping controls stronger than ever. These controls are maintained even though the product-development effort may make some of their most reliable design activities impossible to conduct.

As a result of these difficulties, consulting organizations work hard to educate their clients and to help them understand that they can reduce costs and improve quality by involving the technical-communication teams as early as possible. Unfortunately, many development organizations that use outside consultants for technical-publications development believe they save money by ignoring publications needs until the last minute.

The belief statements of Level 3

Here is a list of statements that a Level 3 organization may make about itself.

Writing beliefs:

- We have begun to study our users through site visits, telephone interviews, and surveys.
- We are still surprised when our users know less than we thought or use publications differently than we had hoped.

- Writers are responsible for their own investigations, but they frequently work on teams and share ideas and knowledge.
- Writers are beginning to engage in peer editing and sharing responsibility for some of the implementation processes.

Engineering and marketing beliefs:

- When changes to a product are considered, the developers ask what the impact on the documentation will be.
- Engineers and marketing specialists work together with the publications group to plan. They are no longer encouraged to dictate the content of the publications.
- We are starting to be invited to participate on development teams, although participation is still a novelty and depends upon the individual development manager.
- We are not sure that the rest of the organization understands the importance of the publications as part of the project, but we are working to educate them.

Planning and managing beliefs:

- Every project has a designated project manager, although it is often one of the writers.
- The quality of our project management is inconsistent.
- There is no training in project management, but we are interested.
- We would never start a project without a thorough and complete Information Plan.
- We manage our projects according to the requirements defined in the Information Plans and Content Specifications.
- Everyone on the publications team is committed to the planning process and using the plans as their personal project guides.
- We estimate all our projects and track the projects carefully.
- We have a database of previous projects and keep statistics on all projects.
- We have begun to put control procedures into place.
- We keep to our schedules, although we sometimes fall back into a crisis mode when changes come fast and furious.
- In many cases, we are still victims of someone else's version of the schedule.
- We handle schedule changes with care but are sometimes overwhelmed by their number and lateness.

Quality beliefs:

- We usually try to verify the documentation we write for accuracy and completeness.
- We are beginning to think about instituting usability testing but are concerned about its impact on budget and schedules.
- We are beginning to move from copyediting to developmental editing, but it's still experimental.
- We really believe in developmental editing, but we cannot always get the resources we need to bring in editing specialists.
- If we cannot have developmental editors, we do as much peer editing as we can manage.
- Sometimes we get stuck in our process, and we are not always innovative.

Level 4: Managed and sustainable

> *Creed: We believe in managed projects. Every project is managed, and the development processes are part of our culture.*

My primary difficulty in describing Level 4 and 5 organizations is lack of direct experience. Although I have found individual project managers who are operating at Level 4, I have not found entire organizations working at these levels regularly. Even in some of the top consulting organizations, Levels 4 and 5 are difficult to achieve given the state of most client publications and development organizations. It is rarely possible to promote the long-term involvement in quality that results in a permanent improvement in the process and continuing flexibility. Only occasionally, and then only in the most innovative organizations, are consulting companies able to do the best, most innovative publications work they are capable of doing.

In a Level 4 organization, team members have a strong and sustainable process in place to develop high-quality technical publications that meet customer needs. The publications-development life cycle has been built into the product-development life cycle and is taken seriously by marketing and development managers. They have moved from the plateau of Level 3 and are climbing toward a strong and sustainable process, as illustrated in Figure 3.6.

Members of a Level 4 organization regularly participate on development teams and are considered credible and valued additions. The experienced communicators help with the design of product interfaces or plan how the information will be communicated. Technical publications themselves are considered an integral part of the product and are planned in tandem with other aspects of the product. Some members of senior management consider high-quality technical publications an important strategic advantage.

The stronger members of the publications team take on a public-relations role with others in the organization. Other members of the team are learning this important role and working on their communication skills.

The place of the planning process in Level 4

Project management is a key to the success of a Level 4 organization. Project managers lead every project to ensure that process and standards are maintained. Managers have a number of significant roles, from liaison with internal customers to training new team members in the organization's values and processes. Project managers have significant responsibility for keeping costs under control and managing to their budgets. However, they are beginning to educate their team members about the cost of operation. As a result, the publications organization is beginning to gain credibility with senior management as a full partner in the organization's business.

Figure 3.6 On the journey to Level 4

The teams are interested in controlling their own destinies rather than having them dictated by management from other parts of the organization. As a result, they work hard to communicate about their processes and make the professional quality of their work more visible.

The division of labor into areas of specialization is strongly apparent, although the team members are beginning to cross-train, especially in developmental editing. Development reviews take place from the earliest point in the publications-development life cycle and occur at each major milestone.

The project managers in a Level 4 organization are concerned about the high costs of translation and localization of the publications they produce. As a result they are beginning to investigate ways of reducing the size of hardcopy publications and communicating more information through electronic means. They do not wait for their internal developers and managers to insist on cost reductions before they initiate their own studies. They also recognize that international markets are gaining significance to their larger organizations, and they are preparing to respond to more diverse customer needs.

As a result of their commitment to satisfying customer needs, a Level 4 organization has begun to make a strong commitment to usability testing of its publications. They remain concerned about the impact of testing on budgets and schedules because testing often occurs late in the development life cycle. However, their forays into usability testing have been especially successful in demonstrating the importance of usable design to the larger organization. Their concern for usability affects both product interface and publications.

The role of the publications manager in Level 4

In a Level 4 organization, the manager maintains a leadership role, encouraging innovation, educating new project managers, monitoring the individual development of team members, and ensuring that processes are working effectively. In addition, the publications manager continues a public relations role within the larger organization, ensuring that the publications organization continues to be well represented to senior management. The manager is also responsible for translating the requirements of senior management back to the publications organization so that they do not lose touch with the direction the business is taking.

To help the organization move toward Level 5, the publications manager institutes continuous process improvement at the highest levels. Nothing about the publications-development process is sacred. Every aspect of the job needs to be examined continually. With the leadership of the publications manager, the organization finds better ways to meet customer needs.

The transition events from Level 4 to Level 5

The trigger event that encourages an organization to move from Level 4 to Level 5 is not as clear as in less mature levels. Rather, the transition is gradual as the Level 4 organization develops a consistency of approach that begins to allow time for reflection. Nonetheless, the transition requires that a Level 4 organization has achieved considerable stability in its practices and is known for the high quality of its product.

The transition to Level 5 may never occur, especially if a Level 4 organization becomes rigid. At both Level 3 and Level 4, a rigid approach to process is always a danger when management becomes increasingly afraid of innovation and change. In fact, a Level 3 or 4 organization may become so rigid and inflexible in meeting its organization's needs that senior management dissolves the organization, causing it to revert to Level 1 or 2. The publications organization is decentralized, and the cycle begins anew.

The belief statements of Level 4

Here is a list of statements that a Level 4 organization may make about itself.

Writer beliefs:

- Our communicators are able to measure the percentage complete of their projects with considerable accuracy.
- We do everything we did at Level 3, but we are more convinced than ever of the value of planning.

- We have project managers who estimate, track, and monitor our projects, but all our communicators assume responsibility for meeting their schedules and tracking their own time and effort.

Engineering and marketing beliefs:

- We are equal partners with the developers, and our contributions are respected.
- We always participate on the development teams.
- The publications life cycle supports and is an integral part of the product life cycle.
- Publications requirements are taken seriously as part of project planning as a whole.
- Publications are considered an integral part of the product and may represent a strategic advantage to the company.

Planning and managing beliefs:

- Our project managers are getting the training they need to understand their roles and perform effectively.
- The role of the project manager is clearly defined and well understood.
- We would never consider doing an unplanned project.
- Our projects meet their budgets and schedules.
- We make changes to our projects by estimating their costs versus their benefits.
- We understand our organization's need to keep costs under control, and we are learning more about our role in cost containment.

Quality beliefs:

- We are committed to developmental editing, as well as copyediting.
- Usability testing and other assessment tools are becoming an integral part of our process.
- We are thoroughly committed to understanding our users and their needs.
- Our staff members frequently visit customers sites and participate in interviews and surveys of our users.
- We're learning how to be innovative and not let the process control us.

Level 5: Optimizing

> *Creed: We are finding ways to improve our process and our products to better serve customer needs.*

Organizations at Level 5 do everything in Level 4 to maintain a sound, managed publications-development process, but managers and staff members have processes so finely tuned that they have the leisure to stand back and look carefully at improving those processes. Level 5 managers work at finding better ways to manage, especially through encouraging the establishment of self-managed teams. They are attuned to the need for continuous process improvement, as illustrated in Figure 3.7.

Figure 3.7 On the path of continuous process improvement

In addition to fine-tuning management processes, the technical communicators in a Level 5 organization have time to explore innovative techniques. They invite team members who are interested to develop technological specialities by getting the training they need. Even though specialties are encouraged, a strong team approach gives a Level 5 organization considerable flexibility. In many cases, the technical communicators work in a cooperative and supportive manner that is most reminiscent of the work style of the medical operating room. A group of fully trained professionals cooperates by supporting one another to develop the best possible information products.

In some ways reminiscent of a Level 1 organization, the professional communicators on the team serve as consultants and members of development teams. But Level 5 differs from Level 1 in that each technical communicator embraces and communicates the values of the publications organization as a whole.

The belief statements of Level 5

Here is the list of statements that a Level 5 organization may make about itself.

Writer beliefs:

- We have an organizational structure that is heavily matrixed and cross-trained.
- We believe in a division of labor among specialists but can support one another as needed.
- Our people know how to work effectively with all types of internal and external customers.
- Our team members are diversifying and assuming many different types of responsibilities on the development teams, especially interface design and usability.

Engineering and marketing beliefs:

- We are viewed as a team of professionals by others in the organization.

Planning and managing beliefs:

- We have had a very strong publications-development process in place for some time.
- We are committed to project management; however, so many of our people are good at project management that we're moving to more self-managed teams.
- We are looking at new project-management models so that we have a better way to manage complex projects.

Quality beliefs:

- We are always working to improve our development process.
- We have developed a strong partnership with our users.
- We are fully committed to usability assessment, but we are working to move the assessment processes to positions earlier in the life cycle.
- We are finding more time in our schedules for innovation.

Managing in chaotic environments

What happens in a publications organization that is trying to institute a process when the larger organization does not itself believe in planning? What happens when you are trying to develop Level 3 process maturity when the rest of your company is happily in Level 1 in its product-development process? What happens when the company is bought, sold, or reorganized and all the managers are eliminated?

The tenets of quality management remind you to change what you are capable of changing rather than worrying about changing everyone else. If you are trying to manage in a chaotic environment, do whatever you can to change your own processes. In time, the larger organization may recognize the possibility of process change as well.

In a chaotic environment, planning is your only protection. Use it effectively.

The Roles of the Project Manager

A project manager is like the conductor of an orchestra. The conductor sets the tempo, ensuring that all the musicians are working together at the same rate and going in the same direction. The conductor assumes that all the musicians are proficient in playing their individual instruments and know their individual parts, but need leadership to work together most effectively. Although the conductor knows something about playing each of the individual instruments, he or she is not a specialist in any one of them. However, the conductor knows what each musician is capable of producing with his or her instrument. Finally, the conductor envisions how all the individual sounds must fit together to result in a pleasing whole that delights the audience.

If your goal is to be an effective project manager, think about the role of the conductor. You must understand the score, know each of the individual roles intimately, understand the capabilities and weaknesses of each member of your team, and be able to encourage them in their best work. You must also know when to start a project and when to stop, and be able to monitor every possible milestone in between. You must be constantly aware of all the details so that you can tell exactly when something goes wrong or strays from the initial plan. You must control the response to outside demands for change, dampening the effect of management, development, and marketing people on your team so that they can continue to produce their best work.

"Project management is the process of managing, allocating, and timing resources to achieve the desired goals of a project in an efficient and expedient manner. The objectives that constitute the desired goal are normally a combination of time, cost, and performance requirements" (Badiru, 1993). Badiru's definition implies two goals for project management. The first is the efficient and effective operation of the project itself, in terms of handling your resources carefully. The second goal relates to performance. Not only is it important for a project manager to ensure that a project is completed efficiently, within budget, and on schedule. You must also ensure that the people working on the project perform effectively. The more effectively your team members perform, the easier you will find them to manage.

Like the conductor of an orchestra, a project manager is a leader, encouraging every member of the team to do the best job they are able to do. To lead your team in the development of high-quality publications, you must ensure that

- Your goals are well defined in meeting the information needs of the users and the performance requirements of your organization.

- Your specific project objectives are made concrete through a detailed and comprehensive specification of the project's scope.
- Your project's scope is communicated effectively to those who control the allocation of resources (people, time, and budget).
- You get the resources your team needs to meet the goals.
- Resources continue to be available to meet the changing needs of the project.
- You control your resources so that your team works as efficiently and effectively as possible.

To succeed, a publications project manager must be able to lead a team to do the research and planning necessary to specify correctly the publications required for the project, estimate the resources required to complete the specified project on budget and schedule, communicate the specifications and resource requirements to senior management, and ensure that every team member understands how to produce the desired publication products.

The characteristics of a good project manager

An effective project manager plays many roles in an organization, with responsibilities to manage the content of the project, as well as manage the people and other resources necessary to perform the project. In a publications project, some of the roles you will need to play well are

Communicator:

- The ability to communicate with team members, senior management, and managers in peer organizations
- A thorough understanding of and empathy for the publications-development process

Estimator:

- The ability to estimate the scope of a project from very little information and to continue to revise the estimate of scope as new information becomes available
- The ability to relate your estimate of scope to the resources required to complete the project on time and within budget

Leader:

- A continual engagement in the development process as you work side by side with your team members
- The ability to guide a team to produce appropriate levels of quality that meet customer requirements

Visionary:

- The ability to help others stay on track
- A clear vision of what the track is and where it is going
- A clear vision of what constitutes a high standard of quality in technical publications

If these requirements sound challenging, they are meant to. Project management in competitive business environments is not an easy job. It is rarely a job for the faint of heart who lack confidence in their own ability to learn and communicate what they have learned to others. It is a wonderful job for the individual who has vision, enjoys a leadership role, is an effective communicator, enjoys working with people, and becomes adept at monitoring project details and controlling change.

Good project management also requires that you learn to understand and handle your numbers. The quantitative aspects of project control are extremely important to ensuring that you stay within your budgets and schedules. It is not enough to be a good publications designer or a good editor or even to like working with people. You must know how to estimate and allocate time and costs. You must monitor time and costs on a continual basis, never allowing the details to get out of control.

Because they have so many diverse responsibilities, project managers tend to find themselves in the middle—pulled in a variety of directions by compelling and often contradictory forces.

- Pulling from one direction is your senior management, who want you to keep costs under control and meet schedules.

- Pulling from another direction are your team members who want you to support their need for professional satisfaction in their achievements, to buy them the latest tools, and to ensure that everything is working.

- Pulling in still another direction are your external customers, who demand publications that are easy to use, short, comprehensive, and technically accurate, among other conflicting requirements.

- And, finally, pulling you are your peers, those who manage other aspects of the project— from product development and testing, to training and customer service.

All of these groups insist that you respond to their demands and meet their requirements.

To play all the roles at once (Figure 4.1) and to respond to the requirements of so many masters requires that you become a very accomplished individual. Bob Lamons, in an article in *Marketing News*, quotes an old acquaintance who describes some of the challenges of effective project management (Lamons, 1993).

Figure 4.1 A project manager playing many roles

A wise man of the business world (Charles L. Lapp) once said, "There are three kinds of people in organizations: rowboat people, sailboat people, and steamboat people. Rowboat people are those who always must be pushed or shoved along. Sailboat people move quite nicely when there's wind. Steamboat people, on the other hand, move continuously through calm or storm. They are usually the masters of themselves, their surroundings, and their fate."

Project managers need to be steamboat people, able to set their own courses and work to achieve their visions of successful and productive organizations that produce excellent technical publications. Without that vision and leadership, you will not easily succeed.

Project managers need not only to understand the needs of team members and customers, but also understand the needs of the larger organization. Brooks asks us to consider the model of the producer/director, especially for large projects. The producer handles all the communication upward and sideways, finds budgets and resources, handles schedules, establishes the patterns of communication within the team, and responds to changing circumstances. You have a producer's job in keeping your project under control.

In most organizations you must also assume the role of the director. The director is responsible for designing the content and organization, specifying the details of the design, and supervising the implementation. As director, you must find solutions to individual problems and set limits on their design innovations. You need to communicate with your team, keeping them on a sound design and technical course.

To be successful in all of these ways, you need, as project manager, to

- Understand corporate priorities
- Prepare your own marketing-communication plan
- Take initiative to get things accomplished
- Be an advertising specialist
- Be a strategist for change

The details of this book describe what it feels like to be an effective publications project manager. It also describes the steps in a comprehensive publications-development life cycle. Look upon these details as guidelines and indicators of the path you may want to follow. Develop your own process from the details presented here. Find the process that works best in your organization as it is today. Yet, set your sights on process improvement. Review the five levels of process maturity in Chapter 3, deciding where you are and where you want to be.

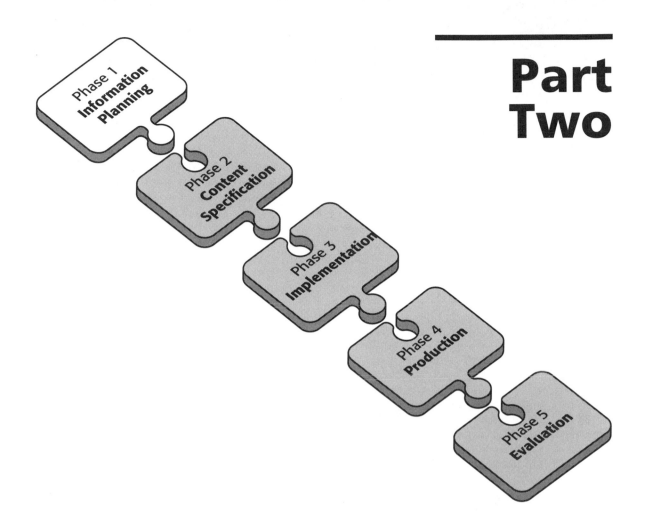

Phase 1
**Information
Planning**

Phase 2
**Content
Specification**

Phase 3
Implementation

Phase 4
Production

Phase 5
Evaluation

Part Two

Starting the Project

The Information-Planning Phase

For too long, many publications projects have gone essentially unplanned by technical-communication professionals. Others in the organization, from marketing to development, have defined the publications to be produced, often without regard to quality and usability for the customer. As publications project manager, your job is to take charge of the publications projects and to guide them so that customer needs are met and schedules and budgets are maintained. To do so, you need first to ensure that sufficient time is spent on front-end research and planning so that the most efficient and effective publications are produced.

In Phase 1: Information Planning, you learn the steps involved in planning a publications project and the decisions necessary to ensure that the project is a success. You take a hard look at the need for documentation, including paper, CD-ROM, online, and other media. In the present climate of reducing development costs and shortening time to market, you need to understand the realities of the business environment in which your projects exist. It is essential that you direct your team to do the front-end research to plan the project in detail and justify the plan in terms of customer requirements and market focus.

Just as publications planning is not the business of marketing or development, publications planning should also not be the sole responsibility of individual writers working independently. Individual writers must be guided by the overall goals of the corporation, as well as the goals of the publications group. As a publications manager or as the manager of an individual project, you will need to review information plans to ensure that they are appropriate to the corporation's goals, represent sound design principles for the user community, and are fiscally responsible. You cannot afford to permit individuals to create their own documents without regard to requirements, specifications, economics, and corporate philosophy.

In Phase 1, you learn a step-by-step approach to produce an Information Plan and its accompanying Project Plan. In the planning process, you consider ideas for initiating and managing audience and task analysis, overseeing the discussions of design implications, and planning the required budgets and schedules to implement the plan.

Contents

Five chapters provide detail about Phase 1: Information Planning.

Chapter 5: Starting Projects on Time

- When does a project start?
- Getting publications in the communications loop
- Participating on cross-functional design teams
- Getting an early start
- When is early too early?

Chapter 6: Defining the Need for Information

- The tradition of needs analysis
- When do we *not* need technical publications?
- Taking a minimalist approach
- The project manager's role in needs analysis

Chapter 7: Creating the Information Plan

- Defining the purpose of the Information Plan
- Understanding the purpose of the development project
- Determining the publication goals and objectives
- Analyzing the audiences for the publications
- Developing a high-level task inventory
- Selecting media

Chapter 8: Creating the Project Plan

- Timing early planning activities
- Setting up the planning team
- Finding early indicators of project scope
- Using page-count metrics
- Making a preliminary estimate of required resources
- Estimating project costs
- Creating a resource spreadsheet
- Creating a preliminary schedule of milestones
- Assigning roles and responsibilities to team members
- Selecting publication tools
- Planning for translation and localization

Results

After reading and thinking about the information in the Phase 1 chapters, I hope that you will know how to direct the design of a front-end research effort, oversee the development of an Information Plan, and estimate budget and schedule for the project in a Project Plan. You will gain insight into the process of negotiating for significant resources in a corporate environment that emphasizes metrics. And you will learn how to use metrics effectively to shape a publications proposal and to delineate clearly the tradeoffs between the proposed plan and its alternatives.

CHAPTER
5

Starting Projects on Time

"You won't believe what just happened," exclaimed Fred. "Dan Oliver just called and asked me to attend the Q2 project kickoff meeting on Monday. He wants technical publications to be part of his development team."

"That's great," said Eleanor. "We've been working on Dan for months, educating him about the importance of starting the publications effort on the same schedule as the product development. Looks like he's finally come around."

"He's been the last holdout," said Fred. "You've done a good job of convincing management that publications is an integral part of the process and that we save money and produce better-quality documents when we start early."

If this story sounds unfamiliar and strikes you as an impossible dream, it should no longer. In this chapter, you learn how to make sure you know when projects start in enough time to develop high-quality technical publications. You will plan how to involve the publications team at the beginning of the product life cycle and how to define your role as a member of a development team.

As you begin the process of changing from a Level 1 to a Level 3 publications organization, a key ingredient will be the full involvement of your team in the product-development process. But it's up to you to take action. As a Level 1 or 2 publications manager, you'll continue to be forgotten or considered a necessary evil unless you do something to advance your cause and grow your organization. In this chapter, you learn tactics for becoming informed and influencing others in your organization in a positive way.

When does a project start?

When we look at the environment for technical publications, it's pretty obvious: Publications projects don't stand alone. They are closely linked to other activities in the development organization. Engineers and programmers design products that require information that explains how to use and repair them. Scientists work on research that needs to be reported to the scientific community and the funding agencies. Management develops policies and procedures that must be communicated so that employees understand and follow them.

In fact, there are few situations where a technical communicator would suddenly decide: "I feel like writing a manual this week." Inside a company that makes products for sale, an organization that does research, or a group running a business, technical publications are part of somebody else's project.

Because technical publications are tied to development projects, the key question that you need to ask is: "What's going on around here that I need to know about?" Figure 5.1 illustrates the questions to ask yourself.

You can't plan what you don't know

Most of us have a hard time planning in the face of uncertainty. We really like to know what's coming along—it makes us feel more secure. However, in many Level 1 and 2 publications organizations, from managers and writers in large departments to independent consultants, you have learned to live with an atmosphere of uncertainty. You often do not know that a development project is going to start until someone walks in the door. You learn that the product is already behind schedule, and you have to be ready to start immediately.

There is no reason, especially in an inhouse technical-publications organization, for such uncertain conditions to continue.

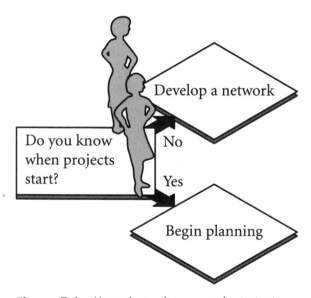

Figure 5.1 Knowing when a project starts

 How do you know what projects your staff will be working on over the next year?" I asked the publications manager in a large, respected manufacturing company.

"I don't," she said. "Somebody will call from marketing or engineering and tell us that they need a writer assigned to a project because they're planning to ship in three months. We run around trying to rearrange schedules so that somebody can cover the assignment."

"Well, maybe a year is too long," I replied. "Surely you know what's happening in the next three months?"

"Maybe some of the writers know. I have a list from marketing about the proposed projects for the year, but most of the projects on the list have no start dates, or the indicated dates have already gone by with no start in sight."

"How can you possibly plan ahead? How do you know if you have the staff to handle all the projects that you'll be asked to do this year?"

"I don't.

As this manager explained her plight, it was clear that she was trying her best to function in a very difficult environment. No one in her department had a firm idea about future projects. New projects arrived at random. A few of the staff had better contacts then others, which helped them learn about new development activities a little earlier. The product developers were themselves functioning like a Level 1: Ad hoc publications organization. Very little planning was taking place anywhere in the organization.

In product-development organizations of this type, the actual beginning of a project can be very fuzzy. Some projects get their start as individual efforts; engineers, programmers, or scientists have an interesting idea and begin to investigate its feasibility independently. The same developers build something that is useful for themselves or is needed by a small internal group. Then the internal product is targeted as a full-scale product for public release. People "just work on things" until management decides to put the projects on an official list.

In *Quality Software Management*, Gerald Weinberg labels development organizations of this type, "Pattern 1: Variable" (Weinberg, 1992). A variable pattern of development is characterized by a simple expression: "We do whatever we feel like at the moment." Pattern 1 organizations have not discovered that project management is actually part of the development process. Instead of an effective and well-managed process, they rely on the abilities of individual superdevelopers. They believe they succeed because the superprogrammers save the day. Their point of view is illustrated in Figure 5.2.

You won't find simple solutions to managing publications projects if you're in an organization that doesn't believe in managing its development efforts. Nonetheless, you'll find it worthwhile to manage your own organization as effectively as possible, even if all around you is chaos. Unless, of course, your own department is at Level 1.

Pattern 1: Variable
"Who needs to plan anyway?
Planning stifles creativity."

Figure 5.2 A Pattern 1 development organization

Weinberg's Pattern 1 corresponds to Level 1 in the publications process-maturity model described in Chapter 3.

Weinberg's five patterns for software-development organizations are roughly parallel to Levels 1 through 5 of the publications process-maturity model. A Level 1: Ad hoc publications organization is often chaotic, with everyone charging off in individual directions. In a Level 2: Rudimentary publications organization, planning and process are new. Even though they are often enthusiastic about the new process, managers and writers who are inexperienced in using a process will tend to abandon it as soon as the projects become difficult. In a Level 3: Managed and Repeatable publications organization, as in Weinberg's Pattern 3, the processes are always followed, not because someone is enforcing good practice but because the managers and most of the staff believe that the processes are successful in producing quality and controlling costs. Levels 4 and 5 are just as rare in publications organizations as they are in software, possibly because many publications organizations are so closely tied to development processes.

If you are managing a Level 1 publications department, you often find that your individual writers will learn about projects as the news reaches them. If you keep a list of who is working on what, you can add the newest project to it—until, of course, it is abruptly canceled.

If you are a manager who is struggling to build a Level 2 organization and instill some order in the chaos around you, you may begin by

- Developing your own network independent of the writers in your group
- Enlisting the help of your writers to extend the network and find out what is going on
- Enlisting the help of mentors in your organization to learn more about how projects get started
- Letting the people in charge of deciding project startups know that you need to be in the communications loop

Knowing what projects are in the pipeline helps publications in two ways: First, if you know early enough, you may be able to involve one of your writers in the planning process. Second, you will have time to plan the publications project. You and your staff need sufficient lead time to ensure that you can adequately plan a project and assemble the resources required to complete the project on time. With early involvement, you will be able to staff your projects at an appropriate and cost-effective level.

If you are not notified until the last minute, planning time may feel nonexistent. You may have only the resources at your disposal to do a less-than-high-quality job. Or you will find that your costs increase through overtime pay and increased sick time from meeting impossible deadlines.

Consider if any other key components of the product are permitted to be "forgotten" in your organization. Does anyone regularly "forget" about manufacturing? Yet, in many organizations, product developers are permitted to forget about technical publications. This deliberate forgetfulness may occur because developers notice no difference between starting publications early or starting them late. They seem to get the same publications in either case. Consequently, there is no obvious cost for not planning.

To change this perception, you need to communicate the consequences of failing to start publications at the beginning of the development process. The best way to communicate the consequences is to show how much better the publications can be if you start early.

 Guideline: If you are not in the project startup pipeline, use all the resources available to you to communicate your need to know when projects are starting so that you can plan the resources needed to produce high-quality publications.

The contract starts the clock

In organizations where technical projects occur in response to customer demands, projects may start in a more rational way than in organizations that develop for less obvious customers.

- Internal customers ask that a particular product or service be developed to meet a defined need.
- A customer contracts for a specific product, service, or investigation.
- A government agency issues new or changed regulations that require a new or revised product or procedure. Although the lead time may be short, at least you have a well-defined time to start the clock.

In each of these cases, there's a clear procedure, and it's followed without fail.

We try to find out what's in the pipeline," explained the publications manager at a financial institution. "We'll know far ahead that Congress or the state legislature is working on new banking legislation. For example, we knew almost a year ahead that they were working on a new banking service. We just didn't know exactly when it would be approved."

"What if it wasn't approved?" I asked.

"There's always that chance. But we have to be prepared. One service wasn't approved by Congress until November, with a January 1 start date. If we hadn't been

Pattern 2: Routine

"Routine procedures are very important. That is, until everything falls apart."

Figure 5.3   A Pattern 2 development organization

working on the software months in advance and preparing the policies and procedures and the marketing information, we would never have been ready for the first of the year. Missing that date would have cost us millions of dollars."

"But you might have had to throw out all your work."

"Right. But we didn't. We were ready. We have experts who decide what risks are worth taking. They have great networks in the government. They know all the representatives on the banking committees, and they're plugged into the staffs.

There's an obvious lesson here: Networks count. Just as the banking experts have their feelers out among the legislators, you need to put your feelers out in your organization. As your organization becomes interested in planning, you will find it easier to be included.

Weinberg labels software-development organizations that believe in planning "Pattern 2: Routine." The creed for a Pattern 2 organization is: "We follow our routines (except when we panic)." A Pattern 2 development group depends, not on its superstar programmers, but on its strong managers and processes. The managers are supposed to have everything under control, following an established routine. Unfortunately, when things go wrong, Pattern 2 managers tend to abandon routine procedures, chiefly because they don't really understand the purpose underlying the procedures. Figure 5.3 illustrates the point of view of a Pattern 2 organization.

Pattern 2 developers often recognize that good management is important to achieving quality, but they are unwilling to spend time and money on it. They are afraid to abandon their strict procedures because they aren't convinced that a new way will work. They often believe that they will succeed if they push people hard enough.

For an organization dominated by routine procedures, an external event, such as an outside contract, is a convenient trigger to start a project. Unfortunately, once the start date occurs, the rest of the planning process may be inadequate to keep the project under control.

If you manage in an organization that leaves everything until the last minute and quickly abandons planning, you may want to begin by

- Ensuring that you have a strong information network in place
- Helping to develop a better early planning process for all projects, not just publications
- Reassuring people who tend to panic, so that they don't abandon the procedures under pressure
- Providing a model of the planning process in the publications organization

Projects that are contract-dependent may also have inadequate lead time. The less adequate the time to do the project, the greater the need you will find for planning and project control. Planning will work—even for the shortest project. In one case, my staff went through all the planning steps, abbreviated of course, for a project that had to be completed in six days. We conducted an audience and task analysis, learned how the machine worked, wrote the installation manual, created the graphics, and verified the accuracy of the procedures in those six days. We even discovered that the calibration procedure was incorrect and created a new one without slipping the deadline. The project was done on time and on budget and produced a useful publication.

If you are in an organization that is beginning to think about planning, work hard to ensure that planning always occurs, even under the least favorable circumstances.

 Guideline: The worst time to abandon a good process is when things get tough. Manage your publications department so that planning always occurs, especially when schedules are short.

Product marketing plans are step one

Some organizations always plan projects in advance. When you talk with publications managers in these organizations, they are surprised that anyone needs to ask the question: "How do you know when a project is going to start?"

"That's obvious," explained the publications manager of a large electronics firm. "When marketing releases their product marketing plan."

Marketing, in this organization, has been meeting with external customers to identify the need for a new product or product enhancement. They are aware of current market trends and sensitive to clues about the competition's activities. They attend trade shows and user-group meetings, trying to assess the customers' moods and anticipate emerging needs. Or they simply know that the market demands a new release once a year. All this marketing activity rolls up into approved marketing plans for new or enhanced products.

Before the beginning of a new fiscal year, managers are given a preview of the plans that are in the pipeline. They plan the budget and staff they will need to handle the coming projects. Or they figure out how to work with the staff they already have to meet project needs. Either way, enough initial planning takes place so that they prepare—until plans change or projects are delayed or canceled. The more mature the organization, the better the planning process works. The more experienced the managers, the better they understand the lead time required to operate a development project effectively.

Weinberg labels these well-oiled organizations "Pattern 3: Steering." In a Pattern 3 development group, everyone follows a development process because managers truly understand the purpose of the process. All projects begin with planning of some kind. The resources required to complete the projects successfully are estimated, and the milestone schedule is calculated and communicated. Figure 5.4 illustrates the point of view of a Pattern 3 organization.

```
┌─────────────────────────────────────────────────────────┐
│                    Pattern 3: Steering                    │
│   "Planning is the only possible way to produce high-quality │
│            work on budget and on schedule."               │
└─────────────────────────────────────────────────────────┘
```

Figure 5.4 A Pattern 3 development organization

Weinberg goes on to describe "Pattern 4: Anticipating" and "Pattern 5: Congruent" in his scheme for software-development organizations. Managers in a Pattern 4 organization not only follow their processes but also have instituted steps to anticipate and drive process improvements. In a Pattern 5 organization, everyone is involved in improving the process all the time. Weinberg also explains that, like Crosby (1979) and Humphrey (1989), he has found little evidence of Pattern 4 or 5 organizations. Occasionally, an individual project or part of a project is managed in a manner similar to Pattern 4, but not an entire organization.

If you are working with a Pattern 3, 4, or 5 development organization, you will find that projects begin in a reasonable way. You will be given many opportunities to institute and improve your own development process for publications.

Networking counts in project startup

Whatever the circumstances surrounding project startup in your organization, it is your responsibility as a manager to keep in close touch with the ideas, initiatives, schedules, and decisions of the groups that ordinarily start projects. If you're in an organization where projects are formally initiated and placed on a development schedule, you definitely have an easier task, as long as you're part of the distribution of startup information.

If you're in an organization that has no formal planning process (development Pattern 1), you have a harder task. You need to build your network among the people who know about work in the idea stage or work in progress. If you want to schedule and staff adequately to meet project requirements, you must be in the communications loop.

In too many organizations, publications project managers are the last people to know about projects that are starting. Projects are initiated and schedules determined without regard to publications development. Projects are half or fully completed before anyone remembers that publications are needed. Products are even released to unsuspecting customers without the publications the customers need.

You can't control the actions of others in the organization, but you can show them the cost of neglecting publications. If people don't think publications are important, they'll wait until the last minute before informing you about their project needs. In many organizations, the view is still too prevalent that publications are a necessary evil to be put off until the end. Your task becomes one of continuous education, gathering evidence that successful publications save money and promote the image of the organization among the customers.

When it comes to judgments about the importance of publications, you're not going to change everyone's mind overnight. You'll always find a few diehards who will never change. But some minds will change, especially as people learn about the cost of mediocre technical publications.

At the same time, you cannot afford to sit back and wait for a miracle that will completely change how your organization operates. Establish your network, and make sure that people who can be persuaded to include publications in the planning process do so. Follow the dictum of "managing by walking around." Find out what is going on, and act on your information.

 Guideline: Networking is the most important skill for the publications manager who wants to avoid surprises in starting projects. Find out who knows, and make sure that you're on their distribution list.

Getting publications in the communications loop

If your organization does not recognize the significance of quality publications to product success, you have the difficult task of establishing and maintaining original lines of communication. To begin the process, you need to

- Discover which people or groups are most often responsible for starting projects.
- Develop mentors in your organization who know how startup decisions are made.
- Discuss the communications problem with your managers, and get their ideas about possible strategies.
- Establish a network of people who will keep you informed.
- Enlist the help of all your staff in the information-gathering effort.

Admittedly, the process of forging new communication links will take time and persistence. But without a strong network, you're at the mercy of anyone who forgets that publications are important.

Getting in the communications loop will also require a fairly high degree of political savvy within your organization. It cannot be done by isolating yourself or communicating mainly with your subordinates.

Even if your organization has a well-established process of initiating new projects, you need to cultivate your network. You need to know about projects while they are still "in the wind" so that you can begin making contingency plans and be ready to get your staff involved as early as possible.

One effective manager makes a point of meeting people in other departments. Every evening from 5:30 to 7:30, rather than heading out the door, she walks in and out of the engineers' offices, chatting with people who ordinarily work half the night.

"She goes out of her way to know what's going on at our company," one technical communicator explained about this manager. "She's one of the most effective managers I've ever known."

This manager spends a few hours nearly every evening talking with developers and marketing people.

"She's genuinely interested in their work and their problems. Once people find out she wants to know what they're working on, they really open up. She knows more about the projects that are in the works than the CEO."

This manager cultivates her connections in the organization with the people who start projects. She's included in company planning, and people let her know what is going on. You will often discover that once you're willing to listen and you have good questions and ideas, people become enthusiastic about keeping you informed. Conversely, when you're not interested, when you don't know anything about "all that technical stuff," no one will bother you with information.

To maintain your communications network, you must be ready to respond to change. Reorganization means that you will have to establish the communications links all over again. The new players may not be aware of your role in the product-development process or the contributions you are prepared to make.

 Guideline: If you want to know what's going on, make sure you're seen as a person whose ideas and opinions matter.

Participating on cross-functional design teams

Although many publications teams are left out of the mainstream of product planning, the publications group has a significant role in organizations that have an advanced product-development process in place. These organizations recognize that to introduce a product or service successfully to internal or external customers requires many diverse skills. If you are in a progressive organization, you may already be serving on cross-functional design teams.

A few years ago, technical communicators on a development team discussed their role during the critical early development of a product. The developers would try a new way of presenting the operating system. Their job was to write the appropriate section of the user's guide.

Whenever the text got too complicated, or it took too many words to explain how to perform a function, the programmers would redesign the function. The user's guide served as a check on the complexity of the design.

Cross-functional teams include representatives from every internal group that is responsible for a part of the product, from development and manufacturing through customer support. Teams may include representatives from

- Marketing and sales
- Development
- Field service
- Customer support
- Manufacturing or production
- Distribution
- Quality assurance
- Training
- Publications
- Users

On the best teams, each representative plays a significant role to ensure the success of the development effort. If your organization is considering cross-functional design teams, get involved. The publications group plays an integral part in ensuring that customer needs are met. Especially in the absence of human-factors specialists, technical communicators are often the most skilled and effective advocates for the user. Attend project meetings as often as possible so that you can watch the development process unfold.

 Guideline: Make publications an integral part of the product-design process. The publications organization will benefit, and so may the product design.

Getting a seat

Unfortunately, instituting cross-functional design teams does not guarantee technical communicators a place. You may need to fight for a place by helping others understand the role of publications in product success. In the literature on cross-functional development teams, the publications organization is rarely included. Few authorities on the product-development life cycle include publications as a regular player in the earliest development phases. Even in cases where publications are defined during a feasibility phase or a requirements definition, they may be defined without the contribution of the publications professionals.

More enlightened views of the development life cycle include publications at the beginning of the process. In my experience, between 5 and 10 percent of publications organizations are involved from the initial feasibility study phase. Under the best conditions, the publications are planned in concert with the rest of the product, not as an afterthought. Whenever the question "Where do publications fit in?" is asked, as in Figure 5.5, the answer is the same: at the beginning.

Product-development life cycle

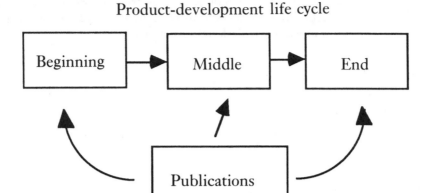

Where do publications fit in?

Figure 5.5 Fitting publications into the product-development life cycle

If cross-functional design teams are being planned in your organization, take a leading role to ensure that the information for the user is prepared in a timely and effective manner. Argue that being on the team allows you to

- Serve as advocates for the user
- Have the publications ready in time for the product release
- Learn the product as it is being developed
- Use less of the developers' time for interviews and questions later in the development process
- Contribute to developing a consistent interface for the product, producing less documentation and saving production costs
- Contribute to the early development of a policy and procedure or a major report or proposal, and eliminate major revisions required when you discover inconsistencies or omissions late in the cycle
- Conduct usability studies to ensure that customers can use the product quickly and easily

These are only a few of the arguments you can make to be included on the development team. The key is to show that your contribution will save time and money. Your next responsibility is to demonstrate that the savings do indeed occur.

Guideline: Become part of a cross-functional development team so that you can influence the usability of the product, and develop publications that are closely targeted to meet user needs.

Sometimes you only need to ask

Ten years ago, it was more difficult to convince groups of technical communicators of the importance of playing an integral role in the development effort. Many were convinced that they had no chance to be included in their companies' design activities.

In one workshop I held in Los Angeles, a woman in the group had an exciting announcement. She had become convinced that a place on the design team was essential.

On the way home after class, I rehearsed all the arguments we discussed that I could use on my manager to convince him to give me a chance," she explained. "I was almost sure I could get him to agree when I went back to work on Monday."

"Once I got home, I realized that my manager, who always works late, was probably still at work. I decided to call him immediately, before I lost my nerve."

"I described what had happened in class and started to explain how I could contribute. Before I got more than a few words out, he said, 'Great. The new development team is meeting on Monday morning. Plan to be there.'"

"I was so surprised by his response that I just thanked him and hung up. Later on, I was sort of disappointed that I didn't have a chance to use all those great arguments that I'd been rehearsing.

Sometimes, all you need to do is ask. Too many technical communicators are so convinced that they'll be turned down that they never ask to contribute. And if you have not convinced yourself that you have something significant to contribute to the development effort, others are unlikely to invite you to take part.

To make the best contribution and become an effective team member, prepare yourself and your staff members to perform new and different activities. If you believe that your primary responsibility is to edit the work of the developers or fix the mechanical and stylistic problems in the scientists' writing, others on the development team will give little support to your membership. If you are going to work on a cross-functional development team, you need to contribute to the development process. That means understanding the product, the market, and the customers as well as or better than the other team members.

If you or your team members are invited to take part, be active and enthusiastic contributors. Maintain your interest in the technical discussions, and stay abreast of the product changes. Beware of becoming the team scribe or editing the team's documents. Be certain that everyone considers you a publications-development expert, an equal contributor to the process. Work hard to avoid the traditional stereotypes of writers and editors (more interested in commas than content). Start a new stereotype that identifies publications experts as those who understand how to communicate effectively with a wide range of audiences.

Guideline: *Be prepared to serve as an effective team member so that your contributions are valued and your expertise is acknowledged.*

Getting an early start

Many publications professionals have long argued the importance of becoming involved early in the product-development life cycle. The arguments go this way:

- Publications are an integral part of the product and need to be planned at the same time as the product.
- Publications prototypes facilitate early and informed user participation in development.
- Early publications drafts are part of detailed user-interface specifications.
- Publications staff members are often the strongest advocates for product usability from the customer's point of view.
- Publications staff members need to understand the rest of the product thoroughly to plan the best publications to support the user.
- Publications staff members can perform early user and task analyses and develop accurate and complete user and task profiles to aid product development.

Once you've convinced the rest of the organization to involve the publications group from the beginning of the development life cycle, you have to know when the projects begin. Make certain that you're in the communications loop so that you're there when the projects start. Ensure that, as illustrated in Figure 5.6, publications startup is parallel to product startup.

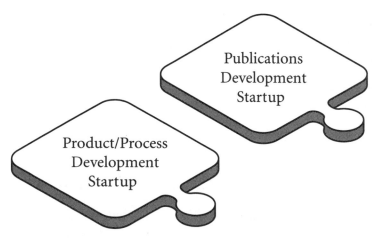

Figure 5.6 Product and publications — starting in tandem

If publications professionals are involved early, you can help to ensure that

- Users and tasks are studied thoroughly and early enough to influence the development process.
- Ease of use is maintained through all elements of the product interface, including the publications.
- Sufficient time is available in the schedule to assess the usability of the planned publications.
- Publications are fully integrated with the product.

When is early too early?

It is never too early to begin developing publications that are successful in helping users accomplish their goals. However, you must carefully plan your involvement so that you do not perform publications-development tasks at the wrong time in the development life cycle. Too often, technical writers believe that being on a project-development team means immediately starting to produce document drafts. People who view their primary task to be "writing" want to begin writing immediately. That's a serious mistake—one that needs strong management to prevent.

In projects where writers begin to produce drafts too early, there is often a great deal of rewriting to do as the project evolves. Costs increase, and frustration builds. Writers feel they should have waited until the development effort was farther along before committing words to paper.

That's right. No one should be creating draft documents at the early stages of the development life cycle.

As project manager, your job must be to ensure that *writing* does not begin too early and that publications' involvement in the project is carefully staged. Insist that planning continue until you reach the right time to begin producing drafts. Some of your team members may still believe that planning is a waste of time; they'd rather be writing and editing than planning. They need assistance, in the form of effective management, to understand the development life cycle and their role in it.

Part of the problem may be an overcommitment of resources in the early stages of the development life cycle. Managers assign writers to design teams full-time when they have only part-time tasks to perform. To fill in the gaps in their schedules, the writers move ahead too quickly with writing tasks and sometimes ignore the planning tasks that need to occur early.

In the rest of Part Two, you will look at the tasks that your team might perform in the early stages of the publications-development life cycle and relate them to the product-development activities occurring simultaneously.

Guideline: If you have the opportunity to start early, be prepared to take full advantage of the time for thorough planning. A thorough planning process will mean that the publications you create maintain a high standard of quality and are produced on time and on budget.

Defining the Need for Information

An effective way to begin a publications-development life cycle is with a needs analysis. To conduct a needs analysis, the publications team needs to ask key questions about the audiences:

- What is the prior experience of the audiences in using the product, performing the process, or evaluating the information?

- What is the existing subject-matter knowledge of the audiences? Expert? Novice? Somewhere in between? All of the above?

- What data exists in the development community about the audiences' need for information and training? Have focus groups been conducted? Has data been gathered about existing products and processes?

- What indicators exist that audience needs are not being met? Customer complaints of missing information? Large volume of help calls?

- What indicators exist that audience needs are not being exceeded? Information that goes unused?

- What profiles exist about the information needs of the audiences? Are they based on data or assumptions?

The goal of these questions is to start a new planning process with data gathered about past successes and failures. The challenges of a needs analysis may begin with a requirement to reduce the cost of publications. The challenge may come from rumors that existing information goes unread. Or from irate audiences who are unable to perform tasks successfully, find solutions to problems, or find the information they need to make decisions.

As project manager, follow as many leads as you can to set the stage for a thorough analysis of audience needs. Answers to the questions will come during the information planning phase and the audience and task analyses. But the direction for these planning activities needs to be set early, often long before formal development activities begin.

The tradition of needs analysis

Needs analysis has long been a traditional part of the product-development life cycle, or should be. The essential question marketing asks in a needs analysis or feasibility study is

Does anyone need this product?

In the context of traditional training development, instructional designers ask a variation of the product-needs question:

Are there people in this organization who need to improve their job performance?

In both cases, if the answer to the basic needs-analysis question is *no*, we seriously consider not developing the product or providing training. But products continue to be developed that no one needs. The same holds true for technical publications. If we neglect the basic needs-analysis question, we are more likely to produce publications that few, if anyone, needs and uses.

In conducting customer site visits, many technical communicators discover manuals still in their original shrink wrap or packing boxes. Of course, a few examples do not mean that everyone finds the information irrelevant to their tasks. In fact, we have to be careful about generalizing from a few examples, especially if those examples come from the super specialists in the field. The standard user publications may never have been intended for them.

We do, however, know that much information is published that is rarely used. We publish information that is interesting and relevant to those who have developed the product. We include information required to understand how the product was built. We create documents intended to teach task performance that include histories of the development of the service or process. In one instance, a cooking manual for a fast-food franchise organization included the history of the founder's development of the recipe. Nice to know, perhaps, but clearly in the way of the new employee who needs to get the fried potatoes on the customer's plate immediately.

In this era of shrinking staff and budgets, you can ill afford to produce publications that are not directly relevant to the user's successful performance of his or her tasks. Therefore, you need to include a needs analysis in the earliest phases of the publications development process. Figure 6.1 illustrates the questions to ask.

When do we *not* need technical publications?

Are there any circumstances when technical publications are not needed to support a product or process? Certainly,

- All users are already trained in the correct process and have performed successfully.
- All users already have the required skills and abilities to use the product or perform the process and require no additional training or support.

If you are an experienced driver and have driven more than one type of automobile, you will be able to drive another automobile without referring to the owner's manual. The user interface (controls) in the new automobile will be sufficiently similar to the

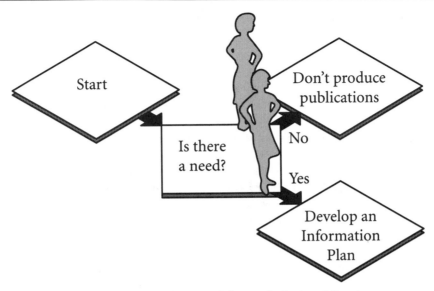

Figure 6.1 Considering the need for technical publications

interface you have experience using that you will be able to figure out how to drive without assistance from the user manual.

At issue is the familiarity of the interface and the process required to drive the automobile. If users have sufficient prior experience and knowledge of a similar product or process, they will need no assistance in performing known tasks. It is only when there is a gap between the user's prior knowledge and experience and the product or process that you need to provide assistance through an instructional text (or other instructional media).

Many competent users of technical products or processes expect to use their prior knowledge and experience to figure out how to perform tasks with a new product. Only when they encounter problems or become confused do they feel it necessary to consult some instructional medium. In fact, if a more experienced person is nearby and can be consulted, one-on-one training is often preferred to consulting the documentation.

We have evidence from usability testing as well as the evidence of user interviews, response cards, and anecdotes to make the following generalization. Many people prefer to figure something out themselves first, consult another person second, and read instructional text third.

Of course, these generalizations don't apply to everyone. We all know individuals who read manuals from cover to cover before touching a product or who would never ask another person for help. There are the independent types who figure out what to do on their own even if it takes them considerable time.

As a result of diverse patterns of use and different learning styles among audiences, technical communicators may have a difficult time doing a needs analysis. Because the users are diverse, the answers to the needs questions will also be diverse. Some users need little supporting information; others need a great deal.

Nonetheless, you will encounter situations in which little if any technical information is needed to enable users to perform their tasks successfully.

Often, we make such decisions in a vacuum, based upon our internal assessments rather than on data about our users. Once you have gathered data about your customers' need, you may decide that user manuals can be eliminated.

If you can eliminate information that users do not need, you may find that you have time to do a better job on the information they do need. If you continue to produce unnecessary information, you will often reduce the overall quality of the publications when you run out of time.

 Guideline: Consider a careful needs analysis so that you have enough time to do an excellent job producing information that is needed.

Taking a minimalist approach

Perhaps the critical decision in the needs analysis is to decide exactly how much information your customers need. You have options to

- Provide instructions for using all product features and functions
- Provide instructions for using only the most frequently used features and functions
- Provide instructions for using only those features and functions that the user will have difficulty understanding and using
- Provide only enough instructions to get the user started on learning
- Provide more detailed information at additional cost

In *The Nurnberg Funnel*, John Carroll explains that "new users are not inclined to read training material. As one person we observed put it while flipping pages in a manual: 'This is just information.' People seem to be more interested in action, in working on real tasks, than in reading" (Carroll, 1990). Carroll suggests eliminating information from manuals, information that gets in the way of learning—an approach he calls "minimalist."

A needs analysis should be designed to help you investigate a minimalist approach to publications design. Search for ways to reduce the volume of information as you conduct audience and task analyses for the project. Be prepared during the development process to produce and test minimalist versions of the information. While the needs analysis questions should be addressed as early as possible, information that supports a minimalist solution may need to be gathered during the early phases of the publications development process.

Remember that the less information you produce, the less it will cost to publish and maintain. In general, we produce too much information for our customers because we lack detailed information about the characteristics of the audience and the tasks they need to perform. A thorough needs analysis allows us to target information specifically to meet customer needs.

In one case study, a publications group decided as part of a paper-reduction goal to reduce the size of their hardware installation manuals from over 100 pages of text and illustrations to approximately 20 pages. They eliminated redundancy and cut unnecessary information in the process, but they never consulted the users. All the decisions to eliminate information and redesign the installation books were made by the technical writers and the developers.

The users, 98 percent of whom were trained company technicians, were asked to review the content of the new, shorter manuals for accuracy. They carefully corrected errors in the existing text. Finally, they inquired why anyone in their group needed 20 pages of text to install the hardware.

Once they were asked, the technicians explained that all they needed was a picture of the board to verify that they had the right piece of hardware. They wanted lists of the jumper and cable connections and pinouts. They also admitted that, to conform with legal requirements, the text should include a warning about wearing a wrist strap for protection against electrical shock. All the users' needs could be addressed on a single sheet of paper.

They also asked that the instruction sheet be printed on poor-quality paper so they did not feel so guilty when they threw it away.

The point of the story is this: Find out what your audience really needs—don't assume that you know. This organization was able to substantially reduce the cost of producing installation instructions by reducing the original 100-page manuals to a 1-page instruction sheet. The same possibility may be available to your organization.

Guideline: Investigate the possibility of developing the least possible information to satisfy audience needs.

The project manager's role in needs analysis

As project manager, consider a needs analysis as a method of making an initial assessment of the overall scope of the publications project. The Information Plan described in Chapter 7 includes a statement about the goals of the publications project, a statement that is derived from an early needs analysis.

You will often be asked to estimate the cost of a project and the required resources before you have much, if any, information about the project scope. Use the needs analysis to help you make that early assessment or postpone the estimate until after the Information Plan has been completed.

Include a needs analysis even if your task is to revise existing publications. The needs analysis provides a way to look at the revision with an eye to what the users absolutely need to know.

A revision project presents a significant opportunity to reassess the need for the publications produced in the past.

- Are there opportunities for a reduction in volume of text?
- Should the media selection be reconsidered?
- Should hardcopy books be reorganized into different libraries?
- Should several small volumes be created from one behemoth?
- Are there opportunities to improve the quality of the publications?

Too often we simply make changes to existing text, perpetuating whatever problems existed in the original information and continue to produce volumes of information that no one may need.

As project manager, ensure that a needs analysis occurs, either as an integral part of the information planning task or as a prior step. As an early decision stage, needs analysis lends direction to subsequent research by setting the limits in which the publications team will work.

Guideline: Decide carefully about opportunities to minimize the volume of information produced while better satisfying audience needs.

Creating the Information Plan

The first milestone of Phase 1: Information Planning of the publications-development life cycle is the Information Plan. The plan records the information you gathered during the needs analyses and the publications decisions you made. It is the primary document you will use to plan how to manage the publications project, providing the basis for your preliminary estimates of the schedule and budget needed to complete the project. Once you have completed the Information Plan, you are ready to develop the Project Plan, the second milestone of Phase 1, described in Chapter 8.

As Figure 7.1 illustrates, the Information Plan and the Project Plan are the major components of Phase 1 of the publications-development life cycle.

The Information Plan describes the scope of the publications project, and the Project Plan describes the schedule you will follow and the resources you will need to complete the project.

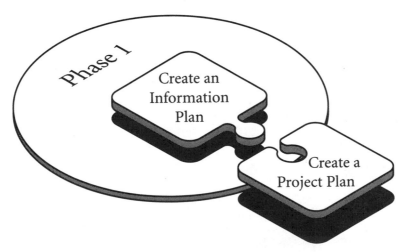

Figure 7.1 Phase 1 of the publications-development life cycle

In this chapter, you will learn how to direct your team in the following activities to produce a strong plan:

- Understanding the purpose of the development project
- Determining publications goals and objectives
- Analyzing audience and environment
- Developing a high-level task inventory, including a user/task matrix
- Analyzing design implications
- Selecting media, including nonprint (online, interactive compact disk, video, audio, and others)

The activities for the first part of Phase 1 are illustrated in Figure 7.2.

Defining the purpose of the Information Plan

The Information Plan documents the basic organization and content of the publications you intend to build. The plan is the end product of your research effort to gather the information about your audience, their tasks, the market, and the product.

To produce a sound and comprehensive plan, you must spend adequate time on information gathering. I recommend that for many projects, information planning

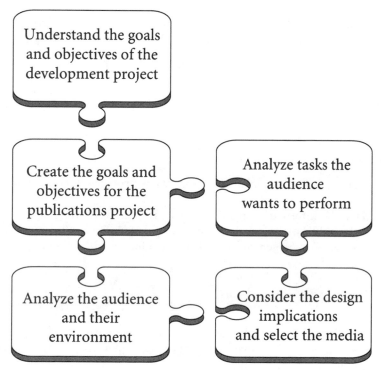

Figure 7.2 The information-planning process

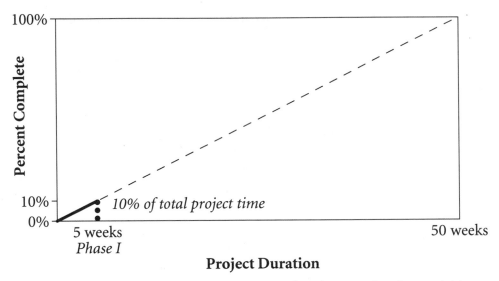

Figure 7.3 Percentage of total project time for Phase 1 planning activities

should take at least 10 percent of total project time. For complex projects, the percentage may be higher. To illustrate, the 10-percent goal for early information planning means that for a one-writer project that takes a calendar year (50 weeks) to complete, you should spend 5 weeks on information planning (Figure 7.3).

The Information Plan, at minimum, should contain the following sections:

- Goals and objectives of the development project
- Goals and objectives for the publications
- Preliminary user profile
- High-level task analysis
- Design implications and publications strategy
- Preliminary media selection

The Information Plan template in Appendix A provides a model and an outline for these sections.

To manage the information-planning process effectively, you must be convinced of its value to the publications-development life cycle. The following case study illustrates how a publications manager succeeded in introducing information planning into her organization.

Diana was the manager of a small publications group in a software-development company. She instituted information planning a few years ago because she was convinced it would make them better organized as a department and help the writers create more successful documents.

"Everyone in the development group was surprised when we produced our first Information Plan. For some reason, they didn't expect pubs to be so well organized," she explained. "We needed a document that would give us direction and let everyone else know what we were doing."

"At first, we sent out copies of our plan as information only. Then, we started to get comments like, 'This is the best explanation that we've seen of what the development project is about.'"

"People wanted to comment on the plan, to suggest changes. We held a walk-through of the plan to give them a chance to respond. The walkthrough was an opportunity to get all players in one room and talking to one another. It was possible to solve problems on the spot, rather than waiting for someone to sift through a lot of written comments."

"The first successful plan caused quite a stir around here. Some of the other development groups asked if we could help them develop their own planning documents.

Information Plans are valuable from at least three viewpoints: They provide direction for your staff, communicate to others in the organization, and provide a basis for communication among those engaged in other parts of the development activities.

For your staff, the Information Plan

- Focuses the early efforts of the publications team and sometimes of the development team
- Provides a repository for data collected during information gathering
- Helps the publications team organize its ideas about the publication design for the project
- Ensures that the publications team reaches a consensus
- Sets the stage for the project plan and the resource estimate
- Ensures that incoming publications team members can come up to speed quickly
- Creates an outlet for the creative activities of the publications team and keeps them from writing draft documents too soon

For the larger organization, the Information Plan

- Clarifies the publications team's understanding of the total project
- Communicates your analyses of the users and their tasks
- Communicates the reasoning behind your design decisions and media selection
- Provides an opportunity for the complete project team to discuss and possibly resolve issues about the direction of the project, sometimes right in the review meeting

By communicating its planning clearly to the rest of the organization, the publications team may eliminate much of the debate that occurs in many organizations about the role technical publications serve. If the publications team has no plan, others in the organization will fill the vacuum. The Information Plan helps the publications team express its point of view in a positive, rather than in a defensive, manner.

Most important, the Information Plan communicates to the rest of the organization that publications follows a concrete process to ensure high-quality results. It demonstrates the quality of the data collection and thinking that professional technical communicators bring to the publications effort. It implies that no one else in the organization is prepared to produce professional technical publications in such a well-defined way. It also implies that technical publications are not arbitrarily based on the personal whims of individual writers (or the company treasurer) but are built through a careful planning process.

Guideline: Demonstrate the importance of the Information Plan by doing it well, distributing the drafts widely, and holding a review meeting.

Understanding the purpose of the development project

The first section of the Information Plan calls for a brief explanation of the goals and objectives of the development project (see Figure 7.4). But the brief discussion is only a by-product of a significant effort by the publications team to ensure that you understand and will contribute to broad organizational goals.

By understanding the overall project goals and objectives, your team can better plan publications that assist marketing and contribute to the success of the development efforts. By investigating and understanding your organization's goals for the project, you communicate your willingness to provide value to the larger organization.

Senior managers of many organizations do not believe that the publication teams understand the goals of the organizations. Consequently, they lack respect for the activities of the publications people because they believe technical communicators show little interest in or understanding of the business significance of the projects. You must work hard to dispel this image.

As a publications project manager, one of your most important jobs is to understand your organization's goals and objectives for a new development project and to establish a leadership position in the company.

On a recent project, my publications team discovered, by keeping our ears open and cultivating our engineering contacts, that the new company president was concerned about maintenance costs for the company's product. The service costs involved in sending field engineers out to repair machines exceeded revenues from the maintenance contracts.

One solution was to raise the fees for the maintenance contracts. However, maintenance contracts were an important revenue source. In addition, the company was in competition with independent maintenance organizations who would be delighted with an increase in fees by the original manufacturer.

The best solution was to reduce the costs of field service by reducing the number of maintenance trips and the average time spent in making repairs. During the cost-

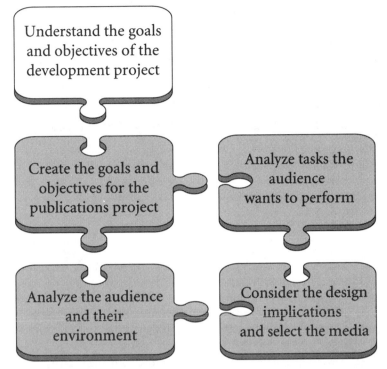

Figure 7.4 Understanding development project goals and objectives

assessment study, the field engineers complained that many of the repair visits were caused by a manufacturing defect in the product. The defect made it very difficult to repair the machine at the customer's site.

As a result of the complaints, manufacturing eliminated the service-causing defect from the assembly process.

Those responsible for producing the maintenance manuals also wanted to contribute to the cost-reduction efforts and increase customer satisfaction. By interviewing field engineers, the project manager discovered that they had difficulty reading the small print in the maintenance manuals. They typically placed the manuals on the floor or on a chair while repairing the machines. The 10-point Times Roman was difficult to read at a distance of 3 feet or more.

A point-size font change in the manuals wasn't dramatic, but the discussion of the usability issue in the Information Plan demonstrated that technical publications understood the company's goal and was prepared to contribute. The cost relationship between a larger font and the length of a service call might be difficult to quantify, but the field engineers were pleased with the change and believed their jobs were made a little easier. They also were pleased that someone in publications had bothered to ask them what they needed.

Managers win respect in an organization when they are perceived as understanding the objectives of senior management. As a publications project manager, you need to demonstrate that you understand and appreciate the need for

- Timely release of products to the market
- Cost controls on the production of publications
- Greater efficiency in processes

 Guideline: Find out the direction that the rest of the organization is going and align yourself with it or contribute to the direction in the first place.

Asking the right people

How do you get your staff to find out about the organization's strategy for a new product? You may have to model the process, especially with team members who do not have strong interviewing skills. Set up and perhaps conduct interviews with key people who understand and establish policy. These key people may include product marketing, sales, engineering, and senior management. Finding the key people means using the communications network you established before the project began. In a Pattern 3: Steering development organization, the sources will be fairly well established. In Pattern 1: Variable and Pattern 2: Routine organizations, you may have to do some creative digging to find people who can articulate their sense of the organization's direction.

Unfortunately, in Pattern 1 and 2 development organizations, you may find considerable disagreement about strategy. In one project for a scientific research organization, we thought we had done our homework in asking the department leaders in the local and national offices to help us define the purpose of the report we were preparing. They wanted to promote their work in establishing small, cost-effective power plants in rural communities. What we didn't know was that some national officials were adamantly opposed to this development work and had withdrawn funding for it. Only after we'd produced a first draft of the report did someone raise the alarm and withdraw the project. It seemed to us that the right hand didn't know what the left hand was doing. But that's the nature of many Pattern 1 and 2 organizations. At least, the project was canceled before the client had spent money on final production.

The lesson is to find the right people, all the right people, before drawing conclusions about the nature and intent of the development project. In the course of asking questions, you may discover that you have contributed to clarifying the purpose of the development.

 Guideline: Identify the key people who set the organization's direction.

Asking the right questions

Once you've helped your staff identify the right people to talk to by making good use of your communications network, you can help them further by discussing the questions to ask. Open-ended, short interviews usually work best in establishing an information base. In many cases, when you ask people about their ideas and their strategies, they are more than eager to tell you. Or they many turn red from embarrassment. But that's information, too.

In a product-development organization, such as a computer software or hardware developer, the general direction of questioning might include

- Why is the company thinking of introducing this product?
- What niche will the product occupy relative to the competition?
- Who are the competitors? What are their strengths and weaknesses? What publications do they provide?
- What are our strengths and weaknesses?
- Who are our customers, and what are they asking for?
- Do we have any direct information from our customers? Do we know what they want or how they use or regard our product?
- What have we learned from customer support on previous products?
- Have we held focus groups or used other information-gathering techniques?
- How will the product be marketed?
- Who is most likely to buy the product?
- Are there any problems that the new product must overcome?

In an information-development organization, such as a scientific research laboratory, the general direction of questioning might include

- Who will receive the information?
- Why is the information important to them?
- What will they do with the information?
- What impression does the organization hope to make on the customers?
- What barriers exist to a favorable impression?
- What advantages exist for a favorable impression?

In a process-development organization, such as a provider of services to external or internal customers, the general direction of questioning might include

- Why is the new policy or procedure needed?
- What is the organization's purpose for the procedure?
- Was there an old procedure? What was wrong with it?
- How do the users feel about the old procedure?
- How are they likely to feel about the new procedure?

In any case, work to consider as many positions and opinions as you can in the time you have to ask the questions. Your goal should be to find out what management is thinking about the product or process so that you can plan a strategy that helps achieve the organization's goals.

Guideline: *Ask the right questions to uncover goals, objectives, and strategies.*

Sorting through the answers

The information gathering can be interesting, even exciting, but it also has an element of risk involved. Different members of the organization may have different agendas they hope to pursue in developing the product. You may find yourself in the middle of a controversy if you're not careful about sorting out the various points of view. That is another good reason for the project manager or other more experienced team members to role-play the interviewing process in advance and carefully debrief the team afterwards.

The product manager doesn't think they'll be able to provide customers advance training for free, and they can't charge the customer for it," the writer explained after several interviews. "But training is adamant that the customers won't be able to install and use the product without a training course. I think we should plan the documentation so that it is dependent on prior training."

"Wait a minute," the project manager replied. "Explain to me why can't we charge for training."

"A training fee would make our product more expensive than the competition's. Marketing thinks that will be a deal-breaker."

"That sounds like a serious problem. Can't we design the documentation so that a training course won't be necessary? And what about the new interface? Is it really going to be that difficult to use?"

"We could plan a tutorial as part of the documentation package. Or we could include a training video demonstrating the installation process. But I think we should support training."

"Training's position doesn't appear to be very realistic. We can present that alternative in the Information Plan and open it up for discussion in the review, but let's plan our strategy around the no-training option.

Since information planning is a strategic process, your team members should ask the questions. But as manager, you may have to provide a perspective on the answers, as well as encouragement during the process. That means you need a broad understanding of the organization's goals and the politics of the decision-making process. If you're in doubt yourself about how to handle a complicated political situation, you may want to consult your management, your mentors, and your network as well. It might also be helpful to have on hand your crystal ball, a psychic, and your astrologer, just in case.

 Guideline: ***Don't send your publications staff out unprepared. They may be pushed around by the big guns in the organization.***

Composing the project goals statement

Teamwork is needed throughout the information-planning process, but it is essential when you are attempting to analyze organizational strategies and plan your own. The close coordination and support between publications management and staff members will strengthen the process and foster skill building.

Once your staff has asked the right questions of the right people and together you've sorted out the answers, you are ready to compose the first section of the Information Plan: the statement of project goals and objectives. The statement should include the information and perspectives gathered and your conclusions about their relative weight. It should also include a brief description of the product and its market to clarify and communicate your understanding. If there are conflicts among various groups involved in the development effort, you may choose to point out these conflicts for discussion. Indicate that different decisions will result in different publication strategies.

Remember that the project is defined at this point as the greater project, the total effort in the organization of producing a new product, process, or document. In the next section, we will discuss how to turn the project goals into publications goals and objectives.

In a Pattern 3: Steering organization, development teams that take planning seriously will respect publications' objective statement as a further refinement of the planning process. They will be interested to know what publications is planning and contribute their own understanding to the process. In fact, parts of the strategy you document in the Information Plan should already have been laid out in a product-marketing plan.

In Pattern 1: Variable and Pattern 2: Routine organizations, your Information Plan may represent the first time that members of the development team see their project goals and objectives in print. In Pattern 2, development managers may view your statement as an effort to tell them what to do. They may resent the intrusion and remark that their strategies are none of your business. You'll have to make a strong case that you need the statement for your own project-management process, a concept they're likely to accept because it mirrors their own practice of telling people what to do. For a Pattern 2 organization that is flirting with Pattern 3, your Information Plan statement may help to push them into a new process model.

In a Pattern 1 organization, people will likely view your Information Plan as unnecessary, a waste of time, another attempt to curtail the freewheeling creativity of individual team members. They will often be too busy to read the document. Of course, if you're trying to be a Level 3 publications manager in a Pattern 1 development organization, you have your work cut out for you. Value the effort for your own staff and planning process, if not for the feedback you're hoping for from the rest of the company.

In addition, be aware that if you are a Level 1 or 2 publications organization, you are likely to find resistance among your own team members to the planning process. If they have learned from the organization's culture, they will resent having their thinking open to scrutiny and discussion. You may want to begin by introducing the concepts and asking your most cooperative and interested team member to develop the first plan. Early adapters are those who are eager for new challenges and opportunities and are more open to change. You may also write the initial Information Plan yourself and invite your team to critique your plan. In doing so, you broadcast the message that everyone's work should be reviewed to ensure that the publications group is producing the best-quality work it can.

 Guideline: Clarify the purpose of the development project so that you can build your publications strategy in tandem with the goals of your organization.

Determining the publication goals and objectives

Once your team understands the goals and objectives of the greater project, direct them to an analysis of the goals and objectives they need to establish for the publications project (see Figure 7.5).

Although the discussion of publications goals and objectives is the second major section of the Information Plan, it is not necessarily written second. Publications goals and objectives are heavily influenced by an analysis of the audience and the tasks they want to perform. Therefore, your staff may not be ready to complete this section of their plan until they have a clearer view of audience and task. Nevertheless, to the extent that project goals and objectives need to influence your planning process, you may find it useful to open the discussion of general goals and objectives early.

In the case of the maintenance manual, our investigation of the problems that the field engineers experienced in using the manual led to a publications objective. The objective stated that

The maintenance manual should be designed and organized so that the average time needed by field engineering to find, read, and execute a procedure is reduced by 20 percent.

Figure 7.5 Creating goals and objectives for the publications project

A concrete objective of this sort has many advantages. It directs the writers to produce a document with a very specific goal in mind. All formatting and organizational decisions need to be focused on the objective of reducing the time the audience spends using the document. Planning decisions, based on this criterion, become less arbitrary and better directed.

A concrete objective also sets the direction for possible testing of the maintenance manual. You could compare the average time needed by a field engineer to find, read, and correctly execute a procedure using the old manual with the average time using the new manual.

A concrete objective demonstrates that publications do make a difference in a user's performance. A maintenance manual that is easy to use and read may result in an average reduction in the cost of a field-engineering visit. A visit that succeeds in bringing a customer's equipment back into working order more quickly will also result in a more satisfied customer.

Many managers view publications as expensive add-ons that are required as part of the sale but contribute little to the success of the product. It is your obligation to educate them by producing publications that make a difference. You can begin this education process by stating in your Information Plans how the publications organization intends to contribute to product success and customer satisfaction and to state your goals and objectives as concretely as possible.

In the following example, the publications goals are clearly linked to the product and marketing goals of the organization:

In the publications designed for the ABC product, users must be able to find the information they need to perform their tasks as quickly as possible. Since users will interact with the system infrequently and will have no time for learning, the information must be presented simply and briefly with little discussion of concepts. The users of this product are general aviation pilots who will appear at the airport a half hour to an hour before their intended takeoff time. They need to file a flight plan and obtain up-to-the-minute weather maps, as well as ready their planes for the trip. They will spend no more than a few minutes with the system. The documentation must make this brief interaction possible.

In this objective statement, the writer stresses the need for simple and short information, organized for quick access. The "getting started" structure suggested by this objective might be implemented in a small pamphlet. Concepts and more difficult tasks need to be reserved for those few users who allow themselves more time with the system.

Establishing usability goals

Wanderly "Van" Diehl, in his presentation on usability goals (Diehl, 1992) for documentation, argues that not only should we state the goals and objectives for the publications project in our planning document, but we should also emphasize, in a separate section, the usability goals that we believe the documentation will accomplish. Usability goals stress the importance of making our documentation as usable as possible under the conditions that we identify in the audience, environment, and task analyses. Usability goals provide the basis for documentation-usability testing during the development life cycle. Goals set early need to be tested to judge whether they have been adequately accomplished.

It should be quite clear that your publications staff cannot produce sound goals and objectives until they understand the users, the environment in which users must work, and the tasks they want to perform. Therefore, while you may ask them to state tentative goals and objectives early, they will need to revise the goals and objectives as they gain more information. Although most information gathering about users, environment, and tasks will occur early in a project's life cycle, new information will continue to surface during implementation. Whenever new information appears, you need to assess its impact on the overall goals and objectives of the publications.

The Information Plan is not a document that is written once, signed off on, and shelved. It should be a dynamic document that is changed as the project is better understood. Although a formal revised plan may not be issued, communications describing the changes are part of the project-management process. While any project manager wants to minimize late changes to a project, new information may require course adjustments later on. You often make such adjustments to respond to changes in the product. You should also evaluate the need for adjustments as your staff gains experience with the product and increases its understanding of the users. A stubborn refusal to change in the face of new information will result in an unsuccessful publications project.

Guideline: Establish publications goals and objectives that support the users and their tasks and contribute to the organization's overall goals.

Analyzing the audiences for the publications

The third step in the information-planning process is the development of a detailed profile of the audiences for the publications (see Figure 7.6). The audience profiles established will inevitably inform the goals and objectives of the publications. Although Figure 7.6 shows the analysis steps occurring after goals and objectives are set, in fact they often occur simultaneously with the investigation of development project goals and objectives.

Audience analysis is one of the most widely accepted parts of the publications planning process and one of the least effectively performed. Audience analysis sits in

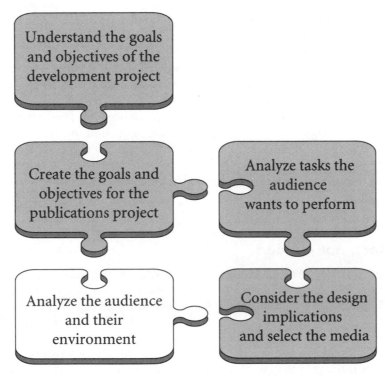

Figure 7.6 Analyzing the audience and their environment

the heart of a fundamental controversy between publications specialists and others in the organizations. The controversy revolves around a very significant question:

Do technical writers need to have direct contact with users to write effective documents?

Publications managers themselves contribute to the controversy by acknowledging the importance of audience analysis but discouraging writers from performing it. They tend to argue that there is not enough time and money in the publications budget to permit writers to conduct interviews, visit customer sites, and otherwise gather direct information about the people who will use the documents they produce.

Despite genuine restrictions on time, budget, and access to users, we must recognize a simple truth. Without firsthand knowledge of the audience, without a rich picture of the people who will be reading and using a document, you are very likely to design and build documents that are of limited success in meeting your audience's needs. There is no substitute for direct experience with the audience. And there is no way to construct a rich picture of the audience without some firsthand contact. Any substitution, even if it includes at best the firsthand experience of other people in the organization, leaves open the possibility of miscalculation. The reports your audiences give you of their difficulty in reading and using the documents you painstakingly produce are their own best evidence. Even given talented and dedicated technical communicators, you may fail to produce high-quality information products if you don't know who you are designing for. In fact, good, usable design is always a reflection of the depth of the designer's understanding of those who will use the product.

You know that developing a viable rich picture of the audience for your work is not a simple task. It is not a task that can be done adequately with a single brief interview. It is a task that will take time and can profit from a gradual learning process. As a manager, you should also recognize and communicate to your staff that audience analysis activities need not all be done at the same time or for the same project. Understanding your organization's audience is a long-term and cumulative process that results in an increasingly rich picture. All audience analysis need not be budgeted to one project; it can be spread among the budgets of several projects and over longer periods of time.

Designing from fact, not opinion

Every Information Plan must contain a profile of the audience for the planned information. The project manager's task is to see to it that the profiles are based more on fact than on opinion. We already know that many people in the organization will have opinions about the audience for the documentation. Marketing, sales, research and development, training, field engineering, service, and others will all have opinions, occasionally based upon direct interaction, about the characteristics of the audience. Although it is possible to plan publications based on the opinions of others, a plan that contains more opinions than facts may be seriously flawed.

Perhaps the most damaging opinion is based on the assumption that the audience has as much experience with similar products or processes as the product designer. Designers, whether they are engineers, computer scientists, or technical communicators, often portray the audience in remarkably personal tones.

"The user is a programmer. I'm a programmer. Therefore, the user is just like me," goes the most common refrain. From a technical communicator, the refrain sounds something like this: "I like to understand the whole concept before I do anything. Therefore, the user needs to have a detailed conceptual overview before he or she begins to perform a task."

Unfortunately, it is highly likely that many of our assumptions about the audience are wrong. What we find instead, when we conduct careful audience analyses, is that the users are quite different from us and have very different needs and objectives.

Consequently, it is extremely important that as a manager you find ways to permit your writers to survey, interview, and observe members of their audience directly so that they gain a rich picture of exactly who the audience is.

In one case, the software-development team for the US Department of Agriculture's brucellosis project had an unusually deep understanding of their users. By its well-organized and readable screens and neatly designed reports, the software design clearly demonstrated that the developers recognized that their users were not computer experts. When I asked the development manager how this unusual degree of empathy came about, she explained that when the project began, she scheduled time for the programmers and analysts to visit veterinarians' offices around the country. They met with the people who ran the small offices, learning that the office staff had little computer experience and frequently worked part-time. They returned with individual portraits of the people they had to design for. As they worked on the user interface, many of the developers had specific individuals in mind, individuals they had met on their site visits. That direct contact with users had made all the difference.

Why should you want to fight for time and money to support audience analysis? Primarily, because a fact-based audience profile will enable your publications staff to produce better publications that are more closely focused on audience needs.

Why will a better analysis of the audience enable you to product better publications? Some people may argue that their audiences are too complex and diverse—that there is no point in studying a few customers if you cannot afford to study hundreds. I believe that even small studies of real users can provide significant information to the publications-development process.

If you think of technical publications as tools that people use to perform a task, rather than as compendiums of information about a product or process, then you can clearly define the need for a rich understanding of the audience. To be effective and useful, tools must be designed to match the capabilities of the people who must use them. People designing can openers must know if their intended users have the strength and physical dexterity to operate the handle and gears they design to open the can. If the handle is too difficult to turn or too small or large to hold, users will return the opener and purchase a competitor's product, or they may discard the opener and decide never to buy another product from the designer's company.

So it goes with more sophisticated products. The manuals we write to support products and processes, the documents we produce to convey information, all must be designed as tools for convenient and productive use. Without knowing the basic characteristic of our intended users, how can we possibly design effective tools?

Convincing management of the need for direct audience analysis

Now, it is certainly easy to state that better-defined audiences will enable you to produce publications of higher quality. But audience analysis takes time and costs money. How do you convince your own management that this time and money are well spent?

One publications manager argued that by studying the audiences for their publications, they would gain

- A better understanding of the audience that might help reduce publication costs
- Direct knowledge of audience characteristics that would permit the publications group to argue more effectively for the learning needs of the audience
- The specialized information about the audience that is not necessarily relevant to the needs of other development groups
- The ability to contribute to everyone's better understanding of user characteristics and requirements

You can argue that understanding the audience actually has the potential not only for an increase in publications quality but also for a reduction in publications cost. An organization that has comprehensive data about its audiences is better able to target publications for their needs. By adequately targeting information, you may be able to eliminate information that is unnecessary to the audience.

In many instances, publications organizations produce more information than the audience needs to know. When they do not know enough about their prospective readers, writers feel they must include sufficient information to cover all possible contingencies. As a result, audience members frequently complain that they feel buried under too much information in too much detail. The critical information that they need to know is difficult to find when it is mixed with "nice to know" but unnecessary information.

Yet, you cannot fault the writers or others inside your organization for including everything. In the absence of data about the audience, it may appear safer to include too much than to include too little. Unfortunately, a publications strategy that errs on the side of too much information is costly. Unnecessary information must be reviewed, edited, printed, and distributed. It must also be maintained, perhaps for many years, by legions of maintenance writers.

In short, publications that are designed for well-defined audiences are often less costly to produce and maintain than publications that simply broadcast all the information we have in hopes that someone will find what they need.

A publications department that roots its decisions in fact rather than opinion will be better able to forestall unproductive arguments among the members of the product-development team. Since many people in an organization have opinions about the users of a product or process, they often indulge in long and unproductive arguments about the needs of the audiences for publications. Without hard data, a publications organization has little ability to counter these arguments. You might say that without data, all opinions are equal and that the loudest opinions voiced by the most powerful people are more equal than others. However, nothing argues as loudly as facts. Hard data enables you to base your designs upon fact rather than opinion and to produce strong arguments in favor of your designs.

Of course, other members of your organization may argue that they have already profiled the audiences for their products or information. Marketing departments often conduct comprehensive studies of the potential buyers of a product. Product-marketing and development groups may produce audience profiles during the requirements-definition process. The information developed by these groups is valuable and contributes to the understanding needed in technical publications to design information. To the extent that any audience information is based on data and contributes to our understanding, it will be useful. Unfortunately, the data collected by other groups about the information users is often inadequate for detailed information planning.

Marketing organizations that do important and useful studies of potential buyers and users of a product may focus on the characteristics of the buyer rather than the characteristics of the user. Indeed, there may be similarities between buyer and user; they may, in fact, be the same individual. However, the publications team needs to know about the users, not as buyers, but as people who interact with many types of information, from hardcopy books to online tutorials. Information about the learning styles of the audience is not necessarily relevant to the marketing effort and is often not collected.

Development organizations that do extensive user profiles to develop user-requirements documents may also provide significant information needed by publications. However, software and hardware user requirements are often focused on system interaction rather than user profiles, and the user profiles neglect aspects of the user characteristics that relate directly to publications. For example, the age of the average user may not be significant to the development of a machine tool but may be significant to decisions about book design.

The focus in arguing for direct user contact should be that publications has unique questions that you must address if you are to plan effectively for information that meets user needs. You have questions to ask and perspectives to gain that are unique to publications. And in a larger organization that has not adequately studied the characteristics of its users, you may have a significant role to play in developing data that will be valuable for the entire product-development and sales cycles.

If your organization does not already conduct user analyses for requirements definition and planning, you can argue that allowing the publications staff to conduct the analysis will be cost-effective and produce wide-ranging benefits.

In one instance, we learned late in the product-development life cycle that the intended users of a complicated computer system lacked one extremely important characteristic: They could not and would not learn to type. Yet, the computer system required extensive data entry through a keyboard. Without strong typing skills, the users were likely to find the time needed to perform a task greatly increased. The lack of typing skills had a impact on our design of a training program for the users. But it had a more significant impact on the design of the computer system itself. We did not believe that we could or should include basic typing skills in the user training. The better solution was to redesign the user interface so that minimal typing was required.

In this case, the audience analysis conducted by technical communicators led to a significant change in the user interface for the product. Without that change, the product might have failed in the market because of user resistance.

Getting help from others in the organization

If you are fortunate enough to work for an organization that values the customer's role in the design of products and processes, you may be able to use information gathered by others. In particular, as a project manager, direct your staff to have discussions with those people in the organization most likely to have direct contact with the audiences for your publications. These groups may include

- Training
- Customer support
- Field engineering
- Sales and retail

Training organizations are especially valuable sources of audience information because they have the same interest in detailed user profiles as publications. In fact, instructional designers in your training organization may have already conducted a comprehensive user analysis as part of their training-development process. Such information will be extremely helpful in developing a user profile for publications, although it may have to be supplemented by specific details about publications use.

As a strategic-planning consultant, I strongly recommend, in fact, that training and publications be closely aligned in the development of documents and job aids. It may be most cost-effective to do a single analysis of the audience with enough focus on specific details to satisfy the planning needs of both groups.

In addition to the training organization, others who have direct customer contact should be part of the audience-analysis efforts. Enlist the help of customer support. They listen to audience questions and problems all day and often have a detailed perspective on the capabilities of their callers. Do not forget, however, that customer support often views users with a jaundiced eye. They only interact with those customers who call for support. These customers may have significant characteristics that place them in a particular user group, such as less experience and knowledge or fewer problem-solving skills.

A frequently heard statement in many organizations is that users will not read documentation but prefer to call for answers to their questions. This declaration often comes from customer support. One might ask: What percentage of customers call customer support, especially after the first few days or weeks of use? Often, the percentages are low—somewhere between 10 and 25 percent. Who are the customers who do not call? In a user analysis, we may want to discover why some customers call customer support and others do not. We need to plan publications for both groups.

Field engineering and direct sales and retail are other possible internal sources of information about customers. Both of these groups interact directly with customers and experience their questions and problems. Direct your project team to find out as much as possible from these sources before they plan their direct contact with the audience.

Deciding how much audience analysis to do

When your project team has limited time and money to spend on audience analysis, what should you choose to do? Here is a list of possible activities in order of least to most expensive.

- Contact internal sources of information, especially those groups that have direct contact with the audience for your publications.

  Learn as much from internal sources as possible before performing additional studies. With a limited budget, internal sources may be your only source of information. Just be certain that you direct your inquiry to those who have facts rather than opinions about your audience.

- Consult internal and external written sources of information about the audience.

  Has your marketing department conducted focus groups or user surveys? Has the development organization conducted a user-requirements study? Is there a human-factors group that has gathered experimental data about the audience?

  Are there external sources of information in the trade publications of the industry in which you work? In many specialized markets, you may be surprised to find extensive library information about your audience. When we studied nurses, we discovered several important books and a journal devoted to discussions of nurses' interactions with computers. These sources helped to direct our site visits and interviews and corroborated information we gathered in the field.

- Develop a survey questionnaire, and send it to a selected (or random) sample of your users.

  Questionnaires, unfortunately, are the least productive way to develop the detailed information we need to understand our audiences. They are also difficult to plan, execute, validate, and interpret and take more time than you may imagine. If you are considering a survey, I strongly suggest that you find expert help either within your organization or outside. Don't waste money on an invalid survey. Poor results can cause extensive damage by suggesting changes to your publications that you might find inadvisable if you have better information.

- Conduct a telephone survey of your audience members.

  A carefully planned telephone survey can be cost-effective and produce a significant amount of information in a short period of time. However, any survey must be carefully planned if the results are to be valid. Get help in planning a questionnaire from people in your own marketing organization or from outside experts in survey design. Decide carefully on your sample size and which individuals you will call. Be certain to get permission from the appropriate people in the organization before contacting customers directly. Sales and marketing may be concerned about the professionalism of the survey and want to protect customers from harrassment.

Fax or mail the questionnaire before interviewing if possible, so that your user is prepared to answer the questions. Set up an appointment for your call; don't expect people to interrupt important tasks to answer your questions. Finally, leave time for more open-ended comments. Your users may have things to tell you that were not covered in your questionnaire.

- Meet with human resources.

If you are developing a user profile for an inhouse group, you may find it very useful to discuss hiring and performance issues with the human resources department. We have found that human resources can provide solid information on hiring requirements and often has information on test results of new or potential hires that can be very informative. In one instance, we discovered that tellers in savings and loan companies were frequently hired for their friendly manner and their ability to make customers feel comfortable, rather than for their computer skills.

- Interview customers when they visit your site for demonstrations, discussions, training classes, or user groups.

Make sure that your staff takes advantage of every inexpensive opportunity to interact with the real audience. We frequently find, when we ask, that customers often visit a company site. It may take only a brief phone call to arrange for a visit with publications. You might offer to meet during a lunch break or at the end of the day, so that you don't interfere with other customer activities. Company visits offer access to customers who may be difficult to meet otherwise. In one instance, we were able to interview a customer from an important site in South America because he happened to be attending a user conference nearby. He spent nearly two hours with the publications staff and was happy for the opportunity to voice his concerns about the quality and appropriateness of the documentation.

Customer training classes also present valuable opportunities for your publications staff to interact with their audiences as they are learning to use the product. Not only do technical communicators profit from taking part in a training class by learning new information, they also have an opportunity to listen and watch members of their potential audiences as they experience the product for the first time or in a new situation. Training classes also provide opportunities for informal, low-key exchanges of information with audience members. These exchanges are invaluable to the development of a rich audience profile.

User-group meetings provide excellent opportunities to meet customers en masse. At one user group, we developed a panel on documentation that included members of the publications staff. The organization was amazed at the response. More users attended the documentation panel than any of the other panels scheduled. They were anxious to ask and answer questions. Although they used the opportunity to criticize poor publications, they seemed pleased that their concerns were being heard.

You might also find it possible to attend conferences or conventions where your company is exhibiting. Members of your audience will need product demonstrations, that present opportunities for you to experience their confusion and their needs directly.

- Conduct site visits.

There is no better way to develop a rich picture of the audience than to visit them in their own environment. People at work behave differently than people around a conference table being interviewed or people being interviewed over the telephone. The interviewers get a feel for the workplace, the environment in which the audience members must function. But most important, the interviewers get to know their audiences as individuals rather than as stereotypes. By meeting users directly, we recognize their needs and their challenges; we see them as Sam or Mary rather than as clerks or engineers.

Although you must be careful about potential bias, even a few site visits can help the publications team become more aware of their audiences, especially of their diversity. Of course, several site visits are better than one, but one site visit is better than none.

Overcoming objections

As a manager, your task is to help team members make the arrangements and smooth the path through the maze of marketing and sales restrictions on customer contact. To do so, you must understand the reasons for the objections you may encounter. People in marketing and sales organizations are genuinely concerned about the impression your staff members may make on the customer. They are afraid that someone will reflect badly on the company and its products or may inadvertently provide advance information about a new product before it is released.

Perhaps the most effective way to counter such arguments is to invite the marketing or sales person to take part in the site visit or listen in on the telephone conversation. I have encountered very few instances in which the customer is not pleased to be asked about publications. They are often very interested in obtaining easier-to-use and more accurate information and appreciate an opportunity to make their needs and problems known to technical communicators.

At the same time, we need to take concerns about professional conduct seriously. You must ensure that your staff members behave professionally and are aware of the restrictions on what they may say about forthcoming products. If you are beginning the process of site visits, you may want to accompany staff members, in part to gain information yourself about the audience but also to guide your staff in their approach to the customer. You may want to select carefully the staff members who interact with customers; not everyone makes a good impression or is an effective interviewer.

You also need to ensure that your staff members are well prepared for any interaction they might have with customers. That means working with them on the questions they will ask and how they will conduct themselves during the customer meeting.

Appendix B contains a short list of the categories of questions that may be relevant to your audience analysis. These categories represent guidelines only, however. Your staff will need to develop the specific questions most relevant to the audiences you are working with. In general, you will need to know something about the abilities that your audiences bring to their interaction with your company's processes or products and the methods they use to solve problems, as well as any personal characteristics that may challenge their use of the product or the learning materials you produce.

Guideline: Create opportunities for your publications staff to interact directly with the audiences to develop a rich picture of whom they serve.

Including an environment analysis

An integral part of an audience analysis is an analysis of the environment in which the audience functions. The physical and operational environments may significantly influence the ability of audiences to learn new tasks and solve problems. Difficult or unusual working environments are likely to influence the way you organize and package publications.

You may discover that some audiences work in difficult physical environments, ones that are dark, dirty, or noisy. You may discover that some audiences work in difficult operational environments in which publications are hard to use. They may face constant interruptions of their work flow that make learning new information difficult. They may not have immediate access to hardcopy manuals, or their access to critical information may be limited by company policy. Once, we found the only copy of a manual in a supervisor's office with the door locked.

You may even discover critical social environments that create barriers to an effective learning process, including coworkers who are threatened by individuals who spend "too much time with their noses in a book." Your task, as manager, is to ensure that you staff members are on the lookout for environmental challenges to the users. In Appendix C, you will find a brief checklist of the types of questions you might ask about the user environment.

Environment analysis is best conducted at the same time as audience analysis. However, it is difficult to obtain a comprehensive view of environmental challenges unless your staff has access to the audiences' actual working world. Site visits are thus critical to gaining the information you need to make good decisions about publications.

Guideline: Ensure that you know the challenges your audiences face in their actual working environments.

In the example in Figure 7.7, the audience and environment have been carefully analyzed.

This analysis resulted from a combination of internal discussions with development, marketing, training, and service and visits to customer sites.

Sample audience profile

Before we can determine how best to organize and design Locust 1234 user-support materials, we must determine who the audience is. We need to develop an audience profile that begins to identify

- The types of audiences we must address — Are we possibly looking at multiple audiences who have different backgrounds, use the product in different ways, or perform at different levels?
- The environment they work in — What is the actual physical location like, and what background issues come into play as a result of the environment?
- The audience's needs — What does the audience expect and require of the documentation to learn how to use and service the product as quickly and efficiently as possible?

The rest of this section presents the results of our audience analysis and provides answers to these questions.

Types of audiences

There are two basic audiences for the Locust 1234 instructional documentation: end users of the product (user audience) and service technicians who will service and repair the product (service audience).

According to Locust's marketing research, approximately 80 percent of the user audience for the Locust 1234 product-support materials is made up of lab technicians and machine shop mechanics, most of whom will have little or no experience using technology for the task and are unaccustomed to using computers. Approximately 20 percent of the user audience consists of engineers, scientists, and others, most of whom will have had experience with similar products. Although the specific needs of individuals in each of these groups will undoubtedly vary, for the purposes of this plan we are dividing our user audience into two general types: novice users and experienced users. To some degree, then, each of these two major user groups will include all segments of our overall user audience.

The service audience consists mainly of Locust-trained service technicians.

Novice users

Typical novice users — mainly technicians and mechanics — present a number of challenges that the documentation must adequately address. For example, these users, according to the project manager, are older "computer phobics" who are experienced in machine shop techniques but highly resistant to

Figure 7.7 Sample audience and environmental analysis

computerized systems. Therefore, they will need extra support ("hand-holding") to make the transition to using software-controlled laser technology for calibration.

Novice users typically will not have participated in the buying decision, a decision that is typically made by an executive (or economic) buyer at a higher level of management (and with whom shop personnel normally have no direct communication). These users consequently receive the equipment without having been sold on its value and very often do not even know the extent of the product's capability. All they know is that they must use the product to do what they formerly did manually with simple, easy-to-use techniques. This situation tends to inspire not only resistance but also fear of making mistakes. If mistakes are made by novice users because of their resistance to the new technology or because they have not been adequately trained in its use, they will avoid using the machine to its full capacity and blame it for any failures to achieve the desired results. Therefore, it is important that early in the learning process these users understand the extent of the product's capability and are convinced that the product is easy to use.

Also, because they are the accepted experts in their own environments, these typical novice users have the power to pass unfavorable judgments on equipment performance back to the original buyers. Therefore, this group represents the greatest opportunity for achieving one of the marketing objectives: to ensure that these novice users are as completely sold on the product as the original buyers. Their needs must be met through project-support materials and training, and the materials themselves must be designed to ensure that they will provide the stand-alone sales appeal capable of overcoming the characteristic resistance to new techniques.

The challenge is to excite and motivate these novice users so that they will want to learn the new system and take pride both in the quality of the new system and in their own expertise in using it. User pride can be developed when performance improvements can be demonstrated through their own performance of specific operational tasks. As these users develop mastery of the new system, they will be transformed from passive task performers to active product promoters.

Experienced users

The primary audience of experienced users is made up of engineers, scientists, and the minority of technicians and mechanics who have more product-related experience than those in the novice user group. Experienced users have some knowledge of the technology, training on similar equipment, and experience with computer software. Their need is for easily accessible overview and reference information so they can quickly learn the specifics of how this system differs from others they have used and start performing new tasks.

Figure 7.7 (Continued)

Service technicians

This audience is made up primarily of the service technicians who have received training in servicing this product and products like it.

Audience environments

This section first identifies the user-audience environment. It then identifies the service-audience environment.

User-audience environment

The most common user environments are laboratories (such as QA labs) and production floors (for the majority of applications). Laboratories present no special requirements impacting user documentation, but the typical production floor environment does present specific requirements for document design.

Typically, users in the production floor environment must set up the equipment on the production line and accomplish the procedures while the machine is down. They must perform the work quickly and accurately to reduce production downtime to an absolute minimum. To achieve this aim, users must know the procedure before they get out on the floor. Once there, they won't have much (if any) time to access and review detailed information in printed documents; and in most cases, if training is adequate, they won't need to. By necessity, any instructional information users might need to complete the work must be in the form of quick-reference documentation, whether it be a quick-reference card or guide or online screens.

The necessity for user expertise on the floor means that training must be done prior to operation, preferably in a locale dedicated to the training process. The use of training materials, including printed materials and videos, would be geared appropriately to a training environment.

Service-audience environment

The service technician works in a service center. This environment presents no special requirements impacting the document design.

Audience information needs analysis

Based on our audience analysis and product assessment, we have identified the following major information needs for novice users, experienced users, and service technicians. (See the next section of this report, "Task descriptions," for an analysis of general tasks users must perform with the product.)

Figure 7.7 (Continued)

Novice users

User documentation should fulfill the following needs of the novice user:

- Information in a "friendly design" that is easy to access and understand (not intimidating), so that users can efficiently and painlessly adapt to a new way of doing their job
- Brief overview information that "sells" the capabilities of the product with an emphasis on ease of use and quickly acquired product expertise
- Easy-to-follow step-by-step instructions that include the detail necessary for novice users to fully understand what they are doing and why

What novice users don't need are

- The theory
- In-depth information on how the system works
- In-depth troubleshooting or servicing information

Experienced users

User documentation should fulfill the following needs of the experienced user:

- Overview information that succinctly describes the unique features of the product
- Procedural instructions that are easy for the reader to access and review without getting bogged down by rudimentary support information
- Detailed information about the system that allows the experienced audience to perform analysis tasks that might not typically be performed by the novice audience

Service technicians

For service technicians, the service documentation should provide task-oriented information that is easy to refer to and follow. It should include all the information the technician needs to troubleshoot and service the product.

Figure 7.7 (Continued)

Developing a high-level task inventory

In comparison with audience analysis, task analysis is a more complex and difficult process. If you and your staff members are embarking on your first attempt at a task analysis, I strongly recommend that you obtain some training in the techniques to use and that you refer to the reference material in the field (see Figure 7.8).

Task analysis, or an understanding of how and why the audiences will interact with a product or a set of informational publications, provides the database needed by the publications group to support a useful Information Plan. Task analysis is your primary source of data to counter the interests of those who would orient the publications toward the interests and needs of the developers.

At the information-planning stage, it is most likely that you will develop only a high-level inventory of the major tasks that your audiences will want to perform. A high-level task inventory is generally sufficient at this early stage in the development process, when you are trying to produce a broad view of project requirements. However, you need to develop the task inventory sufficiently to be able to select the types of publications needed for the product and to make an early assessment of their scope.

As a manager, you need to be aware of the need to develop sound task-related information as an integral part of the planning process. Abundant evidence exists that

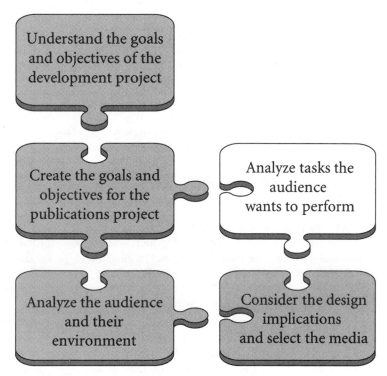

Figure 7.8   Conducting a task analysis

the vast majority of users profit from information that is designed to support their performance. Information that is organized according to the tasks users want to perform, rather than according to the design of the product, is easier to access and to use.

Managing the task analysis

As a manager, your task is to help direct your staff members toward the development of a library of information that best supports user needs. Your own familiarity with current best practices is essential if you are to provide the appropriate guidance and direction. In many organizations, writers are directed by researchers and developers, whose tendency is to focus on the product rather than its use. As a result, far too much technical documentation presents a description of the product. We continue to see publications that are reformatted versions of the specification documents, detailing menus and fields but containing little information on how to use the product efficiently and effectively.

In producing such product-oriented documentation, writers are often strongly influenced by the point of view and expertise of developers. In learning about the product under development, they talk to developers, who are primarily interested in the design of the product. In fact, developers may have very little direct information about how people intend to use the product. In many cases, product-marketing specialists translate user requirements into design specifications. The developers interact with the design specifications, never experiencing the users' needs firsthand.

The lack of an understanding of user needs among researchers and developers, as well as the strong influence of developers over the design of publications, often results in a library of publications that are mistargeted. Such publications are often a compendium of information about product development, often fulfilling the role of product-maintenance documentation rather than meeting the needs of the audiences. Writers who have little experience or training in the development of publications that meet user needs are very likely to take the path of least resistance. It is far easier to comply with the ideas of the development team than to resist them and strike out on a different path, a path designed to meet user needs. The publications manager's job is to lead the way and set the tone for the development of publications. Task analysis is a key ingredient in establishing the autonomy and authority of the publications group over the selection of the best library for the product.

In one project, we had studied the patterns of use that were likely to occur in the audience's environment. We knew that the product was to be installed by the dealer and only reinstalled by the user in an emergency. Consequently, we decided to place minimal installation instructions in an appendix to the user's guide. Developers, thinking more in terms of the product logic than of users' needs, argued that "all installation instructions should be at the beginning of the manual, since installation is the first action required of the product." The head of development referred to his own experience in seeing installation instructions at the beginning of some manuals for products he owned. However, by bringing into the discussion the analysis we had done of the users' environment and the distribution of user tasks, we were able to convince development that installation instructions were of secondary importance to using the product effectively. The users, we argued, were more interested in getting their jobs done than in learning about an installation task they were unlikely ever to perform.

The same holds true for much conceptual information about a product. We know that a majority of users simply want to get a task done; they are not ready to learn the hows and whys of what they are doing. Yet, many publications are planned as if the audience members will read the entire document from cover to cover. One technical writer insisted to me that the users would only be successful if they read the entire manual three times.

A task analysis that demonstrates the most probable patterns of use for publications can help you support an argument to place beginning or commonly used tasks in prominent positions in the documentation and minimize the conceptual information.

Armed with a good task analysis, one that stems from close interaction with the user in the user's environment, a publications team is better able to hold its ground and argue for the primacy of the user's needs in the design of publications. A rich picture not only of user characteristics developed in the audience analysis but also of the user's goals, attitudes, and current tasks can provide the basis for all design decisions during the course of the project.

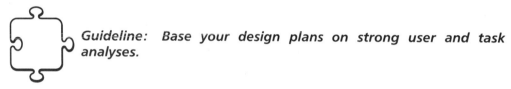

Guideline: Base your design plans on strong user and task analyses.

Using task analysis to determine scope

Besides directing your thinking about how to meet user needs, the high-level task analysis your staff performs at this early stage in the document-development process is essential for an initial definition of the scope of the project. By looking at user tasks as well as user needs for reference-oriented information, your team can actively begin to outline the scope of the project as a whole.

It is essential that you be able to produce some task information in the information-planning phase to determine the project's scope. To estimate the effort required to complete the documentation project, you must define how much work is to be done. By looking at user tasks, you have a method for defining that work.

One approach at this early stage is to combine information gathered about the product or process itself with a generic task taxonomy. A task taxonomy is a standard list of tasks that people tend to perform. For examples of detailed taxonomies of tasks and behaviors, you may want to consult Galitz's or Berliner's work (Galitz, 1984, and Berliner, 1965). You may want to begin with any of these lists of standard tasks and compare the lists with what is known about your users' requirements. A very simple but useful standard list we have used includes such generic tasks as

- Planning
- Installation
- Administration

- Configuration and customization
- Diagnosis and troubleshooting
- Maintenance

Out of the generic task list, we can derive specific tasks handled by the product in addition to the critical list of user-oriented tasks. The more user-oriented tasks often fall under the generic category of operation or end use. Most of your responsibility will be to analyze the operational tasks the user needs to perform. The category of operational tasks includes all the goals that users have for the product or process they need to perform.

Guideline: Begin your task analysis with a generic task list, and expand the list by performing a high-level task analysis.

Sample task description

In Figure 7.9, the user tasks are prominent, although several generic tasks, such as installation, are included.

It is easy to see that the users of the system are most interested in gathering, analyzing, and reporting data. They must also learn to install, troubleshoot, and maintain the equipment. User- and product-related tasks such as these are derived from direct user contact and from discussions with individuals who have themselves studied the users and are developing the product requirements.

A number of techniques are available to your staff in studying user tasks, including

- Surveys and interviews
- Direct observation of user performance
- Protocol analysis
- Simulations and prototypes

To learn about these techniques, review some of the major texts on task analysis, such as Jonassen, et al. (1989).

Turning your task research into a task description

For your staff to turn their understanding of user tasks into a full Information Plan, they need to evaluate the interrelationships of tasks and user characteristics and the effect of these interrelationships on the design of the information. The results of their evaluation and analysis become the sections in the Information Plan called the user/task matrix and the design implications.

In publications groups that produce information that is not related to products or processes, task analysis may not appear to be directly relevant to identifying the needs of the audience. Indeed, if we define task analysis broadly enough to include the

Task description

Once we have established who will be using the Locust 1234 documentation (and how), we must identify all the essential tasks required to accomplish a meaningful outcome using and servicing the product. And this list must be coordinated with the audiences identified in the previous section, "Audience profile." Our intent in this Information Plan is to establish a high-level listing of tasks so that we can begin to determine how information should be organized and designed. A more detailed listing of low-level specific tasks will be developed for, and included in, the individual Content Plans.

High-level tasks

We have identified the following high-level tasks required for Locust 1234 users and service technicians:

- Initially installing the hardware and software (novice users, experienced users, and service technicians)
- Gathering data (novice users and experienced users)
- Analyzing and reporting the data (experienced users)
- Troubleshooting the system (novice users and experienced users at the user level, service technicians at a more comprehensive technical level)
- Maintaining and servicing the system (novice users and experienced users at the user level, service technicians at a more complex technical level)

Initially installing the hardware and software

This high-level task includes all the subtasks required to install the hardware and software for the system and connect components. It may be performed by novice users, experienced users, or service technicians.

Gathering data

This high-level task includes all the subtasks required to prepare the hardware and software for operation, set up the hardware, and actually gather the data. It may be performed by either novice or experienced users.

Analyzing and reporting the data

This high-level task has yet to be fully defined and developed by Locust. Once developed, it will include subtasks for using computer-generated data for evaluating, planning for, and maintaining other equipment as part of the user

Figure 7.9 Sample high-level task analysis

company's operations-management and facilities-development functions. These tasks will be performed only by experienced users and are not likely to become part of our effort for the April release.

Troubleshooting the system (user level and service level)

This high-level task includes subtasks for two different audiences: users (novice and experienced) and service technicians. Users need user-level instructions to perform rudimentary troubleshooting on the system. Service technicians need more in-depth information to perform more comprehensive technical troubleshooting procedures.

Maintaining and servicing the system (user level and service level)

This high-level task includes subtasks for two different audiences: users (novice and experienced) and service technicians. Users need instructions to perform user-level routine maintenance procedures. Service technicians need more in-depth maintenance information to perform complex maintenance and servicing procedures, including removal and replacement procedures.

Figure 7.9 (Continued)

cognitive tasks of analyzing and evaluating information, then most users of business publications have tasks to perform. By understanding the nature of the users' cognitive tasks, we are better able to plan publications that meet their needs. We can direct writers to ask such task-related questions as

- What will the users do with the information provided?
- How will they make their decisions about the validity and strength of the arguments presented?
- How will they apply the information received to their own work?

This question-based technique I have long referred to as a discussion outline. It applies as well to scientific papers as it does to proposals and technical reports. To plan the organization and style of a particular document, we must know what the audience intends to do with the document and how they will be influenced by what the document contains. By attempting to anticipate the audience's questions about the subject matter, we are better able to focus the information design on answering the questions. A series of user questions, turned later into a series of informative headings, helps writers focus on user needs rather than on a logical presentation that conforms to the subject matter or to the interests of the researchers. The discussion-outline technique facilitates the development of user-oriented rather than subject-oriented publications.

If you are managing a writing staff that produces proposals and reports and other information-based publications, consider directing them to produce discussion outlines that reflect the questions the audiences are most likely to ask. Then, turn the potential audience questions into a user/task matrix, described in the next section.

Guideline: Use the discussion-outline technique to identify the questions that your text must answer for the audience.

Creating a user/task matrix

One of the best ways to illustrate the results of a high-level task analysis and its relationship to user characteristics is through the construction of a user/task matrix. In Figure 7.10, you see a simple user/task matrix for a device that allows manufacturing personnel to analyze the cables coming off the assembly line.

In analyzing tasks at a very high level, the company identified three major tasks:

- Installation
- Operation
- Maintenance

They also discovered three potential audiences:

- Engineers
- Technicians
- Operators

In the user/task matrix, they evaluated the probability on a scale of 1 (low) to 10 (high) that a particular user group would perform a particular task.

This graphic illustration of the interrelationship between user group and task allowed them to define more accurately the purpose and organization of their manuals.

Not only does the user/task matrix show which users are likely to perform which tasks, it also includes a probability assessment. Users and tasks are not an either/or proposition. Many writers complain that the tasks and processes they document are performed by individuals with a wide range of abilities and prior experience. By

User Task	User type		
	Engineers	*Technicians*	*Operators*
Installation	10	8	2
Operation	0	1	10
Maintenance	5	10	4

Figure 7.10 User / task matrix

evaluating the probability that a particular user group will perform a task, you can take into account this diversity of skills. A rich picture developed with a user/task matrix can help you make the decisions necessary to produce the most effective set of publications.

The probability scale in the user/task matrix can also help you plan a strategy for publications. For example, you may have a user group with a low probability of performing a particular task. You may decide not to provide support for this user group in your Information Plan. A typical instance of a strategy of nonsupport occurs when the writers of a document state their assumption that anyone reading the text must have previous experience of some sort. We often see such statements in the prefaces of technical publications:

> *This book has been designed for users who have training and experience in C programming. If you do not have C-programming experience, you will need to refer to additional texts before using this book.*

Such a declaration of nonsupport is perfectly acceptable and frequently made. To teach C programming to a group of novices would require a far different text than is produced by assuming that the users already have programming experience. Establishing this baseline of required characteristics is facilitated by the user/task matrix. And the decisions you make from the user/task matrix influence enormously the publications strategy you choose. How much the users already know and how much we have to tell them are at the heart of nearly every significant decision about the nature of a publication. User baseline characteristics determine the organization of the library as a whole, the organization of particular units of information (books, online help, computer-based training), as well as the selection of detail and the writing style. Even the choice of graphics and the page design should be influenced by the user characteristics.

Guideline: *Analyze the result of your user and task analyses by constructing a user/task matrix.*

Preparing the design implications

In terms of articulating a publications strategy for a project, the design implications are the most important part of the Information Plan (see Figure 7.11). By asking the members of the writing staff to fully describe their thinking about the organization of the publications, you gain two advantages:

- The writers have to clarify the reasoning behind their recommendations.
- The writers have to communicate that reasoning to those who will review and approve the Information Plan.

Figure 7.12 is a sample of design implications. In this sample, the writer describes her analysis of the data gathered by audience and task analyses, stressing the need for a diverse publications strategy. It illustrates what a design analysis may include.

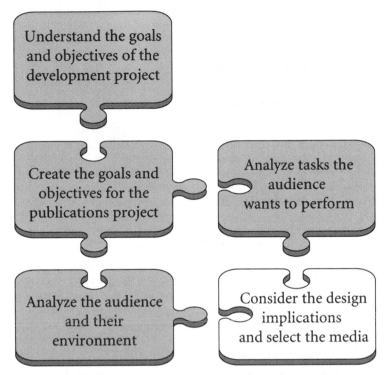

Figure 7.11   Considering design implications and selecting media

In the design implications, the writers focus on the issues that affect the success of the publications strategy. Because the users lack computer experience and may be somewhat prejudiced against using computers in their jobs, the design implications discuss how best to provide basic training and to alleviate the negative attitudes. In this instance, hardcopy manuals plus online help that is both context-sensitive and task-oriented appear to provide the best combination.

If there are issues to be discussed and resolved by the entire development team, it is best to introduce them in the design implications. Especially when budgets may be inadequate to produce the publications that will satisfy user needs, the design implications should present the trade-offs. In the plan in Figure 7.12, we strongly recommended online documentation, although the original budget allocations only financed the development of a hardcopy user manual. As a result of our recommendations and the discussion of publications strategy that took place during the team review, the development team was successful at finding the extra funding to produce the online documentation.

An Information Plan is really a proposal, the statement of your team's analysis of the information solutions that will best meet user requirements. The design implications, as well as the statement of purpose, are the sections of the plan in which you argue your case. The audience and task analyses, as well as your understanding of the product, are the evidence you produce to substantiate your case. Encourage your

Sample design implications

This section discusses the design implications we have identified after completing our front-end analysis. The implications are presented here in the context of our two main project objectives:

- Reduce the size of the user library.
- Fulfill the user's need to learn how to use the product quickly and efficiently.

Reducing the size of the user library

The Locust project team began with an initial objective to reduce the user documentation-page count from 908 printed pages for the Locust 1234 to 156 printed pages and 234 pages of online or video copy (390 pages total) for the Locust 1234. However, the scope of documentation requirements has expanded to include additional software functions and hardware options that could significantly increase the documentation scope. These are seemingly contradictory requirements that must be resolved in the final design of the Locust 1234 user documentation.

Ultimately, our ability to reduce the size of the documentation depends on two issues: (1) the extent to which we can minimize redundancy and unnecessary detail and (2) the ease of use of the product. Although we can, in this plan, begin to make high-level recommendations to eliminate redundancy between library elements, the issue of unnecessary detail will need to be more fully addressed in the individual Content Plans.

Also, we are not certain at this point how easy the product really is to use. We cannot effectively reduce the page count if the result will be that the product is perceived by the user as difficult to use. Simply stated, products that are difficult to use require more user documentation than those that are easy to use.

Fulfilling users' needs

From our analysis, it is clear that all users must be thoroughly trained on the product prior to actually using it on the production floor; otherwise, downtime could be increased to an unacceptable level. Ideally, all users would receive formal training that is the result of a well-developed training program. For novice users particularly, formal training would enable them to gain early success in using the product, thus minimizing fear and anxieties and gaining confidence. We must acknowledge, however, that some users will not receive formal training; these users must be provided a mechanism for self-training.

Figure 7.12 Sample design implications

If the software is truly designed for easy use, experienced users would not require the extensive training novices would require. (For example, they should already be familiar with the mechanical setup procedures.) They would need to know how this product is different from similar products they have used; then they could zero in on how they must modify their technique to use the Locust 1234 to its fullest extent.

Assuming users (novice and experienced) will learn how to perform tasks prior to doing them in a real situation, their only need in the plant would be for quick-reference information to refresh their memory or clarify a procedural detail. Since it is most likely that their need for such information would come up after the system is turned on and they are online, the best place to put this information might be in the online help screens. This depends on the help screens being designed so that they are easily accessible and extremely usable.

Figure 7.12 (Continued)

writing staff to use their most persuasive writing techniques to frame the design implications. They may not win everything they propose; but without a strong argument advocating the users' needs, they are more likely to be overridden.

 Guideline: Present your analysis of the relationship between the users and the tasks they want to perform in your discussion of the publications design implications.

Selecting media

If the user/task matrix is a two-dimensional representation of what you have learned about the contemplated audience for your information, the media selection adds a third dimension. Your staff should be able to lead from well-articulated design implications directly into their media recommendations. The third part of the matrix illustrates their decisions (see Figure 7.13).

As a manager, you may have to encourage your team to look beyond hardcopy solutions. You may have to explore the new media yourself or develop study teams to do so. However, those roles, while important and exciting, are all extraneous to your role as project manager.

As the project manager, your jobs in media selection are to be convinced of its thoughtfulness and to ensure that you can move from the media to a definition of project scope. If your team decides that the information needed includes both hardcopy manuals and nonprint media, then you must have enough information about the scope of each to use it to estimate the time and resources it will take to complete each project.

User task	User type/Media selection		
	Engineers	*Technicians*	*Operators*
Installation	quick-reference card	quick-reference card	video
Operation	none	online help	online help, manual
Maintenance	manual	manual	caution against

Figure 7.13 Media-selection matrix

You also may have the responsibility of guiding your team members away from selecting media that are not technically feasible in your environment or are unreasonably expensive for the project. You walk a fine line at this point between stifling an important solution that will best meet the audience's needs and recommending a solution that is not supportable by others in the organization. It's a political line and should be made with considerable understanding of the possibilities open to you. Sometimes, a more costly solution has no chance of success and should probably be discussed and rejected within your writing team. In other cases, you may want to propose media that, although initially costly, will end by saving your organization considerable expense in the long term.

There are no easy decisions when you have a limited budget and limited time to produce publications for a complex project. You need to make the best decisions that you can and then work to accomplish them. It is important to recognize, however, that you will never get what you don't ask for. Even if you don't get approval for all your recommendations, you have at least introduced the ideas. Approval may come the next time around.

Guideline: Once you have analyzed the implications of your research for the design of the technical publications, use the results of your analysis to select the most effective media to meet the needs of your audience.

Creating the Project Plan

In Chapter 7, you learned how to construct an Information Plan. The Information Plan presents an early picture of a publications project by specifying the product or process, the audience and their tasks, and your initial ideas about the publications to be designed. Through the media selection, you described "What" you hoped to build. To produce the second milestone of Phase 1, the Project Plan, you move on to the "How."

When you designate a team (project manager, writers, editors, graphic artists, and production specialists) to build the required publications for a project and predict how much time and money they will have to do the job, you create the Project Plan. The Project Plan takes the creative ideas of the Information Plan and sets a course for their development (Figure 8.1).

For Phase 1: Information Planning to be complete, you must produce both plans: the specification of what to build and the course you have charted to build it. Too often, technical communicators create plans that outline the book they will write or the online documentation they will build, but do not establish how they intend to accomplish their goals. They lack a concrete plan for accomplishing their goals or the goals of their organization within the allotted time and budget. In like manner, a supervisor may assign a writer to a project without a clear idea whether that writer will be able to create a high-quality publication by the deadline.

One fairly experienced writer once told me that he never planned his work or estimated how he would meet a deadline. Instead, he insisted, "I just keep writing until I run out of time." I suspect that such a scenario is more common than many of us would like to admit. We assign someone to a job—one person seems a likely choice. A nice compact, inexpensive number is one. Then that one person dutifully tries to create something useful in the allotted time. Sometimes it works; sometimes it doesn't. Sometimes we get excellent publications; sometimes we don't. The writer fills the available time, adding evenings and weekends to the schedule, in an attempt to fulfill his or her own or the technical team's idea of completeness and quality. It's a fine, mysterious process. Or, a risky one.

A Project Plan that carefully specifies what can be built in the allotted time and at the designated level of quality removes some of the risk. Of course, it also removes some of the mystery. It evens out the field, enabling the average player to succeed but also taking some of the potential glory away from the star. That's why project planning is resisted in a Level 1: Ad hoc organization. When a concrete plan is in place, the stars are not as likely to show once again that they can save the day against all odds. In a

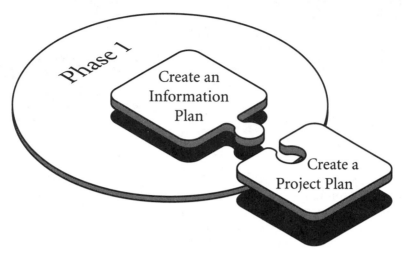

Figure 8.1 Creating a Project Plan

Level 3 (Managed and repeatable) organization, project planning is an essential part of the process. In such an organization, people recognize that the only way to maintain quality standards and to manage resources properly is by accurately estimating the duration and complexity of a project.

In response to the high-level specification in the first milestone of Phase 1, the Project Plan contains the following:

- An early estimate of the scope and complexity of the project
- An early estimate of the time and budget required to complete the project by the deadline
- An early estimate of the resources required (people, equipment, and tools) to produce the specified level of quality
- A schedule of milestones
- A description of the roles and responsibilities of the team members, including those who are not members of the publications organization
- A list of the technical and other reviewers and their responsibilities and estimated times for the review activities
- A plan for the final production of the publications, including printing or disk duplication
- A plan for the localization and translation of the publications, if applicable
- A plan for usability and validation testing of the publications
- A plan for ongoing maintenance of the publications

These requirements are illustrated in Figure 8.2.

The thorough delineation of this information allows the project manager to set the stage for the development effort and to maintain control of the project during its course. It allows the project manager to staff the project properly from the beginning and to anticipate the degree of change expected during the development process. It sets

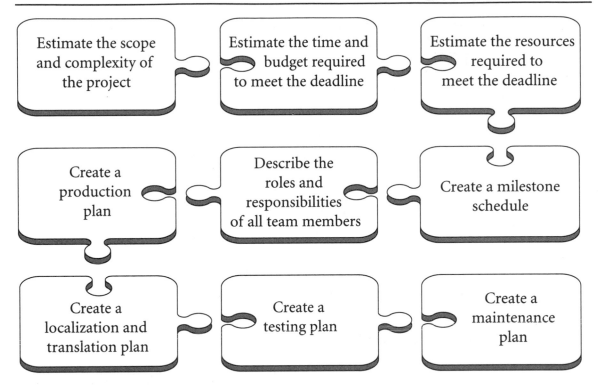

Figure 8.2 The project-planning process

out what must be accomplished so that it can be scheduled to minimize demands on the personal time of the team members. And it provides a basis for later negotiation of changes during the development project that cause the project to exceed early predictions of scope.

Without a well-thought-out project plan, the publications team becomes a victim of events. It's like starting out a long and complicated journey without a map. You have a vague idea of where you want to go but no idea of how you are going to get there. As a result, you make many wrong turns, requiring time-consuming backtracking and sometimes covering the same path twice. Meeting your schedule becomes more a matter of luck than of clear progress. And you never know how close you are to the end—or how far away.

With a good Project Plan, the path may still be rocky and full of pitfalls. But at the very least you will have charted a course to follow until a new one becomes necessary. With a good Project Plan, you will be better able to anticipate the need for a revised or new course as early as possible during the development process.

Guideline: Invest in a carefully thought-through project plan to ensure that you are able to produce the information you have described in the Information Plan.

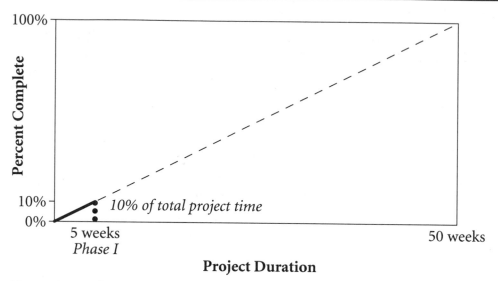

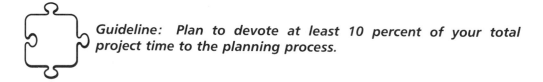

Figure 8.3 Allocating time for the project plan

Timing early planning activities

In Chapter 7, I suggested that you should devote at least 10 percent of total project time to creating the Information Plan. However, early in the publications-development life cycle, you may have a difficult time estimating total project time and figuring out just how much 10 percent is of that unknown total (Figure 8.3). How do you plan to spend 10 percent of total time when you don't know what total project time will be?

Although there is no simple answer to this question, there are a few early indicators that you might use to ease the confusion.

Guideline: Plan to devote at least 10 percent of your total project time to the planning process.

Using elapsed calendar time

In many cases, we have information (or at least a guess) about the total duration of a project. Marketing may require that the new product by ready for release in 6 months or a year. Engineering knows it will take 10 months or maybe 15, but often does not make its estimates public. In any event, we can use calendar information to make some rough guesses. If you have a year, that means with a 2-week vacation and no other time off, you can anticipate 50 weeks of work on the project. If 50 weeks is your schedule, you might plan to devote at least the first 5 of them to the Information Plan. If five people will be working for a year on a project, then information-planning time may go as high as 25 person-weeks. That virtual 6-month total may seem huge, but a project that will require the work of five people for a year is a huge project and deserves to be carefully and thoroughly planned.

A calendar-time guess such as this one, however, generally requires a project of long duration, in the neighborhood of 6 months or more. Shorter projects are more difficult to estimate early because the time for any activity is so compressed.

Using what you already know about an existing publication

In most high-tech organizations, we find more projects based upon the revision of existing products than projects that start from scratch. If you are working on a revision of existing material, you may already have considerable data about the audiences for the publications and the tasks they need to perform. Revision projects based on existing data may require less time for the preparation of an Information Plan than new projects. To estimate the time you need for the Information Plan, decide how much new information you may have to gather and analyze and how much time you will need to develop it into a plan. However, recognize that the time you can devote to a revision may be limited when you divide it among the other projects you are responsible for. Information planning, even for a small revision project, is still likely to be 10 percent of the whole, even though the 10 percent may be less than a full day's work.

Deciding how much time we can afford to give

I strongly advocate using the full 10 percent of total project time for information planning. If you shortchange initial planning time, you are likely to have a project that begins with an inadequate plan. If you think you can write an Information Plan without gathering information, you are not thinking about the planning activities correctly. A strong Information Plan requires outside research—customer site visits, phone calls to people who know the customers, exploration of project options, an understanding of user tasks, old and new.

Even if you can budget only a few days or hours on planning, do not omit the planning process. Avoid being pressed by others in the organization to produce draft pages. We know that planning is a mental activity, and we often feel pressed to produce something tangible. Without a plan, those premature words and sentences are the most likely to be revised, thrown out, and written all over again.

Nonetheless, in short projects, including durations of three months or less, you may have to compress the amount of time you can devote to information planning. Ten percent of total time may result in only a few days or a few hours to gather information that may be difficult to get. Any process that involves calling on people, especially customers, quickly becomes time-consuming. And, the process is exacerbated by communication barriers like voice mail. In these cases, my advice is to do what you can, finding out as much as possible so that you begin your design process with more facts than assumptions.

 Guideline: Include planning in even the shortest projects. They require the best plans to succeed.

Avoiding early project pressure to write

An important justification for the Information Plan itself is that it helps the publications team produce something concrete for review reasonably early in the project life cycle. It helps to quiet the concerns of others who want to know what writers are spending their time on. It also gives members of the publications team the satisfaction of producing something tangible.

However, it is also important to think of the planning process as primarily consisting of data-gathering activities. Actually writing the plan is the least important part of the process.

I find that writers often become overly concerned with the composition aspects of the job, to the neglect of the information gathering. Avoid the trap of spending most of your time perfecting the writing in your Information Plan. Spend most of your time interviewing, researching, and asking questions. Explain to those who want to see words on pages that you are working on a planning document and you cannot write anything useful without first knowing what it is that will best satisfy customer needs.

Guideline: Never begin writing drafts until the planning process is complete. Substitute writing the plan for writing supposedly final text.

Setting up the planning team

A number of options are available to a project manager first creating a planning team for a publications project. With a sound estimate of the total project scope, it may be possible to put the entire team in place and ask all writers to work on aspects of the Information Plan. With a single writer assigned to a project, then that writer, being the entire team, is responsible for creating the Information Plan. However, many large projects, especially when the overall scope has not yet been established, are more manageable when they begin with a smaller team at first and add team members as tasks become better defined (Figure 8.4). In addition, many organizations set up a senior-level planning team that is responsible for all project planning. Only after the Information Plan (and sometimes the Content Specifications) is complete does the project get turned over to individual writers.

You may sometimes find it advantageous to assign senior staff members to do the information-planning phase of an important project, small or large. In choosing senior staff members, pay most attention to communication skills. The activities involved in information planning require the ability to

- Communicate with diverse groups in a professional manner
- Seek information from customers or others outside your organization
- Understand the political nuances that play an important role in specifying a publications project

New, inexperienced writers, individuals new to your organization, and those who have better technical than communication skills may have difficulty breaking down the

Figure 8.4 Setting up a planning team

barriers that often spring up around information gathering. A good information planner for a new project will have political savvy as well as a strong sense of the overall design options available and the ability to assess the link between the publications product to be defined and the needs analysis.

A project team that includes one or more key senior members may then be supplemented with individuals with less experience, newer to your organization, or with special technical expertise in the project content. The presence of senior planners will help in training newer people while making effective use of the technical skills of the project specialists. The team members learn from one another and a better plan results from the collaboration.

Unfortunately, not all projects call for a large team of communicators and few organizations have an overabundance of people with strong information-gathering and project-planning skills. As overall department or project manager, you may find yourself in demand as a project-planning leader. If you have assigned a more junior individual to the planning task, strongly consider serving as a coach and mentor.

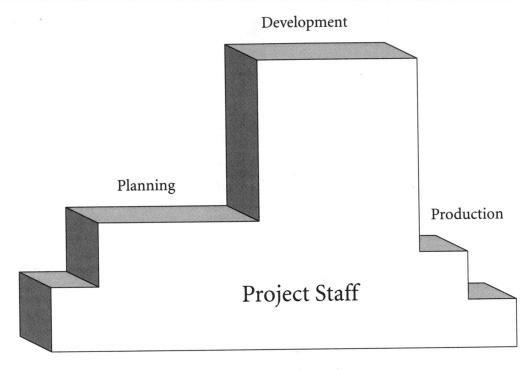

Figure 8.5 A typical project pattern

Suggest information sources that a newcomer to the organization may be unaware of. Review information gathered and discuss the design implications. Offer suggestions for media selection, especially when project budgets may exclude some effective but expensive alternatives to paper. Bring your understanding of company politics into play by helping the staff member assess the input received from various parts of the organization. Help your less-experienced staff members learn the difference between offhand remarks and comments that will affect the success of your project proposal.

In creating the project team for the early planning stages, carefully consider the overall staffing pattern for the project. Many projects follow a pattern like the one in Figure 8.5. This project begins with a small staff during the planning phases, adds staff during the development phase, and then ends with a smaller team to prepare final camera-ready copy and oversee the production activities preceding delivery.

In this example, the smaller planning team sets the stage through the tasks of information planning and sometimes the Content Specification. Then, more writers are added, along with graphic designers, illustrators, photographers, layout specialists, and others who contribute to the complex task of development.

In another scheme, you may need senior staff members to review and support the work of the individual responsible for information planning, but once the plan is prepared and signed off, staffing drops to the one person responsible for development

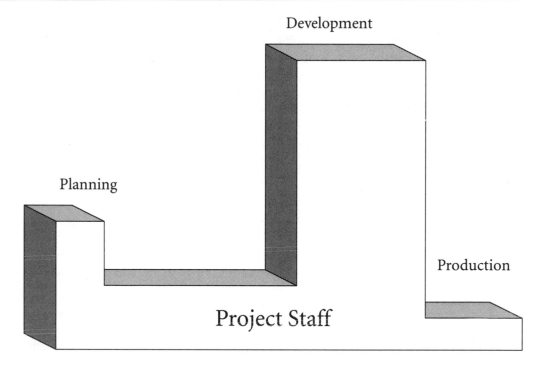

Development

Planning

Project Staff

Production

Project Duration

Figure 8.6 An alternative project pattern

(Figure 8.6). In the second scenario illustrated, a single writer is supplemented with editing and production help at the very end of the project, as well as planning help at the beginning of the project.

Whichever scenario best suits the needs of your project, ensure that the right team of people is in place and that help is available for those who want to discuss problems and try out ideas on their team members before the Information Plan draft goes outside the publications organization for review.

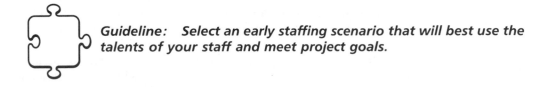

Guideline: Select an early staffing scenario that will best use the talents of your staff and meet project goals.

Finding early indicators of project scope

Once you have worked through the media selection section of the Information Plan, you have, in fact, established a great deal of the data needed to determine the scope of

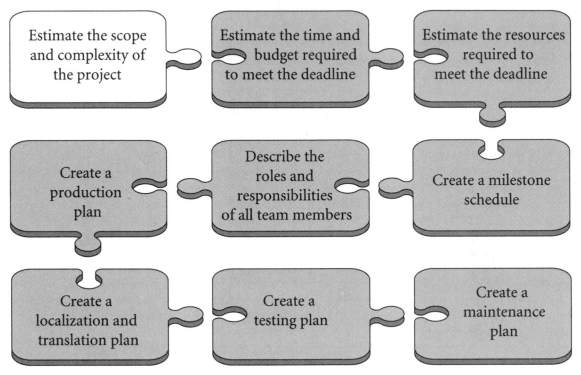

Figure 8.7   Creating an early estimate of project scope

the project. A project that lays out the development of several hardcopy manuals, online documentation, a training class, and an instructional video clearly has a more ambitious scope that a project that calls for a single user's guide. Unfortunately, the mere delineation of a list of media titles is not enough information on which to base a project budget and schedule. As project manager, you will need to know more about the scope of the proposed project if you are to create a valid early estimate (Figure 8.7).

In looking for early indicators of the scope of a project, we are, at the information-planning phase, primarily looking for reliable ranges. Is the user's guide going to end up containing 500 pages of new writing, replete with explanations of difficult concepts and tasks, many time-consuming illustrations, and data-rich reference information, or is it to contain a maximum of 50 pages of simple task instruction with a few views of a dozen computer screens?

There is nothing simple about estimating scope. The estimate is most difficult to make early in the publications-development life cycle when little information about the size and complexity of the product may be available. Several years ago my company attended a bidders' conference on a project for the planning department of our county government. They needed several publications to encompass the policies and proce-dures to be followed by developers and home owners who needed county approval for new projects. At the conference, the bidders were attempting to establish the scope of the project so that we all could work with the same baseline information. We asked the county representative for a rough estimate of the scope of the large policies and procedures book they were envisioning. His reply was, "I have no idea; that's for you to determine."

We explained that we could not estimate the size of a manual that we knew nothing about. Yet, the request for proposal required that we present a firm price. By comparison, we said that omitting an estimate of scope was the same as asking a construction company to guarantee a firm bid on a highway project without specifying the length of the highway. His answer, "I know it's hard."

We ended up defining the scope of the policies and procedures manual that we were willing to develop for the price quoted. Of course, like most publications projects, the scope changed many times during the course of the development activities. The Information Plan gave us a basis on which to estimate the impact of those changes. But the early estimate of scope gave us a place to start.

Fortunately, many requests for proposal are better defined than the one from, of all places, the county planning department. Nevertheless, every project manager has been faced with having to produce an "off the cuff" estimate of a project with little data on which to base the estimate. Consequently, we seek early indicators of scope on which to base early resource estimates. If you are placed in a position of determining too soon how many people will be needed for how much time to complete a development project, here are some suggestions for new projects:

- Base your estimate on previous projects of apparently similar scope.
- Compare competitors' documentation for similar projects.
- Develop a metric based on other project indicators, such as the number of developers who will be working on the project.
- Create an estimate based on acceptable size.
- Produce a "guess"-timate.
- Delay estimating the project until after the Information Plan and Content Specifications are complete.

For revision projects, do all of the above, but also attempt to estimate the number and type of changes to the publications that will result from engineering changes to the product.

Basing an early scope estimate on previous similar projects

Some of the best estimators are those who have considerable experience estimating and tracking many projects. Their skill comes from having worked on many projects that are, to various degrees, similar or dissimilar to the new project. Not only do these estimators carry in their heads the experience of similar projects, they also have often developed a database of information on how long it once took them or others to complete those projects successfully (Figure 8.8). The best estimators are defined by the accuracy of their projections at the end of the projects.

In searching their database of information, the best estimators begin with a comparison of the new project with projects that have come before. In one project, we were

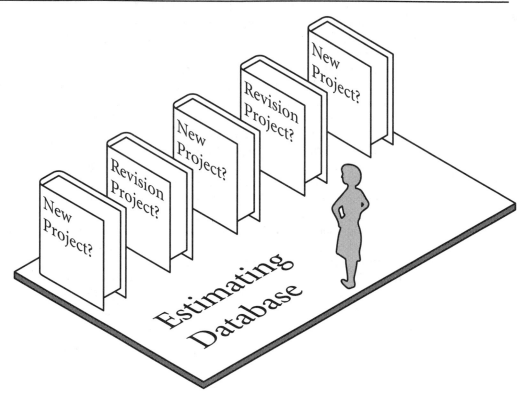

Figure 8.8 An estimating database

asked by the marketing and engineering managers to estimate how many manuals of what size we thought might have to be produced to support a new product and a very new technology. We had less than half a page of information about the technical content of the product, which was still being defined. After a number of discussions with the developers and the product-marketing people about the envisioned product, we decided to use a project we had recently completed that had a similar scope. That appeared to be as good a place to begin as any of us could devise.

If you have kept data about previous projects, as I suggest you do in Phase 5: Evaluation, you will have a database of information for comparisons. If you have not kept data, you may have to recreate information from previous projects. For example, you may look at three previous projects and discover that the user's guide for all three products averaged about 150 pages, plus or minus 10 percent. That might be a good indicator that the new project will also require a 150-page user's guide produced at the same level of quality.

You might discover that a previous manual produced for an earlier version of the product contained nearly 280 pages of information. However, you know that the new version of the product is supposed to be easier to use. You also know that, according to customer reports, the old manual contained too much extraneous information about the engineering-development process. You might then estimate that with better plan-

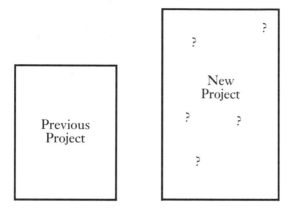

Figure 8.9 Comparing new projects to previous projects

ning for the user's needs, you should be able to reduce the new manual to 170 pages of task-oriented instruction.

The same process applies to different types of publications projects. For example, you may know that the previous year's annual report for your division had 78 pages and described 14 important projects. This year, the division needs to report on 12 projects, which suggests that the annual report will be about 85 percent the size of last year's report—or about 67 pages.

Two years ago, the release of the company's new operating system was accomplished by the development and delivery of three 5-day training courses. The new operating system is bound to be equally complex and to contain a number of new features and functions. The training courses will be at least as long as those developed for the previous version.

Previous projects provide you with a place to begin a new scope determination (Figure 8.9). They also give you a strong base of assumptions to state in the Project Plan.

Guideline: Use the size and scope of a vast array of previous projects as guidelines for your estimate of the scope of a new project.

Using competitors' publications as a guide

In the absence of similar projects in your own organization or from your previous experience, competitors' publications may provide a useful guide for early scope estimates (Figure 8.10). The additional advantage of reviewing competitor's publications is that you also develop a perception about the competition that may be useful in the development of your Information Plan. Since many consumers of high-tech products equate length of manual with difficulty in learning a product, you may want to suggest that your company produce shorter manuals than your competitors. Of

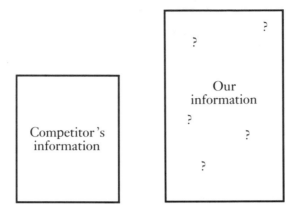

Figure 8.10 Comparing competitive projects to your project

course, shorter manuals of equal or better quality require better product design, not just fewer words or smaller type.

If your company is developing a new product that has established competition, investigate the scope of the publications the competition has produced. Discuss the success of these manuals with product marketing or others familiar with the reception of the competitors' products by the customers. Also read trade reviews that discuss the competitors' documentation. Reviewers may note that the documentation is useful or useless, giving you some assessment about the adequacy of the scope and quality.

If you are to produce a policies and procedures manual, call companies where similar functions are performed and attempt to find some basis for your estimate of scope. Six volumes of instructional procedures to explain how to handle materials at one public utility may suggest that you will need six volumes at your public utility as well.

 Guideline: Use competitor's information as a guide for your early estimate of scope.

Developing a new metric based on other project indicators

Even if you have already looked at comparisons with previous projects, you may want to consider developing a metric based on other aspects of the developing project. The earlier you are involved in the product-development life cycle, the more difficult it will be to identify useful metrics. Just remember that engineering and software development are having as much difficulty as you are coming up with their scope estimates (DeMarco, 1982).

In the last few years, some software developers have suggested that technical communicators should be able to develop a metric based on some aspect of the code being developed. They believe that there should be some point of comparison between the number of objects created in an object-oriented language with the number of pages of documentation to be written. Until we have an opportunity to research the points of comparison, we have no way to know if such a metric could be developed. A problem inherent in the software-developers' suggestion, however, is the implied relationship between software objects and user tasks. One could speculate on a metric that related numbers of objects or lines of code to documentation if the documentation's purpose was to describe the code being developed. There is certainly a correspondence between the scope and complexity of code and the scope of programming maintenance documentation. But most technical communication today is more concerned with providing information for customers, rather than developers. Consequently, numbers of objects or lines of code are unlikely to relate well to user tasks and the gap between previous knowledge and experience and the skills and knowledge required to perform using the new product. We know that a single line of code changed may ripple through a library of publications and require hundreds of changes.

Despite the assessment that shortcuts based on engineering metrics may be unachievable, other aspects of project requirements definitions may provide useful early predictors for publications. If a requirements definition provides information about user tasks to be supported by the product, you may use a combination of a task list and previous documentation projects to develop a custom metric for a new project.

I suggest that you start with a task list, especially one as extensive as possible in light of the general lack of information that you now face. For example, you may learn that the new human resources software will permit users to add and delete employees and change employee information. A small hierarchy of these tasks will give you a reasonable early estimate of scope.

The next step is to investigate the data architecture for the project. How many pieces of information about employees do the system designers expect to collect? Pieces of information may lead to data input fields of various types. Raw counts of data and tasks may help you estimate the number of pages needed in a user's guide or reference manual.

The same counts based on user tasks can occur with hardware as well as software products. In designing manuals for typical consumer products such as convection ovens, cellular phones, or laptop computers, you can develop an early scope indicator based on what needs the equipment will be designed to meet.

If you can review previous manuals for your own or competing products, consider the following questions. How many user tasks are addressed? How many pages are devoted to the average task? Will we need the same number of pages in the new manuals for the average task?

Unfortunately, at very early stages of the product-development life cycle, you may find very little information about user tasks in the development documents. In fact, in a Pattern 1: Variable organization, there will probably be no development documents to address. Under those circumstances, you may find yourself depending more heavily on previous similar projects.

In a Pattern 3: Steering organization, your team may be involved in the process of analyzing users and tasks. The resulting information will be used by the development team for the requirements definition as well as for the Information Plan. You also should not be expected to produce a project estimate until after the Information Plan is complete.

Guideline: Investigate the possibility of using product-size information as an early indicator of publications scope.

Estimating based on acceptable size

As I mentioned earlier, consumers frequently draw conclusions, faulty or otherwise, about the learning difficulty of a product based on the size of the publications. This fact of life suggests to many marketing organizations that sales of a product may be enhanced by having smaller publications. In one discussion about such an indicator, the marketing organization explained that they strongly believed a getting-started guide longer than 50 pages would be viewed negatively by potential users. They asked us to find a way to write a 50-page guide.

In another scenario, the development team agreed that users for the product being developed would be frightened away by an introductory manual longer than 30 pages. In such a short manual, we had to plan to cover only very simple tasks that were easy to learn to achieve the marketing goal.

In developing the instructions for a board game, the publications team as well as the game designer felt strongly that anything longer than a 16- to 20-page 3″ × 5″ pamphlet would be unacceptable. In other cases, you may have to plan a manual that will fit in the previously designed product box or online documentation that would take no more than some predetermined amount of disk space. Such external requirements, once they are recognized, provide extremely useful guidelines for predicting the scope of a project.

With or without the benefit of analyses from others in the organization, you also need to use common sense in determining an acceptable size. In the process of looking at the gap between the user before the new product is introduced and the user afterward, you need to search for indicators of the challenge. A user who faces a great many new, detailed, and complex ideas and skills to learn may require more supporting information than someone who is already an expert.

Not only does the intrinsic nature of the information to be conveyed influence your determination of publications scope, so does the marketplace. Today, people have little time to spend laboring through long and difficult documents unless they are highly motivated. The market assessment you have already conducted as part of the information-planning process should give you a context in which to estimate information that will sell.

 Guideline: Investigate the preferences and needs of the audience that may limit publications to a designated size and scope.

Producing a "guess"-timate

No one likes to produce a pure guess in estimating a project, but sometimes a "guess"-timate is the only way to storm out of the corner someone has maneuvered you into. The point of a "guess"-timate is not that you hold a wet finger to the wind to discover which way it is blowing. Rather, even a "guess"-timate can have some basis in a series of assumptions.

You may feel that your assumptions have no basis in fact. Fine. Most likely no one else involved in the project is working with any facts either. Just state your assumptions thoroughly and clearly.

In one such project, the lead software developer was approached by the subject-matter expert.

"I need to know if you can get this new project done by October 1," announced Ed.

"Well, give me some information about the project, and I'll let you know if we can do it," said Bill.

"Just tell me if you can get it done. That's all I want to know," replied Ed.

"I need to know what the project is and what work is involved first," said Bill.

"I don't want to waste time telling you what the project is about until you tell me if you can get it done," said Ed.

"Fine," answered Bill in an exasperated tone, "we can get it done by October 1. Now, tell me what the project is.

I hope that you do not find yourself in many situations like this one, which actually happened. Some people, we find, avoid logic whenever possible.

In more reasonable organizations, to come up with an early estimate of project scope, you may have to state assumptions like the following. You will be able to produce a 150-page user's manual if

- The product has no more than ten new functions added to the existing functions.
- The names of the data input fields are consistent from screen to screen.
- Error capture routines are included that keep users from entering numbers in alpha fields.
- Data input routines no longer require that users count the number of characters they type.
- The screen design enables users to correct errors in input fields immediately.
- No writers get sick or leave before the project is completed.

Assumptions and qualifications such as these help you define the relationship between a rough guess of publication scope and the promises made about software or other product usability. The assumptions define the basis for your earliest guess and, I hope, will enable you to revise your "guess"-timate at the earliest possible opportunity in the development life cycle.

Whatever you estimate, on whatever basis, always state your assumptions. The more doubtful your assumptions—the more they are based on guesses rather than data—the less reliable your early estimate of scope will be.

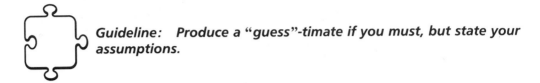

Guideline: Produce a "guess"-timate if you must, but state your assumptions.

Delaying the scope estimate

If no reliable indicators of scope are available for your project at this early stage, I strongly recommend postponing your estimate until the Information Plan is complete. Postponing gives you enough time to do some real data gathering on the project—including valuable user and task analyses. Postponing is a responsible response to an irresponsible request. Postponing helps you avoid being intimidated into making an

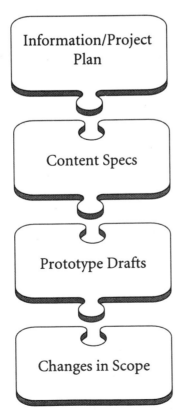

Figure 8.11 Estimating milestones to include in your schedule

"off the cuff" guess at the beginning of a project. People tend to remember that initial guess despite everything else you do later to justify the changes in your estimate.

If you are forced into a premature estimate of project scope, at the very least, schedule new, more reliable estimates into your project plan. New project estimates must follow the review and acceptance of the Information Plan and the Content Specifications. Project estimates should be scheduled for revision at each major project milestone and should be instituted whenever a major change occurs in the product development that has an impact on publications scope (Figure 8.11).

Thoughtful comparisons with previous projects, studies of competitors' publications, predictors based on development metrics or marketing goals, even pure guesses based on assumptions rather than facts will all give you useful early predictors of project scope. However, they may not give you much assistance in analyzing the second significant ingredient to your estimate of the resources you need to do the job. The second ingredient is the quality of what you intend to produce.

Guideline: *Include times for re-estimates as a standard part of your project milestone schedule.*

Using page-count metrics

In the examples in this section, I have defined scope chiefly in terms of final numbers of pages for hardcopy publications. Page counts are easy to compare with previous and future projects and provide numbers that are easy to track during the course of the project. Consequently, page count is the most common metric used in publications to indicate project scope. In addition, the page-count metric is the most reliable basis for estimating the resources required for a project. However, many technical communicators object to a metric based on page count because they argue that all pages are not the same. Some pages are more difficult to write than others, some easier. An extensively researched, carefully planned and executed, and thoroughly tested 50-page user guide may be more costly to develop than a 250-page reference manual that consists largely of reformatted engineering notes. But, given the same standard of quality, the same type of information (reference, tutorial, etc.), and the same starting assumptions, a 250-page book is likely to take longer to produce than a 50-page book.

If we agree that quality differences exist among different publications in the same company, among publications in different companies, and even among publications prepared by the same people in the same department, do we simply abandon page count as a useful estimating metric? Or, do we combine page count with a definition of quality as a refinement of the notion of scope? To place the appropriate emphasis on the size of a project and to define the quality, we must understand the relationship between size and quality. Like the two-faced god, Janus, size and quality might be viewed as two faces of the concept of scope (Figure 8.12).

To be comprehensive, the concept of a publication-project scope requires not only an early estimate of the size of the project but also a determination of the level of

Figure 8.12 The two-faced god of quality and scope

quality to be produced. Unfortunately, quality is notoriously difficult to define. I do not intend this to be a comprehensive discussion of quality metrics, but good project management should not only be designed to ensure that something is ready to hand the user at the deadline but should help to ensure that the "something" is as useful to the user as we can afford to make it. Hence, the need for some means of measuring quality as part of project management.

In publications projects, we recognize that quality is determined not only by a set of external criteria that we use to judge the success of a publication but by the resources (time, money, people, equipment) that we have available to do the project. While many technical communicators would like to believe that everything they produce is of uniform quality, we also recognize that we must and do cut corners, often late in the project life cycle as well as late at night or on the weekends following 60-hour work weeks.

One of the goals of good project estimating is to ensure that we have the resources we need to maintain the level of quality required by the customer and the market. If we estimate a project incorrectly, especially if our estimate results in inadequate resources, we are affecting quality. While we often rely on the commitment and expertise of individuals, an overworked, overwrought staff is ultimately going to perform less effectively than a staff that has the right amount of time to do the job well (and at the appropriate level of quality).

I recommend that in estimating the scope of a project, you define the level of quality to be achieved and set your resource requirements according to that quality level. In defining a level of quality, it is important to recognize that all projects are not the same and that we may not always be asked to achieve the same level of quality.

At Los Alamos National Laboratories (LANL), the technical editing staff established four levels of quality for the editing work they perform in preparing scientific and technical manuscripts for publication. Much like the nine levels of edit first developed at the Jet Propulsion Laboratory, the four levels of edit at LANL establish quality goals for the editors and those who engage their editorial services. The quality criteria for the levels of edit are based on the types of document analysis and correction that the editor will perform in the time allotted as well as on external criteria measuring certain aspects of the completed manuscripts.

The four levels of edit were determined both by the criteria that the editorial staff believes define the quality of a published document and the internal customer's assessment of what the end reader requires. For example, if an internal customer, such as a research scientist, determines that the document being produced will end up in a government file cabinet in perpetuity, he or she may decide on a minimal level of editing quality (Level 1). In a Level-1 edit, the editor ensures that the words are spelled correctly, most of the punctuation is correct, all the figure references are accounted for, page numbering is correct, and so on.

In a Level-1 edit, the publication receives such a minimal review that it is often very frustrating for the professional editor. A Level-1 edit requires that the editor avoid marking some obvious errors and avoid the temptation to revise awkward sentences and incomprehensible organization. Levels of Edit 2 through 4 permit the editor to achieve higher quality by doing more to improve the document, including substantively reorganizing the structure and recasting paragraphs and sentences for maximum readability and comprehensibility.

However, when the internal customer has neither the time, money, nor inclination to contract for the highest levels of quality, the editors have agreed to do only what is contracted for. That is not to say that the technical editing department does not promote higher levels of quality. Their job is to know the quality standards demanded by the greater organization for certain types of publications and to argue for the needs of the external customer. But they also recognize that every publication does not require the same level of quality nor are internal customers always willing to listen to arguments about the needs of the external customers.

Other technical-publication organizations would be wise to follow LANL's lead and outline the levels of quality they might expect to produce given the resources available. The danger, of course, is that other members of the organization, representing interests insensitive to the information needs of customers, may elect the lowest levels of quality. But they already do so by insisting on inadequate schedules and people. At least with clear definitions of levels of quality and analyses of the consequences of not producing the highest quality, we can manage projects knowing what our quality goals should be. Instead, we cut quality quietly, at night and on weekends, when we accept badly done reviews, avoid verifying and testing our work, and go along with restrictions on contact with users and direct understanding of their tasks.

A combination of two indicators of scope—project size and level of quality—provides a valuable response to those who distrust counting pages. We can produce excellent pages or poor pages; they are still pages that we can use as a basis for estimating project resources. Figure 8.13 illustrates possible quality levels expressed for a 150-page user guide.

 Guideline: Establish the scope of a publications project in relationship to the quality to be achieved.

Creating a quality metric

In establishing a quality metric for your publications, a good place to start is at the top. It is easier for many of us to define what we would consider to be a great job than to

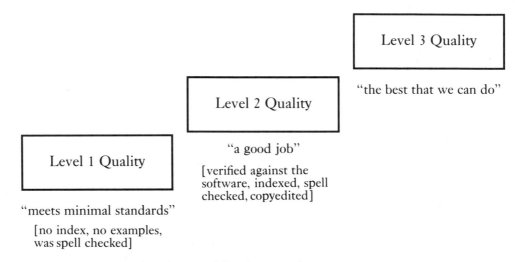

Figure 8.13 Setting levels of quality for a publications project

define something less. Once you have defined levels 3 or 4 of quality, or as many levels as you want to use, then work your way down the levels of quality by removing attributes from the quality list. Stop when you reach Level 1 of quality. Level 1 should represent the minimal level of quality acceptable in your organization. If you have defined it correctly, Level 1 should feel somewhat uncomfortable, but it should be the discomfort that comes from a recognition of reality. Level 1 quality should represent a level that members of your group have produced under pressure of time and resources in the past. If your Level 1 feels comfortable, yet members of your publications group have at times been forced to forego even these minimum standards, then your Level 1 is too high.

In establishing your quality levels, take into account both product and process measurements. Product measurements describe attributes that can be judged by reviewing the finished document. For example, some publications groups feel that books can be published without indexes, although everyone recognizes that indexes are important tools for users. If your organization will permit a book to be released without an index, you might make "no index" one of the attributes of a Level 1 quality standard. If your organization never permits any book to be released that lacks an index, then the Level 1 attribute list must include a basic index.

Identify other product measurements that you can evaluate through a careful review of the finished document—including attributes of organization, style, and accuracy. Then, add process measurements to your product measurements.

Process measurements are often more appropriate indicators of quality than product measurements, but they require good project management and a well-trained staff to accomplish. For example, Level 4 quality in your organization might require that the technical writer perform a user analysis by interviewing customers, visiting user sites, and meeting with people who regularly interact with a wide range of customers. In such an organization, a project that does not have the time or resources to permit a comprehensive user analysis will never achieve Level 4 quality. If the writer has to be content with a one-line user definition by engineering ("the user is an electrical engineer"), then you might have a process measurement for Level 1 quality.

In addition, to product and process measurements, you may want to include in your quality-level definitions measurements that include customer satisfaction surveys, the results of usability testing, or increases or decreases in the volume of customer-service requests. These external measurements of quality rely upon data gathering outside of your organization. In keeping with the requirements of Total Quality Management (TQM), they focus on the customers' response to the product.

The point is to define levels that are appropriate in your organization, given your customer base, the competition, and the corporate culture, and stick to them when you define the scope of a project. If you have one writer and 2 weeks, you might be able to produce 50 pages at Level 1 quality, but never 50 pages at Level 4 quality. However, you might suggest that the writer work on 16 top-quality (Level 4 quality) pages in those 2 weeks and produce the other 42 pages when there is sufficient time to do a good job.

Size and quality—two faces of the same problem. As a project manager, you need to state in your Project Plan how much you intend to produce and what level of quality you hope to achieve, given the budget and schedule available.

Once you have established levels of quality, then you can move on to set the hours per page needed to produce the quality required for a particular project.

 Guideline: Define the levels of quality by comparing the realities of project demands with the goals you hope to achieve.

Cost/benefit analysis

I'm sure the danger flags are now flying high among many technical communicators. What if my company only wants Level 1 quality? Well, lots of technical communicators produce Level 1 quality regularly. Many companies have their technical experts produce what we might label Level 0 quality by compiling stacks of development notes, stuffing them into binders, and calling them user documentation.

Here is a story that may illuminate your choices. When my family and I were living in west Texas, we had a terrible weed problem in our yard. Nut grass, a common high-plains noxious weed, had invaded everywhere, including the flower and vegetable gardens. It produced a hard, spiked "nut" that penetrated most shoes and all skin easily. One evening, we were having dinner with friends who had been west Texas pioneers back in the thirties. We were complaining about nut grass. At a break in the complaints, our friend, Al, exclaimed, "I can tell you how to get rid of nut grass." We stared at him in disbelief, waiting on the edges of our chairs for his critical advice. "Move," he stated.

If you are in an organization that only cares to deliver Level 1 quality to its customers, and you have your heart set on producing documents with Level 4 quality, either move or be prepared to fight hard for change. It is possible to convince people with a willingness to listen and open minds that Level 2, 3, or 4 quality is desirable. The technique is called a cost/benefit analysis.

In a cost/benefit analysis you compare the cost of creating better quality with the benefits likely to accrue as a result. In one case, we were able to recoup the cost of redesigning the installation guides in less than 6 months because of reduced costs of customer service.

In a cost/benefit analysis, you can use several indicators of benefit including payback period, the ratio of cost to benefits, or a calculation of return on investment. Each of these methods provides an acceptable data set for management to make sound decisions about the quality of publications. If you do not have actual data about cost savings or revenue increases before the publications are actually released, you may want to construct what-if scenarios.

For example, employees at one company were spending between 4 and 14 minutes to find information in poorly designed publications. We calculated the cost of those search times for a conservative number of searches per month. If each employee spend 14 minutes twice a month looking for information, it was costing the company over $3 million dollars per month to pay for the search time. What if we could redesign the publications to reduce the search time by 10 percent for a potential savings of $300,000 per month? Would that return justify the investment in the redesign effort? A what-if scenario can be a powerful tool in a cost/benefit analysis. Even if you are not able to acquire reliable numbers for every benefit, your audience will know better than you may imagine just what your hypothetical numbers represent.

Include a cost/benefit analysis in your discussion of levels of quality, as well as in the Information Plan for a project in which you argue for a high level of quality to meet customer requirements.

 Guideline: Conduct a cost/benefit analysis to demonstrate the value added by publications to your organization and its customers.

Developing metrics for each publication type

With the size of the project predicted from the early indicators and a level of quality established in terms of the needs of the customers and the constraints on resources and schedule, we need only one other piece of information to develop an estimate of the time needed to complete a project. The last piece is the hours-per-page estimating metric. In 1975, the Society for Technical Communication reported that the average hours per page to develop technical information was 5 hours (STC, 1975). That 5 hours included data from many industries types and averaged in all kinds of publications. Across a variety of industry from computer software and hardware through internal policies and procedures, this estimating metric of 5 hours per page appears to continue to hold. However, if we look only at those organizations known to produce

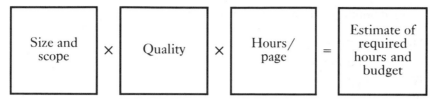

Figure 8.14 Producing an estimate of required project hours and budget

publications that their customers need and use, the 5 hours per page appears low. A more likely average across all types of high-tech information appears to be 7 hours per page. Figure 8.14 illustrates that the hours required to complete a publication depend upon the size and scope of effort, the quality level required, and the average hours per page in your organization to produce this level of quality.

If you do not have internal data on previous projects on which to base your estimate for a new project, using 5 hours per page will give you a place to begin. If you have a comprehensive database of projects, you may discover that the average hours per page in your organization is less or more than the industry average.

The sources of a baseline hours-per-page average are thorough project histories. Project histories that discuss the size, quality, and risk factors involved in particular projects provide a solid basis for comparison with the size, quality, and risk factors associated in developing a new product.

For example, the network communication division of a major computer hardware and software manufacturer had tracked its information-development projects for several years. They found that their projects averaged 8 hours per page to complete, counting all activities from project initiation through the delivery of the final manuals to those responsible for distribution. Projects ranged from 6 to 10 hours per page in this division, depending upon a variety of risk factors that influenced development time. The quality levels in this publishing organization are very high. They produce information that is considered an industry leader for quality. Their publications also have very high production values, including carefully planned and well-executed color illustrations, spot color for text emphasis, and thorough information inspections for accuracy and completeness of content.

To estimate the hours required to complete a project of a particular size and quality, you must either have a history of similar projects to compare or you must use an industry average. You can discover averages for your industry by discussing project histories with colleagues in other organizations. Consider, however, that you must first ensure that you are thinking about an estimating metric in the same way.

The key question in comparing project metrics is inclusiveness. One project manager may include peer-editing time in calculating the total number of hours to complete a project; another may include only writing time. Some writers think only of the amount of time they actually use in composition tasks, sitting in front of the word processor. Other writers include the time it takes them to interview people and research the product as part of the total writing effort. I recommend that you include all the time spent by people whose effort you can control. This means counting in your average hours per page the time it takes to

- Manage the project
- Research and interview
- Write and edit
- Illustrate
- Proofread
- Translate
- Prepare for publication
- Attend project meetings
- Attend review sessions

All of these activities are usually performed within the publications organization and should be included in determining how long it takes to complete a publications-development project in your organization.

At 3 hours, 5 hours, or 7 hours per page (depending on the quality goals) in my organization, we are able to perform all of these activities to complete the project. The differences in the averages depend upon three elements: the quality desired, the risk factors involved in completing the work, and the type of hardcopy publication being produced.

If your organization develops more than one type of publication, you will need to gather data about each of these types as you develop your estimating metrics. For example, you may develop a set of estimating metrics like those in Figure 8.15, depending on the media to be produced. This hypothetical set of estimating metrics demonstrates how estimating units change with the type of media to be produced. Different parts of the information-development industry use different metrics, but the

Information type	Hours per estimating unit
user guide	5 hours per page
software applications reference manual	4 hours per page
hardware maintenance and troubleshooting manual	8 hours per page
classroom training	40 hours per deliverable hour of training
context-sensitive help	4 hours per topic of help information
comprehensive help	4 hours per topic, including hypertext links
videotaped instruction	30 hours per finished minute of production time
computer-based training	60 hours per finished hour of training

Figure 8.15 Sample estimating metrics

metrics usually depend on some measurement of the completed work plus the additional elements of quality and complexity of the job. For example, a producer estimating the time required and the cost of a training video will include the amount of travel required to film at remote sites, the type of equipment needed to light and control difficult shots, and the amount of computer-generated graphics, animation, and special effects needed. The producer may be able to develop a simple video for 20 hours per finished minute or a complicated, elaborately animated video for 80 hours per finished minute. Each level of quality will represent a different amount of work to complete the job.

What should you do if you have no records of previous projects to use as a starting point in your organization? First, vow today to begin tracking projects so that you can develop a database of your own. Second, use a industry-standard estimating metric such as 5 hours per page to begin. Then, evaluate the accuracy of your estimate against actual project data at the completion of the project.

 Guideline: Develop a metric to use to estimate the hours required in your organization to complete different types of projects at different levels of quality, and develop guidelines to track project histories.

Making a preliminary estimate of required resources

With a complete Information Plan in hand, an understanding of the level of quality that you need to achieve, and the hours-per-page metrics of previous projects, you are ready to make a preliminary estimate of the resources required to complete your project. The only missing ingredient is an evaluation of the difficulty of completing the project on time, on budget, and with the scope and quality desired.

Calculating risk factors

Earlier in the descriptions of Phase 1 activities, I referred to the risk factors associated with a project. Risk factors are the elements that may occur during a project to increase the difficulty of performance. In many publications projects, you may know from the start that the project will be challenging. Your most experienced writer just quit, and you have doubts about the performance of the replacement. The technical development team is 4,000 miles away, and the team leader has a reputation for being difficult to work with. Your department has just acquired a new desktop-publishing system, and no one knows how to use it effectively. You may be an inexperienced project manager and be unsure of your own abilities in keeping a large project team on track.

Complications like these may turn a nice 3-hours per page project into a 10-hours per page debacle. In estimating the resources you will need to complete a project, you need to assess the potential risks.

Many individuals who try to estimate the amount of time they will need to complete a project assume that nothing will go wrong. You hear them explain, "I can write that

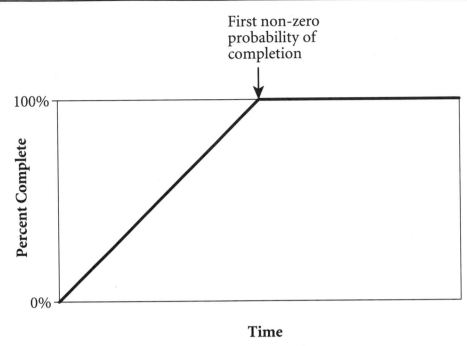

Figure 8.16 The non-zero estimating technique

manual in 3 months if everything goes exactly right. Why, I could probably complete it in half the time if it weren't for all the interruptions and complications." Well, how often does everything go exactly right? Fewer times than we would like to admit.

Optimistic estimates like these are not real estimates at all. Rather, they are examples of wishful thinking. The estimator is trying to predict the *first non-zero probability* (Figure 8.16) that he or she will be able to complete the project. The first non-zero probability refers to the first possible date that the estimator believes the project might, with great good luck, be completed. You can tell an overly optimistic estimate is in the works if you ask the writer what the chances are that this project will be done 2 weeks early or 2 weeks late. If the writer replies, "There's no chance it will be done 2 weeks early. But it's highly likely to be done 2 weeks or more late," you know you are dealing with an eternal optimist.

A second version of a nonestimate of this sort comes when a project manager or a writer explains that his or her estimating method is to guess at an optimistic time and add a factor. For example, the writer who explains that projects always take twice as long as he or she thinks is using a *guess factor* to estimate.

A third version of a nonestimate occurs in organizations in which management does not want a real estimate but wants a guess that will make everyone happy. We can call this an estimate of *devoutly desired results*. If we present managers of this type with realistic estimates, they become unhappy, even belligerent. They want us to say that we will have the 500-page reference manual for the new software done in 3 weeks, even if everyone in the organization knows that is impossible. At best, such organizations challenge creative people to find new solutions, like preparing an 8-page quick reference card instead of the 5-pound tome requested. At worst, such organizations gain a reputation for producing vaporware, making extraordinary demands of their employees, and failing to meet their announced release dates.

In organizations that appear to prefer inaccurate estimates, you may encounter managers who appear to have the answer they want from you written on a scrap of paper they have buried in their pockets. Every time we provide a real estimate, they consult the scrap of paper and exclaim, "Wrong! Go back and try again." After enough of these episodes of attempting to guess the hidden number, project managers eventually either learn the game or leave. It's an annoying little game of one-upmanship, but it has nothing to do with estimating.

A real estimate is a study in probabilities. Instead of a politically popular guess, a real estimate indicates the time when it is equally likely that we will complete the project before or after a particular date (Figure 8.17). For example, with a good estimate, the project manager should be able to state with confidence that the project will be as likely to be completed 1 week before the due date as 1 week after. Or, the project is as likely to be 1 month early as it is to be 1 month late. If you question a good estimator, he or she will be able to say with confidence, "We won't finish 2 weeks earlier than this date, but we won't finish 2 weeks later either."

If you intend to produce a realistic estimate that has a strong probability of accuracy, you must evaluate the risk factors associated with your project in your working

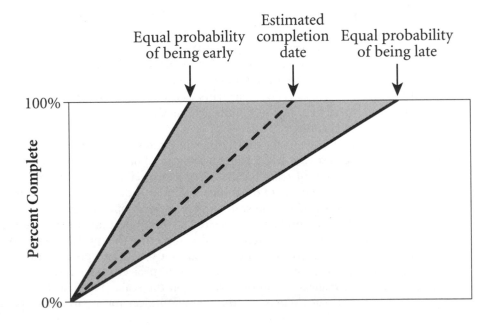

Figure 8.17 Equal probabilities estimating technique

environment. From your evaluation of the risks, you can determine the complexity level of a particular project.

Guideline: Understand the difference between real estimating and wishful thinking. Then decide what is most appropriate to communicate in your organization.

Evaluating complexity

In any decision-making process, of which estimating is an example, we evaluate the risks associated with each possible decision. For example, when I decide to build a new house and apply for a mortgage, potential lenders evaluate the risk of the investment. They estimate the probability that I will be able to repay the loan. In this estimate, they may include such risks as the likelihood that the government will change the tax laws and disallow the deduction for interest payments. If this happens, what is the chance that I will still be able to repay the loan? They consider the likelihood that property taxes will increase or insurance costs go up.

For complex decisions of this type, it is possible to use probability calculations for each of the risk factors and look at the effect of the accumulation of risk factors on the ability to repay a loan or to make money on an investment.

In determining the risks involved in completing a publications project on time and on budget, some years ago my organization developed a simple assessment tool that we call a Dependencies Calculator (Figure 8.18).

The Dependencies Calculator uses straightforward linear relationships that are weighted according to level of importance to allow a project manager to assess the risks involved with a project. The Calculator asks the project manager to assess nine dependencies, or factors, that may influence the success of a project or make it easier or more difficult to perform.

To assess a dependency, the project manager rates the dependency on a scale of 1 to 5, where 1 is the best case and 5 is the worst case. For example, if the project manager knows that the technical team on the current project rarely completes its reviews on time and review comments are often incomplete or indecipherable, then he or she may choose a factor of 4 or 5 on the scale for the review dependency.

This means that the problems associated with publications reviews in the organization are likely to increase the difficulty of completing this project in comparison with other projects in which reviews are handled in a timely and professional manner.

Deciding that, in terms of reviews, the current project is about average for his or her organization, the manager would choose a 3 on the scale. The 3, as the center point of an odd-numbered scale, represents the average project for a particular organization. A 1 or 2 represents a better than average project; a 3 or 4 represents a worse than average project.

The first five dependencies in the Dependencies Calculator are labeled external dependencies because they describe risks outside of the publications organization and

Fateful User Guide

Average Hours/Page: 5.50

	1	2	3	4	5	
Product Stability	1	2	3	**4**	5	x 1.10
Information Availability	1	2	**3**	4	5	x 1.00
Subject Matter Experts	1	2	**3**	4	5	x 1.00
Review	1	2	3	**4**	5	x 1.05
Writing Experience	1	**2**	3	4	5	x 0.95
Technical Experience	1	**2**	3	4	5	x 0.95
Audience Awareness	1	2	**3**	4	5	x 1.00
Team Experience	1	2	**3**	4	5	x 1.00
Prototype availability	1	**2**	3	4	5	x 0.95

Hours/Page Projection: 5.45

Figure 8.18 The Dependencies Calculator

the project manager's sphere of control. The external dependencies are

- Product stability/completeness
- Information availability
- Prototype availability of the product
- Availability of subject-matter experts
- Effectiveness of reviews (information inspections)

The four internal dependencies are those that may be within the project manager's ability to influence. The internal dependencies represent the publications staff's

- Technical experience
- Writing and document design experience
- Audience understanding
- Team experience

Figure 8.19 lists each dependency and provides an interpretation of its meaning. Let us look at an example of the application of the dependencies to a project. At Fateful Software Company, the publications project manager, Eleanor, knows that they produce user guides at an average of 5 hours per page at the company's standard level of quality. However, user guide projects vary. Some are easier to complete; others are more difficult than average.

Dependency	Interpretation
Product stability/completeness	The amount of change the product is likely to undergo during the course of the project. A product that changes drastically during the development cycle, especially when major changes occur late in the development cycle, is likely to require frequent changes to the draft publications.
Information availability	The existence and quality of written information about the product, including marketing studies, requirements definitions, specifications, user profiles, task analyses, and other information that will help the publications team understand the audience and product as quickly as possible. A lack of planning information may mean that publications is being included early in the development cycle. It also may mean that little planning has been done for the project — a good predictor of numerous and late development changes. Information availability is one of the factors that may contribute to a reduction in hours per page for revision projects. If the publications team is working with a high-quality earlier version of the documentation, then the job of learning the new information and fitting it into the existing structure is made easier.
Prototype availability	The existence and quality of a prototype of the product under development. The existence of an early prototype often indicates the sophistication of the development team in their planning. It also reflects on the stability of the product design. The lack of a prototype may make it difficult for the publications team to develop an accurate use model (a picture of how the user will perform a task using the product).
Subject-matter-expert availability	The availability of the Subject-Matter Experts (SMEs) to aid the publications team. SMEs, or technical experts, are important sources of information for the publications team. If they are too busy, unavailable, or lack knowledge about the development effort, they may impede the progress of the publications effort. Cooperative SMEs who look upon publications specialists as equal development partners can greatly reduce the difficulty of a publications project.
Review experience	The likelihood that reviews will be thorough, complete, and timely. Thorough and timely reviews or technical inspections of draft documents are essential to the success of a publications-development project. Poor reviews can impede progress or require costly reworking at the end of the project life cycle.
Technical experience	The degree of technical experience your team has with the new product. Every publications team has a learning curve on a new technical project. The writers and others involved in the project must learn the technical subject matter to be addressed. While not every team member needs to be technically skilled in the area of interest, team performance may be accelerated if some team members are reasonably familiar with the technical subject matter.
Writing and design experience	The amount of writing and design experience your team has with the type of publications. Especially when they are involved in designing and writing

Figure 8.19 A sample set of project dependencies for publication estimating

Dependency	Interpretation
Writing and design experience (continued)	documents that represent a new approach to the information and the audience, publications-team members may also experience a writing and design learning curve. When the document types are familiar and the team experienced in their design, this learning curve may be reduced. This dependency may also be used to account for changes in the word-processing and desktop-publishing tools available to the publications team.
Audience understanding	The degree to which your team understands the audience requirements. While we expect the publications team to conduct a user and task analysis at the beginning of the planning phase of a project, the more they already know about the intended audiences, the more effective they may be in designing and conveying information.
Team experience	The amount of experience your individual staff members have working on teams. If you are a project manager of a publications team, the experience you have in working with the individual team members and their experience working together effectively may enhance your ability to complete the project on time and on budget. The less experience you have working with your team members, or they with one another, the higher the risk.

Figure 8.19 (Continued)

Eleanor uses the Dependencies Calculator to decide on the direction and degree of variance from the norm. After studying the risk factors, Eleanor details the current project as shown in Figure 8.20.

Dependency	Interpretation
Product stability = 4	The current project is being handled by one of Fateful's best software development managers, Janice. Janice has a reputation for extensive planning and allowing few changes to the product after initial specification and prototyping. However, the marketing manager is often late in bringing in requirements information, a problem that may affect product stability. In addition, Eleanor's team is new to serving on the development team and will have to learn to react appropriately to the inevitable design changes that occur early in the development life cycle.
Information availability = 5	The publications team will be involved from the first day of the product-development cycle. That means that little if any information will be written about the product. However, the publications team will be involved in the analysis of the audience and tasks and will have sufficient time to learn about the product during the team meetings. While the involvement in early development activities may mean that little information will be available at project start-up, early involvement will have a positive effect on other dependencies and the overall success of the project. The early activities will require more time from the publications team since they have never been involved this early before.

Figure 8.20 Fateful Software's estimate of project dependencies

Dependency	Interpretation
Prototype availability = 3	The product manager, Janice, is well known for designing and testing software prototypes. The publications team will be involved in evaluating the design and recommending changes to decrease the volume of information required to support the product.
Subject-matter expert availability = 2	Janice always insists that her development team cooperates with publications. The SMEs are usually available and genuinely interested in the success of the publications. However, two of the engineers have difficulty communicating in English which may present some degree of risk. And, there's a user group meeting scheduled for Germany that will take three top engineers away at the same time.
Review experience = 1	The reviewers on Janice's projects always do a good job. Careful reviews are part of their assignments.
Technical experience = 2	Eleanor believes that the technical content of the current project is about average for her team. They have worked on similar technologies before. One senior member of the team has considerable technical experience in the area; the more junior team members have less experience. One important point, however, pushes Eleanor's thinking toward a 2 rather than a 3 rating for this dependency. The entire team will be involved in the development of the product from start-up. They will have the opportunity to learn about the product as it is being created.
Writing and design experience = 4	The publications department has designed and written user guides of this type before. Nonetheless, Eleanor wants to challenge the team to think creatively, especially in terms of a more minimalist approach to the information. In addition, Eleanor has a number of new employees to work with who have strong credentials but lack experience with Fateful's design guidelines.
Audience understanding = 3	Marketing wants to direct this product toward a different audience than previous Fateful projects. The team will have work to do in analyzing the new audience and understanding how its needs differ from Fateful's traditional audience. However, they will have the early development life cycle to work on the analysis. Eleanor selects an average value of 3, rather than a higher risk factor of 4 or 5 because of the special circumstances.
Team experience = 5	Eleanor is concerned about the inexperience of several members of her team in working together. The most senior member has been a strong individual contributor but has a reputation for impatience and intolerance for less experienced people. Several of the team members are new to the company. Eleanor knows she has considerable work to do to weld these individuals into a smoothly working group.

Figure 8.20 (Continued)

In summary, Eleanor's choice of dependencies ratings looks like this:

Product stability = 4
Information availability = 5
Prototype availability = 3
Subject-matter-expert availability = 2
Review experience = 1
Technical experience = 2
Writing and design experience = 4
Audience understanding = 3
Team experience = 5

When Eleanor runs the Dependencies Calculator, she finds the current project to be somewhat more than 10 percent more difficult than average. Since 5 hours per page for user guides is average at Fateful, Eleanor estimates that the current project will take 5.6 hours per page.

 Guideline: Develop a dependencies calculator of your own to reflect the situations that are likely to affect the difficulty of getting a project done in your organization.

Using the Dependencies Calculator

To calculate the hours per page (hrs/pg) for the current project:

- Multiply the average hrs/pg by the total composite risk factor.

Or, project hrs/pg = average hrs/pg × total composite risk factor (see the calculation below).

The average hrs/pg is derived from your company or organization's previous experience. Fateful's average hrs/pg for user guides is 5.

To calculate the total composite risk factor:

1. Using the 5-point scale, rate each dependency.
2. For the product-stability dependency (the first factor in Figure 8.19), find the composite score in the table below for the risk level, or factor, you have selected.

Composite scores for the product-stability dependency

Factor	Composite score
1	0.80
2	0.90
3	1.00
4	1.10
5	1.20

Note: The composite scores for product stability are twice the scores for the other dependencies. This indicates that product stability is weighted more heavily than each of the other eight dependencies.

3. For each of the remaining dependencies listed in Figure 8.19, find the composite scores in the table below.

Composite scores for all other dependencies

Factor	Composite score
1	0.90
2	0.95
3	1.00
4	1.05
5	1.10

4. Multiply all nine composite scores by each other. For example, for Eleanor's current project the multiplication appears as follows:

$$1.10 \times 1.10 \times 1.00 \times 0.95 \times 0.90 \times 0.95 \times 1.05 \times 1.00 \times 1.00 = 1.135$$

5. Multiply the composite score by the average hrs/pg. In Eleanor's example, the multiplication appears as follows:

$$\text{Project hrs/pg} = 5.00 \times 1.135 = 5.7$$

For the nine dependencies, each composite score represents an increase or decrease in difficulty of 5 percent from the average. When the rating factor equals 3, the composite score is 1, indicating no change from the average. For product stability, the increments above and below the average are 10 percent. Note that a project that is perfectly average would have ratings all equal to 3 and composite scores all equal to 1.00. Multiplying nine 1.00s by each other yield a product of 1.00. Multiplying this total composite score by the average hrs/pg yields a current hrs/pg exactly the same as the average.

The Dependencies Calculator is based purely on empirical data, the many years of experience I have had estimating projects and comparing actual project data with the original estimates. To find the right mix of dependencies and factors for your organization will also require trial and error. I suggest that you experiment with the values presented here and make modifications as you learn more about the factors that affect the complexity of your projects. If you want to change the composite scores, always be certain that the midpoint (factor = 3) is 1.00. The increments above and below 1.00 need not be equal, but if they are not equal, the relationship among the scores will no longer be linear. Be careful about assuming nonlinear relationships without carefully testing the results.

The nine project dependencies have worked well for years in helping us to assess the difficulty of performing a particular project. However, you may find it advantageous to develop your own list of dependencies. If you elect to do so, look closely at the risks that exist in your organization. What influences project success? Why do some projects go over budget and schedule? Why do others finish on time? What is the difference?

 Guideline: Use the dependencies calculator to evaluate the composite risk factors of your project.

Calculating total project hours

Armed with a dependencies calculation of the relative complexity of the current project and your early indicator of the size of the project, calculating the total hours required to complete the project is now a simple matter. The total hours required to complete the project equals the number of pages in the document times the calculated hours per page (complexity metric).

For example, Eleanor, the Fateful project manager, calculated the hours per page for her current project to be 5.7. Based on the Information Plan, she and her planning team believed that the user guide for the new product would resemble a user guide created for a similar project 2 years earlier. That guide was 168 pages long. Using her previous experience, the team then looked at the functionality of the new project and compared it with the older one. They found that marketing had suggested that the new product would have more functionality than previous projects. The early indicators, then, suggested an increase of about 15 percent. Using this information, they calculated the size of the new user guide to be 192 pages, or 15 percent larger than the old user guide.

Then, Eleanor multiplied 192 pages by the complexity factor of 5.7. She found that she could estimate that it would take 1,092 hours to complete the current project. The total of 1,092 hours would include all the time required for project management, writing, research, editing, illustrations, and production of the camera-ready copy, as well as the time required to see the book through printing and into the correct distribution channels.

Holistic estimating

The technique for estimating total project hours presented here may be new to you. Many people think of estimating as the process of adding up the time required to perform many small tasks. I call this estimating process "bottom-up" estimating. Bottom-up estimating is typical of many production-oriented industries. Building contractors estimate the time and cost of a new project by adding up the time for each individual activity, from digging the foundation to putting up the drywall. Printers estimate the time and cost of a printing job by adding up the time it will take people to prepare mechanicals, make plates, prepare the press, run the press, and more. In each of these industries, estimators use "estimating bluebooks," published schedules of the experience of thousands of projects over many years. They add up all the individual tasks to be performed and arrive at a total estimate of hours and cost.

Publications development, unlike printing and construction, is not a production-oriented activity. It is a creative activity, working the intellectual activity of many people. If we try to produce a bottom-up estimate for a publications project, we quickly run into trouble. We have to estimate the time it will take for the writer to "interview Sam, the subject-matter expert." But we don't really know when Sam will be available or how talkative he will be. We have to estimate the time it will take the writer to understand the new concepts and learn how to perform the new tasks. But how long does it take someone to understand something?

Bottom-up estimating works in industries in which the project is fully specified by a blueprint or a specification, and the nature of the individual tasks is well known. Within a small individual range, laying carpet will take a certain number of hours per square feet and difficulty of the room design. Development projects are rarely that well defined and contain many unknowns. Publications development, like research or product development, is a poorly defined activity that is not divisible into discrete and estimatable tasks. Only a few aspects of a publications project, like Phase 5 production activities, lend themselves to bottom-up estimating.

The estimating philosophy presented in this chapter I call "top-down" or "holistic" estimating. Holistic estimating is appropriate for development activities in which the overall scope of effort can be defined more easily than the duration of individual tasks. As you can see by the dependencies calculation, instead of adding up the duration of multiple small tasks, you instead create an overall estimate of the duration of the project by predicting the scope, using past experience with similar projects, and adding risk factors, called project dependencies. The final estimate is a total number of hours that will be needed to complete the project.

As you will learn in the milestone scheduling process described in the section "Creating a preliminary schedule of milestones," later in this chapter, once you have the estimate of the whole project, you will be able to divide the time into individual milestones and tasks. Instead of adding individual tasks up from the bottom, you will assign time to individual tasks from the top. You will determine how much time your team can afford to devote to a particular task, such as interviewing Sam or learning the technology, to complete the project on schedule and within budget.

I believe that you will find such holistic estimating to be much more accurate and successful than bottom-up estimating because it takes into account your previous experience and your assessment of risk in a much more direct manner. It asks you to view the project as a whole rather than as the accumulation of detail. The estimating philosophy presented in this book, however, requires that you monitor and control project activities to ensure that you meet your milestones. It also requires that you adjust your early estimates continually throughout the project life cycle as you gain more understanding of the project's complexity and as the project changes to accommodate the risk factors associated with the product-development process.

Making frequent adjustments

How accurate is such an early estimate as the one you make during Phase 1: Information Planning? The earliest estimates for a development project are always the least accurate. The less information that the project manager has and the more assumptions and guesses that have to be used, the more inaccurate the initial estimates of size and complexity. Estimates become more accurate as the project proceeds. For that reason, you should plan to re-estimate a project as you learn more about its size and complexity.

One thing an experienced project manager never assumes is that a project will not change. A responsible project manager takes every opportunity to revise earlier estimates based upon knowledge about the project. Estimating the resources required for a project and ensuring that quality goals are met takes constant adjustment to changing circumstances. The whole point of good estimating is not to achieve a great "guess" at the beginning of the project, but to track the project carefully against the estimates and be able to make informed decisions about adjusting the course as you go.

Dewitt Jones, a photographer for *National Geographic*, during a presentation on creativity, recounted an experience he had flying in an airliner. He was invited to visit the cockpit and talk with the pilots. The plane was on auto pilot during the visit. As the pilots explained how the controls worked, Jones noticed a constant, annoying beeping. When he asked what the sound was, the pilots explained that the beep sounded every time the auto pilot was off course. Alarmed, Jones wondered aloud whether the pilots weren't concerned that the plane was off course. They explained that the plane was always off course. The auto pilot detects tiny course fluctuations and makes constant adjustments to ensure that they reach their destination.

The same is true in project management. You may discover that you are always somewhat off course. However, if you know what the goal is (a publication that meets the needs of the audience), then you can make informed and thoughtful course adjustments throughout the project. The ability to adjust course, however, depends on entering a reasonable course setting at the beginning (the initial estimate) and monitoring progress carefully using a sound tracking mechanism.

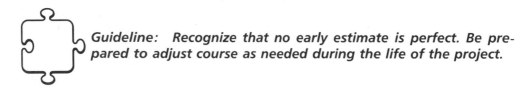 *Guideline: Recognize that no early estimate is perfect. Be prepared to adjust course as needed during the life of the project.*

Handling art, production, and other external estimates

The basis premise of the total project hours calculation is that all project activities conducted by members of the publications team are included in the total. Not included in the total, although they might be, are activities that occur outside the publications team. We have not counted, for example, the time spent by the developers and marketing people talking about the project with the writers, providing written source information, reviewing document drafts, and so forth. We also have not counted the time spent by the people who run the print shop, especially if the printing is vended outside the organization. We simply include the printing estimate in our calculation of the total cost of the project.

Whenever you examine the validity of an initial project estimate, you must decide whose time will be included and whose will be excluded. You may decide to exclude all externally subcontracted activities and simply include the dollar totals in your cost estimate. Or, you may decide to make your own estimate of external time so that you can evaluate bids more effectively. For example, your organization may decide to subcontract all illustrations for a project. However, you will need to communicate with your vendors about the number, size, and complexity of the illustrations needed for the project. If you know the number of hours it took to create illustrations inhouse, you might compare the hours with the hours proposed by the vendors. If you do not know how to estimate illustration time, you may have to rely entirely upon the judgment of your outside vendors.

The problem occurs for project managers when the rules change on a project. For past projects, you may have done all illustrations inhouse but cost-cutting measures now dictate that illustrations will be subcontracted outside. If you have good project records, you know how much time it took for your internal illustrators to do similar work. You also may know how much time it took for your writers to work with the illustrators in planning, creating, reviewing, and revising the art. Consider, however, that the amount of time needed to coordinate the efforts of outside vendors may be greater than the amount of time needed when you worked with insiders.

For example, the writers at one company had always worked with inhouse illustrators until downsizing cut the illustrators out of the budget. Previous projects had included art estimates, resulting in averages for hardware maintenance manuals of 10 hours per page. Fifty percent of that time was devoted to producing illustrations. As a result, it appeared to the project manager that new projects could be estimated at 5 hours per page, excluding the vended art. Unfortunately, that assumption failed to account for the additional time required by the writers in coordinating with illustrators who were across town rather than down the hall. Using experience working under the new conditions, the publications group would have to revise its average hours per page for maintenance manuals upward.

The same might be true under circumstances in which specialists such as illustrators or production coordinators are eliminated from the publications team, and writers are expected to add these activities to their writing responsibilities. You will have to determine if the writers are able to produce the illustrations in more or less time than the professional illustrators and at more or less the same quality standards. In most instances, you will discover that it takes amateur illustrators more time than the professionals and that the quality declines. In any event, you will have to budget the most time when you ask writers to make the transition. Conscientious writers will spend a great deal of time learning their new area of responsibility to ensure they don't encounter problems later on.

The same may be true in looking at the work of production specialists. As tools for publishing become more complex, the skills required to produce sound camera-ready copy become more difficult. If we expect all writers also to be desktop-publishing experts, we may find that the production hours for a project need to be increased or the quality of the finished work will decline.

I am a firm advocate of specialists performing specialized work. I would rather have professional artists creating high-quality illustrations than amateurs creating poor illustrations or eating up time that might better be used in research and writing. The same is true for production and editing tasks. I prefer to leverage the experience of senior writers with a support staff who add special skills to the project.

Depending on how your company is organized, you may find yourself managing the work of a team of specialists who can assist one another if necessary, or you may find yourself with generalists who have to do everything. In terms of estimating, however, the important ingredient is consistency. Be certain that your current project estimate includes the same activities done by the same people as the projects recorded in your database. If some of the elements change, you must collect new data and adjust your estimating assumptions to remain accurate.

 Guideline: Include estimates of work done by all team members, including those responsible for art and final production activities.

Estimating project costs

Once you have calculated the total number of hours needed for a project, you can produce a rough estimate of the dollars needed. Publications projects are primarily labor intensive; few costs are associated with equipment or outside resources. For that reason, the majority of the dollars needed for your project will be people costs. This second activity in producing a Project Plan is illustrated in Figure 8.21.

In one organization, publications, working closely with the finance department, has established a uniform billing rate for all publications personnel. Calculating the cost of a project like the one described for Fateful Software is simple. The project manager simply multiplies the total hours by the hourly cost.

If the estimate calls for 1,094 total project hours and the uniform billing rate is $55.00 per hour, then the total labor costs of the Fateful project will be $60,170.00. Added to the total labor costs will be any external costs, such as printing, binding, photography, art, illustration, and other costs that are contracted for with an external organization.

If your organization does not have a uniform billing rate already established, you will have to calculate one yourself to find the labor cost of your publications. The total labor costs include not only the cost of the salary paid to individual employees, but also the cost of direct benefits, such as health benefits, pensions, and tax payments, as well as the indirect costs, such as the cost of equipment, office space, heat and light, and training. These total costs are referred to as "fully burdened costs."

One of the best ways to determine the fully burdened costs of your employees is to work with the finance organization in your company. But be clear about the numbers you are given. The tendency will be to give you only the salary and direct costs, rather than the fully burdened costs. Direct costs are usually somewhere between 25 percent and 40 percent of salary, especially if holidays, vacations, and sick leave are factored in. That means, if you have a writer who is paid $40,000 per year, the total direct cost of that writer may be $50,000 to $56,000 per year. See Figure 8.22 for an example of calculating full costs.

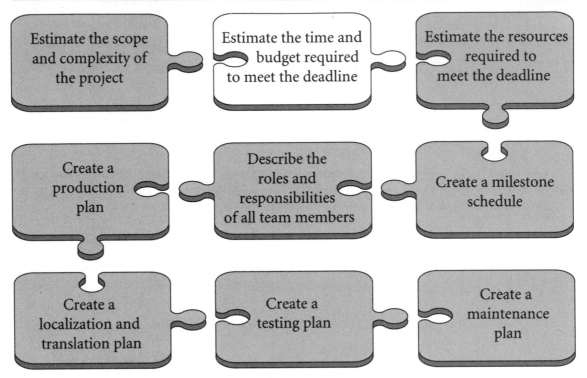

Figure 8.21 Estimating the budget required to complete the project

Job Title	Yearly salary	Factor	Total cost
Project manager	$60,000	3	$180,000
senior writer	$50,000	3	$150,000
senior writer	$48,000	3	$144,000
writer 2	$40,000	3	$120,000
writer 2	$38,000	3	$114,000
writer 1	$30,000	3	$90,000
writer 1	$28,000	3	$84,000
illustrator	$35,000	3	$105,000
illustrator	$30,000	3	$90,000
production	$25,000	3	$75,000
Total cost	$384,000		$1,152,000

Figure 8.22 Sample labor costs for a publications department

Added to the direct costs associated with payroll are the indirect costs associated with operating the company. When fully burdened costs are calculated, everything the company spends money on is included. For many US companies, the indirect costs plus the direct costs represent 2.5 to 3.0 times salary. That means, if your writer is paid a salary of $40,000 per year, the full costs of supporting that writer may be $120,000 per year or more. Companies can run as lean as 2 times salary or as much as 5 or 6 times salary, especially in manufacturing. To find a uniform billing rate for your publications, you need to include all the fully burdened costs to find an average cost per employee.

In Figure 8.22, you see the total cost of a publications department of 10 people. In this sample department, the average cost per employee is $115,200. To determine an hourly rate, you must divide this amount by the total number of hours worked in a year. The total number of hours worked equal the full-time hours in a year, less the time for vacation, holidays, and average sick days. For US employees, the total hours can be expressed as 1,896. That total is calculated as follows:

Total hours available = 52 weeks × 40 hours per week   = 2,080 hours
Less
   an average of 8 holidays   =   64 hours
   an average of 10 vacation days   =   80 hours
   an average of 5 sick days   =   40 hours
Total hours worked   = 1,896 hours

For the sample department, then, the average hourly cost is $115,200 divided by 1,896 hours, or $61 per hour.

Instead of calculating an average hourly cost for the entire department, you may prefer to calculate individual hourly costs per employee. To do so, divide each salary by the hours worked. Figure 8.23 displays the individual hourly costs for the sample

Job title	Yearly salary	Total cost	Hourly cost
project manager	$60,000	$180,000	$95
senior writer	$50,000	$150,000	$79
senior writer	$48,000	$144,000	$76
writer 2	$40,000	$120,000	$63
writer 2	$38,000	$114,000	$60
writer 1	$30,000	$90,000	$47
writer 1	$28,000	$84,000	$44
illustrator	$35,000	$105,000	$55
illustrator	$30,000	$90,000	$47
production	$25,000	$75,000	$40

Figure 8.23 Sample estimate of hourly costs for publications personnel

department. To use this information to estimate costs, you must first know how many hours of the project to assign to each individual involved.

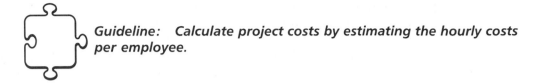

Guideline: Calculate project costs by estimating the hourly costs per employee.

Creating a resource spreadsheet

Once you have estimated the total number of hours needed for your project, you are ready to allocate resources. This third activity in developing your Project Plan is illustrated in Figure 8.24.

To allocate the total hours you have estimated for a project to the appropriate individual, create a spreadsheet for the project. The spreadsheet provides an effective mechanism for allocating hours to various project activities.

To set up a project spreadsheet, begin with the number of months originally scheduled for the project. If your project is very short, you may want to use weeks

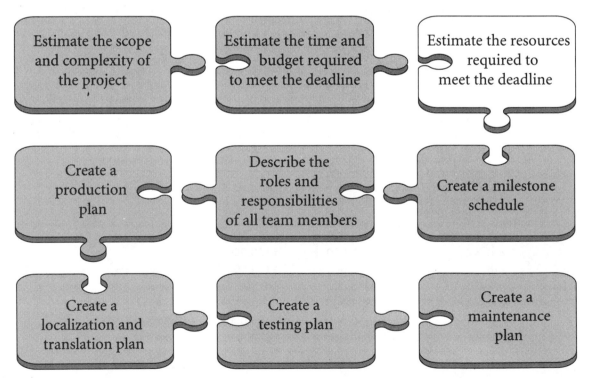

Figure 8.24 Allocate resources to complete the project on time

instead of months on the spreadsheet. Assign each month of the project to a column on the estimating spreadsheet.

To clarify the resource estimating, we will use Eleanor's project as an example. Eleanor had calculated that she needed 1,092 hours to complete the project. She anticipates beginning the project on March 1 and assigning one writer, Doug, full time to the project, with no authorized overtime. Consequently, she creates an initial spreadsheet as shown in Figure 8.25.

Note that Eleanor has assumed that a writer working full time on one project will be able to devote an average of 6 hours per day to the project, 5 days a week, after deducting time for departmental meetings, sick days, training, and other interruptions to project work. She has counted the number of working days in each month, excluding holidays and vacation days for the writer, to arrive at the available hours per month. The available hours appear at the bottom of each monthly column on the spreadsheet.

Eleanor also knows that in her organization, which has a separate group responsible for producing the final camera-ready copy, to prepare approximately 200 pages for printing takes about a week. To prepare final camera-ready copy, the production group takes the files prepared by the writer; checks for conformity to the company style; completes a final copyedit; reviews graphics placement, sets page breaks, inserts index tags, and runs and edits the index; runs the table of contents and other tables; and prints the final copy on special camera-ready paper.

To account for the work of the production group, Eleanor has allowed 40 hours for production on her spreadsheet after the final writing and editing have been completed. She also knows that printing a user guide in Fateful's usual first-run quantities ordinarily takes 10 working days. That means the Fateful user guide will not be ready to ship until at least 3 weeks after Doug has completed his work.

In working out her initial spreadsheet (Figure 8.25), Eleanor recognizes that she has a problem with her preferred scenario. Doug, working full time on the project, cannot complete the user guide until early November. With three weeks for production and printing, that means the manual will not be ready to ship until early December. The marketing department has set a date of early September for release of the new product, in time for a major user's group meeting after the Labor Day holiday.

Eleanor meets with Doug to discuss the project. They usually estimate that Fateful user guides will have some sort of illustration for every two pages of text, discounting front and back matter. They estimate that the new manual will contain approximately 75 illustrations, many of which will be screen shots. If the department's graphic artist can handle the computer screen shots and work with Doug to produce some effective conceptual illustrations, Doug believes that he will be able to save about 150 hours of work time. Eleanor decides to assign that 150 hours to the graphic artist.

Eleanor revises her spreadsheet to account for transferring the art work to the graphic artists (Figure 8.26). Although the situation is improved, Doug still cannot complete the manual on time. Under this second scenario, production will be completed in early October, with delivery of the printed manuals by late October. The marketing department will not be happy with this scenario.

From their experience in tracking projects at Fateful, Eleanor and Doug know that writers spend anywhere from 7 percent to 12 percent of their time in project-manage-

Fateful User Guide
Projected Hours Worksheet

Book Name Factor	Skill Level	Projected Mar-93	Projected Apr-93	Projected May-93	Projected Jun-93	Projected Jul-93	Projected Aug-93	Projected Sep-93	Projected Oct-93	Projected Nov-93	Projected Total Hours	Projected Hours/Page
User Guide		Page Count: 192										
0.00	Project management	0	0	0	0	0	0	0	0	0	0	0.00
	Writer	138	132	120	132	126	132	126	126	20	1052	5.48
0.00	Editor	0	0	0	0	0	0	0	0	0	0	0.00
	Illustrator										0	0.00
	Production									40	40	0.21
	Subtotal	138	132	120	132	126	132	126	126	60	1092	5.69
	Total Hours	138	132	120	132	126	132	126	126	60	1092	5.69
	Hours/Month	138	132	120	132	126	132	126	126	120	522	
	Full-Time Equivalent/Month	1.00	1.00	1.00	1.00	1.00	1.00	1.00	1.00	0.50		

Figure 8.25 An initial spreadsheet shell for the Fateful project estimate

Fateful User Guide
Projected Hours Worksheet

Book Name Factor	Skill Level	Projected Mar-93	Projected Apr-93	Projected May-93	Projected Jun-93	Projected Jul-93	Projected Aug-93	Projected Sep-93	Projected Oct-93	Projected Nov-93	Projected Total Hours	Projected Hours/Page
User Guide		Page Count: 192										
0.00	Project management	0	0	0	0	0	0	0	0	0	0	0.00
	Writer	138	132	120	132	126	132	122	0	0	902	4.70
0.00	Editor	0	0	0	0	0	0	0	0	0	0	0.00
	Illustrator					75	75	0	0		150	0.78
	Production					0	0	0	40	0	40	0.21
	Subtotal	138	132	120	132	201	207	122	40	0	1092	5.69
	Total Hours	138	132	120	132	201	207	122	40	0	1092	5.69
	Hours/Month	138	132	120	132	126	132	126	126	120	522	
	Full-Time Equivalent/Month	1.00	1.00	1.00	1.00	1.60	1.57	0.97	0.32	0.00		

Figure 8.26 Second scenario for the Fateful estimating spreadsheet

ment activities. These activities include scheduling meetings, planning agendas, writing progress reports, tracking the budget, and doing the myriad other tasks that keep a project on track and running smoothly. Eleanor suggests to Doug that she take responsibility for some of the project-management duties to free Doug for research, planning, and writing. They agree that the new project will have some project-management challenges. The development team is large and inexperienced in working with publications, and the development schedule is very tight. They decide on a 12 percent factor for project management. Eleanor will assume responsibility for 10 percent, Doug for the remaining 2 percent.

In working through this third scenario on her spreadsheet (Figure 8.27), Eleanor manages to push the schedule back a month, with project completion coming at the end of September. They still cannot meet marketing's requirement. Doug has another suggestion. On the last project, he had the opportunity to work with Jeannie, a senior-level contract editor.

"Jeannie really helped me save a lot of time. I didn't have to spend as much time rereading my own work," Doug explained. "Jeannie started reviewing with my first draft and pointed out problems in organization and style that I then incorporated into later drafts. It really saved me rework time."

Eleanor agrees that Jeannie might be hired again to work with Doug. On the last project, Jeannie's time represented 12 percent of Doug's total writing time. Doug suggests they increase the percentage to 15 percent for editing so that Jeannie can take over the mechanical edits before the second and third drafts. Eleanor works out the details in the spreadsheet (Figure 8.28). The project will now be completed by the first of September, in time to meet marketing's schedule.

In analyzing the project requirements, Eleanor had enough flexibility to add resources to the project to supplement Doug's research and writing. If she did not have the ability to hire an editor to contribute to Doug's work, or if she did not have a graphic artist on staff, she might have alternative approaches to consider:

- She could ask another writer to work with Doug. Two writers working on the same book would, however, increase the coordination problems and conceivably require additional copyediting to straighten out any lack of consistency, all requiring additional time.

- She could meet with the development team to consider reducing the size of the project so that Doug working alone might meet the schedule.

- She could suggest that a beta draft might be sufficient for the user group meeting.

- She could ask the marketing group to consider extending the project schedule so that the complete user guide would not need to be ready until December.

- She could work with the development team to reduce the complexity level of the project so that the hours per page rate might be reduced.

- She could work with the development and marketing teams to reduce the quality level of the project to accommodate a difficult schedule. However, any time that quality is compromised the consequences must be carefully examined. Reductions in the quality of publications will often result in increases in other costs of supporting customers, like customer service, warranty repairs, complaints, lost referrals, and others.

Fateful User Guide
Projected Hours Worksheet

Book Name Factor	Skill Level	Projected Mar-93	Projected Apr-93	Projected May-93	Projected Jun-93	Projected Jul-93	Projected Aug-93	Projected Sep-93	Projected Oct-93	Projected Nov-93	Projected Total Hours	Projected Hours/Page
User Guide		**Page Count: 192**										
0.10	Project management	14	13	12	13	20	21	6	0	0	99	0.52
	Writer	138	132	120	132	126	132	23	0	0	803	4.18
0.00	Editor	0	0	0	0	0	0	0	0	0	0	0.00
	Illustrator					75	75	0			150	0.78
	Production					0	0	40			40	0.21
	Subtotal	152	145	132	145	221	228	69	0	0	1092	5.69
	Total Hours	152	145	132	145	221	228	69	0	0	1092	5.69
	Hours/Month	138	132	120	132	126	132	126	126	120	522	
	Full-Time Equivalent/Month	1.10	1.10	1.10	1.10	1.75	1.73	0.55	0.00	0.00	0.00	

Figure 8.27 Third scenario for the Fateful estimating spreadsheet

Fateful User Guide
Projected Hours Worksheet

Book Name Factor	Skill Level	Projected Mar-93	Projected Apr-93	Projected May-93	Projected Jun-93	Projected Jul-93	Projected Aug-93	Projected Sep-93	Projected Oct-93	Projected Nov-93	Projected Total Hours	Projected Hours/Page
User Guide		**Page Count: 192**										
0.10	Project management	16	15	14	20	23	11	0	0	0	99	0.52
	Writer	138	132	120	132	126	50	0	0	0	698	3.64
0.15	Editor	21	20	18	20	19	8	0	0	0	106	0.55
	Illustrator				50	85	15	0			150	0.78
	Production				0	0	40	0			40	0.21
	Subtotal	175	167	152	222	253	124	0	0	0	1093	5.69
	Total Hours	175	167	152	222	253	124	0	0	0	1093	5.69
	Hours/Month	138	132	120	132	126	132	126	126	120	522	
	Full-Time Equivalent/Month	1.27	1.27	1.27	1.68	2.01	0.94	0.00	0.00	0.00	0.00	

Figure 8.28 Final Fateful estimating spreadsheet

With any of these alternatives, Eleanor is in a position to negotiate from a clear understanding of project requirements and a sound strategy to guarantee project success. The first part of the Information Plan provides the project requirements; the second half provides the basis of a well-reasoned strategy.

Summary of the resource estimating process

1. Using an early indicator of size, calculate the target hours required to complete the project by multiplying size by the complexity factor.
2. Based on the number of hours available per day to work on the project, calculate the total calendar hours available for the project each month.
3. Starting with one writer, assign enough writers to the project to meet the schedule.
4. Factor in time for editing as a percentage of total writing time assigned if editing is performed by an assigned editor or a peer editor.
5. Add time for final production of camera-ready copy if this activity is performed by a production specialist.
6. Add time to produce graphics if this activity is performed by a graphic artist or illustrator.
7. Factor in the time for project management as a percentage of the total time devoted to the project by writers, editors, graphic artists, and production specialists.
8. Adjust the resource time until the total hours equal the number of hours originally targeted for the project and the final schedule requirements are met.

I have found it useful to track project management and editing time as percentages of the time assigned to writing and total project. Some typical results are illustrated in Figure 8.29. Depending on the complexity of the project, project management and editing percentages may vary.

Project management and editing may also be calculated as absolute values rather than factors. For example, substantive editing through mechanical editing and proof-reading in some organizations are calculated at a standard rate. In one organization, simple proofreading is estimated at a rate of 50 pages per day, while substantive editing may done at a rate of 4 pages per day. Another editing team calculates that they are able to edit final drafts at a rate of 3 pages an hour.

Remember that project management and editing occur on a project even if they are performed by individual writers. The tasks involved in these activities are handled by the writer, although sometimes less effectively than if specialists are assigned. Simple graphics may be produced by a writer, but more complicated graphics are better handled by a professional. The professional takes less time and creates higher-quality work. The same is true for production tasks. As desktop-publishing systems increase in complexity, the ability of individual writers to handle all the diverse capabilities effectively is reduced. Production specialists become skilled in using the systems and decrease the time that must be devoted to final production.

Editing is a more serious issue. Many publications organizations have no editors or have eliminated editors. Writers are expected to edit their own work. However, most

Resource	Variance	Tasks	Notes
Project Management	7% – 12% of total project time	Supervising the development of Information Plans and Content Specifications; estimating project resources; negotiating trade-offs; handling project meetings; setting agendas; tracking and reporting progress; reviewing prototypes and drafts; ensuring schedules are met; and more.	The percentage of project-management increases in relationship to the number of people assigned to the project, the amount of paperwork required, the difficulties of negotiation, the experience of team members, and other factors.
Developmental and Mechanical Editing	15% – 25% of writing time	Review Information Plans and Content Specifications; develop and maintain project style guide; review prototypes and drafts for organization, completeness, and style; proofread and perform a full mechanical edit on all drafts; coordinate the styles of all writers on the project; and more.	The percentage of editing increases depending on the number of writers assigned to the project, the writing experience of the writers, the complexity of the style, the types of editing assigned from substantive to mechanical, and more.
Production tasks	15 – 45 minutes per page	Conduct final copyedit and style check to ensure accuracy and consistency; place final index tags and edit index; place final page breaks; generate final index and table of contents; generate title and copyright pages; check page numbering; place final art and ensure proper labels on art; print camera-ready copy and produce page guide for printer; and more.	The time devoted to final production tasks depends on the complexity of the style, the amount of copyediting required, the amount of art and its complexity, and the amount of art to be placed, adjusted, labeled, and printed. The production time is also highly dependent on the type of desktop publishing software used.

Figure 8.29 Sample estimating scenarios for print-based publications project tasks

writers know that they cannot effectively edit their own work because they are too close to it. They lack the perspective of an outside reader who is trained to find weaknesses in organization, sentence structure, consistency, and style. A professional editor ensures a uniform treatment and style among various writers on a project and ensures that company requirements are met and effective writing employed among individual writers working on diverse and unrelated projects. See Part Four for a detailed discussion of adding an editing function to the development life cycle.

Although project management activities can be handled by individual writers working on individual projects, they are more effectively performed by one leader for a team effort. I find that project management encompasses a unique set of tasks that must be learned by new writers. Some individuals are better at the estimating, tracking, and negotiating activities than others. Project management specialists can save a complex project from disaster and ensure that a broad corporate perspective is represented on less complicated projects. Project managers may have more political clout in the organization.

The tradeoffs among project size, complexity, and available resources and schedule should be apparent in the Fateful example. Analysis of the type suggested in the example is required of all projects to ensure that quality objectives are met. If Eleanor did not have the option of adding support staff, she would have to consider reducing the scope of Doug's project or reducing the quality. A shorter manual might have been planned, or Doug might have had to shortcut his research into the product features and functions, the amount of time for reviews, the number of reviews, the amount of editing time, the time spent on indexing, or other activities that enhance the quality of the documentation.

To examine these alternatives, Eleanor would try out different approaches on the project estimating spreadsheets. Each scenario could be estimated and the strategic tradeoffs explained in the Information Plan. If there were inadequate resources in either people or time for the project, the tradeoffs must be clear to all involved so that careful decisions are made.

Guideline: Create a project estimating spreadsheet to assign resources to a project.

Creating a preliminary schedule of milestones

With an estimating spreadsheet in place, you are ready to develop a preliminary schedule of project milestones (Figure 8.30). A milestone schedule records the expected date of completion for each deliverable at each phase of the project. For example, if your deliverables include prototype chapters of a manual, first draft, second draft, and camera-ready copy, each of these needs to be given a scheduled date of completion. Milestone schedules are dependent on activities in the product-development life cycle or other events in the larger project schedule. You may need to plan for a draft of a user manual to be completed in time for a beta test of the product. Or, you may not be able to complete a second draft of a technical reference manual until all remaining engineering issues have been decided in the development of hardware. For a policies and procedures project, schedule dates may be dependent on the required implementation date for a new company process.

While milestone schedules for publications projects are certainly dependent on external schedule requirements, they are also related to the ability of publications team members to have sufficient resources to complete their own activities on time. Some managers believe that publications schedules are infinitely compressible. We only need ask people to work faster, put in more overtime, or add more people to a project if we want it to be completed sooner. Unfortunately, development activities, which include

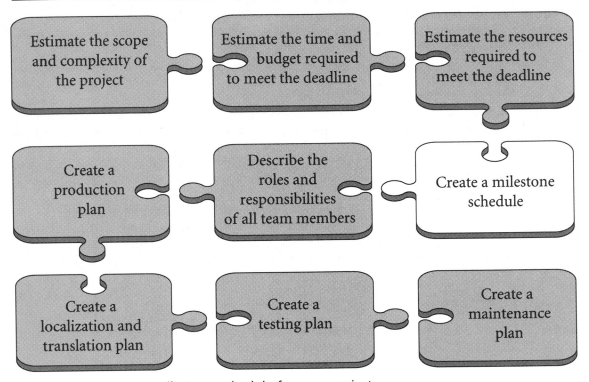

Figure 8.30 Create a milestone schedule for your project

such unknown factors as research, understanding, interviewing, and composition, are not infinitely compressible. Frederick Brooks, in *The Mythical Man Month*, explains that one cannot simply double the people assigned to a project and expect it to be done in half the time (Brooks, 1982). As we increase the number of people, the time needed to manage them, review their work, provide tools, or give them access to the product also increases (Figure 8.31). The more people we add, the more problems we have, and the more people we need to solve the problems. Unlike mechanical time for a machine, people time cannot contract to meet all schedule demands without a decrease in the quality of the product.

Even simple demands on the use of equipment will limit the number of people you can use to staff a project. If you have only one old, decrepit printer to support an entire department, consider the delays to the project schedule if the printer decides to break down on the day all of your writers need to print drafts to meet schedule requirements.

In looking at an example of the obvious dilemma facing publications project managers, we can again turn to Eleanor's user guide project. Using the fourth estimating spreadsheet, Eleanor has figured out how to staff the project so that the manual will be finished in time to meet Marketing's release date of early September as long as they can get started by March 1 and no one takes any vacations this summer. Because Eleanor has had experience tracking projects, she uses the following guidelines to calculate a schedule for project deliverables (Figure 8.32).

Figure 8.31 The effect of adding people to a project

Deliverable	Percent of total time	Milestone date
Content Specification	30%	April 28
Complete first draft	60%	June 21
Complete second draft	85%	July 27
Camera-ready copy	100%	September 3

Figure 8.32 Fateful project milestone guidelines

Eleanor knows enough about Fateful's development style that she can use these guidelines at the beginning of most projects. Although she may have to revise them later, they provide a useful starting point for the Information Plan. A fairly high percentage of Fateful's projects correspond to the scheduling guidelines.

However, when Eleanor presents the schedule to Marketing, the product manager is visibly upset. "We have already promised Gargantuan Banks, our biggest customers, that we'll have a beta release to them by May 28," she exclaims. "You have to have the first draft ready before that date."

Eleanor explains that producing a complete first draft 3 weeks early is impossible given that she has only one writer to assign to the project. She also doubts that enough of the software will be ready by the end of May to permit all of the user guide sections to be drafted and reviewed by that time. Eleanor explains to the product manager that her team will be 160 hours short of a complete first draft at the end of May. That represents a full 25 percent of the total 655 hours needed on a project of this scope and complexity to produce a first draft. With a 25 percent schedule deficit, the publications team will only be able to produce 75 percent of the scheduled first draft. Eleanor asks the product manager to sit down with her to decide which 25 percent of the first draft of the user guide might be postponed until June 21 and still meet the delivery requirements to Gargantuan Banks. Together they can decide what will be necessary, what would be nice, and what can be left until later in the schedule. They will also consult with the development manager to ensure that the development schedule also corresponds to the parts of the product needed for the Gargantuan beta site.

When a project manager calculates a schedule based on reasonable guidelines for the completion of milestones, then that schedule can be reasonably negotiated to meet other schedule demands. Such an approach to scheduling is far different from schedule promises based on wishful thinking rather than data and experience. In many cases, writers, as well as other developers, will make schedule promises based on what the other party wants to hear.

To calculate a schedule, use the following guidelines:

1. Estimate the total hours needed to complete the project.
2. Create a spreadsheet of the required resources to complete the project on time.
3. Using guidelines developed from your own experience or the guidelines listed here (Figure 8.33), calculate the calendar dates for completion of major project milestones. Remember to take holidays, planned vacations, and training into account.

For example, if you estimate that you need 60 percent of total project hours to

Milestone	Cumulative % of total project
Information Plan	10%
Content Specifications	25 – 30%
Complete first draft	60%
Complete second draft	80 – 85%
Camera-ready copy	100%

Figure 8.33   Guidelines for project milestone estimates

complete a first draft, multiply the total project hours by 60 percent (1092 × .6). Then, add all the hours for the entire team for every month of the project until you exceed the 60 percent hours. Finally, calculate the percentage needed of the partial month and find the nearest calendar date that represents that percentage.

These scheduling guidelines are based upon experience and a clear definition of the deliverables required at each milestone. Your experience may be different. However, if you track project milestones in terms of percentages of total effort, you may find, as I have, that there is a remarkable consistency in the time needed to complete each set of activities to meet a milestone. Yet, the consistency will occur only if you have defined the deliverables required at each milestone and those deliverables remain consistent across projects.

Measurable milestones

The concept of clearly defined, or measurable, milestones is critical to the effective management of the schedule and resources for a project. Too often, project managers regard milestones as dates on a calendar rather than defined events in a project life cycle. Without clearly defined deliverables, you cannot judge if you have met a milestone. Some writers think about milestones casually—a first draft is whatever one prints out from the word processor on the required date.

To track a project and determine if it is on schedule, a project manager must know if milestones have been met. To control a project and guarantee that it will be completed on time and on budget, a project manager must measure milestones. To measure a milestone, one must have something to measure. Measurable milestones require clear definitions of required deliverables.

DeMarco states that in project management, "you can only control what you can measure" (DeMarco, 1982). To be able to measure milestones, you must define what those milestones will require from your project. For example, you may define a measurable milestone for a first draft of a document in the following manner.

First draft milestone

The first draft of the user guide will be complete when

- 90 percent of all the technical information is complete.
- 90 percent of the graphics are in freehand sketch form.

- A table of contents and sample title page have been generated.
- Development editing is complete, meaning that the organization meets the needs of the audience and all information is comprehensible.
- A preliminary copyedit (for misspellings, punctuation errors, etc.) is complete.

Note that no index has been produced for this definition of a first draft. Perhaps the most difficult part of measuring the completeness of a first draft, given a definition such as this one, is the issue of what represents 90 percent complete technical information. How are you to tell if the technical information is 90 percent complete? While each project may be defined differently, consider that the completeness of information can be judged by the number of pages drafted, the number of queries remaining in the text for the technical experts, or the number of information holes remaining. Except for the number of pages drafted, each of these measurements has a degree of subjectivity. It is difficult to judge the relationship between the number of queries remaining and the total number of possible queries, for example. But it is nonetheless possible for the writers and project manager to do an assessment of milestone completion that is more meaningful than if no measurable milestones were ever defined. Practical estimating does not have to be perfect to be better than a guess and much better than nothing.

When you are asked to establish milestone dates for a project, consider the percentage of total time and the likelihood of meeting the defined deliverable for each

Milestone	Definitions
Information Plan	The information Plan template is complete. The research required to complete the template is sufficiently comprehensive to meet planning needs and quality requirements for the project.
Content Specifications	The Content-Specifications template is complete. The research required to complete the template is sufficiently comprehensive to meet planning needs and quality requirements for the project.
Complete first draft	The first draft meets the defined first-draft deliverables for the project. All support activities (editing, production, graphics) have been completed as defined.
Complete second draft	All review comments from the first draft have been incorporated and any additional information added as defined for the second-draft deliverables for the project. All support activities (editing, production, graphics) have been completed as defined.
Camera-ready copy	All review comments from the second draft have been incorporated and any additional information added as defined for the camera-ready deliverables for the project. All support activities (editing, production, graphics) have been completed as defined.

Figure 8.34 Milestone definition guidelines

milestone. Even if they may be difficult to define, establish lists of deliverables for each milestone at the outset. If you have done so, you will be better able to determine if the milestone has been met. Figure 8.34 provides tentative definitions of each milestone.

If you have thoroughly defined your milestone deliverables for a project, then you can negotiate changes from a position of understanding and a clear strategy. If you are asked to move a milestone date up or back, you can do so with full knowledge of the impact of the change on your ability to complete the deliverables and the total project on schedule and on budget. You can also calculate exactly what the additional cost will be.

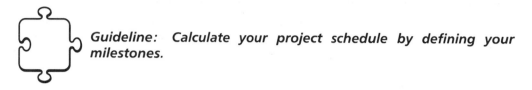

Guideline: Calculate your project schedule by defining your milestones.

Planning to re-estimate

As a project manager, you often find yourself responding to changes in schedule. A set of defined and measurable milestones allows you to re-estimate as needed during the course of a project. In fact, I strongly recommend that you include your plans to re-estimate the project in the Project Plan portion of Phase 1. In general, you will find it important to re-estimate a project at each major milestone. At Phase 2: Content Specification, for example, you and your team are likely to find that you have learned much more about the development project and are better able to estimate the size of the final deliverables. At first draft, you may discover that your estimates of risk in the form of project dependencies do not reflect reality. The project may have become more complex due to factors beyond your control.

The best estimators recognize that the worst estimates they will ever make are the estimates they make early in a project life cycle. At the beginning of a project, we are working with many unknowns and many assumptions about the future. As the project unfolds, we learn much that will influence the final schedule and resources required to complete the project. As Emerson told us, "A foolish consistency is the hobgoblin of little minds." Never feel that you need to stick to your initial estimate if the opportunity occurs to refine and increase the accuracy of that estimate. Too often, project managers and senior management stick by initial estimates as if they were set in stone.

Early estimates have a high probability of being too high or too low. Later estimates become increasingly accurate the closer we come to the end of the project. In fact, our best estimates are usually near the end of the life cycle. We can often predict with great accuracy that a project will be completed next week unless some major catastrophe occurs.

In short, be prepared to re-estimate using your early estimate in the Project Plan, plus the thorough analysis of assumptions that you have included with the dependencies calculation and the measurable milestones, as a guide.

Guideline: Always plan to re-estimate as you learn more about the nature of the project and when the project scope changes.

Assigning roles and responsibilities to team members

For a publications project, you need to specify the people who will participate in the project and the roles and responsibilities they will need to assume (Figure 8.35). You may find that you need to list at least three groups for every project: the publications team, the development and marketing team, and the team of technical reviewers and subject-matter experts. Some projects, especially those with highly complex and diverse publications deliverables may include training development teams, teams for developing online documentation or performing usability testing, or teams responsible for product localization and translation of documents.

The publications team should include all individuals who will be contributing to the development of the publications, including project manager, writers, editors, graphic

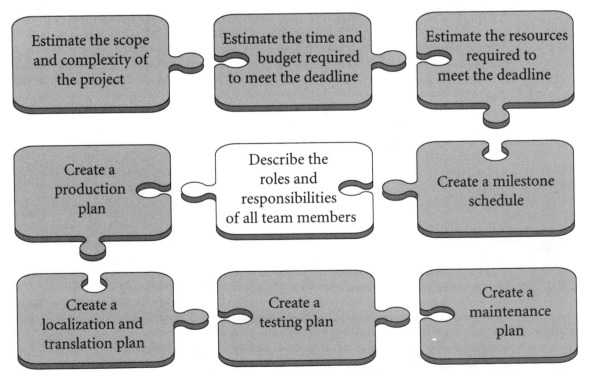

Figure 8.35 Describing the roles and responsibilities of all team members

artists, production specialists, and any one else involved. List the team members and state each of their roles and responsibilities.

The development and marketing teams include those individuals who will contribute to the definition of the publication set for a project and contribute audience research and technical source information to the publications team. List the team members and state each of their roles and responsibilities.

The review team includes those individuals who will be responsible for providing technical and other reviews of the publications during the development life cycle. List the names of all reviewers and state which publications they will be responsible for reviewing. If at all possible, designate a technical owner or team for each type of document. The technical owner is responsible for reconciling conflicts among reviewers and presenting one response to the project manager/writer for that document. The technical owner consolidates review comments into one document so that the writer has only a single set of comments to work with.

The advantage of specifying the team members for various parts of the publications process is to minimize surprises late in the development life cycle. Every publications manager has experienced the chaos that can occur when reviewers are added late in the life cycle. Writers find they have to respond to the ideas and interests of individuals who have not participated in any of the planning phases.

Late reviewer additions can completely derail an otherwise successful project. In one case, late reviewers insisted that information be added to manuals that earlier reviewers and the publications team had decided would be best omitted. If these reviewers had been involved earlier, their point of view might have been taken into account during the planning phases. Instead, the project schedule was disrupted, the new information was hastily put together, and the consistency and continuity of the publications (hence their quality) suffered immensely.

While the system may not be perfect, listing the roles and responsibilities of all the diverse team members, especially the review teams may help you to avoid calamities later on. You may want to state an assumption in the Project Plan that the list of reviewers is complete and will not change in any significant way.

Selecting publication tools

In most projects that are conducted by inhouse publications teams, the publication tools are established by company policy. The word-processing systems, desktop-publishing systems, graphics tools, online documentation tools, and others have been set long in advance (Figure 8.36).

For projects conducted by outside publications teams, or in organizations where there are distributed publications teams, the tools to be used are best settled upon in the information-planning phase. No project team should be asked to shift tools midstream; it is bad enough if you must learn new tools at the beginning of a project.

In the current environment of new, more powerful tools, every project manager may have to make early decisions about what can and cannot be introduced. You may find yourself obligated to select a tool for multi-platform, context-specific help or a tool for the development of a demonstration tutorial or a computer-based training package. If

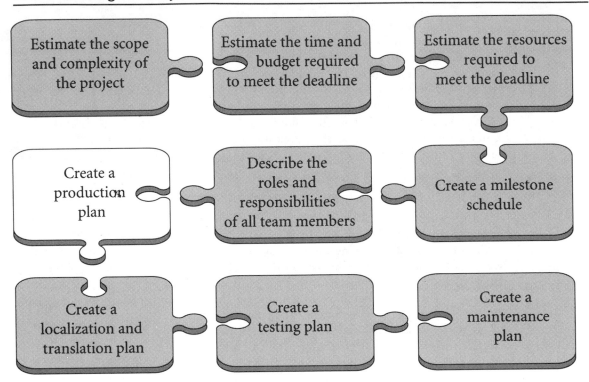

Figure 8.36 Create a production plan by selecting the best tools

you have a group assigned to investigating tools, rely on them to help in the decision-making process. If you do not have such a group, use your network of professional colleagues to gather information.

Remember that the introduction of a new tool will increase the complexity of a project by an unknown amount. While we do not include tools as a standard risk factor in the Dependencies Calculator, they nonetheless present significant deterrents to successful project completion. If you introduce a new desktop-publishing system, you may find your hours per page for a project going up by 10 or 20 percent above the average. Calculating the effect of a new tool is difficult. It presents you with the same degree of uncertainty as the introduction of a new language, platform, or operating system presents to a software development team. You may encounter problems that will be very difficult to resolve and may require extensive reworking or working around. My recommendation is simply to be prepared and allow sufficient schedule and resources to change course.

Another advantage of defining the tools to be used on a project is to account for the input coming to the publications group from other parts of the organization. In many organizations, graphics or computer-screen captures may be produced using a wide variety of tools, many of which may be incompatible with the publishing tools. If you suspect that the tools will be incompatible, discuss in the Project Plan whose responsibility it is to ensure transfer from one tool or medium to another that will be compatible. It can take enormous amounts of time to convert a computer-screen graphic from its original system to a publishing system and may, after that expenditure of time, prove impossible. It would be wise to anticipate such problems and discuss the potential routes to solutions in the Information Plan.

Planning for translation and localization

Many more of the publications we produce will be used by people who speak and read a wide variety of languages and live in cultures with different traditions for the exchange of information than our own. We find that not only must we translate publications into many languages, but we must also consider the redesign of publications if they are going to be successful in meeting the learning and information needs of people whose cultures differ from our own (Figure 8.37).

Much information is available to help publications teams respond to the needs for translation and localization of their products. Organizations both inside and outside your own can provide expert assistance in planning for translation and localization. Project managers would be wise to consult with these organizations as early as possible in the publications life cycle and follow their recommendations. If the translation and localization experts are involved in the information-planning phase, they can help to reduce the costs of their activities by proper advanced planning.

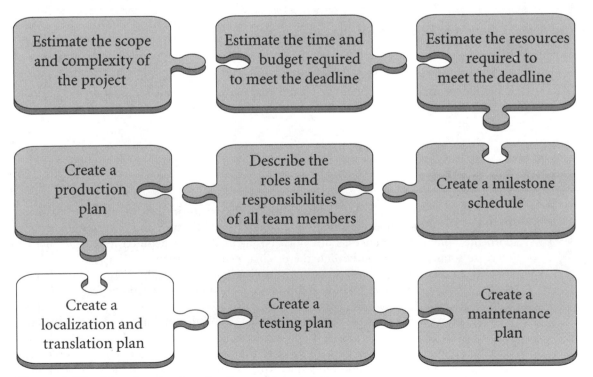

Figure 8.37   Planning for localization and translation

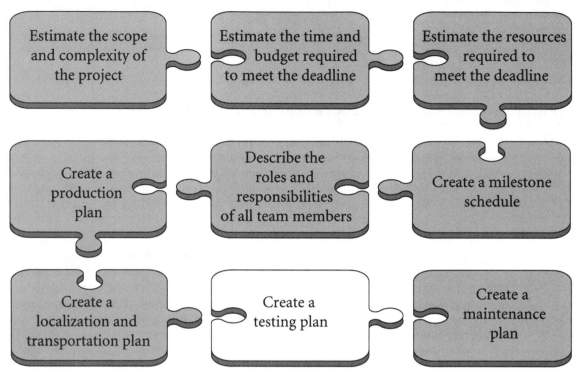

Figure 8.38 Create a testing plan for the publications

In the Information Plan, you need to describe the plans you have made and the schedule you have developed to ensure that translation and localization occur in a timely manner, are carefully and thoroughly planned, and are conducted in such a way as to minimize cost.

Planning for testing

Two types of testing exist for publications: validation testing and usability assessment. Both are significant in establishing the quality of a publication and ensuring its success with the potential audiences. Both must be planned and scheduled if they are not to increase total project time beyond the original estimate. In the sections above, I have mentioned the traditional milestones of a publications life cycle. In more quality-focused life-cycle plans, we now include publication validation and usability testing (Figure 8.38).

Validation is the process of ensuring that the information in the publications matches the products described. If you are writing an instructional manual such as a user guide, that means you need to validate the manual by performing each task with the finished product. In the validation, you ensure that the instructions accurately reflect the product in its final form. If the instruction says to push the red button in step 5, then indeed the user must push the red button before proceeding to step 6.

Validation occurs in several ways for publications, some of them as part of the traditional life cycle and already planned. Validation occurs during some reviews when subject-matter experts test the instructions against the product or consider the technical content in light of their own product or process knowledge. Validation occurs during product testing when the test teams use the documentation as part of their process. They verify that the instructions and the product match. Validation also occurs when the technical writer tests his or her own instructions against the product to ensure that all the steps are present and accurate.

In the Project Plan, you may find it valuable to describe exactly how validation of publications will occur in your project. If validation steps are omitted because the product is behind schedule or testing is cut short or does not include publications, then the specified quality level is unlikely to have been reached. If validation does not occur, technical accuracy cannot be guaranteed.

Usability assessment is a more recent introduction into the publications-development life cycle, although growing in importance and application. Usability assessment can take many shapes and sizes and can be scheduled to occur at a number of stages in publications development. While I do not discuss how to conduct usability assessment in this book, there are several excellent sources available for learning more about when to schedule testing and how to conduct it. Part Four contains a more complete discussion of presenting the benefits of usability assessment to the development team.

In the Project Plan, you should describe the methods your team will use, if any, to assess the usability of the publications produced and ensure that quality standards are met. You may decide to include a customer-survey card at the end of each printed manual or to conduct a customer-satisfaction survey after the publications are released. You may decide to bring in outside expert evaluators to assess the compliance of your publications with industry standards of quality. You may decide to schedule a full-scale usability test and study the audiences' ability to find and use the information they need to perform tasks. You may have developed a set of guidelines that help you assess the quality of a document, such as a standard for indexes or one for task-oriented headings. In any case, describe the methods you will use in your plan.

Planning for maintenance

The final part of the Project Plan contains the plan for maintaining the publications products once the current project has been completed. Technical publications have a long life, frequently being revised and updated during the many years a product is available and being updated and maintained in the marketplace or in an organization. As project manager, you need to explain what plans you have made for maintaining the publications (Figure 8.39). For example, policy and procedure publications may be reissued on a regular schedule with emergency updates issued on an ad hoc basis in more ephemeral publications.

If your organization calls for frequent and regular updates of publications, you need to explain how those maintenance cycles will be managed. A brief statement of your maintenance plan will be effective in setting the stage for regular maintenance if it has never been done.

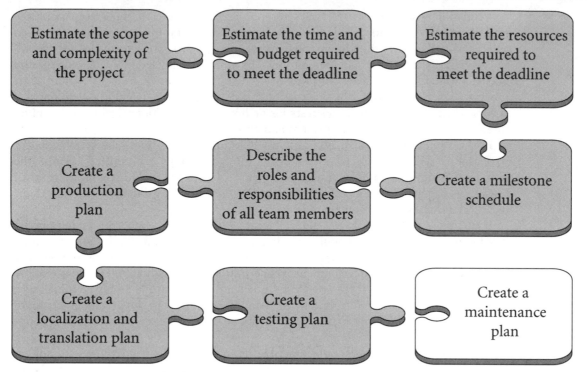

Figure 8.39   Planning for maintenance

Summary

In Phase 1: Information Planning, I introduced project managers to the myriad decisions to be made in the process of starting a publications project. The products of those decisions are the Information Plan and the Project Plan. The Information Plan describes what is to be built and is planned in light of the information gathered from user, task, product, and market analyses early in the development life cycle. The Project Plan describes the project managers' strategies for getting the job done, including the early estimate of the size of the project, the calculation of risk factors or dependencies, the early estimate of the total time needed to complete the project, the assignment of hours to people, and the calculation of a schedule. From the Information Plan, the project managers set goals that they can measure for completeness, appropriateness to audience, and quality. In the Project Plan, the project managers set goals for schedule and resources to ensure they can actually produce what they set out to produce in the first part of the plan.

If the Information and Project Plans appear to be proposals for the rest of the publications project, they are. Based on the information you and your team can gather in a short period of time, they should contain your best analysis of the needs of your audience and your organization and the evidence that you have planned thoroughly and carefully to ensure success.

I have stated that producing Information and Project Plans should take approximately 10 percent of total project time. Although 10 percent is a significant fraction of a project's activities, it still represents a short time and may represent a very short duration in calendar time. Nonetheless, it is an important effort and needs to be given the complete attention of the project manager. Never shortchange Phase 1: Information Planning. You will regret it later in a project. You cannot manage and control an unplanned project.

The advantages of taking the time to plan carefully and early are clear from both research and anecdotal evidence. Thorough plans can and do reduce total project time by reducing the need for changes in course or frequent reworking to undo bad decisions made earlier. Research by the federal government into environmental impact statements showed that the total project time could be reduced by at least a third through careful upfront planning.

If planning is unknown in your organization (a Level 1 or Level 2 organization), you may encounter difficulties in having your planning activities accepted by others. If that is the case, I recommend that you do as much as you can to introduce your plans and demonstrate their effectiveness. If planning is unknown in your organization, you will often find that the best laid plans in your publications organization are undermined by the lack of planning elsewhere. Take the changes in stride. With a careful plan, you will be better able to respond to changes and make good decisions.

Finally, consider that planning is in itself an exciting and highly creative activity. It does not stand in the way of writing activities; it is a "writing" activity in itself. You may discover that you enjoy planning even more than creating publications.

Managing the Phase 1 Review Process

Once an Information Plan has been drafted, it is ready for review. Figure 9.1 illustrates the relationship of the reviews to the first two milestones in Phase 1: Information Planning.

Like any effective review activity, the review of the Information Plan should be carefully staged by the project manager. Effective staging means setting a time and place for a discussion of the plan; ensuring that all concerned parties attend or send representatives; creating an agenda, preparing a presentation of the high points of the plan, with assumptions, tradeoffs, and strategies; and sending out advance copies prior to the meeting.

You may note that sending out advance copies to review team members is the last activity on the list, rather than the first. The review of an Information Plan is not like the review of chapters of a manual. Although you may find it useful to send advance copies of your plan to members of the review team, it is more important that you present the plan to them orally. If you think of the Information Plan as a proposal for the publications part of a product or process development, you will recognize that a review meeting is an opportunity to present your proposal and explain its benefits. You will also recognize that a review meeting permits you to listen to and respond to questions and concerns and to negotiate vital tradeoffs.

Too often, publications project managers view the Information Plan as just another part of the product or process documentation. Consequently, they treat the review process much like the review process that customarily occurs for document drafts. The Information Plan is shipped to the reviewers, and they are asked to return their comments in writing. The project manager then incorporates the changes into the draft plan, often without considering their impact on the proposal as a whole.

An Information Plan is not the same as a draft of a technical publication. The plan is a proposal that links what will be produced with how the publications team will perform its tasks. The review process should be viewed not as an opportunity to improve the style, clarity, or organization of the plan's text but as an opportunity to clarify the assumptions and goals and to give all team members an opportunity to commit to the proposed strategy. If you send out an Information Plan for review and receive only stylistic comments in response, the review process has been ineffective. In many cases, ineffective responses occur because the project manager has not adequately communicated the purpose of the Information Plan and the objectives of the review.

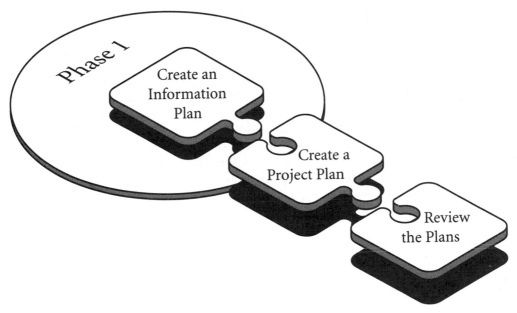

Figure 9.1   Phase 1 review

The objectives of the Information Plan review include reviewing and either accepting or revising the following:

- User profiles
- Results of the task analysis
- Assumptions about the purposes of the product or process
- Usability objectives for the product and the publications
- Assumptions that inform the resource estimates and schedules
- Details of the resource and cost estimates and the schedule
- Analysis of the risk factors (dependencies) that threaten project success

If the review team members are to contribute to a discussion of the plan and agree that it be implemented, they must be prepared to consider each issue raised and activity planned in light of their own understanding of the development project. If such thoughtful and informed consideration is to take place, the publications project manager must communicate the objectives of the review meeting and impress its importance upon the participants.

I recommend that you include the list of objectives in your cover memo for the review, especially if you are planning the review meeting. The bulleted list will alert team members of your intentions for the review.

In many business settings, you may find it difficult to ensure that other members of the development team have read thoroughly and thoughtfully a long, detailed, and complex Information Plan. Instead of complaining about this seeming lack of attention, sympathize with everyone's busy schedules and prepare an executive summary and short, well-structured presentation of plan highlights and major assumptions. In the presentation, be especially careful to make all tradeoffs clear.

In a recent presentation of an Information Plan, the publications team knew that our full media proposal would require more than the budgeted funds to implement. Yet, we were concerned that the budget limitations would cause us to seriously compromise the user needs we had identified. For the presentation, we created overhead slides that detailed our media selection and showed the correlation we had established between the selections and our user and task research. We also presented our budget estimates for the proposed media and carefully explained the tradeoffs in terms of fulfilling customer needs. Each member of the review team received not only an advance copy of the plan but a copy of the slides used for the presentation.

Our plan was given a full and careful hearing by the team, which included members from engineering, programming, marketing, graphics, and training. Their questions clearly demonstrated that they had read the plan and thought about the recommendations. They were also convinced that our analysis was correct. However, those who controlled the money for the publications project reiterated the budget restrictions and asked us to establish our priorities within the restrictions. Because we were prepared to negotiate, we gave our priority list as follows:

1. Hardcopy user's manual
2. Electronic context-sensitive help
3. Training video

The immediate result of the presentation was the approval of the user's manual, our first priority. At the same time, marketing and engineering agreed that the online help should be done if the money were available. A few weeks later, they had found the funds and approved the development of the help system. Had we not presented the alternatives and demonstrated the value of our recommendations, we would never have had the chance to create the online help. The video was delayed until a subsequent version of the product.

In most cases, it is worth presenting what you want even if you know you will not get it this time. Next time, the members of the development team will be prepared because they have heard the ideas before and have had time to consider them informally. The third time, you may even get agreement.

As this case indicates, an oral presentation of your proposed plan can be extremely valuable. Potentially controversial recommendations should never be left to the mercy of reviewers who have their own priorities. I find that whenever I am unable to present the issues in person, the likelihood that my proposal will succeed decreases substantially. Complex recommendations are too often misread or misinterpreted. Too often, reviewers tend to focus on bottom-line numbers and miss the critical data that informs the bottom line. During an oral presentation, you can clear up misinterpretations and ensure that your high points are not overlooked.

As you ready your Information Plan for review, concentrate on the following:

1. Schedule the review meeting to ensure that as many members of the review team as possible are able to attend. Send an electronic mail message scheduling the meeting and ask for return commitments to attend. If you cannot ensure the presence of key players, reschedule the meeting.

Sample cover memo

Project: Mercury

Project manager: Miguel H., Manager — Publication Services

Start date: January 13, 1993

This Information Plan outlines the documentation recommended for the Mercury project. It describes the project, audience, and each piece of the library and evaluates the resources required to complete the library in a timely fashion.

We are delivering this Information Plan in first-draft form for your review. Please review the plan carefully and come prepared with your comments to the meeting on February 8, 1993. If you are unable to attend the review meeting, send a delegate who can represent your viewpoint. Please recommend changes or additions as necessary, and send them to Miguel by February 5, 1993.

At the review meeting, we will consider all recommendations. After the review, we will incorporate those changes agreed upon in a second draft of the Information Plan. You will receive the revised plan for final review and signoff.

If you have any questions about this plan, please contact Miguel.

Figure 9.2   Sample cover memo for a Phase 1 review

2. Distribute an agenda for the review meeting that is respectful of people's time commitments. Keep the meeting short and decision-oriented.

3. Prepare your presentation with overhead slides and handouts. Emphasize the data you have collected, your interpretation of it, the resultant media selection, and the assumptions that you have included in your estimates of time and budget.

4. Distribute copies in enough time for careful reading but not so early that people put them aside without reading them or forget what they read a few weeks ago. Include a cover memo that explains what the Information Plan is and what role you expect it to play. Figure 9.2 presents a sample cover memo.

5. Advertise the upcoming review meeting at the product team meetings that precede it.

6. Hold the review meeting. Serve refreshments, and be sure that everyone knows about the refreshments in advance. At the review, gather information from other members, and listen to alternative ideas. Be prepared to change your course if necessary.

Presenting alternative plans

People who know how to control meetings never go into a meeting without lobbying for their cause ahead of time. Talk to as many people individually about the plan as you can before the meeting. Get a feel for their objections, and try to provide responses. If you know there will be objections remaining, consider alternative approaches.

Every project manager needs to consider how and when to present alternative approaches. Sometimes you will find it appropriate to present alternatives in the Information Plan, especially when you believe that the tradeoffs involved in alternatives need a wider base of support among your colleagues. In other cases, presenting less expensive alternatives too early may stack the deck against your carefully honed recommendations. You will need to consider how the review team will look at alternatives. If they have always opted for the least expensive alternative in the past and have given little consideration to quality, you may want to hold the alternative approaches in abeyance until after you have the opportunity to make your case.

On the other hand, you do not want to present an Information Plan that is so expensive and unrealistic that you lose credibility. Yes, it would be great to have a 15-minute computer-based training piece with full animation and lots of hypertext links, but the price tag for such a production is far beyond the project budget. There is a distinction you must draw between a "neat idea" that costs a fortune and a carefully represented argument for a special publication that you strongly believe will add considerable value to the product.

If you are going to propose an unusual combination of media or an expensive redesign project, you must be prepared to present a cost/benefit analysis. Sometimes it is possible to persuade the most tradition-bound people that an up-front investment is worth the cost in comparison with the savings to the customer and the gain in company reputation.

While I do not advocate proposing impossibilities, if you never propose anything different from the standard package you have always built, you are wasting an opportunity. A persuasive proposal may gain you increased credibility in your organization and an unexpected acceptance of your plan. If you never propose anything innovative, you continue to reinforce the status quo.

Communicating tradeoffs

The discussions that emerge during an Information Plan review present an opportunity for the project manager to explain the tradeoffs to be made if insufficient resources and schedule are available to produce high-quality publications. To prepare to present tradeoffs, you need to be aware of the benefits that will accrue with the development of publications that meet audience needs and the costs that will be incurred if they are not developed. Some of the benefits of producing high-quality publications are obvious.

- A strong, consistent, and attractive corporate image is portrayed to the public.
- Customer requirements for information are satisfied.
- Customers have fewer complaints about the usability of information.
- The number of information requests from customers (customer-service calls) is reduced.
- Customers are able to achieve their goals of productivity and knowledge more quickly and with less training and support.

- Customers become independent more quickly.
- Satisfied customers make more referrals.
- Trade reviewers give high marks to the publications.

Many more arguments could be made to show the value added by high-quality publications to an organization's product sales, internal productivity, or exchange of technical information.

However, general statements about the value added by publications may not be enough to convince those in your organization who place a high value on reducing the immediate costs of developing publications. To convince the doubters that high-quality publications are worth producing, you must develop evidence of costs and benefits that are directly relevant to your organization.

To develop your own evidence of the value added by publications, you may want to

- Create and administer customer-satisfaction surveys.
- Track customer complaints associated with publications.
- Estimate the cost of one minute of your user's time.
- Track the number of calls for help associated with publications.
- Ask your customer-support people to calculate the average cost of a call.
- Track the number of unnecessary field-engineering visits (due to inadequate or missing instructions).
- Consult trade reviewers and comparative analyses of your publications and your competitors'.

In each case, you are seeking information that may help you improve the publications and demonstrate a correlation between publications quality and cost of servicing customer problems.

If you know how long it takes to create publications that meet the highest standards in your organization, you will be able to demonstrate the effect of having insufficient resources and schedule to produce your highest-quality work.

The quality / scope tradeoff

As you have already seen, every development project faces tradeoffs between quality and scope and the resources and schedules available. To produce work of high quality, you need a defined amount of resources in the form of qualified people to perform necessary activities and sufficient calendar time to carry out the activities. If the resources and time are not available, then one of two things can occur: Either the quality or the scope of the development project will have to be reduced.

As a project manager negotiating tradeoffs during an Information Plan review, you should be prepared to explain the effects of lower quality. In most cases, you may find it effective to recommend that scope be reduced rather than quality compromised.

For example, if you have insufficient resources and schedule to create both a user's guide and a technical reference for a software project at the quality level required by the customers, you have the choice of producing either one of the publications at the quality level required or both publications at a lower quality level. In a recent project, a client lacked the resources to allow the publications team to produce the publications originally proposed for the product. The team examined the Information Plan and suggested ways in which the project could be scaled back to accommodate the budget and schedule. Management was unhappy about the cutbacks but was convinced by the argument that a smaller publications package with higher quality was preferable.

In the Information Plan review, be prepared to make changes. Have a clear list of the priorities in the proposed publications package. Know what is essential and what might be left for another time or eliminated completely. If you know that tradeoffs are likely, have estimating spreadsheets prepared with several different scenarios. By being prepared, you will be able to focus the discussion and manage the decision-making process.

In many instances, you will discover that the reviewers become involved in their own issues during the review meetings. The review meeting may be the first time all the team members are together in the same room at the same time. Then, they may discover that they disagree about the direction the product is taking. If these discussions seem important and will affect the decisions about publications, you may want to let them go on. But eventually, it may be best to call time and ask that such discussions continue elsewhere. Your responsibility is to obtain decisions about the publications, but the opportunity to influence the product direction will frequently present itself.

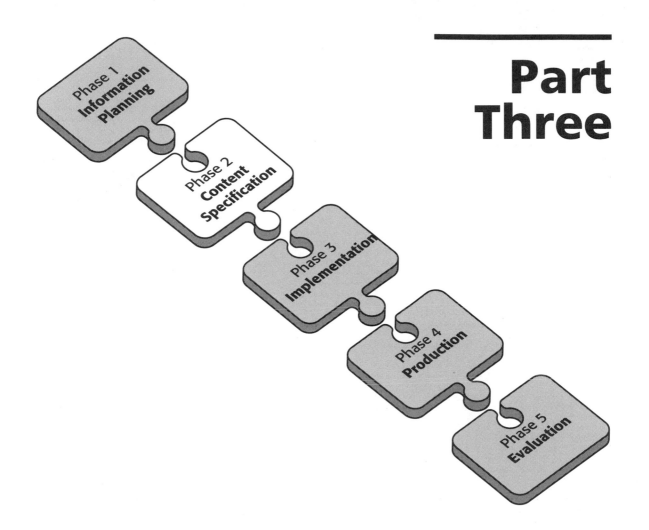

Phase 1
Information
Planning

Phase 2
Content
Specification

Phase 3
Implementation

Phase 4
Production

Phase 5
Evaluation

Part Three

Establishing the Specifics

The Content Specification Phase

In the transition from Phase 1: Information Planning to Phase 2: Content Specification, the project manager moves from defining the publications project as a whole to the detailed design of the individual parts of the project, from books to online documentation. In Phase 2, as you gain more information about the project, you evaluate your earlier Information Plan to decide if it is still accurate in predicting project scope. During Phase 2, you may work alone or with a full team of writers, editors, instructional designers, graphics specialists, illustrators, and others.

As you progress between Phase 1 and Phase 2, you may find a problem in your approach to the project. Your publications team established an Information Plan but then fails to update the plan as they learn more about the product. As the project focus shifts, a publications team at Level 1: Ad hoc or Level 2: Rudimentary of process maturity may shelve the plan and proceed without a real plan in place. Rather than abandon the original plan as the scope of the project changes, in Phase 2 you move on to a more detailed and updated plan instead, updating the original Information Plan in the process.

In Part Three, you learn to create a second and highly significant planning tool, the Content Specification. You learn about the benefits of a detailed specification process and about working with your team members in creating the detail.

As part of the specification process, you need to consider the possibility of reducing the volume of information your team will create. In many cases, members of the product-development team view publications as historical artifacts that record all data about the development project. In contrast, our audiences ask for the appropriate information to meet their needs, rather than volume. Complete information about the product-development process is often much more information than the user requires—or wants. In considering how to "downsize" current publications or find new ways to target information more appropriately, you need to take into account research suggesting that "less" may be "more" for the audience. Some audiences learn and perform better with less but more targeted information.

After you complete your Content Specifications, re-examine your original Project Plan to ensure that you continue to have the resources and schedule necessary to produce high-quality publications. In revising your Project Plan, you work with team members to develop detailed estimates of page and graphic counts so that earlier estimates of project scope (resources, schedule, and budget) can be confirmed or modified early enough in the publications-development life cycle to avoid substantial cost or schedule over-runs later.

In Chapter 12, you learn to create a tracking system that allows you to efficiently collect information about the development process. You will use the tracking system during Phase 3: Implementation to monitor and control progress. At the end of the project, you will use your tracking information to review productivity and success and to create better estimates for future projects.

If such processes are not already in place in your organization, you learn in Chapter 13 to establish development standards for the style and design of the publications you are producing. You also begin to plan in earnest for the production process.

Finally, you learn to manage the process of publications reviews by experts in other parts of your organization. By managing the review process, you help to ensure that the initial project goals are maintained.

Contents

The chapters in Part 3 focus on the following issues:

Chapter 10: Creating the Content Specifications

- Understanding the purpose of the Content Specification
- Determining goals and objectives
- Analyzing product, audience, and environment
- Performing a detailed task analysis
- Organizing the publication
- Estimating pages and graphics
- Downsizing the publications
- Combining the Information Plan and Content Specifications

Chapter 11: Revising the Project Plan

- Reviewing the Content-Specification estimates
- Estimating revision projects
- Revising resource requirements and schedules
- Leveling resources
- Scheduling the next phase—Implementation
- Planning for production

Chapter 12: Creating a Tracking System

- Creating a new project spreadsheet
- Creating a project-reporting spreadsheet

- Instituting weekly staff progress reports and time sheets
- Writing monthly progress reports

Chapter 13: Creating Project Standards

- Creating style standards for text and graphics
- Creating an information-control plan
- Establishing a security plan
- Tracking graphics
- Establishing a document-control function

Chapter 14: Conducting the Content-Specification Reviews

- Managing the content-review process
- Negotiating changes in resources and schedules
- Adding to your Project Management Notebook

Results

As a result of completing Part 3, you learn how to work with team members in producing comprehensive and detailed Content Specifications for the parts of the publications library. You will better understand how to respond to the challenge of downsizing the publications both to save costs and time during implementation and to meet customer needs more effectively.

Additionally, you learn the steps involved in creating implementation standards and the importance of early planning for the production cycle, including planning and negotiating with outside vendors. Inexperienced publications project managers often learn too late that the text and graphics you have created so carefully in a desktop-publishing system do not reproduce well with the typesetter's or printer's more sophisticated system. Good planning can help you avoid such pitfalls.

Finally, you understand the necessity of the Content-Specification reviews and their relationship to the continuing process of negotiating responsible budgets and schedules.

CHAPTER 10

Creating the Content Specifications

The Content Specifications are the second planning documents that your team creates during the publications-development life cycle. In Phase 1 of the life cycle, you created an Information Plan and Project Plan to give shape to the publications project. In Phase 2, you continue the planning process by specifying in greater detail what you will construct. While you created one Information Plan and one Project Plan in Phase 1, you will create many Content Specifications in Phase 2. You and your team members will specify the content of each individual document or other media outlined in the Information Plan.

The deliverable for Phase 2 is a complete package of Content Specifications. If all parts of the project are synchronized, it may be possible to produce all the Content Specifications on the same schedule. However, you may determine that different schedules are needed depending on the availability of resources to staff the project and the availability of technical information about the product. For example, installation procedures may not be specified until late in the project's life because the installation process is often the last to be designed and developed. Or, the online help may be scheduled to begin after the printed documents go into production but may need to be planned earlier.

The Phase 2 deliverable is defined by the Content-Specification template, presented in Appendix D. Once the template is completed to the satisfaction of the project manager and the rest of the team (including the outside reviewers), then Phase 2 of the project is also complete. The primary parts of Phase 2 are illustrated in Figure 10.1.

In this chapter, you learn how to direct your team in the following activities to produce strong specifications for each document in the Information Plan by

- Understanding the purpose of the specification process
- Determining goals and objectives
- Analyzing audience and environment
- Developing a detailed task analysis
- Analyzing organizational strategies

Figure 10.2 illustrates the steps in the process.

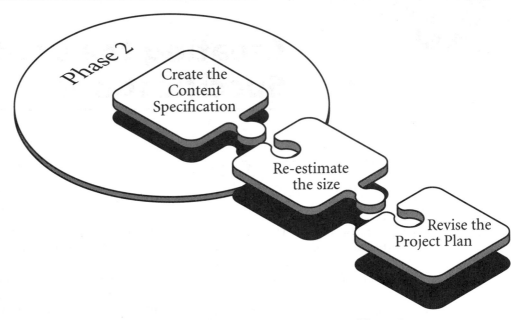

Figure 10.1 Phase 2 of the publications-development life cycle

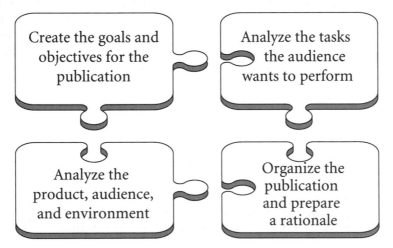

Figure 10.2 Creating the Content Specification

Understanding the purpose of the Content Specification

The Content Specification documents your writers' detailed analysis of the content they plan to develop and how they intend to organize it. The writers produce Content Specifications for each document defined in the Information Plan. That means your team will produce Content Specifications for each

- Printed book
- Online help system
- Classroom training program
- Computer-based training course
- Quick-reference tool
- Other media included in the publications project

As you begin to manage the Content-Specification phase, you must allocate time in the schedule to produce the plan, convince your team members that the time is well spent, and decide which team members will participate in the specification process. If you are introducing a new development process in a Level 1 or 2 organization, it is especially important that you have lots of good reasons to spend the additional time planning, the support of all your team members, and a clear set of directions and examples for the team to follow in creating their Content Specifications.

Allocating time for planning

To produce the detailed specifications necessary for each project element, you must spend adequate time analyzing the tasks to be supported and organizing the information you have gathered. For many projects, specifying the content of publications should take between 15 and 25 percent of total project time. For complex projects, the percentages may be higher. A 20-percent goal for Content Specification means for a one-writer/one-calendar-year project, you should expect to spend 10 weeks on the Content Specification. The 10 weeks follows the first 5 weeks of information planning, which means a total initial planning time of 15 weeks, representing 30 percent of total project time, as illustrated in the graph in Figure 10.3.

As project manager, protect your planning time. It is essential for laying the groundwork for a successful project. The less time you devote to planning, the more likely that you and your team members will have to reorganize and rewrite significant portions of the documentation. Avoid the temptation to shorten or eliminate planning time, especially when the project is very short and you feel deadlines pressing on you. The shorter the project calendar time, the more you need sound planning. On a very short project, you have no time to do anything wrong and no time to do anything over. Remember that managing a project without a plan is like setting off on a trip without a map and no destination.

 Guideline: Devote about 30 percent of total project time to the planning phases to ensure project success and a high-quality result.

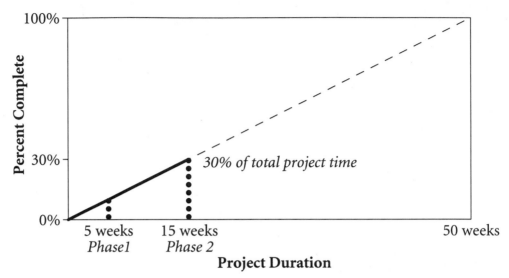

Figure 10.3 Percentage of total project time for Phase 1 and 2 activities

Consider that each Content Specification, at minimum, should contain the following pieces of information and analysis:

- Overview of the entire library and the role of the individual publication in the library (goals and objectives)
- Description of the product or process
- Usability goals of the individual publication
- Audience profile for the individual publication
- Objectives of the publication
- Organization of the publication
- Annotated outline of the publication subsections
- Predicted page and graphic counts (or other scope metrics).

The Content-Specification template in Appendix D provides instructions for producing these sections. To produce detailed information on each of these topics will require considerable effort by your team. If you plan the content thoroughly, you may come to the conclusion that 25 to 30 percent of total project time is far shorter than you originally thought. A complete Content Specification is not the same as a simple outline of topic headings. Substantial time is required to achieve the level of detail presented in the template.

Why specify content so completely?

If you hope to successfully manage the Content-Specification process, you must be convinced of its value to the publications-development life cycle, and you must be able to convince others. In the following case study, an experienced project manager effectively communicates the importance of detailed planning to an inexperienced writer.

$\bigodot\bigodot$ I can't spend 30 percent of my time planning. I need to get started writing my manual," announces Sam, a new writer on the project. "I'll do a quick outline at home tonight and show it to you tomorrow."

"I know how you feel, and I really appreciate your dedication to meeting your deadline," Eleanor commiserates, "but planning is a very important part of our process. We can't afford to start writing before we know what it is we're going to write. We also need the agreement of the reviewers as early as possible. If they agree to our planned organization of information now, they will be less likely to suggest major changes later."

"I really want to plan, but I just don't think I have time for it," explained Sam.

"You know," continues Eleanor, "when I was a new writer here, I had trouble making time for planning, too. It made me feel like I wasn't producing anything. But I promise that you'll find the actual writing does not take as long as it may have before. With a good plan, you may even find the writing less difficult and more fun."

"But how am I going to convince Cindy that I need to spend time planning. She's the engineer I'm working with, and she said yesterday that she wants to see my chapter on installation as soon as possible. She'll go crazy if I tell her I won't be able to start the installation chapter for 2 months."

"Well, I can help you talk to Cindy if necessary. But, you know, she's one of the more dedicated planners in the engineering group. Besides, how can you write about installation, when the installation procedure hasn't even been designed?" asks Eleanor.

"Installation was going to be the first chapter in the user's guide. Cindy told me to just write up something that sounded plausible, and we would change it later when she figured out how the software would be installed," Sam explained.

"That's exactly what I'm talking about when I insist that we need to plan. Why would you put installation in the first chapter of the user's guide? According to marketing's plans for the product, the installation is going to be handled by the dealer," explained Eleanor. "Janice will probably include the installation instructions in the dealer's kit she's working on. Your book is intended for the office manager who'll have nothing to do with installation."

"Cindy thinks that all user's guides need to start with an installation chapter. It's a standard piece," insisted Sam. "I was just going along with her ideas."

"This is a chance for you to contribute your own ideas. You'll understand the issues better once you've tackled the audience profile section in the Content Specification," explained Eleanor. "You'll want to ask which tasks the office manager will want to perform with the product. How about spending some of those 10 weeks finding out?"

"But I'll waste so much time when I could be writing," protested Sam.

"You just said you'd likely have to write the entire installation section over again once the process is worked out," explained Eleanor. "At this point, writing would really waste time for you. Planning saves you time. Once the Content Spec is done, you'll be surprised how quickly the writing will go—you'll have built a sound knowledge base to draw on as you write."

"OK, I'll try it. But I really don't know where to start," explained Sam.

"Let me dig out one of my old Content Specs for you to look at," explained Eleanor. "Then, we can go over the template together. You might want to start by getting a good understanding of your user. Talk to Joe in marketing. There's also a training class coming up for new office managers on the old system. Talk to the trainer and arrange to sit in on the class."

"I can do that. But what about the product? I really don't know much about the new release yet. Cindy says she's going to approach the manager activities in a totally new way," questioned Sam.

"Then schedule time to work with Cindy and find out what she's planning. She is probably working on her own design specification now. Why don't you read it as she's writing it—you could even volunteer to edit it," said Eleanor. "By the time your Content Specification is done, you'll know a lot about the product. The other writers will tell you that writing from a thorough Content Spec is like filling in the blanks of a form. All the structure is in place. I know it sounds hard to do a Content Spec. But once you've done one, the others get easier."

"You mean it's like creating a map of exactly where I'm going?" said Sam. "I can do that. Maybe by the time I've got a complete Content Specification, Cindy will have the interface designed. She's said she's going to create a prototype for the user groups to review."

"Right. By spending time on planning, you delay writing until more of the details are in place. That means less time rewriting in the future," explained Eleanor.

As you can see from the case study, the purposes of the Content Specification are to

- Understand how the product will work and how it will support user tasks
- Organize the details of the publication
- Confirm the earlier audience and task analyses and extend them with more information as the project develops
- Delay writing the detailed text until the product is sufficiently designed to write about
- Avoid rewriting because of product changes
- Obtain early agreement about the organization of the publication from all team members, including internal publications management
- Avoid reorganizing the publication late in the development cycle
- Position the publications team as the primary designers of the publications

Getting value from Content Specifications

In addition to these primary purposes for the Content Specification, the development of a complete specification provides you with flexibility to manage the project. It also enlarges the range of options that you can use to respond to changing project needs.

With a thorough and complete Content Specification in place, you can, if necessary,

- Split assignments among several writers
- Add writing staff during the implementation cycle

What happens if a writer leaves in the middle of a project? A good Content Specification allows a new writer to come up to speed on the assignment more quickly and with fewer disruptions to the rest of the team. The new writer can review the specification and evaluate the work completed in light of the specification, a more efficient process than plowing through random notes on the writer's desk.

What happens if the assignment begins to grow and a single writer is not able to complete the project by the deadline? A good Content Specification allows you to assign another writer to part of the project without jeopardizing the organization of the publication. Continuity is more effectively maintained because several writers are working from a single, unified plan. With a good Content Specification, you may also be able to help a senior writer devise tasks for a more junior writer to accomplish. Without a thorough plan, a senior writer who needs assistance often finds it difficult to make effective assignments for someone new to the project or newer to writing. With a good plan, pieces of the work activities that could be handled by a teammate are more easily identified and are defined in context for the newcomer.

In addition to its project management role, a thorough Content Specification provides the project manager and the developmental editors with an opportunity to review the organizational thinking of the individual writers. Such a high-level organizational review ensures that all publications in the library are coordinated and consistent and that each publication is effectively organized to best meet audience needs.

In terms of its impact outside the publications team, a thorough Content Specification communicates to the reviewers and others in your organization that you have carefully considered customer needs in organizing the information. Many reviewers seem to think that the organization of a publication is a matter of personal preference. In the case study above, Cindy, the engineer, has an opinion about the placement of installation instructions in a user guide. A carefully structured and documented Content Specification, however, can counter this opinion with a logical, data-supported argument. By understanding that the office manager will not be installing the software, Cindy is more likely to agree to omitting installation instructions. Thus, you avoid an opinion battle between engineering and publications by focusing on customer needs.

Finally, many reviewers, including publications-project managers, have difficulty responding effectively to a simple topic outline. The Content Specification, which includes a rationale for the organization and an annotated outline, communicates more effectively and elicits a more thorough response. By clearly understanding the publications team's position, reviewers can better evaluate their own positions. Frequently, a Content Specification reveals major organizational flaws in the product design because reviewers see for the first time exactly how the product will be used in the context of user tasks.

Guideline: A solid Content Specification provides a detailed map for the rest of the publications-development life cycle.

Setting up the Content-Specification team

On most publications teams, an individual technical writer is assigned to develop each Content Specification, although one writer may develop more than one spec. Less frequently, more than one writer may be assigned to a large spec. An individual writer appears to provide the coherence and consistency needed during this phase of the development life cycle. Nonetheless, other members of the publications team have important roles to play in the development of sound Content Specifications. These roles are described below.

Project manager. Just because one writer has primary responsibility for a Content Specification does not mean that the writer has sole responsibility. As project manager, you are responsible for ensuring that all the Content Specifications are coordinated and that no gaps or unnecessary overlaps occur among them. Carefully review all Content Specifications before they are released for review by developers and marketing to ensure that the goals and objectives established in the Information Plan are being met.

Team members. If possible, all publications team members involved in a particular development effort should have the opportunity to review all the Content Specifications together. In this way, everyone learns how the entire project fits together and is aware of what other team members are charged with accomplishing. In addition, the insights gained during information gathering are shared among team members, strengthening the overall approach taken in the design and specification of the publications library.

Developmental editor. If a team review is not possible, or in addition to a team review, a publications team that has a developmental editor should also ensure that the editor reviews all Content Specifications. The editor, as a senior member of the group and as an individual overseeing many publications, will often have a broader perspective than individual team members. The developmental editor will also be a superb organizer, able to bring the latest ideas about organization to bear on the project.

The developmental editor should also ensure that not only is there coordination among the diverse Content Specifications, but that there is coordination with other publications being developed elsewhere in the organization. This coordination ensures that the audience receives a unified view of the product or process.

Graphics. In addition to the developmental editor and other members of the writing team, you may also want to include those responsible for graphics and illustration on the Content-Specification team. Since graphics and illustrations will be specified in Phase 2, the inclusion of the graphic artists on the team ensures that their expertise is taken into account and that they know the extent of their tasks during the rest of the publications-development life cycle.

Localization and translation. If you have individuals responsible for localization and translation, you may also want to include them in the internal review cycle to ensure that decisions made in Phase 2 will not cause problems later. By participating in defining the purpose and the organization of each element of the publications library, the localization and translation professionals will be better able to plan their own function.

Indexer. If you have an individual responsible for indexing, that person should review the Content Specification to gain a firm understanding of the project direction, the subject matter, and the intended audiences. The indexer can begin planning the style and content of the index from the beginning of the project.

Guideline: **Create a team for Content Specification that represents all those affected by the decisions made.**

Determining goals and objectives

The first part of the Content Specification closely resembles parts of the Information Plan. The Content Specification template calls for statements of goals and objectives, audience and task analysis, and organizational strategies that have already been addressed in the Information Plan. As a result, many project managers may be tempted to eliminate the first part of the Content Specification and ask for only the annotated outline. Resist this temptation.

If the writers on the team have not participated in the initial information planning, they need to thoroughly understand the thinking and decision making behind the plan. Even if they have participated in the initial planning, individual writers are planning single publications at this point and are planning in considerably more depth. More time has gone by in the product-development life cycle, which means that the product design may have changed since the Information Plan was written. The writers need to take these changes into account. And, with the passage of time, writers have had an opportunity to learn more about the project, the product, and the audience than was known in the first phase of the publications life cycle.

In many publications organizations, initial information planning is done by senior members of the team, including the publications manager or the project manager. Because the goals and objectives of the library of publications are defined in the Information Plan, individual writers may not be aware of the goals until the Content-Specification stage. During Content Specification, each writer needs to review the Information Plan thoroughly, talk with its designers, and reflect on how the goals and objectives of their individual publications can mirror the overall goals and objectives. For example, while the goals and objectives of an entire library of documents will include meeting the needs of many diverse audience members, the goals and objectives of a system-administration manual will focus on the needs of system administrators alone.

The goals and objectives section of the Content Specification should, therefore, reflect each writer's understanding of both the project as a whole and his or her individual contribution to the project. This section should state clearly how the writer intends to meet the goals in the design and organization of the publication, as illustrated in Figure 10.4.

The starting point for the writers is the goals and objectives section of the Information Plan. Call a planning meeting for the entire publications team to convey

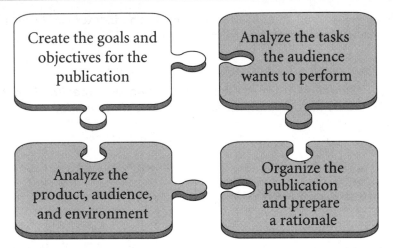

Figure 10.4 Creating goals and objectives for the publication

the decision-making process used in the Information Plan. The meeting focus should be to ensure that all team members grasp the rationale for the plan and are able to express their understanding in their own planning documents.

The project manager should direct the team members to conduct some of the same activities discussed in detail in Chapter 7:

- Determining publications goals and objectives
- Analyzing audience and environment
- Developing a detailed task inventory
- Analyzing design implications

The only difference is in the focus on an individual publication. Suggest, as well, that the goals and objectives section of the Content Specification, while it is the first section of the document, may be the last section written. The goals for a publication are developed in light of the writer's understanding of the audience and tasks.

Figure 10.5 presents the goals and objectives for a project that included two manuals to support a software product for a training organization. This Content Specification is for one of the manuals.

Note that the writer has learned a great deal about the user expectations for the documentation and the product from the focus groups. She has established an effective goal for the developer's guide to ensure that the product is viewed positively.

Guideline: Ensure that the goals and objectives of the publications focus on the needs and requirements of the audience.

Purpose of the Guide

The PARROTT Test Developer's Guide is intended for test developers. It will provide an overview of the PARROT system, complete descriptions of the various screens displayed, and step-by-step instructions for:

- reviewing information in the PARROT database
- starting ACD on a PC
- getting an NBO ID
- developing and linking NBOs in ACD
- developing and linking test items in ACD
- storing and printing test information in ACD

The test developer's guide will also briefly explain how students take tests and provide an overview of how administrators maintain the PARROT database.

No training is planned for the test developers. The Guide must stand alone in supporting their learning and use of the system.

In preliminary focus groups held with potential customers, the participants strongly indicated that they would not use a system that they perceived as difficult. They were very critical of the initial design presented to the focus group. Development has made changes to the design in response to the criticism; however, it will still be important for the documentation to create a positive impression of the software and to help users clearly understand how to use the product to their benefit. As much as possible, the publications group must produce a set of instructions that makes the product easy to use.

Figure 10.5   Sample goals and objectives for a publications project

Analyzing product, audience, and environment

Before defining the goals and usability objectives for the publication, the writer of the Content Specification must first have researched the product, the audience for the publication, and the environment (Figure 10.6) in which the publication will be used. Although product, audience, and environment are also described in the Information Plan, the writer needs to study them from the point of view of the individual publication. The processes used in the study are the same as those discussed in detail in Part Two.

Since more time is available for this study than for developing the Information Plan, the writer has a chance to learn more about the audiences and their environments. Site visits that were not feasible in the first few weeks may become feasible now. Some development teams may already be developing prototype interfaces for the product to evaluate in early usability testing or to present in focus groups. The more the audience

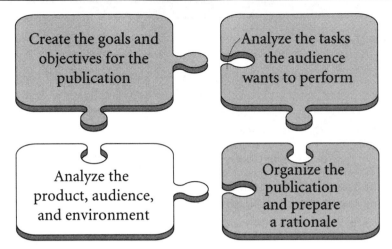

Figure 10.6 Describing the product, audience, and environment for the Content Specification

is involved in the design process, the more access the publications group has to them. It is important to use the opportunity to learn as much as possible about the audience characteristics.

The Content-Specification phase provides the time needed for the writer to become familiar with the product as well as the audience. While the final details of the design may not be in place, the broad outlines of the design should be clear by this time. Many technical projects have a steep learning curve. Writers are often asked to come up to speed quickly on products that have been in development for years. Although the developers had many months to understand the requirements and specify the design of the product, the writer may have only a few weeks or days to understand complex processes. By spending time specifying the publication, the writer gains the time needed to learn and understand the product well before committing words to paper.

The audience profile in Figure 10.7 comes from the PARROT project introduced in the "Goals and Objectives" section.

Note that the writer has paid special attention to the audience preferences and their previous experience working with similar products. The information was acquired both through direct interviews and analysis of the focus-group videos, allowing the writer to achieve a complete picture of the audience and their needs.

Guideline: Find out as much about the audience as possible to ensure that the organizational strategies on the Content Specification respond to audience needs.

Product Description

PARROT is being developed for use by three different audiences:

- Test Developers (authors) who develop and link new ICDs and test information.
- System Administrators who install and maintain the system and control access to the PARROT database.
- Students who use the system to register for tests, take tests, and access their test results.

Test developers will use the SFD tool to develop online tests for students. Although SFD will be installed and used on PCs, test information developed in SFD will be uploaded to the PARROT database (by the system administrator) for online testing, compiling, and reporting. Test developers will be able to review information in the PARROT database using the operating system, but any changes they wish to make to existing tests or SPOs must be made on their PCs in SFD; the files they wish to modify are simply downloaded (again, by the system administrator) to SFD.

System administrators, in addition to installing and maintaining the system, will manage the PARROT database. They will have the authority to review and manipulate database information, accept or reject pending student registrations, provide and change lockwords, and upload and download information between SFD and PARROT.

Students will be able to sign on the PARROT system to register for testing, take tests, and receive their test results quickly. They will also find out where to go to find information covering an ICD they might have missed. Students take tests to (1) prove a course prerequisite skill, (2) waive a course, or (3) successfully complete a course.

Audience Profile

Note: The following analysis is based in part on the two SFD Beta test videos and the SFD Usage video.

The PARROT Test Developer's Guide is primarily intended for test developers: division engineers and instructors. This audience has a lot of experience with mainframe computer systems and PCs, and they are familiar with standard computer procedures. Except for PARROT-specific terminology, all of the computer terminology used in the guide will be familiar to these people.

In addition, this audience is very familiar with training and testing procedures. They know what an "ICD" is and they understand the principles of online training and testing. More importantly, they have developed clear

Figure 10.7   Sample audience profile

objectives for their training and testing needs and are quick to evaluate the usefulness of a new tool.

In general, we can assume this audience does not require (or appreciate) lengthy explanations of computer usage or training and testing procedures. They want information that will enable them to get started as quickly and efficiently as possible. These people typically prefer hands-on experience to in-depth explanations and are eager to see if a program really works the way they think it should.

The PARROT Test Developer's Guide must also accommodate a second smaller group of users — administrative assistants (or data entry clerks). This group may include temporary personnel who only perform data entry tasks and do not have extensive computer or testing experience. However, these people will receive at least basic training from the company before they are required to perform data entry in SCD. This audience requires clear, complete instructions and a minimal amount of in-depth background information. They need to know exactly how to perform a task (no shortcuts!); they don't need a detailed explanation of what's taking place behind the screens.

Figure 10.7 (Continued)

Performing a detailed task analysis

With an understanding of audience and environment as a baseline for further investigation, the writer proceeds to collect data about the user tasks supported by the publication (Figure 10.8). While not all publications are task oriented in their explicit design details, most publications are intended to support some task that the audience wishes or needs to perform. Even purely conceptual information needs to be designed with the audience goals in mind. Most people read technical conceptual information to increase their ability to solve practical problems.

As the project manager, your most important role is directing the writers to perform a task analysis and suggesting the type of investigation that the project schedule will permit. As the individual writer, your most important role is to use whatever means at your disposal to view the publication from the audience's point of view.

Too often, technical documents mimic the organization of the product or the original research, rather than support the needs of the audience. By structuring the publications more effectively, you can avoid audience complaints that the publications don't help them learn what they need or perform their tasks, that they have to figure out how to perform the tasks by fitting together bits and pieces of information.

Task-oriented publications support audience tasks directly, rather than indirectly. Only for experienced audiences do we find that reference information or even concep-

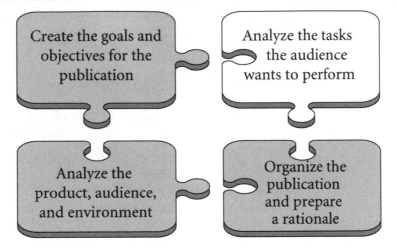

Figure 10.8 Analyzing the tasks the audience wants to perform

tual information is the best solution. Even reference information, however, must be designed with audience tasks in mind. The user of a command reference manual needs to know not only a definition of the command, but also how to use it in a real application. Information describing a command will be better written and more useful if the writer understands how the user is likely to use the command.

Policy and procedures information should be designed with the audience tasks clearly in mind. Certainly, a procedure is a step-by-step account of the actions and decisions to be made. But a policy should also be designed so that it may be acted upon effectively by the intended audience.

Even marketing information such as data sheets, product brochures, and other sales aids, should be designed to support the audience's task of evaluating the product and making a favorable purchase decision. Only a very rare technical publication has no use that might be identified. Sometimes frustrated writers will refer to "file-cabinet" documents, reports that are sent to people who do not read them, have no use for the information, and simply file them away. If some documents are clearly destined for the file cabinet (rectangular or circular), then a professional technical writer has no role to play in their publication other than ensuring that it meets corporate standards.

Performing a task analysis

In the design of documents that the audience will use to operate, administer, or maintain a product, a task-oriented approach to information is essential. We know that task-oriented information

- Reduces training time
- Enhances productivity
- Decreases customer-support costs
- Increases audience satisfaction with information

However, to be presented effectively, tasks need to be studied from the viewpoint of the audience. Perhaps the greatest danger for the writer is to spend more time studying tasks from the perspective of the product than from the perspective of the audience. While some tasks, like installation and configuration, are performed strictly from a product perspective, end-user tasks need to be understood from the audience's viewpoint.

It is difficult for a writer to understand the audience's perspective without having any contact with the audience. The writer works in a vacuum, isolated from knowledge of how the tasks fit into the audience's world. By spending time interviewing audience members, the writer is better able to

- Design from a task perspective rather than a product perspective.
- Create headings with task names that the audience knows.
- Group headings together in ways that are logical for the audience.
- Place procedural information within the context of a larger task environment.
- Write only the information the audience needs to perform the task, rather than all the information that the writer knows.
- Present information so that the most-used information comes first.
- Provide more explanation for difficult tasks and less for simple tasks by knowing which tasks are difficult and which are simple from the audience's perspective.
- Account for the audience's environment in writing procedures.
- Prepare a better index, using synonyms that some audience members are more likely to know.

A thorough task analysis is the route to minimalist publications, those that have only the information needed to perform tasks and not extraneous information that may have been included to meet the needs of internal audiences.

The better the task analysis for the Content Specification, the better defined the publication is and the less likely it is to change substantially during the course of the project. Many major organizational changes occur in publications late in the development life cycle because tasks are not adequately defined. The lack of definition occurs in part when marketing and development do not have the detailed understanding of human performance issues required to develop high-quality publications.

In conducting the task analysis, the project manager and the writer need to work together to focus the information gathering. Decide whom to talk to about audience tasks, including the audience members themselves and others who understand their working environment. Decide whom to talk to about the product-specific tasks, including the marketing and development organizations that are designing how the task will look and feel in the new environment created by the product. If there are prototypes available, study the prototype and become familiar with the look and feel of the product. Perform as many of the tasks as possible yourself.

In the course of the task analysis, discuss not only which tasks can be performed with the product but also evaluate how the tasks will affect the audience environment. Ask questions such as

- What skill level is needed by the person performing the task?
- What prior knowledge is needed to perform the task well?

Task Analysis

The PARROT Test Developer's Guide is intended for test developers. It will provide an overview of the PARROT system, annotated illustrations of the various screens displayed, and step-by-step instructions. With the aid of the Guide, the test developer will be able to

- review information in the PARROT database
- start SFDs on a PC
- get an ISD ID
- develop and link ISDs in SFD
- develop and link test items in SFD
- store and print test information in SFD

The test developer's guide will also briefly explain how students take tests and provide an overview of how administrators maintain the PARROT database.

Figure 10.9 Sample task analysis

- How often is the task performed?
- How difficult will the task be for the "average" audience member?
- How critical is the task? What are the consequences of doing it wrong?
- Is it possible to recover?

Ask audience members to identify tasks they perform by naming them and then grouping them together with other tasks that seem similar to them. This information, while not providing a final design, provides good data for the writer in the organization of the publication.

In the Content-Specification phase, sufficient information must be gathered about tasks and information needed in support of tasks for the writers to create two or three levels of heading for their outlines. Such depth of analysis requires more information than was gathered in the information planning phase but not as much information as will eventually be required to write the procedures themselves or create the final text of reference, conceptual, or marketing information.

In the excerpt from the PARROT project in Figure 10.9, the writer lists the test-developer tasks that the guide is intended to support.

Doing a task analysis for noninstructional text

Many technical communicators are involved in preparing papers, reports, proposals, and other documents that are not based on tasks. How then does task analysis apply? Many technical communication texts discuss the organization of information according to a number of traditional and some not-so-traditional patterns. The patterns are intended to be arranged to meet audience needs. For example, a proposal is organized to follow the requirements in the Request for Proposal or, if none exists, to answer reviewer questions in an order that meets their needs. A report might be organized to answer the reader's need for information regarding conclusions, methodology, and references. In each case, the audience needs should supersede the needs of the writers, the internal reviewers, or the organization.

Technical communicators often find themselves in the center of disputes about the organization of information, whether it is task oriented or not. The Content Specification is designed to help avoid or at least settle those disputes in a rational way. If you have no overt audience tasks to support, consider substituting a section in the Content Specification that describes in detail how and why your audience will use the information in a particular publication. The more data you can present about audience requirements, the more prepared you will be to counter objections and consider valid alternative plans.

Guideline: **The task analysis for the Content Specification should be thorough enough for the writer to develop two to three heading levels for the proposed text.**

Organizing the publication

Once the writers have completed their data gathering on product, audience, and tasks, they are ready to develop an outline of the book or other information source they will produce (Figure 10.10). Every media developed to support the audience requires some type of outline. For a training program, you might produce a list of the objectives and

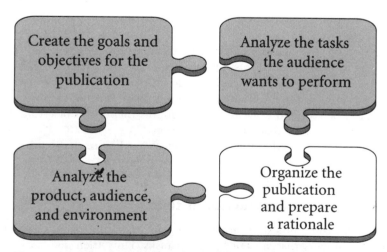

Figure 10.10 Organizing the publication and preparing a rationale

the training modules that will address the objectives. For an online help system, you might produce a visual map of the topics to be included in the help system. For a video production, you might produce a storyboard, an outline of the topics that will be addressed in the script, and the suggested order of those topics.

The most significant characteristic of any outlining device is the organizational strategy implied. The organizational strategy anticipates how the information will be revealed to the audience and how they will access the information they need. For example, most of us have encountered this guideline for people planning a speech:

- Tell them what you're going to tell them.
- Tell them.
- Tell them what you've told them.

The strategy implied by this guideline takes into account the way people remember information they hear. We tend to remember best what we heard last. While the introductory material sets the stage and provides an organizational pattern to help the listeners make sense of the talk, the conclusion organizes the information once again so that it is more likely to be remembered.

Many organizational strategies are available to writers planning the structure of a publication. Text may be organized according to

- The frequency with which information may be used, from the most frequent to the least, or vice versa
- The difficulty of the information for the audience, from the simplest to the most complex
- The chronology of use from the first information needed to the last
- An alphabetical or numerical listing for ease of access by experienced users
- A network of grouped topics, especially in online information
- A learning order, from the information that is easiest to learn first to more difficult information that builds on the earlier learning
- Categories of information (name, purpose, usage notes, example) with labeled paragraphs

The writer's job is to find an organizational strategy that will serve the needs of most members of the audience and is, itself, easy to understand. Whatever pattern is selected, the pattern should be made obvious. Structural devices, such as item names, parallel grammatical structures, visual mapping devices, icons, headers and footers in hardcopy, menu systems online, advanced organizers in overviews, numbering systems, and others should all advance the cause of revealing the organizational strategy the writer has chosen.

The project manager's role

The role of the project manager is to review that writer's strategy with other members of the team, ensuring that the writer has taken into account all relevant information about the product, audience, and tasks. The project-team review also ensures that individual strategies for each type of publication and each individual publication are coordinated.

In many cases, the project manager needs to oversee the emerging organizational strategies for a project. Perhaps you can suggest better strategies to new writers or to writers who are new to task-oriented design. Because the product structure often dominates the thinking of developers and influences the thinking of writers, many first attempts at an organization are strongly product oriented.

The dominance of a product-oriented strategy appears to occur because of the history of computer software documentation. The very term *documentation* suggests that the information is designed to record the details of product design. Originally, computer documentation was intended to describe fully the software so that maintenance programmers would understand its structure and be able to make changes carefully. Such documentation remains a necessary part of the product. Even in the hardware world, engineers need documents that record what was created and how that creation is organized.

Unfortunately, the documentation strategy has been carried over into the information provided to users of the product. Users are supplied with descriptions of software menus and screens and lists of field definitions. Or, in hardware, they encounter descriptions of the parts and lists of button and knob definitions. In most cases, this information is not organized in a useful way and has little to do with the tasks the user wants to perform with the product.

A sound organizational strategy for an instructional text can mean the difference between a happy customer and an angry, frustrated one. Many readers of technical publications complain that they cannot find what they need in the publications. More than likely their frustration comes from a poor organizational strategy.

Not all organizational strategies are task oriented. In a scientific publication, the strategy may be dictated by the standards of the professional field. Where such standards exist, it is best for the technical writers to follow them. Members of the audience have been trained to expect a particular strategy of presentation and to associate this strategy with the technical author's membership in the profession.

Too often, however, technical authors lapse into a chronological organization of reports and similar documents. A chronological organization is easy to produce since it is simply a record of what occurred in a project in the order of events. Unfortunately, such a strategy is rarely appropriate for the reader who is looking for results and conclusions rather than a historical narrative.

 Guideline: Finding the best organizational strategy is the responsibility not only of the individual writers, but also of the project manager. In managing a publications project, the manager is responsible both for the content that is built and the strategy used to do the building.

Creating an outline

The outline is the obvious starting point for illustrating the organizational strategy of the publication. The Content Specification template calls for a detailed outline. This depth in the levels of heading ensures that the writer has gathered sufficient information about the tasks or topics at this stage in the development life cycle. If the outline can only be written to one heading level, the Content Specification is not complete. The project manager should suggest that the writer gather more detailed information about tasks or topics to complete the specification.

Perhaps the most significant part of the outlining process is the selection of the best words to use for headings. The audience analysis should provide the writer with some insights into the words most likely to be used by the greatest percentage of the audience. The words in the headings should be easily understandable to the audience. They should not be the words used by the development organization to describe the tasks and topics. Consequently, the writer may discover a conflict between the words used for the product and the words that will work best in the publications. The best solution is to change the words in the product to be consistent with the audience's vocabulary. If that change is not possible, then the project manager and the writer may have to design a compromise system in which both terms are presented. The compromise will affect both the table of contents and the index of hardcopy publications, as well as the topic lists and synonym searches available on line.

If the writer does not select the right words to label sections of the publications, the audience will become frustrated. Inadequate labels lead readers to the wrong information or present information that the reader cannot understand or misinterprets.

For example, in a cellular phone manual, the writer starts off with good task-oriented headings. The first headings are gerunds such as

- Placing a call
- Storing often used numbers

These are clear and understandable from the user's point of view. However, things get worse quickly. Three subsequent tasks are described as follows:

- Discontinuous transmission mode
- STO/P1,P2 RCl/P1,P2 One-touch dial memory
- DTMF

The most frustrating part of the bad headings is that the user may need the information under the DTMF heading, but doesn't know it. The acronym DTMF is never defined.

Annotating the outline

Once the headings are worked out, the writer should annotate the outline, explaining what objectives will be met in each section and what type of information will be included to meet the audience's needs. The annotations are very important to the specification process and need to be developed carefully. The annotations explain to the reviewers exactly what the writer intends to include in a section. They should be considerably more informative than the headings alone.

In the example from the PARROT project (Figure 10.11), the writer states the objectives for Chapter 1 and describes what will be covered in the chapter.

Chapter 1. Reviewing Information in the PARROT Database

Chapter 1 objectives

After reading Chapter 1, users will know:

- how to access archival material in the PARROT database
- how to review information
- what their options are if they want material printed or modified

Chapter 1 organization

Chapter 1 includes the following sections:
Finding the PARROT database — explains the step-by-step process the user follows to locate the database by navigating the program's menu structure.

    A. Locating the proper equipment — describes the equipment users need
    B. Finding archival information — outlines the steps they take to access PARROT archival material

Reviewing information in the PARROT database — describes the different kinds of information the user can access in the PARROT database and explains how to review the information.

Figure 10.11   Sample annotated chapter outline

Note that the information is complete enough that the reviewers and members of the publications team can tell exactly what the writer intends. The level of detail suggested here enables reviewers to gain a much better understanding of the organizational strategy. As a result, their reviewers are more thorough and their agreement with the plan more stable. In general, I do not recommend that reviewers be presented with a topic outline alone. Topics outlines do not ordinarily contain enough information to make the organizational strategy for the publications sufficiently clear.

As project manager, you will also find the annotations to be more informative than an outline alone. You will be able to understand the writer's intent and communicate it to the publications team. As a writer, you will be more secure in your estimates of page and graphic numbers if you have developed sufficient detail for your outline. By writing the annotations (objectives and descriptions), you will find that the section takes on a more substantial quality than with a heading alone. It is remarkably easy to forget what you meant by a heading after weeks or months of writing.

Many writers who have learned to create detailed Content Specifications also report that the planning process is very thorough. Once they begin to write the section, they feel as if they are filling in the blanks of a form. All the organization has been worked out in advance.

I do not want to imply, however, that once the Content Specification is complete and signed off, no changes will occur. The business of technical communication embraces constant change. Structure changes as the product becomes better understood; details change as problems are encountered in the product development and worked around. Strategies change as we learn more about the audience and tasks become better defined. The Content Specification is likely to change but the first presentation is essential to the smooth working of the development life cycle.

The better the initial specification, the better the Project Plan. As changes occur, the project manager can evaluate those changes in light of the initial plan and determine the effect of change on resources and schedule.

Developing a rationale

Obviously, the organizational strategy needs to be planned in order for the writer to create and annotate an outline. It is also useful to explain the strategy in the Content Specification. Figure 10.12 displays an excerpt from the PARROT project, explaining the strategy behind the organization. The organization is explained carefully, especially the placement of information at the end of the guide. The writer uses as general chronological order of tasks, including finding the information that supports a task (Chapter 2) before the users will perform it (Chapter 3).

Both writer and project manager should ensure that the rationale in the section called "organization of the publication" is well argued. A well-argued rationale may help to dispel arguments later among the review teams. At the very least, it will set the tone for the argument. If someone wants the organization changed, they will need a persuasive reason based on audience needs.

Guideline: Present your organizational strategy as persuasively as possible to forestall arguments among the various review teams.

Estimating pages and graphics

Once a detailed annotated outline has been produced, re-estimating pages and graphics from the original Information Plan becomes much simpler than it may at first appear (Figure 10.13). As they develop the detail for the annotations and learn how tasks will be performed or information must be presented, individual writers should find themselves visualizing the number of pages or other information units (screens of online help, minutes of video, hours of training) they will produce. At this juncture, the

Publication Organization

The organization of the PARROTT Test Developer's Guide reflects the user-friendliness and clear task orientation of the SCD software. The guide takes test developers through the process step by step, presenting tasks in the order that they are most likely to be performed. The order is basically chronological, from installing through printing and saving. The section of troubleshooting follows the chronological sequence.

Additional information about student use of the system is included at the end of the volume. The users may not need this information initially, but may find it valuable as they become more experienced. The volume ends with a comprehensive glossary of PARROT terms.

The chapter-level organization is as follows:

- The preface, "Introducing PARROT," provides a brief overview of the PARROT system and identifies the test developer as the primary audience. It also lists and describes all the chapters in the book and provides a brief glossary of the most important terms users need to know.
- The first chapter, "Getting Started in SFD," helps users get started with SFD by showing them how to start the program. This chapter also includes a chart that allows users to quickly find and use special key functions such as the zoom key and the help key.
- The second chapter, "Reviewing Information in the PARROT Database," provides users with the information they need to access the PARROT database and review information within it. They will use the database as part of developing ICDs in Chapter 3.
- The third chapter, "Developing ICDs in SFD," provides users with the information they need to create, edit, and delete an ICD. It also explains how to get an ICD ID and how to link ICDs to courses and to other ICDs.
- The fourth chapter, "Developing Test Items in SFD," provides users with the information they need to add, edit, and delete a test item. It also shows users how to relink, copy and preview a test item.
- The fifth chapter, "Printing and Saving in SFD," provides users with the information they need to print a full bank of questions, print a list of questions, print a randomized test and an answer key, and copy a set of SPOs to a floppy disk.
- The sixth chapter, "Troubleshooting SFD," provides users with the information they need to troubleshoot SFD. It includes a chart showing SFD error messages and explaining what users can do to solve problems.
- The seventh chapter, "Understanding How Students and System Administrators Use PARROT," provides users with information about the roles that system administrators and students play in using the PARROT system.
- The PARROT Test Developer's Guide includes a comprehensive glossary of terms that test developers need to know to use SFD and to communicate with system administrators. It also includes a task-oriented index.

Figure 10.12 Sample organization rationale

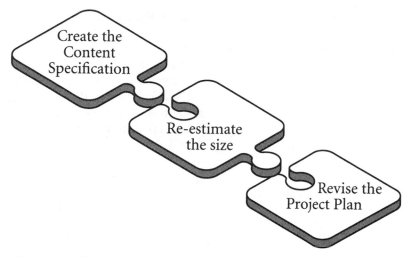

Figure 10.13   Re-estimating the page and graphics counts

writers may find it especially useful to coordinate with graphic artists. Their participation in determining which types of illustration to use and how often will be invaluable to the estimating metric.

To writers who haven't done it before, estimating pages accurately from the Content Specification may seem impossible. As project manager, you will find yourself guiding the process and educating the writer about visualizing scope. The following case study illustrates how you may want to work with your team members and anticipate their confusion about page-count estimates.

I don't think I can estimate pages for the Content Specification," announced Sam. "I'm just guessing. It's impossible to tell in advance how many pages you're going to write."

"The page-count estimates are very important," explained Eleanor. "You need to make them as accurate as possible. I need accurate estimates to use in evaluating my Project Plan. If the scope of the project looks different from what we estimated for the Information Plan, I'm going to have to revise my Program Plan."

"What if I just start writing," asked Sam. "I'll find out how many pages we'll have when I finish a section. You could revise the Project Plan then."

"The Content Specification is a major milestone in the publications-development life cycle," explained Eleanor. "Everyone on the development team expects us to tell them if we can make the schedule now that we've had real time to plan. I can help you learn to estimate page counts. Let's sit down this afternoon and work on an estimating metric and some thumbnail sketches."

"If you can help me understand how to estimate, that'll be great," exclaimed Sam. "I'm having a hard time seeing how this will work. You know, maybe you should just do the estimate yourself."

"I don't know the information in the depth that you do now. And, if you don't do your own estimating, you won't have any ownership of the results," said Eleanor. "I expect you to stick to the estimates once they're in place."

"You mean—if I say a chapter is going to be 10 pages, I can't go over that?" questioned Sam. "But what if the information is more complicated than I thought?"

"The page-count estimates are part of our contract with the development team," Eleanor replied. "Yes, I definitely expect you to follow them closely. If the information needs to change, you need to let me know immediately, so that I can either help you reduce the volume of information or assess the need to re-estimate the project as a whole."

"In my last job, I just kept writing until I thought I had covered the topic," explained Sam. "We had some rough estimates, but nobody paid attention to them."

"We used to do that, too," admitted Eleanor. "Books just got bigger and bigger. Everything was out of control. We found that we were writing everything we knew about a topic, rather than what the customer needed. We had to get the process under control and stick to our estimates."

"Today, it works pretty well. On a book I wrote a couple of years ago, I did thumbnails that set the page count at 178 pages. While I was writing, I rearranged some of the information but the major form of the book didn't change. The final book had 182 pages."

"That's amazing," said Sam. "You must be a great estimator."

"No," said Eleanor. "I just stuck to my plan. The goal, about 180 pages, really represented the level of detail we had decided the customer needed. More pages would have been overkill. Usually when I find writers exceeding the page count dramatically, they are writing for the wrong audience, with too much explanation of things the users already know how to do. I once had a writer who produced eight pages of text and graphics just to explain how to turn on the machine. All it had was a simple toggle switch, one of those 1/0 types. And the users all worked in a computer center. They didn't need a dissertation on flipping a switch. We cut the whole thing back to one sentence and a picture locating the switch. Now, let's work on those estimates."

Accurate page-count estimates, as Eleanor tries to make clear to Sam, are critical to the successful completion of the Content-Specification milestone. As project manager, you might suggest a combination of strategies to the writers to help them visualize the size of their projects. The first method involves dividing the tasks or topics in the Content Specification into categories. The second method, an additional step, involves creating thumbnail sketches of the pages or screens, including elements of both text and graphics.

In the first method, the goal is to divide the topics or tasks into categories according to the difficulty of the task or the complexity and size of the topic. For example, in looking at 50 tasks that users might perform, you may envision some to be simple to perform, some difficult, and some in the middle. You might create a matrix of task difficulty as shown in Figure 10.14.

Task Difficulty		
Simple	Medium	Complex
IIIII	IIIII	IIIII
IIIII	IIIII	IIIII
IIIII	III (13)	IIII (14)
IIIII		
III (23)		

Figure 10.14 Difficulty matrix for estimating pages

The tic marks represent the 50 tasks allocated according to a difficulty measure. Difficulty might represent the number of steps in the task, the level of detail required to understand the steps, the number of illustrations needed, the number of screens and menu items to move through, the number of decisions required, or other issues that require more words and illustrations to become clear to the reader. Difficulty might also represent how complicated the task is for the writer to describe.

In one case, a subject-matter expert on the development team, someone who had been a user of the ultrasound equipment we were documenting, helped the publications team allocate tasks in the difficulty matrix. She knew a great deal about the difficulty levels because she knew how difficult some of the tasks were to learn and how many steps were required for other tasks.

The same process of allocating items to different categories may be used for topics in reference information or proposals and reports. As a guide in the allocation process, the project manager may want to recalculate pages from an existing publication. Look at the number of pages associated with each task or topic. Rather than averaging them all together, divide the tasks or topics into categories and calculate the average number of pages per category. Use the average number of pages in each category to estimate the page counts for the new material.

Guideline: Develop the Content Specification in sufficient detail to allow for accurate estimates of the size and difficulty of individual tasks.

Using thumbnail sketches and an estimating metric

In addition to accounting for task difficulty, the project manager may want to recommend that the writer produce a miniature version of the storyboard—thumbnail sketches. Using thumbnail sketches, the writer envisions each page of text and graphics for every topic and subtopic in the outline. The more detailed the outline, the easier thumbnail sketches will be to visualize.

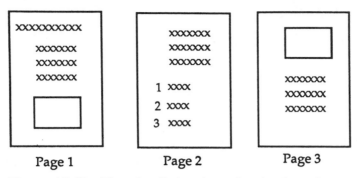

Page 1   Page 2   Page 3

Figure 10.15   Thumbnail sketches of a simple task

The more structured the document, the easier the thumbnail sketches will be to create. When a document is well organized, it is easier to predict what will appear on each page. Once you know what topics will be covered for each type of information, you need only multiply the number of pages for one topic by the total number of topics.

Once they have a difficulty matrix in place, the writers should be able to draw a picture of text and graphic blocks per page for each of the categories you have identified. A set of thumbnail sketches for a simple task might look like Figure 10.15.

The sketch indicates that a simple task may take approximately three pages of text and graphics to explain. Do the same for the other categories of task or topic. Then use the results to estimate the page counts of the major sections of the publication. Be certain to estimate the pages required for front and back matter. Include glossary, index, tables of contents and figures, title pages, copyright notices, warnings and cautions, and any other required parts of the publication. All of these items, while they may include boilerplate, still take real time to produce, review, coordinate, edit, and revise. They represent real pages that require time to complete.

 Guideline: Use a difficulty matrix and thumbnail sketches to create a page-count estimate.

Developing storyboards

In very basic terms, storyboards are thumbnail sketches made large. However, storyboards are usually intended to serve many more purposes than a page and graphic estimate. The storyboard is a process that you may want to recommend when the writers are presenting a new idea or a new mode of development to the other members of the development team. A storyboard puts life into the annotated outline you have produced for the Content Specification. Storyboards work especially well for online documentation projects.

To produce a full-fledged storyboard, ask your writers to expand their annotated outlines by the number of pages of text and graphics they have estimated. One writer simply added page breaks to the outline. You might want to include placeholders in your word-processing copy for graphics and text that resemble the thumbnail sketches. With "greeked" text (nonsense words) in place and boxes to represent graphics, you run the whole thing through the word processor. Voila! Instant storyboard.

After your writers have produced their stacks of paper, tape them to display boards and attach them to the wall of the review room. Then, ask the review team members to attend a storyboard presentation. The writer's job is to explain the storyboard and invite comments. The reviewer's job is to stroll through the storyboard presentations, visualizing the content, making comments on individual boards, and discussing issues of overall presentation strategy. As project manager, you may discover that team members will understand the proposed structure better through storyboards than through reading the Content Specification. Most people have difficulty visualizing something that is new and unfamiliar. Yet, we want them to "see" what the publications will look like early in the life cycle, so that they are less likely to suggest major structural changes late in the life cycle. Storyboards produce this effect.

 Guideline: Use storyboards to help the publications and development teams visualize the Content Specification.

Estimating size for publications that are not books

Can thumbnail sketches and storyboards be used for publications that are not intended as hardcopy or softcopy books? Certainly. In fact, storyboards originated in the film industry to invite feedback on the sequence of scenes to be developed for a film. Since so much of the effect of film is visual rather than verbal, the development teams produce storyboard pictures of what the frames will look like to supplement the text of the script.

Since online help systems and other forms of computer-based information have a significant visual component, you may find you can communicate your design ideas much more effectively through a storyboard than through a planning document. The more tangible you can make a presentation, the better response and the less confusion you will get from the review teams. Good visual planning devices like storyboards can help to overcome conceptual problems. Without a good visualizing tool, reviewers may be surprised when they review final drafts of an online help or computer-based training project. The drafts may look quite different from what they had envisioned.

Online help that is closely tied to the design of screens, menus, and dialog boxes can also be effectively prototyped through a storyboard. The storyboard may be linked with the screen displays to show exactly how the user will access the online documentation and how a clear relationship will be maintained between the screen object in question and the online help.

 Guideline: Use storyboards to visualize the organization of other aspects of documentation, including online help, other online documentation, tutorials and computer-based learning.

Creating the page-count matrix

Once your team has worked through its page and graphic estimates, the final results should be presented in table form at the end of the Content Specification. For the Content Specification, include only the estimated counts. But for tracking purposes, you may want to leave columns for actuals that you record as the project progresses (Figure 10.16).

Chapter	Estimated Pages	Actual Pages	Estimated Graphics	Actual Graphics
Preface				
Introducing PARROT	5			
Who uses PARROT?	2			
How to use this guide	5			
Important terms for test developers	2			
Chapter 1				
Accessing the PARROT database	11		3	
Reviewing information in the PARROT database	9			
Printing and changing information in the PARROT database				
Chapter 2				
What you need to run an ISD	4			
Starting up ISD	5			
Using the ISD main menu	2			
Using the ISD function keys	2		1	
Chapter 3				
Getting an FSD ID	10		1	
Creating an FSD	13		2	
Editing an FSD	10		2	
Deleting and FSD	9		2	
Linking an FSD to courses and to prerequisite FSDs	15		4	
Chapter 4				
Adding a test item	13		2	
Editing a team item	11		2	
Deleting a test item	9		2	
Moving a test item	9		1	
Copying a test item	9		1	
Chapter 5				
Printing a full bank of questions	10		2	
Printing a question bank	10		2	
Printing a test	11		2	
Bundling FSDs	2		0	
Chapter 6				
Problem solving in ISD	14			
Error messages in ISD	8			

Figure 10.16 A page/graphic-count matrix

Downsizing the publications

Much has been made in the last few years about reducing the volume of information provided to audiences. John Carroll's research suggests that user of computer software may actually learn more effectively with less rather than more information (Carroll, 1990). Less information encourages users to explore on their own, and this exploration enhances their ability to learn. In addition, many organizations are concerned with the cost of publications, especially those that accompany products or are designed to support policy and procedures. In many instances, the cost of the publication package is the highest portion of the cost of goods. As a result, many publications-project managers find themselves challenged to reduce the volume of pages produced.

A number of strategies are available to the project manager faced with downsizing the documentation on a product or process. In fact, the approach suggested here directly lends itself to producing publications specifically targeted for an audience. In creating the right size for a publication, consider the following:

- Investigate audience needs thoroughly so that you develop and produce only what is needed to get the job done.
- For software projects (and some hardware projects), seriously consider placing information in online help and avoiding duplication in the hardcopy manuals.
- Design the user interfaces so that less information is needed for the audience to learn the product.

Develop a strategy for downsizing during the planning phases, not later. The first, and simplest solutions, are internal.

Internal solutions

Internal solutions begin with the premise that many publications contain clutter, poorly designed elements, and redundancy that should first be removed. Typically a 30 percent reduction in volume may be achieved in many publications simply by wielding a sharp pencil. Of course, you may disturb a few sacred cows, so be prepared for a battle.

1. Eliminate all information that is not directly needed by the target audience. Publications are often repositories of information someone developed in the past and no one ever thought to remove. Cut a wide swath through the historical artifacts. They cost money to maintain, reproduce, and disseminate, and probably no one ever uses them.

2. Consolidate information that is repeated in more than one place. Don't tell the user over and over again how to type the customer's name in a field.

3. Reduce or eliminate information the audience is likely to know. Does anyone need to be told how to type the customer's name? Many publications contain relics of earlier technologies that make no sense today.

4. A picture is often "worth a thousand words." Find ways to use well-labeled graphics to describe actions, rather than lots of lengthy text.

Online solutions

Once the internal solutions have been exhausted, look into new media to support the audience and reduce the cost of publication.

5. Consider placing all reference information in the computer system for software products and many hardware products. Build online help that explains how to enter information into fields and respond to choices in dialog boxes.

6. Include online task-based help if it is feasible. If tasks become too difficult for brief sets of instructions, refer the user to the hardcopy documentation.

7. Deliver your hardcopy manuals in softcopy form if your audience, environment, and task analyses support the feasibility of this alternative.

8. Establish documentation databases that audience members can access directly through query languages.

9. Eliminate from hardcopy documents everything that exists online.

10. Redesign the interfaces so that less supporting information is needed.

More radical solutions

Placing information on the computer screen reduces only the cost of production and distribution. While substantial, these costs may not be as high as the costs of developing information that is not needed, or at least not needed by all audiences. More radical solutions, like some of the solutions suggested by Carroll's research, require careful planning and testing before implementation but may reap substantial benefits for both the audience and the development organization. Minimal manuals may take longer to create than traditional manuals, a fact you need to take into account when estimating hours per page.

1. Consider minimalist "getting started" and "tutorial" information.

   Minimalist, in this context, means giving the audience enough to get started and then leaving them on their own to explore. In one manual we designed, we got the user to the primary input screen. Then, we suggested they pull down the menus and open the dialog boxes and generally explore the screen on their own. We provided no details about the fields and options available.

   Eliminating information is a calculated risk, available only for certain special and well-analyzed audiences. It is a solution that may not be available to the primary manufacturer who feels obligated to document everything. A minimalist approach also demands thorough testing and evaluation. A wrong decision about the audience, one not supported by usability testing, may result in a dramatic increase in requests for customer support and service.

2. Deliver to the audience only the most commonly used information. Make less commonly used information available on demand.

   Consider the possibility of making some information, such as the 20 percent used infrequently or by only a few members of the audience, available only on demand. The on-demand system might work through special orders or even by FAXed copies sent through a voice-mail-based inquiry system or directly through a customer-service representative. The point is to find out what the 20 percent is and then identify better ways to deliver this information only to those who need it.

3. Provide electronic performance support systems that aid in diagnosis, troubleshooting, and decision-making tasks.

Many of the tasks that users have difficulty with are those that require analysis and response. Software and hardware systems produce error messages or report problems in the product. Users of a product report problems to a system administrator. Systems crash and need to be restored. Employees have difficult problems to solve and need the right answers quickly. Computers provide us with the capability to help these audiences find the solutions they need directly, rather than by hunting through books. However, sophisticated performance support requires new designs for software and hardware and a much better understanding of what the problems might be in the first place. Developers and writers often lack the resources and the knowledge to develop such solutions.

As a project manager, your role is to investigate the possibilities and be prepared to suggest solutions to difficult audience problems. First, of course, you need to know what the difficult problems are, which requires audience analysis. You must also work with customer support people who know what the most commonly asked questions are. So we come back full circle. We can develop innovative solutions and reduce the amount of paper produced, but only if we do the work correctly the first time—that is through a "rich picture" of the world in which a product or process is used.

In most instances, you will find that a minimal manual is a second manual for the same product. Unfortunately, many products change so drastically that we do not get to write second manuals.

Combining the Information Plan and Content Specifications

In some short projects or in projects that are primarily revisions of previously designed publications, you may not need to produce both an Information Plan and Content Specifications. For short projects, you may find that the schedule may be simplified if the first two phases of the publications-development life cycle are condensed into a single design document. That does not mean that you should neglect the issues of defining the audience, environment, and tasks or the need for a well-conceived publication strategy, but you may be able to shorten the review process by combining the Information Plan issues with the Content Specification (annotated outline and page-count estimates). Combining the two documents may be feasible if you are able to answer all the questions in a shorter period of research time. Combining may also be feasible if you are defining only a single deliverable for the project.

For projects that are primarily revisions, an Information Plan in place from the last version of the project may remain sufficient to describe the strategy adopted by the publications team. In that case, you may want only to update the Content Specifications and leave the Information Plan as is. However, after many revisions, you should revisit the Information Plan and consider if the audience, environment, and tasks have changed. Too often, organizations continue to update publications that have lost contact with their audience. It is simply easier to continue to revise rather than rethink the organizational strategy or consider new information about the audience. Remember that audiences change too. Maintenance tasks that for years were performed by factory-trained personnel may now be performed by office workers in an effort to reduce costs. Operations tasks once performed by long-time employees may now be performed by part-time workers who are less thoroughly trained and lack some of the basic skills you may once have assumed. A changing workforce, where more and more workers are part time, temporary, or do not speak English as their first language, increases the need for well-designed, thorough, and complete information. Be careful that your audience hasn't changed since the last version of the product.

If the audience and tasks remain the same, however, Content Specifications need only be updated rather than begun anew. Writers should indicate with change bars (vertical lines printed in the margin next to added text) which sections of the publications will be changed to accommodate new procedures, new functions, or substantially changed functions.

For a revision project, the document-change matrix described in Chapter 11 leads to a revision of the Content Specification. This revision process helps your team judge the extent of the revisions and the amount of work required to accomplish them. In the Content Specification, they should indicate what new sections will be added, where major changes and minor changes will occur, and what type of global changes will have to be made to bring the publication up to date.

Guideline: In some short projects and many revision projects, you may want to combine the Information Plan and the Content Specification into a single document.

CHAPTER 11

Revising the Project Plan

When the writers have completed their Content Specifications, the project manager has the opportunity to review and revise the Project Plan. The Content Specifications are complete once the writers have completed their research on the product, audience, environment, and tasks and have filled in the template (see Appendix D). Depending upon the relationship of information planning activities (Phase 2) to the development process, the writers may have less than a complete understanding of the product design. Consequently, the Content Specifications will likely contain tentative organizational structures that may have to be modified as more information about the product emerges.

Once more information is available about the design of the product, the Content Specifications will become more complete and stable. Nevertheless, with approximately a third of the publication project complete, writers should have sufficient information to address user tasks coherently and to suggest the organization of more descriptive information. As project manager, assisted by the team members and the editor, you will need to decide that the Content Specifications are sufficiently developed to be presented for consideration by external reviewers.

If the Content Specifications are too incomplete, little will be accomplished by a premature review. You may want to suggest to the writer that more time be taken for research to make the specifications firmer. If a third of the project time has been expended with little concrete information available about the product, you may want to suggest that staffing be reduced until more information is forthcoming. By this time, it may be clear that the total project time will inevitably be extended.

However, if the Content Specifications appear reasonably complete and user tasks are well understood although their technical implementation in the product has not entirely been worked out, you are ready to analyze the specifications and revise your Project Plan.

A thorough and thoughtful job on the Content Specifications will allow the writers to develop the page and graphic estimates with confidence. These estimates should have sufficient input for the writers and you to believe that the final publication will be plus or minus 10 percent of the estimates if no subsequent major changes occur to the product or to the audience and task analyses. Certainly, the product may continue to be changed, but at the Phase 2: Content Specification milestone, you will have to assume a temporarily stable project scope.

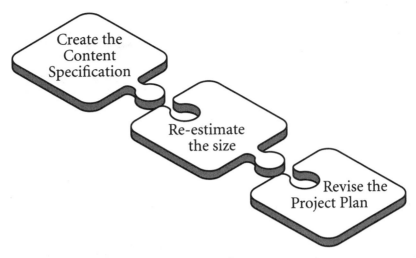

Figure 11.1   Revising the Project Plan

Reviewing the Content-Specification estimates

Once the page and graphic estimates are in place, you are ready to re-evaluate the "rough-order-of-magnitude" estimate done in the Information Plan phase (see Figure 11.1). With an additional 15 to 20 percent of the project time expended and more research completed, you should be prepared to determine if the estimate was in line with the realities of the product and project or if a new estimate is needed.

In reviewing the Project Plan in light of the Content Specification, you face at last three possibilities:

- The Content Specification is virtually identical to the size predictions made in the Information Plan, and no change to the Project Plan is needed.
- The Content Specification suggests that the size predictions in the Information Plan were too high, and the resources or schedule determined for the project should be cut back.
- The Content Specification suggests that the size predictions in the Information Plan were too low, and the resources, quality level, and schedule determined for the project should be increased.

The first possibility is, of course, the simplest. The Project Plan remains in force, and the project proceeds as initially indicated. The second and third possibilities indicate that you need to re-evaluate the requirements to complete the project and provide a new estimate and schedule. The third possibility is the most likely, given the underestimating of product scope that is typical of the high-tech industries.

Before you consider revising your Project Plan based on the page-count estimates in the Content Specification, you must be certain that the estimates are reasonable. You and the team of writers need to review the reasonableness of the estimates in light of the audience and task requirements and the marketing and budget requirements of your organization. For example, for a complicated piece of hardware, the writer and the engineer decided that the maintenance manual needed a lengthy section called "Theory of Operation." They felt that the field engineers would need to understand exactly how the electronic components were designed in order to troubleshoot effectively. However, the original Information Plan called for the maintenance manual to be written for less skilled field engineers. These individuals were expected to make only board-level repairs and needed diagnostics that would help them identify the correct board to replace. They did not need a theory of operation. The plan had been to make the theory of operation available on an as-needed basis for the more senior field engineers, rather than publishing it in all copies of the maintenance manual. The project manager discussed the plans with the writer and the engineer. They agreed that the original division of information was more cost-effective.

As project manager, you need to evaluate any increase in page count from the Information Plan to ensure that the original design philosophy has been maintained. However, it is highly likely that increases will occur between the Information Plan and Content Specification phases due to a more thorough understanding of the product and the requirements of audience and task.

 Guideline: Review the page-count estimates to ensure their compliance with the information design begun in the Information Plan.

Estimating revision projects

I have left the discussion of revision projects until Part Three because many revision projects begin at Phase 2, rather than with an Information Plan. Often, a valid Information Plan exists from earlier versions of the project, although it should be periodically re-evaluated. If the original Information Plan continues to be useful, then revision projects are more likely to begin with the Content Specification phase.

Two possibilities exist for handling Content Specifications for revisions: Revise existing ones, or build new ones. The simplest route is to revise the existing Content Specification by indicating what changes will occur for the new version of the publication. The writers may find that they have to add new sections, delete old sections, and make major and minor changes to some or most of the original publication to account for product or process changes. The second possibility occurs when either there was no Content Specification for the previous version or the old version of the publication needs to be redesigned from scratch. In this case, the writers should treat the Content Specification as a totally new project but indicate what might be preserved from the older version. If there is no Content Specification at all, ask the writers to create brief ones from the existing publication with the changes indicated. In that way, you will have a complete set of Content Specifications for future reference.

The most difficult job in specifying a revision project is estimating the impact of the changes in the product or process on the publication. We know that many changes in the product will filter through an entire publication or library of publications. What looks like a small product change on the surface may have a profound effect on the publications. For example, at one company, the marketing department decided that they wanted to change the name of the product. The publications library consisted of 12 volumes of information, every one of which mentioned the product name. The marketing department viewed the change as a modest one, calling for a simple search-and-replace routine in the document files. Unfortunately, as the project manager demonstrated, the change was by no means simple. The 12 volumes of information occupied several hundred computer files that would have to be searched individually. The new name required a change in the use of words in the sentence structure, so no global change procedure could be invoked. Each instance of the name change would have to be assessed individually. In addition, the product name existed in hundreds of illustrations, each of which would have to be changed. And finally, the product name appeared on every computer screen. Not only would all the screens have to be reprogrammed, but the screen images in the publications would also have to be redone. The project manager calculated that the work would take a minimum of 2 weeks and would cost $20,000. The marketing department decided that the change wasn't worth the cost.

As project manager, how might you suggest that individual writers on your team go about investigating the changes to the existing publication and estimating the cost of the changes? I recommend a procedure called the Changed Item Matrix. It works as follows:

1. Make a list of the engineering changes in the product or process.
2. Calculate the number of pages to be added as a result of each change.
3. Calculate the number of major changes to existing pages as a result of each change.
4. Calculate the number of minor changes to existing pages as a result of each change.
5. Calculate the copyediting changes required for all existing pages.

Use a table to record the changes, as illustrated in Figure 11.2.

A major change is defined as a change that affects more than half of a page; a minor change is defined as a change that affects less than half of a page. A copyediting change affects a word or a phrase at the sentence level and may include correcting spelling, punctuation, or grammar errors that remain in the previous version of the publications. Add other categories to the matrix as needed for your projects. We often use a category of "reformatting only" to describe projects in which we take source material and

Engineering Change	Original Pages	New Pages	Major Changes	Minor Changes	Copyediting Changes
EC 1	0	20	0	0	0
EC 2	75	5	40	20	15
EC 3	50	0	0	45	5
EC 4	60	25	30	10	0

Figure 11.2 Changed Item Matrix for calculating changed pages for a revision project

simply style it to look like the rest of the publications in the library. You may also want to include categories for editing of source material, from a light copyedit to a major substantive edit or a category for illustrations.

To calculate the pages affected by each engineering change, your writers should sit down with the developers and the marketing people, whoever is responsible for defining the requirements for the new product or process. This change team should work page by page through the original publications and "redline" the pages that will change. Only by using such a disciplined process can you hope to have an accurate page count of a revision project.

Once the Changed Item Matrix has been organized, the writers and project manager need to decide how much time should be devoted to making each type of change. The most systematic way of estimating the hours for each activity is to look at the dependencies calculations for each type of activity. For example, a new page for a revision project may take as long to develop as the average new page takes in your organization for a new project. If projects of this type average 5 hours per page new, a new page for a revision project may be the same. However, when you apply the dependencies to a revision project, you need to account for the existence of the original publication. With a well-written original publication in place, the writer may find it easier to come up to speed on the technical content. You will have to decide if this factor offsets the other factors associated with the new material to be learned.

A major change might easily require the same hours per page as a new page in a revision project. It depends on the nature of the work to be done to develop a major change. You need to evaluate the dependencies separately for each type of change—major, minor, or copyediting. While a new page and a major changed page may require 5 hours of effort to develop, a minor change may require less, perhaps 2 or 3 hours per page.

Copyediting changes may be small enough to be considered as a part of the editing tasks rather than writing. If you have calculated editing as a part of writing in determining the resources needed for a project, you may want to apply the editing factor to the pages that need copyediting. Or you may want to use an editing metric instead of a writing metric. Some organizations calculate that they can perform a light copyedit at the rate of 10 to 15 pages in an hour. More complex editing, ranging from a major copyediting or sentence and paragraph organization, through a substantive edit, may require anywhere from less than 1 hour per page to more than 4 hours. In Chapter 8, you will find the Los Alamos National Laboratories editing metrics to use as a starting point if you have none of your own.

Once you have established the hours per page or hours per item for each of the categories you have included in the Changed Item Matrix, apply the metrics to the total page estimates in the table. The result may look like Figure 11.3.

According to the calculations in the sample Changed Item Matrix in Figure 11.3, the total hours for the revision project are 809. To this total, you may also want to add hours to revise the front and back matter for the new version of the publication.

If no one on the development team has any idea what the engineering changes are going to be, then you may find it extremely difficult to produce a Changed Item Matrix. Nevertheless, I recommend that you guess your way through one and use it to estimate the size and difficulty of the revision project, even if you may only be able to achieve a

Engineering Change	Original Pages	New Pages	Major Changes	Minor Changes	Copyediting Changes
EC 1	0	20	0	0	0
EC 2	75	5	40	20	15
EC 3	50	0	0	45	5
EC 4	60	25	30	10	0
Total pages		50	70	75	20
Hours / page		5	4.5	3.2	0.2
Total hours		250	315	240	4

Figure 11.3 Changed Item Matrix with hours-per-page calculations

rough order of magnitude. At least you will have a starting point to use to schedule the project, and you will be able to evaluate the progress as you learn exactly what needs to be done.

Even when estimating is difficult, I recommend strongly that you create an estimate and base it on a systematic analysis of the project. Even if the basis for your analysis is incorrect, you will know why you estimated the way you did. A rough order of magnitude is better than nothing. If you have no estimate of the scope of work, you have no way to manage and control that scope during the development process.

Guideline: Estimate a revision project by creating a Changed Item Matrix of the number and nature of the changes that will occur.

Revising resource requirements and schedules

In revising your resource requirements and schedule for a new project, first consider the relationship between the data produced for the Content Specification and your original Information Plan. If the Content Specification accurately suggests a smaller publications set for the project, you will need to revise your resource requirements downward and adjust your schedule. You may be able to shorten the deliverables schedule if the rest of the project schedule will permit it. Or you may be able to stretch the project schedule by reducing the resources devoted to it during the development phase. Stretching the schedule occurs when you do not want the publications life cycle to get too far ahead of the product life cycle.

If the Content Specification suggests a larger publications library for the project (see Figure 11.4), you will need to revise your resource requirements upward and lengthen your schedule accordingly. Or you may have to find a way to produce the larger publications on the same schedule as before, either by increasing the staff or by reducing the quality. Or you may have to find a way to reduce the page-count estimates so that the publications can be completed by the existing staff on the original schedule.

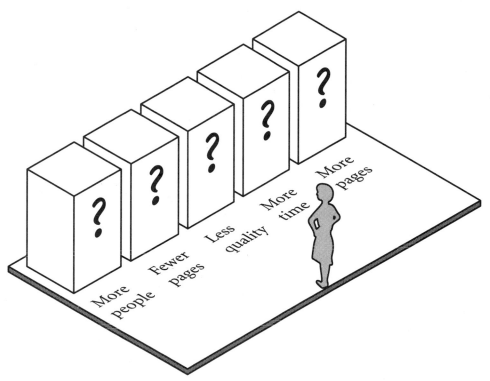

Figure 11.4 Larger project options

Reducing an initial estimate

The first possibility, that of cutting back the publications project, requires some careful thinking. Presumably, the effort to produce the Content Specification has been in keeping with the original determination of staffing and schedule. For example, for the 50-week project, a team of people began developing the Content Specification after the fifth week and proceeded through the fifteenth week (or 30 percent of total project time). Sometimes, when a project appears much smaller soon after content planning begins, the project team is able to complete its work faster than expected, well before the original 30 percent mark. However, many projects that are originally estimated too high require considerable effort to determine that they should be smaller, which means that the full 30 percent of the larger project may be used for the Content Specification.

An early estimate that is too high is likely to occur because of misconceptions among the marketing and development teams, as well as the publications team. High early estimates often occur because the product originally looked bigger or more complex than it turns out to be. Or the developers and marketing wanted information to be included in the publications that, on closer examination of the audience, turns out to be unnecessary or undesirable to publish (see Figure 11.5).

In one such case, our original estimates were based on a mistaken notion that a great deal of in-depth information about the product design was to be communicated to a

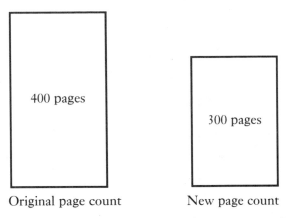

Original page count   New page count

Figure 11.5   Reducing an early resource estimate

sophisticated audience. In the development of the Content Specification, we began to question the reasoning behind giving so much product-design information away. As a result of our questions, development and marketing realized that they did not want to reveal so much about the product. Development, in fact, had been thinking more in terms of its own need for documentation than the customers'. Consequently, the Content Specification indicated that we would develop about half the pages of the original estimate.

Since we were able to cut in half the original page count for the project, the product manager expected that we would then cut in half the resource estimate for the project. However, two issues had to be taken into account to determine how much the resource estimate could be reduced. After verifying that the new page count was indeed reasonable, the project manager had to reassess the risk factors, or dependencies, associated with the project through the Content-Specification phase.

In reassessing the project dependencies, the project manager should ask the following questions:

- Was the original Content Specification milestone date met?
- Were more or less hours expended in meeting the milestone?
- Have any of the original assumptions on which the dependencies were calculated changed?

If the milestone date was missed or the hours increased, that should suggest to the project manager that the degree of difficulty of conducting the project may have also increased. Even if the milestone was met and the hours remained the same, that should also suggest that the degree of difficulty has increased. In this second instance, reaching the second milestone for a smaller project has taken more time than you would have predicted had your original estimate indicated a smaller project in the first place. Let's look at these situations graphically in Figure 11.6.

In Figure 11.6, you see a typical 50-week project with 15 weeks allocated to the combined planning Phases 1 and 2. After 15 weeks, the project should have been 30 percent complete. At 5 hours per page, we had predicted that the average technical

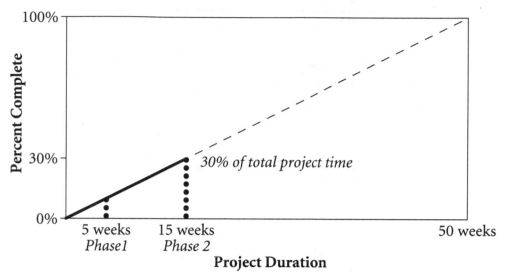

Figure 11.6 Re-estimating a smaller project

publications team would be able to produce a 400-page user's guide in this time. What if the user's guide appears to be only 300 pages long, based on the detailed analysis in the Content Specification? Then, the entire project should be completed in 1,500 rather than 2,000 hours, or 37.5 weeks rather than 50. If the full 15 weeks have been used in planning, then the new graph looks like Figure 11.7.

Note that the curve has gotten a lot steeper for the remaining part of the project. That is because the writers will have to develop the 300 pages in less time than they might have had because they have used up 30 percent of their original hours already.

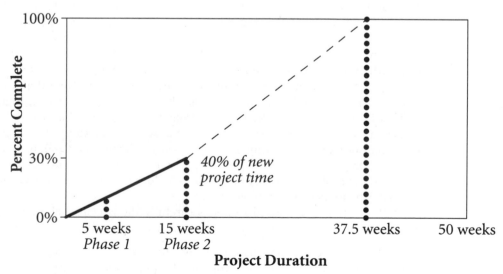

Figure 11.7 A shorter project with a higher level of productivity

Original project	New Project
400 pages	300 pages
2,000 hours @ 5 hours / page	1,500 hours @5 hours / page
600 hours for Phases 1 and 2	600 hours for Phases 1 and 2
1,400 hours remaining @3.5 hours / page	900 hours remaining @3 hours / page
	1,050 hours remaining @3.5 hours / page
	new total = 1,850 hours

Figure 11.8 Analysis of the new project requirements

Had the 300-page user's guide been predicted from the first, the team would have had 30 percent of 1,500 hours, or 450 hours, for Phases 1 and 2, rather than the 600 hours that they have expended. In fact, the team is already behind as a consequence of the mistakes in the original plan and will have to work faster to catch up. However, it is highly likely that the new predictions reflect a change in risk factors.

If we look at this scenario numerically, we can analyze the project as shown in Figure 11.8.

Note that the remaining hours mean a decrease in the hours per page from 3.5 to 3 for the rest of the project. That means that the writers will have to work about 20 percent faster to complete the project in the same number of total hours. An alternative, particularly if the original schedule is still in place, would be for you to calculate the remaining hours on the basis of 3.5 hours per page instead of 3 hours per page. Consequently, the hours remaining to complete the 300 pages following Phase 2 would be 1,050 hours rather than 900 hours. The total hours for the project would be 1,850 instead of 2,000.

As a consequence of this calculation, you should be aware that while the size of the publications decreased to 75 percent of the original, the scope of the project decreased to only 92.5 percent of the original. Because more hours were consumed in Phases 1 and 2 than might have been necessary, overall efficiency has decreased on the project from 5 hours per page to 6.2 hours per page. This typical loss of efficiency demonstrates the importance of good early estimates in keeping productivity under control.

What if the Content Specification phase had taken more time than predicted? The resulting graph of the project might look like the one represented in Figure 11.9.

This scenario also indicates that the project is in trouble. You have taken more than 30 percent of total project time to reach the second milestone. In Figure 11.9, a full 45 percent of total project time has been used producing the Content Specification for a smaller project. In both scenarios, the writers will have considerably fewer hours to complete the project than they ordinarily should have spent if you want to keep to the original 5-hours-per-page estimate.

At this juncture, you need to assess carefully the reasons behind the problem and decide how to respond. Once again, a number of possibilities exist. The first two are:

▪ The Content Specification phase took too long because the project manager was not paying enough attention to the work of the publications team or the team was not reporting adequately. The project manager should have seen more quickly that a

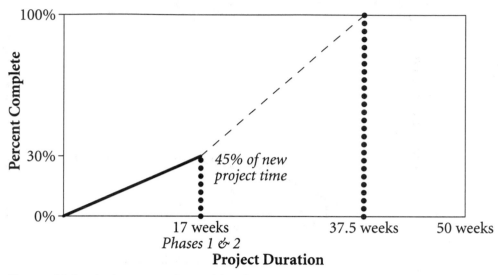

Figure 11.9 A shorter project with a late second milestone

smaller project was emerging and either reduced the work effort (fewer hours and resources devoted to the planning) or shortened the schedule (moved up the Phase 2 due date).

- Even though a smaller project seems likely, the publications team had to work harder than expected to get the information needed to find out that the project was smaller. Perhaps the team had difficulty getting the information needed, or the developers and marketing people were unavailable for interviews and questions, or lots of misinformation was provided, so that work had to be rethought and redone.

If the second possibility seems to be the case, the project difficulty has increased and you need to reassess the dependencies. As project manager, you may find that instead of a 5-hours-per-page project, the dependencies calculation now indicates that your team is doing a 6-hours-per-page project. Then, instead of 1,500 hours to produce a 300-page user's guide, you will need 1,800 hours, or 45 weeks instead of 37.5. The resulting graph would look like Figure 11.10.

As Figure 11.10 indicates, the pace will have to be picked up somewhat to complete the project in 45 weeks, but not impossibly so. Or you can reduce the level of effort by reducing the work assignments of the team members and continue to work toward the original calendar due date of 50 weeks. The remaining weeks will have, not a full 40 hours per week devoted to the project, but 34 hours per week, based on stretching the remaining 28 weeks of project time over 33 weeks of calendar time. The same possibilities are available if the project time is reduced to 37.5 weeks. In the case illustrated in Figure 11.10, however, the team's resource level will be reduced to 25 hours per week.

If you decide to reduce the hours per week for the team, be careful. If you have staff members who are not experienced at handling multiple projects simultaneously, you may find that their efficiency decreases as they learn to switch gears from one project to

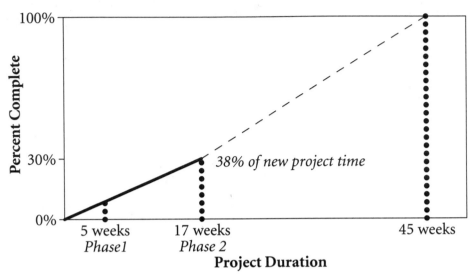

Figure 11.10 A shorter but more difficult project to complete

another during the day or week. In general, people working on multiple projects are less efficient in their use of time than are people working on single projects. It has been estimated that a full 20 percent of productivity is lost when someone works on two projects at the same time (Weinberg, 1992). Be certain to take the decreased efficiency into account on your project. And if you do have writers who are not used to handling multiple projects, be prepared to offer them assistance while they are learning.

A third scenario is also possible in looking at this project. What if the project manager caught on quickly to the emerging smaller project and reduced the level of effort in the planning phase, or if the team caught on and informed the project manager that the effort should be reduced? In that case, fewer hours were expended to meet the deliverable, and sufficient hours remain to complete the project in an efficient and timely manner at the reduced level of effort. The new project looks the same as a 300-page project would have looked from the beginning.

Another alternative available to the project manager is to examine the quality level for the project. Because more time is now available to prepare the publications than was originally thought, it might be appropriate to take action to increase the level of quality. To do so, the project manager may consider the following options:

- Adding additional audience interviews and site visits
- Including usability testing
- Adding a validation step to ensure that the information in the publications is accurate and complete
- Planning a more thorough editing cycle
- Adding graphics and examples
- Devoting more time to the index

Any number of possibilities might suggest themselves, depending on what activities were omitted in the original quality level set for the project. Increasing the quality level is always a pleasant decision to be able to make. Increasing quality will increase the hours per page for the smaller page count while allowing more to be done to ensure that audience requirements are met. Increasing the quality level will also boost morale for your team.

Finally, before reducing the level of effort on the project, the project manager may also want to assess the likelihood of changes occurring during the remaining project phases. With the additional experience on the project through the first two phases, the project manager may be better able to determine how well the larger project is going. If product changes appear imminent, you may want to preserve your original team in anticipation of future problems. You may be able to add some quality steps at this point or temporarily reduce the resource level by assigning people to a special project. In any event, do not disband a team that has gotten this far along the learning curve without serious consideration. Remember that experienced writers may leave or get sick.

On the other hand, do not keep people idle or unnecessarily increase the hours expended on a project by having your team simply fill the available time. As project manager, your role is to increase project efficiency, not reduce it. You and your team are more likely to be viewed as effective and efficient if you keep your productivity and quality high. Recall your list of important standards-building activities that your staff might work on. Use the opportunity to improve procedures or write and expand style guides.

 Guideline: Carefully evaluate how to handle a project that is smaller than originally projected, but remember to keep productivity as high as possible.

Handling a growing project

You will perhaps find it more common that a project looks larger, not smaller, after Content Specifications are complete. Projects tend to grow for many reasons.

- Inadequate information was available during Phase 1 to correctly estimate the volume of work to be produced.
- Management insisted that you underestimate the size of the project during Phase 1.
- The product or process was inadequately defined during the early stages of development.
- The functionality to be designed into the product has increased or changed.
- The audience is now better understood, and its need for information is greater than first thought.

Because new development projects tend to change drastically, especially during the early phases of the life cycle, you will likely find yourself trying to respond to a growing project that requires additional resources to complete (see Figure 11.11).

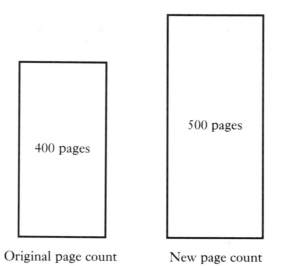

Original page count   New page count

Figure 11.11   Increasing an early resource estimate

Once again, verify the new page count carefully to ensure that the project really is as large as the writers believe from the Content Specifications.

If you are convinced that the new estimates are justifiable, you have four avenues of attack:

- Change the schedule by revising the deadline
- Increase the scope of the project
- Decrease the size of the publications
- Reduce the activities that produce quality

Remember that an increase in schedule represents an increase in the resources required for the project (same people for a longer period of time). Be certain to check vacation schedules. A schedule extension may mean that you will run into vacation time for several team members.

Using a Project Equation to assess project scope

In Figure 11.12, Project Equations represent an effective way to look at the factors that affect the success of a publications project. The primary factors are people (resources), schedule, size of the project, and level of quality. In evaluating how to increase or reduce a project, you have five equations. The first two equations are the simplest because both of the key factors, resources and schedule, are flexible. The first equation assumes that you can add people (within reason). The second equation assumes that you can add time to the schedule.

Equation 3 presents considerable difficulties to the project manager but is often the equation one has to work with. You can neither increase your staff nor alter the schedule. As a result, either reduce the size of the project, or quality will suffer. The response in many organizations to Equation 3 is to demand more and more overtime

Project Equations

Equation 1—If schedule is constant, then increase the resources.

Equation 2—If resources are constant, then increase the schedule.

Equation 3—If resources and schedule are both constant, then either reduce the size of the project or reduce the level of quality.

Equation 4—If the level of quality is constant, increase the schedule and resources or reduce the size.

Equation 5—If the increased size is necessary and quality is constant, increase the schedule and the resources.

Figure 11.12 The Project Equations for quality

and to pressure the staff to work harder. To some extent and for a limited time, more pressure will result in higher productivity. However, if you continue to push in a stressed environment, productivity and quality will begin to decline. The decline occurs when there is increased sick time and when people make more mistakes and leave out critical steps in the process just to get by.

Equations 4 and 5 are the responses of a Level 3 organization that believes that quality is significant for customer satisfaction. The difference between Equation 4 and Equation 5 is cost. If the quality remains high, then it may be necessary to reduce the information delivered in order to maintain costs at a reasonable level.

The equation most project managers would prefer to invoke is the last. You are able to increase the size of the publications to meet the revised product requirements, and you have sufficient resources and schedule to maintain the quality level originally desired.

All the other equations require difficult tradeoffs and careful thought and planning from the project manager.

 Guideline: Consider the effect on quality and your staff of increases in project size and resulting reductions in resources and schedule.

Evaluating the Phase 2 effort

When you decide on a Project Equation, first consider the amount of time already devoted to Phase 2. Has Phase 2 already taken longer than predicted at the end of Phase 1? Or if it has not taken longer, is the research completed adequate to define the rest of the project? When a project begins to expand, the writing staff often meets the expanding needs through additional work effort. We often first notice an expanding project when the amount of overtime increases during Phase 2. People are putting in extra time gathering information that is beyond the scope indicated in the Information Plan.

Remember that the work effort for a life-cycle phase may increase even if the schedule is maintained. In your original schedule, you may have allowed 600 hours for the Information Plan and Content Specifications to be done by a particular calendar date. You may discover that your staff has used more hours to meet the same date. Instead of working a 40-hour week, they have been working a 50-hour week or more. To assess the level of effort adequately, you must ask your staff to keep track of overtime hours. If they do not and you are unaware of the amount of overtime being spent, you may underestimate the duration of the rest of the project.

After assessing the work done for Phase 2, you again have three possibilities to consider

- Has the project size increased but the level of difficulty remained the same?
- Has the project increased in difficulty as well as in size?
- Has the project decreased in difficulty as size has increased?

Your writers may have worked more efficiently in producing the Content Specifications and maintained the original 600 hours in their work schedule. As a result, you have good Content Specifications for a larger project, and you are still on schedule. In fact, in the previous example, the project increased in size by 25 percent, from 400 to 500 pages. If you maintain the work level of 3.5 hours per page for the remaining phases, you should now predict that you need an additional 350 hours to complete the project, for a total of 2,350 project hours. If your writing staff is working more efficiently, you may want to predict only a 17.5 percent increase in hours. Remember that if you originally estimated a 500-page project, you should have also estimated a total of 2,500 hours, rather than 2,000.

How will you find those 350 additional hours? You can increase staffing on the project by adding writers, you can ask the existing writers to work additional hours, or you can add approximately 9 weeks to the schedule. In many cases, when a publications project has grown as much as this one has, the rest of the development project has grown as well. The schedule for the entire project may already have slipped, or it may soon.

If the schedule has not slipped, you may request an increase in staffing or ask your existing staff to work longer hours. In fact, overtime hours seem to be the norm in many organizations, especially those that do not pay overtime compensation. The advantage of overtime work by the existing staff is that you avoid having to break in a new member of the team. The disadvantage is that your existing team loses efficiency. They may also experience an increase in health problems, more sick leave, and a decrease in morale. Overtime may also affect the budget in states that require overtime pay or compensatory time off. It's a lose-lose situation.

If you decide to add a new member to the team, you must be careful to consider the effect of the new person's learning curve on the rest of the team. Growing projects produce lots of strain on everyone and increase the communications overhead. With new team members coming in, you will find yourself increasing the amount of time for project management as you orient the new people. Existing members of your team may

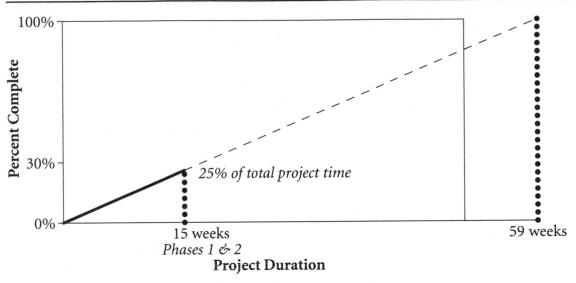

Figure 11.13 Re-estimating a larger project

also lose efficiency as they, too, spend time orienting and educating the new members in the project requirements. In *The Mythical Man-Month*, Brooks argues that the project manager should expect only 80 percent efficiency from any additions to the team during the course of the project (Brooks, 1975). That means the predicted addition of 350 hours may have to be increased to 437 hours to account for the 20 percent decrease in efficiency. That means you'll need more project-management hours and your staff will need more hours to educate the newcomers.

Let's look at the graph in Figure 11.13 of the new project estimate given the situation just outlined.

In the graph, you have extended the curve to 59 weeks, approximately 350 hours more than the original project estimate. This graph implies, however, that the project's difficulty level has remained the same even though we have added to the schedule and maintained the original team.

What if you cannot add to the original schedule but must increase the size of the team to respond to the needs of the project? In that case, the additional 9 weeks will represent an increase to the 40-hour workweek. You will need to spread the 350 hours across the remaining 35 weeks of the project by adding 10 hours per week. If you account for the 80 percent productivity level, those 10 hours are likely to increase to 12.5 hours per week if you are to achieve a productive 10 hours. You have gained a quarter-time additional team member, but you and the rest of the team are putting in extra hours to compensate.

Suppose that the project appears to have become not only larger but also more difficult. In one such project, we had been assured that the source material was in excellent shape and would only have to be copyedited and reformatted to produce one of the books scheduled for the library. Once we got the information, we saw that not only was it barely readable but it was also no longer up to date. The task changed from

Original project estimate	New project estimate
400 pages	500 pages
2,000 hours @5 hours / page	3,250 hours @6.5 hours / page
600 hours for Phases 1 and 2	950 hours for Phases 1 and 2
1,400 hours remaining @3.5 hours / page	2,300 hours remaining @4.6 hours / page

Figure 11.14   Analysis of new project requirements for a larger project

editing and formatting a 200-page book to rewriting a 300-page book. The original Information Plan estimate was incorrect, and the project needed to be totally re-estimated and rescheduled with a larger staff.

Once you have re-evaluated the dependencies for the project following the work done on Phase 2, you are ready to look at re-estimating the development phases. In Figure 11.14, note that the 500-page project now is estimated at 6.5 hours per page rather than the original 5 hours per page.

This calculation indicates that you need 900 additional hours for the project. If you have to meet the original schedule, that means increasing the level of effort to 66 hours per week rather than 40. You will most likely need a new half-time writer to work on the project, plus additions to project managing and editing time. Be aware the project management and editing tasks always increase with the assignment of additional staff members to a project. It is more difficult to manage two people than one, and the editing work increases with the need to coordinate the styles of different writers.

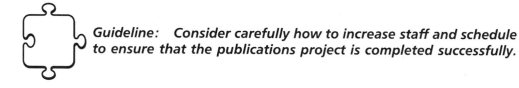

Guideline: Consider carefully how to increase staff and schedule to ensure that the publications project is completed successfully.

Decreasing size and quality

In the previous section, you learned how to respond to the need for an increase in staffing for a project. You also considered extending the schedule if needed to avoid increasing the staff. But what happens if neither of these options is available? Project Equation 3 suggests that two alternatives are available: cutting the size of the project or reducing the quality level.

If the resources are not available to complete the larger project in the time originally scheduled, then it is best to recommend that the size of the publications be reduced. For example, you might be able to produce a user's guide but not a reference manual in the time available. Or you may be able to do a good job of addressing the getting-started needs of the audience but produce a reduced-size user's guide. In one such project, we recommended that the manuals be limited to addressing the needs of experienced users. Then, once the first version of the product was released, we could create the set of manuals needed by new, less experienced users. The compromise worked well, particularly since the first product to be shipped was going to existing customers.

Marketing's plans for a new, more novice market segment would not begin to bear fruit until we had enough time to design and develop new manuals.

In effect, by scaling back the project after the Content Specification phase, you are returning to the original scope of work (in the example, that was 400 pages). You and your team will need to scrutinize the specifications to find opportunities to cut 20 percent of the estimated pages. In general, you will have to eliminate some information or reduce the information provided in particular sections.

The solution of decreasing the scope of the project is generally preferable to reducing quality. However, reductions in quality do occur and will continue to do so as demands on time and staff increase. To decrease the quality of a publications project, you may

- Eliminate illustrations or reduce their number.
- Reduce the number of review cycles and editing passes.
- Eliminate the index or reduce its quality.
- Eliminate a separate step to verify the accuracy of the information.
- Document the screens rather than respond to the audience's tasks.

All these activities, and many others that publications groups frequently find themselves forgoing, reduce the customer's satisfaction with the information, increase the amount of time and money spent for customer service, and potentially reduce referrals and sales because of declining customer satisfaction.

I hesitate to recommend decreasing the quality of a publications project. We should be convinced that it's worth the money and time to do the right job—that is, to satisfy the needs of our audiences for accurate, complete, and usable information. I would much rather reduce the scope of a project than reduce quality. I am aware, however, that quality tradeoffs do occur in many organizations, including my own. They occur whenever projects are not adequately controlled from the beginning, not because we have inadequate resources to do the job. They occur because some of the people in control of budget and schedule do not understand the quality tradeoffs or prefer not to listen and recognize them.

 Guideline: Reduce the size of a publications project before you reduce the quality.

Handling threats to quality by decreasing publication size

Perhaps the best solution to increases in the size of publications between the Information Plan and the Content Specification phase is to reverse the effect. As a project manager, you are responsible for ensuring that you have the resources to do the job. If the resources cannot be increased, then the job sould be decreased. Most of the time, recommendations for reducing the scope of the project are well received. Sometimes, they are not.

We recommended such a cutback to one of our potential clients when they cut the budget for technical publications from $100,000 to $60,000. We searched carefully for ways to set priorities and discussed with them what we could produce for the smaller amount of money. Their response was to throw out all the planning work we had done with them for several months and hire one freelance writer to do the work. Careful planning demonstrated that it was not a one-person job, but the client was unwilling to set priorities. A single writer faced with this task is going to make significant compromises. He or she will have to turn out some sort of user's guide, but it won't be well designed, it won't be complete or accurate, it won't even be well written. None of those quality goals can be met by one person in the time allotted. There will be some words on paper; the result will look like a book. But customers will call with problems and complain that they cannot use the product they purchased. I suspect the client's engineers will be bombarded with problems because they have no other customer-service organization.

If you have the ability to control the scope decisions rationally, look carefully with your team at the Content Specifications. Are you including information that would be nice to know but is not essential? Are you planning more detail than is needed by the average audience? Are you providing multiple alternative paths to perform the same action when one path is sufficient? Is there any way to cut the volume of information and decrease the workload on the writing staff?

In most instances, you can set priorities and make rational decisions. Avoid promising to do a bigger project than you are capable of with a reasonable schedule.

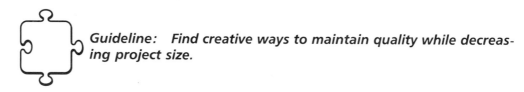

Guideline: *Find creative ways to maintain quality while decreasing project size.*

Handling schedule slips

By the end of the Content Specification phase, your team may already be faced with schedule slips by the rest of the development team. As project manager, you need to respond to these slips and still achieve your original goal of keeping the project under control. One of the hallmarks of a Level 2 organization is its reaction to crisis. In a Level 2 organization, managers are likely to abandon procedures as soon as things begin to break down.

Here's how the story goes. The product schedule slips; the publications group is forced to respond. Writers start rewriting because the information changes continuously. Draft after draft is produced, and costs skyrocket. At the last minute, pressure builds to "get something out the door." As a result, morale declines and stress increases. People burn out, get sick, leave.

The best that the publications project manager can do under the pressure of a disintegrating product-development process is to maintain control and keep calm. In some instances, the best decision is to wait until some control is restored. Another decision is to keep planning without committing too much of the work to its final form. Especially avoid endless rounds of copyediting.

When schedule slips go unannounced until the last-possible minute, be aware that this is a sure sign that the project is deteriorating. Some managers devoutly believe that the way to keep the pressure up and avoid further slippage is simply to declare that the original schedule will be met. That holds until the scheduled date passes and a new one is set. Or it holds until someone decides to ship a product that isn't ready and is full of errors.

How do you handle your project when everything else is deteriorating? By concentrating on morale-building activities for yourself, by keeping your team sane, and by responding in an orderly manner. You just might set a good example.

 Guideline: *Don't let schedule slips drive you into abandoning your process. Keep your part of the project under control even if everything else is deteriorating.*

Leveling resources

In Chapter 8, I discussed the idea of starting a project with a smaller planning staff and adding people during Phase 2 to produce Content Specifications. As the project moves into Phase 3: Implementation, you must consider the staffing mix once again. You may have assigned a team member to prepare the Content Specifications for each publication or even several publications. Now, in light of the new page-count estimates, you need to look at the staffing levels for the rest of the project.

You may find that you will be able to use a matrix organization to increase the flexibility of your team members and add less experienced members as assistants. In a matrix organization, team members may take on individual pieces of the publications library, or they may take on roles that cut across the library. It might be useful to have a single writer handle user, reference, and online documentation for the same part of the product, rather than handling only the user documentation. By cutting across the library, you can leverage product learning effectively through different media. Or you may want media experts who know exactly how to handle online documentation, thus decreasing the learning curve for everyone else on the project. Or you may want one person to handle localization for all pieces in a given language.

The idea is to arrive at an optimal staffing level as early as possible. Once you get into Phase 3, you will decrease the effectiveness of your team if you add additional people during development. Some managers seem to be reluctant to add people early in the project life cycle because they are unsure of their staffing requirements. They are afraid of spending time training people who don't remain on the project. They need to remember that it's better to have trained people available and working than to have the work and no people. Managers need to spend sufficient time managing to make the right staffing decisions at the right time.

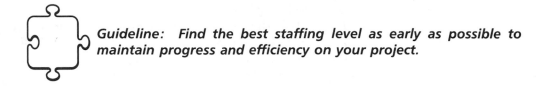

Guideline: Find the best staffing level as early as possible to maintain progress and efficiency on your project.

Scheduling the next phase — Implementation

Once the Content Specification is well established and you have revised the Project Plan to account for changes, you are prepared to design the next phase of the project. Before the Content Specifications were done, too little was known about the details of the project to be much concerned about the details of the Phase 3 schedule. At the end of Phase 2, you should be ready to put in the detail and to include schedules for the production of graphics, the localization and translation of the publications as needed, and the final production activities on the project.

As I described in Chapter 8, it is entirely possible to use scheduling rules of thumb to establish the primary milestones. These milestones include first and second drafts of the publications, as well as the due dates for the camera-ready copy. As you begin to track the parts of Phase 3, you will need a much more detailed picture of the milestones. For example, you may have a book with 10 chapters to be developed, all of which will go into final review at the first-draft milestone. Figure 11.15 illustrates the 50-week project in light of a 60 percent first draft.

Continuing the example of the 300-page user's guide, your team now has 15 weeks to develop 300 pages of first-draft text. If you have already established the definition of

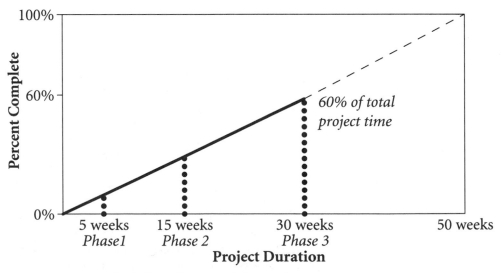

Figure 11.15 Scheduling Phase 3 of the project

your measurable milestones, you will know exactly what needs to be included in the first draft. Now you need to look at the details of how you will reach first draft.

 Why do I have to bother prioritizing the chapters and setting all these detailed schedules?" asked Sam. "I'm never going to be able to keep all of it straight. I'd rather just start writing from Chapter 1 and go to the end."

"Look, Sam," replied Eleanor, "you already told me that Charlie, who knows about the material for Chapter 5, is going to be out of town in March. Either you meet with him earlier, or you'll miss your first-draft deadline. Besides, how do you expect to tell me if you've completed a section on time unless you know how much time to spend on it?"

"I usually have a hunch if I'm on schedule," replied Sam. "On the last project, I made the first-draft deadline."

"Right. But only because you got help on the last three chapters. You spent entirely too much time on the first two chapters. Then you ran out of time at the end," said Eleanor.

"But I won't do that again. It was because I really like working on the getting-started information," said Sam. "OK, I get it. You want me to decide up front how much time I can afford to spend on each chapter. I have a total of 15 weeks. With 10 chapters, I could spend a week and a half on each. That would add up to 15 weeks."

"Sam, the chapters aren't all the same length, and they're certainly not all equally difficult to write," said Eleanor. "Chapter 1 is only 10 pages of introduction. You probably should schedule that for last. What if you take all the page counts and divide by the number of hours you have? Then, we can add extra hours to account for the most difficult sections and delete from the easier sections. How about that?"

"Sure, I'll take a first cut and show you what I've come up with," said Sam.

By dividing the writing effort into smaller pieces and evaluating the difficulty and priority levels of each piece, you and the writing team will be able to work together to set interim deadlines. The interim deadlines may certainly be flexible; but by starting with them, you will be better able to evaluate the percent complete of the project than if they do not exist.

In many publications organizations, project managers ask for interim drafts of small sections so that they can get faster feedback to the writers and ensure that the team is on the right track. Early interim drafts ensure that the writers are conforming to company style and adhering to best practice in the detailed organization of the information. Once they are reviewed internally, early interim drafts may go outside the publications group for review, but only to a few individuals directly responsible for the technical content of the smaller subsections.

To prepare for interim reviews and to schedule the smaller pieces, you need to use the page-count estimates in the Content Specification plus additional information about the schedule. What if the writer has 10 chapters to produce in 15 weeks? How much time should be devoted to producing each piece? Should one piece be developed at a time, or is it better to have all the pieces progressing on the same schedule?

In looking with the writer at the individual chapters, ask two kinds of questions. What chapters will have information available earlier than others? What chapters are most critical to the success of the publications project and need the most thorough review? From these two decision points, set the chapters in priority order. If necessary, review the priority order with members of the larger development team. They may have information about scheduling difficulties that your team is unaware of. On one project, for example, we learned that the critical subject-matter expert would be out of town for several weeks. That meant we either did his section earlier or waited until he returned. Such contingencies are extremely important to the detailed scheduling.

As the detailed schedule emerges, you may want to create a schedule diagram that shows all the pieces in place. With a good visualization of the schedule, other members of the publications team will be able to schedule their own activities. The graphics people will be able to figure out from the Content Specifications the type and number of graphics they will have to produce for each publication. They can plan their own time and ensure that first-draft graphics requirements are met. Or if you are confident that the writers can produce acceptable sketch graphics or screen dumps, you may want the graphics people to postpone their efforts until after first-draft review. If that is the case, you will want to ensure that the appropriate resources are available when they are needed.

A detailed schedule for the subsections of a project is usefully illustrated in a Gantt chart (see Figure 11.16).

A schedule of subsections can also be produced on a calendar with different activities indicated in different colors. Whichever method you choose, distribute the schedules to all involved team members, including the product-development team. Then, ask the writers to give you information in terms of the detailed activities in their weekly progress reports.

Guideline: Develop a detailed schedule of activities, and help the team members plan how they will meet the schedule.

Planning for production

If you have revised the Project Plan as a result of the Content Specifications and other changes to the project schedule, be certain to consider production requirements once again. If you are planning to translate the publications, you will also need to revise your translation schedule to match the new Project Plan. Most important, inform all the relevant players in the publications process, especially those who are outside your organization. It is your responsibility as project manager to assure that they are prepared to meet the schedule. Also, be aware that external organizations have

Project Activities	Project Time Line in Weeks													
	1	2	3	4	5	6	7	8	9	10	11	12	13	14
Write Chapter 3	█	█	█	█	█									
Edit Chapter 3						█								
Revise Chapter 3							█							
Write Chapter 4				█	█	█	█	█	█					
Edit Chapter 4										█				
Revise Chapter 4											█	█		

Figure 11.16 Gantt chart illustration of a detailed schedule

commitments to other clients. If you change your schedule at the last minute, they may not be able to respond with the promised turnaround or may need to charge for overtime to meet your new schedule. To avoid a disaster at the last minute, be certain that everyone is alerted to potential problems in the schedule and has an opportunity to make their own internal changes.

CHAPTER 12

Creating a Tracking System

Once the Content Specification is complete and you have evaluated the effect of the new project information on your original Information and Project plans, your next step is to create a new project estimating spreadsheet. In this chapter, you learn how to revise the spreadsheet to take into account new information on the project and to turn the spreadsheet into a project-tracking tool.

If you have not already created tracking mechanisms during Phase 1: Information Planning of the project, during Phase 2: Content Specification all the formal tracking mechanisms should be in place. In this chapter, you learn to institute weekly time sheets, weekly progress reports, and weekly tracking spreadsheets. From the data gathered and assessed weekly, you next produce a monthly or periodic progress report for your project as a whole (Figure 12.1).

Creating a new project spreadsheet

In the information-planning phase, you created a project estimating spreadsheet that indicated the hours, people, and schedule you had calculated for the Project Plan. For Phase 2: Content Specification, you need to revise the spreadsheet so that you can begin to use it to track progress. In fact, you may already have begun to track progress (hours and activities) during Phase 1.

If the project has not changed substantially from the rough-order-of-magnitude estimate in Phase 1: Information Planning, there is no need to revise your estimating spreadsheet. However, if the project has changed in size or complexity, you need to change the spreadsheet to reflect the differences. Your team may also have recommended changes in Phase 2: Content Specification to the library plan itself, rearranging publications, as well as adding and subtracting from the media selections. As a result, you may find that you have to revise the project estimating spreadsheets to reflect these changes.

In Part Two, you learned how Eleanor estimated the hours and resources she needed to complete her publications project by the September due date. Let's look again at this project following the development of the Content Specification for the user guide.

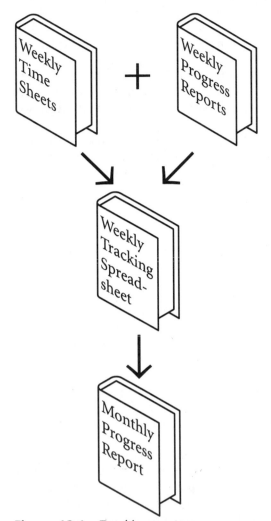

Figure 12.1 Tracking system

In Eleanor's final version of the estimating spreadsheet, she estimated that Doug and the rest of the team needed 1,092 hours to complete the 192-page user guide. In her schedule, she allocated 30 percent of that time to the Content Specification. That meant that Doug had about 328 hours to gather detailed information about product, audience, and tasks and to come up with an organizational plan for the guide. Doug expected to be finished with the Content Specification by April 28.

By mid-April, the requirements for the product have gone through a substantial change. Doug tells Eleanor that he believes the user guide is going to increase, possibly by as much as 10 percent. By the end of April, Doug, Eleanor, and Jeannie all agree that the user guide will definitely be larger than originally planned. Marketing has identified several new features that were important to potential customers. By the time Doug finishes the Content Specification, the user guide has grown to 225 pages, a 17 percent increase.

I don't see how we can make this book much smaller," said Doug. "It's already a very lean design."

"I agree," said Eleanor. "Your estimate looks pretty good. Jeannie agrees, too. We're going to have to add time to the schedule. Luckily, the two of you were able to stick to the original estimate for Phase 2: Content Specification. At least we're not behind already."

"I think we're OK," replied Doug. "I feel confident about the Spec. I just don't see how I can get the user guide done by the middle of August. And, with all the extra work going into the product-design spec, I can't get the programmers to talk to me. They're getting behind, too."

"Sounds like some of the dependencies are changing." said Eleanor.

Eleanor talks to the head of development about the schedule issues and finds that the programmers are stressed and working a lot of overtime. It's going to be difficult, at least for the next few weeks, to free them up enough to talk to Doug. Eleanor decides she needs to change the dependency rating on subject-matter-expert availability from 2 to 3. She still feels her original rating on product stability of 4 will hold. The hours per page for the project has increased from 5.7 to 6 hours per page.

At 6 hours per page, the 225-page project should take 1,350 hours, an increase of 258 hours. At the current staffing level Eleanor has in place, the new project will require 2 more months to complete. However, they are slightly ahead of schedule because of the shorter hours for Phase 2: Content Specification. If they had spent the full 30 percent of the larger project on Phases 1 and 2, they would already have used 405 hours, rather than 328.

If Eleanor considers that Phase 2: Content Specification is complete, the remaining 70 percent of the project should take 945 hours, for a total of 1,273 hours, rather than 1,350. She gives Doug the remaining 70 percent of the 6 hours per page, or 4.2 hours per page for development. That means they only need an additional 181 hours, rather than 258. That's about 6 weeks. Eleanor's new spreadsheet looks like Figure 12.2.

Because of the efficiency Doug achieved in Phase 2, they are able to maintain the original productivity estimate of 5.7 hours per page even in light of the larger book and the increase in project difficulty. However, they don't expect to deliver camera-ready copy until mid-September.

Eleanor discusses the new estimate and schedule changes with the marketing and development managers. Marketing is very unhappy but they really believe that the new features are key to the success of the product. Development says they need the extra time to add the new features, too. This time, development and publications prevail and the decision is made to extend the delivery until mid-September, with product release on October 1.

If Eleanor had been unable to reach agreement on a new schedule, her alternatives would be to

- Add additional staff to the project.
- Cut the size of the user guide back to 192 pages while adding the new features.

Fateful User Guide
Projected Hours Worksheet

Book Name Factor	Skill Level	Projected Mar-93	Projected Apr-93	Projected May-93	Projected Jun-93	Projected Jul-93	Projected Aug-93	Projected Sep-93	Projected Oct-93	Projected Nov-93	Projected Total Hours	Projected Hours/Page
User Guide		Page Count: 192										
0.10	Project management	16	15	14	20	23	17	11	0	0	116	0.60
	Writer	138	132	120	132	126	132	60	0	0	840	4.38
0.15	Editor	21	20	18	20	19	20	9	0	0	127	0.66
	Illustrator		0	0	50	85	15	0	0	0	150	0.78
	Production				0	0	0	40	0	0	40	0.21
	Subtotal	175	167	152	222	253	184	120	0	0	1273	6.63
	Total Hours	175	167	152	222	253	184	120	0	0	1273	6.63
	Hours/Month	138	132	120	132	126	132	126	126	120	522	
	Full-Time Equivalent/Month	1.27	1.27	1.27	1.68	2.01	1.39	0.95	0.00	0.00		

Figure 12.2 Fateful spreadsheet 5

The advantage of adding staff would have to be balanced with its disadvantages. A new writer would have to come up to speed quickly in order to be effective in working with Doug. And, since Doug is new, he might not know how to use help. Most likely, they would not achieve the productivity level they hoped for but would experience a further increase in hours per page. Cutting the size of the user guide while adding the new features would mean less complete information in all the sections, not just in the new ones. Customer satisfaction might be threatened by the cutback. Eleanor might also consider cutting the quality of the effort by eliminating the editing hours. That's been suggested to her before. That would definitely decrease Doug's efficiency and also jeopardize the effectiveness of the documentation. The best solution is to lengthen the schedule to accommodate the changes to the product.

 Guideline: Revise the spreadsheet to reflect the new picture of the project that emerges following Phase 2: Content Specification.

Creating a project-reporting spreadsheet

As project manager, you should begin tracking the hours used by the team members as soon as you have an initial rough-order-of-magnitude spreadsheet for the Information and Project plans. You can easily use the original estimating spreadsheet to create a project-reporting spreadsheet for the project. Simply add columns to the spreadsheet in between the estimated-hours columns to record the actual hours expended by each person. Figure 12.3 shows a project-reporting spreadsheet for Eleanor's project, based on the changes made after Content Specification. The spreadsheet shows the 328 hours that already have been used on the Fateful project to complete Phases 1 and 2.

 Guideline: Create a project-reporting spreadsheet to track the hours expended on your project.

Instituting weekly staff progress reports and time sheets

Tom DeMarco notes in his book on managing software development projects (DeMarco, 1982):

You can't control what you don't measure.

It's impossible to manage a project responsibly without knowing how many hours have been expended and what has been accomplished with those hours. To measure

Fateful User Guide
Monthly Hours Tracking Worksheet

Book Name / Skill Level	Actual Mar-93	Projected Mar-93	Actual Apr-93	Projected Apr-93	Actual May-93	Projected May-93	Actual Jun-93	Projected Jun-93	Actual Jul-93	Projected Jul-93	Actual Aug-93	Projected Aug-93
User Guide Page Count: 192												
Project management		16		15		14		20		23		17
Writer		138		132		120		132		126		132
Editor		21		20		18		20		19		20
Illustrator		0		0		0		50		85		15
Production		0		0		0		0		0		0
Subtotal	0.00	175	0.00	167	0.00	152	0.00	222	0.00	253	0.00	184
Total Hours	0.00	175	0.00	167	0.00	152	0.00	222	0.00	253	0.00	184
Hour/Month	138	138	0.00	132	0.00	120	0.00	132	0.00	126	0.00	132
Full-Time Equivalent/Month	0.00	1.27	0.00	1.27	0.00	1.27	0.00	1.68	0.00	2.01	0.00	1.39

Skill Level	Actual Sep-93	Projected Sep-93	Actual Oct-93	Projected Oct-93	Actual Nov-93	Projected Nov-93	Actual Total Hours	Projected Total Hours	Actual Hours/Page	Projected Hours/Page
Project management		11		0		0		116		0.60
Writer		60		0		0		840		4.38
Editor		9		0		0		127		0.66
Illustrator		0		0		0		150		0.78
Production		40		0		0		40		0.21
Subtotal	0.00	120	0.00	0	0.00	0	0.00	1273	0.00	6.63
Total Hours	0.00	120	0.00	0	0.00	0	0.00	1273	0.00	6.63
Hour/Month	126	126	126	126	120	120	126	126		
Full-Time Equivalent/Month	0.00	0.95	0.00	0.00	0.00	0.00	0.00	0.00		

Figure 12.3 Project-reporting spreadsheet 6

the progress of a project, or its lack of progress, you and your team members must keep track of all of your project-related time.

You can define project-related time as all time, during the work day or in the evening or on weekends, that is connected to the project. Project-related time includes time spent

- Gathering information
- Interviewing
- Learning the product
- Organizing
- Composing
- Formatting
- Editing
- Revising
- Illustrating
- Printing, and more

It also includes time spent waiting for people to become available, planning and attending meetings, talking on the telephone—everything that is project related, including regular breaks. Writers also experience down time—waiting for printers, network crashes, desktop-publishing problems. Project time includes the time it takes to complete time sheets and weekly progress reports.

In tracking project-related time, it is especially important to account for extra hours spent in the evenings or on weekends. If you don't count these extra hours, they will never be credited to your team and you will not be able to make accurate estimates of future projects. If you use overtime hours and don't count them, future projects will also require overtime because these extra hours have never been entered into the record.

As project manager, you also need to know if your team members are spending extra hours on the project. If you are unaware of the overtime, you may be surprised by decreased morale or increased sickness. You'll be under the impression that everything is going well when it is not. That doesn't mean that team members will never have to put in extra time to complete a project. The deadline crunch experienced on most publications projects makes overtime seem inevitable. However, you don't want to be in a position of asking people to put in an extra effort to meet a deadline when they have already been putting in many extra hours that you know nothing about.

On a project a few years ago, the writer did not record the time he put in driving across town to the development office to work on the product or talk to the developers. He considered his driving time to be his own time. On the next project, unfortunately, the project manager scheduled the same hours per page as the writer had reported on the previous project. Everyone expected him to maintain the same efficiency as he had previously. This time, however, he had to count his driving time because it severely impacted a second project he was working on. He could not meet either of the new project schedules.

Hiding project time, for whatever reason, will have negative consequences on the current and future projects. Some writers believe they should not report the hours they spend at home on the weekends working on their books. They believe they'll look bad if they need extra hours. Perhaps if they had discussed the extra time demands with their project manager, they would have made everyone aware that the project was actually increasing in difficulty. Their tendency to blame their own productivity rather than the project results in inaccurate records and less time for the projects in the future.

Promoting time reporting

Many project managers find that their team members resist keeping track of the time they spend on a project. They are afraid that the time records will be used to evaluate their abilities as writers. They also believe that it will take too much time to keep track of hours. They conclude that the costs of tracking time outweigh the benefits. They also argue that hours expended do not equate to progress or to quality. As project manager, you need to understand and be prepared to counter these arguments.

- Time records will be used to evaluate the relative productivity of team members.

It is certainly possible for an inexperienced project manager to use time expended to evaluate the effectiveness of a particular writer and to make comparisons among writers. However, experienced and skilled project managers know how dangerous such a practice can become. First, no two projects are exactly the same. An individual writer may have a difficult time getting information, communicating a complex procedure, or understanding a difficult concept. Individual circumstances will account for much of the variation on projects. It is not fair to compare apples and oranges or one writer to another in terms of the details of the project hours.

As project manager, you should make it absolutely clear to your team members that the record of hours is for tracking and estimating purposes only. And, you must resolve to avoid using hours as a productivity measure. If you want good data for tracking and estimating, you will have to forego any hint of using hours in any other way. If you do, the data you receive will simply be wrong, made deliberately so by team members who are trying to look good.

You must also be careful never to reward individuals based on hours they have spent or have not spent during a project. Save the evaluations for personnel reviews—keep them out of project analysis.

Hours per page are a good way to estimate project requirements. They are not a good way to estimate quality of effort. Just because an individual spends more hours, does not automatically mean that he or she improves the quality of output. Remember the saying, attributed to everyone from Agricola to Mark Twain: "I'm sorry this letter is so long; I didn't have time to make it shorter." You cannot equate hours per page with quality. A very fine writer may indeed take more hours to produce fewer, high-quality pages than a weaker writer. A weaker writer might succeed in keeping the hours down with the help of an experienced developmental editor.

 Guideline: Completely divorce tracking time from quality and productivity measures if you want accurate records of time expended on a project.

- It takes too much time to track hours.

Keeping track of and recording your work hours does take time. However, if you design an efficient reporting scheme and if your team members learn to write down their time frequently during the day, the amount of time spent accounting for hours can be minimized. It is especially important to find a convenient method for recording hours. You may want to institute a computer-based time sheet, or you may simply want team members to keep record sheets on their desks. Monitor the process closely. If the record-keeping time gets to be too much, do what you can to reduce the burden. In general, I estimate that it takes no more than 30 minutes a week to record time and keep a weekly progress report up to the minute.

- The cost of tracking and recording time outweighs the benefits.

The costs of tracking and recording time can be kept as low as possible, but the benefits are great. With accurate information about the time it takes to complete a project, your entire team will benefit. Every publications team member wants to have sufficient time to do a first-quality job. Anything less damages morale and causes enormous professional frustration. However, the only way you will be able to argue effectively for the time needed to achieve quality is to know what the cost of quality is today.

 Guideline: With accurate data, you will be able to justify the requests you make for the time you need in the future to do the best job you can for your audience.

Setting up time sheets

Once you have team agreement to track hours expended, you need to create a simple record-keeping system. I recommend using a spreadsheet form so that you can add rows and columns automatically (Figure 12.4).

1. Create a row for every day in the month, including weekend days.
2. Create a column for every project.
3. Create sub columns for the types of activities that you want to track.

Keep the activities you track to an absolute minimum. Track only those activities that will be helpful in analyzing the progress of your project and creating the data you will need for future estimates. I recommend tracking only five activities:

- Writing
- Editing
- Illustrating
- Project management
- Formatting and production

Name _____   **Monthly Time Sheet**
Month _____

Day	Date	Proj 1	Proj 2	Proj 3	Proj 4	Proj 5	Proj 6	Proj 7	Proj 8	Proj 9	Total hrs

Day	Date	Proj 1	Proj 2	Proj 3	Proj 4	Proj 5	Proj 6	Proj 7	Proj 8	Proj 9	Total hrs
Sun											
Mon											
Tue											
Wed											
Thu											
Fri											
Sat											
Weekly											

Day	Date	Proj 1	Proj 2	Proj 3	Proj 4	Proj 5	Proj 6	Proj 7	Proj 8	Proj 9	Total hrs
Sun											
Mon											
Tue											
Wed											
Thu											
Fri											
Sat											
Weekly											

Day	Date	Proj 1	Proj 2	Proj 3	Proj 4	Proj 5	Proj 6	Proj 7	Proj 8	Proj 9	Total hrs
Sun											
Mon											
Tue											
Wed											
Thu											
Fri											
Sat											
Weekly											

Day	Date	Proj 1	Proj 2	Proj 3	Proj 4	Proj 5	Proj 6	Proj 7	Proj 8	Proj 9	Total hrs
Sun											
Mon											
Tue											
Wed											
Thu											
Fri											
Sat											
Weekly											

Day	Date	Proj 1	Proj 2	Proj 3	Proj 4	Proj 5	Proj 6	Proj 7	Proj 8	Proj 9	Total hrs
Sun											
Mon											
Tue											
Wed											
Thu											
Fri											
Sat											
Weekly											

Monthly total											

Figure 12.4   Monthly time spreadsheet example

Some organizations also track research time, as differentiated from writing time. By separating research time, you may be better able to assess the relationship between investigatory activities and the quality of the outcome. At other times, it may be useful to track something that is causing everyone trouble. At one company, the publications team might have justified the cost of an additional printer if they had tracked the hours spent troubleshooting a printer that had frequent breakdowns.

Once you have decided on the types of activities to track, meet with your team to decide how to interpret each type. Without agreement on what to include or exclude from each type of activity, the individual team members will not produce comparable

Activity type	Tasks
Research	Interviewing, telephone calls, using the product, reading development reports, studying the specifications for the product, reviewing previous manuals, creating flow charts and matrices, creating storyboards, waiting, being confused.
Writing	Composing, initial formatting, self-editing, copyreading, organizing, preparing progress reports and time sheets, preparing Information Plans and Content Specifications, revising, entering edits and comments, attending meetings, setting meetings, resolving conflicts in information, making additions to the style sheet, indexing, creating tables of content, printing copies for review, maintaining backup copies, archiving, waiting, feeling frustrated, losing files.
Editing	Reviewing style sheets, revising style sheets, setting up editing checklists, reading drafts of documents and plans, attending meetings, marking drafts, reviewing markup with writers, copyediting text, and copyediting index entries.
Illustrating	Discussing illustrations, sketching, creating original illustrations, obtaining feedback, editing illustrations, revising illustrations, moving illustrations from source files to text files, making backup copies, archiving, attending meetings.
Project management	Planning, hiring staff, making staff assignments, coordinating among team members, creating spreadsheets, revising spreadsheets, setting meeting agendas, attending meetings, discussing progress with writers, negotiating with clients and other departments, tracking hours and progress, reviewing planning documents, revising planning documents, negotiating with translators and localizers, preparing materials for translation and localization, checking translations and localizations.
Production and formatting	Editing final formats, correcting formats, running tables of contents and indexes, printing files, doing final copyediting, inserting graphics, copyediting graphics, creating final page breaks, making late corrections, coordinating with printers and other vendors, supervising printing activities, reviewing blueline copy and color keys, doing press checks, creating press dummies, negotiating with printers and other outside vendors.

Figure 12.5 Division of work activities

data. In Figure 12.5 is a list of some of the tasks that you may want to include under a particular activity type.

It doesn't really matter what goes into the various activities types, as long as everyone on the team puts the same activities in each category. In addition to work activities, include categories for vacation, training, sick leave, department-wide activities, and any other miscellaneous activities that are not project related. Your team members may be interested to find just how little of a work day they can devote to actually working on their projects. They may even recognize why they seem to put in so much overtime. Keeping track of time may create the occasion to eliminate some activities that unduly interfere with project work.

It is best to advise team members to keep their time sheets current. If they wait until the end of the week, or even the end of the day, to record time, they will introduce much inaccuracy. It is difficult to remember what you have done after even a few hours, let alone several days. The best practice is to record hours hourly, perhaps when you take a break or make a telephone call.

As project manager, your role is to ensure that everyone is keeping their time sheets current and understands the types of activities they should record. It is worth reviewing the time sheets with anyone who seems not to be recording all of his or her time.

Guideline: Create time sheets that are easy to complete and are produced accurately and regularly to help track the course of a project.

Weekly reporting spreadsheets

At the end of each week, collect everyone's time sheets and transfer the data to your project-reporting spreadsheet. If you have created a monthly reporting spreadsheet like the one illustrated in Figure 12.3, you may find it advantageous to divide the month into weeks and record your time data weekly. Figure 12.6 shows an example of a weekly tracking spreadsheet.

With a weekly tracking spreadsheet, you can monitor activities more closely than you might if you analyze them only on a monthly basis. I frequently find that discovering a problem at the end of the month means finding the problem too late to solve it simply. I originally instituted weekly tracking because of the difficulty project managers had keeping abreast of problems. On a weekly basis, you are more likely to account for small changes before they become large changes to the project schedule. You are also able to address schedule anomalies such as sick time and vacation or time for training and ensure that the project demands for time and effort are still being met.

Guideline: Record all hours expended in a weekly tracking spreadsheet.

Fateful User Guide
April: Week 5
Weekly Hours Tracking Worksheet

Book Name Factor	Name Skill Level	Week 1 4/1-4/3 Actual	4/1-4/3 Projected	Week 2 4/4-4/10 Actual	4/4-4/10 Projected	Week 3 4/11-4/17 Actual	4/11-4/17 Projected	Week 4 4/18-4/24 Actual	4/18-4/24 Projected	Week 5 4/25-4/30 Actual	4/25-4/30 Projected	Apr to date Actual	Apr to date Projected	Apr to date Variance
User Guide														
0.10	Project management		1		4		4		4		4	0.00	17	(17.00)
	Writer		12		30		30		30		30	0.00	132	(132.00)
0.15	Editor		2		5		5		5		5	0.00	22	(22.00)
	Illustrator											0.00	0	0.00
	Production											0.00	0	0.00
	Subtotal	0.00	15	0.00	39	0.00	39	0.00	39	0.00	39	0.00	171	(171.00)
	Total Hours	0.00	15	0.00	39	0.00	39	0.00	39	0.00	39	0.00	171	(171.00)

0
132

Figure 12.6 Weekly reporting spreadsheet

Completing weekly reports

The records you and the team members keep of the hours expended are only a small part of the picture of assessing your progress. The activities scheduled and completed, the success of the activities, the progress toward interim and milestone goals are most important if you are to keep the project under control.

A weekly progress report that discusses accomplishments, plans, and problems should accompany every time sheet. The progress report should provide details about what was done in relationship to the hours expended.

In Figure 12.7, the progress report sample identifies activities with each project. Note that the project manager is concerned with the reviews he has been receiving from one group of reviewers. He is attempting to resolve the problems through the discussion in the report. Note also that the project manager has some editing responsibilities on his two projects, although an editor has also been assigned to the team.

The weekly progress report enables the project manager to assess explicitly what has been and will be accomplished and compare this assessment with the schedule of activities. The report provides the information that the project manager needs to evaluate the percent complete of the project on a weekly basis.

The weekly progress report may also include in the problems section the team member's assessment of his or her own morale. I find that a project manager can gain a better sense of the well-being of the people on the team if they have an opportunity to write their concerns weekly. If they wait to tell the project manager in person, the problem may have already escalated. Since many writers are introverts, they are often more reluctant to tell you about a problem in person than if they have a chance to write about it (Hackos, 1988). Your role is to respond quickly before problems are allowed to become worse.

If you ask team members to report problems or morale issues on their weekly progress reports, you should ensure that the reports remain confidential. You do not want personnel-related information to be available for everyone to read.

Many project managers consider it important to schedule weekly "one-on-one's" with each team member. At the meeting, the writer has the manager's complete attention. The writer has a chance to voice concerns directly, and the manager has the opportunity to discuss issues that were raised in the weekly progress report. The manager who has a tendency to stay in his or her office too much, isolated from the team, will be encouraged to communicate. The writer will have the opportunity to learn from the manager about how to handle the project more effectively.

One-on-one meetings may also be extended in weekly team meetings. These meetings, which help to promote team unity, are discussed in detail in Chapter 16.

 Guideline: Be sure that you receive weekly progress reports from all publications team members that record their accomplishments, plans, and problems at the end of each week on the project.

Weekly Time Report (5/15)   Week of 3/15 – 3/21

Name _____ John Doe

Progress

Project	Activity	Duration	Description (by chapter and draft, if applicable)
Sun.			
Mon.			
Prime	w	1	Go over 5/15s and file. Go through mounds of source material and organize into notebooks. Talk to Ann about prime.
Prime	edit	6	Edit administration content spec (4.5). Begin edit of customization content spec.
ML	edit	1.5	Go through 4.3 source material received (Implementing material and part of Reports). Distribute to writers currently working on these chapters and explain how to incorporate these changes into these almost completed chapters.
Tues.			
Prime	edit	9.5	Completed edit of Customization content spec (2). Fussed with primary plan the rest of the day, brainstorming with Joe about an approach that would work. Finally, decided on approach similar to the Operation. Went over that approach with Harry and Sam for a sanity check. Then wrote rough outline with Joe, giving a lot of details about the tutorial and sketching out the reference for Gene and Ann to flesh out given their exposure to the actual system.
Misc		.50	Computer problems kept me from accessing the server properly. Worked with Jane to figure out the problem: I was missing my apple prep file.
Wed.			
Prime	edit	6	Final pass through admin and customization Content Specs for delivery today. Asked Harry to edit them as well in the absence of anyone else with time. Worked on problem that arose late Tuesday regarding the number of menus the primary actually has. Tried to maintain task reference despite poor menu organization.
Prime	w	1.5	Talked with Lane about the primary nightmare. Explained our new organization and talked about how 17 menus with no task orientation would make our job very difficult. Asked for a menu tree so we could at least understand everything under each menu. Later, Lane called to say the developers were not devoted to current menu organization and would be open to our suggestions. We decided to keep primary task chapters as already outlined and include a document with menu organization suggestions with the Content Spec. Delayed delivery of primary Content Spec until next week.
ML	w	1.5	Received first three chapters reviewed by ML. Called Tom to discuss them. I was unhappy with some comments and explained our rationalization behind the decisions. As always, Tom agreed with what I had to say, but whether he can communicate that to the reviewers remains to be seen. Discussed edits with staff so they could adjust some style guidelines to avoid review comments on future chapters.

Figure 12.7 Weekly progress report

Project	Activity	Duration	Description (by chapter and draft, if applicable)
Thurs.			
ML	edit	8.0	Edited chapter 15, Cross reference files, and gave to Harry for final edit. Began Quality Assurance nightmare chapter. Source material includes large amounts of information not needed by this audience, so I had to sort out that information and make sure it went to the appropriate book.
Prime	w	.5	Talked with Joe and Ann briefly about progress on prime Content Spec. Offered suggestions for organization. I felt that their current organization was too specific — our h1s should be more generic (for example, Logging in Hoods, rather than Logging in Hats, Logging in . . .)
Fri.			
ML	edit	7.5	Completed Quality Assurance chapter and had Harry edit it. Went over the chapter with Pam to help her understand audience analysis. Input Harry's edits on Cross Reference chapter. Prepared cover letter and review sheets for each chapter. Sent package to ML.
Prime	w	.5	Made more suggestions for organization of prime Content Spec. Still not generic enough in some chapters, making it very obvious that system itself is organized poorly. While our documentation can't be much better than the product, I feel we can help the audience somewhat by identifying main tasks with h1s, then subtasks under that main task as h2s and so on. The problem is, we don't necessarily know all the main and subtasks.

Accomplishments

- Delivered two chapters to ML. These chapters incorporated our new style and included information gained from the 4.3 reference material and ML's edits of our prototype chapters.
- Delivered admin and customization Content Specs to RP. Delayed delivery of prime Content Spec to next week due to the large amounts of information learned this week.
- Brought PM notebooks for ML and Prime back up to date.

Plans

- Deliver another set of chapters to ML. I hope to make up for a two-chapter week last week by delivering at least four this week. However, these chapters are more and more convoluted and I'm not convinced my writers are completely in touch with the audience needs. I'm trying to teach by going over my edits with them, even though I'm entering these edits due to our tight delivery schedule.
- Deliver first draft prime Content Spec.
- Discuss schedules and budget with Sam when Content Specs are signed off. There are several people at RP who are worried we can't do our job in the current budget, but that's all they have. Page counts have shrunk considerably since our original proposal and despite the instability of the product and all the other problems we're having, I don't anticipate any problems meeting the budget. The schedule may be another issue — we can't write the entire prime book two weeks before beta. I've given RP deadlines of April 10 for information they have to have in the beta draft. We'll see how well they do.

Figure 12.7 (Continued)

Problems

- ML

  The first set of review comments from ML was heavier than I had been expecting. However, the bulk of the comments I disagree with. And yet, I'm not convinced they're catching the important stuff.

  First, the bulk of the trainers' comments addressed our examples. They seem to be very attached to the "brown" pages in their current books. We've cut the number of examples significantly. While examples are important, there's no need for 20 pages of them for each code being defined. They seem to want to include all the examples with their footnotes. We've taken greater care to ensure that any important information found in the footnotes of the examples was included in the step-by-step procedures, a better place than lost in the examples that many people won't even read. And we've told them from the start that one of the ways we were reducing page count was by cutting some of those examples.

  They also object to the examples we are using. In several cases, we have not used any of the examples in their source material, but made something up. This is because the examples show how to define a code that is already defined in the included starter database. A user who followed the examples like a tutorial would not get the prompts shown in the example because the code is already defined. They would either get an accept, modify, reject prompt or a warning that the code is already defined. Therefore, we have chosen examples that are not in the starter database and also referred the user to the starter database whenever it includes some of those codes. Another problem with some of their examples is that they are real places. For example, the reference lab examples gave real lab names with real addresses and real phone numbers. I felt this was inappropriate and gave the examples 555-prefixes and so on. ML was divided on this issue — some had no problem with it, some were still attached to the original examples.

  The second problem is even more serious. I don't feel that they are catching important issues. The more I review our chapters, the more I learn about the system. And either the system is entirely inconsistent (and maybe this is more of a possibility than I want to admit), or the source material is inconsistent. I really suspect the latter, in which case, ML is not giving us good feedback. Their solution was to staple the appropriate pages of the source material to the chapter and tell us to incorporate the changes.

  The 4.3 source material is another problem. Jane told both Sara and me that 4.3 didn't change much from 4.2 in the way the user accessed the system. However, the big difference is that 4.2 supported a line editor for text entry; 4.3 supports a screen editor if the customer has a particular type of screen. That's a big difference in my book!

- Prime

  The prime is a mess and we continue to get conflicting stories. One day we're told the prime has 7 menus, the next day 17 menus, the next day we're told nobody's really decided what the menu tree will be (or even the tasks that the prime will encompass), the next day we're told the tasks are decided but the organization is still up in the air. We are doing the best we can, but to get a usable draft by beta, they have to have a usable product. I envision us documenting the prime the way it currently is (17 menus) and then having them change everything after beta. Of course this would be a scope change, but it's still a messy situation.

Figure 12.7 (Continued)

Assessing percent complete

Weekly time sheets and progress reports enable the project manager to assess the percent complete of a project regularly. Each week, enough information should be summarized in the various reports to give you a good idea of the health of your project. If you compare the weekly information with the original plans, you should be able to tell if you are behind schedule, doing well, or ahead of schedule. Of course, you can only judge the percent complete of a milestone or an interim deadline if you have defined exactly what should be accomplished at the milestone or deadline. Without fully defined milestones and interim deadlines, all you will know is what has been accomplished to date. You will not know how much you have achieved in terms of meeting the milestones or deadlines.

Managers who are out of touch with their progress are most likely to shrug off requests to assess the percent complete of their projects. We have all heard about managers who insist for weeks and even months that their projects are 90 percent complete (see Chapter 21 for a more detailed discussion of the rework cycle). Generally, repeated claims of being "almost done" are simply a way of admitting total confusion. Even if a project is far behind schedule, you should have a new schedule that makes some sense or a plan to accomplish the remaining activities to complete the project.

A manager in a Level 2 organization is most likely to abandon controlling a project when things go bad. The Level 2 manager will decide that "everything" is out of control and, therefore, careful decisions, assessments, and controls are no longer possible. Quite the contrary. The worse a project gets, the more need there is for management controls.

 Guideline: Determine the well-being of your project by comparing the weekly progress report information with the original schedule of activities.

Writing monthly progress reports

If you have been tracking your project weekly, reviewing time sheets and progress reports from your team, and assessing the well-being of the project on a weekly if not a daily basis, you should be well prepared to roll your information into a monthly progress report. Monthly progress reports, or other periodic progress reports, are sent to all members of the project and publications teams. The reports let everyone know the status of the project and alert them to problems that require joint resolution.

Monthly progress reports, like weekly progress reports, detail the accomplishments of the team, your plans for the next reporting period, and any problems or risk factors encountered. You may also want to include a monthly spreadsheet that shows the hours expended and dollars spent to date.

Progress Report for
PASS
2/01

Progress (1/1 – 1/31)

- Jane Jones began work on the PASS Information Plan. She identified potential problems that could arise without a local editor/manager to provide guidance to the writers on the project. John Doe began work in that capacity toward the end of the month.
- Jane and John completed the PASS Information Plan as far as they could with the information available. They submitted a first draft of the plan with many embedded questions for the reviewers to consider while looking over the plan.
- Due to the tight development schedule for the first phase deliveries, John made initial assignments based on the first draft of the Information Plan. Assignments were made based on the elements we perceived as the most stable; that is, we do not expect the material to be affected by any changes made to the Information Plan.
- Jane and Harry began chapter-level Content Specs for the chapters assigned to them. Ann began documenting the administration tables (due to their nature, we felt it unnecessary to write Content Specs for these chapters).

Plans (2/01 – 2/28)

- Jane, Harry, and Ann will complete their first phase assignments by March 1. We will submit these drafts, as completed, for review. Depending on the speed with which Ann can complete the tables, we may need an additional writer to assist with the tables to meet this deadline.
- We will incorporate any changes on the Information Plan for final approval and sign-off.

Other issues

- We are concerned about the appropriateness of the page design for PASS. First, it is for a standard 8 1/2 × 11 sheet. How will it translate to A4 for European use? Second, we have received documentation standards from PASS that have no similarity to the current word-processing template. Should PASS be conforming to Germany's standards?
- We are concerned about the stability of the product. At the weekly project meeting, we learned that major changes had been made to the database. Since the engineers did not feel these were the last major changes, they initiated a database change tracking process. We are currently documenting the administration tables that were just changed for the first phase. We are concerned that if the tables continue to change, we will be using time inefficiently and as a result our hours/page will increase.

Hours Tracking

Projected hours for PASS project (based on initial Information Plan)

Project mgt/editing	579.00 hrs	
Writing	2,632.00 hrs	
Total projected hours for PASS project		3,211.00

Hours for 1/1 through 1/31

Project mgt/editing	40.00 hrs	
Writing	151.50 hrs	
Total hours for 1/1 through 1/31		191.50

Hours remaining

Project mgt/editing	539.00 hrs	
Writing	2,480.50 hrs	
Total remaining hours for PASS project		3,019.50

Figure 12.8   Monthly progress report sample

Figure 12.8 shows an example of a typical progress report. Note that the progress report details the activities that were completed given the hours expended (191.5) and discusses in detail the concerns of the publications team and the apparent escalation in the risk factors affecting the project. The project manager suggests that another writer may have to be added to the staff to accomplish one of the tasks by the deadline.

A progress report is an important project activity and needs to be carefully thought through and diplomatically written. To write an effective progress report, the project manager needs to know enough about the politics of the project to avoid confrontation and yet make issues sufficiently clear that they gain the attention required.

If the organization also promotes monthly or periodic progress meetings, the project manager should definitely present the accomplishments and problems to the entire development team. A progress meeting provides an opportunity for everyone to discuss any issues that have emerged and to resolve them if possible.

Guideline: Ensure that you prepare carefully thought-out progress reports regularly for your project. Discuss the accomplishments, plans, and problems of your team.

CHAPTER

13

Creating Project Standards

In this chapter, you learn to set standards for the text and graphics for your project. You also consider the issues surrounding the loss of data in your organization. In each case, you are trying to ensure that information appears in the right place at the right time and that critical project time is not lost. Information-control procedures minimize the time you spend recreating damaged or lost files; recovering from inadequate backup procedures; searching for misplaced, lost, or stolen documents that you are responsible for; and losing track of graphics and documents through the review processes.

Creating style standards for text and graphics

Many organizations have established standards for the publications they produce. In fact, one of the primary activities differentiating a Level 1 from a Level 2 publication organization appears to be the development of style standards. The standards usually include requirements for the following:

- Use of the company logo and other identifiers
- Design of the title pages and other packaging
- Page design for hardcopy publications
- Screen design for softcopy and online documentation
- Use of acronyms and abbreviations
- Correct use of grammar and suggested writing style

Other standards, including information on the publications-development life cycle, may be included in an organization's style guide.

As a project manager, one of your responsibilities is to know thoroughly and to enforce your organization's standards. However, many of the decisions your team will have to make in the creation or revision of a library will not be included in the organization's standards. You should be prepared to develop and maintain a project-specific style guide to record the decisions you will make during the course of the project.

Some of the items to include in a project-specific style guide are

- Spelling of project-specific terms
- Abbreviations and acronyms for the project
- Rules of capitalization and other highlighting techniques
- Styles for numbered and unnumbered lists
- Styles for step-by-step procedures
- Styles for code samples
- Writing conventions for prefaces, overviews, introductions, notes, and other special sections
- Other issues specific to the project and not addressed in the organization's style guide

In addition to special standards for the writing of text, you may want to include special standards for the design of graphics. You may want to specify line weight, font for labels, arrangement of callouts on illustrations, style of art for specific uses, and other items not covered in the standard style.

If you have an editor assigned to the project team, you may want to make him or her responsible for developing and maintaining the style guide. Otherwise, one person on the team should assume this responsibility so that conflicting styles do not emerge. However, everyone on the team should be responsible for contributing to the style guide by bringing style decisions to the team's attention. During team meetings, you may find it useful to discuss style issues to ensure that individuals are not going off in their own directions and making decisions without sufficient input from others. For example, one writer might need to use an abbreviation that has not been defined. The writer should bring the problem and a recommendation to the team meeting. Once everyone agrees, the new abbreviation should be recorded in the project-specific style guide. If no agreement can be reached, the manager should be prepared to make a decision.

The style guide should be updated often and made available to the entire team on the file server or some other central location for project information. Once the new style information is in place, all team members should be responsible for ensuring that they have edited their writing to comply with those standards before turning their work over to the editor or the reviewers.

If a standard for the formatting of different publications on the project does not already exist, the formatting standards should also be documented in the project-specific style guide. The standards for typography and layout should all be included. If possible in the publishing systems used, these standards should be incorporated into the tagging system. All heading levels, types of text, lists, numbered steps, notes, warnings, cautions, and other elements should be defined in the publishing-system style sheet.

Once a publishing-system style sheet is defined for a project, every team member should be required to use the standard style. It is your responsibility as project manager to ensure that the standards are being followed. You may want to institute periodic file reviews to ensure that all team members understand how to apply the style tags correctly. You may also want to institute a policy regarding the introduction of new style tags. In many cases, individual publications require a few special style tags that have not been defined for the entire project. However, if individual team members create their own styles, those styles may not be designed in accordance with the overall publication style. Each publication in the library will take on its own look. I recommend that someone on the team, possibly the editor or the production specialist, be responsible for updating the style sheets. If a writer needs a new style, he or she should discuss the need with the editor or other individual responsible. Then, the editor plans the new styles and updates all style sheets used by the entire team so that all the publications remain in sync.

Without such a control system in place and a policy about changing the styles, you may find the individual publications in the library deteriorating into individual styles. At one company where style standards were not enforced, major problems occurred when the publications groups attempted to convert their documents from hardcopy into a computer-accessible form. All the style differences had to be treated as individual design elements so that the conversion program could read and translate them accurately. As a consequence, the company experienced a large cost overrun for the conversion.

Toward the completion of a milestone that requires an outside review, the project-specific style guide can be used as a copyediting checklist for the project. The checklist ensures that all pieces of the library follow exactly the same style conventions.

If your organization does not have a general style guide, a project-specific style guide can serve as the catalyst for a general development effort. By creating the style guide as needed during a project, you can devote resources to this effort without affecting project deadlines. Once the project-specific style guide is in place, other teams can begin adding to it, eventually generating a nearly complete organization style guide.

 Guideline: Create a project-specific style guide, and enforce its use during your project.

Creating an information-control plan

With several people working on a publications project, or even with a single individual, you need to establish a plan for controlling the in-progress publications. It is extraordinarily easy for disasters to occur if plans are not carefully made in advance. Perhaps the most common disaster occurs when a writer has more than one copy of a document and makes changes to an old copy rather than to the most recent copy.

To avoid disaster, consider the following actions:

- Develop a naming convention for all project files so that they can easily be located by everyone on the team.
- Use plain-English naming conventions if at all possible.
- Avoid using chapter numbers in the file names in case you need to rearrange chapters.
- If you have to use cryptic names, plan to include a file that lists all the names in English and records the cryptic names as well.

If the project files are stored on a file server, ensure that the files are properly organized for easy retrieval by team members. You may want to set the levels of permission needed to access each file, with people allowed to write on only their own files.

In addition to the file-server storage, you may find it helpful to require that team members retrieve an active file to work on each day on their own workstations and replace the file at the end of the day on the file server. Then, ensure that the file server is backed up every evening. In this way, you have never lost more than a single day's work.

To avoid losing even a single day's work, you may also have to establish a policy on saving current work. Today, it is possible to set saving requirements and reminders into a publishing system's software. If this is not possible, create a policy that requires that team members save files frequently during the day. Think about how much work you are willing to lose. Eight hours? Four hours? Fifteen minutes? Five minutes? Although experienced team members may understand the importance of saving their work frequently, new team members may not. Since the final responsibility for the work is in the hands of the project manager, you may want to ensure that the policies for saving work are followed.

If you do not have a system of automatic backups for a file server or individual workstations, it will be your responsibility to ensure that backups are made on a regular basis. Daily backups are really a necessity on any project, not a luxury. If your team has back up files on floppy disks, consider instituting odd and even backups. That means you have two sets of backup disks, one for the even-numbered days and one for the odd-numbered days. Therefore, you always have a set of disks that is untouched and no more than one day out of date. In this way, you avoid the chance that both the work disk and the backup will be destroyed by a bad sector or a disk crash.

Establish a central location for storing working and backup disks so you can reach them if you need to. The data on your project is company property and your responsibility. It is also your valuable product. Find ways to ensure that it isn't lost or doesn't disappear with a disgruntled employee. Consider off-site storage of a second or third set of disks or tapes to ensure that a serious mishap does not result in lost data.

 Guideline: Establish procedures ensuring that all computer files are safeguarded and backup copies regularly made.

Establishing a security plan

As you can see, by establishing a set of naming conventions for project files, you are immediately involved in establishing a security system for your project data. A critical part of any security system is ensuring that data is not destroyed or inadvertently lost during a project. For that reason, you create naming conventions for files and directories and establish and enforce a sound backup system.

A security plan may also need to be in place to ensure that hardcopy documents are not lost, misplaced, or stolen during the course of a project. Documents often are lost when there are inadequate processes to ensure that they are always returned to a secure location after regular use. Documents are misplaced through simple carelessness or an inadequate file-control system. Some documents are deliberately stolen, especially when they involve critical projects.

Consider establishing a central filing system for all hardcopy documents associated with your project. If you have multiple publications to track, you may have to designate a file cabinet or two simply to keep track of key information. With the filing system, devise a checkout system, which can be as simple as a control sheet for each file that has been removed, with the name of the item removed, its approximate content, the number of pages or sheets, the name of the person who has the file, and the date it was removed. When a file is returned, the return date is added to the control sheet.

Periodically, especially for a long project, the project manager should review the filing system to discover if documents have been checked out for long periods of time and not returned. It would be wise if you tracked down critical documents from time to time to ensure they have not been misplaced. Some organizations conduct official audits of all documents under a project manager's responsibility to ensure that they are not lost and to impress the importance of document control on the team members.

Finally, if you are working on a sensitive topic—a company proposal or a new product or company-significant data—you need to ensure that information is not deliberately stolen. We don't like to believe that corporate espionage occurs, but it does. You do not want to be the one responsible for the security breach if one occurs. A secure system may require filing cabinets with locks and few keys. You may need to ensure that your computer systems are secure or that floppy disks are locked up each evening. You may also be responsible for ensuring either that trash is carefully collected and secured or that it is shredded. I know of at least one critical government proposal worth millions of contract dollars where document trash was searched by spies for the competing organization. When information may be worth millions of dollars in contracts or competitive advantage, it is worth keeping it secure.

We do not like to think that our team members will take critical information with them when they leave the company. Nonetheless, it does happen. Many companies direct project managers to carefully account for information assigned to an individual who has resigned. In addition, many companies require that immediate steps be taken to ensure that computer files are not damaged or erased when someone chooses to leave or is laid off or fired.

Whatever the situation in your organization, remember that publications files contain critical information that may have serious repercussions if lost, misplaced, or stolen. You have a role in keeping it secure. Write down your security procedures, review them with senior management or others involved with company security, and ensure that the procedures are followed by all your team members.

If you are dealing with information that contains life- or data-threatening warnings and cautions, you may also want to consider keeping copies of drafts that were marked up during reviews. In some litigation, the paper path of review comments, ensuring that safety information was carefully considered by engineers or members of the legal staff, will be subject to subpoena by a court. Someday, you may want to prove that the warnings and cautions in your publications were adequately reviewed by specialists to ensure that people or data are not at risk. Discuss processes for information control with your organization's attorneys or senior management.

 Guideline: Ensure that the information for which you are responsible is secure from loss, misplacement, and theft.

Tracking graphics

Not only do text files have to be well organized and secure; so do graphics files. Perhaps the most frustrating mishap with graphics files occurs when changes are not controlled. A graphic is created for a single use in one publication. Then, the author of another publication decides that the same graphic would be appropriate for his or her text. Now, the graphic is to be used twice or any number of times. No problems occur until one of the authors decides to modify the graphic in some way. The modification is made to all the occurrences of the graphic. Unfortunately, the other authors do not like the modification and either modify the graphic again or return it to its original version. Soon, the whole graphics operation is out of control. You are left with multiple, slightly different copies of the same graphic and no one to sort out which goes where.

Establish a system for controlling graphics, just as you would control text. However, be certain to anticipate multiple uses of the same graphic. You may need a control tool that records every use of a particular graphic anywhere in the publications library. Each unique graphic is given a graphic ID. If an instance of the graphic is modified, then it takes on a unique but related graphic ID. That way, subsequent modifications that affect every instance of the graphic continue to be made without deleting the original modification.

Establishing a document-control function

Not only do you need to control modifications to individual graphics, you also need to control the location of every graphic and text element in your publications library. Consider setting up a document-control form with blocks to identify the name of the element, its author, date of origination, review activities, and dates of all revisions. Figure 13.1 provides an example of a document-control form.

The document-control form should be as complete as it needs to be to ensure that you know where each element is in the life cycle. It is especially important to record when a document is out of your department for review and when it is expected to be returned (revision date). Then, you can track late reviews and the effects they have on your team's ability to progress.

Document element	Author	Origination date	Review one	Revision date	Review two	Revision date	Alpha review	Revision date	Beta review	Revision Date

Figure 13.1   Document-control form

The document-control form, especially one that contains review dates, should be communicated to managers of other parts of the development organization. Managers often do not know that their staff members have scheduled review dates and dates on which the review comments are due. The document-control form may give them the information to plan their own schedules more thoroughly and ensure that their own team members meet their publications responsibilities.

Other project managers may not care if publication responsibilities are met or not met by their team members. In that case, you have information about what was supposed to happen during life-cycle reviews and what did not.

Guideline: Establish a document-control process to account for the whereabouts of every element produced by your team.

Conducting the Content-Specification Reviews

Like the review of the Information Plan, the reviews of the Content Specifications are significant milestones in the publications-development life cycle. The Content Specifications set the stage for the entire implementation phase. If the development team understands how you plan to organize and convinces itself that you have included all the tasks the user needs to perform and data the user needs to use the product or process, then you are unlikely to make major structural changes to the publications later in the development process. In the same way, if the development team fails to understand the organization plans laid out in the Content Specifications, you are likely to face continuing arguments about organization and content, arguments that may result in costly reorganizations of individual publications or the entire library late in the development life cycle. The better the Content Specifications are understood, the more successful the review process will be in establishing the direction for the Implementation Phase (Figure 14.1).

Managing the content-review process

To manage the review process, especially the first time that anyone among the reviewers sees full Content Specifications, you need to educate the reviewers about their responsibility. Full-fledged Content Specifications may seem daunting to reviewers. They will need preparation and direction. In the cover memo for each Content Specification, suggest that reviewers

- Read the introductory material over quickly before beginning to concentrate on the organizational plans.
- Consider that the introductory material outlines the sources of the decisions about organization and content.
- Note if they have different conceptions of or information about the audience, topics, and tasks covered by the publication in question.
- Read the organizational strategy carefully to get a full picture of the writer's proposed structure.
- Spend more time thinking about the content sections, especially in terms of omissions.

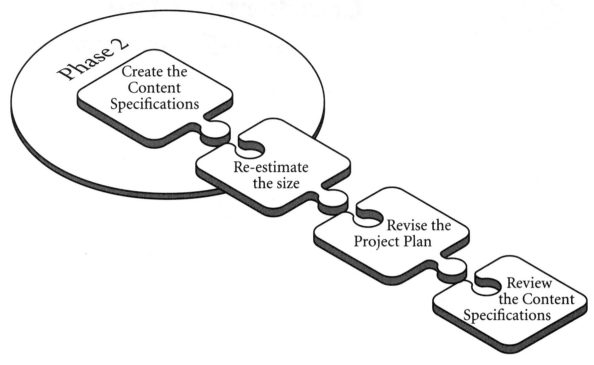

Figure 14.1 Content-Specification review

At some companies, the publications organization holds brief classes on how to review. They get better reviews as a result.

Since many of the reviewers will be experts in the particular content items to be discussed in each section of the publication, they may have their own notion about what someone may need to know to use the product or perform the process. In this light, they need to see themselves as responsible for discovering topics or tasks that have been omitted by the writer, as well as topics or tasks that need not be discussed or might be restructured for easier access.

Reviewers must especially be alert to finding information that has been omitted. It is very easy for writers to omit minor or even major pieces of information about the product and the audience's tasks or the topics that need to be included. Not only are the writers trying to find a usable structure for the information; they are, at the same time, trying to understand the product's capabilities or the extent of the process domain. The reviewers have the important and difficult job of finding the missing pieces. Point out to the reviewers that it is much easier to respond to what is in the Content Specification rather than what has been left out. They will have to use more imagination to uncover omitted information.

Of course, they also have the responsibility of pointing out information that should be included for the audience in question or may be inappropriate to be disclosed to the recipient of the publication. Some reviewers, especially those involved in the marketing and sale of the product, must decide how much should and should not be disclosed. Other reviewers, especially those involved in the design of the product, must help to decide what is necessary for the audience to know and what is true but unnecessary. They must bear in mind that they are responsible for considering the interests of the organization as a whole, not simply their own interests.

As much as possible, the publications-project manager must impress upon the review team that their job is to serve the needs of the audience, not themselves. It is important to remind reviewers that the company's publications are not meant to be compendiums of all information known about the product or process. Some information is meant for internal use only. Other information may be presented in forms other than official publications, especially if that information will only be used by a small minority of the audience. Still other information may be critical to the needs of the designers of the product or process but irrelevant to the needs of the users. Even the most highly educated and skilled audiences want information that is tailored for their needs, not the needs of the designers.

Prepare the review team for the strenuous effort of reviewing Content Specifications by introducing the subject in a good cover memo and sufficient time for a thoughtful review process. Figure 14.2 offers an example of a cover memo for a Content Specification. Note that the memo directs the reviewers to offer advice on the specification. You may find, however, that first-time reviewers of a detailed Content Specification may be surprised at the volume of information you ask them to consider carefully. To avoid some of the shock effect of full-fledged Content Specification, you may elect to shorten the versions that go to the review team, saving the complete versions for the publications team itself. However, decide carefully if all the information should be included for the specification to be adequately understood.

As we discussed for the Phase 1: Information Plan review, leave sufficient time between delivering the Content Specification to the reviewers and the time for a review meeting. Too much time invites neglect; too little time threatens thoroughness. In general, however, you may find that one week is sufficient for Phase 2: Content Specification review.

Guideline: Direct the Content Specification review process to ensure that the organization and content of each publication is carefully considered and agreed upon.

Staggering the reviews

For many projects, the Content Specification will not be prepared according to identical schedules. It is more likely that the schedules will be staggered to accommodate different development schedules for parts of the project. For example, there is no point in specifying an installation procedure when the details of installation are not scheduled to be addressed until the end of the product-development life cycle.

If the Content Specifications are on a variety of schedules, the project manager needs to work out these different schedules after the information-planning phase. Then, the schedule start dates must continue to be tracked so that writers are assigned

November 2

PARROT Project

PARROT Test Developer's Guide

Project Manager: Ed Smith

Introduction and Review Notes: The following is our first draft of the Content Specification for the PARROT Test Developer's Guide. This Content Specification describes the content of the PARROT Test Developer's Guide. The specification includes a discussion of the overall organization of the guide and a detailed description of each section. It also identifies graphic elements and provides an estimated page count.

Many of the factors we considered when preparing this specification are discussed more fully in the "PARROT Documentation Information Plan." These factors include:

- objectives for the PARROT project
- purpose of the PARROT documentation
- audience analysis
- user tasks analysis
- design implications
- media selection
- documentation development
- project assumptions and dependencies

Together, the documentation Information Plan and the Content Specification comprise the learning products group's comprehensive plan for producing the PARROT Test Developer's Guide. We need your advice on the thoroughness of the specification. Please pay careful attention to anything that we may have omitted.

Please review this information carefully and come to the review walkthrough meeting with concerns and recommendations. Thank you!

Figure 14.2 Content Specification cover memo

to them at appropriate times. It is easy to forget the start dates in the general rush toward deadlines.

If your schedule calls for different deadlines for Content-Specification reviews, be certain that you publish the schedule for the entire developmental team. Reviewers are justified in expressing dismay when they are surprised by review copies on their desks. One reviewer explained that she had been out of town for a week. When she returned, she found a massive review copy in her inbox. It had been there a week and was scheduled for return on the next day. She had had no warning that it was coming because the publications team never announced review dates in advance. Of course, she missed the deadline and the schedule slipped.

Be certain that you treat members of the review team with courtesy. While some people will always be out of touch with schedules and fail to pay attention to announcements, that is no reason to omit schedules completely. If your schedule slips, immediately notify the review team and include a new date for the review as soon as you know it. If reviewers have scheduled their time around your schedule, they may have to make adjustments or find other team members to take over their responsibilities.

 Guideline: Stagger the Content-Specification deliverables and reviews in accordance with the timing of various parts of the product-development life cycle.

Handling the review meeting

The Content Specifications, like the Information Plan, are not ordinary documents to be commented upon in the margins and returned to the writer for revision. The Content Specifications are a significant milestone that must be handled thoroughly and carefully to ensure that decision making occurs and sign-off is something more than a mechanical process.

To stage the review process:

- Invite all those responsible for supporting the development of information for the publication.
- Prepare a presentation of the organizational strategy for the publication.
- Clarify the relationship between the strategy and the particular implementation in the content sections of the Specification.
- Emphasize changes that have been made in the overall strategy from Phase 1: Information Planning.
- Emphasize all changes that will affect the resources and schedule required to complete Phase 3: Implementation.

The most significant agreements to reach during the Content-Specification review are those that affect the resources and schedule for the remaining phases of the project. If the Content Specifications suggest that the publications are larger in scope and more difficult to produce than first estimated, that fact must be clearly explained and considered. If key members of the development team are not prepared to support the changes in resources and schedule, then the publications team must be prepared to recommend reductions in scope so that the original schedule can be met with the existing resources.

Negotiating changes in resources and schedules

As we discussed earlier in the revision of the Project Plan for Phase 2, there are several possible scenarios that the project manager may want to bring to the attention of the review team. None of these scenarios need be presented, however, if the Content Specifications indicate that the publication is the same as originally indicated in the Information Plan and the degree of difficulty in completing the project is also estimated to remain the same. More likely, however, there will be change—change that results in the need for more resources or more time to produce the same quality as originally proposed.

At the review meeting, consider the following scenarios. If the review team accepts the writer's estimate of scope and difficulty, then they may either

- Agree to add the additional time in the schedule needed.
- Agree to finance additional resources (more people) for the project.
- Agree to decrease the quality of the publication if no additional time or resources are available.

If the review team does not accept the writer's estimate of scope and difficulty, then they may either

- Decide how to cut the scope to accommodate the schedule and resources.
- Decide how to cut quality or scope to accommodate the schedule and resources.
- Decide to provide additional assistance and agree to modify the level of difficulty (especially if they are responsible for some of the difficulties that have ensued or are predicted).
- Decide to do nothing and agree to nothing, whereby the quality and scope will be affected by the degree to which the schedule is beyond the ability of the given resources to meet.

The last scenario, of course, reflects an ostrich mentality. Keep your head in the sand and all problems will appear to go away. Unfortunately, the denial of reality will simply exacerbate the problems. The publications team will attempt to comply with the latest round of unreasonable demands, find that they must cut the quality of their work beyond acceptable levels, and spend most of their off hours sharpening their resumes. Or, the publications team will play the game and wait for the product-development schedule to slip so that once again publications are on schedule. However, the wear and tear on the publications team playing this cat-and-mouse game may be sufficient to destroy team morale for some time to come.

The project manager's role is either to

- Oversee the development of a new and sane schedule with adequate resources (not a cast of thousands) to complete the job
- Cut the scope of the project sufficiently so that team members feel some sense of control, if not satisfaction over the quality of the job

The best case, of course, is to be as convincing as possible, to make the best business case you can for the changes you believe are needed. Most teams are made of reasonable people who will work with you to find an acceptable solution to the problem. And, fortunately, at the end of Phase 2, you are early enough in the publications-development life cycle to be able to add resources and schedule or make cuts without unduly jeopardizing the success of the project.

 Guideline: Negotiate the changes in resources and schedules as effectively as possible during Phase 2 reviews. Frequently, this is your last chance to make changes that will not affect product quality.

Adding to your Project Management Notebook

Once the Phase 2 reviews are complete, add the Content Specifications in their final form to the Project Management Notebook. Also include any relevant minutes from the review meetings, including discussions and decisions on major points of disagreement. You may also want to file the marked-up copies of the Content Specifications to ensure that you have documented all points of view or decided some did not apply or could not be considered.

After the reviews, it may be worthwhile for the writing team to revise the original drafts of the Content Specifications, especially if there were points of contention. Then, the revised Specifications should be distributed with change bars in place and another cover memo pointing out the modifications that were agreed upon. Later changes in the project that may affect the Content Specifications will more likely be handled by change memos rather than by revisions of the original document. Only at the end of the project are you likely to bring the Content Specifications in line with the final publications design. The final versions of the Content Specifications become the starting point of the next release of the product.

 Guideline: Revise the Content Specifications and place the revised Specifications in the Project Management Notebook.

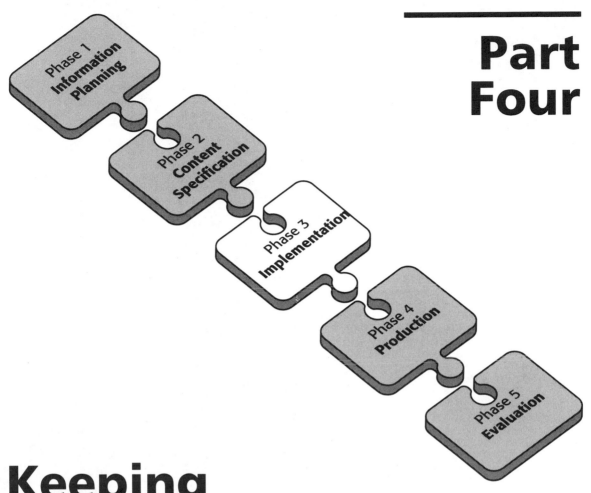

Phase 1
Information
Planning

Phase 2
Content
Specification

Phase 3
Implementation

Phase 4
Production

Phase 5
Evaluation

Part Four

Keeping the Project Running

The Implementation Phase

During the implementation process, project managers need to take responsibility for keeping the project operating smoothly. Perhaps the greatest challenge you have during this phase is to ensure that the project team communicates thoroughly and regularly. Traditionally, project teams seem to communicate very little, much to the detriment of the project's success.

Experienced publications project managers know that projects do not manage themselves. They set meaningful and measurable milestones to ensure that their teams are successful. Perhaps the greatest continuing difficulties during implementation are the inevitable changes that take place in the corresponding product-development process. Many project managers, as well as many technical writers, feel at the mercy of continual product changes and shifting development schedules. It is difficult for project managers to control the publications-development life cycle when the larger project is not being adequately controlled.

In Part Four, you learn some of the strategies that a publications project manager can use to keep control over the publications-development process even when the rest of the development activities are changing and appear out of control. You learn to monitor your team's progress closely in both quantitative and qualitative terms, recognizing early signs of schedule changes, keeping careful track of schedule dependencies, and learning to communicate progress or lack thereof to team members and other managers in the organization.

As part of the management process, however, you also need to maintain the good will and sanity of the publications team. It is not sufficient to manage by the numbers. Team members need continuous feedback on their own progress in reaching project goals. They must also learn to manage their own time and set their priorities. You can help them monitor and control their own processes.

In addition to the discussion of managing the implementation process, you learn that usability testing is an effective way of monitoring and ensuring the quality of publications for the audience. You and your team may want to develop early prototypes for testing, conduct early paper tests of ideas, and finally, establish formal usability testing as part of the publications-development life cycle. You develop strategies for introducing usability testing to the larger organization and establishing it as a standard part of the product-development process.

Contents

The chapters in Part Four focus on the following issues:

Chapter 15: Managing Phase 3: Implementation Activities

- Establishing Phase 3 milestones
- Scheduling Phase 3 milestones
- Managing Phase 3 milestone reviews
- Adding to the Project Management Notebook

Chapter 16: Keeping the Project Operating Smoothly

- Communicating with your team
- Promoting team unity
- Helping writers manage themselves
- Establishing an internal review process using peer editing
- Instituting copyediting and developmental editing
- Instituting productivity measures

Chapter 17: Tracking Progress

- Producing interim drafts
- Tracking interim project milestones and progress
- Reporting project progress
- Adding to the Project Management Notebook

Chapter 18: Managing Change

- Tracking changes to the product and schedule
- Managing changes to the publications project
- Evaluating percent complete at the first-draft milestone
- Adding resources to complete a project in Phase 3
- Negotiating changes in scope
- Negotiating changes in quality

Chapter 19: Developing Prototypes

- Using the Content Specification as an early prototype
- Developing a complete prototype
- Establishing the details of the format
- Establishing the details of the writing style
- Establishing the details of the graphic style

Chapter 20: Introducing Usability Assessment

- Managing usability assessments
- Conducting tests during the planning phases
- Conducting early prototype and formative testing of drafts
- Conducting evaluative testing

Chapter 21: Anticipating Changes in the Development Life Cycle

- The publications rework process
- Anticipating the amount of rework
- Changing the rework curve

Results

By the end of Part Four, you will know how to monitor the project schedule and track milestones. You will understand the importance of managing the change process and how to work with others in the product-development organization to help reduce excessive change or at least mitigate its effect on publications development.

You will learn about the importance of team building and team management, including essential team communications, a process often challenging for introverted writing professionals.

You will learn how to work in an environment that demands rapid prototyping, as well as how to use prototyping to design more effective publications for your audiences. You will also learn how to plan and schedule usability tests of early prototypes and how to negotiate the introduction of usability testing into the publications- and product-development life cycles.

Finally, you will learn how to approach late changes in the development process and maintain control of the publications-development process throughout.

CHAPTER 15

Managing Phase 3: Implementation Activities

Phase 3: Implementation of the publications-development life cycle begins as soon as the Content Specifications developed in Phase 2 have been revised and approved for implementation. When Phase 3 begins, about one-third of the total project hours have been expended. Another 55 to 60 percent of total project hours will be devoted to Phase 3. By the time camera-ready copy of the publications is ready to be sent to the printer or to the developer of compact disks or is ready to be compiled as online documentation, only 10 to 15 percent of the project time will remain for internal production activities and evaluation.

In Part Four of this book, you learn the issues associated with managing the development cycle, starting with establishing major and minor milestones for Phase 3 activities. In every phase of the development life cycle, you must try to develop a clear and detailed picture of what you expect to happen. Only then will you be able to track progress and determine if the project is on time, falling behind, or actually ahead of schedule.

Unfortunately, you may be faced with issues that you have not handled before. At the end of the project, when little time is left in the schedule for changes, you may find your team placing documentation online for the first time, learning about disk-to-film production methods, or handling a conversion to CD-ROM. Changes in production technology will be especially challenging to manage. But other changes, including the introduction of translation into your process, may also occur. The best you can do is plan as thoroughly and carefully as possible but be prepared for the uncertainties that new technology will introduce to your process.

There is an old project-management saying that should govern your thinking about Phase 3 activities. "What is not tracked does not get done." You must be continually alert for subtle changes in the schedule and changes in the level of difficulty of performing the project (dependencies), in addition to changes in the product or process you are documenting and in the scope of the publications your team is developing.

Establishing Phase 3 milestones

The milestones for Phase 3: Implementation are not as clearly drawn as those for Phases 1 and 2. Individual organizations have different numbers of development

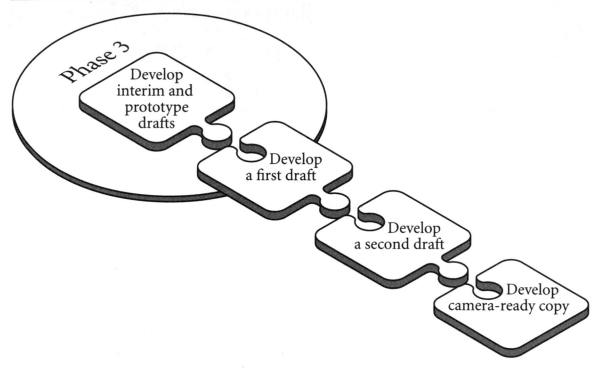

Figure 15.1 The Phase 3 implementation process

milestones and label them with different names. In Figure 15.1, I suggest that a publications team develop four stages with milestone dates and definitions for Phase 3 if no other stages are required by your organization. These stages can be renamed or changed to accommodate the needs of your organization. A major milestone provides an ideal opportunity to reassess the project scope, its dependencies, and the likelihood of success.

The four stages within Phase 3 are

- Interim and prototype drafts
- First draft
- Second draft
- Camera-ready copy

The interim- and prototype-draft stages can be divided into two parts: the large number of interim drafts and a single prototype draft for early testing.

Guideline: Use a four-stage process in establishing the milestones for Phase 3.

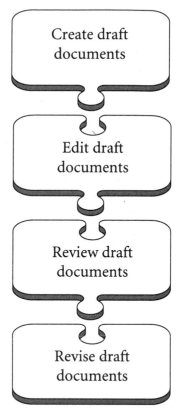

Figure 15.2   The writing-development process during Phase 3

The interim draft

The interim drafts, described fully in Chapter 17, represent the informal cycle of writing, developmental editing, and reviewing that occurs throughout Phase 3. The writers and graphic artists prepare text and graphics of small sections of a publication, such as chapters or online topics. These are reviewed by the developmental editor and by the subject-matter experts (SMEs) on the technical team. The writers and artists then implement the recommended changes as appropriate. Figure 15.2 represents this cycle, which is repeated throughout Phase 3 for all the writing milestones.

The number of interim drafts is flexible but should be controlled. Too many interim drafts, including review and revise cycles, may seriously affect the ability of the writers to move forward to the first-draft milestone. They will also increase project costs. To monitor and control the interim-draft process, you and the writers, editors, and artists need to determine milestone dates to be met and definitions of what is supposed to be achieved by those dates for each subdivision of the development task. These subdivisions may represent chapters, sections, topics, modules, or other units but should be small enough so that they can be monitored closely for early warnings of increased project difficulty, increased project scope, and consequent schedule delays.

Guideline: Schedule interim drafts and reviews to help ensure that the details of the publications-development process are on track.

The prototype draft

A prototype draft differs from an interim draft only in its intended purpose. The purpose of a prototype draft is to present a new strategy for a publication that can be tested early in the development life cycle. For example, an organization interested in moving from a topic-oriented to a task-oriented approach to its documentation should produce a prototype draft. Likewise, prototype drafts may be used to investigate

- A new organization for a publication
- A new page or book design
- A new publication for a library
- Quick-reference tools
- A minimalist approach to documentation
- A mix of paper and online documentation

Although interim drafts may be used to fulfill the edit, review, and revise cycle of an existing publication design, a prototype draft represents the development of something new. In most cases, I recommend prototype drafts for all new approaches to publications (see Figure 15.3).

Prototype drafts are simply interim drafts carried through to a more complete state. The prototype should include all draft text and graphics and a complete page design. The prototype should be complete enough to go through usability testing to study and verify the viability of the new design. I discuss prototype drafts and their testing in detail in Chapters 19 and 20.

Guideline: Create a prototype draft to develop and review new ideas in publications design.

The first or alpha draft

The complete first or alpha draft represents the culmination of all the interim-draft milestones into the first formal milestone of Phase 3. The first draft is marked by a

Figure 15.3   Planning the interim drafts

formal milestone definition formulated in Phase 2 (see Figure 15.4). The first-draft definition may include descriptions of

- The number of estimated pages to be in the draft
- The number and degree of completeness of the graphics
- Front matter and back matter to be included in the draft
- The information expected to be missing from the first draft

In some organizations, a formal first draft is replaced by a series of interim drafts. There is no stated milestone by which all interim drafts must be completed, edited, reviewed, and revised and put together into an entire publication or series of publications. Although a formal first draft may be omitted in an organization that basically maintains existing publications, I recommend that it not be omitted from most publications life cycles.

The first draft represents the first time that the entire product-development team, in addition to the publications team, is able to review publications in their entirety. If the publication is never reviewed as a whole, members of the team may find that they have lost track of the relationship among the parts. When the team reviews only a series of small pieces, the lack of a formal phase review means no group approves of the direction taken by the publications team as a whole.

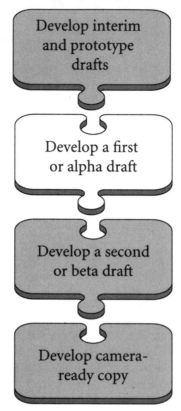

Figure 15.4 Planning the first draft

The formal first-draft review also provides a significant opportunity to ensure that the publications project is on track. Frequently, the first-draft review of the publications also represents the first time many members of the product-development team actually see all parts of their own project as a whole. During first-draft reviews, you will almost always encounter technical experts who are surprised by the design that has emerged for the project as a whole. First-draft reviews of publications often generate arguments about the direction of the technical project among the technical experts who have suddenly recognized that they have not conceptualized the product in the same way. To omit a formal first-draft review is to lose a significant opportunity to maintain the integrity of the product itself.

As a result of first-draft reviews, you will frequently face a reconceptualization not only of the publications but also of the product as a whole. Certainly, that means changes will occur that you will have to accommodate in a new project plan. But the product and the publications are likely to be better designed as a consequence.

Guideline: Always include a formal first-draft milestone to ensure that the product- and publications-development processes are on track.

The second or beta draft

The second- or beta-draft milestone is often associated with the beta release of a product. At a beta release, an early version of the product with its documentation is shipped to certain select customers for a trial run. The customers are expected to use the product in their own environments, test it as thoroughly as possible, and communicate to the developers their problems and concerns. It is often hoped that these beta customers will also comment on the publications.

A second draft, illustrated in Figure 15.5, should include all information missing from the first draft, in addition to all changes, insertions, and deletions of text and graphics produced in the first draft. The writers and artists will create the second draft following the comments from the first-draft review. Frequently, new information is added, information is changed to make it more accurate and more usable, and information is deleted that the audience does not need to know.

In a standard definition of the second-draft milestone, you may require that

- All technical information is complete, with 100 percent of the text in place.
- All technical illustrations are complete and in place.
- Developmental editing and copyediting are complete and changes entered.
- Tests for the accuracy of the information are complete, and all information is accurate.

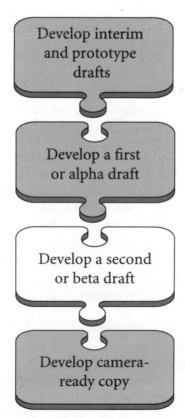

Figure 15.5 Planning the second draft

- The index is complete.
- All front and back matter is complete.

In short, the second draft is a complete publication that needs only to be checked one more time by the development team for completeness and accuracy.

If there are holes remaining in the technical content of the second draft when the milestone date is reached, then the second draft is not complete. Consequently, you will have to revise the schedule for the production of the camera-ready copy. If information is missing from a second draft, you will have to schedule reviews of the missing information, which will almost certainly cause the schedule to slip.

In many organizations, translations are scheduled to begin during the second-draft development, although preliminary work on translation occurs much earlier in the publications-development life cycle. This preliminary work includes translation estimates and the development of glossaries of technical terms in all the target languages. As organizations move into the simultaneous worldwide release of products, translations cannot be delayed beyond the second-draft stage without delaying the release of the product in some markets. If simultaneous release is not planned, then translations can be scheduled following camera-ready copy.

Guideline: Ensure that the second draft is intended only to make corrections to the first draft. If significant new material is added or material is deleted or substantially rearranged, your next milestone will likely be behind schedule.

Camera-ready copy

Once the second draft is reviewed, the writer, graphic artist, copy editor, and production specialists work together to produce the copy that will be put into production. The term "camera-ready" comes from the offset printing process, in which a photographic copy is made of the original pages and art and then turned into a paper or metal plate. Today, many printing processes bypass the photographic copy and proceed directly to plates, but the term remains useful for the publications organization.

At the camera-ready copy or final-approval draft (see Figure 15.6) everything is ready for the process or for any of the other electronic production methods used today.

- Final art is in place and accurate.
- Table of contents and index page numbers correctly correspond to the text copy.
- Final page breaks have been placed to avoid unsightly gaps as much as possible or to create gaps so that headings start on new pages and paragraphs and tables do not break across pages.
- Final copyediting is complete, and all corrections are made.

Many managers use a copyediting checklist at this final stage to ensure that a single publication is internally consistent and that the publications in a library are also consistent with each other. In addition, production specialists will prepare collating sheets that enumerate each page in the publication so that it can be collated correctly by the printer. Finally, the production specialists will monitor the production process to ensure that the publications are correct.

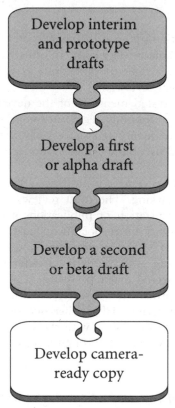

Figure 15.6   Planning the camera-ready copy

The camera-ready draft is usually signed off as a last step before it is turned over for reproduction, assembly, and distribution. If changes are made at this final-approval step, they are guaranteed to cause slips in the production schedule. They are also likely to cause unexpected errors elsewhere in the publications because thorough consistency checking could not take place. Changes made in camera-ready copy are the most expensive changes made in the publications-development life cycle because much of the final production checking will have to be redone. The only changes that are more expensive are those that take place after the publications are in blueline form or have been printed.

In some organizations, a typesetting step comes between the second and the camera-ready drafts. More often, however, final type is run or printing plates are made directly from the final softcopy of the publications. Few technical publications today are typeset from paper copy.

Guideline: Consider the camera-ready copy milestone to be the last approval step before the production process begins. Changes following camera-ready copy preparation are extremely expensive and can result in substantial schedule delays.

Phase 3 reviews

Formal reviews during Phase 3: Implementation occur at the conclusion of each of the writing cycles: first draft, second draft, and camera-ready copy. Informal reviews occur during the development of interim drafts preceding the first draft. If you produce a prototype draft, that, too, will require a formal review.

As in all previous formal reviews, all interested members of the development and marketing organizations, plus members from training, legal, customer service, field engineering, and anyone else interested in the quality and success of the publications, take part in the review process. The intended users of a publication may also take part in draft reviews.

Once again, I recommend that formal draft reviews within Phase 3 take the form of walkthroughs rather than individual copy marking. The draft reviews are significant opportunities to review the content and organization of publications and to reassess life-cycle schedules and plans. Walkthroughs of entire documents may be extremely time-consuming, however. You may decide to conduct comprehensive walkthroughs of user's guides and tutorials but faster-moving walkthroughs of reference material, concentrating on areas where reviewers uncovered major problems.

Interim draft reviewers need not be formal nor associated with walkthrough meetings. In many cases, interim drafts are reviewed by either one or a very small number of SMEs who have already been working closely with the writers. Often, the writer accomplishes an interim-draft review by walking through a copy with the SME directly.

 Guideline: Schedule formal reviews of the last three stages of Phase 3—first, second, and camera-ready drafts. Schedule a formal review of a prototype draft but only informal reviews of interim drafts preceding first draft.

Usability assessment

In addition to the traditional technical reviews of draft publications, you may want to include usability assessments as part of each development stage. The traditional placement of usability assessments has been following the second-draft review. At this point, the publications are complete, and the product may be sufficiently operable to allow for simultaneous testing. Potential users are able to perform tasks using the product and the appropriate documentation together. The usability assessment measures the user's success at performing tasks, as well as success in finding and understanding supporting information.

Unfortunately, if major usability problems are uncovered in the product, the documentation, or both, you have little time to make substantive changes and still meet the camera-ready copy milestone. Either the deadline must be extended and the product and documentation released late, or substantive changes must be forgone until the next version of the product. There is usually only enough time for small-scale changes to be made as a standard part of the second-draft revision. In addition, major usability problems almost always require rethinking the user interface. Doing this rethinking after beta testing has already occurred is usually "unthinkable" (which means that it is likely to be discouraged by upper management). The cost of very late changes and the consequent delays in release to market are often so high that an organization cannot afford to make them.

Instead of waiting for after the second draft, usability assessment may begin much earlier in the life cycle. Prototype drafts, particularly those that match prototypes of the user interface, are prime candidates for early usability testing. Interim drafts of small sections of the documentation can be tested, either with working sections of the product or independently. Following first-draft technical review, substantial pieces of the documentation should also be ready for testing.

During Phase 3, you should consider making usability assessment a standard part of the process and schedule it at the first opportunity. I discuss usability assessment more fully in Chapter 20.

Guideline: Schedule usability assessment at frequent intervals during Phase 3: Implementation.

Scheduling Phase 3 milestones

You need to schedule carefully each of the Phase 3 stages following the approval of the Content Specifications. With the Content Specifications in hand, you will be able to work back from the date for delivery of camera-ready copy to production. Your first step is to schedule the major milestones for first draft, second draft, and camera-ready copy. Then, you can schedule the interim drafts and a possible prototype draft in preparation for the first draft.

As I described more fully in Parts 2 and 3, you may find a rule of thumb useful to schedule the first-draft milestone: You should find yourself able to complete a first draft after you have expended approximately 60 percent of your total project hours, or 30 percent of the hours following Phase 2: Content Specification. Figure 15.7 illustrates the positioning of the first-draft milestone for a 50-week (one year) project.

Although the 60 percent–complete rule of thumb is a good starting point, be certain to use your own experience to revise the rule. You may find that in your organization, a 70 percent–complete first draft is more appropriate because of later changes in the product. Always leave sufficient time, however, for reviews and subsequent drafts.

If you need to schedule an earlier first-draft due date because of the scheduling of alpha releases of the product, you may have to negotiate a first draft with only certain sections complete, as explained in Chapter 8. If there is insufficient time between the end of Phase 2 and the need for a first draft, you may have to cut sections out of the first draft that are not needed to support the alpha release. You may also want to schedule interim drafts to accommodate the needs of scheduled product-development activities.

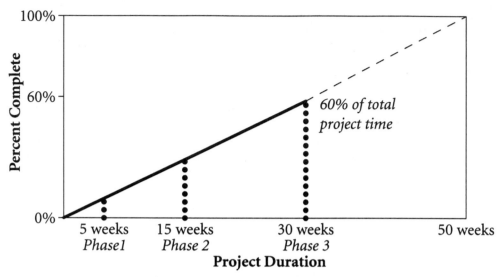

Figure 15.7   Scheduling the first-draft milestone

Once you have scheduled your first-draft milestone, schedule interim milestones together with the writing and editing team members. The realities of the product-development process will dictate which subsections of publications can be completed in a particular order.

If you are planning to produce a prototype section of a publication, consider which parts of the product will be sufficiently complete to allow for a full presentation in the prototype. You may want to schedule a prototype draft to be completed in tandem with a prototype of the user interface.

While you may want to delay creating a final schedule for the second-draft milestone until you have completed the first-draft review, you may need to schedule a second draft to coincide with the beta release of the product. Again, be aware that a second draft should take anywhere from 20 to 30 percent of the total project hours between first draft and release to production. Figure 15.8 illustrates a second-draft schedule when 90 percent of project hours have been expended.

Note that the time to develop the first draft following Content Specification is equal to the time between the first draft and the second draft. This schedule allows for changes in the information later in the development cycle. Most publications project managers know that product changes seem to increase as the product life cycle gets farther into development and implementation. Toward the end of Phase 3: Implementation, when system testing is taking place, bugs are encountered that may necessitate major product changes, especially if the product was insufficiently specified during the planning phases.

Scheduling for the camera-ready draft is also heavily dependent on the success of the second draft. Delays in completing the second draft will almost certainly result in delays for the camera-ready draft. The tendency in many organizations is to leave insufficient time in the schedule between second draft and camera-ready draft. When

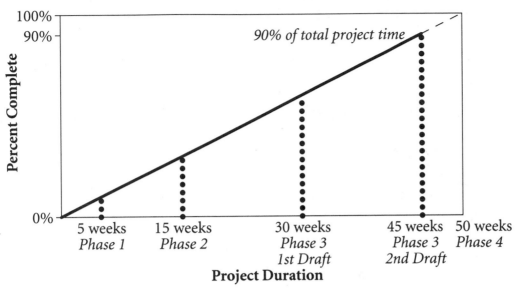

Figure 15.8 Scheduling the second-draft milestone

the final-stage schedule is shortchanged, the project almost always experiences schedule slips. Many final-stage tasks are sequential. For example, you cannot complete the index until all the page breaks are set unless you are using an automated indexing system. Some checklist activities can be accomplished in parallel but will depend upon the resources (people and equipment) available to do all the tasks that are necessary to bring a publication up to camera-ready standards.

As illustrated in Figure 15.9, the stage between the second and camera-ready drafts represents about 10 percent of the total project hours. Some time will be devoted to project wrap-up and evaluation, but that time can be scheduled during production or afterwards if necessary.

 *Guideline: **Work backward and forward between the end of Phase 2: Content Specification and the date that the camera-ready copy is due to be released to production to schedule the major milestones of Phase 3.***

Managing Phase 3 milestone reviews

Like the reviews that you managed following Phase 1: Information Planning and Phase 2: Content Specification, the Phase 3: Implementation reviews need to be carefully scheduled and planned. Only the interim reviews that are handled by individual writers may not need your intervention unless they begin to delay the overall project. All the major phase reviews following first, second, and camera-ready drafts should be managed.

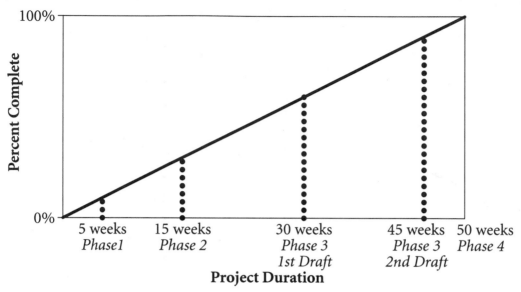

Figure 15.9 Scheduling the camera-ready milestone

The first step in managing the review process is to schedule the reviews and publicize the schedule. By working with the product-development manager, try to schedule reviews for times when the product team is not overly occupied with their own deadlines. Once you and the product-development manager have decided on a review schedule, create a chart of the schedule and send copies to all involved team members, both product and publications. Be certain that your own team members are aware of the commitment you have made to the product team.

As the review times approach, send a memo reminding everyone involved of the upcoming review. Let them know when they will receive copies of the publication and how many days they will have for the review. Remind them of the length of the publication, and suggest a time in hours per page for the review process. Many technical experts do not realize how long it will take them to review a publication thoroughly. They fail to leave sufficient time in their schedules to do a good job. Also remind the product-development manager of the schedule, and ask that he or she notify team members to plan sufficient time to review the draft copy.

You might even consider splitting up large sections or chapters and assigning smaller pieces to different reviewers. Only a few people, such as the product manager, need to review the entire publications library.

When the draft copy is ready to send out, include a cover memo that explains what the reviewers are supposed to do and reiterates the review schedule. Include the time and place of the review walkthrough, and state the amount of time the walkthrough is expected to take. Figure 15.10 shows a typical first-draft cover memo.

In the cover memo, let the reviewers know what you expect them to look for. In this memo, the project manager reminds everyone that they are reading for technical content. Some reviewers think they should mark everything.

To: Review team members
From: Publications project manager
Subject: Review of the Fateful User's Guide, first draft
Date: January 2

Dear folks!

I'm certain you've been waiting with bated breath for this first-draft review copy to arrive. Well, here it is. Let me explain what you're getting.

The first-draft of the Fateful User's Guide contains 150 pages with

- All the text of the main body of the guide, except for Chapter 7 on installation
- Sketches of all the graphics and all the screen dumps (attached to the end of each chapter)
- A table of contents

You do not have the index or the preface or the final title page.

Here's what we need from you.

- Read each section thoroughly.
- Focus on the technical content.
- Look out for missing information in addition to reviewing what is there.

If you note information that is incorrect or missing, either

- Attach the information we need, or
- Write the information in the margins.

If you only mark something as incorrect or missing and don't give the new information, the writer will have to interview you for the information. That takes more time.

If you note that something should be deleted, please state why. Don't just cross something out.

We'll be happy if you find any typos as you read, but you don't need to worry about them. We have several more copyediting rounds scheduled, and we'll catch everything eventually.

We predict it will take you about 8 hours to review 150 pages. That's about 20 pages per hour. Please leave yourself enough time.

The walkthrough is scheduled for Tuesday at 9:00 A.M. in the Chippendale conference room. We expect the meeting to take at least 6 hours.

If you cannot attend, please give your marked copy and any other comments to Joe. He'll consolidate the comments before the meeting, so get them to him by Monday morning. If you find a lot of problems, I'd appreciate it if you'd call me in advance.

If you need any more information, call me at extension 7852. I'll be near my office all week.

Figure 15.10 Sample cover memo for a first-draft review

Many people think of reviewing as similar to grading a college paper. They make comments that are like the ones they got from their college composition teachers. Unfortunately, cryptic comments like "Wrong!" or "Unclear" are no help to the writer. In one organization, the technical writers held a workshop for reviewers on how to review. It was a great success in improving the quality of reviews and saving everyone significant time. The reviewers stopped marking commas incorrectly and making critical remarks on the quality of the writing and the writer. The reviews went more smoothly, with less ill feeling on both sides.

You may also find it useful to help the reviewers understand that someone on their technical team provided information to the writers and may have already reviewed an interim draft. Include a list of those who are the technical contacts for each section and those who conducted interim reviews. This may forestall some of the nastier comments about the technical content because a peer has had a hand in developing the information. Reviewers who want to challenge the content know that they must also face a colleague who may not agree with the challenge.

Guideline: Carefully manage the process of Phase 3 reviews so that they are as efficient and productive as possible.

Handling reluctant reviewers

Many project managers find that reviews in their organizations rarely go smoothly. Some technical experts never get around to reviewing at all. Others wait until the last minute, in part because they do not know what to expect and only have time to skim the draft. Still others wait until they are in the review meeting to begin reading the draft.

In many organizations, reviews are notoriously late. The technical experts ask for a week's turnaround time but take a month. When they finally turn in a marked copy, they have often done a cursory job or reviewed only part of the draft.

Some of these problems may be solvable with better advance planning. Other problems may not be solvable without major changes in corporate philosophy. Work on the problems you can influence.

The sample cover memo in Figure 15.10 illustrates one tack you may take in communicating more effectively about the review process. But the cover memo alone is not enough to change some ingrained ideas about documentation reviews. Plan a strategy that begins in Phase 1: Information Planning.

- Meet with the product-development project manager to discuss the importance of the reviews.

- Schedule the reviews in relationship to project milestones with the assistance and cooperation of the product-development manager.

- Make a presentation at a product-development meeting to explain the review schedule.

- Point out that if review schedules slip, all the rest of the development schedule will slip.
- Conduct a short workshop for the review team on how to review a draft.
- At least a month before the Phase 3 reviews, send out a review schedule, and note who is supposed to attend which reviews.

Just before the scheduled reviews, you should do the following:

- At least one week before the Phase 3 reviews, send out a brief reminder.
- Write a cover memo detailing the review activities, expected time for the review, and the schedule of the walkthrough.
- Provide alternatives for those who cannot attend a walkthrough.
- Ask one person to consolidate the comments of several reviewers so that the reviewers resolve their differences.

One technique to ensure attendance that is often mentioned by project managers and writers is to have food available at the review meeting and announce it in advance. People are frequently willing to attend a meeting at which they get free food. Recognition of the need for sustenance acknowledges that intellectual labor is real work.

During the review walkthrough, do the following:

- Plan an agenda that sets limits on the time you want to spend on each section, and stick to it.
- Keep everyone on task as much as possible so that the walkthrough does not go overtime.
- Suggest that discussions about the product be conducted elsewhere.
- Ensure that the comments remain positive; don't allow people to attack the writer.
- Have someone other than the writer responsible for creating a master copy of all changes in the text.
- If disagreements arise about the technical content that cannot be resolved at the walkthrough, ask someone to take responsibility for resolving the conflict in a set time frame.
- Thank everyone for participating.

After the review meeting, send a brief thank-you memo to the reviewers that

- Focuses on the usefulness of the walkthrough and the good information provided by everyone
- Lists all action items, who is responsible for each, and the due date
- Briefly reiterates the plans for the next draft and the upcoming review schedule

Following such a strategy will not guarantee that an uncooperative group of reviewers will suddenly fall into line and become cooperative and productive. However, it represents the best job you can do to ensure that reviewers are treated with courtesy and respect, as you would treat any customer.

If reviews still go badly or fail to happen despite your best efforts, the next strategy would be to escalate your concerns to the next level of management. Be prepared with an analysis of the costs of failed and late reviews. Include an analysis of the effect of poor reviews on quality. We know that to our customers, one of the most important documentation attributes is the accuracy of the technical information. The technical-review process is intended to promote accuracy in the documentation and is one of our primary quality-assurance processes. By accepting poor review practices and permitting poor reviews to occur, senior management is seriously jeopardizing customer satisfaction.

Guideline: **Plan a strategy to manage the draft-review process to ensure that reviews are timely, complete, and useful to the publication team.**

Adding to the Project Management Notebook

As you develop your project-implementation schedule, include the schedule information in your Project Management Notebook. You may want to include a calendar of milestone dates, as well as Gantt charts or other chart types that may be useful in conveying information to members of the development team. As usual, include meeting minutes, your telephone log of project discussions, electronic mail records, and other documents that show how the project is progressing.

Keeping the Project
Operating Smoothly

Although you should be concerned about the smooth operation of your project from project startup, in this chapter I discuss the issues of team building and team maintenance because I find that many new project managers start neglecting their teams in Phase 3: Implementation of the publications-development life cycle. Phase 1: Information Plan and Phase 2: Content Specification naturally lend themselves to more communication among team members. During the first two phases, the project is being planned; everyone is involved in the early decision making; team members should be concerned with understanding the goals of the publications project. Once Phase 2 is complete and the Content Specifications accepted as revised, individual team members have their assignments and are ready to begin the process of preparing first drafts. The pace of the project naturally becomes more hectic, and some of the team unity achieved during the planning phases falls off as team members set individual courses.

At this time in the project life cycle, it is especially important that, as project manager, you work hard to help team members coordinate their efforts and maintain communication. Project quality will suffer if team members disperse and communication suffers. While the rare team will seem to cooperate of its own volition, it is more likely that you will have to encourage and facilitate communication among team members. As everyone becomes busier, they may begin to feel that team meetings are more intrusive than productive (Figure 16.1).

As project manager, you need to schedule regular meetings and ensure that these meetings are as short and productive as possible. You need to communicate regularly with each team member and ensure they communicate with you. Your team members need to feel confident that they can report problems to you as soon as they emerge without fear of repercussion. They need to know that you will take action to help resolve problems even though you may not always be successful. You need to promote not only two-way communication between yourself and the team members but also communication among the team members. Since you cannot be everywhere and see and hear everything, you need to depend upon team members to talk to one another and coordinate activities on their own.

While you may have a few experienced and skilled team members whom you can count on to act independently, you should be prepared to help those who are less experienced and less skilled in managing their own time and scheduling their own activities. In addition, even experienced team members may need help from time to

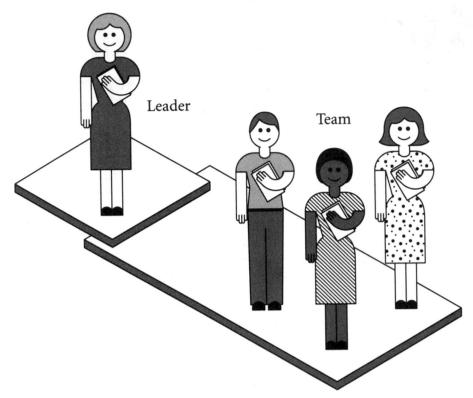

Figure 16.1   Creating a publications-project team

time, and you need to assure yourself that they have not gone off on unfortunate tangents. You should take responsibility for assignment changes among the team members. By being able to pull resources from some activities to aid others, you are helping your team members be alert themselves for opportunities to lighten the load. They are prepared to look for parts of the job that others might handle, so that they can devote themselves to those parts that no one else is prepared to do.

Finally, while all the team members may have reviewed all the planning documents produced in Phases 1 and 2, you need to put a continuing review process in place. Through peer editing and the work of a development editor during Phase 3, the team will be able to maintain corporate and project standards as well as achieve the quality goals established during the project. Each piece of a publication project must work together and support the whole. Consequently, both peer and developmental editing emphasize to team members that building an excellent library of publications is a team responsibility, not an individual one. With a well-managed process, everyone should be heading in the same direction. Individual spurts of creativity are frequently out of place in a managed process unless their outcome is accepted by the team. Equally inappropriate is a jealous ownership of one's work that manifests itself in an unwillingness to adhere to standards and an unwillingness to be open to the comments and critique of others.

In this chapter, you learn to keep lines of communication open between yourself and your team and to establish the review mechanisms that will maintain the process and promote the achievement of a high-quality product throughout the development life cycle.

Communicating with your team

Communication and coordination among members of a development team is essential to the successful outcome of any complex publications project. Without strong communication, the likelihood is high that individual schedules will slip, publications will drift away from a unified team standard, and the final result will fail to serve the needs of the audience. With strong communication, the likelihood is equally high that the resulting publication library will appear as a unified whole, with consistency maintained across all individual units, and that team members will support one another in ensuring that all schedules are met and quality maintained.

Unfortunately, the normal mode of operation in a Level 1: Ad hoc or even a Level 2: Rudimentary organization does not promote communication. In a Level 1 organization, individuals working on a project consider themselves independent contributors who make their own decisions about their work. They view themselves as "creative" writers who own the text or documents they are developing. Such independent contributors populate many product-development teams and often provide a model that publications organizations tend to follow. Individuals work on their portions of a project and do not regularly communicate what they are doing. Only when their individual portions of a project need to be integrated do they discover that they have been designing and implementing in an incompatible manner.

Even in Level 2 organizations, many product- and publications-development team members often do not know what other team members are working on, nor do they understand how the entire product fits together. They focus on their individual portions to the exclusion of others. In software projects, these individuals engage in repeated cycles of coding and testing without a plan that establishes a unified direction. In publications projects, the same individuals start writing and only stop revising and reworking a text when the deadline appears. They may go through repeated cycles of writing and revising, changing the organization of publications and the details of the text many times over to respond to the latest ideas of individuals from development and marketing.

 Guideline: Communication is essential to the success of your project. Ensure that it takes place regularly and fruitfully.

The best people for the job

Many managers in Level 1 and 2 organizations believe that communication is not necessary for the success of their projects. All they need is a team consisting of individual contributors who can work on their own without help from anyone, as illustrated in Figure 16.2. Quality will occur because all the individual contributors will already know exactly what quality means and automatically produce it. If managers believe that everyone should be a star who can work completely independently and achieve consistent and repeatable success, they are likely to be disappointed.

On many occasions over the last few years, Level 1 and 2 publications managers have expressed to me great difficulty filling vacant positions on their staffs. They have such extensive requirements that they are unable to find people who meet them. Frequently, the requirements include knowledge of a very specific technology and experience with a very specific set of tools. They keep searching for people who can work entirely on their own from the beginning of the project. Everyone else is so busy putting out their own fires and completing their individual publications that they believe they have no time to communicate and coordinate with new team members. A new team member who might profit from some help is unacceptable.

These publications managers believe that the quality of the product their teams produce is highly dependent on the talent of the individual members. And, in fact, given the lack in their organizations of a repeatable and learnable process, they are

Figure 16.2 An organization of individual contributors

probably correct in their belief. Yet, even the best writing teams they can put together, including people whose resumes reflect the most stringent requirements, will end up exhibiting a variety of skills. Some people will be strong individual contributors with a talent for communicating and bringing the disparate parts of a development project together. Others, with equally strong resumes, will turn out to be followers who wait to be told what to do next and have the tendency to copy previous work. Still others will be marginal contributors who feel safest simply rewording the source material given them by the engineers, programmers, and scientists. These last may be accused of changing the meaning of the original text into incomprehensible nonsense because they take no responsibility for understanding the meaning in the first place.

Even in a Level 1: Ad hoc organization, managers may sense the divergence of skills on the team and make assignments accordingly. But, more frequently, managers are unaware of the differences until complaints come from developers or customers. One manager discovered rather late that a writer with more than five years of experience had written a system concepts draft that demonstrated clearly to the entire engineering team that the writer had almost no understanding of how the system worked. Another manager learned near the end of the project that the writer handling the "theory of operations" had entirely left out any discussion of the new components of the product. This writer, with more than 20 years of experience, had simply edited what had been written for the previous version of the product.

The weakest members of the team are not the only ones likely to make mistakes. Even the most talented people on the team can go off in the wrong direction or have a bad day. In a Level 2: Rudimentary organization, a writer completed a large part of a publication before the development team, which included actual users, observed that the project had taken a direction they had not expected and were uncomfortable with. The lack of early and frequent communication with members of the development team resulted in wasted effort and many extra hours to do the work over again.

Since the project manager's responsibility is to produce a quality product despite the individual skills of the team members, the project manager has to know a great deal about the progress of the work and the activities of all contributors. In fact, an organized manager can often produce a better product with a team of good writers with a variety of skills than an unorganized manager can produce with a team of stars.

 Guideline: A team of "stars" is not a substitute for strong communication and coordination. Problems just remain hidden longer.

Managing the team you have now

The realities of the marketplace also work to the detriment of the star system. We all know that "stars," the best people we might include on a publications team, are notoriously difficult to find. You may not be convinced that they are unnecessary and sometimes undesirable to the success of a project. However, even if you intentionally

Figure 16.3   Building a team from a group of individuals

decide to use a star system, you will probably fail in the attempt. You are more likely to end up with a team with mixed skills, people who can perform well if they are well managed (Figure 16.3).

Some of the individual contributors on your team may be independent and skilled enough to carry off a project entirely on their own. Equally likely they will be prima donnas who cannot or will not get along with anyone else on the team. They hide their own work, but spend lots of time criticizing others. They lack a team spirit of cooperation because they believe that weaker team members will drag them down and jeopardize the success of their project. Instead of supporting the weaker team members, they spend much of their time being negative.

As a project manager, you might prefer to avoid a cast of stars and work with a mixed group of people who are enthusiastic about working together. Certainly we would all like to have the best team we can put together for a project. You will find, however, that people with modest skills or a lack of experience can produce excellent work if they are properly directed and supported. Such direction often occurs in a Level 2: Rudimentary or, most likely, a Level 3: Organized and repeatable organization. In fact, bright and enthusiastic people who simply lack experience will often produce extraordinary work in a Level 3 organization with strong management, a sound development process, and frequent, well-planned, and well-executed communication activities.

A sound process that is effectively communicated and tracked in a Level 3: Organized and repeatable or Level 4: Managed and sustainable organization through even better communication will support the efforts of the weaker team members and

Figure 16.4 Fostering team communications

enhance the efforts of the stronger ones. However, it is not enough for the project manager to have the process in his or her own mind. Everyone on the team should understand what needs to be done so that they are able to monitor their own efforts and help their team members achieve their goals. The best teams turn out uniformly good and occasionally superb work. Even the weaker team members do well, often exceeding their own expectations of themselves.

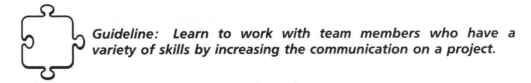

Guideline: Learn to work with team members who have a variety of skills by increasing the communication on a project.

Organizing team meetings

As project manager, your role in fostering strong communication begins with the recognition that appropriately scheduled and well-orchestrated communication among team members will result in higher-quality publications (Figure 16.4). Many new managers become so involved in their own tasks that they forget about communicating with the team. Many new managers believe that time for team communication activities is time poorly spent—that team members would be better off using that time working on their documents. New managers who don't understand the type of communication activities that will most benefit the team become bored by the team meetings they themselves schedule. They find that they would rather be doing desk work than communicating. New managers who are reluctant communicators (possibly devoted introverts) may have been successful writers but are uncomfortable with the demands of managing.

I hate meetings. I can't get my own work done when I have to be in meetings with everyone," exclaimed Becky, a new project manager. "Why can't everyone just get their work done on their own?"

"You have some good people on your project team," mentioned Andy, an experienced manager. "But they still need to know what you're doing and what you expect from them."

"But when I call a team meeting, I always ask them if they need to know anything," said Becky. "Usually they just sit there and don't say a word."

"Maybe you are asking them in the wrong way," said Andy. "A few of your people have mentioned to me that they don't know what you expect from them. My team members really want a lot of feedback on their progress, and they want a better idea of what I need them to accomplish. If we're going to meet our quality goals, we all have to work together."

"But I'm really busy meeting the quality goals. I have to go over everything anybody writes," said Becky. "They don't know the project standards, and they don't follow through on getting their work done."

"Sounds like you're taking all the quality responsibility onto yourself. How about preparing a set of issues and questions to hand out for each team meeting?" offered Andy. "You could hand them out in advance so that everyone will come prepared. Ask the questions that you need to have answered if you're going to ensure that everyone is on track. Also use the meeting to go over the standards for the project. Have people explain how they incorporate the standards into their own work. Maybe they just lack a process."

"I really think they should be responsible for doing their own work properly," answered Becky. "But maybe you're right. I could go over the standards again."

"Don't just go over them," explained Andy. "Find out more about the processes they each use to write and figure out why the standards aren't being applied. Then the team members can work out a way of ensuring that standards are met. If you really want them to work effectively and independently, you may have to help them develop ways to do so."

"I never thought about it that way," said Becky. "Maybe they really don't know what to do. I just assume that everyone works the way I do. That's probably not a very good assumption. I'll try your idea and see if it works.

Becky, like many new managers, assumes that her team members can read her mind and that they have the same work style and understanding of the tasks that she has. Instead of assuming, every project manager needs to ensure that a common level of understanding exists for the project. The best method of developing this understanding comes from well-constructed team meetings.

If you want to develop sound communication practices among your team members, begin with your own communication skills:

- Set up a regularly scheduled team meeting as often as necessary for the project duration.

  Weekly or at least biweekly meetings are possibilities, but on very short projects with difficult external deadlines, more frequent meetings may be needed. Do not be afraid to call an ad-hoc meeting of two or three writers who share a common issue. Always balance the need for a team meeting with the need for team members to get their work done.

- Create a plan for the regularly scheduled meetings.

  The worst thing you can do is hold a meeting simply because one is scheduled or not hold one because it is not previously scheduled. Since you should know at what point in the milestone schedule your team members are supposed to be, you may want to use some part of a regular meeting to ensure that everyone is on schedule. If anyone is behind schedule, the team can help build a plan for getting back on track. Then, you can plan the next week's activities and milestones.

- Develop an agenda of points to cover the issues that concern you.

  A written agenda will help you keep the meetings focused, especially if the agenda consists of questions to be answered and issues to be resolved. Once you've developed the agenda, distribute it to the team members so that they come to the meeting prepared to deal with the agenda items.

- Set a time and length for the team meetings and stick to it.

  Avoid letting meetings get longer and longer. People can easily begin to eat into their productive time by spending too much time in meetings. Always set a time limit for the meeting and partition the meeting time as needed. Be vigilant in keeping to the schedule.

- Keep team meetings focused on the work to be done.

  Hardly a team exists that does not like to complain about something. Team members may complain about one another, sometimes in a team meeting. They may also complain about others in the organization, especially the development and marketing teams. They can be depended upon to complain about upper management's lack of sensitivity to their needs. If your project meeting begins to deteriorate into a gripe session, turn it off immediately. Not only is the complaining counterproductive but it has a tendency to infect team members who are not complaining. They decide that if a few key people appear to be dissatisfied, they should probably be dissatisfied too.

If a team meeting goes well, everyone on the team should feel that they have learned something and made progress toward accomplishing their project tasks more efficiently and effectively. Team members should feel that they are supported by the manager and each other. To show your support, be certain that when a positive event occurs, you recognize the individual who has performed well and remind everyone that the event is typical of what will occur in a successful project (Cantando, 1991). If a negative event occurs, be certain that your comments are restricted to the specific event and encourage others to see the problem as a fluke and not as the failure of an individual or of the project as a whole.

By the time the meeting is over, everyone should be clear about the status of the project as a whole and feel free to bring their individual problems to the team for solution. They should not feel they will be criticized for having problems. Also, by hearing about the issues, problems, and successes of more experienced team members, team meetings assist in the process of educating new and less experienced members.

Take every opportunity to model problem-solving processes and supportive, guiding comments. Demonstrate how you believe everyone on the team should behave toward one another and members of the larger development team by modeling good practices yourself.

 Guideline: Construct team meetings to make them as effective and constructive a learning and communication process as possible.

Communicating outside of the team meetings

Only a small portion of the business of project communication will take place at regularly scheduled team meetings. Much communication will take place one-on-one between a team member and the manager or through small groups working together on parts of a large project (Figure 16.5). Encourage team members to come in to talk to you at least once a week, alone or in small groups. Review their weekly reports and be prepared to ask detailed questions about their progress.

In setting up these small meetings, ensure that you are getting the same level of information from all team members. Some may be outgoing and talkative, others taciturn and reluctant. You may enjoy working with some team members more than others. However, you need to ensure that personality differences don't get in the way of the smooth operation of your project. As the manager, you need to adjust your style to the needs of each team member (Hackos, 1990).

It's highly likely that some of your team members will spend too much time in your office while others will spend too little. Both types can become problems. The team member who is constantly asking for direction and reassurance needs to be helped to understand that more independence of action is appreciated. While you want to know

Figure 16.5 Communicating on an individual basis

what everyone is doing, each team member is ultimately responsible for getting his or her work done and finding ways to solve minor problems independently.

On the other hand, team members who never talk to you about what is going on are an even greater potential problem. You never know quite what they are doing. If they are getting into trouble, you won't know until it is too late to do something about the problem. Some team members will tell you they do not want to worry you with a problem they have encountered. Tell them that you would rather worry about a small problem than a catastrophe.

Some of the reluctant communicators may tell you that you always look busy and they are uncomfortable interrupting you. Of course you look busy; you have a great deal to do. However, make clear that one of the most important things you have to do is communicate with them. If they feel uncomfortable just breaking into the middle of an activity, ask them to send you an e-mail or a note or drop in to make an appointment. Then, make sure they understand that keeping the appointment is their responsibility. You should not have to go searching for them.

Many team members seem to feel that it is the manager's responsibility to initiate any communication. That's simply wrong. In fact, more of the responsibility is on the team member. You can use a regularly scheduled meeting to help reluctant communicators become more structured in their communication routines. You can also ask them to be more assertive in ensuring that their needs for information, guidance, and reassurance are met. Often, reluctant communicators believe that you expect them to do everything on their own. They are concerned that you will view too many questions on their part as a lack of competence.

Assure all your team members that you value communicating with them, since discussions are the best way for you to learn how well they are doing. If you have a tendency to become annoyed when your own work is interrupted, ask people to schedule times with you that are mutually convenient. In any case, don't close off their access to you to such an extent that you appear to discourage communication. Your project will suffer as a consequence.

Guideline: Plan for individual communication with all team members, including those who are reluctant to discuss issues with you.

Promoting team unity

A unified team is one that has a common goal. Actions taken by individual members of the team are calculated to advance progress toward the goal. Everyone on the team supports the goal and is united in reaching it and maintaining quality. Without a common goal, teams really do not exist—they are simply collections of individual contributors going in their own directions and working toward fulfilling personal agendas or personal conceptions of the project goals.

Personal agendas

Sometimes a manager is faced with a team member who has a personal agenda to achieve that has nothing to do with the goals the team is trying to achieve. As project manager, you need to recognize the signs of personal agendas and work hard to keep them properly controlled. Certainly, every team member wants to do well and be recognized for individual as well as team achievement. But sometimes the goal of individual recognition gets out of control. Occasionally, writers may be working for themselves, not for the team, the organization, nor the customer (Figure 16.6).

In one project, an individual writer made it quite clear that he was working on a personal agenda. Every time the editor asked to see a draft of a small section, the writer was ready with excuses: "The draft isn't ready yet." "I have only a few more items to add." "I want to work on the wording one more time." When the project manager approached the writer on the frustrated editor's behalf, the story was the same. Nothing was quite ready enough.

As a result of the delay tactics, the manager couldn't pry the draft copy away from the writer until the day before the client's review. Once the editor looked at the draft, it was clear that the writer had misinterpreted the purpose of the project and organized the information in a manner contrary to the project goals. The project manager knew that the client would be unhappy with the results. The project manager told the writer to revise the draft in very specific ways in the few hours before the client arrived.

The writer, continuing to know better than everyone else on the team, selectively revised the draft. Unfortunately, the editor and project manager had no time to review the changes before the client arrived. As a result, the client was unhappy with the work, and the writer looked foolish. Instead of achieving his personal goal of impress-

Figure 16.6 Discouraging personal agendas

ing the client by ignoring his team and his manager, the writer had succeeded in convincing the client that he was not competent.

If you have a team member who has a personal agenda and prefers individual to group achievement, point out the disservice this attitude does to the customer and to the other team members. Ensure that the team members get a lot of praise for their individual contributions but also ensure that team members who cooperate with one another get more praise. You have to be certain that you do not encourage use of the "star" system by your own actions.

Carefully explain the consequences of personal agendas to the offending team member. If the team makes a mistake together, then the whole team and the project manager will share the responsibility. If the project manager supports the team member's case on a controversial issue or has reviewed the team member's work, then the project manager shares the responsibility for any mistakes. However, if the team members and the project manager are kept in the dark, then they will be unwilling to share any blame. Writers who want to get all the praise must be aware that they also will get all the blame if something goes wrong. Are they willing to take that chance?

Guideline: Ensure that all team members recognize that a unified team will present a united front and protect the contributions of individual team members. The team will receive the rewards as well, even as they recognize the importance of individual contributions.

A feuding team

One of the most destructive elements caused by a lack of team unity is reflected in the scenario described above. The client, whether internal or external, sees the team in chaos, fighting among themselves. The project manager presents one direction; some team members take another. And they air their differences publicly (Figure 16.7).

Figure 16.7 A feuding team reflects a lack of common goals

Certainly, team members need the freedom to disagree with one another and with the manager. Constructive argument often results in better decisions when alternatives are fully examined. But sometimes, despite the best efforts on everyone's part, consensus cannot be achieved. The project manager then must make the decision and inform all team members of the reasoning behind the decision. If the decision is important enough and the project manager sees legitimate reasons for alternative positions, the manager may want to involve others in the organization in the decision-making process. Or, the manager may want to go outside the publications team to collect data to resolve the disagreement.

Whatever method the manager uses to resolve the conflict, once a decision is reached, all team members are obligated to present a united front. Unfortunately, when a team lacks cohesion, dissident team members may feel that they have the right to lobby others in the organization to support their points of view. The dissidents present their minority views at development-team meetings, in front of their manager and other team members. The result is to undermine the manager and the team and to destroy the confidence that the developers should have in the publications team by undermining their hard-won credibility. Such grandstanding behavior is inappropriate and should be dealt with quickly and firmly.

At one level, you may be able to deal with dissident members bent on causing trouble by firmly insisting that the behavior not be repeated. In most instances, a reprimand is enough. Often the offending team members are not aware of the way their behavior appears to outsiders. If the behavior continues, your next step is to make the entire team, including the dissident, aware of the effect of the feud on the publications organization. Credibility is difficult enough to achieve without having that credibility undermined by internal dissent. Although all decisions might not satisfy everyone, once the decisions are made, everyone is responsible for supporting them. The danger is that the responsibility for the decisions will be usurped by the development team. Then a decision might be made that no one likes.

Finally, you may have to take more decisive action. A formal letter that outlines the team member's behavior and its consequences is an unfortunate last course to take. However, such a step may be inevitable. The final step may be the separation of the team member from the team or the organization.

As the manager, you may find that occasionally a team member will be upset enough about a decision that he or she goes over your head and speaks to senior management. First of all, if the team member is so convinced of his or her position and so certain that you are not open to hearing about the problem, then it might be a good idea to assure yourself that you have been open to all alternatives. With your own management now involved, you may find that the best course is to be reasonable rather than defensive. Outline the situation as you see it, and make your reasoning clear. In most cases, upper management will support its project managers' decisions. If they do not, they are undermining the entire project-management process. If you find yourself unsupported, you have several alternatives:

- Find a compromise solution.
- Ask that the team member be assigned elsewhere.
- Begin a search for a new position.

A feuding team, especially when the feud becomes public knowledge, does no one any good in the publications organization. Credibility is threatened, and opportunities are closed for contributing effectively to the larger development process. As much as possible, keep all conflicts inhouse and respect the need for consensus.

Guideline: *Be alert to early warning signs of team problems. If the situation gets out of your control, work to regain control over your feuding team and avoid making the feud public.*

Lack of respect for team members

While a team feud may have as its source a genuine disagreement over methodology or the quality of the end product, some team feuds appear because team members do not respect one another (Figure 16.8). Personal prejudices due to social and cultural differences among team members may also cause problems in the team's working relationships. Often such a dispute occurs when one or a few team members begin to feel superior in their skills and contributions to other team members. Often a weaker or less experienced team member may become the victim. The project manager's job is to nip the dispute in the bud.

Figure 16.8 Every team member needs to respect the others

"I don't think you know what a poor job Jack is doing," said Dan. "He doesn't understand the product at all, and his writing is really terrible."

"Well, Dan, I appreciate your voicing your opinion to me rather than to your team members," said Eleanor. "But, you have to realize that everyone on the team is contributing to the project's success. Jack's contribution is as important as yours. It's my responsibility to see that everyone is successful."

"Sure, that's fine. But I've been finding errors in Jack's work. Usually I can get them fixed before anything goes out for review," said Dan. "You just don't know how bad things are."

"I don't think it's appropriate for you to change Jack's work without his knowledge or mine," replied Eleanor. "If you have a comment about the technology, you should make it at the team meeting so that everyone has the benefit of your understanding. Let's leave the editing to Sally and the reviewing to me and the team. We'll catch problems before they get out."

"It's just that I'm really getting tired of having to spoon-feed information to Jack. He's always asking me to help him out. He doesn't even know how to use the word-processing system."

"If Jack is having a problem with the word processor, I will ask him to speak to Helen, our production support person. You don't have time to be training anyone else."

"OK, I guess I can do that. But that isn't going to solve the problem."

"If there is a problem with a team member's performance, it's up to me to resolve. Your job is to get your work done and support your team members. Let me know when you're having a problem. Leave everyone else's problems to me.

Eleanor has to be careful not to undermine Jack. Dan is tattling, a pretty reprehensible behavior in the first place and inappropriate for an adult. Listen to the complainer but scrupulously avoid taking sides against the team member or letting your own point of view become public. It may be that Dan is correct in his assessment of Jack's problems. But as the manager, you need to first consider the unity of the team and the effect that tale-telling may have on morale and productivity. You want everyone to do well, and you may already be working with Jack to solve his problems. What you don't want to do is lead Dan to believe that his troublemaking has been successful.

The Dan's on your team will always find the weakest link to single out for criticism. They believe they enhance their own standing by making others look less competent and dedicated. They are wrong. They only succeed in making themselves look unprofessional and immature.

Undercutting team members by the manager

You need to ensure that team members have respect for one another's different abilities and contributions to the project. The best way to do that is by respecting each team member yourself. If you discover that an individual is not capable of understanding the technology, has problems with writing, or is unwilling to do his or her share of the work, you will have to take your own action. First, work with the individual to solve the problem through training, support, or better understanding of his or her responsibilities. Be certain to use neutral language and describe the behavior that presents a problem, not blame the individual.

Guideline: Ensure that all team members respect each other's contributions to the project and support one another fully.

Helping writers manage themselves

We have heard in recent years about the importance of self-managed teams. Self-managed teams are supposed to consist of individuals who understand the project goals and are able to monitor and control their team progress toward those goals. Self-managed teams do not mean, however, teams without skilled project management, although that is often how the concept is interpreted. In fact, it is the project manager who has the responsibility for helping the teams achieve self-management. Since you cannot possibly watch over everyone's shoulder at all times, you need to establish a process that ensures that everyone knows what to do and how to do it. Your best solution is to help your team members achieve self-sufficiency while remaining contributing members to the team.

Project managers sometimes get into the habit of overdirecting their team members, managing every step they take. This practice is the opposite of one used by a project manager who relinquishes all knowledge of and responsibility for the project's success. Neither extreme is satisfactory. By overdirecting, you will find that your team members cannot do anything unless you are there to direct. They appear to have no idea what is happening with the project and will refuse to assume the simplest responsibilities. By helping your team members assume responsibility for their own activities, you will lighten your own workload and protect your project from your inability to do everything yourself.

Team members need lots of support and teaching. Their progress may be slow, and they are likely to make mistakes. The alternative—ignoring the team—however, is worse. They will never learn how to do a better job, and you will always be stuck redoing their work and salvaging a mess. Not only will they not appreciate all your valiant efforts, they will resent them.

Guideline: Ensure that your team assumes responsibility for its own work without the need to constantly direct every effort.

Figure 16.9   Encouraging a self-managed team

Achieving a self-managed team

To achieve a self-managed team (Figure 16.9), you may want to

- Ensure that everyone knows the steps of the development process and understands how to achieve them.
- Help each member of the team develop his or her own detailed work schedule.
- Ask team members to explain to each other how they will meet their schedules and maintain quality.
- Use team meetings to share time management and tracking skills.
- Affirm that team members are responsible for doing their work well the first time, not waiting for someone else to redo it.
- Work with those team members who have difficulty managing their own time.
- Work with team members to explore the root causes of problems in meeting schedules and maintaining quality.
- Ask the team to find ways for everyone to avoid the problems in the first place.

Like any quality process, if you find yourself fixing the same problems over and over again, you are not doing a good job of training your team members and asking them to take responsibility for their own work. If they do not understand and support the process of project development and control, they will have a difficult time understanding what you are trying to achieve. Without knowing the goals, they will not be able to identify paths they can take to achieve the goals.

Guideline: Achieve a self-managed team by giving everyone as much responsibility as he or she can handle. Make team members responsible for their own success.

Helping team members schedule their time

One task that seems to be difficult for many writers is scheduling their own activities (Figure 16.10). Because many writers have never tracked their own time, they have little feel for how long a task has taken them in the past. Even some experienced writers are notoriously bad at estimating their own time and scheduling activities. They always approach a deadline by putting in a great deal of overtime to catch up.

It is difficult for anyone to estimate how long each small task will take to complete a project. A set of review comments could take five minutes to incorporate in your text, or you may find yourself with comments that raise cascading issues with ramifications in five chapters. The only way to predict this in advance is through your experience working with a particular group of reviewers.

Estimating the overall effect of individual events is difficult. The difficulty does not mean, however, that it should not be done. Like any estimating I have discussed in this book, the first attempts will be the worst. As you track actual projects and monitor the effects of dependencies, your estimating will get better. Remember especially that it is easier to estimate larger chunks of work than every small detail.

Figure 16.10   Helping team members schedule their time

If you have team members who have difficulty estimating and scheduling their own time, you may want to

- Help them make a detailed list of the activities they will perform to reach a milestone.
- Divide the allotted time among the listed activities.
- Set interim milestones that they can use to judge their progress.

Then, you need to work with them to monitor their progress. What if you have set a project milestone for the end of a month? You may have enough experience working with some writers on the team to rest assured that they will achieve the milestone or tell you early enough that they are having problems. Other writers may have a poor record of meeting schedules; you may lack experience working with others. In either case, work with both groups to establish interim milestones.

Be vigilant about checking work progress. You may find it advantageous to check on writer progress every 2 or 3 days to ensure yourself that they are accomplishing the activities they have set for themselves. With frequent progress checks, you will be better able to spot difficulties either in the writer's activities or the project itself. Once difficulties become apparent, you can work together with the writer to decide on a course of action.

A good technique is managing by walking around. Stop by your team members' offices and casually ask if they need anything from you. Give them a chance to ask a question or even tell you that everything is going well.

Guideline: Work with writers to establish and monitor interim milestones to ensure that the larger project milestones are being met.

Establishing an internal review process using peer editing

Some project managers design teams that include people with distinct editing responsibilities, either at the developmental or copyediting levels. Other project managers design teams in which writers are responsible for editing each other's work. The best design includes both types of editing resources to ensure that quality standards are maintained and project time used most productively.

Relying on self-editing

Some managers decide that external editing is unnecessary and that each writer should be responsible for editing his or her own work. Self-editing, a popular label for a lack of external editing, is both expensive and often likely to fail. Failures result because people run out of time to edit their own work and lack the perspective to do so effectively (Figure 16.11).

Figure 16.11 Experimenting with self-editing

Many years ago, English composition instructors recommended that students draft an essay and then put it into cold storage for a week or at least a day or two. Using this technique, the students could read their draft from a fresh perspective and identify problems that might have gone unnoticed immediately after the draft was complete. Unfortunately, most students completed their first drafts a few hours or a few minutes before the essay was due to be turned in to the instructor. Not only did they not leave themselves time to edit, they usually did not leave themselves time for anything except a first draft. The quality of the work suffered immensely as a result.

Many people who go into writing as a career have been brought up in the "first draft equals final draft" tradition. They are uncomfortable reviewing their own work, and they frequently fail to reserve time in their own schedules for a self-review and editing cycle. The pressures of deadlines appear to the writer to disallow any type of review and editing process at all. Technical communicators rarely have time to put a draft away for a week or even a day. Given the pressure of deadlines, they will quickly recognize the value of a good editor or peer editor to work with.

Other failures result because self-editing is simply not an adequate method for ensuring product quality. The notion of self-editing so popularized by traditional writing instruction rests on the basic assumption that reviewing and editing one's own work is an adequate method of achieving quality. We know from practice that writers are often their own worst editors. When you have been working on a text for hours, days, or weeks, you are rarely able to find evidence of inconsistencies, gaps, redundancies, or the other early warning signs of a decline in quality. You get so close to your own work that you fill in between the lines and make sense of sentences and paragraphs that leave everyone else struggling for meaning. The same is true for much creative effort—we are our own worst judges.

We tend to resist editing our own work because we recognize the futility of the activity. By the time we have produced a first draft, we are sick of the material and ready to go on to something new and more interesting. Revisiting the same old stuff is annoying and frustrating. We are willing to review that last few pages, but the very thought of reviewing tens or hundreds of pages leaves us cold. Anyway—there will always be a technical review. Perhaps the technical experts will pick up errors and omissions. Besides, what's the point of editing something that is just going to change. We'll have time for revising after the draft returns from technical reviews. That way we can incorporate the engineering comments and fix the problems we find at the same time.

In addition to the sense of futility and wasted time, many writers find it difficult to believe that their writing has any problems. If they have done a careful job of investigation and carefully worked through the text, perhaps including self-editing, then everything should be perfect. They fail to see what will be gained from an outside review. Besides, no one knows the subject matter as well as they do. An outside reviewer will change the meaning and create more work for the writer in the long run.

 Guideline: Recognize the limitations of self-editing in ensuring the quality of the finished work.

Editing as quality assurance

Most publications organizations give considerable lip service to the importance of quality in their work. Technical communicators decry the product changes that make it difficult to maintain the accuracy of publications. They are frustrated by the lack of quality in the product and the difficulties caused by software bugs, engineering inconsistencies, and functions that are awkward to use. At the same time, however, they maintain that publications quality will occur automatically through individual efforts to "do a good job." Or, they believe that existing methods of assuring quality, primarily self-editing and the technical review, are adequate.

When you learn scuba diving, one of the cardinal rules impressed upon you is the importance of always diving with a buddy. Relying on a self-contained breathing apparatus at underwater depths of 20 to 100 feet for recreational divers and deeper for professional divers can be quite frightening. If anything goes wrong with your equipment, your life may be threatened. Considering the essential need for quality in a potentially life-threatening situation, scuba diving buddies are taught always to check each other's equipment before a dive. For novice divers, the dive instructor carefully monitors every step and checks to ensure that all the equipment is connected and working properly. No one objects to these quality-assurance checks. Everyone works hard to be as careful as possible, but the system assumes that everyone is human and will make mistakes.

If we are genuinely serious about quality in publications, then we will also assume that writers are all human and will make mistakes. We need to put a quality-assurance system into place that ensures that standards are followed and the best work is accomplished considering the circumstances governing the project.

 Guideline: Quality assurance is essential to the success of any publications project and cannot be accomplished through self-editing alone.

When is self-editing important

Despite the clear disadvantages of self-editing as the only quality-assurance mechanism, individual writers should not feel that they are "off the hook" in terms of reviewing their own work. I have alluded to the altogether human reluctance to revisit our own copy. However, turning in an unedited mess to a project manager, a copy editor, or a developmental editor should also be considered unacceptable. As project manager, impress upon all team members their responsibility for checking their own work, at least to avoid the most egregious copy and formatting errors. At the very least, every team member should feel responsible for running an automatic spell check of a text. It is a waste of the editor's time to have to deal with errors that could be more easily caught by a machine.

All writers on the team should be responsible for reading their drafts before they turn them in for editing. They will find the most obvious errors and omissions easily on their own, saving time for the editor. The following guidelines were developed by Comtech Services (Figure 16.12) for our internal use.

The manager as editor

On very small projects, with no more than five team members, it may be possible for the project manager to monitor all the work closely enough. Of course, such monitoring assumes that the project manager is a skilled editor. In my organization, one of the requirements for project management is the ability to do both developmental editing and copyediting as necessary to ensure that quality is maintained.

As projects become larger and staff size increases, project managers will need to spend most of their time on management activities, not on quality assurance. At that point they can either claim to rely on self-editing, set up a system of peer editing, or invest in an editor to assist the team.

As we have already seen, self-editing is the least desirable solution. In general, when a project manager insists that all their writers edit their own work, I assume that they have decided that quality is not important or they do not have enough experience themselves with the editing process to understand the implications of this decision.

All writers will use the following guidelines for editing or implementing edits on any document pertaining to the project, including content specifications, reports, external memos, and, especially, drafts.

When preparing a draft

- While writing original material, follow the conventions established in the Style Sheet and Style Guidelines.
- Establish boilerplate text for repeated or similar information. Present similar information the same way each time.
- Record all significant style decisions on your copies of the Style Sheet and Style Guidelines.

Note: Save your document frequently. Develop a system so that saving becomes second nature. For example, save every time you complete a certain number of paragraphs or after you enter a certain number of edits. Make it a habit to save your document whenever your work is interrupted. Set the required save command in your system for every 15 minutes.

Before printing or submitting a draft

- Check your headers and footers. It's easy to forget to correct headers and footers, particularly when using a template. It's also frustrating (and wasteful) to have to reprint an entire draft because of an incorrect footer.
- Check for bad page breaks. Page breaks are not a big priority during first drafts. However, we should catch the most blatant bad breaks, such as breaks between a list and its introductory text. Use the Keep with Next Paragraph option to prevent such breaks.
- Run spell checker on your document immediately before printing a document.

Note: The publishing system allows you to create a user dictionary. While this feature is attractive, it is also potentially dangerous and should be used with discretion. Avoid adding dictionary words that could be misspellings of more common words. For example, adding the abbreviation "ANS" to a dictionary may prevent you from catching misspellings of the word "and.")

- Check your draft for "cleanliness" before submitting it for editing. Check for missing or misspelled words, formatting errors, incorrect headers or footers, and so on.
- When submitting a draft for editing, include the following materials:
  - the draft
  - the most recent copies of the Style Sheet and Style Guidelines
  - a table of contents for the draft

Figure 16.12 Editing guidelines for the writer

When implementing edits

- Mark off edits as you implement them. Use a pen or pencil (in a color other than that used by the editor) to indicate which edits have been entered.
- Address all edits. If you do not understand or agree with an edit, discuss the issue with the editor. Do not simply disregard an edit.
- Do not introduce new material or make changes to an edited draft. If you spot an error not caught by the editor or see a need for additional changes, discuss the issue with the editor. If both you and the editor agree that the change is warranted, add the change to the mark-up as well as the revised draft.
- Check the revised draft to make sure all edits were implemented.

Figure 16.12 (Continued)

Guideline: If you are managing a small group and have editing experience, do the quality-assurance editing yourself.

Introducing peer editing

Another solution is to institute a program of peer editing. In a peer-editing system, writers in the group are assigned to review the work of others. Everyone has an editing responsibility that is built in to the project schedule. From a technical viewpoint, peer members of the team are well suited to review one another's work. They all know the subject matter fairly well, even if they work on different aspects of the product. From an economic standpoint, no outside people need to be added to the team. Team members support one another, working together to assure product quality (Figure 16.13). Peer editing can work in one of two ways:

- Individual editing activities
- Group editing activities

With individual peer editing, the peer editors make time in their schedules to review and mark up the drafts of other members of the team. Once the review is complete, the writer goes over the edits and, if time permits, discusses any disagreements with the peer editor.

With group editing, all the team members review the draft documents. Then, they meet as a team to discuss problems and raise questions with the authors. It is a good idea to have a senior writer or the project manager serve as a facilitator of a group review to ensure that everyone remains objective and keeps overall project goals foremost in mind. A good facilitator will keep the group reviews from deteriorating into writer-bashing sessions. The point is not to beat up someone for not doing a perfect job, but to work together as a team to ensure that quality is maintained.

Figure 16.13   Introducing peer editing as quality assurance

The advantage of peer editing is that all team members get to look at one another's work. They all learn from the errors and omissions that are discovered and profit from knowing how all aspects of the project are coming together. They profit from observing other writers' skillful approaches and solutions to writing problems. Without peer editing, individual writers may have no idea what others are working on. They fail to profit from someone's understanding of a difficult technical concept or the solution to an especially difficult procedural or instructional design problem. With peer editing, the entire team learns from one another, and the quality of the project is maintained and enhanced.

Of course, peer editing also has to be managed. You may discover that some peers make few comments because they are afraid of hurting another writer's feelings. As a result, major problems go unmarked. Some peers may be ruthless, making scathing remarks in their comments that cause morale problems on the team. If you institute peer editing, it is a good idea to monitor the editing activities by shadow editing. You may even have to institute some training in the techniques of good editing and editing protocol to keep the process from deteriorating and discouraging everyone. Remind all the peer editors to take every opportunity to comment on parts of a draft that are particularly well done.

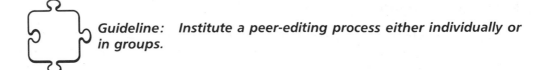

Guideline: Institute a peer-editing process either individually or in groups.

When peer editing does not work

Unfortunately, peer editing also has its disadvantages if not managed correctly. Four problems are most apparent:

- The peer-editing system breaks down under the strain of too much work and difficult deadlines.
- The peer-editing system is not adequate to ensure quality because the peer editors are not sufficiently skilled.
- Peer editors lack the clout to enforce standards.
- Peer editors may become too harsh and personally judgmental in their comments to the author.

As soon as schedules become too demanding, peer-editing systems do not work well. Even though peer editors feel responsible for reviewing each other's work, their own schedules always seem to get in the way. I hear many groups sheepishly admit that they are supposed to do peer editing, but they never seem to have the time. Consequently, no editing occurs at all and everyone feels badly about it.

In organizations where everyone is expected to be an editor, the quality of the editing activities will vary dramatically. Those peers who are skilled editors will find their services in demand, at least by those writers who want their work to be edited and know how valuable good editing is. Those peers who are weak editors either find themselves with little to edit or sought out by those who really don't want to submit their work to the scrutiny of a strong editor.

If management decides to remedy the inequities by giving everyone editing chores, then the weak editors may fail to recognize both major and minor problems or be afraid to bring major problems to the attention of stronger writers. In general, they resort to simple mechanical editing, pointing out typographical and punctuation errors. The original goal of quality assurance gets lost.

Finally, some writers become so attached to their original drafts that they feel insulted by peers, especially less experienced peers, who find errors and omissions in their work. They decide to ignore any edits they disagree with and frequently accuse the peer editor of failing to understand the technical content of the work. The peer editor lacks the organizational clout to enforce standards unless he or she complains about the writer to the project manager. Complaints, which work against team unity, may be difficult for the project manager to handle. If the peer editor lacks editing skills, the project manager may have to override the editor's comments and decide in favor of the writer. Any action of that sort will essentially destroy the peer-editing process. No one will feel safe in editing another's work for fear of the project manager negating the edits.

Enforcing peer editing

If a peer-editing system is to work, the project manager must first set ground rules for the activity with the team. You may want to establish the rules similar to those that are useful in working with a full-time editor:

- The editor is right unless proven otherwise.
- The writer will accept all edits.
- If the writer disagrees with an edit, he or she will negotiate with the peer editor until they reach an agreement.
- If no agreement can be reached, the writer and the peer editor will take the matter to the project manager for resolution.
- The writer and editor will accept the final resolution.

With rules in place, you are less likely to find yourself settling disputes. The team has a standard process to use, and you have a process to enforce. Personal likes and dislikes are avoided.

Be careful that peer editing does not become editing by committee. The committee may not be able to resolve problems, and much bad feeling may result.

Of course, you also need to work to ensure that the quality of peer editing is maintained. That often means working on editing skills with the team or obtaining outside training. Even after the team has been trained, you will find differences in skill level and will have to serve as a backup for less skilled and less experienced team members.

However, despite having a good process in place and obtaining training for the team members, you will likely experience an unevenness in quality. Eventually, unless everyone is continually vigilant, peer editing will deteriorate and quality-assurance activities will be abandoned.

 Guideline: Establish a rigorous process to ensure that peer editing is successful.

Instituting copyediting and developmental editing

Many publications organizations who do no other editing during the publications-development life cycle, do include final copyediting in the quality-assurance process. However, copyediting alone implies that the only level of quality worth assuring is at the word, sentence, and format level. A more comprehensive quality-assurance activity will extend well beyond copyediting to ensure that

- Standards and procedures are maintained for the publications and the publications-development process.
- Final publications quality occurs by monitoring the quality at each step of the process.
- Problems with the product and the process are brought to the attention of the project manager.

In some organizations, copyediting is the first step toward assuring quality and may be easier to institute. Few technical communicators will argue with the need to ensure that all the details of the copy are correct. While upper management may wonder why individual writers cannot do their own copyediting, copyediting by an independent group or individual will save writer time as well as ensuring that the copyediting is done well and consistently. Copy editors, in general, earn less than technical communicators who have extensive technical subject-matter knowledge and experience in constructing complex documents. One copy editor can easily leverage the time of 8 to 10 writers. If your group does not have 8 to 10 writers, then the copy editor can also provide services to other parts of the organization.

Establishing copyediting

An independent member or members of the team may be added to take on the responsibility of editing the publications for mechanical problems before they are released for review by outside groups or before the publications are printed. A copyediting staff is responsible for checking for such items as

- Spelling errors that are overlooked by the automatic spelling checker
- Punctuation and grammar errors
- Errors in formatting
- Inconsistencies in terminology, organization, structure, and approach within a single document and among the many documents that constitute a product library
- Compliance with organizational standards
- Omissions of words or sentences
- Confusing and unclear words, sentences, or paragraphs

A trained copy editor, armed with a corporate style guide, a project-specific style guide, and a checklist, can do much to ensure that the publications organization does not release publications for review or printing that have major and minor structural errors. Figure 16.14 details some of the typical guidelines that a good copy editor uses in proofreading a publication.

The advantages of instituting formal copyediting procedures, from the project manager's point of view, are that

- Copy quality will be consistent across all publications
- Standards will be maintained and enhanced
- Writer time will be saved
- Embarrassing errors will not find their way into review and final copies of documents

We know that technical reviews can often be derailed because of copyediting problems (see Chapters 9 and 14 for more information on the review cycles). Reviewers seem to like nothing better than taking out their frustrations with their old English teachers' inflexibility by wielding a red pen to the work of technical communicators. They will spend time marking copy errors rather than looking for technical errors and omissions. Even if the technical reviewers know their responsibilities in the review

Problem	Look for	Examples or details
Small words	Wrong words	an change, a ordinary (a vs. an)
	Missing words	The goal is to make sure that you the bank . . .
	Extra words	Next field in the Amt. field (watch for extra prepositions)
	Inverted words	As the of statement date . . .
Verbs	Wrong tenses	When you will see the product . . .
	Subject-verb agreement	The team members does the work . . .
Plurals	Missing or extra	. . . use for printing check on laser printer . . .
Punctuation	Missing or extra	Use categories to transfer money., Are all parentheses in pairs? Check for closing parentheses. Do all apostrophes and quotation marks face the right way?
Alignment	Spaces	Check for extra spaces before words, especially at the beginning of an item in a bulleted list, in notes, and where index markers obscure the view online. Check for missing space or extra spaces between sentences.
	Align with text	Check that screen shots and notes are vertically aligned with the text.
Inconsistencies	Glaring examples	A screen called "Write blanks," then called "Writing blanks."
	User problems	"Repeat steps 1 through 5," but there are only 3 steps.
Screenshots	Correct content	Is this the right screenshot? Does it belong here?
	Correct dates	All should have the same dates.
	Information on the screens	Roughly reasonable and consistent—no $3,000 utility bills.
	Complete call-outs	Are any call-outs missing the last line of text?
Spacing	Glaring problems only	Problems with too much space after a numbered step or too little space after a stand-alone step.
Footers	Page numbers	Check first and last pages of each chapter for correct numbers and the correct format.
Step procedures	Numbering	Do all procedures start with step 1? Are all numbers in sequences and no numbers missing or duplicated?

Figure 16.14 Copyediting tips

process, badly edited copy will become an annoying distraction. Copyediting errors act as surface errors that obscure the more important errors below. They call attention to themselves and interrupt the comprehension process.

Finally, badly edited copy will reduce the credibility of the publications team. If writing is supposed to be our job, we should at least be able to get it right. A project manager who is able to rely on the talents of a good copy editor knows that credibility will be maintained and that reviews will be more effective.

Instituting developmental editing

Not all editing-related quality problems will be addressed by introducing copyediting. Copy editors, while sometimes very talented and able to find serious problems with a text, are generally not in a position to edit a document for substance and organization. Copyediting often occurs too late for major changes in organization to be implemented. Copy editors may not know enough about the subject matter to suggest changes to the content.

In any quality-improvement process, the most important contributions to quality should occur early in the development life cycle. The later in the life cycle that major problems are discovered, the harder and more expensive it will be to correct them. The job of the developmental editor is to ensure that quality is maintained from the first. The developmental editor, as indicated by the job title, has a responsibility for maintaining standards and recommending substantive changes to documents or to entire libraries throughout the development process. The developmental editor plays a major role in training new writers and ensuring that the highest standards of work are maintained (Figure 16.15).

Frequently, the developmental editor is the individual who reviews all the Information Plans and Content Specifications before they are reviewed by the project manager and the technical reviewers. The developmental editor is responsible for working with early prototypes and first drafts to ensure that consistent approaches are in place, that writers are adhering to standards, and that the latest developments in best writing practices are introduced to the project. The developmental editor plays one of the most significant roles in assuring the consistent quality of publications (Figure 16.16).

To fulfill such a comprehensive role in the publications-development life cycle, it should be clear that the developmental editor must be a highly experienced and highly skilled individual. Perhaps the best candidate for the developmental editor's job is a senior writer who enjoys editing and is already viewed by team members as a mentor and an authority. The peer-editing process will frequently reveal the best editors. If a job category can be established that is senior enough and attractive enough, some senior writers will find developmental editing an attractive career path.

As project manager, be on the lookout for skilled editors on your team. These are the people who have the best suggestions during team meetings, are sought out by team members for peer reviews, are able to notice errors and omissions that are invisible to others on the team, can get to the heart of a problem quickly and identify viable solutions, or are able to catch technical problems even when they are not working on the exact technology. Good developmental editors are a rare breed and should not be allowed to get away.

Figure 16.15   Educating writers through developmental editing

Once you are convinced that your team and the quality of your work will benefit from developmental editing, how do you convince senior management to approve the elevation of a senior writer to new rank or the hiring of a new member of the team as a senior editor rather than hiring another writer? One manager was successful at creating the position of developmental editor by using the following pointers:

- Impress upon senior management that the senior developmental editor will help to ensure the quality of the team's work.
- Demonstrate that the developmental editor will reduce publications-development time by ensuring that serious errors and omissions are discovered early in the life cycle when they are less expensive and easier to fix.
- Establish the position at a senior level, clearly differentiating it from copyediting.
- Elevate an experienced writer who knows the technology to the first developmental editor's position.
- Make the editor's services available to senior management for their own work.
- Clearly explain the developmental editing process.

Title: **Developmental Editor**

Duties and Responsibilities

Responsible for quality assurance and establishing company writing and editing guidelines and standards, with the assistance of the project managers and senior management. The responsibilities include, but are not limited to, the following:

- Maintaining documentation quality
  - Edit documents as requested for content, style, copyediting and proofreading accuracy
  - Conduct substantive edits of the organization, style, completeness, and consistency of draft documents
  - Understand the technical material on projects well enough to ensure that the documentation is consistent and logically developed
  - Ensure that projects maintain an up-to-date and adequate style guide
  - Discuss editing style and corrections with writers to educate them on good writing and editing techniques
- Creating Information Plans and Content Specifications
  - Help writers develop Information Plans for a documentation library, as appropriate. Produce these plans independently for short projects or projects that must start up before the writer has been assigned
  - Help writers to develop Content Specifications for individual books, or develop Content Specifications independently for short projects
  - Work with clients and management to determine the types of documentation that are required for particular projects
- Maintaining style standards
  - Prepare style standards with the help of the publications manager and senior project-management staff. Ensure that these are communicated regularly and frequently to the writing staff.
  - Maintain the Style Guide in response to requests for additions or new discoveries
  - Determine when to deviate from the style standards to meet client standards or special requests
- Teaching new people about the standard style
  - Review the style expectations with new people as part of the new employee orientation
  - Teach writers what belongs in a style guide and how to maintain one
  - Explain to new writers what belongs in Content Specifications and how the publications-development life cycle works
  - Train lead writers and senior writers to maintain editing quality by reviewing their edits of other writers' work

Figure 16.16 Job description for a developmental editor

- Quality assurance
  - With the project managers and publications manager, share responsibility for ensuring that the material released to clients meets quality standards. In some cases, this will mean helping to ensure that the writers adjust their efforts to meet the quality standards dictated by the budget and schedule obligations
  - Bring problems to the attention of the project manager
- Project management
  - Serve as project manager on short term projects or projects for which no project manager is available
  - As requested, oversee the work of senior writers or lead writers on projects to help ensure that they perform their project management responsibilities properly
  - Identify scope changes with the lead writer or senior writer and bring them to the attention of the project managers
- Supervising Senior Writers, Writers, and Editorial Assistants
  - Help maintain the progress of persons supervised in attaining required job skills and aid the learning process
  - Help write periodic and annual performance evaluations
  - Keep staff members apprised of their performance on a regular basis
  - Maintain morale of persons supervised during projects
  - Meet regularly with persons supervised
- Communication
  - Communicate effectively with writing staff
  - Communicate effectively with management
  - Bring problems to management's attention
  - Support company policies

Other duties and responsibilities as assigned.

Reporting

The Developmental Editor reports to the Publications Manager.

Entry-Level Skills

Must have acquired the skills of a project manager. Must be an expert substantive editor, copyeditor, and proofreader. Must understand and apply a thorough knowledge of grammar and style standards.

Acquired Skills

Must develop the ability to work tactfully with writers to help them restructure their work, as appropriate. As project manager backup, must learn when to intervene with lead writers/senior writers to avoid contractual difficulties.

This job description is a guideline only. Changes may be made to the description at any time, with or without notice.

Figure 16.16 (Continued)

Although many developmental editors are also responsible for a lot of copyediting, having a developmental editor on the team does not preclude having copy editors. The roles and the timing are different. Developmental editing is formative, because the editor works with the writers as they are forming their strategies and trying out alternative approaches. Copyediting is, in part, evaluative, ensuring that all the *is* are dotted and the *ts* are crossed before the publications go out the door. Both activities have a role in maintaining quality.

However, if I had to choose between the two, I would always choose developmental editing. As a project manager, you are responsible for meeting the needs of your audiences for the most accurate, accessible, readable, and usable information you can produce. Developmental editing, as well as frequent communication among team members, will go a long way toward helping you meet those responsibilities. Copyediting, although important to the image of your organization and influential in removing the most egregious errors from a document, is of less importance to the customer. While the customer may be able to tolerate, albeit with annoyance, typographical and formatting errors, he or she will not be willing to tolerate documents that are inaccurate or unusable.

 Guideline: Work hard to institute developmental editing as the single most important quality-assurance mechanism in the publications-development life cycle.

Validating the accuracy of publications

Though developmental editing should ensure that publications standards are maintained and quality is built into the process, editing of any sort often cannot ensure that the information written is technically accurate. In the publications-development life cycle, we use the technical-review process to help ensure that inaccurate information is not sent to the customer. We have discussed the technical-review process in Chapters 9 and 14. However, the technical review is often not structured to ensure that all the technical information is correct, especially the information that delineates procedures to be followed by the audiences of each publication.

Many organizations include the verification of the content of technical publications as part of the standard quality-assurance activities. Independent testing groups are responsible both for

- Testing the product's functionality to ensure that no bugs exist
- Ensuring that standards are maintained
- Testing the documentation

Frequently, the quality-assurance testing groups will use early drafts of the documentation to test the functionality of the product.

However, if your organization does not have a quality-assurance testing group or if that group is unwilling to test the documentation as well as the product, you still have a responsibility to ensure that the information that your team produces is accurate. A system of validation testing should ensure that every procedure is executed with the software and hardware being developed before the documentation is released. This validation may be done by publications-team members or by individuals specially hired for this purpose. An individual validating a document performs every procedure exactly as written using the product. If an error is found (either the instruction is incomplete or incorrect, or the result is different than expected), the validator documents the error as thoroughly as possible, in particular explaining how the product differs from the instruction.

All errors found during the validation process are reported to the publications team. Individual writers are often responsible for correcting the errors and removing the defects from their documents.

Unfortunately, even the best managed team sometimes find themselves with no time left to validate their procedures. As a result, incorrect information gets out to the customers and invites them to call customer service. With difficult schedules, we should plan as much validation time as possible and bring to the attention of upper management what the consequences are when this step is omitted.

 Guideline: *Ensure that all publications are validated so that they accurately describe the functioning of the product and the activities to be performed by the users.*

Instituting productivity measures

The productivity of your publications team is dependent both on the volume of work they produce within a given time, as well as the quality of the resulting publications and the quality of the process used to produce them. The simplest measure of productivity at the end of a project is represented by the number of pages published. However, measurements of pages produced can vary greatly depending on what is counted. Has your team documented an entirely new product from scratch, designing the form the publications would take and completely departing from any previous standards? Or, has your team made minimal changes to a previous set of publications? In most cases, we find that publications teams, in the course of a year, produce both new pages and changed pages with wide variations in the time required. If we count both blank pages and pages that contain extremely complex theories of operation, we may have variations in hours per page of 10 times or more.

Because the process of counting pages is not uniformly defined across organizations or even within the same organization, it is impossible to compare the productivity of one group with another by depending solely on page counts. Only if the data gathered is identical would such comparisons begin to be meaningful. However, even if the data is identical, the circumstances under which the publications teams have worked and the complexity of the tasks they performed will also be different.

Measurement	Purpose	Action
Dependencies (see Chapter 8)	to evaluate team productivity	compare the original dependencies predicted for a project with the final results
Customer requirements	to evaluate the success of the team's process	focus on the quality of the final product to determine how well it met customer requirements
Process	to improve the process	assess the adequacy of the publications-development process

Figure 16.17   Methods for evaluating productivity

The problem with counting pages produced as the only measure of productivity is that the final count ignores the dependencies, the factors that contribute to the ease or difficulty of a particular project. Such a simplistic measurement as hours per page, while extremely valuable for estimating the size of a project, should not be used to evaluate individuals or compare projects.

To evaluate the productivity of publications teams, we need more complex measuring systems that take into account the dependencies of the project and the quality and complexity of the product. Figure 16.17 includes some possible productivity measures.

Defining team productivity

A system of measuring team productivity should be put into place early in the publications-development life cycle. In the Information Plan phase and again in the Content Specification phase, we have the basis for evaluating the team's success in developing what it said it would develop with the time and resources allotted. If the requirements do not change and the dependencies remain the same, working together, the team should be able to complete the project in the time required with the defined resources, as illustrated in Figure 16.18. That is, if you said you will write three 300-page manuals in 9 months with four team members, you should be able to do so unless something changes that causes you to redefine your assumptions. Thus, a fundamental measure of productivity is doing what you said you would do.

Such a productivity measure is meaningful, however, only if your team also achieved the level of quality that you decided was needed to satisfy the customer. If you produced those three manuals in 9 months, but half the information in them is incorrect, the organization of the information makes it difficult for the customer to find anything, and you use terminology that the customers do not understand, then the simple measure of effort is meaningless. If you were unable to maintain an acceptable level of quality, then your team has probably been less efficient than expected.

Most likely, you have had to change your estimates of the project's scope and duration in response to changes occurring in the product-development process. Under changing circumstances, how then do you measure the productivity of your team? One possibility is the success of the team in monitoring and controlling the project while responding to changes. Although features may have been added and the schedules

Figure 16.18 Defining team productivity

shortened, was your team able to respond with reasonable success? If so, the project may be evaluated as a success, if the process remains under control. You may also decide that the team has been productive if the process has been controlled to the extent that work is done only after it has been approved. That is, no one member of the team or the team as a whole has deviated from the plan and exceeded expectations. They have not put in more hours on the project than predicted during the course of the project. They have not done work on their own volition that was not approved. A team and a project manager able to control their actions, even in the face of seeming chaos around them, may be judged highly productive.

Measuring productivity

In addition to measuring productivity in terms of adherence to the original plan or the revised plans, you also need to look at the quality of the work produced and the quality of the process. During Phase 3 of the project, you must set expectations of quality and process so that they can be measured as the project develops, as well as measured at the end.

Your measurements of the quality of the process will depend upon the expectations of the team in meeting the project milestones. You may want to use the editing process described above as a first step in the measurement process. The second-process measurement step will involve the technical review process and any customer reviews that may take place.

Of particular interest is to measure productivity in relationship to the percentage of editing time required. For example, you predict during Phases 1 and 2 that your team will require approximately 15 percent editing time as a factor of writing time. That means, for every 100 hours of writing, you expect the editing activities (peer editors, developmental editors, copy editors, team reviews) to account for another 15 hours. Within that prediction is, of course, an allowance for individual differences among team members in terms of dependencies such as technical, team, audience, and writing experience.

What if, during Phase 3 of project development, it becomes clear that the team is exceeding the 15 percent factor for editing. In fact, the editors find that they need 20 percent of total writing time to maintain the quality of the drafts. The editing factor may increase for several reasons. Some writers may have difficulty with the following:

- Understanding the level of the audiences (writing at a level that is judged too difficult for the audience to understand or too simple for a more sophisticated audience).
- Maintaining the original page estimates either by writing too little or too much. In either case the editors have to spend time helping the writers adhere to the original scope estimates or work with them and the project manager to revise the scope based on product changes.
- Maintaining a consistent structure for a document. For instance, they may change how they write an instruction each time they write one. Or, their chapters are all organized differently when they should be adhering to a pre-established pattern.
- Maintaining consistent terminology. The editors find that terms change constantly from section to section and even within the same section.
- Maintaining consistency when they add information. They appear to be unaware that changes to one part of a document affect information in other parts of the document.

All of these issues and others like them will drastically affect the ability of the editors to maintain the initial estimate of editing time. Editors will often be the first to notice that certain team members require far more editing and coaching to create an acceptable first draft than others. Those individual differences are also serious enough to affect the overall productivity of the team. The team is using more hours than estimated to achieve a milestone, not because the information is changing or the external dependencies have changed, but because earlier predictions of productivity levels are not being achieved.

Remember to be very careful about deciding what to measure. In general, you will affect what you measure. If you do not measure some attribute, it will likely go unchanged.

 Guideline: Measure team productivity by evaluating the amount of editing time required to meet the quality standards for each project milestone.

In addition to the internal measurement of overall editing time, you may be interested in the possibility of quantifying the types of errors that are uncovered during the editing process. In terms of a severity hierarchy, you may be able to rate types of errors. For example, one rating scale may look like Figure 16.19.

The four levels suggested in Figure 16.19 begin with the most severe errors and decrease in severity through Level 4. The severity is a factor of the amount of time needed for the editor to identify the problem and recommend a fix, and for the writer to complete the revision to the editor's satisfaction. Note that errors that involve larger portions of the document are judged more severe than those affecting words or sentences only. If the developmental editor finds that she needs to perform only a light copyedit on a writer's initial draft, then the writer may be considered very productive. This productivity is achieved, however, only if the original schedule has been maintained.

A writer who has difficulty organizing information and maintaining coherence from section to section and paragraph to paragraph will require many more hours of editing and revising (as well as guidance and instruction) before a satisfactory result is achieved. If no editing occurs in the development process, then errors of the type mentioned here may be detected by the technical reviewers (who feel that they should have written the information themselves) or may go entirely undetected until they negatively impact the customer.

As project manager, you need to work closely with your writers, developmental editors, and copy editors to set standards and watch for major problems with the team's internal productivity. The point is not to punish people who are less productive, but to find ways to make them more productive while at the same time maintaining the quality of the drafts.

Although defects in the structure of the information should be detectable by the editing process, defects in the technical accuracy of the information should be detected by the technical-review and validation processes. Your team may want to institute a method for quantifying the number and severity of the errors detected during technical reviews and validation, as well as through the internal editing processes. Severity levels may depend upon the consequences to the customer of having the incorrect informa-

Severity of error	Consequences	Frequency
Level 1a: organization	major reorganization of information required at the book or section level	more than 25 percent of the total information provided
Level 1b: organization	major reorganization within a sub-section	more than 25 percent of the total information provided
Level 1a: coherence	major pieces of information missing or repeated randomly	more than 25 percent of the information provided
Level 1b: coherence	transitions between paragraphs and sentences missing or inappropriate	more than 25 percent of the information provided
Level 2a: organization	minor reorganization of information required at the book or section level	less than 25 percent of the total information provided
Level 2b: organization	minor reorganization within a sub-section	less than 25 percent of the total information provided
Level 2a: coherence	minor pieces of information missing or repeated randomly	less than 25 percent of the information provided
Level 2b: coherence	some transitions between paragraphs and sentences missing or inappropriate	less than 25 percent of the information provided
Level 3: sentence structure	sentences require restructuring for readability	more than 25 percent of the total number of sentences need revision
Level 3: terminology	terminology inconsistent	more than 25 percent of the terms need revision
Level 4: sentence structure	minor grammar and punctuation errors	less than 25 percent of the sentences need revision
Level 4: spelling	minor spelling errors	less than 10 percent of words are misspelled; no errors that could have been detected automatically
Level 4: formatting	minor formatting errors	fewer than 10 percent of the formatting codes are misapplied

Figure 16.19 Possible structure for evaluating the severity of problems identified during the editing cycle

tion in the text. For example, if the name of a particular input field in the text does not exactly match the name of the field in the software, the customers may never notice or be able to figure out the variance on their own. However, if the installation procedure leaves out critical steps in the process, the customers may be completely unable to install the product.

By categorizing the severity of defects, you will be able to establish which changes must be made, especially if there is not time enough to make them all. Given too little time in the schedule, minor defects will have to go uncorrected until the next version of the publication.

Correcting defects is important to the success of the publication with its users. However, be certain that defects are not used as a club to penalize the writing team. In evaluating defects in the publications, you need to take into account the circumstances under which your team members are forced to work.

The importance of both the internal and external productivity measurements during Phase 3 is that problems are being identified and corrected before they become problems for the customers. Once problems are detected and corrected, the team has the potential of going the next step. That next step, seen in a Level 4 organization, includes the activities involved in identifying root causes for the defects and improving the process so that the number and severity of the defects are reduced before internal and external edits and reviews occur. Remember, of course, that many defects result when the product changes and information that was once correct now no longer matches the product.

Guideline: Establish methods for quantifying the number and severity of errors detected during the review and validation processes.

Promoting increases in productivity

If all you are counting to measure productivity is the number of pages produced, then it is quite simple to increase the productivity of your team. All you need to do is produce more pages in less time. That is relatively easy if you just stuff the pages with information that is irrelevant to the audience. More pages, less quality.

If you really want to promote quality and productivity in your team, you will have to work harder. Start by ensuring that everyone understands the publications-development process and promote the value added by the editing process. By far, the best way to increase productivity while improving quality is through education, training, and an excellent editing and review process. If individuals are having difficulty with their design and writing skills, find ways to help them improve. If they are having problems understanding the technical material, get them into training classes so that they master the technology to the extent necessary to write well. Increase the communication among team members and between you and team members so that the team's productivity is not hurt by its weakest members. Help the strong team members find ways to support those who are less experienced or less skilled. Assist the strong team members in strengthening their own skills and adding new areas of expertise.

To raise the productivity of your entire team, you must ensure that team members work together. The team should never compromise the quality of its work because some team members are having a more difficult time meeting the project demands than others.

Guideline: Increase the productivity of your team by examining your process, providing education and training for team members, and working together to maintain quality among the team as a whole.

CHAPTER

17

Tracking Progress

In Chapter 12, you learned to create the components of a tracking system for your projects. You created templates for weekly time sheets and progress reports from all your team members. You established a method of recording weekly data in a reporting spreadsheet and put in place a system for producing periodic reports. During Phase 3: Implementation, you should be ready to put the tracking system into full use.

During Phase 1: Information Planning and Phase 2: Content Specification, you may have found it reasonably straightforward to keep track of progress. The entire team, or a smaller planning team, is completely directed toward a common goal—gathering sufficient information about the project to result in comprehensive and detailed plans for the publications library.

During Phase 3, the unity established during the planning phases becomes more difficult to maintain because the team members have their individual assignments for separate publications or even parts of a publication. The team members move on to their own processes of data gathering, composing, verifying, editing, and revising. In most cases, team members work with different SMEs on the development team. More than in the planning phases, team members become dependent upon the availability, cooperation, and understanding of individual experts. If your experts suddenly leave for Germany for two weeks, your schedule may be seriously disrupted.

Consequently, the tracking process during Phase 3 becomes much more complex and time-consuming than it was during the planning phases. As project manager, you have many diverse threads to follow to ensure that progress is being made according to the original project plan. To track progress, you need to have a clear understanding of the types of activities that your team members will pursue during implementation. In the table in Figure 17.1, larger categories of activities are detailed and the possible types of output delineated.

Each of the detailed activities in Phase 3 should be scheduled with agreement between you and the individual writers. The initial activities to place on the schedule are the interim drafts that together will become a complete first draft. The writers produce interim drafts so that a limited number of SMEs will have an opportunity to conduct preliminary reviews of the content in small pieces. Generally, interim draft reviews are casual—simple readings of the ideas that the writers are working with. Reviewers must be limited to a few key people who are working most closely with the writers on the subject matter.

Category	Activities	Output 1	Output 2	Output 3
Writing	Data gathering Composing Self-editing Revising	Interim draft	First draft	Second draft
Editing	Substantive editing	Organizational changes to the interim draft	Changes to the first draft	Changes to the second draft
	Copyediting	Copy corrections to the interim draft		
Graphics	Illustration and design		First draft	Second draft
Review	Technical review	Content changes to the interim draft	Content changes to the first draft	Content changes to the second draft
Verification	Technical review		Content changes to the first draft	Content changes to the second draft
Production	Design of style templates	Interim draft	Style additions to the first draft	Style additions to the second draft
Testing	Usability testing		First-draft usability testing	Second-draft usability evaluation

Figure 17.1   Phase 3 activities

Guideline: Schedule and track interim drafts of parts of the planned publications so that major milestones can be met.

Producing interim drafts

If we take the information in Figure 17.2 in a roughly chronological flow, activity begins with data gathering by the writer. The writer produces initial text and ideas for art for subsections of the publication. The resulting interim draft is first reviewed internally by the developmental editor for adherence to standards, conformance with the Content Specifications, and other substantive issues. Before the interim draft is released for an interim and informal technical review, basic copyediting occurs to

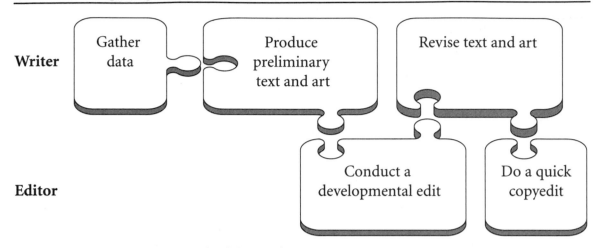

Figure 17.2 Initial writing and editing cycle

eliminate the worst copy errors. This copyediting may be done by an editor or directly by the writers.

At the same time that the writer is composing the interim drafts of subsections, those responsible for the physical format of the document are preparing project-specific format guidelines and an electronic style template (see Figure 17.3). This template may be the standard template used in the organization, a modification of the standard template to account for new design elements needed by the writers, or a completely new template for the publications project. The writer applies the template to the information prepared for the interim draft.

As soon as the project manager believes the interim draft is ready, the writer gives it to the single individual or very small group responsible for an initial technical review. Usually, this interim review is not part of the formal review process; rather, it is an attempt to ensure that everyone on the team is on the same track. The writers learn if they have gained a sufficient understanding of the information to produce the formal first draft, and the technical reviewers gain confidence in the writers' ability to convey the information correctly to the audience.

As much as possible, you should ensure that the interim reviews stay informal. They are really part of the data-gathering process between the writer and the SMEs. Although extensive copyediting is probably unnecessary at this stage, you may want to include a quick copyedit to ensure that the reviewer's process is not interrupted by typographical, grammatical, or formatting errors.

While copyediting may be minimal, developmental editing at this stage ensures that the editor and the project manager agree that the information is well-enough structured to be ready for the SME. You need to assure yourself that the writers are working to the specifications and understand the needs of the audience. Many organizational and structural problems that may not be caught by the SME are likely to be identified by the developmental editor and the project manager.

With skilled and experienced writers on the team, the developmental edit at this stage may be little more than a quick read through. However, if some writers are having difficulty conceptualizing the structure of the information or want to experi-

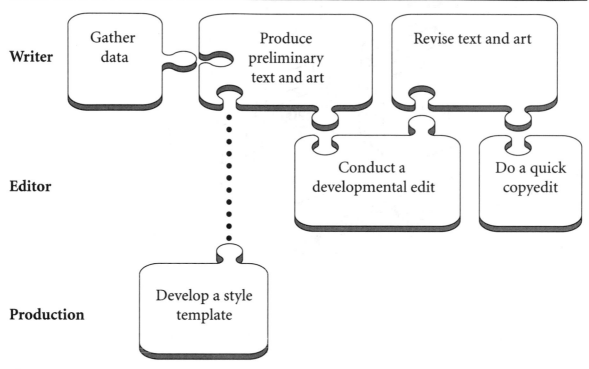

Figure 17.3 Initial writing, editing, and review cycle

ment with alternative structures, they will benefit from top-quality assistance. If writers have uncovered new information that was not included in the Content Specifications, the internal interim review is their opportunity to make this information known to the project manager so that the project plan can be adjusted.

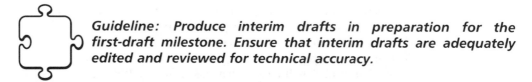

Guideline: Produce interim drafts in preparation for the first-draft milestone. Ensure that interim drafts are adequately edited and reviewed for technical accuracy.

Scheduling interim drafts

Although interim drafts usually do not have strict deadlines, you may find it useful to set tentative schedules for the interim drafts with your writers. The simplest way to set interim deadlines begins with the hours available for the entire first-draft effort. What if you have 15 weeks between the end of Phase 2: Content Specification and the first-draft deadline? The writers might divide their time in the following ways:

- Equally divide the total first-draft time by the number of pages to be produced.
- Add extra time for more difficult sections and subtract time for easier sections.
- Schedule individual sections according to the availability of SMEs.

Figure 17.4   Scheduling interim-draft deadlines to keep the project on track

- Schedule individual sections according to the completeness of the product design and implementation.
- Schedule detailed sections before overviews.

At this detailed level, the exact interim schedules are unlikely to be strictly adhered to. Availability of SMEs and product completeness will vary and be difficult to predict. But in a general sense, the interim schedules serve as a guideline for determining progress. If the writers get too far behind early in Phase 3, they may not be able to catch up later. People have a normal human tendency to view a vast expanse of time at the start and believe they will have no problem meeting their schedules. They proceed at a leisurely pace until the deadlines loom.

To manage the project effectively, you will want the writers to create many minor deadlines that, if met, will ensure that the major deadlines are met (see Figure 17.4). In this way, you keep your team focused on immediate and tangible goals, rather than on vague and distant ones. You establish a mild sense of urgency that should help everyone avoid the schedule crunches that tend to emerge as major deadlines approach.

"I thought I had lots of time," explained Doris, one of Eleanor's most experienced writers. "I always seem to underestimate my time."

"I know what you mean," replied Eleanor. "At the beginning of a project, I always feel that there's plenty of time to get the job done. I start right off procrastinating. It's easy to forget that you have to make progress from the beginning. Otherwise, by the time you think things need to get serious, the slightest schedule breakdown is going to be a disaster."

"Right," said Doris. "I thought I'd be able to get three chapters written last week. Instead, I had to spend an entire day getting the printer working again. I didn't accomplish nearly as much as I had expected. Now, I've got to work all weekend to try to catch up."

"I wish I had some of that leisurely schedule back that I frittered away three months ago," groaned Eleanor. "Now I'm getting desperate and putting in all sorts of extra hours."

"I guess that's what planning is all about," concluded Doris. "Next time, I'm going to figure out what I need to accomplish during each week of the project so I don't do this to myself again."

"Maybe we can work together to keep each other on track," agreed Eleanor. "I have a tough time disciplining myself until it's almost too late."

If this sounds like a familiar scenario, that is because it is normal for those of us who are procrastinators. You always regret the wasted time after it's too late. By the time the deadlines loom, you have to start cutting out tasks you would really like to perform. Unfortunately, you have only enough time remaining to do the minimum.

In evaluating the importance of setting small interim deadlines with your writing team, you may actually be acknowledging that some project delays or stressful overtime schedules are not caused by product changes. We contribute to the delays and stress ourselves by procrastinating. I once had a senior writer who always worked on weekends. When she complained to me about her resentment of the constant weekend work, we reviewed her weekday schedule. Because she preferred to write without interruptions, she spent her 40-hour week in meetings, discussions, and interviews. She was subconsciously saving the weekends for writing. To decrease the perceived overtime, we worked out a method for her to have uninterrupted time during the week.

Detailed interim schedules allow writers to schedule their time effectively and decrease the effects of procrastination. But even the most detailed schedule will not account for delays that occur because of overly committed schedules among the development-team members. Much of the lack of progress on the many small pieces of a publications project occur because of a lack of communication and coordination of effort among members of the larger team.

You may have assumed, for example, that certain development events would be completed on schedule, only to discover that they have been delayed or rescheduled. You may have assumed that SMEs would be available to explain their designs to the writers only to discover that they have not factored publications time into their schedules. You may discover that development managers have told their team members to protect their development schedules and ignore writers' requests for interviews. Although these schedule shifts may not affect the due dates of major milestones, they will make regular, organized progress difficult for the writing team. Interim-draft schedules will have to be adjusted to take delays of this type into account.

Not only will alterations in the development schedule require changes to the microscheduling of the publications project, the process of learning new and sometimes difficult technology may also produce delays among your own team members. You will find instances in which your writers experience difficulty in understanding the subject matter. You must be especially alert to these delays because you may need to shift team resources. You may have to ask senior team members with more product experience to assist newer team members with their product learning.

In the constantly shifting sands of interim drafts, you need to watch closely the hours expended compared with hours estimated and to monitor these in terms of the percent complete of the project.

Guideline: Microschedule interim drafts, and be alert to shifts in the schedule that may adversely impact the success of the publications project.

Turning interim drafts into a complete first draft

The activities involved in producing myriad interim drafts eventually roll up to a complete first draft, as defined by the milestones established in the Information Plan and detailed in the Content specifications. As a rule of thumb, I suggest that the first draft represent approximately 60 percent of total project time (see Figure 17.5).

With 15 weeks in the schedule to complete the first draft, every week counts. You need to make progress consistently from the very first day if you are to meet the deadlines with a minimum of overtime.

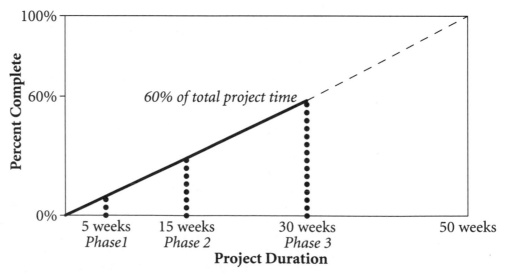

Figure 17.5 Phase 3 milestone schedule

Guideline: Ensure that your team makes regular progress toward the first-draft milestone.

Tracking interim project milestones and progress

As the implementation activities proceed through Phase 3, the processes you have put into place will allow you to track progress. As project manager, you receive weekly time sheets and progress reports from each team member. Review the accomplishments carefully. Based on your understanding of the overall schedule, ask yourself if the writer has accomplished what was needed during the week. If the writers are tracking their own progress, the problems section of the weekly reports should alert you to any deviations from the overall schedule. The problems section provides an opportunity for the writers to identify areas where they have not accomplished what they expected and to explain what has caused the deviation from the schedule.

However, you cannot rely on the writers' assessment of progress alone. You also need to know what you expect each writer to accomplish weekly and to track those accomplishments carefully through the progress reports. In addition to matching the accomplishments reported with those in the original plan and following problems closely, you should pay careful attention to the plans section of the progress report. The plans should give you a good idea how the writers are envisioning the immediate next stage of activities. Do the activities appear to be advancing the project? Are the writers waiting for others to produce work so that they can meet their own schedules? Is everyone too optimistic?

If you and the writers have determined interim deadlines, use the schedules to track progress. If some of the promised work cannot be accomplished for legitimate reasons, the writers should immediately fill in the time with other scheduled items. As the project progresses, some interim sections may be ahead of schedule and some behind, but the overall project will appear to be on track (see Figure 17.6).

As you review progress reports, be especially careful to watch for downtime. Are the writers having difficulty with important equipment or software? Has time been lost to network or equipment failures? On one project, we had a mainframe crash at exactly the wrong time. A few days before a critical deadline, the mainframe was down for about 48 hours while the team did whatever paperwork they could. Remember that all teams have system and equipment problems that may result in schedule slips. If the schedule is sufficiently critical, make contingency plans for backup systems.

In addition to unscheduled and annoying downtime, you should track sick leave and other time lost to training and similar activities. Although you cannot control for sick leave, you need to estimate the impact sick leave, especially extensive sick leave, may have on the progress of the project. If a team member loses a lot of time, how will the schedule be maintained? Once the team member returns to work, you should discuss plans to get back on track with the interim schedule. If some team members have taken

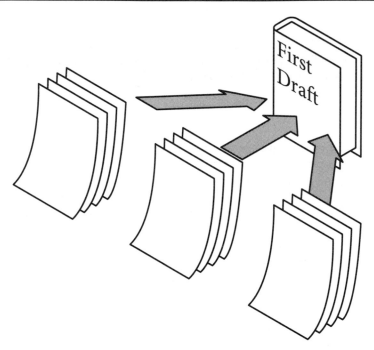

Figure 17.6   Interim drafts become the first-draft milestone.

extensive time off, they may need help to recover lost time. In addition, team members who have been sick may lack the energy to put in extra time. Explore the possibility of bringing in temporary help or enlisting the aid of other team members in the crisis.

Downtime, sick leave, interminable departmental meetings, personal time, unscheduled short projects—all these interruptions can have a negative effect on your team's progress. In some teams, these activities can account for 50 percent of the total workweek. No wonder projects come in 100 percent over schedule. What is essential is always knowing the status of all the writing activities occurring in your team—you never know when a crisis will occur. Consider what you will do if your only experienced writer is hit by a car and cannot type for eight weeks right before beta release.

Guideline: Track interim progress carefully, ensuring that time used for extraneous activities does not interfere with your potential for meeting your schedule obligations.

Picking up the pace

If members of your team are sufficiently behind schedule and you cannot attribute the delays to any outside sources, you may have to rearrange assignments and call in emergency help. Sometimes, it is possible to increase the pace of writing by moving your best performers into areas that are behind. In one such case, we had to assign the strongest member of a team to work with a writer who was having real difficulty with a complex piece of information. In a few weeks, the senior writer was able to produce a detailed outline that the less experienced writer could use as a template.

A more drastic solution might be to switch assignments, giving the strongest writer the more difficult assignment and putting the weaker writer on an easier task. Or you may want to take part in some of the data gathering so that you can understand the subject matter and help the writer master the difficult sections. To provide help at this level, however, you must know who is having difficulty and why.

Most of your information about writers in trouble should come from the weekly progress reports. Not only will the writers be aware of problems and note them in their reports, but you may also become aware of schedule slips before the writer does because you are tracking interim schedules. Be sensitive to reports of difficult interactions with SMEs or reports from the developmental editor. Early signs of problems may first emerge as writers complain about a lack of cooperation from the experts. Other signs of impending problems may be noticed by the editors who are concerned with the writers' interim drafts. If you are reviewing drafts yourself, even if only by spot-checking, you may become aware of problems more quickly than if you wait to read about them in progress reports.

Guideline: Find ways to increase the pace on a project so that the team gets back on track.

Supporting your team members

The most difficult situations occur when you get complaints from the subject-matter experts or other members of the development team. When outsiders complain about a writer's progress or apparent lack of understanding, you must take immediate steps to control the damage. You do not want your writers to lose credibility. Investigate the problem immediately. However, do not assume that the writer is at fault. The SME may be especially difficult to work with, or the development team may be hostile to the contributions of an assertive writer. Nor should you always assume that others are always responsible for problems. Find out as much about what happened as possible. If the writer is indeed having comprehension or communication problems, work closely with the writer to find solutions to the problems and to repair the damage that may have been done.

The worst action you can take is to abandon the writer. Not only will you lose credibility among your team members, but you will eventually lose credibility with the development team. If the writer has been following all the rules of the life-cycle process and following your instructions, you have an obligation to maintain your support. If you always give in to the demands of the development team, you will lose the support of your own team.

If your job is to support your team with the rest of your organization, you need to know enough about what they are doing to provide the required support. If anyone questions the actions of your team members, you must know enough about what they are doing and have enough confidence in their work to support them fully.

Guideline: When the going gets tough, support your team outside your organization. Solve your problems inside your organization.

Reporting project progress

As the interim drafts continue to be produced during the early stages of Phase 3, your job is to track whether or not progress is being made and the schedule is under control. Your information comes from your own assessment and the weekly reports of your team members. The data from the weekly time sheets is transferred to the weekly reporting spreadsheet, where you can compare actual hours expended with estimated hours. The qualitative assessments of progress, including the percent complete, become part of your regular project progress reports.

In Figure 17.7, the sample progress report shows that the project is on track even though the team got a later start than they had hoped. The Information Plan and Content Specifications have been delivered following revisions. The first draft of the training plan is in the hands of the reviewers, and a number of chapters are in the interim-draft stages. Note that the chapters are reviewed internally in the publications group before they are sent to outside reviewers. In this way, the project manager ensures that they meet internal standards first.

Progress reports of this type keep the larger development team informed about the activities being pursued by the publications team. Far-flung members of the team, including an overseas group in this example, maintain contact with the publications part of the project. When some members of the team are confused about publications plans, the project manager makes sure that their confusion is dispelled by better information. Note that the project manager is using the Content Specifications to further inform Rene about the division of information.

In addition to distributing progress reports to those outside your organization, you should distribute the reports to your team members so that they are aware of your assessment of their progress, your plans for the next project interval, and your concerns about problems that have surfaced and need to be solved. If your team members know what you are thinking, they will be better able to respond to and support your plan.

All this reporting in addition to the documents created in the planning phases and those created weekly by the team members may make you feel as if you are about to be buried in a sea of white paper. It can indeed become that if you let the reporting become routine and uninteresting to you, your management, and your team members. As you become more practiced as a project manager, you should begin to recognize that the key documents of the publications-development life cycle, among them your

Progress Report for
ATF
April 2

Progress (3/1 – 3/31)

- Delivered final versions of the Information Plan and Content Specifications for the user's and system administrator's guides. Dave will be sending these plans to Rene in Ukraine to clarify our plans to Lata. There appears to be some confusion about exactly what a system administrator's guide is — Rene keeps asking for separate user's guides for each audience; we suspect that she doesn't realize that the system administrator's guide is the "user's guide" for a system administrator. So we hope to clarify the contents of the books by showing her the Content Specifications.
- Delivered preliminary training plan. Although training is not due until September, Lata wants to ensure that we have the right concepts for training. Therefore, we have developed this training plan outlining the materials and methods we are using. Dave is currently reviewing this before sending to Rene.
- Drafted several chapters in the system administrator's and user's guides. They are in various stages of review, either inhouse with us or with Dave.

Plans (4/01 – 4/30)

- Continue drafting system administrator's and user's guides. All chapters should be complete by April 19 for integration testing.
- Write online help as corresponding chapters are completed and approved.

Other issues

- Although off to a late start, I think we have everything under control. We are still running under our projections, but I expect that we'll catch up some this month with the PASS team working on ATF. However, I don't expect that we'll go over our projections despite this temporary staffing increase.

Hours Tracking

Projected hours for ATF project (based on final Information Plan)		
Project mgt/editing	304.00 hrs	
Writing	1,373.00 hrs	
Total projected hours for ATF project		1,677.00
Hours through 2/28		170.00
Hours for 3/1 through 3/31		
Project mgt/editing	31.50 hrs	
Writing	310.75 hrs	
Total hours for 3/1 through 3/31		342.25
Hours remaining		
Project mgt/editing	225 hrs	
Writing	939.75 hrs	
Total remaining hours for ATF project		1,164.75

Figure 17.7   Sample interim progress report

periodic progress reports, represent your opportunity to focus your thoughts and maintain control of the project. The progress report functions as a status report of the project, a list of activities completed and those remaining, and a database for future reporting and analysis.

Periodic progress reports provide you with a checklist for your activities, a method of stopping to look at exactly what has occurred and, in particular, to look at what has changed. If you are too busy fighting fires and attending to detail to analyze and report your progress, then you are neglecting your responsibilities as project manager.

 Guideline: Analyze and report project progress thoroughly and regularly to ensure that you are paying sufficient attention to the relationship between everyday details and overall project success.

Adding to the Project Management Notebook

The tracking spreadsheets and progress reports that you develop should all be added to the Project Management Notebook. Your project information is part of the record that you establish during the course of the project. The information includes

- Meeting minutes
- Telephone logs
- Memos and electronic mail
- Weekly and monthly tracking spreadsheets
- Any other information that may help you track the project

It is especially important to record all decisions you make about handling changes in the project. Changes in scope, resources, schedule, and quality are all significant to the project's success and will impact your final analysis of the project's success and productivity.

CHAPTER
18

Managing Change

Slips in schedule occur not because of disastrous calamities but because of small deviations from the original plan. A writer is sick for two days, a programmer gets behind on coding, a printer breaks down. Each of these small events is the stuff of change. Schedules slip one day at a time. Before we know it, the April 1 deadlines cannot be achieved before May 15.

In Chapter 17, I suggested that the most significant part of managing and controlling a project is to set many small, achievable, measurable interim milestones. These small milestones eventually roll up into major milestones, represented in the publications-development life cycle by publications drafts. We call them first and second drafts or alpha and beta drafts—the names make no difference in the nature of the event.

In this chapter, you learn both how to track a project in detail during Phase 3 and how to estimate the effects of changes to the product scope or efficiency. You also learn how to respond effectively to changes that will affect the publications schedule by calculating

- The level of resources required to maintain schedule
- The amount of schedule slip required to maintain resources and quality
- The amount that will have to be trimmed from the publications if schedule and resources cannot change

Tracking changes to the product and schedule

As project manager, your job, as we have described it, is to track all changes, no matter how seemingly small and inconsequential, to the project schedule. To do so accurately, you may want to prepare a tracking chart in which you record the date that every interim draft item is expected to be complete. The granularity of your choice of interim draft items depends upon your need to keep the details under control. The more complex the project, as defined by the changes that occur in the development of the product or process, the difficulty of obtaining information, and the difficulty of the information itself, the more need you will find for smaller divisions for tracking purposes.

Section	Respon-sibility	Initial interim draft complete	Develop-mental edit complete	Preliminary copy edit complete	Interim review complete	Revisions made	First draft text complete	First draft graphics complete
Chap 1	Sam	11/5	11/8	11/9	11/16	11/19	11/25	11/25
Chap 2	Sam	11/8	11/12	11/13	11/20	11/23	11/29	11/29

Figure 18.1   Schedule tracking table with estimated dates

Developing a tracking table

Figure 18.1 shows a brief example of a tracking table that has been divided by chapters in a book. The tracking table may be divided into subchapters or even into larger sections if applicable to the needs of a project. The dates on the sample schedule are the dates that the project manager, the writer, the SMEs who are responsible for the interim review, the editors, and the graphic illustrators all agreed upon at the beginning of Phase 3. This particular example takes the project manager all the way to the first-draft deliverable. Other events to track may be added, depending on the needs of the project.

As the work progresses, the project manager adds the actual dates that events occurred to the estimated dates. Figure 18.2 shows that the writing and editing for a project is well on track, but the SMEs are not getting their reviews done on schedule.

Note that the example shows that both interim reviews were completed on the same day, 6 days and 2 days past the schedule. These dates may point to a timing problem. The reviewers may have had other deadlines to meet in mid-November, may have been unaware of the need to adhere to pre-established deadlines for publications reviews, or may have been unaware that the deadlines existed at all. No matter what the situation that caused the problem, as project manager, you now have a problem to analyze.

Obviously, your team members have worked hard to ameliorate the effects of the late reviews. Rather than being 6 and 2 days behind schedule, they are 2 and 4 days behind for the two chapters. However, meeting these scheduled deadlines may have

Section	Respon-sibility	Initial interim draft complete	Develop-mental edit complete	Preliminary copy edit complete	Interim review complete	Revisions made	First draft text copyedited and corrected	First draft graphics complete
Chap 1	Sam	11/5	11/8	11/9	11/16	11/19	11/25	11/25
		11/5	**11/8**	**11/9**	**11/22**	**11/24**	**11/27**	**11/27**
Chap 2	Sam	11/8	11/12	11/13	11/20	11/23	11/29	11/29
		11/8	**11/12**	**11/13**	**11/22**	**11/26**	**12/3**	**12/3**

Figure 18.2   Schedule tracking table with estimated and actual dates (in boldface)

caused other parts of the project to fall behind. It's up to you to understand the entire range of interim deadlines and to evaluate the effects.

 Guideline: Develop a mechanism like a tracking table to account for all the small deadlines in your project.

Analyzing the effects of small slips

Many project managers and team members tend to avoid analyzing the effects of numerous small slips. They are optimistic that they will be able to catch up. In fact, they may be able to catch up if the changes are small enough. An enterprising team, alert to the delays occurring on the reviews for the first two chapters, will have moved up work on later sections. An enterprising team knows the importance of "hustle," that quality of working hard at all times so that one is prepared to meet emergencies. Using hustle means avoiding opportunities to procrastinate.

A procrastinating team is one that does not display hustle in a situation like the one described in Figure 18.2. A delay caused by external reviewers is viewed as an opportunity to slack off, to purposively avoid looking for more work to be done. These small slack times, especially when they can be easily blamed on someone else, are the sources of disaster.

Of course, it is very difficult for individuals to maintain the discipline to work hard when other members of the development organization are behind. We all look forward to small respites in the daily grind. However, we have project managers exactly because of the normal tendencies of team members to look for opportunities to delay. Your responsibility is to remind everyone of the looming deadlines ahead and suggest that it is far smarter to work steadily today rather than put in a lot of overtime later. Regular meetings with your team provide motivation to finish small sections on time because the deadlines are looming.

 Guideline: Maintain a steady pace of work, in line with the detailed interim schedule created, to avoid schedule catastrophes at the end of the project.

Responding to schedule slips

What if you discover that the small schedule slips are indeed adding up to a large schedule slip later in the project? You first need to assess the effect of the slip and decide exactly how much it will be. The best way to make this assessment is to use the past as your guide. For example, Figure 18.2 shows a small schedule slip in the first

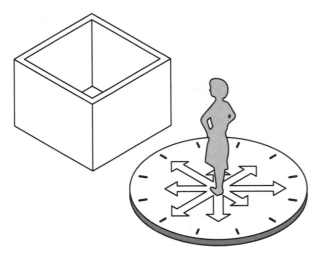

Figure 18.3 Schedule continues to slip as the project develops

two chapters of a book, a slip of between two and four days. If no other changes have occurred in the overall schedule, then you may want to predict an overall slip in the first-draft milestone of 2 to 4 days.

In many cases, such a slip of less than a week will be in line with other schedule changes occurring within the work of the entire development team. The late reviews that we saw in Figure 18.2 are often the product of changes occurring within the development team's own micro-schedule of the project. Investigate that possibility with the development project manager. The publications project may continue to be moving in line with the larger project schedule as illustrated in Figure 18.3. Unfortunately, we often find that the project managers involved in larger development efforts seem unwilling to admit to the existence of small schedule slips and insist that the original deadlines must be achieved.

At such a juncture, you need to take your sense of organizational politics into account. If no one ever announces schedule slips until after they have occurred, then continue to watch your schedule carefully and document the changes in your periodic progress reports. If others in the organization do assess the changes to their schedules, sit down with them and discuss possible changes to the relationship between publications and product. It may be possible for writers to work in areas that skirt major problems occurring in the product-development process. Your team may be able to move ahead on other areas of the publications development to alleviate the pressure on the technical team members. Your team may also be able to do more to help the technical team provide information in a time-effective manner.

Many solutions are no doubt available as long as everyone is willing to cooperate. If no one appears to be willing to cooperate and would rather insist that all is well, you may have to be content with documenting the schedule slips in your progress reports. However, you may find it more satisfying to find the schedule work-around on your own. The danger, of course, is that working around problems in the schedule will increase the total project time for the publications project. In the face of many false claims, the increase in project time may be inevitable.

Guideline: Find creative and cooperative ways for the publications team to respond to schedule changes.

Understanding product changes

In the examples discussed above, the changes to the project schedule have occurred because the planned work is taking more time than originally estimated. Many development efforts experience changes of this sort. A hardware component does not work as expected; software modules that passed module tests suddenly sprout problems when they are integrated with other modules in early system tests; bugs that everyone thought could be ferreted out in a few days take weeks of frustrating effort. Nothing is being added or taken away from the project. It is all just taking longer than anyone thought.

Schedule slips based on increased technical difficulty are common enough in development efforts. Some of them are, of course, due to poor project management and coercive estimating. But even more common in development projects are changes to the original project requirements and specifications (Figure 18.4). Requirements are always tricky to get right. We work hard to understand user needs and desires during the design phases, but we understand them only incompletely. We begin a design effort, only to discover that needs are different than we had originally thought. We begin to implement a design, only to find that technical limitations and technical opportunities reveal design options that we had not considered before.

Development organizations, including publications, generally recognize the inevitability of change to the original design of a project. In fact, we have institutionalized the idea of change through a design process that includes the development and testing of early prototypes. The difference between organizations that handle change

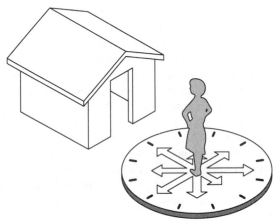

Figure 18.4 Schedule changes as the product changes

successfully and those that allow change to dominate and control them is found in their response to and management of the change process.

Controlling change

In an organization that is dedicated to controlling change, all changes to requirements and specifications are handled in an orderly manner. Each proposed change is recorded by some formal mechanism, and all affected parties are asked to respond to the proposal. Publications, as well as development, testing, manufacturing, training, fulfillment, and others, are asked to evaluate the impact of the change request on their operations and their ability to deliver in keeping with the existing schedule deadlines. Either the deadlines are extended to accommodate the change, resources are increased to make the change possible within the original schedule, or the proposed change is rejected.

The intent of a managed change process is to ensure that the full impact of any proposed change is well understood throughout the organization, and all players agree to assume responsibility for accommodating the change. A managed change process is based on the assumption that all changes, including small and seemingly insignificant changes, may affect the design of a product or process in fundamental ways. The purpose of managed change is to preserve the integrity of the original design and to ensure that changes are reflected in all development documentation, including user publications.

A managed change process is not intended to stifle creativity nor to continue designing a product that fails to meet the needs of its proposed users. As we proceed into the depths of a development project, we hope to learn more about our users' needs and better understand how to meet them effectively. However, the original design of project requirements was based not only on the organization's understanding of the needs of its customers, but also on a calculation of how much time and money could be expended to meet these needs.

Changes always have the inherent danger of substituting a desire to include everything anyone claims they want and to achieve perfection for the requirement to keep costs and schedules under control. A tension always develops between those who want to do more and do it better and those who want to keep costs under control. The tension is exacerbated by the tendency for most creative people to appreciate others' desire to do outstanding work. That human creative tendency ends up pitting the cost and schedule managers against those who espouse beauty and truth.

A formal and well-managed change process helps to reduce the tension and reduce the conflict. To be successful, however, project managers need to devote sufficient time to the initial planning phases so that requirements are better understood before design begins and design is thoroughly worked out before implementation begins. Project managers also need to devote time and effort to controlling and tracking the changes.

One manager of a programming project described to me how she handles the creative impulses of her programming staff. Every idea for a change that will affect any other part of the project must be evaluated and approved before it is implemented. If a programmer makes a change that has not been approved, she insists that it be removed before it can be considered.

Guideline: Help institute a formal change-control process.

Responding to a controlled change process

Many publications-project managers are surprised when they learn that some organizations work in such an orderly fashion. Publications-project managers who work in an environment where changes are controlled are amazed that other organizations fail to understand the advantages to the entire development process. They cannot imagine how someone can work in an unmanaged environment. They are noting the fundamental differences between Level 1, 2, and 3 organizations. Level 1 organizations ignore process altogether and Level 2 organizations institute process but abandon it when things changes, whereas Level 3 organizations manage and control change.

In a Level 3 organization, when a change request is circulated, the publications-project manager needs to evaluate the impact of the change on the publications cost and schedule. The impact on publications is added to the overall impact assessment when a final decision is made to approve or not to approve the change.

Guideline: Respond to formal engineering change requests by assessing the impact of the change on the publications.

Monitoring project changes in an unmanaged environment

Unfortunately, a large percentage of publications-project managers do not work in organizations that have a managed change process, or the publications activities are not included as part of change control. The second situation is easier to correct. It means convincing those responsible for tracking changes and assessing the impact of change to include publications in the process. Not that the convincing process is necessarily simple. In many organizations, schedules and deadlines are managed, except for publications. No one in the larger development organization appears to appreciate the time and energy needed to change publications. While other groups involved in development are credited with being able to evaluate the effects of changes on their budgets and schedules, publications' pleas for more time and budget are ignored. Publications organizations are expected to adhere to budgets and schedules that change only in response to other development needs.

Managers may ignore the effect of schedule changes on publications because they do not understand how the publications process works. This lack of understanding can be remedied by developing and publicizing a well-managed publications-development process. The effect on publications may also be ignored because the publications organization lacks credibility. A lack of credibility is more difficult to remedy because it is usually of long standing. To change a credibility problem requires a forceful and determined leader in publications who has the support of his or her own senior management. The place to begin the attack on a credibility problem is the development of a managed process accompanied by the gradual education of the rest of the development organization. This educational process will work, but if development management changes, it may have to begin again.

Publications-project managers often work within organizations that lack a change control process. In this case, you need to monitor changes occurring without the aid of a formal process. Your network and your team members become key elements in monitoring and controlling change. Your informal network in the development organization will help you learn of changes that affect the publications process. By "hanging around" the developers, you may be able to discover what they are changing in enough time to respond.

Despite your best network, you may not have access to all the diverse parts of a large project. For that reason, you need to enlist the support and assistance of your team members. They are more likely to be in frequent contact with developers than you are. They need to be very attentive to news of changes and to report those changes immediately to you. Too often, publications team members learn about changes and agree to implement changes in the publications without informing their project manager and fellow team members.

The danger involved in having your team members respond personally to changes is a loss of project control to the detriment of the schedule, the budget, and the quality of your product. Some team members appear not to understand or appreciate the ripple effect of small changes on the success of the entire project. A few pages added here and there, late changes that fail to be reviewed by editors, all of the small effects of change can easily mushroom into large effects for the entire team. Cheryl Herfurth, manager of a publications group in a network development firm, requires approval by the project manager of any change request that will take more than one-half hour of writer time to handle.

66 Mike told me that he was changing the installation screen because he wanted to add a new function he thought that the users might want," explained Ellie. "I went ahead and changed the installation chapter to add the function. It only took me a couple of days to rewrite the procedures."

"I know you meant to be helpful and accommodate Mike's request," said Eleanor, "but you added 15 pages to Chapter 7, a 100-percent increase. You're also about 4 days behind schedule on Chapter 8."

"But I'll catch up. I can work this weekend," answered Ellie. "And we only added eight pages."

"You've been working a lot of weekends lately," replied Eleanor. "Aren't you starting to get tired? That's going to affect your work soon if it hasn't already. But more importantly, we need to think about the impact of the change on the rest of the project.

"You need to give Chapter 7 back to Harriet. I know she edited it once already, but we need to consider the new information you've added in light of the entire design. Then, it needs to go to Bruce for copyediting and to the reviewers who already have the earlier version. In fact, I'm going to have to put a memo together to explain why we're sending them a late change.

"Then, I'll need to revise the page counts for the translators. Remember that they based their estimates on the original page counts we gave them. Finally, I want to find out if the additional pages will fit into the binders we've ordered. Your book was almost at the maximum count for a 2-inch binder already."

"Wow! I didn't realize so much might have to change because I added a few pages," said Ellie. "I'm really sorry I've caused so many problems. I guess I should have asked you how to handle the change before I went ahead and just did it."

"Well, there's always a first time," replied Eleanor. "Now you know why I'm so fanatical about change control. I know you'll be more careful in the future. By the way, do you know if Mike's manager knows about the change to the installation screens? Is there any chance that he's going to change them back again?"

"I don't know, but I better find out," said Ellie. "Mike usually doesn't tell his boss what he's doing.

Eleanor's conversation with Ellie is a good example of the educating you will have to do with your team members, especially new ones. Even experienced people will get trapped into making changes to the publications project. I once had a project manager agree to take on the responsibility for tracking all graphic changes without evaluating the effects. This change in responsibility of the publications group resulted in a 30-percent increase in the total project hours charged against publications. The manager who had convinced the project manager to agree was also the first to complain about publication cost overruns.

Guideline: *Be alert to unmanaged changes that enter the project by the individual actions of your team members.*

Instituting change-control procedures

Even if the rest of your organization seems unable and unwilling to manage and control changes to the project, you have an opportunity to institute a simple change-control procedure for the publications team. I recommend creating a change-request form and widely disseminating the form among the development team. People outside your team may choose to ignore the change-request form, but ensure that your team members do not. Every publications team member should have a stack of

Publications Change Request

Project name_____

Initiated by_____ Date_____

Description of the change_____
_____
_____
_____

Publications affected_____
_____
_____
_____

Number of affected pages_____
_____
_____

Number of affected illustrations_____
_____
_____

Estimate of page-count increases/decreases_____
_____
_____

Estimate of illustration increases_____
_____

Start date_____ Completion date_____

Effect on resources
  people resources_____
  schedule_____
  localization and translation_____
  manufacturing_____

Approval signatures
  publications project manager_____ date_____
  development manager_____ date_____
  marketing manager_____ date_____
  other_____ date_____

Figure 18.5 Sample publications change-request form supplied by Cheryl Herfurth

change-request forms or an online version to print from. Whenever anyone asks them to make a change that is outside the normal review process, they must complete the change-request form and bring it to you for review. They should also explain to the individuals asking for the change that publications has a change-control process. They will have to get the change request signed off by their manager before they can respond.

In Figure 18.5 I have included a sample change-request form. Be sure that your team members know how to complete one. Once you have reviewed the request and evaluated the impact, meet with the team member, the individual initiating the request, and that individual's manager so that everyone understands the impact of the change. Even if you are unable to influence the overall process of change in your organization, you can affect the process used in your own organization. Using a publications change-request form will make control easier.

The change-request procedure described here is primarily for use during Phase 3 of the publications-development life cycle, although it may be useful during Phase 2. However, during Phase 3 changes to the project specifications, redefinitions of audience, and changes in the implementation of the specifications, may greatly affect the publications schedule and resource allocations. The earlier you are in the publications life cycle, the easier and less expensive it is for you to respond to changes.

The change-request procedure is also best used during interim-draft development rather than at the major project milestones of the first and second drafts. Changes made during the draft reviews are appropriately handled as part of the review and revision process.

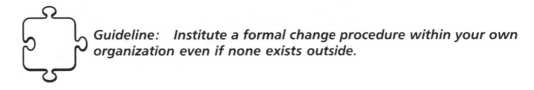

Guideline: Institute a formal change procedure within your own organization even if none exists outside.

Reporting project changes that affect publications

You must carefully report all changes that affect the budget, schedule, and resource allocations in your periodic progress reports. For many projects, monthly and bi-monthly progress reports from the publications project manager to the department manager and various development managers are sufficient. However, for projects that are experiencing a high degree of change, you may need to institute more frequent, possibly weekly, progress reports to ensure that you are communicating your concerns and needs. The example in Figure 18.6 shows how one project manager is accounting for project changes.

Note that the project manager has documented the changes that are affecting the publications and has estimated that, for the time being, the overall estimate of the scope of the projects will not change. She leaves open the possibility, however, that events prior to the mid-April report will require that she once again evaluate the impact of the changes to project scope.

Progress Report for
PASS
April 2

Progress (3/1 – 3/31)

- Completed and delivered first phase documentation to Germany for integration and acceptance testing. These drafts are clearly marked as drafts, since many chapters are incomplete (since they also cover later phase functionality) and they are in the writer's, as opposed to the production, template.

- Completed first phase online documentation and delivered to Denver technical staff for installation and to "piggyback" on a bug fix tape for Germany. Online took much longer than expected (102.5 hours so far) due to many experiments with the formatting to get it to convert back and forth between the A and B platforms. In addition, it was not a simple edit as we ended up planning for; the programmers' source material was so inconsistent and minimal that we ended up starting from scratch. Hopefully, things will improve since we provided a template to the programmers outlining the information to provide for their future screens.

- Drafted first phase training materials. We will be finishing these materials for final delivery by April 6. Dan is very happy with the materials; he has never had such detailed materials before. Since it now appears that he will not be the actual person to do the training, it's a good thing the materials are so clear.

- Attended several meetings about the business screens. It was readily apparent that most of the information was still in a great state of flux. This may have been the final straw that brought about the design schedule slip for April.

Plans (4/01 – 4/31)

- Complete first phase training materials by April 6.
- Work on ATF until PASS design phase is complete in Germany. This should take most of the month — the review meeting for the design is not scheduled until April 26 – 28.

Other issues

- We are well over our projections for first-phase budget. I have identified the following reasons for this overage:
  - I had little control over the hours Donna was putting into the project. In the two months she worked on the project, she produced only four table descriptions. Although I informed her of the hours I had allotted for the work, she kept putting me off. She claimed that WNET was taking most of her time, which was true, but still the number of hours she did spend on PASS far exceeded my projections. This will no longer be a problem since Donna is no longer on the project.
  - We spent a lot of time with template issues. Files were first put in the two-column format. Then, when it became obvious that our technical people didn't like the style, we switched to DRS until the new template was resolved. And since switching back to DRS, we've received three updates to the template and know that more are coming. I've given the writers instructions not to convert any files to a new template until either we get word that it's the final template or until right before our next delivery to avoid spending excess time in this area.

Figure 18.6 Reporting project changes in periodic progress reports

- The hours for first phase include the hours spent on the planning stages, writing the Information Plan. However, when I divided the hours into projections for each phase, I did not first subtract that planning time. Therefore, all planning was done up front, but scheduled in phases. This time will definitely be made up in the later phases since the Information Plan is complete.

- As I mentioned earlier in this report, online help took much longer than expected due to formatting issues and the quality of the programmers' initial attempts at writing the help. I expect the time required to improve since the programmers now have both examples and a template for their future writing. And, we've ironed out all the formatting issues and can therefore deliver the files in the right format from now on.

- Information has been changing continually. Typically, I would assign an information cut-off date after which no new information can be included until the next draft. However, the phased delivery means that each phase must be as technically correct as possible since it will be used for acceptance testing. Therefore, we've had to make every last change, up to the last possible minute. For example, we learned only the day before first phase delivery that the ST Report had once again been removed from the product. This report has been on-again, off-again for several weeks. The information changes have significantly added to time spent as we continuously update the chapters and send them through additional review cycles. Completing the design phase in April should help stabilize the information.

- Screen dumps have really slowed us down. We've had to retake them due to information changes, due to the RX bug, and due to the fact that the original database we were using contained a lot of "bogus" data. And we suspect that the screens will all have to be retaken again before we're through. Typically, I would not take screen dumps this early in the project, but again the phased delivery requires it. Ideally, we should not tie up writer time to complete these screens, but George's illness and other time demands required it. In addition, I'm not sure it would help for George to be doing this, since the screens are changing. To help address the extra time, we will not take screen dumps until the last possible minute.

- There was some confusion about first-phase deliverables. For example, we did online documentation for TT tables, rather than TS tables. This was not wasted time as we can use this information in second phase; however, it does show up as overage in the first phase.

- Some hours shown in first phase were spent on second-phase activities. For example, initially we thought Starting and Stopping the Examples would be in the first phase. A draft was written for my review before we discovered it was a second phase deliverable. Again, these hours will be made up in second phase since it doesn't need to be done again.

Unfortunately, I do not project that most of the time will be made up in later phases. However, we do expect that ATF will go more smoothly—it is more stable and we can draw on the experiences from PASS. Therefore, I think we can still fall within the projected 4000 hours for the two projects; it's a little early to say for sure. I will generate another report on the hours spent on the two projects in mid-April after the ATF SOM deadlines have been met.

Figure 18.6 (Continued)

Guideline: Carefully note all changes that affect the publications project in your regular progress reports.

Managing changes to the publications project

The process of monitoring changes that occur during the course of a publications project constitutes only half of your responsibility for managing change. Once you are aware of a change, either through your network, informal reports from your team members, or through a formal change process, you must next evaluate the impact of the change on the publications project.

Chapter 12 describes in detail how to evaluate changes that occur at the Content-Specification milestone. You need to use the same type of evaluation process as changes occur during Phase 3. Your starting point remains your previous Project Plan, hopefully one that was updated after Phase 2. Once again, you must review the percent complete of your project against changes that may affect project scope and risk factors (dependencies).

You may discover, as Eleanor did in the scenario above, that a change in the installation screens for the product has resulted in a 8-page addition to one of the publications. To evaluate the cost of an addition, you must take into account two significant factors:

- The change to the size of the original publication
- Possible changes in the project dependencies

Calculating the effect of an increase in publication size

Many changes that occur to the product or process you are documenting result in additions to the publications (Figure 18.7). Changes to software or hardware, additional detail in a process, and more thorough explanations or examples tend to increase the size of technical publications. The following steps point to the issues you must consider in evaluating the effect of increases.

1. Compare the new size of the publication with the original size.

   Perhaps the best way to think about additions is in terms of percentages. If the original estimate of size had been 150 pages, then a 15-page addition would represent a 10-percent increase.

2. Review the original hours per page estimate.

   If the original hours per page estimate was 6.63, as it was for the Fateful User's Guide, consider carefully the history of the project through the first two phases and into Phase 3. If the writer has been on schedule and has not been working overtime, the estimated

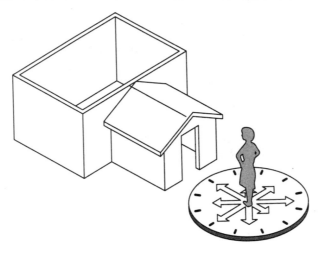

Figure 18.7 Changes to the product affect the publications life cycle

hours per page for the publication will likely remain in effect. If the writer is behind schedule on parts of the project other than the addition or has been putting in excessive overtime, you are most likely exceeding the hours per page estimate. Consult the actual hours on your weekly and monthly tracking spreadsheets to calculate the new hours per page.

3. If you find that the hours per page has increased, evaluate why the increase has occurred.

   Hours per page will increase on a project in response to changes in the project dependencies. The product specifications may be changing more than originally anticipated, SMEs may be less available than originally agreed upon, the writer may be less experienced in the technology or the writing process than you had calculated.

4. Re-evaluate the project dependencies and recalculate the hours per page using the dependencies calculator.

   If your data converges, the new dependencies calculation should predict an hours per page that is similar to the actual hours per page you are experiencing on the project. If the hours per page predicted by the dependencies calculation is not the same as the actual hours per page you believe you are experiencing on the project, you may not be tracking percent complete carefully enough or you may be evaluating the dependencies incorrectly. Check all of your data and decisions again. If the results still do not converge, use the actual hours as a guideline to re-estimate the project. However, watch the results carefully over the next few weeks. You may find that your dependencies calculation is really not as far off as it appeared.

5. Use either the original (if it is still accurate) or the new hours per page to calculate the number of hours needed to handle the additional pages.

If your new dependencies calculation indicates that hours per page have increased to 7.0 from 6.63, multiply the 15 pages by 7. This means that, had the 15 pages been in the original Content Specification, you would have added 105 hours to the project plan.

6. Take into account those phases of the project already completed.

If an addition to the total pages occurs during Phase 3 of the project, consider that you have already completed Phases 1 and 2 for the original 150 pages. If you have spent about one-third of your total project hours on the planning phases, as recommended, then you have already accounted for approximately one-third of the 7 hours per page. For the 15-page addition, that suggests that one-third of 105 hours, or 35 hours, have already been expended. That leaves 70 hours of work left to be done on the addition. That work includes writing, editing, graphics, translation preparation, production, and others.

Be careful at this point. If the addition is simple, isolated to a single new section with no impact on the rest of the publication or on other publications in the library, then the 70-hour estimate may be reasonable. However, you, the writer, and the editors may have to reconsider the overall organization of the publication and even the overall organization of the library in response to the seemingly small change. In this case, you may want to allocate the entire 105 hours to the addition, or some number of hours between 70 and 105.

7. Evaluate the effect of the additional hours on schedule and resources.

A number of strategies are available to you in deciding how the additional work will be accommodated within your project plan:

- An increase in hours close to the end of the project life cycle will almost certainly extend the deadline on the project or necessitate overtime to maintain the original schedule. Be careful. Overtime may be accumulating to a totally impossible and unacceptable level.

- A small increase in hours earlier in the project's life cycle may be accommodated by an increase in hustle. That means that the entire team will have to pick up the pace of their activities to absorb the change without changing the overall schedule. Be careful again. A change in pace almost certainly will have an effect on the quality of the project. A change in pace means completing project activities in less time than originally projected. That means that all of those activities will be done less carefully.

- A large increase in hours cannot be accommodated by small increases in hours or an increase in hustle. You will have to decide if and how you need to add resources to the project to accommodate the extra work. Be careful here, too. As I discuss later in this chapter, adding people to a project in midstream is problematic. Usually additions of people indicate that a project is out of control.

- A large increase in hours may have to be accommodated by extensions of the schedule. During Phase 3, schedule changes may occur without substantial changes to the primary milestones. If a function has been added by engineering, you may ask the engineering team to shorten their review time or make people more easily available to compensate for the increase in size by changing the "SME availability" dependency.

- If the schedule cannot be extended and you have no additional resources available, you may have to consider how to make cuts in the original Content Specification to accommodate the additional information. Perhaps all other sections could be shortened in some logical way so that the new function will not change the overall project size. Be aware that changes of this sort will themselves add to the number of hours you need to complete the project. A re-evaluation of scope takes time.

- If you cannot cut the scope of the overall project to accommodate the additions, you will have to consider cutting the quality of the final product. Since quality is produced by the thorough and careful activities of the entire team throughout the project, then decreasing the time available for those activities by stretching them over more product will decrease quality.

As you proceed through this evaluation and decision-making process, consider that one small change occurring today may be an indicator of more changes coming. A re-estimate is always an opportunity to reconsider the project as a whole.

 Guideline: Systematically estimate the effect of a product change on publications size and on the difficulty of performing the publications work.

Evaluating the impact on size of an engineering change

In evaluating the effect of an additional function on the publications library, you may not have as simple a situation as Eleanor faced. The additional function in the example affected only a single section. Product or process changes are more likely to affect sections of text and graphics throughout a publication library. In many cases, you will have to begin with the change itself and estimate the number of pages affected.

As soon as your team discovers that a change is planned or has already been made to the product, ask team members to investigate whether the change will affect their individual parts of the project. Seemingly innocuous changes to hardware and software may have a great impact on publications. In one instance, we found that a change in a naming convention required that all software screens had to be re-inserted into the documentation, and all references to the screens had to be revised in the text. What amounted to the revision of a few lines of code resulted in more than 100 extra hours of work for the publications team.

Be certain to take into account all aspects of the project in evaluating the effect of a change. Remember that small increases in publication size may have drastic consequences for the timeliness and cost of translation, the cost of printing and binding, and the cost of distribution. Changes to text may require changes in graphics. Changes in text will require additional review time and more time for developmental editing and copyediting. It is always best to take into account the full cost of the change. You should avoid making many small adjustments to a project. It is much more effective to make one large change to the schedule or resource level.

Guideline: Evaluate carefully the full effect of a product change on the publications.

Tracking revision cycles

As seemingly small changes begin to emerge during the implementation phase, be alert to the possibility that the number of revision cycles is increasing. I find that many technical experts ask writers to give them another opportunity to review a draft document after a change has occurred. These reviews occur in addition to the regular interim-draft and first-draft reviews. The request to review a new section of text seems reasonable, and writers are often eager to comply. The technical reviewers have made comments to a draft or added some information; they want to see how the writers have handled the changes.

Unfortunately, the request for additional reviews is not innocuous. Preparing a draft, even a quick, interim draft, takes project time. When sections are added or changed substantially, they need to be copyedited, possibly reviewed by the developmental editor, checked for formatting, and printed. All of these activities take time.

Alert your writers to the problems of adding review cycles to a project. Additional reviews do affect project dependencies, especially the reviews dependency. The point remains—track everything to ensure that the project dynamics are not changing. A project that generates additional review cycles will quickly fall behind. Even small changes produce dramatic effects to the percent complete.

Guideline: Guard against additional review cycles that decrease team efficiency and productivity.

Getting help in tracking change

If the task of monitoring changes to your publications project seems like a difficult and time-consuming process, you may be correct. While a project manager will be able to monitor change adequately on a small project, one involving about five or six writers, on larger projects you may not be able to keep up with all the management activities you need to accomplish plus track all the details.

For large projects, some organizations add a position called planner. The project planner is responsible for helping the team develop estimates, keep records of the estimates and actuals for previous projects, and assist the project manager in tracking the details of ongoing projects. One of the distinct advantages of a planner is independence. Without a major role in the projects, a planner remains objective, whereas the team members and the project manager have a vested interest in claiming project success.

If your organization has many complex projects and the projects tend to be large, long, and involve many writers, you may want to give someone the responsibility for tracking projects and reporting progress to the project managers.

 Guideline: Use a tracking specialist when projects become very large to assist the project manager in watching all the details.

Evaluating percent complete at the first-draft milestone

Chapter 12 presented the concept of percent complete and discussed the effects of change on the completeness of a project. The percent-complete calculation continues to be one of your most useful tools during Phase 3 (Figure 18.8). To evaluate percent complete, you must know exactly what you expected to have done on a project, not only at major milestones but at all the small milestones you have established in Phase 3.

Ask your team members to evaluate their percent complete in every weekly report. Look at each individual evaluation in terms of your own evaluation of progress. If the project is falling behind, be prepared to take action quickly. Do not wait too long. A project that is behind only a few days may offer opportunities for recovery. But a few days quickly become a few weeks or a month.

Although you should be evaluating percent complete weekly, if not daily, on a changing project, the most significant opportunity for evaluating percent complete will come at the first-draft milestone. This milestone represents a very significant point in the project, a point at which the publications project should be more than half done. The first-draft milestone is also a point at which you should have a very detailed statement of what should have been accomplished.

If you created your milestone schedule during Phase 2 to include a detailed definition of first draft, then you should be prepared to do a thorough evaluation of project status. Begin with your milestone definition and the number of hours you predicted to reach that milestone.

Look at an example of a first-draft milestone evaluation. Consider that you have a project plan in which you estimated that it would take 1,000 hours to complete a 200-page manual. At the end of the first-draft milestone, you predicted that the project would be 60-percent complete and you would have used 600 hours.

You defined the first-draft milestone in the following way. At first draft, you expected to have written and edited between 180 and 190 pages of text, have sketches of all the graphics and markers for all the software screens you will use as illustrations. Within the 180 pages, you expect to have holes in the information representing no more than 10 pages of text. The remaining 10 pages will be used for the index at

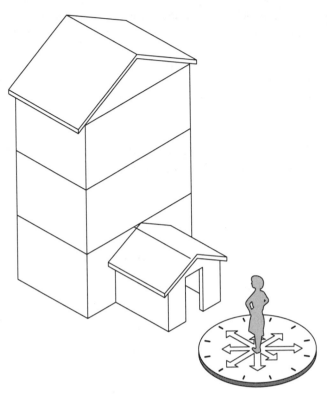

Figure 18.8 Evaluating the percent complete of a project

second draft. You are also expecting that no more than 10 percent of the text and graphics will change following the first-draft review.

As you prepare the first draft for review, you note that one section of about 8 pages has not yet been written because the information is not available. The holes in the text, represented by embedded questions, represent information that the writer was unable to obtain from any of the technical experts. Embedded questions may also represent information in conflict among several technical experts with no resolution in sight. By reviewing carefully the incomplete work and the embedded questions, you decide that approximately 10 percent of the existing text is unfinished. As a result, you estimate that approximately 15 percent of the first draft is incomplete in relationship to your first-draft definition.

To calculate how many additional hours it will take you to complete the first draft so that it is ready for review, consider the following:

- You originally expected to use 300 hours to complete the first draft, after you completed Phases 1 and 2 of the project.
- You are only 85-percent complete with the first draft but you have already used the full 300 hours.
- The hours you need to complete the entire first draft are unknown.
- However, you do know that 300 hours represents 85 percent complete.

▪ Set up your equation as follows:

85 percent × total first-draft hours = 300

total first-draft hours = 300/.85

total first-draft hours = 353

You need an additional 53 hours to complete the first draft according to your original definition. If you are using a 6-hour day for your average project day, your writer will need 9 working days to complete the first draft once the information is available. That means the first draft will be almost 2 weeks late for review, the writer will have to work 53 hours of overtime to complete the first draft on schedule, or you will have to find additional resources to help the original writer.

All percent-complete calculations work in exactly the same way. The most difficult part of the calculation is deciding exactly how complete or incomplete your project is at a particular point in time. Certainly, there is a degree of subjectivity in a percent-complete calculation based on estimating how much work is left to be done. But this degree of subjectivity is much less subjective than the ordinary optimistic estimates that many writers and project managers make. You are nearly 2 weeks behind on your project with no way to make up the schedule without additional resources or considerable overtime work.

In many instances, we take a project into first-draft review believing that we have met the first-draft milestone. At the review the entire development team is present and looking at the publications project as a whole. Frequently, the team begins to realize, perhaps for the first time, that the development project has taken a new direction and the once complete draft is now incomplete. Once again, you need to make an assessment in relationship to the first draft, even though the new work or changes will be included in second draft. It is the first draft that is no longer 100-percent complete. Fixing the first draft will add hours to the second-draft milestone, which means the second draft is likely to be behind schedule.

Be alert to the casual optimism of creative people. Your writers are likely to claim that they can catch up, and to a certain extent they may be able to hustle and compress the schedule. It is smarter to estimate based, not on worst case, but on a realistic case. A realistic case means that the future will be influenced by the past. That 2 weeks of additional time will not magically materialize, and, in fact, more changes are likely to occur that will necessitate more additions to the estimated project hours.

Guideline: To evaluate the percent complete of a project at a major milestone, compare the current level of work with the original milestone definition.

Adding resources to complete a project in Phase 3

Once you discover that you are behind schedule on the publications project, you have a number of alternatives. The simplest alternative is to keep the team intact and extend the schedule to account for the additional work.

In *The Mythical Man Month*, Brooks quotes the menu of Restaurant Antoine in New Orleans, "Good cooking takes time. If you are made to wait, it is to serve you better, and to please you" (Brooks, 1975). Development work, too, takes time. To maintain quality, we need sufficient time in the schedule to perform all of our testing and quality checks. Adding more content to the project generally means adding more time.

However, this alternative of adding more time may not be so simple if you have other projects waiting for the same team members. You cannot start a new project until the original project is complete.

In many cases, you have no alternative but to extend the publications schedule. The entire development project is likely to be behind in its schedule. Your team has to wait until information is available, portions of the software or hardware are complete, or problems in the development effort are resolved. Since all the project activities are interdependent, you can do nothing but extend the schedule as you wait for activities on the critical path to be completed. All later projects will fall behind schedule, like dominos tipping over once the first one is knocked down.

Either you recruit additional staff to begin the new projects that are waiting, or you postpone their start dates. If you recruit new staff, through hiring or contracting, then you may have insufficient work for your existing team once the original project is done. Unsolvable dilemmas of this sort tend to age project managers prematurely.

Schedule slips are not fault-free solutions to changes in a publications project, although they are most satisfying in terms of maintaining the original quality goals. They also allow you to maintain the efficiency of a consistent staff. Team members now know the product, know the players, and are able to be most efficient in responding to changes.

Unfortunately, schedule slips are not always possible. Many projects have rigid deadlines, based upon external customer requirements, market forces, and budget limitations. If original schedules and deadlines must be maintained, one alternative available to you is to add resources to your publications team.

If people were interchangeable parts, adding resources midstream during Phase 3 of a project would be simple. You started with 3.0 full-time equivalent writers; you now need a 3.5 full-time equivalents to complete the project. All you have to do is add half a person. Some senior managers apparently believe that human resources can be exchanged in this way. They are wrong. The creative tasks that occur during a publications project are not easily divisible into smaller and smaller pieces (Figure 18.9). We cannot take a 100-page book and divide it among 100 writers and expect to complete the book in 5 hours. The tasks the writers perform are interdependent and require communication.

Adding people late in the project life cycle is never a simple matter. That is one of the reasons we spend so much time in Phases 1 and 2 trying to plan and estimate the project as accurately as possible. You need to staff correctly from the outset rather than add people in the middle.

When you add people in the middle of the project, you have two problems to deal with:

- New people must be trained.
- Increasing the number of people increases the number of interactions that must occur to keep the team on track.

Figure 18.9 An infinitely divisible project is unlikely

Interactions can become so complicated and numerous that adding people to a project may actually lengthen the project rather than shorten it.

A rule of thumb that is often used to describe the effect of adding people says that each new person added is only 80-percent effective in relationships to the last new person added. Therefore, if you need a new person for 100 hours of work, the time it will take you to train and communicate with this person plus the time the person will use for training will be approximately 20 hours. That means you will need 120 hours of time to complete the original 100 hours of work. The additional 20 hours represents time you, the new person, and others on your team spend in training plus the additional communication time an additional person adds for all team members.

What if you have a 10-month project to which you have assigned a single writer? After 6 months, at the first-draft milestone, you discover that the writer is 1 month behind. If the schedule cannot be extended, you have two assumptions to evaluate:

- You misestimated the work up to the first draft.
- You misestimated the entire remaining project.

If you misestimated only up to the first-draft milestone, you now have 3 months of calendar time remaining to accomplish 4 months of work on Phases 3 and 4. That assumes you have used the additional month needed to complete the first draft. You will now need 1.33 writers to complete the work in 3 months.

If you have misestimated the entire project, then the 1-month increase (or one-sixth of the total 6 months) in Phases 1, 2 and part of 3 will also mean a one-sixth increase in the final 4 months of the project. That one-sixth increase means that you will need $4\frac{2}{3}$ months to complete the project following the first draft. You now have $4\frac{2}{3}$ months of work to complete in 3 months calendar time. That means you will need 1.6 writers to complete the work in 3 months.

These calculations do not take into account, however, the 80-percent rule. Instead of .6 of an additional writer, you will need .72 of an additional writer to be trained and communicated with to complete the project on schedule. As you can see, the project is becoming progressively more difficult to complete.

Adding resources to a project, rather than adding schedule, is only possible without huge decreases in efficiency if you find some way to partition the remaining tasks efficiently. Perhaps an additional .72 team members can be assigned to adding edits to a draft, reformatting pages, collecting screen images, or other more easily divisible tasks. Unfortunately, someone still has to coordinate and communicate even about these more mundane tasks, so that the 80-percent rule continues to apply.

Once you know how many hours of additional work will be needed to complete the project and handle the changes to scope, you can calculate the number of people needed to finish the work on the original schedule. But, before you add a team member, be certain that schedule changes are not imminent.

 Guideline: When faced with an increase in project scope, use your understanding of the original project scope and estimate to calculate the resources needed to complete the project on the original schedule.

Adding new people to an existing team

If you finally decide that there is no alternative but to add team members, be certain that you are willing to spend time training the new people and ensuring that work is well partitioned. You may have to use considerable creative resources to decide how to partition complex jobs effectively. And, you will have to spend extra time ensuring that the original team members understand the roles of the new people and are aware of the demands the new people will put on their time as well as yours (Figure 18.10).

A Level 3 team that works effectively together, sharing ideas and information and assisting each other in making progress, is more likely to be successful in adding team members than teams of independent contributors. In a Level 1 or 2 organization, the

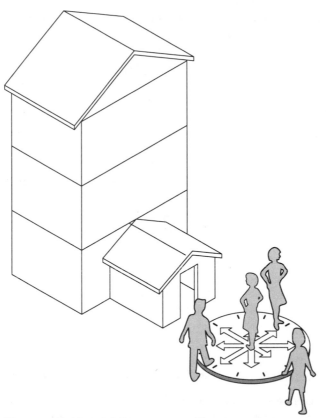

Figure 18.10 Adding new staff to an existing team

result of adding a team member late in the life cycle may sound like the following example.

❝❞ My project really fell apart after Jackie told me I had to work with Jim," complained Barbara. "Jim had no idea what he was doing. I had to explain everything to him and look over all of his work. Most of the time I had to redo it."

"Jackie had calculated that you could not finish the project by yourself and still meet the schedule," replied Alice.

"I don't agree. It took me more time to work with Jim than it would have taken me to do the work myself," said Barbara. "Besides, Jim ruined the quality of the project. I wouldn't want anyone to find out I worked on this mess."

"How did Jim ruin the quality? He's seems like a pretty bright guy," said Alice.

"Oh, he's probably average. But he makes mistakes. There was a lot he didn't know about the project and he kept getting things wrong," said Barbara. "Besides, I didn't have time to look over his shoulder every minute. I told him what he was supposed to do. It's not my fault that he didn't know how to do it."

"What if Jackie wants you to work with an assistant writer again?" said Alice. "I know she really believes in a team approach."

"I wish she'd just leave me alone. I don't like working with other people, especially if they don't know anything," replied Barbara. "If Jackie really wants to make this a team company, I probably will start looking for another job.

Such a scenario is all too common when a new manager tries to introduce a team approach to a Level 1 or 2 organization. Jackie has her work cut out for her in convincing Barbara that she can work effectively with another writer. Jackie's mistake, in this case, was to leave it up to Barbara to decide how to work with Jim. If you are going to introduce new team members late in a project life cycle, you will find that you will save yourself much grief if you work closely with the newly formed team. You will need to help them find ways to work together effectively and to partition tasks in a productive way.

> *Guideline:* **When adding new people to an existing team, help the original team members partition tasks appropriately so that losses of efficiency and quality are minimized.**

Convincing senior management you need additional team members

The best way to convince senior management that you need additional people to complete the project on time is to calculate the effects of the product changes on the publications schedule. Then, present the results of your calculations quantitatively in spreadsheet form. In the following spreadsheet, representing the original estimate of hours for the Fateful user's guide, Eleanor has estimated that the 192-page guide has increased in size by 15 percent to 221 pages because of additions to the software. Of course, since the first-draft milestone arrived before the team found out about the additions, it is now early July, with only $2\frac{1}{2}$ months remaining in the schedule.

Taking into account that the new sections will require re-examining the original Content Specification and training a new writer very late in the schedule, Eleanor has decided to calculate the additional hours needed by applying the original 6.63 hours per page to the 29 additional pages. She finds she needs 150 additional writer hours, plus additional time for managing and editing. She also needs to add to the time allotted for production by 15 percent.

If she could maintain her original one-writer team, Eleanor could ensure that the manual would be completed by the end of October, barring any further additions (Figure 18.11). In this way, she could maintain the original level of quality and avoid the complications of increasing team size.

Unfortunately, Eleanor's boss insists that the original schedule be maintained. He is certain that the software will be completed on time, and he does not want to hold up the release of the product because the documentation is late. At that point, Eleanor presents her second spreadsheet (Figure 18.12), which shows that she can maintain the original schedule only by adding another writer to the team immediately. She also

Fateful User Guide
Projected Hours Worksheet

254

Book Name Factor / Skill Level	Projected Mar-93	Projected Apr-93	Projected May-93	Projected Jun-93	Projected Jul-93	Projected Aug-93	Projected Sep-93	Projected Oct-93	Projected Nov-93	Projected Total Hours	Projected Hours/Page
User Guide	Page Count: 221										
0.10 Project management	16	15	14	20	23	17	15	14	0	134	0.61
Writer	138	132	120	132	126	132	126	84	0	990	4.48
0.15 Editor	21	20	18	20	19	20	19	13	0	150	0.68
Illustrator		0	0	50	85	15	0	0		150	0.68
Production							0	46	0	46	0.21
Subtotal	175	167	152	222	253	184	160	157	0	1470	
Total Hours	175	167	152	222	253	184	160	157	0	1470	6.65
Hours/Month	138	132	120	132	126	132	126	126	120	522	
Full-Time Equivalent/Month	1.27	1.27	1.27	1.68	2.01	1.39	1.27	1.25	0.00		

716   166   882

Figure 18.11 Fateful estimating spreadsheet with an extended schedule

Fateful User Guide
Projected Hours Worksheet

254

Book Name Factor / Skill Level	Projected Mar-93	Projected Apr-93	Projected May-93	Projected Jun-93	Projected Jul-93	Projected Aug-93	Projected Sep-93	Projected Oct-93	Projected Nov-93	Projected Total Hours	Projected Hours/Page
User Guide	Page Count: 221										
0.10 Project management	16	15	14	20	23	32	14	0	0	134	0.61
Writer	138	132	120	132	126	132	54	0	0	834	3.77
Writer 2						132	25	0	0	157	0.71
0.15 Editor	21	20	18	20	19	40	12	0	0	150	0.68
Illustrator				50	85	15	0	0	0	150	0.68
Production							46	0	0	46	0.21
Subtotal	175	167	152	222	253	351	105	0	0	1471	
Total Hours	175	167	152	222	253	351	105	0	0	1471	6.66
Hours/Month	138	132	120	132	126	132	126	126	120	522	
Full-Time Equivalent/Month	1.27	1.27	1.27	1.68	2.01	2.66	0.83	0.00	0.00		

716   167   883

Figure 18.12 Fateful estimating spreadsheet with a new writer added

points out the negative effect of a late change in the team structure, explaining why she needs the new writer for more time than her original estimate using the staff writer.

Since it will take Eleanor some time to bring in a new writer as an independent contractor on such short notice, she hopes to start the new person by the first of August and continue the writer into the beginning of September. She is well aware that it will be difficult to get someone for such a short period of time and on such short notice. In fact, she wants to leave the option open that she will bring the writer in sooner and keep him or her until the writing is done.

If you have to add resources during Phase 3 of a publications project, plan the addition carefully. Leave sufficient time for training and orientation of the new team members.

 Guideline: Add new team members reluctantly when it is late in a project life cycle. Plan the additions well.

Negotiating changes in scope

As you have seen, a re-estimated spreadsheet allows you to calculate both additions to the schedule and additions in resources to complete the work on the original schedule. A carefully prepared spreadsheet will help you establish the grounds for requesting either more time or more people.

However, you will certainly encounter situations where neither time nor people can be added to the project. The original schedule must be maintained, and no funds are available for additional staff. Under these circumstances, the only acceptable alternative is to cut the scope of the project and reduce the amount of work to be done.

Changes in scope during Phase 3 are always painful. The later you get into Phase 3, especially following the first-draft milestone, the more painful the changes will become. Following first draft, changes to reduce the work to be done generally include eliminating some material that has already been written.

In deciding to reduce the scope of the project, you and your team members must look carefully at the work remaining and decide what must be cut. You may even want to involve members of the development team in this effort, because they will have to understand the reductions in scope before the next review cycle. As much as possible, eliminate material that has not yet been developed. For example, the information provided to the audiences on the new functions or features may have to be perfunctory, rather than complete. That produces an unevenness in the text, but such a consequence may be inevitable.

A number of options are available when you are searching for material to cut or not to develop at all:

- Alternative methods for performing the same task
- Illustrations of screens, parts of the product, or conceptual illustrations that have not yet been created

- Conceptual information that is nice to know but not essential to task performance
- Explanations of data-entry fields that may be known to the audience

Make the cuts deeply enough so that you accommodate the new information and produce genuine reductions in scope. If a section, for example, is completely written and copyedited and there have been no changes by reviewers for some time, you should keep that section intact. Reducing it or even eliminating it will take more time than leaving it alone. Look for information that is still undergoing considerable change. Perhaps the original information is sufficient and can remain as is.

With every reduction decision, consider first the effects on the external audience. You may have material in the text that is there to satisfy the needs of an internal audience. This material is a prime candidate for elimination.

Remember that no one will be happy with the changes you are making, but they must be made nonetheless if you are to maintain the quality of the remaining material.

 Guideline: If you must reduce the scope of a project, focus on the needs of the audience. Choose to eliminate information that may be less needed.

Negotiating changes in quality

The least acceptable alternative when you can neither increase schedule or staff is to cut quality. Reductions in quality come when the scope of the project increases with no corresponding changes to time or resources. Brooks believes that more projects fail because of a lack of time than for any other reason (Brooks, 1975).

Reducing quality often does not occur through a conscious decision. Usually, no one comes up to you saying, "Let's reduce the quality of the manuals. Our customers don't need information that is correct, well organized, and well written." Rather, quality is reduced when best practices are abandoned because there is no time for them. In publications projects, quality is reduced when drafts are not edited, procedures are not checked for accuracy, technical reviews are eliminated, indexes are shortchanged, and more.

Sometimes, it is possible to respond to a small crisis by eliminating a few procedures for a short time only. Unfortunately, when good practices start being abandoned, they continue to be eliminated from a team's mode of working. Edits and reviews are completed perfunctorily, if they are done at all. Quick and dirty indexes become the norm. No one has any time to get information about users and tasks because they are always involved in the latest crisis operation.

For a while everyone complains about a loss of quality. Eventually, the strongest team members, who value quality in their own work, find other jobs. The remaining people keep quiet, either because they forget what quality work means or they never know.

If you have a choice, your decision should always be to plan a formal reduction in the scope of work. If you do not, the quality of the work is certain to decrease. If your decision is to reduce the quality of the work, approach the quality reduction with considerable fanfare. Explain how the quality changes are likely to affect customer satisfaction and the costs of customer service.

Too often, publications-project teams and their managers reduce the quality of their work quietly. Procedures are abandoned and known best practices are not followed, because there is not enough time. As a result, no one in the rest of the organization knows that quality has been compromised. If there are problems with customer satisfaction involving publications, it becomes very easy to blame the publications organization. In fact, if you reduce quality without broadcasting the consequences, you may deserve at least some of the blame. Whenever you have to compromise quality, make sure that your decision is well known to the rest of the organization and approved by management.

In the town where I grew up, the townspeople always seemed eager to vote down increases to the school budgets. Whenever a school election was planned, the board of education would present data on the programs to be cut if the new budget were not passed. At the top of the list of program cuts would frequently be the high school football program. Of course, no one in town wanted to cut the football program so they voted for the school budget. If the school board had threatened to cut home economics or the advanced literature programs, probably no one would have gotten very excited. If you are faced with cutting quality, always announce a cut to the football program first.

Guideline: Never abandon quality unless all other alternatives are exhausted. Then, make the consequences of poor quality clear throughout the organization.

Developing Prototypes

We should never be so confident as to believe that our first designs are perfect. First designs share many common flaws:

- They are too long and bulky, containing extraneous information that gets in the way of user performance and understanding.
- They are awkwardly organized.
- They are inconsistent in level of detail, editorial style, writing style, degree of accuracy, and more.

Unfortunately, we are all too willing to test our first design ideas on the customer, with unfortunate results. Bulky publications discourage regular use. Calls to customer service and visits from field engineering increase. Negative reviews affect the publications department's hard-won credibility and the writers' morale.

More effective design methodologies encourage you to assume that the first design not be the last design or even the best design. Rather, they suggest that you build small-scale systems and try them out. In fact, you should be prepared to throw away your first designs. First designs always have flaws. If you do not plan to throw them away early, rather than shipping them off to the customers, you may be forced to throw them away later. Perhaps someone will complain that the publications fail to inform and instruct, perhaps a new team will be hired to find all the flaws that we overlooked, or perhaps you will be asked to downsize to something that customers will want to use and your companies can afford to deliver.

By designing and testing early documentation prototypes, you can better meet the needs of your customers. Prototyping sets the stage for shipping the second version of the design to customers, rather than the first.

Prototypes are working models, like those that architects have long used to help clients understand more thoroughly what a building will look and feel like. Engineers have used models to investigate the feasibility and safety of design ideas. More recently, the traditional physical models of buildings and bridges have moved into the realm of virtual reality. Designers now build computer models of buildings and bridges that allow clients to walk through the space and experience its feel more directly than they might from balsa wood.

Prototypes occupy a place in the development life cycle between the conceptual plans of Phases 1 and 2 and the full-scale development of Phase 3. They permit us to move from our design ideas, which stem from the original user and task analyses of Phases 1 and 2, to early testable models. Prototyping is one reason that technical communicators must be involved at the earliest stages of product development, so that we can develop models of proposed publications as engineers and programmers produce models of proposed hardware and software.

Guideline: Use a prototype of the publications to test your design concepts early in the development life cycle.

Using the Content Specification as an early prototype

The first available prototype, strictly speaking, is the Content Specifications. One of the reasons that you should spend considerable time developing and reviewing the Content Specifications is that they represent an early prototype of how a document will be organized. In Chapter 10, we discussed storyboarding as a way to present detailed Content Specifications and obtain better feedback than might occur from a list of topics alone.

Not only do detailed Content Specifications invite a detailed design walkthrough; they can also be tested for completeness, organization, and language. You can ask users to look up information on performing a specific task and discover if they can find the information in the table of contents. If they cannot, you may decide to revise the organization of the text or the names of sections so that they are more meaningful.

The problem with using the Content Specifications as a prototype is obvious, however. Most reviewers have difficulty responding to a paper-and-pencil design. We know that it is difficult for people to imagine how the end product will look and feel when they are looking at a paper-and-pencil design. The less context you have for reviewing a conceptual design, the more difficult it will be for you to envision the reality from the abstraction. When we were building a new house, I found myself unable to conceptualize the interior design of the kitchen and family room combination that the architect had drawn. I thought it was what I wanted, but the combination of lines and angles did not appear in my mind as an identifiable physical space. It was not until the rooms were completed that I could make the connection between the architect's drawing and the physical space.

In exactly the same way, we find that reviewers, especially users, can review and agree to Content Specifications and yet dislike the final result. As professional technical communicators, we understand the language of our own design world and can visualize the final publications from the plans. Others cannot and should not be expected to. A more complete and fully conceived prototype section or sections of a publication will fill a gap in the process between design and development. It will also allow us to introduce early usability assessment.

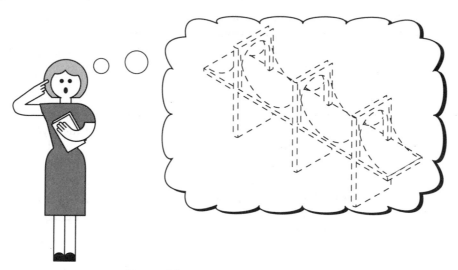

Figure 19.1 Working with a prototype

Guideline: Use the Content Specifications as an early prototyping device, but remain aware of the difficulties reviewers have in visualizing the final design from conceptual models.

Developing a complete prototype

Most prototyping efforts come after an initial detailed design has been suggested and work has begun on a section of the publication. In a prototyping model for publications development (see Figure 19.1), the section of the publication chosen for initial development becomes the trial case for the design ideas being worked out.

The prototyping process includes

- Selecting a sample selection or sections to design
- Gathering as much information as possible
- Fully implementing the design in terms of both organization and layout
- Testing the design with representative users
- Evolving the design through subsequent tests to ensure its usefulness
- Throwing out the first design and starting over

Such a complete prototype allows you to try out your ideas and get better feedback from reviewers and users. You build the prototype, review and test it, then redesign and retest until you are closer to the real needs of the users. In fact, the greatest benefits from prototyping come from the iterative process that prototyping encourages.

"But where," you may ask, "am I supposed to find time for prototyping? With my schedules shorter than ever, how will I find time for prototypes and an iterative design process?"

If you plan to use a standard and familiar design, then you probably do not need prototyping. However, if you are trying to better meet your users' needs with new forms of information design, then prototyping will help you meet your goal. Prototyping can even save you time.

 Guideline: Recognize that early prototyping can save time in the development life cycle by reducing the need for costly last-cycle design changes.

Managing the prototyping process

As project manager, you need to ensure that the prototyping process is accepted in your organization and that it is conducted carefully. To introduce the prototyping process to management, you need to focus on its benefits and analyze its costs. The benefits of prototyping are the same as the benefits that should accrue from good publications design:

- More usable documents
- Decreased search time for information
- Lower training costs
- Greater customer satisfaction

To introduce prototyping to your writers, you need to model the process to help your team learn the new approach. If you use a good example, they will learn that through prototyping you are able to identify and correct design flaws before they become entrenched in hundreds or thousands of pages of documentation.

The advantages to the customer of better publications design are obvious. Prototyping is a method for improving the design process. The advantage of a prototyping methodology to the designers is less obvious in organizations used to a more linear design process. Members of your senior management may feel that you are wasting time building early models to test, when they believe testing can be done more easily and thoroughly at the end of the process. Unfortunately, any activity left until the end of the life cycle is likely to be eliminated entirely as changes occur with ever-increasing frequency. Senior management may be unconvinced of the value of using more time earlier in the process to reduce the time and costs of late-cycle changes. You may want to suggest a trial run to measure the success of early prototyping in comparison with a more standard approach to creating something and then fixing it later.

You may have to convince your own team of the value of early prototyping. They may be uncomfortable with testing something that they consider less than perfect. It may take some convincing to get them to risk testing an early design and then revising rather than waiting until a publication is complete and perfect from the communicator's point of view. With an interested writer, try a pilot project that will serve as a good example for others. Online-help prototypes often work well in convincing writers, as well as programmers, of the value of testing.

You may also find that it is more difficult to estimate the time it will take to complete the design process using iterative prototyping. Perhaps the best way is to use once again an hours-per-page estimate that has been increased to account for design instability. The first dependency, product instability, always has a substantial effect on the difficulty of a publications project. However, publications instability may have the same effect, at least during the planning stages. Try starting with a somewhat higher estimate, perhaps with an increase of 10 percent over your ordinary, linear-process estimate, and use all the extra time for prototyping. Then, look at the effect of the prototyping on the rest of the development schedule, especially the effect on the scope of the project. If you are hoping to reduce the size of the publications by prototyping a new design, you may be in a position to re-estimate the entire project at the end of the prototyping stage.

In planning the prototyping stage within Phase 3, you also need to consider how far you will take the iterative process. It is certainly possible to go through several design and test iterations only to feel that you are no closer to an optimal design than you were when you began. The design issues are complex enough that solutions are rarely obvious and simple. However, it is easier to improve upon something that actually exists than to speculate about design concepts. Even if you will not achieve the perfect design, you will at least have better information about your users to help you make design decisions (see Figure 19.2).

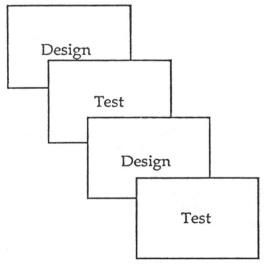

Figure 19.2 The iterative design process

Guideline: Manage the prototyping process by assessing the effect of prototyping on budget and schedule and deciding when to stop the iterative process.

Selecting a project for prototyping

Not every project is a candidate for prototyping. The best candidates are those projects where you are contemplating a major design change to increase customer satisfaction, reduce publications volume, or deliver more information electronically. The worst candidates to prototype are those where there is little likelihood that design changes will be accepted or where you are simply maintaining an existing design. A reference manual as a whole is not a likely candidate for prototyping, but you may find that pieces of the manual are possibilities. You may be considering a new page design for one section or including a new appendix. All these are possibilities.

Think through the issues surrounding your design process and your senior management's support for a new approach. If you decide that prototyping may work, then you are ready to select portions of your publications project for prototyping.

To plan for a prototype, you must first consider carefully which sections planned for the publication are the best candidates for prototyping. Good candidates for prototyping have the following characteristics:

- Representative of larger publication
- Large enough to be tested in a performance context
- Sufficient product information available to complete the text and graphics
- Representative of as many design elements as possible, from numbered and unnumbered lists through heading levels, types of illustrations, tables, and charts

The choice for prototyping should not be a section of a publication that is anomalous, such as an introductory or conceptual section. It should be as representative as possible, possibly a mainline instructional procedure. It should not be a section that represents a portion of the product that is far from being developed. Choose something that is currently in development, preferably the hardware or software product's prototype piece.

Select a prototype candidate for which you can produce a representative section of text and graphics of sufficient size that you can test it thoroughly. Usually, a procedural module is a good choice, because a conceptual module might yield only a knowledge-based rather than a performance-based test. If you want to investigate the interplay between conceptual information and task performance, you may want to produce prototypes of both sections to test. Then, stage the test with two groups, one that reads the conceptual information and one that does not.

Finally, choose a section that includes a number of design elements. A section that has only a single heading level or a simple bulleted list will not give you an opportunity to investigate the effectiveness of your new design elements as they work together to convey hierarchy and importance.

Guideline: Select a prototyping section carefully so that it is representative of the publication as a whole and contains sufficient design elements.

Involving your team members in developing the prototype

Prototyping should not be seen as an individual effort. A number of members of your team should be invited to participate in the planning and development (see Figure 19.3). The writer and the developmental editor have primary responsibility for defining the new structure for the information and a variety of access points for the user. The writer and editor also work together in developing the writing style, including the most appropriate tone, the completeness of explanation, and the use of instructional procedures versus conceptual information. The graphic designer is responsible for creating the page design with appropriate feedback from team members. The page design should fully represent the look of the final publication. The technical illustrator is responsible for defining the style of illustration to be used, starting with distinctions between line drawings and photography and extending into the details of the drawings. Both conceptual and representational graphics should be included in the prototype if they will appear in the rest of the text.

All the elements of design must be considered if the prototype is to be complete and representative of your new design ideas. Once the design elements are in place, the writer and graphic artist build the prototype using data gathered from users during the front-end design of Phases 1 and 2 and from technical experts as the product is being developed. Because product information is an integral part of the prototype publica-

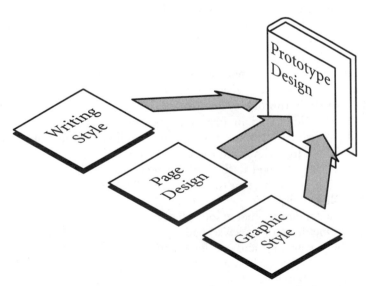

Figure 19.3 Contributions to the prototype design

tion, the writer should gather the most complete and accurate information possible. In the absence of software screens or actual hardware controls, the graphic artist may want to mock up examples that will look like the screens and controls. If prototype software or hardware is available, then photographs, sketches, and screen dumps can be developed directly from the original.

After the prototype draft is prepared, it should, of course, go through a thorough developmental edit as the first line of usability assessment. The editor should look for consistency of presentation, clarity of organization, and other issues that will affect the usability of the information.

After the editor's revisions are made, the prototype draft should go through a technical review to ensure that it represents the prototype product as well as the design concepts being promoted by the product-development team. If the product is also being prototyped, you need to ensure that the prototype information reflects the product accurately. Usability assessment is not a substitute for verification of the information against the prototype interface. If you have technical errors in the prototype, you will waste valuable testing time correcting the errors and attempting to get the test subjects back on track.

 *Guideline:* **Plan for the involvement of the entire publications-development team in the prototyping process.**

Establishing the details of the format

If your team, especially the graphic designers, has not already worked out the details of the page format for the publications, they will have to be designed for the prototype (see Figure 19.4). The designers should begin with a list of the elements to design, from heading levels through tables and lists. Each element should be specified completely and implemented in the publishing system as a series of elements tags.

Ensure that the graphic designer on the team or the person responsible for the design of the format is thoroughly familiar with the audience and tasks identified in Phase 1 and further identified in Phase 2. Too often, designers concentrate on the aesthetics of the presentation rather than on its usability. You may want to schedule a time for the designers to review with the writers how they picture the audience's needs for information access. A good design will decrease access time and make it easier for the users to find their way through the document. Be certain that your designers are in touch with usability issues.

I have found a tendency among some designers to subordinate usability issues to aesthetic issues. One design I reviewed had a preponderance of horizontal lines around illustrations, tables, warnings and cautions, and some of the heading levels. On some pages, there were so many horizontal lines that the pages were impossible to read. The designers liked using horizontal lines; they did not consider the negative impact of the design element on actual publications.

Figure 19.4 Adding the format design to the prototype

In another instance, the designers used a sequence of heading levels all presented in italic type. Because the font was difficult to read on screen, the writers did not notice spacing problems that made the headings difficult to implement. The font was also difficult for the users to read and did not provide them with sufficient differentiation among heading levels. The design, while attractive, was unusable.

As project manager, you are not really in a position to second-guess your designers. However, definitely consider whether or not the graphic design team members appear to be keeping the audience needs foremost. Consider if they are concerned with the ease of implementing the design for the writers. You can tell from the way the designers talk about their design. If they can explain their design ideas in terms of usability and their clear understanding of the audience, then you know your team is thinking about design in a usability-focused way.

Guideline: A complete design of the format of the publication, including page design and screen design, should be part of the prototyping process.

Establishing the details of the writing style

The details of the writing style also need to be established for the prototype sections. That means you will have to ensure that style decisions involving writers and editors are made earlier than they might ordinarily be made in the project. The goal is to make the prototype completely consistent. A consistent style needs to be established and maintained for headings, introductions, lists, tables, step-by-step instructions, descrip-

Figure 19.5 Adding the writing style to the prototype

tions, and more. Consistent terminology and consistent emphasis techniques (boldface, italics, size changes) must be used (see Figure 19.5).

As project manager, you need to make sure that your team members are making the decisions that will result in a consistent and usable style for the prototype documentation. They need to consider how language choices, sentence types, or the use of boldface or other highlighting techniques will affect the audience. Too frequently, decisions about the style of a document are made from an aesthetic point of view alone, just as they are for the graphic design. Listen for the rationale. Are your writers and editors making decisions in terms of user needs, rather than tradition or their own personal preferences. The more good design thinking that occurs during the prototype development, the fewer problems are likely to be uncovered later by the users.

Again, do not try to second-guess your writers and editors. Just be certain that the right kinds of information are being taken into account. As manager, you should guarantee that all members of the team are following the agreed-upon writing style and implementing it in the same way. Although the editor is primarily responsible for the uniformity of the writing style, the project manager makes sure that the editor's changes are implemented. If each team member has total discretion, then the prototype sections will not be the same, nor will the final drafts of the publications.

In addition to facilitating the discussions among writing and editing team members, you also need to play the role of decision maker. Arguments over the details of style are likely to go on indefinitely if they are allowed to do so. Someone will have to make the final decision among alternatives; that person may have to be you or your lead editor.

Guideline: Use the prototyping process to establish the writing style that will be most appropriate for the publication type and audience needs.

Figure 19.6   Adding graphic elements to the prototype

Establishing the details of the graphic style

The final decision that you need to make for the prototype is the graphic style (see Figure 19.6). The graphic style includes the presentation of photography and line drawings in paper documentation and the presentation of line drawings, video, sound, photography, and animation in electronic documentation. Too often, we see documentation produced that appears as if the graphics were created by people from different planets. The line drawings contain different line weights, lettering, perspective, treatment of shading, and more.

Just as the writers must agree on a uniform and consistent writing style for the prototype, so must the illustrators agree on an illustration style. As project manager, your job is to facilitate the discussion and help the team reach consensus. In the absence of reaching consensus, you may have to make the final decisions yourself rather than let the discussions go on interminably.

Once a graphic style is in place, you may need a graphic editor to ensure that it is being followed correctly and completely by all the project's illustrators. Even with an agreement in place, it is quite easy for individuals to deviate from the standard. As project manager, you need to ensure that the deviation is minimal.

Guideline: Establish a style for the illustrations used in the prototype that is appropriate for the publications type and meets the audience needs.

Introducing Usability Assessment

In Chapter 19, I suggested creating prototype drafts early in the publications-development life cycle. One reason to develop prototype drafts is to ensure that the internal reviewers have an early opportunity to see exactly what the publications will look like and how they are intended to be used. A more significant reason is to test the prototype drafts with actual users by using a variety of techniques for assessing usability. Many usability assessment techniques are available that you can use during early stages of the publications-development life cycle (Figure 20.1).

Before you begin any testing, during the development of the prototype drafts, consider reviewing the relevant research in the field. If researchers agree that readable text fonts are between 9 and 12 points, then you may be wasting your time testing the usability of 6-point type. Know the accepted standards in the field and edit your prototype drafts according to the standards. You may not have to test something that experts in the field already agree is unlikely to be usable.

At the earliest design stages, paper-and-pencil tests of various sorts are possible to evaluate such issues as

- The most appropriate and understandable terminology
- The design of tables of contents
- The distribution of topics and tasks within a library of documents
- Document size and configuration
- Readability of certain type fonts
- Clarity of icons and other symbols

As soon as prototype sections of publications are available, tests can be planned and implemented. You can conduct tests of such items as

- Step-by-step instructions
- Introductory text
- Conceptual information
- Reference topics
- Preliminary indexes
- Tables and diagrams
- The combination of illustration and text

and many other issues that will affect the development and success of the information products as a whole.

Phase	Phases 1 and 2 Planning	Phase 3 Implementation Prototyping	Phase 3 Production and Evaluation
Type of tests	formative testing paper-and-pencil examples storyboards outlines previous products competitive products developmental edits technical reviews	formative testing developmental edits technical reviews cognitive walkthroughs performance testing ▪ informal observations ▪ laboratory observations	evaluative testing performance testing ▪ informal observations ▪ laboratory observations ▪ field studies ▪ cognitive walkthroughs
Goals	establish style standards make design decisions plan for later testing	confirm style standards make specific design changes plan for later testing	evaluate style standards revise in critical areas plan for the next release

Figure 20.1 Staging usability assessment throughout the usability testing: schedule table

Once prototypes of the product are available, you can fully integrate information testing with user interface testing (Figure 20.2). If early prototypes are available, then performance testing of information and product may occur early enough to make substantive changes. If prototypes are not available, you may have to wait until late in the product-development cycle to stage performance-based tests.

Finally, once the product and publications are released or shortly before release, performance-based tests can help you evaluate the success of the information in meeting the users' needs. If the tests are performed early enough, you may find that you can revise areas of the text that cause severe problems. If not, you can plan a new approach for the next release of the information.

Figure 20.2 Plan to test the usability of the prototype

In each of these phases, it is up to the project manager to schedule the testing activities as part of the overall schedule and ensure that the test results are taken into account in the design and implementation of the publications. Depending upon the way your company is organized for testing, you may have to help design and administer the test, work closely with your team members as they design and administer the test, work with usability professionals in setting goals and planning the test, and help in all these situations to evaluate the test results.

Working with usability professionals ensures that tests are designed to produce useful results, run with a minimum of testing bias, and evaluated professionally. Usability professionals will also save your staff considerable time and energy. Testing is more difficult and time-consuming than you may believe. If you do not have usability professionals inhouse, consider hiring an outside testing group to conduct the test and participate as an informed observer. Or begin an educational process for your team in usability testing.

 Guideline: Plan to test your prototypes as quickly as possible but do not neglect the requirements of good test design and professional evaluation of results.

Managing usability assessments

As project manager, you have several roles to play in the usability assessment process:

- Educating team members about the possibility of early usability testing
- Educating senior management and members of the product-development team about the opportunities offered by early testing

Once you have been able to establish usability assessment as an integral part of the publications-development process, you will need to help your team members manage the planning, implementation, and evaluation of tests. You may want to

- Act as a liaison between testing professionals and your team
- Provide logistical support to the team in setting up the tests
- Help to evaluate the test results and decide how they affect planning

Involving your team members

During the earliest planning phases, it may not occur to your team members to look for opportunities to test. Early testing can help them define audiences and tasks more thoroughly and resolve differences of opinion among team members concerning the design approach to take.

You can help your team members focus on information they need about their audiences and tasks (Figure 20.3). The better the information they have about their audiences, the better the design decisions they will be able to make. While surveys, questionnaires, and interviews are valuable tools for learning about audiences and their

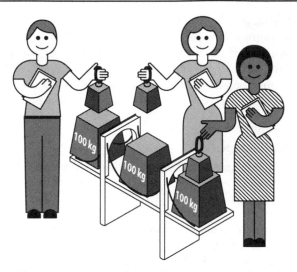

Figure 20.3 Involving the team members in early testing

tasks, usability testing produces a richer picture of how the audiences interact with publications.

You can help your team members resolve differences of opinion by recommending usability testing. You may find that team members get caught up in interminable opinion wars that could quickly and profitably be resolved through small-scale paper-and-pencil usability tests. For example, teams will try to decide by personal preference which terms are more likely to be understood by the audience. They could reach a decision based on direct information from the audience through a simple series of tests. In one case, we conducted a series of iterative tests of part names for a product to find those names that were most quickly understood by the users. The solutions generated would not have occurred to the technical communicators without the assistance of potential users.

Guideline: Encourage the publications team members to take an active role in usability testing.

Convincing your management

Although your team members need to learn to take advantage of opportunities for testing during the planning phases, your management may need education about the entire process of usability assessment. You will find this especially true if you recommend formal tests of previous versions of the publications or tests of competitors' publications. In most cases, you can always conduct small-scale, informal, inhouse tests on your own, unless these tests involve bringing customers inhouse. You must obtain the support of senior management if you want to engage in more extensive testing. At the least, you will need management support to work out confidentiality agreements and agreements for using human subjects.

Convincing management about the usefulness of usability assessment will be easier if you test early in the life cycle. Early testing can often be done with few, if any, additional resources. You may be able to conduct a reasonable test using your existing staff as test administrators and observers. Consider creating a test plan that

- Uses your writing team as the test team
- Uses existing space, such as a conference room
- Requires no special equipment except perhaps a video camera and VCR which are inexpensive to rent or borrow
- Does not disrupt the original milestone schedule

For additional information on documentation-specific usability testing, see *Validating Information Products* (Hubbard, 1989).

Much of the testing that you can do during Phases 1 and 2 can easily fit into this framework of low cost and little disruption. You can do much of the work yourself, although you may need help getting the product set up and running. However, performance-based tests of previous or competitive products and their documentation may involve additional resources and time.

Three strategies are useful in convincing your senior management that usability testing is worth doing. The first strategy calls for you to construct "what-if" scenarios that demonstrate the benefits of usability testing in relationship to its costs. The second strategy calls for you to stage a demonstration test of a company product and its documentation and to ask all responsible senior management to observe the test, view videotapes of the test, or review the results and recommendations. The third strategy simply means that you show that your major competition is already conducting usability tests.

To prevent the "what-if" scenario, start slowly. Clip articles for your managers that discuss the benefits of usability testing and demonstrate that customers demand usable products. Then begin to investigate what might happen to costs in your organization if usability testing led to substantial improvements in the existing documentation. When the Allen-Bradley Company applied a usability-testing approach to redesigning its factory-automation documentation, they were able to reduce customer-service calls from 50 a day to 2 a month, a dramatic change that also resulted in dramatic cost savings for the company (Jereb, 1986). In addition to reducing the cost of customer service, Allen-Bradley also experienced a substantial increase in European sales. They discovered that the European sales force was able to learn the product more quickly and thoroughly with the improved documentation. A better understanding of the product resulted in more effective presentations to potential customers and eventually to increased sales.

By providing your management with this and similar examples, you should be able to prove that substantial cost savings may occur with increased usability of the product publications. But the examples of other companies' success do not necessarily prove that your company will realize similar gains. By investigating your costs of customer service, field-engineering visits, and training, you can construct "what-if" scenarios suggesting that improvements to the usability of publications may have long-range effects on the customer-support costs. Avoid promising a specific return-on-investment, however. The usability of your publications are often inextricably tied to the usability of the products. When customers find a product difficult to use, they often include the publications in their indictment, no matter how much work has gone into ensuring their usability.

A second effective strategy is to stage a sample test that demonstrates to management the value of learning directly from users how to improve the publications. Several companies have even conducted demonstration tests using their senior managers as test subjects. In one case, a computer manufacturer used testing to substantially improve installation procedures and decrease the time and number of errors experienced by customers. To make their point about the value of usability testing, the publications staff invited the CEO to try the new installation procedures himself. He was favorably impressed by the success of the new, more compact installation instructions.

 Guideline: Convince your senior management about the usefulness of usability assessment by demonstrating how your organization will benefit by more effective, more usable publications for your customers.

Developing your management role

Once your management has been convinced that usability assessment may prove valuable or should be a standard part of the publications-development life cycle, you need to consider your role in the assessment process. You can serve as a test designer or even a test administrator to oversee the testing efforts of your team. Or, you may want to play the role of test observer, watching carefully how test subjects interact with the product and documentation and then aiding in the analysis of test results and decisions about which changes to recommend for the publications and, perhaps, for the product itself. If your team members are able to produce good test plans and conduct the tests on their own, you may be able to help facilitate testing by serving as a logistical consultant. If your team will work with usability professionals during the planning, implementation, and evaluation of the tests, you may find a valuable role as a liaison between the team members and the usability organization (Figure 20.4).

If you take on the role of test designer and administrator, you will actually manage the planning, development, implementation, and evaluation of the entire test. As the designer, you will assume the responsibility of developing a complete test plan (goals, objectives, hypotheses, scenarios) and making all test arrangements. As a test administrator, you are responsible for conducting the test with a team of observers, evaluating the results, and making recommendations for change.

If your team members can handle the demands of planning and coordinating the tests, you may want to assume the role of test observer. The test observer works closely with the test administrator to observe and record the actions of the test subjects. Once the testing is complete, the observer works with the rest of the team to evaluate the test results and make recommendations. While test observer is a less challenging role to play than test administrator, it may be the activity that will best fit into your schedule.

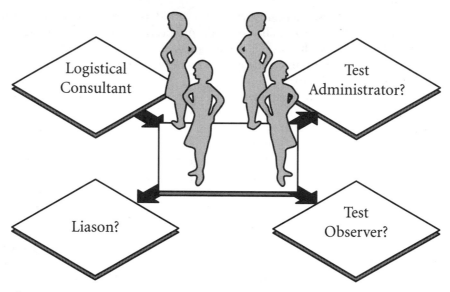

Figure 20.4 Finding your role in usability testing

As a logistical consultant, you may be able to handle a number of responsibilities that will be more difficult for individual members of your team. These include

- Organizing planning meetings with other interested groups, including development, marketing, and training to plan the goals and objectives of the usability assessments
- Ensuring that good estimates are made of the time and resources required to conduct well-planned and carefully designed assessments
- Negotiating with others in the organization to recruit test subjects from internal and external customer communities or from local schools and colleges, employment agencies, or other appropriate sources
- Ensuring that test subjects are paid or given substantial rewards for their efforts in a timely manner and are well treated during the assessment process
- Working with the legal department to develop confidentiality agreements and release forms that will protect the organization in its relationship with test subjects
- Ensuring that the proper hardware, software, or other equipment is available for the duration of the test and that people are at hand to troubleshoot and repair problems
- Ensuring that adequate space for testing is made available for the duration of the test and that suitable test equipment (video camera, videotape recorders and monitors, microphones, and others) is acquired
- Ensuring that technical support is available to the testing team before and during the test
- Organizing a pilot test to avoid problems before bringing in "real" subjects

Because all of these activities consume considerable time and resources and often benefit from having good internal networks, sources of money, and clout, you can contribute by providing this logistical resource to your team. If you arrange for all the problem areas to be handled, your team members will be able to concentrate on planning, implementing, and evaluating the test.

Finally, if your organization has a team of usability professionals who will actually work with your team members to plan, develop, implement and evaluate the usability assessments, you may be able to limit your role to that of liaison. You can arrange for the initial meetings of your team with the usability professionals; you can help the professionals understand the value of testing publications products in addition to hardware and software; and you can help keep the relationship between your team members and the usability staff as friendly and mutually supportive as possible. Many usability professionals do not know how to test and evaluate publications or may be uninterested in publications testing. It will be up to you, as project manager, to obtain their cooperation and encourage their enthusiasm in helping you meet your usability goals.

Guideline: Find the best role for yourself as a usability project manager in your organization, from taking full responsibility for testing to working with usability professionals.

Conducting tests during the planning phases

Usability assessments that you can conduct during the planning phases will range from simple and informal testing and review sessions to formal laboratory-based tests of previous or competitive products. During the planning phases, you need to work with the senior members of your team to decide how usability tests could provide useful information to the planning process. Tests of previous versions of the publications may provide the most comprehensive information for planning. In the early stages of the development process, you will have more writer time available to work on testing. Tests of design ideas, based on the outlines and storyboards produced during Content Specification or of terminology lists or other sample paper-based elements, may give you data on which to base design decisions. The review process itself, especially the combination of a review by the developmental editor and the reviews by the technical experts, can give your team the perspective it needs to develop a more effective design for the publications. Figure 20.5 describes the types of usability assessment that are most effective during the planning phases with a brief description of each methodology and some ideas about the results your team could expect to achieve.

Most of the testing types I recommend for the early planning phases of the publications-development life cycle involve the early involvement of the audience in the design process. Paper-and-pencil tests, storyboard walkthroughs, and formal tests of previous and competitive products all require the involvement of qualified members of the product or process audience. On the other hand, the development edit and the technical-review process are internal techniques that require the participation of experts in publications design and experts in the specification and development of the product. While the information you will gain from experts is different from the

Type of assessment	Methodology	Results
paper-and-pencil test	Tests of individual elements of proposed publications, including • terminology • heading levels • tables of contents • task sequences • modular design • the use of illustrations and examples • possible index entries To conduct paper-and-pencil tests, create sample pieces of proposed publications and ask potential users to run mental scenarios by walking through the design ideas. For conceptual information, ask users to read a brief synopsis of the information you intend to convey and write a summary without looking at your original text.	You will discover early in the publications-development life cycle if you are on the right track with users. Paper-and-pencil tests allow you to answer questions about language choice, the information needed in the tables of contents and heading levels to make access easy, the most useful design of an instruction sequence, the places where illustrations will work better than text, and others.
storyboard reviews	A usability walkthrough of larger design elements, including • library organization • organizational strategies within individual publications • the use of illustrations and examples • division of information into task modules, conceptual modules, and reference modules To hold storyboard reviews, prepare verbal and pictorial presentations of how the larger design elements will look and feel to the user. Ask members of your team, members of the development team, and potential users to review the storyboard and offer suggestions for improvement.	Storyboard reviews give you an early look at the overall organizational usability of the complete library plan and your Content Specifications for various pieces of your library. Storyboard reviews are especially useful for reviewing non-print media such as online documentation, online help, and video.
previous product	Formal, performance-based usability testing of previous versions of the product or related versions of the product.	By testing previous versions of the product and its publications, you will be able to develop better plans for improvements in new versions.

Figure 20.5 Usability techniques during the planning phases

Type of assessment	Methodology	Results
	To conduct usability tests of previous products, develop test plans, generate hypotheses, create scenarios, and ask users to perform typical tasks using the product and the publications.	
competitive product	Formal, performance-based usability testing of competitive products. To conduct usability tests of competitive products, develop test plans, generate hypotheses, create scenarios, and ask users to perform typical tasks using the competitive product and publications. Conduct the usability tests on the competitive products and their publications.	By testing competitive products and their publications, you can gain significant insights into what you should and should not include in your publications. Competitive testing is especially useful when you are designing a new product and publications. It can be used to set usability goals and convince upper management of the importance of usability.
developmental or usability edit	A heuristic-based evaluation of a publication design by the publication quality-assurance team. The developmental editor is a specialist in state-of-the-art guidelines for the usability of technical publications. The heuristic is based upon the developmental editor's experience and expertise. To conduct a developmental edit, ask the senior editor to use guidelines based upon previous experience and knowledge of the latest developments in the field to review a publication plan.	Once you have Information Plans, Content Specifications, and early sections of publications, working with a skilled senior editor can reduce the number of usability problems that will need to be identified later through user testing. There is no point in using more costly testing methods until the standard problems of organization, clarity, consistency, and coherence are cleared up through the edit / revision process.
technical review	A quality-assurance check of the completeness and accuracy of the publications plans in relationship to the current design of the product. To conduct a technical review, ask the members of the development team to review aspects of the publications plan for their relationships to the emerging product design and for their technical accuracy.	Thorough and accurate technical reviews during the planning phases can save considerable time and cost later in the life cycle.

Figure 20.5 (Continued)

information gained from users, both are invaluable to developing an effective early design model for the publications.

Usability assessment that occurs during Phases 1 and 2 of the development process has the greatest likelihood of having a significant effect on the publications design for the least cost. Test results during these phases may require rethinking and reorganization of the detailed specifications of the publications, but do not require wholesale revamping of complete or partial publications. It is always easier for your team to rearrange an outline or redesign a storyboard than it is to rewrite or redesign an entire library of publications when it is in draft stage.

Early testing should be designed to proceed quickly and produce rapid results. Decisions that affect the language and organization of publications can be made before less usable schemes are incorporated into the design and implemented.

 Guideline: Test early, test often. Early planning and testing of ideas can save usability costs and help ensure that usability goals are met with the least possible revision and reconstruction of drafts.

Conducting early prototype and formative testing of drafts

Once your publications project progresses from the planning phases into the implementation activities of Phase 3, you will be able to stage usability assessments of more complete versions of the publications. The starting point is early prototype testing.

In Chapter 19, you learned about some of the issues involved in the development of early prototypes of publications. After your team has developed those prototypes, you are ready to conduct a variety of usability assessments. Some of the assessment methodologies are the same as those you used during the planning phases of the project. Usability assessments that continue from the planning phases through the development of prototypes and drafts include:

- The developmental or usability edit
- The technical review

Other methodologies, listed in Figure 20.6, require more complete publications to be effective and productive.

The information in Figure 20.6 provides a brief overview of some of the most significant testing methodologies available to your team during the implementation phase. Remember that the more testing you plan and conduct early in the development life cycle, the less impact the test results will have on your development schedule. You want to uncover problems with the design and writing of user publications as soon as possible, with prototype sections and early drafts. The earlier you correct the problems, the less rework will be required later in the development process. It is much less time-consuming to find problems early, correct them, and incorporate the new insights into the sections you write later, than to try to make all changes when the publications are nearly complete.

Type of assessment	Methodology	Results
cognitive walkthrough	An evaluation method based on the special skills of a team of experts who understand publication design and the product, and who have studied the user's previous knowledge and experience and have insight into the user's goals. To conduct a cognitive walkthrough, the team of experts attempt to anticipate the user's actions and thoughts while trying to achieve a task-oriented goal. For example, a cognitive walkthrough of a manual begins with a clear statement of the user's objective in performing a task. The user may be looking for information in the index or table of contents to find out how to perform a task or solve a problem. The cognitive walkthrough team moves through the document much as the user would, looking for confusing steps, lack of information when needed, possible places for error, and any other issues they uncover through the walkthrough.	The cognitive walkthrough is intended to supplement or even replace user-based usability assessments. The results will be much the same as those uncovered during user testing, to the extent that the team of experts is able to mimic the actions and mental models of the actual users. The cognitive walkthrough is especially useful in uncovering problems with consistency, terminology, task sequencing, and other aspects of the publication that benefit from a thorough and consistent application of the expert team's experience and knowledge of the field.
informal observation	Informal observation of users performing tasks with the product and its publications. This informal observation may take place in your location with either a single user or a small group of users. However, informal observations may be considerably more productive if they take place in the user's working environment. In this way, you can gain insight into the problems that users encounter in a real setting, with all of its interruptions and awkwardness.	Informal observation, along with questions as the users work, will greatly increase your understanding of the effectiveness of your prototype publications and early drafts. You will gain insight into real use in actual working environments.

Figure 20.6 Usability techniques during the implementation phase

Type of assessment	Methodology	Results
	To conduct an informal observation, provide the users with copies of the prototype publications, with or without the product. Then watch how they use them. Ask questions to clarify behavior and plans as the users work.	
laboratory observation	Formal usability testing is often identified with the use of a special testing laboratory. This laboratory can be a formal and fully equipped lab at your location or the location of your usability consultants. However, laboratory-type observations can also take place in informal settings or at the user's location with the use of portable equipment. No matter what methodology you select for data collection, a formal laboratory test of the usability of a prototype includes a carefully developed test plan, hypotheses, controlled observations with or without talk-aloud protocols from the users, and a thorough evaluation of the results.	Formal, controlled usability testing provides the most thorough user-based analysis of performance with your prototypes and early drafts. You gain significant insight into how users interpret what they read in text, in contrast to what you believe you have written.

Figure 20.6 (Continued)

You will find that it is easier to uncover problems than to know how to fix them. You may uncover problems with the interface that cannot be fixed in the publications at all. You may find problems that you do not understand well enough to be confident that the change you recommend will make things better, not worse. You may concentrate on minor items while neglecting severe problems that are life threatening, may injure the user, or may destroy equipment or data. You may need an entirely new design perspective to change a publications design for the better. If the problems appear to be complex, you may want to enlist an expert information designer to help you find viable solutions.

Guideline: Conduct thorough tests of early prototypes and publications drafts to allow your team to build usability into its design and development activities.

Conducting evaluative testing

All of the testing types discussed in the previous sections are most useful when they are conducted early, during the formative phases of the publications-development life cycle. Formative testing gives your team the information it needs to build more useful publications for the audience.

You may also find it useful, however, to conduct testing during the final stages of the development process to ensure that you have met users' needs and that your publications meet the quality standards of your organization. Late-cycle testing is not as useful for the development process because it becomes more difficult and costly to make substantive changes in the design of publications the closer you get to the production phase. Late-cycle testing is useful in providing statistically significant information that you can then use as a quality benchmark after the product is released to customers and for the next development cycle.

Most of the methods available for evaluative testing are the same as those I have already discussed in the previous sections. Perhaps the greatest difference in the design and execution of evaluative tests concerns the number of test subjects and the types of measurements taken. While we are interested in time on task and numbers of errors made during the early formative testing, in final evaluative testing where we might avoid using talk-aloud protocols, we can accumulate much more meaningful time and error data. With sufficient numbers of test subjects (15 to 20 or more per user type), you can use statistical analysis techniques to set quantitative performance benchmarks or compare with previous benchmarks. For example, you may discover that the mean time to complete a task with the previous version of the documentation was 14 minutes. An evaluative test of your new document design shows that you have been able to decrease the mean time on task to 6 minutes, a substantial improvement in the usefulness of the procedures.

You may be able to show with a well-structured evaluative test that the new organization of publications allows users to find information 50-percent faster than with earlier versions and results in 25-percent fewer calls for help. Such quantitative information is especially valuable in assessing quality and setting goals for later revisions.

Many of the methods shown in Figure 20.7 are the same as those you conducted earlier. However, some of the situations are different during evaluative testing because most of the product is complete and can be tested in its entirety. For example, you may not have been able to test the complete index before the final testing phase because too much of the publication was incomplete. During evaluative testing you can find out if your index is useful.

You may have sufficient time left after evaluative testing to make small changes to the publications, like adding a few words to the index. You are unlikely to have enough time to make substantive changes until the next release. However, if you have planned your testing well, you should have decided what events would cause you to delay the release of the product and publications. Some problems will be so serious that you cannot leave them for the next version to be fixed.

Although not as timely and useful to development as the early phases of testing, late-cycle usability testing gives you an opportunity to determine statistically significant

Type of assessment	Methodology	Results
cognitive walkthrough	The cognitive walkthrough is performed in exactly the same way as described in Figure 20.6. However, for evaluative testing more of the publications will be complete.	Your cognitive walkthrough team should be interested in confirming the usefulness of the changes made since the last walkthrough.
heuristic evaluation	A formal heuristic evaluation is similar to a developmental or usability edit, except that formal heuristic evaluations often include checklists of the guidelines that should have been followed during development. If you have guidelines for publication design in your organization, you can use them to develop a heuristic. The heuristic ordinarily consists of a series of questions that help the evaluation team decide if the publication in question follows the guidelines. Topics might include access points (table of contents, index, headings), language, task orientation, overall organization, and others. The most useful heuristics will include weighting factors for various parts of the publication. The use of weighting factors acknowledges that not every guideline is equally important. A heuristic evaluation works best when it is conducted by a team of experts in publications design. However, some heuristic evaluations are specifically designed to be used by members of the complete design team (development, marketing, publications, customer service, training, etc.).	An evaluative heuristic evaluation can help you decide how well a publication conforms to existing guidelines. To the extent that the guidelines relate to the ultimate usability of the publication, they may help you uncover some of the problems with a publication that might be discovered through performance-based usability testing.
informal observation	Informal observations of the product at customer beta sites can help you evaluate the effectiveness of your publications in the real user environment.	Unobtrusive informal observations may give you information about how your publications are used, or not used, that you cannot obtain in any other way. You will gain insight into the real use, in contrast to what customers say they use in focus groups or individual interviews.

Figure 20.7 Usability techniques late in the development cycle

Type of assessment	Methodology	Results
laboratory observation	Formal usability testing is described more fully in Figure 20.6. At the evaluative phase, you are able to test the usefulness of the entire publication or library of publications rather than small subsections. During the evaluative phase, we often find that usability tests concentrate on the product rather than the publications because the human-factors team wants to discover if the product can be used without reference to the publications. If you want feedback at this point on the publications, you may have to create scenarios that specifically require the use of the publications.	Benchmark information about the usability of your publications is based on the observation of actual users performing real tasks. Evaluative testing provides one of the best opportunities to conduct larger-scale tests that will provide statistically significant results.
field study	Once a product and its publications have been in the customers' hands for some time, you should conduct field studies. Field studies may include informal observation, formal usability tests, and group and individual interviews, as well as customer satisfaction surveys. Field studies enable you to learn how your customers use your publications, especially after the initial getting-started process.	You will be able to discover how publications are used during the life of the product at the customer site. Field studies help you prepare for the next version of the publications, especially when you have a new product and little understanding of actual user tasks could be obtained before the product was introduced.
competitive evaluation	Competitive evaluations can be conducted at the beginning of the publications-development life cycle or at the end. In either case, evaluations of your competitors' publications will give you insights into how to redevelop your own the next time around.	You will be able to benchmark the usability of your own publications in reference to your competition's.

Figure 20.7 (Continued)

quality benchmarks for your publications. Solid, performance-based benchmarks that relate directly to the usability of the product and publications with actual users are the most important benchmarks you can obtain. They are much more significant, from the customer's point of view, than internal benchmarks based on publications guidelines. Guidelines, while moving us closer to good design, are not specific enough to account for all of the problems users will have with our publications. And guidelines enforce the status quo of our design knowledge. If we follow guidelines, we will produce adequate publications that please judging panels but may be completely unsuccessful in meeting user needs. The best guidelines help us produce average publications; performance-based usability assessment enables us to produce excellent publications.

If you are contemplating a redesign of your publications, especially a redesign that includes a minimalist approach to information or involves using new media, I strongly suggest that you invest in usability assessment. We simply do not know enough about our audiences and their environments and needs to intuitively design an excellent set of usable publications. We need to learn how they use the new electronic media, which indicates a requirement for testing online help, softcopy documents, as well as print documents. Only by better understanding our users will we succeed in providing them with the support information they need to learn and use the product successfully.

As publications-project manager, you need to understand the possibilities as well as the costs and logistics of usability assessment so that you can plan such assessment as a standard part of the publications-development life cycle. It is easy to assume that you and your team know enough to design useful publications. The further you are removed in physical environment, experience, knowledge, and learning style from your users, the less likely that an intuitive design will succeed. Begin with the assumption that you must work hard to know your users and plan usability assessments to find out exactly who the users are and how they learn and perform.

It is also easy to assume that there is no time for usability assessments in your busy publications life cycle. As the old saying goes, "There's never time to do it right, but there's always time to do it over." If you have a tight schedule, look carefully at the early-phase usability testing methodologies. Find simple ways to discover the usefulness of your design ideas. Usability testing does not have to take enormous amounts of time. The earlier you test, the better chance you have to fix problems and improve the publications. And, if you cannot test early, consider testing late. As soon as you ship your publications, start testing and use what you learn to improve the next version.

 Guideline: Perform evaluative testing to discover quantifiable usability benchmarks for your publications. Fit usability assessment into the life cycle if you are serious about improving the quality of your publications.

Anticipating Changes in the Development Life Cycle

Software- and hardware-development projects, as well as other highly technical publications projects, all experience a considerable degree of change during the development process. The changes are greatest when the technical challenges are most difficult and when the development effort stretches the developers' level of knowledge and experience. Projects with 50-percent, 100-percent, even 500-percent cost and schedule overruns are not uncommon in high-tech industries.

During the course of the development effort, even when adequate planning has occurred up front, project managers and the members of the development teams inevitably make mistakes. The specifications of the project are imperfect, resulting in rework in early phases of implementation to integrate all the emerging pieces. Requirements are inadequate, resulting in changes to the specifications. The implementation efforts of skilled team members are imperfect, resulting in bugs that are time-consuming to fix. As projects proceed, they appear to increase in technical complexity. Solutions that looked adequate at first turn out to be inadequate.

All the problems that occur in all the life-cycle phases result in work that must be redone to be correct. The amount of rework seems to exist in relationship to the complexity of the technical problems, the skills and experience of the developers, the skills of the project managers, and the ability of all the team members to translate user needs into a usable product. Early prototyping and usability assessment, in addition to traditional validation and verification, uncover problems that have to be rethought, redesigned, re-implemented, and retested. Kenneth Cooper, in his work on development projects in a number of industries (Cooper, March 1993) illustrates the rework problem with the diagram in Figure 21.1.

Every project begins with a certain amount of work to be done. Work progresses during the project. As the work progresses, problems are discovered that require rework. Rework is added to the total amount of work being done, adding to the total number of development hours. Eventually, we hope, all the work is completed and correct, and the project is finished and delivered.

At any point during the development process, a certain amount of rework has been discovered and added to the schedule. At the same point, other rework is unknown and remains to be discovered. Eventually, it will be discovered and be added to the work to

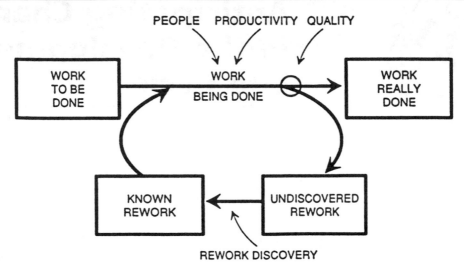

Figure 21.1 The relationship of work done and undiscovered rework. This illustration is reprinted from the *Project Management Journal* with permission of the Project Management Institute, P.O. Box 43, Drexel Hill, Pa 19026, (215) 622-1796, a worldwide organization for advancing the state-of-the-art in project management.

be done. The process continues, with rework occurring several times on the same work, until all work is completed.

The publications rework process

This process of work and rework extends to the publications-development life cycle. Rework occurs not only because of defects found in the publications themselves by peer reviews, copyedits, developmental edits, and technical reviews but also when the product changes in response to rework on the product-development side.

As we have discussed in Chapters 12, 17, and 18, publications project managers, as well as writers and artists, feel frustrated by the lack of progress on projects that seem to be in a continual state of rework. Changes are piled onto previously completed sections of publications. Often enough, the changes are on top of changes already made. And so it goes until someone finally declares that the work and rework are complete and the publications are ready to go to press.

At any point in the development process, the project manager and the team members must be prepared to evaluate the percent complete of the project. To facilitate this evaluation, you have learned in Chapters 17 and 18 to divide the project into many small pieces, work backward in estimating from the final due dates, define milestones in terms of project completion, and take other steps designed to keep projects reasonably under control. But despite your best efforts, you may find yourself declaring that the project is "almost" complete when you have no idea when all the work and rework will actually be finished.

"I'm certain that we are 90-percent complete with the publications. We only have a few sections left to draft. Then, we can complete the reviews and go right into production. We'll have everything done in three weeks," answered John to the vice president's inquiry.

"Fine, but that's exactly what you told me last month, too," said Les, the vice president of marketing. "I need to know today exactly when you'll be done."

"Well, Sam in development says he's 90-percent complete with the code for the new dialogs. If he gets done this week, we'll be OK," said John. "I can promise three weeks."

"Sam has been 90-percent complete with that code for the last four months," answered Les. "I don't know what I'm supposed to be able to tell our customers. I've stopped saying anything that remotely suggests a schedule."

"I guess you're right. On the DRM project last year, we all said we were 90 percent complete in September," admitted John. "We didn't ship until February. I guess none of us is very good at estimating.

If this scenario sounds familiar, it should be. The vast majority of high-tech development projects, including publications, appear to exist in the same state of paralysis. Projects get reported for months at 70-percent complete or 90-percent complete or whatever figure seems palatable to senior management.

Even good publications project managers who work hard at tracking their project activities and revising the schedules will throw up their hands in frustration as the amount of rework and additions keeps increasing. When the changes occur close to the supposed project deadline, the best of managers is likely to give up trying to predict the schedule. The team simply continues to make changes with no end in sight. Teams even put in huge numbers of overtime hours, only to discover that the schedule has once again been pushed out and the crisis is over, at least for a while.

The graph in Figure 21.2 shows a picture of an ideal project. It is similar to the curve we looked at earlier to help anticipate schedule problems. The curve, with a simple 45° slope, represents a perfect project.

On this graph, when a project is believed to be 50-percent complete, it is actually 50-percent complete. When it is believed to be 90-percent complete, it is in reality 90-percent complete. Project managers are tracking everything that needs to be done. The amount of rework is under control, with no surprises late in the development process.

Actual projects are rarely this predictable. More likely, they resemble the curve in Figure 21.3, which shows little correspondence between the beliefs of the project team and reality during most of the course of the project.

Note that at the 60-percent complete point on the horizontal axis, the project team believes that 60-percent of the project is complete, when in reality much less is complete. Only when the project gets closer to actual completion does the belief system begin to merge with reality. The curve in Figure 21.3 represents a project that starts and proceeds slowly. You can imagine the level of overtime devoted to this project

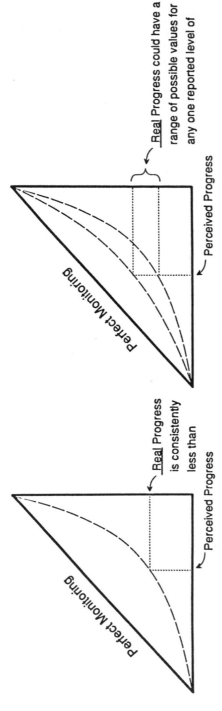

Figure 21.2 A percent complete comparison. This illustration is reprinted from the *Project Management Journal* with permission of the Project Management Institute, P.O. Box 43, Drexel Hill, PA 19026, (215) 622-1796, a worldwide organization for advancing the state-of-the-art in project management.

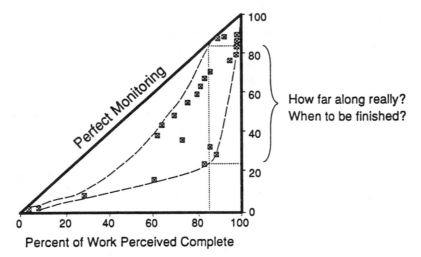

Percent of Work Perceived Complete

Figure 21.3 Percent complete of an actual project. This illustration is reprinted from the *Project Management Journal* with permission of the Project Management Institute, P.O. Box 43, Drexel Hill, PA 19026, (215) 622-1796, a worldwide organization for advancing the state-of-the-art in project management.

during the last stages. The team apparently only makes real progress near the end. The curve is a wonderful illustration of continuing good intentions. No one has postponed their work, everyone is working hard, but what was once done now needs to be done again.

The curve in Figure 21.4 shows a project that gets stuck. It has been proceeding fairly well on schedule until the 50-percent-complete mark. Then, it slows down in

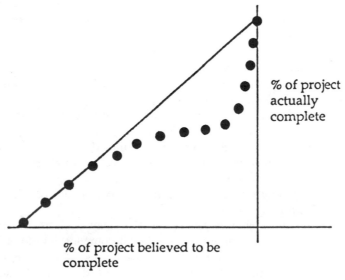

Figure 21.4 Percent complete of a delayed project

reality, although everyone's perceptions get stuck at the 70-percent mark. This is an illustration of a project that has encountered an unforeseen technical difficulty.

Each of the curves represents the actual historical information on the project, reviewed after the project is complete. The percentage of the project actually completed is calculated by knowing the total number of hours needed to complete the project and the percentage of hours used at each time interval (weekly or monthly). The actual percentage of total hours expended at each milestone is compared with the statements about project completion made by the project managers.

 Guideline: Calculate a rework curve by comparing the actual percent complete of your projects with beliefs about the percent complete.

Anticipating the amount of rework

What if you work in an organization that has historical records of project completion that resemble Figure 21.3 or 21.4? How can you use this historical analysis to better predict the future of your current project, especially at seemingly stagnant points in the development process? If you are working in an organization that resembles Figure 21.4, you know that when the development project manager gets to 50-percent complete, the project will begin to experience delays. After three or four months at the 50-percent complete level, the development manager will once again account for progress toward completion, and the development team will finish in a rush.

As the publications project manager, you can use the profile developed from project histories to help predict how much work you have remaining. The work remaining will include not only the work your team is already doing but also the rework that will inevitably occur as the development team tries to solve their problems.

You can use the characteristic rework curve to anticipate the extent of the additional hours that will be needed to complete your current project. Projects that are typically 200-percent over schedule are likely to be 200-percent over schedule again unless some drastic action is taken to change the work/rework process.

Recently, one of our project managers decided that to meet the announced development schedule, she would have to increase her writing staff from 4 full-time writers to 12. Our management team asked about the likelihood of the development team meeting the announced schedule. She explained that, as usual, senior management insisted that certain dates had to be met. Yet, everyone on the development team knew those dates were completely unrealistic. She and the developers both anticipated that the schedule would slip by two months.

In such a situation, how should you react? You may want to ask for additional people to help you advance the publications schedule but not ask for 8 more people. Instead, you may want to extend the 8 person-months across the three months everyone is actually anticipating. That means that you need 8/3 or 2.6 additional staff members right away, rather than 8. You can use historical precedent in your organization to avoid adding additional resources that are unlikely to be needed.

It is always possible, although not probable, that the development team will meet the announced schedule. As project manager, you need to monitor activities closely and be prepared to respond if the schedule speeds up.

Guideline: Use the rework curve to anticipate the amount of change that will occur in your current project.

Changing the rework curve

Just because a rework curve appears to be characteristic of your organization does not mean that it is inevitable. If an organization decides that it must get its development processes under control, the amount of rework that gets done late in the development life cycle can be changed. If requirements can be defined better at the beginning of a project, if requirements can be translated into more complete specifications, if problems with the specifications can be discovered early, the characteristic curve will begin to resemble more closely the ideal project curve.

By instituting a total-quality process, organizations are able to eliminate much rework by earlier testing, more thorough inspections and walkthroughs, rapid prototyping to decrease the number of late-cycle interface changes, and other measures. The sooner problems are discovered, the more efficient the rework process becomes. Teams can schedule rework to fit into the original schedule, as long as the rework occurs early enough.

A development organization that is determined to change its history and decrease the time to market needs to focus on the rework curve to help understand where the process must be improved. The earlier rework is discovered and the more that can be done to eliminate rework altogether, the less time the total project will take to complete.

Guideline: Use the rework curve as a tool to change the development process by eliminating most rework and discovering most of the rework actions early in the development life cycle.

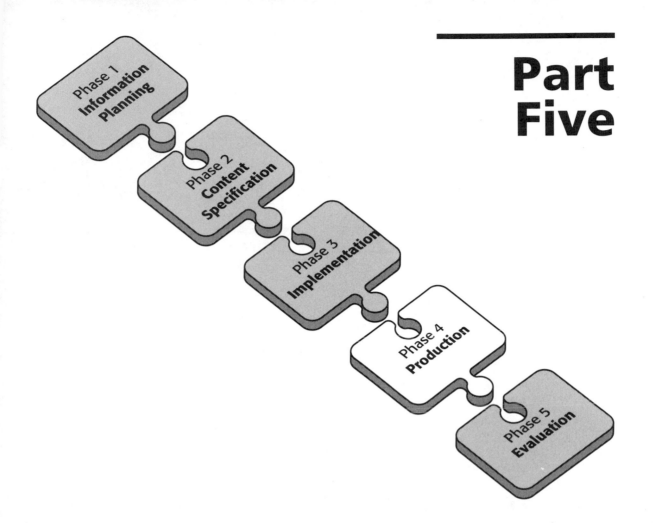

Phase 1
Information
Planning

Phase 2
Content
Specification

Phase 3
Implementation

Phase 4
Production

Phase 5
Evaluation

Part Five

Managing the Production Phase

As a project manager, you need to consider the complicated environment in which you produce publications today. You learn about options open to the project manager in reducing production time, especially through early planning for production. Included in our discussion of the production process are multi-language production issues, multi-platform production issues, graphics, prepress, packaging, and distribution issues from a management point of view. You focus here on the tradeoffs that managers face and the complexities of the decision-making and negotiating process, rather than discussing how to perform production tasks, which is outside the scope of this book.

You also address the issues of managing Phase 4 activities such as indexing and production copyediting. In addition, you consider the demands of translation and localization in a multi-national environment.

Contents

Chapter 22: Managing Production Activities

- Managing the production and review of the camera-ready draft
- Planning for printing, binding, and packaging
- Monitoring the production process
- Supervising distribution
- Adding to the Project Management Notebook

Chapter 23: Managing Indexing

- Selecting a quality level for an index
- Selecting an indexer
- Blocking indexing time into the schedule

Chapter 24: Scheduling Copyediting

- Using copyediting and formatting checklists and electronic styles
- Blocking copyediting time into the schedule

Chapter 25: Managing the Translation and Localization Process

- Finding the best translation vendor for your needs
- Establishing glossaries of key technical terms
- Minimizing translation problems
- Establishing an internal-review process
- Estimating translation costs
- Blocking translation time into the schedule

Results

You will understand elements of the process of working with outside vendors and controlling the production process. You will learn how to schedule and manage the process of translation and localization and to schedule activities such as indexing and copyediting.

Managing Production Activities

Once the second or third (or more) developmental draft has been approved by the review teams and only minor rework is left to perform on the drafts, then you have moved your project out of Phase 3: Implementation activities into Phase 4: Production activities. In Phase 4, the publications are prepared for printing, binding, and delivery to the customers (Figure 22.1).

A number of activities occur during Phase 4 that require careful management if they are to proceed correctly and remain on schedule. Because many of the activities have to occur in sequence rather than in parallel like so many of the Phase 3 activities, the path you must follow to complete the project becomes critical. Each activity must be scheduled, taking advantage of as much overlap as possible. Each deliverable must be carefully defined so that little rework is necessary. The scheduled events must occur as anticipated if the project is not to get seriously behind schedule.

The traditional activities conducted in Phase 4 are summarized in Figure 22.2. These traditional activities have been modified by the introduction of new processes and the addition of activities to the production cycle. In this chapter, you review the activities involved in print production and distribution. Subsequent chapters deal with indexing, copyediting, and translation and localization.

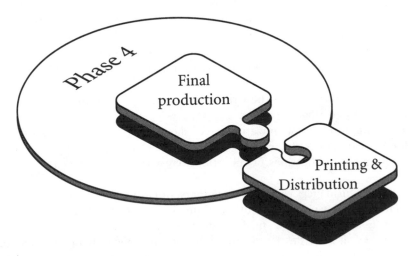

Figure 22.1 Phase 4

Managing the production and review of the camera-ready draft

Traditionally, the final draft of a publications life cycle has been known as a camera-ready draft. The term *camera-ready* refers to the process prior to printing when the type and the graphics were originally pasted up in what is referred to as a *mechanical*. The mechanical was then photographed by a process camera. The output of the camera is a film negative of the page. The paper or metal printing plates were then made light sensitive and exposed with the film negative so that an image of the page appeared on the plate. The plate was then placed on the offset printing press.

Today, most pasteup has been eliminated because we now produce both text and graphics electronically. We can even produce photographic images, in single or multiple colors, with sophisticated electronic publishing equipment. Now, your team members prepare typeset quality text and art. Computer files are used to output pages that are of the traditional typeset quality at 2,400 dpi (dots per inch) or less quality at 300 to 1,200 dpi. Complicated art is constructed electronically. Even gray-tone drawings and four-color art are created electronically and merged with final text. The output from your electronic publishing equipment becomes your camera-ready art.

The output you choose can be either paper or film. If you choose paper, the pages are photographed to produce film negatives. If you choose film, the printer does not need to create film negatives but goes directly from your film negative to exposing the printing plate.

All of these activities, referred to as *prepress*, are designed to reduce the number of steps that were once necessary at the very end of the publications life cycle. In general, the amount of time for final production may have been reduced from the days of pasteup.

Of course, prepress activities are necessary only if a press is involved. Many small-run publications are handled by high-quality copy machines that take original text and graphics directly from the publishing system. For other publications, we eliminate printing altogether, delivering publications as part of the product in software or hardware or publishing books on CD-ROM or computer disk. Internally, in many organizations, we make a copy of a publication available on a file server to be accessed electronically by many people in the customer organization.

Despite all the innovations in the publishing process and the automation of prepress activities, much of the traditional production work is still done within the publications organization by members of the writing staff, assisted by production specialists where it is economically justifiable.

In fact, publications organization have taken over many of the tasks once handled by production specialists in vendor organizations. As a result, the internal production cycle within the publications organization may actually be longer than it was just a few years ago.

As project manager, you need to understand the production activities so that you can plan for their smooth execution. From indexing to copyediting and the development of a copy ready for final production by vendors who are external to your organization, all activities late in the publications-development life cycle must be well understood and scheduled carefully.

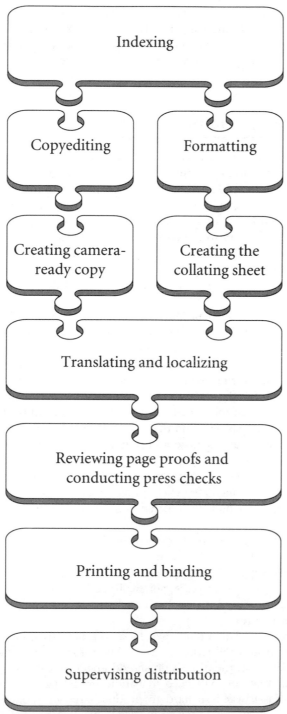

Figure 22.2 Phase 4 activities

The sooner you understand the requirements of Phase 4, the better you will be able to schedule the activities. With the early involvement of production specialists and outside vendors, the less likely a catastrophe will occur that will delay delivery. By understanding the production activities, you will be better able to anticipate problems and find solutions quickly.

Planning for printing, binding, and packaging

In some publications organizations, all activities associated with printing, binding, and packaging of technical publications are handled by a procurement organization that works directly with selected vendors. The project manager, working closely with the production specialists, simply turns over the completed camera-ready copy along with collating instructions and other special requirements to the organization responsible for final reproduction and delivery to the customer or a central delivery facility.

In such situations, you do not need to know much about the processes that occur after your team finishes the camera-ready copy. Your only subsequent involvement may be to check blueline copy from the printer and check the final deliverable copies from the bindery for accuracy.

In large organizations where final production activities are handled by specialists, you may find that you have little control over the process. In one company we worked with for several years, printing and binding ordinarily was scheduled to take 12 weeks. Only through a miracle could the project manager, usually on the product side, shorten that schedule. It took 12 weeks from the time camera-ready copy was turned over until the publications were ready for shipment to the customers. Rush jobs took 9 weeks.

In other organizations where procurement departments handle all relationships with outside printing vendors, you may also find that you have little control over the quality of the work done. Unless you have a close and mutually supportive relationship with your procurement organization, you may find that a well-executed publication is ruined by a printing vendor who did not adequately understand the nature of the job. You may also find that your costs increase when procurement selects an inappropriate vendor who charges extra for a difficult job that could easily be handled by someone else.

However, in many more organizations, you will find yourself totally responsible for all relationships with outside vendors. You will select vendors, provide detailed requirements, obtain bids, supervise the process, and inspect the final deliverables for compliance with requirements. In this case, you will need to know a great deal about the processes of printing, binding, and packaging to ensure that the job is well done and costs are kept under control.

The following discussion is not intended to be a complete treatment of all of the vagaries of managing the print-production process. The topic is much too complex to be treated in full here. However, the discussion should give you some insight into some of the management tasks that you will need to handle or delegate to ensure that the publications your team has worked so hard to produce are not spoiled by late-cycle errors. Many of the problems that occur in print production are the result of inexperience in your organization.

If much of this information is new to you, consider attending a workshop on prepress and print-production techniques, talk to your vendors, call knowledgeable colleagues, and buy books that describe the process more fully. Learn by asking lots of questions. Raise your level of awareness about what can go wrong; you will get better results if you are knowledgeable.

Guideline: If you are responsible for the reproduction processes, become well informed about how they work and understand your role as project manager.

Selecting the best reproduction method for your needs

Your selection of the best way to reproduce your team's publications in hardcopy depends on a number of factors:

- Total cost of the printing method used
- Quality of the output required
- Quality of the input required
- Turnaround time
- Quality of your competitors' publications
- Customer expectations

Some methods, like offset and Webb printing, take more setup time but may cost less if large quantities are needed. Offset printing often produces the highest-quality output. It may be the only method available for the production of multi-color art and spot color to highlight particular features in text and line drawings. Photocopy methods take less setup time, but generally offer lower quality output. However, for small quantities, photocopying provides considerable cost advantages over offset printing.

In addition to the cost of the original printing job, you must also consider the cost of updating and warehousing large quantities of your publications. While offset printing may look less expensive for large quantities than photocopying, if you have to store large quantities of documentation for long periods of time, your long-term costs may actually increase. You may also find yourself with many outdated copies of your publications if changes in the product occur soon after the initial printing.

To determine the best hardcopy reproduction method, you must balance cost against quality. You must also consider the quality of your camera-ready copy. If you are using a 300 dpi draft printer, you gain little quality advantage from using offset printing because of the low quality of the original. In fact, the offset printing process may actually worsen the quality of the original by making the images considerably darker, although offset printing may still be the most cost-effective method. If you are able to produce higher-quality originals, from 600 to 2,400 dpi in laser printers or linotype machines, offset printing may produce significantly better quality than photocopying.

You may also try to increase the reproducibility of your originals by printing them on paper specially prepared for camera-ready copy. A number of paper manufacturers sell paper designed to increase the contrast between your original black text and the white of the paper. The higher the contrast and the cleaner the application of toner, the better the reproduction will be. Once you decide to prepare camera-ready copy from your laser printer or other printing device, ensure that it is in excellent working condition. You want to avoid the streaks and spots that are magnified in the reproduction process. You may also want to have an extra toner cartridge at hand to use only for masters.

You may also want to use a font that results in well-formed dots of toner on the page. Some fonts provide very little ink in areas such as punctuation. These areas of little toner may disappear in both photocopying and offset printing. Other fonts, especially those with small spaces inside closed letters like *a* and *e* (known as the counter), may fill with ink during reproduction, making the text unreadable. You may find it helpful to test various fonts with the reproduction method you select to ensure that text and graphics remain clear and readable.

Another consideration in addition to the quality of the input is the size of the final pages. Most domestic US photocopying equipment uses 8.5″ × 11″ paper. Smaller page sizes will require trimming, which means that you have to position the originals correctly on the 8.5″ × 11″ sheets so that the number of trim cuts is minimized and duplex (front and back) printing turns out correctly placed. Costs increase with the amount of trimming required, and you are paying for paper that will be discarded. For larger paper sizes, your photocopy vendor will need to have special equipment. More hand work may also be required.

To understand the relative costs and decision points, interview several vendors. Ask for a range of costs, depending upon the quality, size, and quantities needed. Use the information you collect to assist your decision-making process.

For nonprint media, you need to understand the decision and price points involved, as well as the reproducibility of your original decisions you made about the print documents. You may need to have CD-ROM disks created, which involves burning a master disk and making copies from it. The cost is greatest for the original; reproduction costs for large quantities of disks are generally orders of magnitude lower than the original. The same is true for video. You will need to have a master videotape created of sufficient quality to make copies. Generally home video equipment in the standard VHS format is totally inadequate for making multiple copies. Your video vendor can advise about the format needed but be certain that the vendor understands your requirements. Some video vendors who quote low prices may produce low-quality output that cannot be copied.

In each case, it is worthwhile to spend time learning about the processes so that you can make informed choices. If your decisions are wrong, you may have to absorb the costs of redoing a reproduction job. Understand what constitutes quality in the output of the process you select, and discuss your quality requirements with your vendors.

 Guideline: Become knowledgeable about the processes from which you choose, especially the quality and price points.

Selecting the best binding and packaging system for your needs

A number of choices are also available for binding hardcopy publications and for packaging a library of media to be shipped with the product. A number of factors will influence your choice:

- Size of the publication (page size and number of pages)
- Environment where the publication will be used
- The users' patterns of use
- Type of updating planned
- Company standards
- The competitions' practices

Among the choices available today, you will find

- Loose-leaf in vinyl or paper-board three-ring or multi-ring binders
- Plastic comb
- Wire-O
- Perfect
- Saddle stitch

Each system involves both advantages and disadvantages. Loose-leaf binders can be updated easily, and tabs can be used to clearly divide sections for the users. Binder covers can either be silk-screened, or slip-in covers can be inserted in clear vinyl sleeves on the spine, front, and back, as needed. The name of the publication is easily read on the spine. However, loose-leaf binders are often large and bulky, take up considerable desk space when open, and can burst their rings if too many pages are inserted. Tabs are expensive to produce, especially in small quantities, and custom sizes may be very expensive.

Loose-leaf binding systems may also require sheet lifters, plastic inserts placed in the front and back of the binder that keep the pages from falling into the rings and ripping. You may also want to consider placing your title page in a sheet protector so that the toner or ink does not adhere to the inside of the vinyl binder.

Plastic comb binding, although not the highest quality, is often the least expensive binding system available. It is often appropriate for inhouse projects and is the binding of choice for proposals and reports and more informal publications. It has the advantage of permitting printing on the plastic binding, which allows you to label the publications and make them easier to find on a bookshelf.

Wire-O bounded books are much smaller and less bulky to handle and can be produced in a wide variety of sizes. They open flat on the work surface and can be turned back on themselves to create an even smaller footprint. Wire-O is often much less expensive than loose-leaf. However, wire-O bindings generally lack spine identification of the publication title, making them difficult to find on the users' shelves. Some companies provide a coverleaf cover that wraps around the wire-O and allows a title to be printed. However, users find the overleafs awkward and frequently do not use them properly. Wire-O books are also very difficult to update.

Perfect-bound technical publications have become increasingly popular in recent years, especially since lay-flat technology has become available. Perfect binding is usually less expensive, especially in large quantities, than either loose-leaf or wire-O. Publications that are perfect bound are difficult to photocopy, often discouraging software pirating. However, perfect-bound publications are impossible to update. A poor-quality job or a publication that gets heavy use may fall apart, leaving the user with a stack of loose sheets. You may also find that the longer translated versions of your publications will not allow for the same binding techniques you chose for the original English version.

Saddle stitch, which uses one or two staples through the center of the publication, is useful for small publications. Anything with more than about 60 pages cannot be saddle-stitched. Saddle stitching is quite inexpensive, but the publications cannot be updated and will not lay flat.

Whatever binding method you select, be certain that you understand the tradeoffs in cost, quality, and usability and that your choice best meets your users' needs.

In addition to binding methods, you also may be responsible for having an entire packaging system designed and manufactured. In this case, you should be working with a graphic artist who can create an attractive and usable package that fits your needs and your users' environment. For a publications library that includes many individual elements, you may want a box or a slipcase that keeps all the elements in one place and is easily identifiable by the users. For software projects, you can also include disks, video, CD-ROMs, and others in slipcases.

You may find that to preserve the quality of your packaging, you must have your hardcopy publications plus the other inserts shrink-wrapped. Be careful about shrink-wrapping, however. The process uses heat to apply a plastic wrap. That same heat can melt parts of your publications.

Guideline: Learn as much as you can about binding and packaging methods so that you can make good decisions and avoid disasters.

Finding the best vendors for your needs

Once you know something about the printing and binding methods you want to use, you are ready to select vendors. In many cases, a single vendor can handle the entire process, but you may also discover cost savings in finding specialists. Many vendors who say they can handle the entire process may subcontract parts of the process to others. Consequently, you pay the subcontractor's markup as well as your original vendor's markup. However, your vendors often gets preferred rates from the subcontractor that you could not obtain independently.

The best way to find good vendors is to use your network. Find out which vendors your local colleagues use, especially project managers who are producing similar types of publications. Referrals are a good place to start. Remember, however, that your quality standards and pricing requirements may differ from your colleagues'. Start with the referrals but always consider looking farther afield.

Visit vendor sites rather than simply telephoning them. When you visit a printing plant, always ask for a tour. Keep your eyes open.

- Does the work area appear to be clean and well organized? A dirty working environment will affect the quality of the work.
- Are there different people responsible for different pieces of equipment, or does it appear that one or two people are running around doing everything?
- Does the printer handle the entire process inhouse? What is subcontracted?
- What type of equipment does the printer have? Ask to see the presses that will be used to run your job.
- What range of work does this printer ordinarily handle? Are they experts at complex four-color jobs for advertising agencies? If so, they may subcontract the small-run black-and-white work elsewhere or charge you high prices for work that is outside their specialty areas.
- What is the average turnaround time for a job?
- What other media, such as disk duplication or CD-ROM, can the printer handle?
- Will the printer store materials for you or handle shipment of publications to the customer (fulfillment)?
- Can provide references, preferably from companies that are doing the same type of work you have in mind? Can you see samples of work that resembles yours?

With these questions in mind, you can find out if the vendors you visit are those who can best meet your requirements. You may also want to be alert to more personal issues. By selecting a vendor who works hard to understand your requirements, has representatives that you find friendly, responsive, and cooperative, and answers your questions, you will find that the entire production process will go more smoothly and produce less anxiety for you.

 Guideline: *Get to know your vendors and how they intend to meet your needs.*

Estimating the cost of printing

You may assume that the simplest method of estimating costs is to ask for estimates from your vendors. Certainly, they will eventually need to estimate the jobs themselves. But, it is worthwhile understanding how the estimating process works so that you can better evaluate the bids (Lillies, 1989).

For photocopying, the costs are relatively simple to estimate. The base cost is a per-impression price with a minimal amount subtracted for duplex printing. There may be a small setup cost, which means the cost per impression will go down as the number of impressions increases. The paper cost is a small part of the overall per-impression cost, so the fact that you are using half the paper does not reduce the overall costs by much, if any. If you photocopy a sheet larger than $8/5'' \times 11''$, you will have to pay for special handling, unless your vendor handles a lot of work of this sort. If you photocopy a smaller page, you will also be charged for special handling and trimming costs. If you ask for special paper, especially paper that has a coating with a higher clay content to reduce show-through, you will be charged a higher per-page rate. Sometimes a cooperative vendor will let you supply your own paper and reduce the per-page cost accordingly.

Offset printing is much more difficult to estimate, especially if you need multiple colors, have a great deal of photography in the publications, or have special effects such as bleed tabs which increase paper and trimming costs. The cost of offset printing is also greatly influenced by the type of paper you select.

The costs of offset printing include the costs of

- Preparing the press
- Setting up the job (mechanicals, plate making, etc.)
- Paper and ink
- Cutting and folding the final sheets so that they are ready for binding

To prepare the press is a one-time cost that is the same for every job that uses the same press. The more elaborate the press, the higher this cost. The setup costs depend upon the number of pages in the camera-ready copy and the amount of work that needs to be done to put graphics in place. If you have only simple line art or scanned photographs embedded in your electronic files, there will be no additional setup charges. The cost of the paper and ink will depend on the price of the paper, the number of pages, and the number of times the paper goes through the press for extra colors. There are also additional costs in setting up the press with additional ink colors.

Because of the high initial cost for preparing the press and setting up the job, the cost of increasing the number of copies printed does not proportionally increase the cost of the job. In fact, the more copies you make, the lower the cost per copy. However, in very large jobs, the original plates may deteriorate enough that the printer will have to prepare extra plates, which increases the cost. And, for very small jobs, your publications may be ganged or grouped with someone else's job so that there is no press preparation charge.

 Guideline: Work with your printing vendors to estimate costs and identify price points for publications, but understand how costs are calculated.

Scheduling the printing and binding

Printing, of course, cannot begin until your camera-ready copy is ready. However, it is wise to be aware of the problems that may occur if you are unable to meet your originally scheduled printing dates. Your printing vendor most likely has a large number of jobs to schedule carefully to make the most efficient use of staff and equipment. Your job, like all the others, will be scheduled for a particular time on press. If you miss your deadline with the printer, you may not be able to get the original turnaround time on the job that you had been promised. Since your job is now late, you must wait your turn in the queue again, which may mean several days before the printer can reschedule your work.

To avoid such delays, be certain that you keep your printing vendor informed about the progress of the project. If you are going to be late, try to estimate accurately when your copy will be ready so that your job can be rescheduled as quickly as possible. Of course, you can always pay a premium to bump everyone else's work, provided they have not already paid the same premium.

Many project managers complain that their senior management does not understand how the printing process works and expects the printing vendors to perform miracles in reducing the time to turn around the job. Miracles are occasionally possible, especially if you are willing to pay for them. But your vendor cannot make the press run faster or ink dry more quickly. Some processes just take a certain amount of time, and no amount of complaining and harassing can change that fact. Explain the process to your management; invite them to visit the vendors; even ask management for special consideration when you are severely pressed.

If you are told that your job will take 1 week, 2 weeks, 6 weeks, or 6 months to deliver, always work backwards in your scheduling process from the day that you must deliver camera-ready copy to your vendors. If the publications have to be in your hands for distribution by the first of June, you may have to schedule camera-ready copy to be complete by the middle of April.

Although printing and binding have to take place at the end of the publications-development life cycle, the preparation of other packaging materials may have to be handled simultaneously with other development activities. One well-known software developer decided several years ago to package their three-ring binders in a clear plastic case. Because of the manufacturing process for the plastic cases, they had to be planned, dyes made, and produced long before the camera-ready copy of the manuals was due to be complete. The cases were planned to accommodate a particular quantity of pages; the publications manager was certain this number would never be exceeded. Sure enough, the final manuals were considerably longer than had been planned but the plastic cases had been built to the earlier specifications. As a result, the technical communicators on the team had to cut words from the final drafts and the graphic designers had to redesign the fonts and page formats so that the manuals would fit in the cases. Needless to say, the plastic cases were not used again.

When you make decisions about packaging during Phase 1: Information Planning, contact your vendors and find out exactly what lead time is needed so that the entire project is finished at the same time. If you do not, you face the danger of cost overruns and delays in delivery.

 *Guideline: **Plan carefully for the scheduling of printing and packaging to ensure that you meet your deadlines and keep costs under control.***

Maintaining good relationships with your vendors

If you have a good working relationship with your vendors, they will cooperate with you, try to deliver the best product in a timely manner, and respond to the occasional emergency. However, do not ask for special consideration too often, or you may run the risk of losing an excellent vendor.

When you do ask for a special job, make sure that the vendor gets paid in a timely manner. I know of one company that was on the blacklist of every printer in the state because they delayed so long in paying their bills. The vendor always had a difficult time getting paid, requiring them to spend lots of time telephoning the company's purchasing department. The publications manager found that he could not get anyone to handle his work.

If your are responsible for dealing with the printing vendors and you want to maintain a good working relationship, do not pass off to the accounts payable department the responsibility of ensuring that your vendors get paid in a timely manner. Here are some of the things you might do to keep your vendors happy and willing to work for you:

- Approve invoices as quickly as possible. Never leave them sitting in your inbox for days or weeks. If you have to approve the invoices, you may want the vendor to send you a copy at the same time one is sent to accounts payable. That way you can review it and make sure that accounts payable sends you the official approval copy in a timely manner.

- Ensure that the vendor has the correct information for submitting invoices, including purchase order numbers, the number of copies required, and exactly where all the copies must be sent.

- Check with accounts payable to find out if your invoices are being handled in a timely manner. Do not wait until your vendor calls after 60 or 90 days to find out that accounts payable has lost the invoice or has some problem that you can resolve.

- If your vendor calls about late payments, research the problem yourself rather than referring the vendor to accounts payable. Find out which clerk is handling the invoice, find out what the problem is and how it can be resolved quickly, find out when the check will be cut, and let the vendor know. You are much better able to navigate through company politics than an outsider.

- If you find that your company has a reputation of never paying until a vendor starts to complain, quietly let the vendor know that they should start calling accounts payable as soon as invoice due date is reached. If this does not help, talk to your senior management about how the policy of late payments is damaging your reputation with your vendors, increasing your costs, and leaving you with few options to get your work done.

On the other side of the process, you should also expect high-quality work from your vendors. Be alert for problems like smudged copies, smeared ink, dirt spots and streaks, lack of uniform color, poor color control on four-color art, and others. All of these problems are avoidable if your printing and packaging vendors have adequate quality controls in place.

To ensure that you get the job done the way you want, be available for press checks and checks of color keys, return bluelines in a timely manner, and answer questions quickly and thoroughly. Once vendors know that you are alert to problems, they are likely to respond by increasing the quality control on your jobs.

If you have a problem with a job, immediately discuss it with your vendor. It is unethical to allow a vendor to wait until they discover that accounts payable will not pay an invoice, to find that you did not like the job they did. If they know about the problems as soon as you find them, they will more likely be able to correct the problems in a timely manner.

Some project managers simply stew about a problem with a vendor, rather than discussing it. If the vendor never knows about a problem, they are unlikely to be able to correct the problem. Make your concerns known quickly and ask how problems will be resolved. Be prepared to accept responsibility for any confusion you may have caused, but also assume that vendors will accept responsibility for their problems.

Avoid turning over a problem to your management until you have tried to deal with it yourself. You may discover that the mistake you consider a disaster is simple to correct and may even have been due to your own miscommunication. Only when you are unable to resolve a problem should you bring the matter to the attention of your management.

 Guideline: Treat your vendors professionally and you will be treated in the same way.

Planning for crisis

Despite all your best-laid plans to manage the production process, crises can and will occur. If your deadlines are completely inflexible, you may have to make contingency plans for printing and binding if something goes awry. On an enormous proposal project several years ago, we planned for a second printing vendor to take over if something happened to the first. If a flood, earthquake, fire, or other natural or business calamity interfered with the printing process, we were fully prepared to move the job. We even paid the second printer to stand by. In this case, however, the proposal, worth several million dollars to our client, could not, under any circumstances, be delivered late.

Be prepared to check everything. On one project, a publication shipped late because the team missed the express-mail deadline by 10 minutes.

If you are prepared for a crisis, given the complexity of your publications project, you will be better able to pursue alternative methods and get the job done in an adequate amount of time.

 Guideline: If you have a particularly complex or urgent project, be prepared for crises by developing contingency plans.

Monitoring the production process

If you now believe that managing and controlling the production process requires great skill and concentration, you are correct. Unlike earlier parts of the process, Phase 4: Production represents a series of parallel and sequential activities that all must be completed on time. If everything is going to happen in the right sequence, you need a clear understanding of all the details of the process. You also need to monitor the production process so that it goes well, everything is done on time, and costs are kept under control.

Some project managers think their job is finished when the last drafts have been revised. In some organizations, all subsequent activities are handled by production specialists who take total control of the processes. However, you are more likely to be responsible for the entire process yourself. Even if you do have a production team handling the details, if you want to ensure the final quality of your team's work, you will choose to monitor the process yourself.

Planning for final technical sign-offs

In many organizations, senior management requires and project managers recognize the importance of a final technical sign-off after all changes have been made to the final draft and the index, table of contents, and artwork, and the front matter and back matter are complete and ready for reproduction. To manage the final sign-off, be sure that only one or two members of the development and the marketing teams have sign-off responsibility. Enlarging the scope of responsibility will cause problems with last-minute changes that someone insists be made. Schedule a sign-off meeting so that you get everyone's agreement at the same time.

No publication is ever perfect. Someone always has one more thing to be said. But in most business cases, we need to accept the lack of perfection as a tradeoff for other values, like timeliness and cost control. The late changes—those that occur after camera-ready copy has been prepared, after bluelines have been created for offset printing, or even after final copies have been printed—are always the most costly. These late changes are often the result of changes to a product that has continued to be fixed and changed long after the publications team must freeze its activities to go into the production phase.

Publications development, like any product-development effort, is largely a creative activity that inevitably will change as the problems are better understood. However, like hardware development, publications development has a manufacturing phase that cannot be shortened. Most of the problems with late changes occur in software-development projects where there is little or no manufacturing process to worry about. Software developers need to understand the nature of the publications manufacturing phase and acknowledge that time must be left in the total project schedule to accommodate it.

Publications project managers also must evaluate the cost versus benefits of late changes to the publications within their own teams. You will always be able to find one more misspelling or one more formatting problem, but eventually you need to sign off the project and allow it to go into final production.

The president of the company just reviewed the final camera-ready draft and he wants some changes made immediately," explained Herb, the marketing director.

"What kind of changes? And who let him review the draft anyway?" replied Andy, the publications project manager. "We go to press in two days. You approved everything on Friday. The president hasn't had any involvement at all with this project."

"Well, I guess I shouldn't have shown him the final draft, but he did ask to see it," admitted Herb. "He wants you to take out all the contractions and to put complete sentences before all the bulleted lists."

"You've got to be kidding," said Andy. "We agreed months ago that we all wanted a very conversational style for the users. Contractions are completely appropriate. And why does he have an opinion about how lists are introduced? If you start with a phrase, then the list items need to be parallel within the grammar of the sentences. You don't need complete sentences every time."

"Well, he feels that you are violating the purity of the English language," said Herb. "Apparently, he was taught that formal writing never contains contractions and all lists must start with complete sentences."

"Do you know what it's going to cost? Whose budget is going to pay for the additional writing and editing time, the time to prepare camera-ready copy all over again, and the printing delays we're sure to face if we miss our due date to the printer?"

"Let me know what it's going to cost. I'll see what I can do."

Andy is probably justified in being upset. The final sign-off process has derailed his planning and put him in an awkward position. In this case, the cost for the time to make the changes was $1,500, which represented a 5-percent addition to the total project budget and made the manuals a week late to the customer.

As project manager, you need to understand the politics of the sign-off process. If Andy had anticipated the president's involvement, he might have met with him earlier to discuss the project and explain the publications-development process. He might also have offered the president an opportunity to review the planning documents and the early prototypes.

Guideline: Involve as few people in the final sign-off process as possible, and ensure that everyone understands the cost/benefit tradeoffs that must be considered with late changes.

Preparing collating instructions and printing dummies

Once the final copy has been signed off and is ready to be sent to the printer, consider asking your team to prepare one or two other documents to communicate to the printer and ensure that the project ends successfully. Collating instructions are tables in which you list every page in a publication with a brief note about the content of the page, especially if the page requires any special treatment or is to be left blank. The collating instructions help the printer build the correct book as the pages are cut from the printing sheet. Offset printing presses print on large sheets of paper that contain many pages that are folded to make up signatures. The signatures are trimmed to create individual pages. The collating instructions explain exactly how the pages are to be sequenced. They detail exactly what the final production is supposed to look like, including page breaks. The page-break information is especially important if you are increasing the dots per inch in the camera-ready copy from your drafts. Subtle changes in the size of identically named fonts may wreak havoc with your page breaks.

Printing dummies are usually constructed for shorter publications, especially for publications that have illustrations that span more than one page. A printer dummy is a sample of the final book with all the pages in the right place. The dummy shows the printer exactly how the publication must appear after it is printed. Printing dummies can help you avoid problems in which the wrong pages are placed back-to-back, illustrations are spread over the incorrect pages, or illustrations are placed on the wrong pages.

Guideline: Create collating instructions and printing dummies to avoid problems in the construction of books after the pages have been printed.

Reviewing blueline and color keys

During the process of preparing a publication for printing, printers are able to produce interim representations that allow you to check the accuracy of the mechanical art. Mechanical art is the mix of text and graphics put together to make images that are ready for the processing camera.

To avoid problems with mechanicals, you may decide to produce film rather than paper output from your typesetting equipment. The film is then used directly by the printer to create the printing plates, without the need for a mechanical step. Be aware, however, that if you go directly to film, you may have considerable difficulty proofreading your final draft. If you have been producing draft copies from your laser printer, you may find problems with letter spacing, word spacing, alignment, and other formatting on typeset quality output that were invisible on lower-quality laser-printer output. If you go directly to film without a paper-level proofreading step on the typeset output, you may find a considerable increase in final costs from having to correct errors and rerun films. If plates have already been exposed, you may have an additional cost in reproducing plates.

In all instances, ask your printer to produce bluelines. Bluelines are made in a blueprint machine that creates a blue-and-white image of the page with all the graphics in place. By reviewing the bluelines carefully, you may be able to find type problems (such as broken type fonts and missing punctuation), as well as problems with misplaced spot color, misplaced illustrations, and others. Turn the bluelines upside down to scan for problems without reading every word. By finding the problems in the blueline copies, you can have them corrected before the presses run.

Your printer will charge you extra if you make changes to the text and graphics in the blueline stage, because the mechanicals will have to be corrected and second plates will have to be produced. The printer will correct at no cost any problems introduced by his process, but anything you want to do differently will be charged. Make only essential changes to bluelines. Do not use bluelines as an opportunity to edit the text.

Like bluelines, color keys provide you with a method of finding problems before you see them in print. Color keys are produced for four-color images to allow you to ensure that the mix of colors will produce the type of final image that you want. Review the color keys carefully. If you do not know what to look for, consult your graphic designer or photographer for assistance, or have them help you review the color keys.

 Guideline: For complicated printing jobs, work with your printer to ensure that problems are caught early in the print-production process.

Doing press checks

Press checks take place as soon as the printer has readied the job for the press. The plates are complete and in place, and the presses are ready to roll. Your responsibility at this point, especially if your publication uses multiple colors or includes four-color printing, is to work with the operator to ensure that the colors are correct. The operator will run the press briefly and pull off a few copies that you can review. Check to be certain that the spot color is exactly as you have specified and that multi-color images are printing in the correct colors.

To perform a press check, you have to be ready when the press is ready. If you keep the printer waiting, you will delay the job and possibly add to the cost. If the project is important enough and color is critical, you may even want to ask the printer to call you in the middle of the night, whenever they are ready to run.

 Guideline: Be prepared to check the first copies off the press on important jobs that use significant amounts of color.

Spot-checking delivered copies

Many new publications-project managers assume that the copies delivered by the printer will be exactly right. With any job, there is the possibility of error. In one case, I found that half of a manual run had been printed on a slightly different paper. We asked that the darker half be reprinted. In another case, we found that a few pages had slipped and been printed at an angle. These pages, in a single-sheet format, had to be reprinted.

If you have hundreds or thousands of copies of a publication, you will obviously not be able to check every one. As you open the boxes or pallets, select samples. Take samples from every box or pallet and from the bottom as well as the top of each box. Look for any changes in the press run. Avoid mixing up the copies; know which boxes they came from. If you find a problem, you will have to check many of the nearby copies to ensure that the problem is not unique.

Some of the items you may want to check are

- Pages printed at an angle
- Faded color on all or some of the signatures
- Smudged pages that were not adequately dried
- Out-of-focus duotone or four-color images (they are not really out of focus—the registration is off)
- Spot color that is not exactly in line with the black text (another registration problem)
- Pages out of order (the signatures were assembled incorrectly)
- Bad trims (your margins, especially the outside margins, are not what you intended)
- Bindings that are already coming apart (perfect bound only)
- Holes misdrilled for three-ring binders

Many of these problems could have been caught earlier if you had checked blueline, provided dummies, checked color keys, or done press checks. But some problems occur even if you have checked everything.

If you find a problem, discuss it with the printer and ask for resolution. You may find that a problem you consider significant is within your company's procurement specification for a job. I had one project in which the second color came out faded. When I objected and pointed out the color was not consistent through the entire book (some signatures were darker and lighter than others), I was informed by the printing broker that the job was within the company's specification for printing procurement. When I questioned this specification with the procurement group, I was told that the printer was correct and we had to accept the job as printed.

In very large organizations you may have no recourse when a problem like this one occurs. However, you may try to work with the procurement group to ensure that the specifications are better prepared in the future. The example is typical of what occurs when the people dealing with the vendors have no idea of the quality requirements of a project. Since they do not recognize the problem, it does not exist.

Also be aware that reprinting an entire run or part of a run of a publication is fairly costly to your printer. Be certain that the problem is serious enough to justify a request to redo the job. Work with the vendor to arrive at an acceptable solution. Remember that you want to maintain a good relationship with a qualified vendor, and you want the job to be ready on time. Consider if the problem will be a problem to the customer and to the company as a whole.

Guideline: Check the delivered copies of a publication to spot mistakes that need to be corrected.

Supervising distribution

In every customer study I have ever conducted, distribution problems with publications result in major usability disasters. Here are just a few examples of problems caused. Customers

- Have the wrong publications
- Do not receive updates for their publications
- Cannot find out what publications are available
- Are missing publications that are critical to their ability to learn and perform tasks
- Have copies of publications that are missing entire sections

and the list goes on.

All of your team's hard work is for naught if the publications do not reach the customer when they are needed.

Many publications project managers are aware of distribution problems in their organizations. They hear about the problems from customers, sales people, and customer service. They also claim that there is nothing they can do about them.

In large organizations where distribution is handled by entire divisions, you may have little influence over the process. But that does not mean that you should not make your senior management aware of the poor reputation that distribution problems give your company. In organizations where senior management thinks that documentation is unimportant, communicate the complaints you receive from customers who cannot find the information they need to function independently.

In smaller organizations, you may be responsible for distribution, or you may want to take over the management of the task. Your first step is to understand exactly how your organization handles distribution tasks:

- Who is responsible for maintaining a database of customer names and addresses?
- How do customers purchase additional copies of publications? How do they purchase publications they do not own already or own only in online copy? Is there a catalog of all publications, organized by product? Is it usable?
- Are noncustomers able to purchase your publications? Are there any restrictions on what can be purchased? Are there any restrictions on which customers can receive certain types of publications?

- How are users of the publications distinguished from purchasers of the product?

- Are new publications sent with the product? Are they packaged together? Shipped separately? Ordered separately? Sent only on request?

- Do the sales representatives know which publications go with which products? Do they complete order forms correctly?

- How are publications identified in the distribution process? Identification numbers? Order numbers?

- How are the publications packaged for shipment? Are binders included? Slip-in covers? Tabs? Shrink-wrapped contents? Is assembly the responsibility of the customer?

- What happens to out-of-date versions of the publications? In one company, these continued to be shipped with new products because distribution wanted to "use them up." What happens to binders that are left over? In another company, 3-inch binders were shipped with 1-inch manuals because they were in stock. Is there a disposal procedure?

- How are updates handled for warehoused copies? Are they immediately inserted? Inserted at time of shipment? What written instructions or checklists direct the distribution staff?

- How long are older versions of publications kept in stock? Are customers with older versions of the product able to purchase older versions of the publications? Who is notified of "out-of-stock" conditions?

These are only a few of the questions you need to ask about the distribution process. The questions represent the decision making that you need to be aware of if you assume responsibility for distribution tasks.

Although you may not have direct responsibility for distribution, you will find it worthwhile to understand the process in your organization and to evaluate its effectiveness for customers. Find out, for example, how long it takes a customer to receive a publication after it has been ordered. Ask if the correct publication arrives. Ask if customers order publications that they do not need because the titles are misleading or insufficiently informative.

If the questions and concerns mentioned above suggest that distribution of publications can indeed be a serious problem, you are correct. Distribution problems can easily derail all your good efforts to meet customer needs. If you cannot solve the problems yourself, bring them to the attention of senior management. Problems with publications distribution usually are a sign of problems with product distribution.

Guideline: Be aware of how the distribution process works or fails to work in your organization.

Adding to the Project Management Notebook

During the production phase, you have a number of items that you will need to add to your Project Management Notebook:

- Final copyediting checklist
- Collating lists
- Specifications for the printing and other production jobs
- Proposals from your vendors
- Copies of all correspondence to vendors, including printers, translators, copyediting, and indexers
- Telephone logs
- Meeting minutes

At the end of the production phase, your Project Management Notebook should contain a record of production activities and an account of the decisions you made. If you do not keep these records, you may be surprised to find that you no longer remember who printed a particular job or what color and paper decisions you made months earlier. At the end of the print-production process, either retain the printing plates in your own organization (if you have a way to keep them clean and safe), or ask your print vendor to retain them. Note in your Project Management Notebook what course you decided on, and be certain that you record the location of all plates, original art, and other source material. When the next print-production comes, you will be thankful that you know exactly what you did the last time and where everything is.

Managing Indexing

Although the introduction of automated indexing systems has made it easier to produce an accurate index, the task of planning, implementing, editing, and revising an index requires the same skills today that it has always required. Some managers and novice indexers believe that the automated systems do the indexing for you. The automated indexing systems simply make it easier to get the page numbers correct and to regenerate an accurate index after the text has been changed. The real job of indexing is not aided by an automated system. In fact, an automated indexing system may make indexing more difficult because you cannot see your entries.

In an article in *PC Computing Magazine*, respondents to an opinion poll noted that they considered a good index the most important element in good computer documentation (Grech, 1992). The index is the major accessibility tool for many users of technical publications, allowing them to find the precise information they need quickly and easily. But not every index achieves this usability goal. At their worst, some indexes appear to be a random collection of words from the text with little thought given to the way users will want to access information. These indexes are often created under the mistaken notion that users come to a technical publication looking for words, rather than information that will answer their questions. A good index takes into account how users will ask their questions, what terminology they will use, and which problems they will have that will bring them to the index. An excellent index anticipates the users' search patterns and provides guideposts to the precise location of specific information.

As project manager, your role is to ensure that your indexers understand how to construct a high-quality index and have enough time in their schedules to do so. The indexers must also know how to use the automated tools available and understand the strengths and weaknesses of the tools.

Selecting a quality level for an index

The quality of an index is dependent upon the skill of the indexer in anticipating the users' search patterns for the text. The more the indexer knows about the user and the product, the better the index will be.

We can measure the quality of an index through usability studies that focus on the amount of time the users take to find the information they need to answer their questions. The shorter the search time, the better the index. For example, we would consider an index to be excellent if the users immediately find the word or phrase that they have in mind and if that word or phrase directs them to the exact page that contains the information they are seeking. We would consider an index to be poor if users are unable to find the information they need, even after they try several different words and phrases and look at a number of pages in the text.

66 I need to take some time off to go to my grandmother's funeral in Indianapolis," explained Harriet. "I'll probably be gone three days. Do I have to use three days of my vacation time?"

"I don't think so," answered Grace, her manager. "The company lets you have some days off for funerals of close relatives. I think grandmothers are included. You might not get all three days, though. I'll look it up in the Personnel Manual." Grace gets her copy of the personnel manual and begins looking for the information that Harriet needs.

"Well, I thought I would find something under 'funerals' in the index," said Grace. There's nothing under that term. Maybe I should try 'leave' or 'family leave.' No, there's nothing there either. I know it's in here someplace. I just can't think of the right word."

"How about 'time off?'" suggests Harriet. "Maybe it's there."

"No, nothing there either. This is frustrating. This index never seems to have any of the words I want to look up. Give me a few minutes. I'll call Sam at the company headquarters in Denver. He always knows where to find information."

After 15 minutes of searching through the index, Grace leaves a voice mail message for Sam in Denver. Three hours later, Sam calls back.

"Hi. I need to know how much time I can give to one of the clerks to go to her grandmother's funeral. Do you have any idea? I can't find anything in the Personnel Manual," explains Grace.

"Sure," replies Sam. "She gets one day for the funeral of a grandmother. It's more for a spouse, child, father, or mother."

"OK, that's fine," says Grace. "But where does it say that in the Personnel Manual? I couldn't find anything on funerals in the index."

"Look it up under 'bereavement'," explains Sam. "It's called the 'bereavement policy'."

"Bereavement? Really?" says Grace. "I would never have thought of that. Why don't they have any cross-references in this index to words people actually use?"

"I know it's frustrating," says Dan. "I think they're working on a better index."

"Well, tell them to talk to me. I can never find anything in this manual. 99

It has taken Grace 15 to 30 minutes to find an answer to Harriet's question in the Personnel Manual. Her search included the cost of a long-distance phone call to Sam, plus Sam's time in calling her back. If the indexer had anticipated the problem that

Index quality level	Characteristics
Level 0	No index or an index with inaccurate page references.
Level 1	An index with accurate page references that includes only references built from the text headings. An index search gets the users to a general area of interest but not to the precise location of the information needed.
Level 2	All the characteristics of a Level 1 index plus index items built from key words and phrases in the text. The index also includes multiple transformations of key phrases and text headings (i.e., "Newtonian model" appears under both "Newtonian" and "model"). The users are able to reach the precise location of the information needed in 3 minutes or less.
Level 3	All the characteristics of a Level 2 index plus cross-references from a synonym known to the users to the word used in the index and the text. You can often find synonyms in your competitors' indexes.

Figure 23.1   Index quality levels

employees were likely to have with the legal term "bereavement," the company would have saved a considerable amount of money.

An excellent index should lead the user to the correct information in 3 minutes or less (Hewlett-Packard, 1990). You can test this benchmark against your team's indexes by giving users specific questions to look up and timing them. You can trace the number of errors made during the search and decide if the users actually succeed in finding the correct information.

The table in Figure 23.1 briefly outlines some of the characteristics of different levels of indexes, with level 0 the lowest quality.

All the levels except Level 1 imply that a human indexer has had a hand in deciding how the index item is to be phrased. Fully automated indexing programs, popularized some years ago, produce index items by including all instances of all words in the text except for those eliminated by the indexing algorithm. Fully automated indexing programs produce, not indexes, but concordances. They list every instance of every word, usually with tens of page numbers accompanying each index item. Some words are eliminated by the algorithms (i.e., the articles "a," "an," and "the"); sometimes, other words can be eliminated by a human indexer. Automated indexes of this sort have minimal use. A user comes to a text looking not for words, but for information—answers to questions. Fully automated indexing programs provide too many target locations, extend the user's search time, and rarely allow the user to separate relevant information from irrelevant information by studying the index.

Simple keyword search mechanisms included in electronic versions of books suffer from some of the same problems as fully automated indexes. Remember the difficulty you once had using the new automated card catalogs in the library. It is never helpful to be informed that the catalog has several hundred or several thousand entries that include the word you have searched on. With somewhat more sophisticated search mechanisms that allow you to include or exclude groups of words from the search, you may find what you need. However, just ask a well-informed reference librarian the same question. The librarian, who understands the subject matter and knows where things are hidden away, is much more likely to suggest a full range of possible titles that relate to your subject. By asking you good questions, the librarian can focus on your needs, separating the relevant from the irrelevant.

A good indexer serves much the same role as a good reference librarian, providing clues to the publications' organization by anticipating the questions you may ask. Good indexing requires a solid understanding of the text, knowledge of the user, and knowledge of search patterns.

Selecting an indexer

Most writers assume that they are the best indexer of texts they have created. Certainly, they understand the organization of the text and the location of critical information. A writer who knows the user and the user's search patterns and who is trained in indexing is a good choice to index his or her own text. Unfortunately, most writers are untrained as indexers and have too little understanding of their users' search patterns to index effectively.

If you want to achieve high-quality indexes, you may have to either obtain indexing training for all your writers, obtain training for certain individuals on your team who like indexing and would like to do it well, or contract with a professional indexer.

In selecting a professional indexer, give first consideration to the indexer's experience with similar types of text. An indexer who has indexed only scientific reference literature may not be the best choice to index user's manuals for high-tech equipment. Then, look for an indexer who has some knowledge of your field. The combination of the appropriate indexing experience plus subject-matter knowledge may be very difficult to find. If the indexer you would like to use lacks subject-matter knowledge or knowledge of the audience, you will have to provide training. Work with the indexer to help him or her become familiar with your field. Provide supplementary texts, competitors' indexes, and user profiles for the indexer to review.

You or your senior editor, as well as the individual writers, should check the indexer's first attempts for subject-matter and user knowledge. It is important for you to expect that the first attempts may have some problems. Give the indexer time to learn and improve.

If your indexers are skilled in creating indexes, understand the users, have sufficient time in the schedule, and have the ability to test the draft index, they will undoubtedly be able to produce a top-quality index. Without these requirements in place, your team will produce indexes of lower quality.

 Guideline: Decide on the best person to index the publications. Unless members of your team are trained in indexing, you may want to hire an indexer from outside your organization.

Blocking indexing time into the schedule

All indexes take real time to construct, even simple keyword indexes or indexes that point only to heading levels. The higher the quality you want to achieve in an index, the more time it will take to construct.

Even if you have skilled indexers who know the audience, you must still allow them sufficient time to create a high-quality index if that is your goal. With less time available, the index quality will decrease.

In my experience, to construct a level 3 index will take 1 hour to mark index items for every 6 to 10 pages of text, depending on the density of the textual material. That means that a 200 page user's manual will take approximately 20 hours to mark for index items. Instructional text with many task-oriented headings and more illustrations takes less time to index than dense text with few headings and illustrations.

If you are using an automated system, once the text is marked with index items, it generally takes another hour for every 6 to 10 pages of text to complete the following:

- Enter the index tags.
- Generate the draft index.
- Edit it for inconsistencies and errors.
- Enter the edits into the tagged index.

That means that your 200-page user's manual will take approximately 40 hours to index thoroughly and accurately.

Given the difficulty of using some of the automated tagging systems included with various word-processing and electronic-publishing systems, I often recommend that indexers create the index manually (in a word-processing or spreadsheet system, of course), sort the index alphabetically, and edit and revise the index draft before tagging the index in the text. In this way, they will know exactly what to enter into each index tag. They will also have a draft with which to edit the final computer-generated index again.

If the text is camera-ready, you may also find that creating an index manually saves considerable time and, if done carefully, is usually as accurate as a tagged index. If the text is likely to change after the index is created, you may choose to enter index tags. However, since most indexes have to be redone if the text is substantially changed in the next version, a tagged index may offer little time advantage.

Once you decide how much time you will need to produce the level of index required by your audience, decide when the indexing will occur in the overall production schedule. You may be able to begin the indexing process, especially if it is going to be handled inhouse, as soon as the second draft is turned over to production. By this time, all substantial changes should have been made to the text and graphics, and the information in the publication should be very stable. In addition, copyediting and proofreading should also be complete.

If you are using an outside indexer, you may want to wait to begin indexing until after the camera-ready draft is complete. You may decide to ask the indexer only to mark the text and have your production staff tag the index items. Or you may ask the indexer to create the final, camera-ready index in a nontagged form. If the indexer has the same text-processing system your team uses, you may even be able to have the indexer tag and generate the final index.

If you keep the indexing inhouse, your team may be able to do some indexing before the second draft has been completely revised. If you are primarily indexing heading levels and the heading levels are reasonably stable, your inhouse indexers can create index tags before the text is complete. In some organizations, writers create index items related to heading levels while they are writing. If the headings are unlikely to change, this may save indexing time at the end of Phase 3. It may also allow you to generate simple indexes earlier in Phase 3 for review and usability testing.

Be careful to review your index if you have rearranged sections of text. You may have to cut and paste index items as well. Edit your index for odd entries that reflect misplacements of index tags.

If you are using an outside indexer, you may also get the indexer started in building keyword and phrase lists from similar publications that can be used in the new index. Lists of keywords and phrases created by your team and your outside indexers can be extremely helpful in reducing indexing time and maintaining consistent indexes across all the publications in a library. Your users will find it disconcerting and frustrating if each of the publications in a set has an entirely different conceptualization of the index. You will also be less able to construct useful master indexes that cross the publications in a library and help users locate the right book before they look for the right page.

Guideline: To produce a Level 3 index, allow 2 hours of indexing time for every 6 to 10 pages of text. Use either inhouse or outside indexers, but ensure that your indexers are trained, experienced with the subject matter, and have a knowledge of the users and their search patterns.

Scheduling Copyediting

Although considerable copyediting takes place during the development of Phase 3 drafts, a final copyedit before the release of camera-ready copy to reproduction will help you ensure that no lingering errors appear in your publications. Copyediting is one of the primary activities of Phase 4, in addition to the preparation of the index.

Many organizations employ people either inhouse or outside who are solely responsible for copyediting. Copy editors need to be experts in

- The organization's standards
- The rules of grammar and punctuation
- Spelling, especially the special terminology used in your field
- Formatting
- The use of trademarks and copyrights
- Bibliography style and format

Copy editors are responsible for the stylistic correctness of the publication and adherence to organizational and industry standards.

Copyediting begins with the first draft, although interim drafts should also undergo quick copyediting to avoid distracting errors for the reviewers. Copyediting continues through the subsequent Phase 3 drafts until the final copyedit before reproduction.

Using copyediting and formatting checklists and electronic styles

You may want to have the development editor, a designated copy editor, or a member of the writing team begin a copyediting checklist while working on the first draft. Into the stylesheet or checklist go all the decisions made about how the team will handle the details of style.

The checklist may also include details of the publications format, although in most cases many of these details will be incorporated into electronic style templates. The use of electronic style templates included as part of most major word-processing packages and electronic-publishing systems decreases the amount of time required for format checks. The electronic style should standardize as many stylistic elements as possible,

Level of edit	Average number of pages / day
Level 1	50 pages / day
Level 2	40 pages / day
Level 3	25 pages / day
Level 4	20 pages / day

Figure 24.1 Time estimates for levels of edit

from the spacing between paragraphs and before and after headings to the emphasis techniques used for special words and phrases, such as bold, underscore, and italic. If the electronic style is applied correctly to a publication, then these elements should be correct. The copy editor need only look for misapplications of the style and places where the style alone does not solve a formatting problem.

Blocking copyediting time into the schedule

Like indexes, the quality of a copyedit increases in relationship to the time available. The more time copy editors have, the more elements they can check and the more errors they can find. Like any quality-assurance effort, the cost of finding errors increases in relationship to the amount of time expended to find the last of the errors. That final error is always the most costly to find. That means any decision you make about the amount of time to devote to copyediting, given competent copy editors, will directly affect the quality of the edit. You will have to decide just how much you are willing to spend to decrease the number of editing defects in a publication.

Los Alamos National Laboratory's (LANL) editing organization has measured the time its experienced editors take to perform four levels of edit and established guidelines for scheduling. The table in Figure 24.1 lists the levels of edit and the associated pages per day.

Each level of edit is fully described in Chapter 8. The averages used by LANL provide a guideline that you can use to measure and establish your own average times for copyediting. The average times in your organization will depend upon the nature of the information, the skill and experience of the copy editors, and the controls you have established throughout Phase 3 to decrease the final copyediting time.

As part of the final production copyedit, you may also choose to include establishing

- Final page breaks
- Illustration edits to ensure that the correct illustrations are in place
- Editing of the index entries
- The development of standard front matter and back matter for the publications, including publication titles, corporate identity, copyrights, trademarks, version numbers, identification numbers, and others

Although page breaks relate only to hardcopy publications, the final production copyedit for softcopy manuals and online help systems should include testing every interaction between software and information and every link within the electronic information for accuracy.

Guideline: *Plan sufficient time in your schedule to allow for the level of copyediting quality required by your organization and your customers.*

Managing the Translation and Localization Process

The translation and localization of technical publications is becoming an increasingly significant part of the publications-development life cycle. As organizations move into global rather than local markets, publications must be translated and localized to meet the needs of diverse audiences worldwide. Some organizations today translate technical publications into 50 to 60 different languages. Often, these translations must all be ready for simultaneous distribution worldwide.

Some organizations have created separate departments that are solely responsible for coordinating translation and localization efforts. More often, the publications department manager or the project manager will be required to coordinate translation activities. As a project manager, you need to understand the translation process so that you can help make it as efficient as possible. You may also be responsible for selecting vendors, coordinating translation activities, and ensuring the translations are accurate and understandable by your user community.

The translation process begins with the decision to translate and localize technical publications for audiences who do not read the original language of the publications. Translation means taking the original language, such as English, and producing the same meaning in other languages. The translation includes all the language in the publication, including the callouts on illustrations. It may also include the translation of all product-related text, including computer screens, hardware displays, error and status messages, and online help. Localization includes taking information that is technically and culturally specific to the original language and changing it into a form that is correct and meaningful in other countries. For example, if your US instructional manual warns people always to drive on the right side of the road, you will have to revise this instruction for countries where people drive on the left side. In one instance, we had to change the name of a character in a scenario-based example because the translation of the name referred to a sacred religious figure whose name could not be printed. Dates, time, currency formats—all these may need localization.

Once you have decided to translate and localize your publications, you should consider the following steps to ensure a high-quality product:

- Select a qualified translation organization.
- Meet with the translation organization in Phase 1 or 2 to discuss the translation requirements and the schedule.
- Work with the translation organization to establish a glossary of terms.
- Discuss the problems that "Americanisms" or any other "-isms" pose to the translators, and plan to minimize the problems.

- Decide in Phase 1 on the text-processing and graphic systems to be used for the translations, taking into account availability of different systems for a variety of languages.
- Clarify the technical expertise required of the individual translators assigned to the project.
- Decide how you will conduct reviews of the translations, especially reviews of warnings and cautions and other legally sensitive information.
- Plan the translation schedule with a full understanding of the schedule dependencies.

Finding the best translation vendor for your needs

Although some technical publications groups contract with individual translators for each language required or have translators inhouse, you may find it advantageous in terms of time, technical accuracy, and project management to contract with a full-service translation vendor. If you are looking at full-service vendors, ask questions about their process:

- How do they locate appropriately trained translators?
- Do they always use native translators who are located in the target countries?
- How do they manage the translation project, especially when there are multiple languages involved?
- What text-processing and graphics systems do they have available?
- How do they handle copyediting of the translated text?
- What other quality-assurance procedures do they have in place to ensure that the translations are accurate and appropriate for your audiences?

The better and more complete the answers to these questions, the more likely you will have found a translation vendor who can meet your quality standards. Remember that you will be unable to check the technical accuracy of the translated information or even copyedit the translation. You must depend upon the quality controls established by your translation vendor.

As soon as you have chosen a vendor, request a kickoff meeting so that you understand exactly how to work with the vendor. By establishing a good working relationship from the start, you can help to ensure that deadlines are met and budgets are maintained. As project manager, you have the responsibility of ensuring that the translators receive the information they need in a timely manner, that they provide you with regular progress and budget reports, and that you are immediately notified if the scope of the translation project appears to be changing. You are responsible for ensuring that the project goes smoothly from your side.

Establishing glossaries of key technical terms

At the beginning of the translation process, you will need to work with your translators to establish appropriate translations for the technical terms specific to your field. Even skilled and experienced translators may not know the most current terms used in their countries for the esoteric vocabulary developed by your marketing and development departments.

The best starting point for a translation glossary is the glossaries your writers produce for the publications in the library. If you already have glossaries in place and you know that all the publications in the library use the same terminology consistently, then you have a valuable head start in the translation process. If you do not have glossaries in place and your publications are inconsistent, you need to know that early enough to establish better consistency through style checklists. If inconsistency reigns, the translation process will be complicated and lengthened.

If you know that your publications are not consistent in their terminology or style, be certain to admit that to the translation organization. It is better that they know about inconsistency problems in advance and plan for them in their schedules and cost estimates, rather than have the problems cause schedule delays and cost overruns later.

If you have no technical glossaries, you will have to ask your team to establish them or request that the translation organization go through the draft publications and create their own glossary lists. Even if you have fairly extensive glossaries in place, the translators may want to do their own review of the draft publications to ensure that all specialized technical terms are accounted for. They will be better able than your team to identify those words that will cause translation problems.

Once the word list is established, you will also be asked to clarify the meaning of specialized technical terms. A term may have a rather vague definition in your publication, especially if the term is already well known to the audience. The translation organization is likely to ask for clarification of the meanings for much of the terminology your writers take for granted.

In large translation projects involving multiple languages, the process of creating the glossaries in all the target languages can take a considerable amount of time.

Guideline: Help your translation organization construct glossaries of technical terms in the target languages.

Minimizing translation problems

Inconsistencies in terminology and treatment of similar subjects is perhaps the greatest cause of translation problems. For the original writers, the relationships between similar sections of publications are clear; for the translator, the dissimilar text can represent entirely different subjects. The translation process reveals many inconsistencies in text that is supposed to treat the subject in similar ways. Good technical writing that follows guidelines for consistency and clarity will translate well.

In addition to inconsistencies, translators can have difficulty with idiomatic expressions and metaphors that are significant in one culture but meaningless in others. There are many stories about problems that translators have with idiomatic expressions that are perfectly clear in their native culture. In one famous story, a Japanese translator is stumped when he has to translate a American general's reference to "being

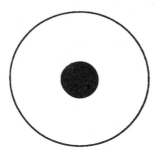

Figure 25.1   European one-way icon

from Missouri." The translator tells his audience that the general has told a joke and asks them to laugh politely.

This particular idiomatic expression might be labeled an Americanism because it uses a stereotypical view of the citizens of Missouri as the base of the expression. Other Americanisms include references to football fields as a measure of length and references to an exercise break as a "seventh-inning stretch." If our words are to be translated accurately into the languages of other cultures, we must try to avoid expressions that are useful but difficult to translate.

Difficulties that readers have with culturally specific expressions do not even require that the languages be different. English as spoken in Great Britain, the United States, and Australia has sufficient differences to cause misunderstandings. When I visited Australia a few years ago, I was surprised that the organization offered only to pay for my "return" trip. I had expected them to pay for both ways. Only after arriving and explaining the problem to a friend did I learn that a "return" trip in Australian English means a trip both ways, the same thing as a "round trip" in American English.

Translators can help you discover Americanisms or other idiomatic expressions in your team's writing. Once you find them, create a checklist to avoid using them in the future. You will make the translator's job infinitely simpler.

We often believe that using more illustrations in place of lots of text will make the translation process simpler. Unfortunately, not all illustrations, especially icons, are easy to understand in different cultures. The European symbol for "One Way—Do Not Enter" (see Figure 25.1) confused me until someone explained it. I kept attempting to go the wrong way down one-way streets.

In a brochure advertising a new telephone system for British customers, readers responded negatively to a photograph that happened to show an American telephone on a table at the side of the picture. They wanted a British product, not an American one.

Not only does your team have to become aware of the problems in translating words, they must also be alert to illustrations and icons that will be meaningless in another culture.

Guideline: Avoid Americanisms or other culturally specific expressions in publications that will be translated.

Establishing an internal-review process

Establishing a process to verify the technical and legal accuracy of translated publications should be an integral part of your publications-development process. Consider the consequences if the translated information is misleading or incorrect. One company with US and Canadian divisions discovered too late that the Canadian-French version of its policies manual did not contain the same information as the English version. An employee who had been fired for failing to follow company policy sued and won his case by proving that he had followed the French version while his manager had referred to the English version. The company had no idea that the two versions were different.

Consider the cost to your company if the translated information in an instructional manual is incorrect. The cost of customer service and field engineering may rise dramatically, and the company's reputation may suffer in the country that gets the wrong information.

If you have information that is legally sensitive or contains warnings and cautions, you may need to institute a technique of reverse translation. The original text is first translated into the target language. Then, the text in the target language is translated back into the original language. The two versions of the original text are then compared so that discrepancies can be corrected.

When information is not so sensitive as to require reverse translation, many companies have instituted review processes in which they ask technical experts in their foreign divisions or even customer representatives who are product experts to review the translated text and verify its accuracy. The technical experts are usually given the original text to compare, especially if they have a reasonable knowledge of the technical aspects of the first language. They may be able to consult the original text with sufficient understanding to note discrepancies in their native-language version.

Technical experts in your field in the countries targeted for translations may also be able to help in developing the technical glossaries that will make the translator's job easier. The technical experts are more likely to know the terms currently in use than the translator.

 Guideline: Establish a system of verification of the technical and legal accuracy of the translated versions of your publications.

Estimating translation costs

The best way of estimating the amount of time needed for a translation is to work with a qualified vendor early in the publications-development life cycle. The translators will be able to use your team's Information Plan and Content Specifications to anticipate the scope and complexity of the translation project. They can then provide you with guidelines to help you anticipate the amount of time needed for translation if the original publications specified change in size.

Most translations are estimated according to the number of words in the original text. As the number of words grows, the translation time and cost also grow. If you have publications that include identical information repeated several times, inform the translators so that they can take the repetition of information into account when they estimate and as they plan their work. Just as your writers save time by copying and pasting identical sections of text throughout a publication or across publications, translators save time if the identical sections are clearly marked so that they, too, can copy and paste.

The cost also depends upon the target language of the translation. Technical translators may be much more difficult to find and in greater demand for languages in countries with smaller technical markets. Although French, German, Spanish, and Japanese technical translators abound, you may find it difficult and expensive to locate a qualified technical translator of Indonesian or Lithuanian. As you work with the translators, be aware that the cost of translations will vary from language to language.

Another consideration to take into account in terms of cost is the difference in word count from language to language. English is one of the most compact technical languages. Some languages, such as German and Swedish, have considerably longer words and sentences than English. Some languages, such as Indonesian, require many more words to communicate the same technical content. If you are intent upon preserving the page counts and producing equal-size publications in every target language, you will have to take the expansion factors of the translations into account. That may require leaving lots of white space in the English version to accommodate the increases. Or you may have to budget for increased reproduction and binding costs for translated versions of your publications.

Of special concern is the problem of translating callouts on illustrations when the space around the artwork has been optimized for English. The German version of the callout, for example, may exceed the space available. Consequently, translators recommend that indirect callouts be used rather than direct callouts. Indirect callouts accompany the artwork in separate lists below or alongside the illustration space. They are linked to the artwork with numbers. Because the callouts are in separate numbered lists, their text can be expanded without damaging visibility of the illustration. Unfortunately, using indirect callouts runs counter to usability guidelines that favor the close proximity of the callout to the feature being identified or explained. As we use illustrations more frequently to communicate instructional steps, the issues of size expansion in translated callouts will become more difficult to resolve.

The problem with translating callouts is exacerbated by the difficulty of using many of the complex drawing software programs now available. Although your translators may be familiar with your electronic-publishing system, they frequently will not know how to use elaborate drawing software. A system that allows you to handle callouts as overlays to drawings may be preferable to hardcoded callouts if you are doing a lot of translation. Then, either the callouts can be translated independently and pasted up, or the translator can change the text of the callout in the electronic-publishing system rather than in the drawing software (see Figure 25.2).

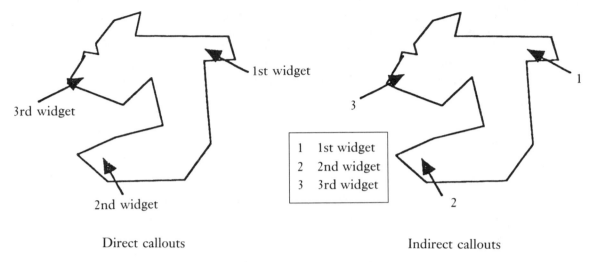

1	1st widget
2	2nd widget
3	3rd widget

Direct callouts   Indirect callouts

Figure 25.2   Direct versus indirect callouts

Just as translation-size expansion will affect graphics, it will also affect online-help systems and the information provided on screen and in status and error messages. If your online-help product or the screen-building tools used by your developers do not allow for expansion of the window size to accommodate more text, you have to plan to create English text that leaves considerable white space.

> *Guideline: Work closely with your translation vendor to esti-mate the cost of translation into different languages, the amount of time needed in relation to the number of words and graphics, and the ramifications of the translation on page counts or screen size.*

Blocking translation time into the schedule

The translation process should begin as early in the publications-development life cycle as possible, preferably during Phase 1: Information Planning. Translation activities will continue through Phase 2: Content Specification and into the first stages of Phase 3: Implementation, when the translators become familiar with the developing text and graphics. The serious work, however, generally begins after the second-draft review. By that time, the text and graphics should be stable. If you believe that they will change considerably before the camera-ready draft, you may want to delay the start of the translation drafts. When translations are in progress, the cost of changes to a publication increases enormously. Every change in the original-language text and graphics has to be communicated to every translator. If there ever was a reason to put some discipline in the change process, it is the cost of translation.

If you want the translations to be ready at the same time that the original text is ready for printing, then you must start the translation process early with planning and glossary building and initiate the full-text translation immediately after the second-draft review.

If you do not plan for the simultaneous introduction of multiple-language versions of the publications, you may want to delay the full-text translation until after the original text has been sent to print.

Guideline: Schedule translations so that their timing meets the needs of your organization's and distribution plans.

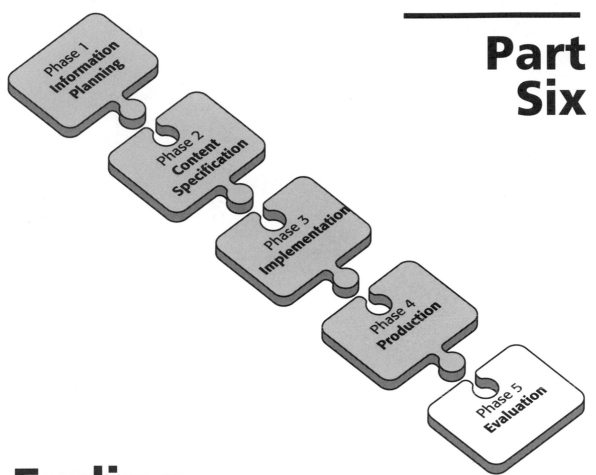

Phase 1
Information
Planning

Phase 2
Content
Specification

Phase 3
Implementation

Phase 4
Production

Phase 5
Evaluation

Part Six

Ending the Project

The Evaluation Phase

Phase 5: Evaluation of the publications-development life cycle is designed to help you bring your project to a successful conclusion and evaluate the results of the publications development process. The importance of your evaluation of the project, the team, and yourself is threefold:

- To learn from both your successes and mistakes so you can incorporate the lessons learned into future projects
- To review the data you have collected so that you can draw conclusions and implement your ideas in future publications-development efforts
- To help you estimate future projects more realistically and accurately

In this part, you can learn to create wrap-up reports that give you a record of project metrics and review the successes and mistakes of the publications-development effort. You also learn to develop a database so that the records of completed projects are saved for future reference.

Based on the results of the wrap-up report, you learn to plan and conduct a project wrap-up meeting so that your own staff members and others in the organization can review the project and air their concerns and ideas for improvements. Project wrap-ups meetings can contribute significantly to reducing the animosities that often emerge among publications team members and others in the organization because of a lack of understanding of each other's needs and goals.

Although the most effective usability testing of a publication and the accompanying product takes place during earlier development stages, you may also want to consider evaluative testing at the completion of the project. Evaluative testing enables the publications team to assess the usefulness and quality of the completed documents for the customer. Evaluative testing provides important data for the next iteration of the publications. It may also provide you with an opportunity to train your staff in administration and monitoring when there is more time available than in the midst of a development project.

To extend evaluative testing into customer satisfaction, you also learn to institute methods for collecting data about user responses to the publications produced. In this section, you consider user-comment forms, user surveys, data collected in customer-response centers, and other methods of learning how well the publications serve the needs of customers.

The results of customer-satisfaction surveys can lead you to find opportunities for change in the publications to improve their usability. You can also use the results as a baseline of information to study publication problems more thoroughly and to assess the relative productivity of your team and its members.

In terms of team development, you learn the importance of conducting performance evaluations that directly relate to the project. Too often the details of project successes or problems are forgotten by the time annual performance appraisals take place. It is important for the project manager and team members to capture the data and impressions about individual performance before they move on to other tasks or even other managers.

Finally, you review the importance of archiving project materials and records. It is especially important for you to decide what to keep and what to discard, along with how to organize what is kept. Project materials should be organized so that finding and understanding them does not place a burden on a new manager taking over mainte- nance on the project.

If plans for the revision and maintenance of product publications have not already been made during the planning stages or if changes must be made to the maintenance plan, you learn the importance of doing so at the end of the project. As is frequently the case, some information has already changed between the time the publication has been printed and the time it is released to the customer. These changes must be monitored and a plan devised to handle them immediately, if necessary.

Contents

Chapter 26: Evaluating the Publications Project

Chapter 27: Evaluating the Publications Process

Chapter 28: Evaluating the Publications Team

- Conducting project-specific evaluations
- Evaluating the successes and mistakes
- Evaluating the performance of the team
- Evaluating individual productivity
- Evaluating the performance of the project manager
- Developing productivity measures

Chapter 29: Preparing for the Project's Future

- Preparing for maintenance
- Archiving project records and materials
- Preparing for the project end-of-life

Results

By the end of this section, you will recognize the imporance of a well-organized end to the project you have managed for many months or even years. You will be especially interested in evaluating project metrics to see how well you estimated project scope at the beginning and how you can make future estimates more precise.

You will prepare your final project wrap-up report, including information on project metrics, a review of problems and successes, and an analysis of the relationship between initial and final project dependencies.

You will be prepared to offer project-specific performance evaluations to staff working on the project so that the performance information is not lost.

You will also plan to store project records carefully so that those who maintain and revise the publications are not burdened by a lack of information. You will know how to avoid the all-too-frequent problem of lost files and supporting information that requires projects to be started from scratch when the next revision is due.

Evaluating the Publications Project

In evaluating the successes and failures of a publications project, the best starting point is the data you have collected throughout the project-development life cycle. If you have maintained project-tracking spreadsheets, along with weekly progress reports, you should be well prepared to trace the history of the project through its many twists and turns.

If you have not been collecting data through the course of the project, you may have to attempt to recreate the project from whatever records are available. Time sheets, progress notes, and the memories of team members are all possible but frustratingly incomplete sources. Many project managers finally are convinced of the value of careful tracking and recordkeeping throughout the project when they attempt to write a project wrap-up report without data.

In this chapter, you learn how to

- Collect the data required for the project wrap-up report
- Calculate project statistics
- Re-evaluate project dependencies

Once you have the data you need to evaluate a single project, you also learn the importance of creating a database of projects that you can use for future project estimates. Finally, you hold a project wrap-up meeting to discuss with all those involved how to improve the process in the future (Figure 26.1).

Preparing the project wrap-up report

The project wrap-up report should be a complete record of the project milestones as they were actually achieved in comparison with how they were planned during the initial planning phases. In preparing a wrap-up report, ask yourself and your team the following questions:

- Did we do what we said we would do in the project? Did the final publications produced match those designed in the Information Plan and the Content Specifications?

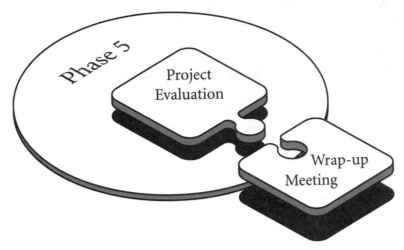

Figure 26.1 Phase 5

- Did the scope of the project remain the same? Were the publications specified similar to the ones that were finally produced in size and organization?
- Did the final product resemble the one described in the original product specifications?
- Did the project dependencies remain the same as originally predicted? For example, did the product change more or less than originally estimated in the dependencies calculation? Was the publications team as well equipped to handle the project as originally projected?
- Was the original schedule maintained? Did the major milestones of first draft, second draft, and camera-ready draft occur on the dates originally scheduled?
- Did the original estimates of hours per page remain accurate?
- Did the original estimates of the percentages of time for project management and editing remain accurate?
- Did the estimates for the mix of graphics and text hold? Had you planned sufficient time for translation and production tasks?
- Did the staff remain the same during the project? Or did you experience a gradually disappearing staff that reminded you of the Cheshire cat?

Finally, if the answers to any of these questions was "no," do you know why? What happened to change the project from the one originally planned, estimated, staffed, and scheduled? Were the changes due to mistakes you made in the original planning process? Could you and your publications team have done anything to avoid the changes or better predict them along the way?

If you could improve the process, what would you and your team do to change your own activities? If the changes were beyond your control, what suggestions can you make to the rest of the organization to help the process go more smoothly in the future?

The purpose of the project wrap-up report is to create a thorough assessment of the project so that you can learn

- What went right
- What went wrong
- How to build on the actions that led to success
- How to change the actions that caused problems or failures

You will use the results of the project wrap-up report to plan more effectively in the future and to improve the publications-development process.

In addition to thinking carefully about the successes and mistakes of your current project, also consider the information that you and other project managers will find useful in planning future projects. Many of you began Phase 1: Information Planning without a database of previous projects. As a result, you had to make pure guesses about the amount of time and staff needed for your new project. If you write your project wrap-up report with future projects in mind, you will be more likely to capture the details you will need later. If you do not carefully think through your future needs, you are likely to miss recording or analyzing a crucial aspect of a current project.

For example, in one project wrap-up report, the project manager, short on time as usual, simply combined all the data for the various books developed into a single hours-per-page figure. Unfortunately, the books had been very different, ranging from tutorials and user guides to reference information and online help. In addition, some of the books were developed from scratch while others required extensive revision to original text. As a result of the combined wrap-up analysis, other project managers could not use the wrap-up data to estimate the needs of future projects. They could not tell whether the revised reference manual had taken 5 hours per page or 8.

As you plan your wrap-up analysis, consider what future project managers may want to know about your project. Remember that they will not understand cryptic references to activities or issues. In fact, you may not be able to understand cryptic references to your own project months or years later. A project wrap-up report is an historical document that should be written so that it will be understood when you are no longer around to answer questions.

Figure 26.2 provides an example of a typical project wrap-up report for a complex project. Appendix E contains a template for a standard wrap-up report. The wrap-up report contains the following sections:

- Project name and description
- Project manager's name and team members' names as needed
- Project statistics
- A review of project dependencies
- Milestone and activity reviews
- Discussions of problems and successes
- Recommendations for future projects

The project description contains a brief but thorough description of the entire project, emphasizing the major activities conducted, such as interface design, usability testing, and others, as well as the major publications produced, such as hardcopy manuals,

CAT Documentation Project Wrap-up Report

Client name: CAT Software
Project Manager: MR
Senior Writer: RT
Date: 11/28

The following report summarizes the CAT documentation project for CAT Software. We produced a user guide for the test developers and a support guide for the system administrators. For this report, the total numbers for both manuals are combined.

Projected, actual, and billed totals

Item	Projected	Actual
Total project hours	921	851
Total project cost	$60,350.00	$60,055.00
Number of pages	170	185
Hours per page	5.42	4.6

Project hours by task

| | Hours | | Percent of total hours | |
Item	Proj	Actual	Proj	Actual
Writing total	745	654	81	77
Editing	104	113	11/14	13/17
Graphics				
Production	17	18	2	2
Project Management	55	68	6	8
Total hours	921	853	100	100

Project hours by milestone

| | Hours | | Percent of total hours | |
Milestone	Proj	Actual	Proj	Actual
Information plan	88	92	10	11
Content specs	176	154	19	18
First draft	364	303	40	36
Second draft	183	186	20	22
Final draft	110	118	11	13
Total hours	921	853	100	100

Figure 26.2   Sample project wrap-up report

Summary of the CAT project

The objective of the CAT project was to produce two documents: the *CAT Test Developer's Guide* and the *CAT System Support Guide*. The test developer's guide was to contain all of the information a test developer would need to use the newly developed computer assisted testing system (an online testing system for CAT engineers). The system support guide was intended to provide all of the information administrators would need to administer the CAT system.

We prepared both documents in the word-processing system and pasted in the graphics.

The original proposal stated that the documentation would consist of approximately 170 pages, requiring approximately 921 hours to complete (5.42 hours per page). The targeted completion date was October 31.

Although various problems were encountered during the project, none of them warranted a scope change. These problems included changes in the perceived audience for the developer's guide, changes in the product, and changes in CAT personnel assigned to the project (a minor impact).

The project was completed on November 12. The combined documents totaled 185 pages. 870 total hours were needed to complete the project, including: 654 hours of writing, 113 hours of editing, 18 hours of production, and 68 hours of project management. This breaks down to 4.6 hours per page.

Project time by task

Writing

We spent approximately 77 percent of our total hours writing the documents.

Information Plan and Content Specifications

We spent approximately 29 percent of our total hours on the plans for both documents, which included the following activities:

- Reviewing the product
- Reviewing videotapes and source documentation
- Writing and revising the plans

First draft

We spent approximately 36 percent of our total hours writing the first drafts of both documents. Writing first drafts included the following activities:

- Working with the product
- Interviewing subject-matter experts (SMEs)
- Preparing a style template
- Writing and revising the draft

Figure 26.2 (Continued)

Second draft

We spent approximately 22 percent of our total hours writing the second drafts of both documents. Writing second drafts included the following activities:

- Working with the product
- Interviewing SMEs
- Identifying and locating graphics (screen dumps prepared by the engineers)
- Revising the first draft

Final draft

We spent approximately 13 percent of our total hours writing the final drafts of both documents. Writing final drafts included the following activities:

- Working with the product
- Interviewing SMEs
- Revising the second draft
- Sizing and pasting in all graphics

The project was late because of changes in the final draft caused by product changes. The total amount increased to produce the final draft.

Editing

We spent approximately 13 percent of our total hours on editing both documents, which represented 17 percent of total writing time, a considerable increase from the expected 14 percent. Editing was conducted at all levels as was appropriate.

Editing increased because of the late changes in the manuals because of product changes. Information that had been completely proofread had to be proofread a second time.

Graphics

Graphics included screen dumps provided by CAT. We identified them, sized them, and pasted them into final draft. This was considered part of writing time.

Production

The production department set up a style to our specifications. This style was intended to closely match the style typically used by CAT on similar documentation.

Figure 26.2 (Continued)

Project management

We spent approximately 8 percent of our total hours on project management, an increase from the projected 6 percent. Project management was handled mostly by the project manager, with the project coordinator contributing 8.5 hours (12.5 percent of the total project management hours). Project management included the following activities:

- Weekly progress reports
- Maintaining weekly spreadsheets
- Invoicing
- Scheduling

Dependency rating summary

We projected approximately 5.42 hours per page for this project based on the dependency ratings shown in the Original Rating column. Our new rating of 4.6 was based on how the project actually went and is shown in the Revised Rating column. The next section of this report, "Evaluating the project dependencies," explains why we revised these ratings.

Dependency	Original Rating	Revised Rating
Product stability	3	4
Information availability	4	4
Subject matter experts	2	4
Review	3	4
Writing experience	3	2
Technical experience	3	2
Audience awareness	3	4

Note: Dependencies are on a scale of 1 to 5 with 1 the best case and 5 the worst case.

Evaluating the project dependencies

Product stability
The product was less stable than we anticipated. Minor changes were made throughout the project. Revised rating = 4.

Information availability
We suspected that it might be a little difficult getting information and we were right. No revision.

Subject-matter experts
We found out that there were few SMEs at CAT. The ones that were there were sometimes unavailable. Revised rating = 4.

Figure 26.2 (Continued)

Review

Reviews were handled in a timely manner, although they were often somewhat incomplete. Revised rating = 4.

Writing experience

The writer did an excellent job and worked very efficiently. Revised rating = 2. The increase in editing time was due entirely to changes in the final draft and not because of a less experienced writer or inefficient editor.

Technical experience

Although the writer did not have experience with a similar product, she did an excellent job of mastering the subject matter. Revised rating = 2.

Audience awareness

The audience for the second document in this library was redefined during the project by CAT. Revised rating = 4.

What we learned from this project

- Our projections were pretty much on target, with writing hours running slightly below the projections and editing and project management running slightly above.
- Our dependencies, though specifically inaccurate, averaged out to be fairly accurate. In other words, although some dependencies changed, the resulting hours-per-page estimate did not change substantially.
- Despite the problems that arose during this project, CAT proved to be a concerned and competent client and we were able to solve all of our problems in a timely manner.
- CAT was always willing to consider our ideas for the documentation, even when those ideas may have varied from the original plan.
- Our communications with CAT were always open and amiable.

Figure 26.2 (Continued)

online help, computer-based training, and others. You should write the description for readers who may not have access to you or to any other project records or the documents produced.

Following the project descriptions, summarize the project statistics that are the result of your project analysis. The statistics will reflect the nature of the project and the importance of certain activities that you chose to track.

Following the statistics, include an analysis of the project dependencies, comparing your initial dependencies analysis with your analysis of the actual dependencies as they occurred in the project. The dependencies are discussed in detail below.

The descriptive sections that follow the statistical analyses provide background information to support your numbers. For example, if you had originally estimated that editing would represent about 12 percent of total writing time and your project statistics show that editing actually represented twice the estimate at 24 percent, use the descriptive section to explain what happened.

After you have discussed the specific activities and issues associated with milestones, summarize the problems and successes of the project as a whole. Even projects that have experienced problems in specific areas may have been successful overall. Projects that have been successful in the details may end with bad feelings because of a single event that did not occur as expected. Use the summary section to put everything into perspective.

Finally, end the wrap-up report with a list of recommendations for future projects. In a Level 4 organization, you are always looking for ways to improve the process: to reduce costs, shorten schedules, produce higher-quality publications, and reduce the stress on team members. Be prepared to recommend changes to your own process in addition to processes that are controlled by others. For example, you may feel that the review process during the life cycle of your project was not handled well by the technical teams. Reviews may have been late, cursory, or filled with insulting comments. You may be able to get agreement from the technical teams to do better next time.

However, look carefully at your own practices to find areas for improvement. How well are you handling the review process yourself? Do you schedule reviews and keep to the schedules? Do you send cover sheets that explain the review process? Do you give people enough time to review? Do you break long documents into shorter sections and divide the review responsibilities? It is always easier to change your own behavior than someone else's behavior.

 Guideline: Prepare a project wrap-up report that contains a thorough analysis of project progress, successes, mistakes, and recommendations for change.

Calculating project statistics

Your ability to calculate useful project statistics is dependent on the care with which you collected data during the project. During Phase 1: Information Planning, you chose the measures that you wanted to track. You may have decided to track the time devoted to

- Project management
- Writing
- Editing
- Graphics
- Production
- Usability

You may also have decided to break out the time for research and information gathering, meetings with review teams, time spent helping to design a more usable product interface, and others.

On your original estimated-hours spreadsheet for the project, you indicated the total hours you expected to spend on each of the activities you decided to track. In your original project schedule, you also estimated the amount of time that your team would devote to each of the major project milestones.

In the statistical presentation of the project wrap-up report, compare your original estimates with the actual hours expended on the project. Figure 26.3 shows another example of project statistics. If you look at the comparisons on this project between the original and final page counts and the estimated and actual hours, you see that the project grew substantially and proved to be more difficult to accomplish than originally estimated. The hours per page increased by 8 percent from 6.5 hours per page to 7.0 hours per page. All other project activities took longer to accomplish, especially the graphics which increased by 188 percent. In fact, the graphics increase was the major contributor to the increase in hours per page. Note also that the writing hours increased in proportion to the increase in the size of the book, while the editing hours increased from 12 to 14 percent of total project time. Everything about these statistics reveals a project that grew and became more complex.

In Figure 26.4, the project manager presents details about the relationship of the project activities to one another. Note that the percentage of the total for project management and production remained remarkably constant for this project. Editing as a percentage of the total project actually declined, although editing as a percentage of writing time increased from 12 to 14 percent, indicating that the editor had more work to do to maintain quality. The most significant change was in the percentage of time devoted to writing, which decreased from 75 to 70 percent. As a factor of total pages produced, the hours per page for writing actually remained the same at 4.8 hours per page. That indicates that the remaining activities accounted for the increase from 6.5 to 7.0 hours per page. The majority of the increase occurred in producing the graphics, which increased from 3 to 8 percent of total project time.

Project activity	Estimated	Actual	Percent change
Total hours	2,000	2,456	+23%
Project management	200	232	+16%
Writing	1,500	1,720	+15%
Editing	180	240	+33%
Graphics	69	199	+188%
Production	51	65	+27%
Page count	308	352	+14%
Hours per page	6.5	7.0	+8%

Figure 26.3 Project statistics 1

Project activity	Estimated	Percent of total	Actual	Percent of total
Total hours	2,000	100.0	2,456	100.0
Project management	200	10.0	232	9.4
Writing	1,500	75.0	1,720	70.0
Editing	180	9.0	240	9.7
Graphics	69	3.0	199	8.0
Production	51	2.6	65	2.6

Figure 26.4 Project statistics 2

From the analysis of project statistics, the project manager for this project would be able to show that the project was as efficient as originally estimated, perhaps more so. However, the increase in the graphics work, perhaps through the development of more and better graphics resulted in an overall increase in hours per page. The project manager believed that the increase in quality produced by developing a more visual document represented a fair tradeoff against the increased cost of producing the document.

We have looked at project statistics in relationship to the estimated time for each activity compared to the actual time for each activity. We have also examined the relationship between the estimated percentage of total project time devoted to an activity and the actual percentage of time devoted to that activity. We can also look at the amount of time in the schedule estimated for each project milestone compared with the amount of time the milestone actually received.

Figure 26.5 illustrates an analysis of milestone time and percentages for the sample project. The time actually devoted to each project milestone has changed in some interesting ways. Note that the hours devoted to the Phase 1: Information Planning were exactly as planned. That appears to indicate that the project manager did not

Project milestone	Estimate	Percent of total	Actual	Percent of total
Total hours	2,000		2,456	
Information Plan	200	10	200	8
Content Specifications	400	20	491	20
First Draft	600	30	842	34
Second Draft	500	25	547	22
Final Draft	300	15	376	15

Figure 26.5 Project statistics 3

anticipate the later project changes during the first phase. However, during Phase 2: Content Specification the early warnings of a larger project begin to emerge with the increase in actual hours devoted to the specifications. Undoubtedly, the team began to recognize that the book would be longer than originally estimated. The percentage of time devoted to Phase 2 at 20 percent of the total remains the same in relationship to the larger project.

The greatest increase in the project occurs during the development of the first draft, which accounts for 34 percent of total project time instead of 30 percent. The total time devoted to the first three milestones has increased from 60 to 62 percent. It appears that the additional time for the development of graphics occurred during the first draft but was anticipated during the Content-Specification process.

Finally, the last two milestones, second draft and final draft, consumed almost exactly the same percentage of the total time as originally anticipated, with a small decrease for second draft. It seems as if many of the primary issues were worked out during the first-draft development, thereby decreasing the amount of time for second-draft changes. The final draft, including copyediting and indexing activities, remained the same.

The project statistics provide many interesting insights into the changing nature of a publications project. The statistics, however, must be explained in the wrap-up report descriptive section. As project manager, analyze your results and then explain why the changes took place. If nothing changed, simply explain what occurred in each activity and each milestone.

Although it may seem unimportant to account for the activities that occurred during a project, a brief listing of what was included under each category and milestone will help future project managers ensure that they are dividing activities in the same way. Similarly, peer managers or the department head can ensure that everyone is analyzing their project statistics in a similar manner, making comparisons simpler and more useful. Many of the discrepancies in hours per page from group to group and organization to organization can be attributed to differences in accounting for project activities. Some managers count only writing activities; others include editing but not project management. When the basic data is different, comparisons are difficult.

 Guideline: Analyze the results of your project and summarize them in tables. Account for the differences from the estimates to the actuals in your descriptive text.

Re-evaluating project dependencies

In addition to calculating the variety of project statistics above, you should also re-evaluate the dependencies or risk factors that you used during Phase 1: Information Planning to determine your project hours per page. This re-evaluation is especially important if your project hours per page has changed from your initial estimate.

When you first evaluated project dependencies in Phase 1, you made assumptions about many aspects of your project, from the stability of the product and other external dependencies to the skill level and experience of your team members. At the end of the project, as well as in conjunction with project milestones, the reality of the project's complexity replaces assumptions.

For example, you may have decided to rate the technical experience of your team members at 2, suggesting that they were more experienced in the technology of the project than average. However, in the middle of your project, your most technically experienced writer resigns. You have to replace the writer with someone who knows less about the technology. At the end of the project, you re-evaluate the technical-experience dependency at 3. A change in one dependency such as this one suggests that the overall hours per page for the project may have increased.

However, an increase in hours per page for one dependency may be offset by another dependency that has improved. In addition to the technical experience of your team members, you may have evaluated the review dependency at 4 because your prior experience with the development team members suggested that reviews would be difficult to accomplish on schedule and in sufficient depth. Fortunately, a new project manager on the development team recognized the seriousness of the review commitment and made sure that the development team members had time in their schedules to review the documentation. As a result, you are happy to re-evaluate the review dependency at the end of the project at 2.

Examine all of your initial dependencies carefully, taking into account any previous re-evaluation you did at project milestones. Then, create a comparison table in your project wrap-up report, as illustrated in Figure 26.6. If the average hours per page for your organization is 5.5, your initial evaluation of project dependencies led you to a project hours per page of 5.45. At the end of the project, your re-evaluation leads you to an hours per page of 5.38, only slightly less overall than your initial estimate. This result should equal the experience of the actual project. If it does not, be certain that

Project Dependency	Initial	Interim	Final
Product stability	4	4	5
Information availability	3	3	3
Prototype availability	2	2	2
Review process	4	2	2
Subject-matter-expert availability	3	2	2
Technical experience	2	3	3
Writing experience	2	2	2
Audience experience	3	3	3
Team experience	2	3	3

Figure 26.6 Re-evaluating project dependencies

you have thought through the dependencies re-evaluation carefully. You may have overstated or understated one or more of the factors.

If the dependencies have changed during the project, accompany the table you create with brief descriptions of the reasons for the changes. This examination of project dependencies will help you use the hours-per-page data to evaluate new projects, as well as account for changes in project difficulty in the current project.

What if your re-evaluation of the dependencies suggests a project hours per page that is significantly different from your actual project experience? The differences may be caused by an incorrect average hours per page for your team or organization. If you are confident of your evaluation of the dependencies at the end of the project, change the average hours per page in the calculation until the actual experience equals the evaluation. In this way, you arrive at a new, more reasonable average hours per page for your organization.

Guideline: Re-evaluate the effect of the project dependencies at the end of the project and account for the changes in your project history.

Creating and updating the project database

A number of possibilities are available to help you keep track of your project histories. A file of project histories that can be accessed by all project managers will help disseminate information in your organization. You may want to organize the wrap-up reports by project type, type of publication, project manager, or any other categories you may find useful. You may want to put project wrap-up reports in a binder by category or even in alphabetical order by project name. You may want to organize the information by date so that you can more effectively track changes in project experience over time.

While a physical file of project wrap-up reports is useful and easily accessed, you may also want to consider creating an online database of project information. The statistical data you collect for a project might be entered into a database so that projects may be compared over time. One manager created a hypertext script that allowed him to automatically update project statistics whenever a new project was added to the database. His script continuously calculated new average hours per page for his department.

In addition to a centralized location for project statistics and histories, you should include the project wrap-up report in your Project Management Notebook, along with your final tracking spreadsheets and any other records you have created at the end of the project. The completed Project Management Notebook should be centrally located so that the information about each project is available to project managers, team members, and others interested in project history and statistics. I keep Project Management Notebooks in the department library so that anyone working on a project may review previous projects to understand how they were managed.

Note that your project correspondence, including your wrap-up report, becomes public when you put your Project Management Notebook in the department library. You may not want all of the information to be generally available. Create an archive file that is only for you and the publications manager to place confidential information that should not be open to general access.

Guideline: Create and maintain a central repository for project statistics and histories as a basis for overall analysis of organizational productivity levels and trends.

Conducting project wrap-up meetings internally and externally

Once your project wrap-up report is complete, you should quickly schedule project wrap-up meetings with your own team members and with members of the larger development team. The wrap-up report and the meetings should be completed and scheduled quickly before team members are dispersed to new projects and lose interest in the project just completed.

For the internal wrap-up meeting, schedule the entire team and any other members of your immediate organization who may be interested in learning more about the project. You may want to include the department manager or other project managers in the internal wrap-up meeting so that you can each learn from the latest experience. But be careful about inviting too many people, especially if they are overbearing or tend to stifle discussion. In planning the internal meeting, ensure that everyone receives a copy of the wrap-up report shortly before the meeting. At the beginning of the meeting, briefly go over the statistics and the high points of the report.

The greatest benefit of the internal wrap-up meeting is for team members to review their participation in the project and discuss how problems could be avoided in the future. Focus the discussion on process improvement rather than on negative comments about individual team members. Certainly mistakes occur. The important point is to learn from the mistakes so that they do not happen again.

I don't really understand why we came up short on the Dracula project," said Andy. "I thought I had recalculated the hours and staffing needs carefully so that we would have enough people to meet the deadline."

"Let's review what happened and see if we can all figure it out," said Lisa. "I know you were tracking your time carefully. In May, you told me that you needed two additional people because the marketing group wanted to add another book to the library. After you added the two people, you still were one person-month short at the end of the project in July."

"Well, now that I look at the numbers, I see what you mean," said Andy. "We were exactly 160 hours short of what we needed. That's the amount that the rest of the team had to work overtime during the last month to get the project done. How did I miss that?"

"Tell me how you did the May recalculation," asked Lisa. "You added the pages for the new book. Your writing hours should have been all right. It looks like you used more editing and project management hours than you had anticipated."

"I thought that I could decrease the percentage of project management and editing I needed because most of the project was done," said Andy. "I had used 12-percent project management and 15-percent editing for the rest of the project. But I cut that back to 10 percent and 12 percent for the last book."

"But you added two new writers near the end of the project," said Lisa. "That usually means more project management and editing rather than less. Remember the good old mythical person-month. The more people you add, the more project management and editing it will take to get the job done."

"Look at this," exclaimed Andy. "If I had used the original percentages, that would have accounted for half of the 160 hours. If I had increased the percentages to take into account the new writers, I would have been OK. I see what you mean now about the difficulty of adding writers to an expanding project."

"You were lucky that the rest of the team came through for you," said Lisa.

"I know," replied Andy. "I'll know not to shortchange them in the future. You know, I really wanted to blame the two new writers. I felt they should have completed their tasks in the same amount of time the rest of the team would have taken. I forgot that the rest of the team had 10 months to learn the technology and the Information Plan."

"Right. I know it's not ideal to add writers at the end of the project. Their efficiency really suffers along with the rest of the team that has to bring the newcomers up to speed. But, in a situation like this one, adding more writers was our only option. You couldn't negotiate additional time."

"I know that's true—even if I don't like it," replied Andy. "Next time I'll fight harder at the beginning to make sure that marketing has thought through their needs and the information they are getting from the clients. I sure don't like last-minute surprises.

Andy has discovered just how difficult it is to keep a project under control, especially when changes occur at the end. The internal wrap-up meeting becomes a learning opportunity for everyone on the team to better understand how a project needs to be managed.

The internal wrap-up meeting also provides you with an opportunity to review the politics of the project. While you may have some strong feelings about unprofessional behavior among external team members, these need to be carefully written in the wrap-up report to avoid repercussions. It may even be advantageous to create two versions of the wrap-up report, one for internal use only and one sanitized for external consumption. You want to communicate to fellow team members and project managers about problem situations in working with development teams, but you may not want to share all of your views with the external team members.

In addition to the internal wrap-up meeting, schedule an external wrap-up meeting with the members of the complete development and marketing teams. Invite as many team members as possible, but be especially sure that the managers attend. In fact, if a project has been especially difficult, you may want to meet alone with the other project managers, rather than subject your team members to angry criticisms.

At the external wrap-up meeting, once again discuss the project's successes and mistakes. Be certain that problems are placed in perspective without affixing blame. Keeping the meeting under control will require strong leadership, good planning, and a positive attitude. Remember that few problems that occur on a project are the fault of just one part of the process. Usually members of the other teams are partially responsible, not just publications. Work with the team members and managers to find solutions and improve the process.

In one project wrap-up meeting, all sides in the development effort acknowledged that communication between publications and engineering had not been as good as it might have been. The senior members of the publications team explained that their initial planning documents had not adequately communicated their approach to the project. Consequently, the engineering team members were disappointed with the first draft. Unfortunately, they did not communicate their concerns so that the publications team could revise the draft thoroughly

As a result of the wrap-up meeting, the publications team decided that in the future they would provide an early prototype that clearly illustrated their plan for the publications and training. The engineering team agreed that they would review the prototype carefully and provide thorough feedback as early as possible, rather than waiting until the second draft was complete. The two teams worked out a potentially more productive and less stressful relationship for future projects.

Project wrap-up meetings can often be effective in helping you and your team members defuse problem projects. In other cases, you may not even be aware of a problem or of hard feelings until the wrap-up meeting. During a project, all team members are reluctant to complain about problems because they are afraid of creating conflicts or halting the progress of the work.

In conducting the wrap-up meeting, be certain that everyone has an opportunity to express genuine concerns. At the same time, you are responsible for ensuring that the meeting does not turn into a shouting match. Keep the discussion focused on improvements rather than blame.

Guideline: Conduct both internal and external project wrap-up meetings to ensure that all problems are discussed openly and plans are made to avoid them in the future with improved processes and better communication.

CHAPTER 27

Evaluating the Publications Process

In the discussion of the project wrap-up report in Chapter 26, the importance of finding ways to improve the publications-development process was stressed. Every wrap-up report and every wrap-up meeting should result in recommendations for improvement in the process of developing professional publications.

Once you have released your publications products to the customer or delivered them to other intended audiences, you have many opportunities for obtaining customer feedback directly. You can use customer feedback to evaluate and improve the quality of the publications and to improve your development process.

In Chapter 20, you learned about the many methods available for evaluating the usability of a publication. Some of these methods are especially valuable for uncovering usability problems during the development process. Others are useful for uncovering usability problems after the publications have been completed. The types of evaluative testing include competitive testing, evaluative usability testing, and expert heuristic evaluation. Each of these evaluative testing types will provide you with information about the usability of completed publications, either on their own or in comparison with competitors' publications.

Once the publications have been delivered to customers and used in the field, other methods become available to you for collecting data and measuring quality. They include customer-satisfaction surveys, as well as information collected from

- Customer-complaint forms
- Customer-service calls
- Field-engineering visits
- Sales contacts with existing customers

The intent of these methods of collecting information about customers is to find and correct problems in the publications as well as to improve the publications-development process so that future problems are reduced or eliminated.

As project manager, you have intended from Phase 1: Information Planning to design a set of publications that will be useful to your audiences and will help them do their jobs effectively. If you followed the Information Plan template, you included measurable usability goals in your information design. You may have also developed prototype publications and tested them with actual users to uncover usability problems and correct them near the beginning of the publications-development life cycle. You may have also conducted usability tests after your first drafts were reviewed and revised by developmental editors and technical experts.

Throughout the publications-development life cycle, you hope that all the validation and testing processes you have put into place are sufficient to ensure the quality of the publications for the audience. Despite all your best efforts, the race to get the publications to the customer on time may have resulted in publications that have problems serious enough to affect the audience's understanding and performance of their jobs. And despite all your early testing, customers using the publications in their real work environments under widely different conditions may encounter problems.

To develop a program for measuring the quality of your publications, you must first consider how your audience identifies quality. Based on many studies of audience needs for information (see Brown, 1990; Coe, 1991; Dintruff et al., 1988; Dunlap, 1992), technical communicators have identified customer quality requirements, as follows:

- Customers want publications that are technically accurate.

  All the information in your publications must be correct. For example, if you describe the switch settings required on a circuit board for a particular application, those switch settings must be correct. If you provide a step-by-step procedure, each step must be correct and all steps must be in the correct sequence, so that the customer can perform the procedure correctly.

- Customers want publications that are as brief as possible.

  Your publications should be as short as possible. Although customers want all the information they need to perform a task successfully, they do not want more information than they need. Endlessly complete explanations of nice-to-know details interfere with their ability to find the simplest steps. Ensure that customers are not told enough to build their own version of the product.

- Customers want publications that are easy to access.

  Publications have high quality if customers can find the information they need to perform a task or understand a concept quickly and without frustration. Customers want complete indexes, tables of contents that are organized in the way they look for information, and names of tasks and parts that make sense to them.

- Customers want publications that are easy for them to understand.

  Publications have quality if the customers are able to understand the information sufficiently well to perform functions, make decisions, or understand concepts. They want information that is written appropriately for their levels of previous knowledge and experience.

- Customers want publications that help them to solve problems.

  Publications are judged effective if they help customers solve problems quickly and easily. Successful publications contain troubleshooting and problem-solving information that is easy to find and sufficiently detailed for customers to solve their problems without outside assistance.

- Customers want publications that are well illustrated and contain relevant examples.

  Publications have quality if they include useful drawings and photographs that help the customer learn. They are successful if they include typical examples of program codes, procedures, decisions, and concepts that customers can relate to their own experiences.

- Customers want publications that are attractive and free from obvious grammatical, typographical, and formatting errors.

Publications are judged effective if they are neatly packaged, have readable and usable formats, have few typographical errors, and are grammatically correct.

Publications that fail to meet customer expectations in any of these categories lack quality. A lack of quality causes customers to make mistakes, discover problems that they cannot correct, become frustrated, and stop using the publications and, possibly, the product. A lack of quality causes customers to call your customer-service organization for assistance, ask sales representatives to clarify procedures, and request field-service visits. Eventually, a lack of quality will cause customers to purchase competitors' products and recommend against the purchase of your organization's products.

Once you know your customers' expectations of your publications products, you should be prepared to collect information from your customers either directly or indirectly. The information you collect will allow you to correct problems and improve your process.

 Guideline: *Learn what your customers expect from your publications, and measure your success in meeting these expectations.*

Gathering customer usability and quality information

To gather information about your customers' problems with your publications, you need to use a variety of data-collection methods. The methods should be designed so that you find out about customer problems with your publications as quickly as possible. You learn about problems so that you can correct them either immediately or during a scheduled update of the publications.

Customers' problems come in two major categories: those that are reported directly by the customers and those that go unreported. The reported problems are only the tip of the iceberg. Most customer problems go unreported. You have the ability to correct problems that customers report. If they call customer service, they can be walked through solutions to the problems they are having. But if the problems go unreported, they can result in unresolved customer dissatisfaction that may have a severe effect on your organization's reputation.

Because unreported problems can be so significant to the success of an organization and a product, you need to find ways to uncover them. You may want to distribute customer surveys, conduct telephone interviews, attend training classes and user groups, and make site visits. You may also want to conduct usability testing to find the real causes of problems that have been vaguely reported. In any event, you cannot wait for customers to tell you that something is wrong. If you correct only 20 percent of the problems that are reported, the other 80 percent will go uncorrected.

Cataloging reported problems

Some of the processes you may want to include in your information-gathering efforts include

- Tracking the number and types of calls to customer service that result from problems with the publications
- Tracking the number of direct customer complaints about publications either through forms, calls to customer service, or discussions with field and sales personnel
- Tracking the number of problems and errors in the publications found by both external and internal customers (such as field-service and customer-service representatives, product developers, trainers, and anyone else within the organization who uses the publications)

Finding unreported problems

Each of these information-gathering processes, however, depends upon customers reporting problems to your organization. You may also want to include information-gathering processes that you initiate. These may include

- Direct-mail surveys of customers' problems
- Telephone surveys that discuss customers' problems
- Site visits in which you discuss customers' problems and observe their performance
- Panels and discussions at customer meetings that focus on problems with publications

In any systematic study that you initiate, you will need to frame questions carefully and include representative groups of customers in proportion to their mix in the customer base and their importance to your organization.

Many customer-initiated complaints are random. A few customers send in customer-comment forms that mention problems they are having with your publications. Some complaints can be verified and changes made. For example, if a customer informs you that the information in a specification table is incorrect, you can verify and correct it. However, other complaints cannot be easily verified and should be treated circumspectly. If one customer asks that you add more conceptual information to clarify a procedure and you comply with the request, you may later discover that other customers are confused by the additional verbiage and make more mistakes. Customers' comments are just that—comments. They may be biased, representing points of view based on unusual circumstances.

Following up on a problem report

When you receive customer complaints about publications, your first task is to follow up. You want to find out the exact nature of the problem and understand how and why it occurred. Call the customer and investigate. You may find a problem that is immediately verifiable. You may also find a problem that is idiosyncratic. Finally, you may find a problem that you suspect may be experienced by many customers. In this last case, you need to investigate further, perhaps by polling other customers, checking for customer-service calls and complaints or initiating a usability or field study. Be careful, however, of immediately changing something in response to one customer's complaint. You may make all the other customers unhappy and severely decrease the usability of your documents.

Even if you find that the problem is idiosyncratic to an individual customer, the fact that you have called and inquired will have a significant effect. Customers are pleased when someone takes a genuine interest in their concerns. They may continue to experience problems, but they frequently will have a better attitude toward your organization.

Guideline: Decide what information you need to collect about problems customers have with your publications, and establish methods for collecting the information from a representative sample of customers.

Evaluating problem severity

Once you decide how you are going to collect information to identify customer problems with your publications, you need to decide how to categorize the problems you discover. Not all problems are equal. Some cause customers severe difficulties or major inconvenience; others simply cause minor inconvenience or create a poor impression of your quality standards.

A problem with a publication that causes the customer to be injured, to lose data, or to lose substantial work time should be promptly remedied. In one case, because the technical information presented in a manual was difficult for a customer to read and understand, the customer misinterpreted the information. The misinterpretation caused the customer to make a mistake in performing a procedure that led to severe and permanent personal injury. In another case, the backup procedures in a user's guide were not explained properly. The customers thought they were backing up their data on a regular basis. Only after many months of work and a system crash did they learn that they had no backups. In a third case, the installation instructions for pouring a concrete base for a machine were incorrect. As a result, the base had to be torn out and replaced, costing the customer considerable time and expense. Problems like these are severe because of their consequences to the customer; they must be corrected immediately.

Other problems may cause customers considerable inconvenience. If a problem with an instruction causes a customer to fail to install a product, the inconvenience is critical because no further work can take place. If a problem with an instruction causes a customer to perform a procedure incorrectly, the customer may be immediately affected. If the results of the problem are delayed, the customer may not learn about the consequences of the problem for days, weeks, or months. Instructions that are difficult to find or difficult to understand may cause customers to use only a small fraction of the functions they paid for.

Still other problems may cause customers minor inconveniences. The customer may have to reread an awkwardly written instruction many times before performing the procedure correctly. The customer may have difficulty finding information. But at least once the customer finds the information, it is correct. Or a new customer may not understand a concept or procedure at first but may eventually learn the concept or procedure after using the product.

Finally, some problems, such as typographical or formatting errors, may annoy the customer or make your publication unattractive but cause the customer no harm, lasting or temporary. Some problems, especially typographical or formatting errors, may be undetectable by the customer and create no problems at all.

Categorizing the severity of the problems you find

When you begin collecting customer quality information, examine the types of problems that are being reported, and categorize them by severity levels, depending upon the consequences for your customers. Obviously, you will correct the most severe and costly publications problems immediately, especially those that result in an immediate cost to your customer or to your organization. A problem that might result in a personal injury or a lawsuit concerning loss of business requires immediate and decisive action.

But even less severe problems can be costly. A problem that generates a customer-service or field-service call has a high internal cost to your organization. Customer-service calls can cost hundreds or thousands of dollars before the problems are resolved. Frequent field-engineering visits can severely reduce the profitability of a product.

Figure 27.1 illustrates four severity levels to consider using to measure the quality of publications problems.

Severity level	Description
Life threatening	A publications problem may cause someone to be injured or killed. Without resolution, the problem will result in legal action against your organization.
Major	A publications problem may cause a loss of data or a performance mistake that results in lost work or expense to correct the problem. The user's work flow is severely disrupted. Without resolution, the problem may result in legal action against your organization, in addition to loss of business.
Minor	A publications problem causes a minor interruption of the user's work flow. Without resolution, the problem may result in loss of business or loss of your organization's credibility.
Annoyance	A publications problem causes the customer to perceive a lack of quality standards in your organization but causes no harm, lasting or temporary. Without resolution, the problem may cause your organization to lose credibility.

Figure 27.1 . Determining the severity levels of publications problems

The four categories depend, in part, upon the cost of the problem to the company and to your organization. The more costly the problem, the more severe that problem should be judged. Although you must remedy life-threatening problems immediately, how you resolve and respond to major, minor, or annoying problems will depend upon the cost of the solution. Some companies send corrected information to their customers as soon as possible, so that major problems do not reoccur. Other companies wait until the next version of a publication is issued before correcting the problem. Some organizations, because of their own internal problems, never correct problems with their publications. In an organization that takes responsibility for the accuracy and usability of its information, each problem you identify requires that you plan for its resolution.

Even though you can solve an immediate problem by issuing a correction to the publication immediately or within the regular updating schedule, you have not fully solved a problem until you get to its source. Your next step, therefore, is to investigate why the problem occurred.

Categorizing the types of problems

When you investigate the cause of a publications problem, you should first turn to the publication itself. If your customer cannot perform a task using your publication because information is missing, you need to discover exactly what information is missing so that you can correct the problem. If the information is incorrect, you need to learn the correct information and include it in the publication. If the customer gets confused by information in the text because it is difficult to understand, you need to find out more about the problem so that you can correct it.

In Figure 27.2, you have some examples of the reasons you might identify in a publication that result in life-threatening, major, minor, or annoying problems for the customer.

If information is written using terminology unknown to the customer, if background knowledge is assumed that the customer does not have, if the information is written at too difficult a reading level, or if it is organized so awkwardly that procedures cannot be separated from conceptual or background information, your customer will have problems performing tasks, and your publications will have problems. Many organizations fail to account for inappropriately written or badly organized information because problems of this type are more difficult to detect than problems of omission. Yet, they are the most persistent problems and the likeliest to cause considerable difficulty for your users.

You may devise many other categories to account for problems in your publications with your particular user community. Some of the problems noted in Figure 27.2 may be detected through customer complaints and service calls, but many can be confirmed only through direct observation of people using your publications. In one case, we knew from customer complaints during site visits that the customers were having difficulty finding information in the publications. Only after we conducted a quick, inexpensive usability investigation were we able to pinpoint exactly what the access problems were.

Reasons for publications problems	Description
Incorrect	The published information is factually wrong.
Incomplete	The published information is missing steps in a process or complete explanations of procedures or reference material. Entire procedures are missing.
Unnecessary	Information that the customer does not need to know is combined with information that is needed, causing considerable confusion.
Terminology	The user has difficulty understanding the information because the terms used in the text are unfamiliar.
Organization	The user has difficulty finding the appropriate information to perform a task because the information is badly organized.
Reading level	The user has difficulty understanding the information because the sentence structure is difficult to read.
Access	The user has difficulty finding information because the index, table of contents, headings, or other access information does not reflect the user's understanding of the problem.
Task orientation	The user has difficulty performing tasks because step-by-step procedures are not provided that correspond to the user's prior knowledge and experience.

Figure 27.2   Tracing the reasons for publications problems

Finding the source of the problem

Once you have identified the possible reasons for a publications problem and corrected it, your final responsibility is to discover why the problem occurred in the first place. If you understand the source of the problem, you may be able to avoid similar problems in the future. If not, at least you will know where problems in your latest publications are likely to occur. In Figure 27.3, there are several possibilities to consider as you try to identify problem sources. This brief list accounts for many of the typical problems experienced by technical-communication professionals in preparing technical publications. After you have completed the publications and released them for printing, the product developers may continue to change the product. As a result, the published information no longer conforms to the product as it is delivered to the customer. Sometimes, such product changes occur early enough during development to be incorporated into the publications, but product developers and the publications team have such poor communications that the publications team never learns of the product changes.

The other problem sources also point to communications problems in your organization. Source information, such as requirements documents and product specifications, are frequently inaccurate, since they are rarely kept up to date during the

Possible sources of publications problems	Description
Late product changes	Late changes in the product were not included in the publication, resulting in incorrect information or missing information.
Inadequate source material	The source information provided to the writers was incorrect or incomplete.
Poor definitions of users and tasks	The writers did not adequately understand the audience or the tasks that needed to be performed to write the instructions correctly.

Figure 27.3 Tracing possible sources of publications problems

product-development life cycle. As a result, the technical publications may lack information about the product that should have been available. A problem of this sort, however, often results from a lack of communication between developers and writers. If the writers are integral members of the development team, then all the emerging information about the product design is available to them. When writers have to rely on written material as their sole source of information about a product design, they are severely handicapped in their ability to produce useful publications.

When the publications team does not have a firm understanding of the audiences and their tasks, they will have difficulty creating publications that are usable. A usable document must be focused on the specific needs of the audiences and help them in the performance of tasks. If writers know nothing about their audiences or are given little more than one-word stereotypical descriptions (e.g., "the users are engineers"), they will be unable to provide information that the audiences will find usable and useful.

In addition to problems that occur because of communications breakdowns between your team and the developers and users, some publications problems will be caused by errors on the writer's part. Writer errors may occur because

- The writers did not have adequate opportunity to learn the subject matter they were writing about.
- The writers were told to incorporate source material without change.
- The writers had inadequate access to the audience.
- The writers had inadequate access to the SMEs.
- The writers had little time to validate the information they created.
- The writers did not have the benefit of developmental editing or copyediting.
- The writers on a single publications project did not work as a team.
- No one supervised the writers.
- The design of the publications was dictated by marketing or development, and the writers had no opportunity to recommend improvements.

Most of these problems occur because of the organization of the work environment, not because of shortcomings on the part of individual writers. Of course, individual writers may make mistakes, but those mistakes get out to the customers only because of inadequate internal review and project management. In Chapter 28, I discuss how to evaluate an individual's contribution to the team and to assess individual and team productivity.

 Guideline: Evaluate the severity, categorize the types, and investigate the true causes of the problems your audiences find with your publications.

Responding to the problems found

A major problem with a publication may require immediate response. If the problem uncovered is less severe, you may decide to wait to correct the publication until the next version is released.

At the next release of the publication, you may want to consider a major redesign and rewriting of the information, rather than small fixes. Frequently, the problems occur because of a lack of understanding of audience needs. In correcting the problems, your team will need a better understanding of the audience and their needs. Only then will they be able to design publications that really work.

Whatever methods you select to gather, categorize, and respond to customer problems, you will need to examine the problems further. It is not enough simply to correct a particular problem; you must also discover what caused the problem to occur in the first place.

Conducting customer-satisfaction surveys

In addition to the methods already mentioned for gathering information about problems that customers experience, you may want to conduct general customer-satisfaction surveys. Customer-satisfaction surveys are designed to solicit opinions about the quality of publications rather than details about problems encountered. They are also designed to help you discover problems that have gone unreported by the customer. Overall satisfaction measures provide important baseline measurements that you can use to initiate or validate a more detailed information-gathering process.

At one company, the results of a general survey showed that customers were less satisfied with the company's publications than they were with the products. As a result of the survey, the publications group was able to finance a detailed usability study that identified several significant shortcomings in the publications. When the problems were corrected, the customer-satisfaction survey results improved.

In many cases, however, the results of customer-satisfaction surveys are more difficult to interpret. If customers are dissatisfied with a product or service, they may also express dissatisfaction with the publications. No matter how much the publications group does to improve the publications, they rarely are able to overcome problems that customers are having with a product. In one survey, customers complained vociferously about the technical manuals. Upon further investigation, the publications group found that the customers were receiving outdated publications. The shipping department had not included the new publications with the latest product release because they wanted to get rid of the leftovers.

Designing survey questions

Customer-satisfaction surveys should be carefully designed to ensure that the results are meaningful. Questions should be unambiguous. If the questions are clearly stated, customers should be able to give meaningful responses that reflect their opinions accurately. Questions should be ones that the customers are able to answer given their level of knowledge. If the customers know nothing about type fonts, it is not particularly helpful to ask which font they prefer. Questions should be designed to give you information you can use as a baseline of customer satisfaction. If your customers have more than one of your company's publications, a general question about satisfaction with publications may not tell you very much. They greatly dislike the reference manual but think the user's guide is useful.

I cannot give you enough information in this context to help you design a complete and successful survey. If you plan a customer-satisfaction survey, you may want to obtain sample surveys from colleagues in other publications organizations. You may also want to read about survey design at your local research library.

If you are not experienced in survey design, you should consult with survey experts to ensure that the questions you ask will elicit the best information from your customers. Research organizations that specialize in designing and conducting customer surveys on technical products or subject matter are the best choice.

Question	Type of Response
How do you rate Company X manuals in comparison to other manuals you use?	three-point Likkert scale: excellent to very poor
Are you able to find the information you need?	five-point Likkert scale: never to always or yes or no response

Please rate Company X user's guide according to the following:
   Technical accuracy
   Ease of finding information
   Completeness
   Ease of reading information
	four-point Likkert scale: very good, good, poor, very poor

Figure 27.4 Typical customer-satisfaction survey questions relating to publications

In the example in Figure 27.4 you see a typical set of publications-oriented questions from a survey.

Selecting a sample to survey

Once you have designed your survey, perhaps with the assistance of a professional research organization, you need to select a sample to study. A number of sampling techniques are available, from a survey of 100 percent of customers to small samples of representative customers. Depending on the size of your customer base, you may be interested in surveying everyone. If you have a large number of customers, a smaller sample, carefully selected, will give you a sound reading of the entire population. Some organizations choose samples randomly. Others group their customers by size, geographic location, type of organization, and other issues. Then, they select small samples from each grouping. Once again, if you have not designed and conducted surveys, you may want to enlist professional help so that you do not waste your money on an invalid study.

In addition to selecting your sample of customers, you need to select a method for conducting the survey. The most obvious choice is to mail the survey and wait for responses. Unfortunately, you may be disappointed by the number of responses, especially if you do nothing but wait.

Most survey professionals suggest that you work hard to obtain a reasonable rate of return. They may suggest that you offer a discount or a small gift as an incentive to reply to the survey. They often suggest that you send the survey three times to the selected population to encourage a higher rate of return. A rate of return of 40 percent is considered excellent.

If you decide that a mailed survey may not give you the results you want, consider a telephone survey. With the widespread use of voice mail, telephone surveys are much more difficult to conduct than they once were. Potential respondents simply never call back. However, if your customers are genuinely interested in helping to improve the publications they receive, you may find that a telephone survey provides you with a better response rate and more in-depth information. A strategy I have found useful is to call the customer, explain the survey, and set up an appointment to call back. Then, I fax the customer a copy of the survey questions so that they can be prepared for the call. Survey participants appreciate having an opportunity to think about their replies and to collect information rather than having to reply on the spot at what might be an inconvenient time. I use the telephone call to go over the survey and record the answers. The telephone discussion allows me to clarify questions if necessary and to pursue problems to understand them better.

If the survey results are important to your organization, you may want to test your mail or telephone survey for possible bias. Sometimes, the people who respond to a survey have characteristics in common. For example, you may have an inordinately high rate of response from people who represent your largest customers because your large customers are more interested in the results. If your small customers are important to you, find out if they are underrepresented in your survey. To study the relationship between those who responded to the survey and those who did not, you may want to seek out responses from nonrespondents by telephoning them or writing them personal letters. If the results from a small group of nonrespondents mirror the results from the initial group, then your respondents are more likely to represent the entire population.

A mail survey allows you to poll a large number of customers at low cost, but a telephone survey gives you more complete results, albeit at a somewhat higher cost. A series of customer-site visits to discuss customer satisfaction with technical publications provides a richer picture but is more costly and often must be limited to a smaller sample size. The customer-site visit, however, gives you an opportunity to see your publications used in a real working environment and to talk to the customers directly. It allows you to explore issues that you would not have considered asking about in more formal surveys. You also may discover problems that customers have never reported. They may have found work-arounds to solve problems, consulted other users, or even continued to use the product incorrectly and inefficiently. You will never know about these problems unless you interview customers directly and observe them at work.

If you conduct visits to customer sites, you will find it important to plan carefully. Spend time developing the questions you want to ask and reviewing them with colleagues. The written questionnaire will give your visit a more formal framework. There is no need to ask the written questions formally, however, I find it best to engage the customer in a more general conversation about the publications. Most of the time, I find that we have covered the issues addressed by the questionnaire. You can always review the questions with the customer at the end of the interview to be certain all the issues were covered.

Evaluating survey results

After your survey is complete, you are ready to evaluate the responses. Many surveys contain questions that are open-ended and ask for free-form responses. Other questions are closed, requiring a particular response, such as a yes or no answer or the selection of a point on a scale, such as 1 to 5. Average the responses to closed questions, and record the open-ended comments.

In evaluating closed questions, you may find, for example, that 75 percent of your customers are very satisfied with your publications. You may find that 80 percent of your customers consider your publications difficult to use. In one case, we found that nearly 90 percent of the customers surveyed found one publication to be nearly useless to them. They could not find the information they needed quickly enough; if they did locate the information, it was not helpful in solving their problems. Many simply never used the publication at all.

In another instance, we discovered one set of publications that was rarely used by close to 100 percent of the customers surveyed. They considered the information to be so out-of-date and so frequently incorrect that they preferred calling customer service with questions.

When you record the responses to open-ended questions, you will find it more useful to categorize them in terms of the type of problem and the severity of the problem. You may discover that 65 percent of your customers complain that the information they receive does not help them "do anything." You may characterize that response as suggesting that customers want more task-oriented procedures in the publications.

After you have tabulated and recorded responses, explain the method you used to gather the information and the number and type of customers surveyed. Include a summary of the conclusions you reached about the responses. Put all this information into your customer-satisfaction report. With the results of your initial study in hand, you now have a baseline for customer satisfaction that you can use to compare with future surveys.

 Guideline: Conduct customer-satisfaction surveys of publications by designing your questions carefully, selecting a representative sample, using the best method available, and thoroughly analyzing the results. Use the results as baseline data for future survey comparisons.

Conducting evaluative usability tests

In addition to conducting customer-satisfaction surveys, which are largely opinion polls, you may find it very useful to conduct evaluative usability tests. Unlike the formative usability tests you used during the design and early implementation phases, evaluative usability tests are usually too late in the development life cycle to allow for any but the most simple changes. Evaluative tests are intended to tell you if you have succeeded in achieving the measurable usability goals that you set in the Information Plan in Phase 1.

An evaluative test is conducted similarly to the formative usability tests discussed in Chapter 20. However, evaluative tests, especially those that are designed to give you statistically significant results, may require a larger number of test subjects. For example, you may want to learn if the tutorial takes the average user less than 30 minutes to complete. In an evaluative test, you would observe the performance of twenty test subjects without asking them to perform a talk-aloud protocol. Instead, you would ask them to work at their own pace without interruption. As test administrator, you would not intervene during the test unless the subjects were completely stuck. Your goal is good timing data, which you cannot achieve if you ask questions during the test or ask for talk-aloud protocols.

If the test subjects in your group of twenty are able to complete the tutorial in an average of 30 minutes or less, then your timing goal has been successful. Similarly, other usability measures allow you to judge the success of your team's efforts to produce a usable publication:

- Time to find information using an index, table of contents, or other tool
- Number of errors made during performance of a task
- Ability to recover from errors in a minimal amount of time
- Ability to apply learning to new situations

Evaluative usability testing is not for the faint of heart. You may find that your publications do not meet your usability goals. This close to the end of the project, you will have little opportunity to make substantive changes. You can either wait to make the changes at the next release of the publication or argue to delay the release of the product until the problems with the publications are corrected. In either case, someone will be very unhappy. Late-cycle evaluative usable tests generally re-emphasize the importance of doing more testing early in the life cycle.

 Guideline: Use evaluative usability tests to measure your success in meeting your original usability goals for the publications.

Performing a root-cause analysis

Once you have identified customer problems with your publications, the obvious next step is to correct the problems. If you find that information about a concept or procedure is incorrect, you can find the correct information and make the change. If you discover that an explanation is incomplete, you can obtain more information and make the explanation more complete.

Two issues emerge, however, from this approach to correcting problems. Although you correct one problem, you may leave similar problems uncorrected. By correcting the immediate problem, you may neglect the root cause of the problem, which means, in all probability, that the same type of problem will occur again.

The goal of evaluating customer problems with technical publications is simple: Make the publications better by eliminating the problems and increasing customer satisfaction. A second goal is to reduce the cost of the service with which your organization responds to resolve the problem.

If you correct the immediate problem without examining its root causes and looking for related problems, you will fail to meet your goal. Certainly, the immediate problem will be fixed, but fixing one small problem will not increase customer satisfaction. The next customer will find another instance of the problem and be equally dissatisfied.

Finding the global problems

The first approach to uncovering the real problems is to look beyond the immediate problem to the more global problem that it represents. For example, one company found that customers were unable to use the index of a manual to find how to center the headings in their text files. The solution was to add the entry "Headings, centering" to the index. The immediate problem was solved. The particular customer who was unable to find the desired phrase in the index would now be satisfied at least momentarily or until the next missing entry appeared.

Well, that problem is fixed," said Jane. "I thought that referring them to centering paragraphs was enough. I didn't think that they'd look up the word 'headings.'"

"I don't think the problem is really fixed," replied Andy. "Maybe we'd better think about what other terms are missing from the index."

"But how are we going to find that out?" asked Jane. "The customer called in about centering headings. How am I supposed to guess what other words they might use to look something up."

"How did you decide on the index entries?" asked Andy.

"I just indexed all the headings in the manual. The section is called "Centering paragraphs.' The index entry reads 'Paragraphs, centering,'" explained Jane.

"Did you also include the entry 'Centering, paragraphs'?" asked Andy.

"Well, I don't think so," said Jane. "I usually create one index entry for each heading in the text. I didn't really think about flipping the entries over."

"I think that's a pretty standard approach to creating index entries," explained Andy. "But that's not going to get you to the word 'headings' when your title reads 'paragraphs.'"

"I have to choose something for the headings," said Jane. "How many words am I supposed to use? The headings wouldn't be consistent."

"Right," acknowledged Andy. "But don't you talk about centering headings in the explanation?"

"Yes," said Jane, "but I only had time to index the headings, not the explanations."

"But we decided last year that we'd leave enough time at the end of the project for the index," said Andy. "We wanted to be sure we indexed more than just the headings. What happened?"

"I thought I could do the index in one day," explained Jane, "but the manual was 200 pages long. I ran out of time."

"I read somewhere that you can index 10 pages in an hour," said Andy. "Maybe we ought to get some training in indexing.

Andy and Jane have identified a problem that has resulted in a customer-service call. Their indexes are not thorough. By adding one entry to the index, they are unlikely to produce a noticeably better index. They need to uncover the global problem. In this case, the global problem results from indexing only the headings rather than the text and failing to transform the index entries to account for different ways of looking something up. If they can index all the text, rather than just the headings, and add transformations, they will have better indexes.

This example also points out another issue with problem identification. Andy and Jane can certainly improve the index of the user's manual. If they are going to produce consistently high-quality indexes, they will need better training. They need to invest in an indexing course or begin an internal study program.

In addition, Jane has pointed to another cause of the indexing problems. Even though the group had decided to create better indexes, she did not know how much time to leave at the end of the project for the index. A consultant might be able to help them better estimate indexing time. Or they may want to track the amount of time that writers take to do thorough indexes and use that time as a guide for future estimates. Andy may also discover that none of the writers has sufficient time or energy at the end of the project to do a thorough index. That might lead them to better scheduling, more indexing earlier in the development cycle, or a decision to hire an indexing specialist who works in parallel with the writers when they are producing the final draft.

Finding the real cause of a problem

As the problem-source information in Figure 27.3 pointed out, problems with publications have a variety of root causes. The product may have changed after the publications were completed. Information about a function may never have been given to the writers. Technical reviews may have been incomplete. The writers may not have had sufficient time to validate the accuracy of their information.

In performing a root-cause analysis, you will obtain the best results by involving all those who contribute to the quality of technical publications. Some problems can be wholly corrected within the publication organization; others cannot be corrected without the help of outside groups. Beware, nonetheless, of blaming all problems on the rest of the company. It is up to the publications group, and especially the project manager, to find internal solutions. If you never seem to have enough time to validate procedures at the end of the process, consider adding some validation activities earlier. If you never have enough time to create a high-quality index, consider hiring an outside indexer or eliminating some other part of your process that has less impact on the customer.

The movement toward total quality asks us to put the customer's requirements first. Many publications groups have a tendency to put their own requirements first, often arguing that if the customer knew better, all these publications-specific activities would be considered important. If your team is spending much of its time correcting problems that would never be detected by a customer, you are probably neglecting areas that are very important. Re-examine your value system, and be sure that it is as close as possible to your customers' value systems.

Once you have identified the root cause of a problem, work hard to eliminate it. Frequently, a root cause requires a change in your process. Process changes, while sometimes difficult to accomplish and immediately costly, have the greatest likelihood of resulting in substantial increases in customer satisfaction.

 Guideline: Move from correcting immediate problems to identifying global problems and uncovering the root causes of those problems. Change your processes so that root causes are corrected.

Evaluating the Publications Team

Not only should you evaluate the success of your publications project in terms of customer satisfaction, as discussed in Chapter 27, you should also evaluate the success of the process your team used to complete the project. At the end of the project, meet with your team as a whole and with each team member individually to discuss the successes and failures of the publications-development process. To evaluate team and individual productivity, you may want to compose project-specific evaluations for the team as a whole and for each team member, as well as an evaluation of your performance as project manager. With these evaluations in hand, you will then be prepared to measure the productivity of your team and its members in comparison with the productivity of other teams with the same or different members. Your first set of productivity measurements provides you with a baseline of information that you can use to evaluate productivity improvements (Figure 28.1).

Conducting project-specific evaluations

In many technical-publications organizations, performance appraisals occur only once a year. The department manager may be responsible for evaluating everyone in a large department, even though most of the writers' work has been managed by project-specific managers. In a matrixed organization, technical communicators frequently shift from one project manager to another, depending on the demands of projects and schedules. Rarely does a communicator work with the same project manager for an entire year.

As soon as a project is complete, we all have the tendency to want to forget the problems, briefly cheer the successes, and move on to the next project. In many cases, we do not even have the opportunity to finish one project before we have to move on to another. Under such circumstances, evaluation of the performance of teams as a whole, in addition to the performance of individual team members, gets lost in the rush. By the end of the year, or by performance-evaluation time, the writers, editors, and artists cannot even remember how many projects they worked on, let alone how each one of them specifically contributed to the efforts.

How well
did we do?

Figure 28.1 Evaluating the project

I strongly recommend that you consider four types of project-specific evaluation and complete these evaluations as soon as the project is complete. These evaluations include

- An internal evaluation of the project and the development process
- An evaluation of the team's performance as a whole
- An evaluation of the individual contributions of each team member
- An evaluation of the performance of the project manager

In preparing the project wrap-up report, you already did much of the work for the first evaluation—an evaluation of the project's overall successes and failures. However, the project evaluation you do internally, unlike the one shared with your technical team members, should address more fully any problems that have occurred with internal processes specific to the publications-development life cycle. Your technical counterparts are not interested in knowing that team members had to go through several drafts of the Content Specifications because the planning process was new to them. There are some criticisms of process that you should keep within the publications organization.

In the second evaluation, you address the success of the team itself, including your success in managing the team. You may conduct this evaluation with all the team members together, or you may want to handle the evaluation entirely yourself, especially if the team members have developed irreconcilable animosity for each other.

In the third evaluation, evaluate the individual contributions and productivity of each team member. Before the details of the project are forgotten, capture in the project-specific performance evaluation all the positive contributions made by each team member, as well as any problems that may have occurred along the way. The department manager will be able to use the project-specific evaluations as part of the annual performance appraisals.

In the fourth evaluation, consider your own performance as manager and leader of the team. You may want to start with a self-evaluation before you ask for your team's contribution. Use the results to communicate with your own management and to undertake a program of improving your management and leadership skills.

 Guideline: Conduct evaluations at the end of each project so that project successes and mistakes are understood, the team's performance is analyzed, and the performance of each individual is reviewed.

Evaluating the successes and mistakes

Every project has some successes and some failures. Rarely, if ever, does a project come out perfectly. At the end of the project, you and your team should assess just how well everything went. Review your original Information Plan and Content Specifications. Look carefully at your project statistics. And consider the interpersonal relationships that occur within every project.

In your project evaluation, consider the following questions:

- How close did you come to our original estimates of the size and scope of the project? If you deviated from these estimates, were you able to keep track of your activities and predict how changes would affect your performance? If not, why not?
- Did you control your activities adequately during the project? Or did you end up abandoning your process and just write madly to get everything done?
- Did you follow the publications-development process fully? Or did you shortcut the process because of problems that occurred during the project?
- Were you better at some aspects of the publications-development process than others? For example, did you do a good job of production editing but were you unable to obtain a better understanding of your audiences?

In answering these questions, look particularly at the development process. If you decide to track project hours faithfully throughout the project, you should have good data about the amount of time spent on each activity. Evaluate the relationship between the amount of time actually spent and the amount of time you had originally estimated for each activity. If there was a significant discrepancy, analyze the causes. Otherwise, you are likely to repeat the same problems in the future.

Perhaps your original estimate was incorrect because you did not have sufficient data from previous projects to arrive at good estimates. With the new data from your recently completed project, you will be able to estimate future projects more accurately. But more accurate estimates will occur only if you understand the reasons for the hours expended in the current project. You may have completed a project that will be an exception rather than the norm. During your project evaluation, you need to decide how much of the project was normal and how much occurred because of special problems. Be careful, however, that you do not dismiss the special problems. The worst estimates are those that always assume a best-case scenario.

 Guideline: Evaluate the success of the project in terms of the original goals and estimates, as well as in response to changes throughout the project life cycle.

Evaluating the performance of the team

In most cases, the success of the project is closely related to the performance of the entire team in seeing the project through from start to finish. Without the contributions of the team members, the project could not have succeeded. However, every team consists of diverse individuals who contribute to the team in a variety of ways. Sometimes those contributions move the team forward and foster a spirit of cooperation in reaching a common goal. Sometimes those contributions move the team backward and cause the team to experience problems. Even though the project may have been successful as a whole, the team process may not have worked well and may need to be examined and improved.

Most of the time, encourage your team to evaluate its own performance. Team self-evaluation is most productive when team activities have gone relatively well, team members have cooperated most of the time, and the team ends the project with mutual respect among members. Given reasonably cordial relationships and a degree of trust among team members at the end of the project, a team self-evaluation will work well. Team members will be able to focus on problems that occur any time a group of people as diverse and single-minded as writers, artists, editors, and production specialists have to work together to reach a goal.

Working with your team members, consider the following questions:

- Did your team work effectively as a whole? If there were disagreements, were they settled amicably?
- Did team members respect the contributions of each other? Did you treat one another professionally, or did personal attitudes obstruct cooperative efforts?
- Did your team maintain a good relationship with all members of the product-development team? Were your efforts acknowledged and respected? If not, how could the relationship be improved?
- Did each team member contribute to the process? Or did some team members choose to act independently on occasion? What problems, if any, did this cause?
- Did team members support one another? If one team member had a deadline to meet, did the others pitch in? If one member had a problem with some aspect of the development process, did the others help solve the problem?

- Did the team work effectively during each stage of the development life cycle? Were some phases of the process handled better than others? If so, how can you improve the weaker areas?

If your team has been successful, they will find the evaluation process challenging and consider it an opportunity to learn. Their answers to the questions above and others that relate to your specific project will be thoughtfully considered. If a general spirit of cooperation reigns, team members will try to find ways to work even more effectively in the future.

But what happens when the team has not functioned well? As the project manager, you should carefully consider whether a team with problems will benefit from a self-evaluation. Airing serious problems publicly might result in an exodus of writers. If the level of animosity among team members is high at the end of the project, consider doing your own evaluation first and discussing it privately with each team member. You may later feel comfortable holding a team discussion of the evaluation, after you have made it clear that everyone contributed in some way to the problems, including yourself.

If you think the team will be unable to handle the criticism and act maturely, you may choose to forego a meeting with team members. It is not productive to permit team members to engage in a shouting match or to criticize individuals who have caused problems.

If you have ended the project with a dysfunctional team, you should consider the following questions:

- What was the exact nature of the problem? Was one team member at fault, or did several team members contribute to the problem?
- As project manager, what did you do to handle the problem? Were you able to resolve it and move on? Did you contribute to the problem? Did you side with some team members against others? Did you act quickly enough, or did you allow the problem to gain strength?
- If you had the same team to manage again, what would you do differently?
- Is the friction among team members so great that they will have difficulty working together in the future? Is there anything you can do to resolve the problems and re-establish a good working relationship?

In most dysfunctional teams, no one person is totally at fault. Most often, the manager has contributed to the problem by failing to recognize it quickly enough or respond to the problem before it worsens.

In organizations that have never used a team approach, you should not anticipate immediate success. If you are in the process of building teams from a group of individual contributors, you should admit to yourself that the first attempts will be rough. People who are accustomed to making all their own decisions often have difficulty when they have to adhere to the decisions of the group. You may have to give them time to accommodate to the change.

If you feel up to the challenge, I strongly recommend that you give your team a chance to evaluate its own performance, even if the team has been dysfunctional. If you genuinely want the team to improve its performance, the incentive for improvement must come from each of the members, not from you alone. If they are permitted to ignore the problems, they will never find more effective forms of cooperation.

Guideline: Help your team evaluate its own performance. If the team has been severely dysfunctional, consider doing the evaluation yourself and sharing your evaluation individually with each team member.

Evaluating individual productivity

Individual performance appraisals at the end of a project might be viewed as mini-versions of annual performance appraisals. For your evaluations, you may want to include the same categories that your organization includes in evaluating overall job performance. The advantage of conducting a review at the end of the project is to ensure that the successful contributions of the individual writer, editor, artist, or production specialist are not lost and that the individuals are given opportunities to correct any problems that have emerged.

In the following scenario, Anne learns how to use a project-specific performance evaluation to work with a difficult team member.

I don't know if we should keep Jane in the department," explained Anne. "Her performance on the Krypton project was terrible. No one on the team is speaking to her at this point."

"That's a pretty strong indictment," replied Allen, the publications-department manager. "Tell me more about the problems she had."

"She seemed to have a real difficulty grasping the technical information. Don had to correct the technical errors in her drafts before we could send them out for review," said Anne. "And then she challenged him on every edit."

"Perhaps she needs help in understanding how to work with an editor," said Allen. "If I recall her previous experience at Semicol, she never worked with an editor. But she should have the technical background to understand the Krypton material."

"Well, Don isn't always the easiest editor to work with, I'll admit," replied Anne. "Perhaps I could get them to sit down together and develop a working relationship for the next project. But the technical stuff worries me. She really should have no problem with the information. I reviewed her drafts after Don mentioned the problems, and Jane had made some really serious mistakes. She even got the name of the product wrong. Luckily, we caught it before it went out for technical review."

"What was Jane's explanation?" asked Allen. "Did she realize the name was wrong?"

"She said she had forgotten to change the name from the previous project," explained Anne. "But she shouldn't have been using the previous project as a template in the first place. Krypton is entirely different. I don't think she recognized that."

"She might need to attend the training class that we give to introduce the customers to data analysis," said Allen. "After she has the class, we'll watch closely how she does with her next project. But what about the fact that no one is speaking to her? What happened?"

"Well, you know that the last 3 weeks have been pretty rough," said Anne. "We've all had to put in a lot of extra time to meet the deadline with all the product changes that came in. Jane made sure that she couldn't stay late or work over any of the weekends. She always had an excuse for leaving at five, whether her work was done or not. Everyone else had to take up the slack and do her work as well as their own."

"That's the most serious problem I've heard yet," replied Allen. "I expect everyone in this department to contribute. Sure, you can have a previous obligation occasionally, but not every night. Why don't you write up a performance evaluation for Jane's role in your project. I'll discuss the schedule problem with her. Perhaps there were extenuating circumstances this time. But she should have explained them to you."

"I think that's a good solution," said Anne. "Once she understands something, Jane can be a pretty good writer. I'd like to see her succeed. Maybe it was partly my fault for not making the schedule requirements clear. When she said she couldn't work on the weekends, I didn't say anything about it. I have a tendency to fume privately."

"I don't like confrontations either," explained Allen. "But sometimes if we let something go, it gets worse rather than better. I don't mean that you have to jump on someone immediately if they do something you don't like. But you and I should talk about how to present a problem without delaying it. Maybe we can come up with a better strategy."

"I like that idea," replied Anne. "I'll schedule a time with you next week, after I write Jane's review. If it's OK with you, I'd like to go over it with her first. Maybe you won't have to deal with it at all. How's that for handling a problem quickly?"

"Great. Go right ahead.

If Anne writes an effective performance evaluation, and Jane takes it to heart, she may become a productive member of the department. If Jane simply moves on to the next project, by the time her annual appraisal is due, she may be in serious trouble. Performance problems need to be identified and solved quickly. Project-specific performance evaluations will contribute to building stronger individuals who succeed as strong team members.

 Guideline: Conduct individual performance evaluations at the end of each project so that successes are not forgotten and problems are not allowed to become worse.

Evaluating the performance of the project manager

Perhaps the most difficult evaluation is the evaluation of yourself as project manager. You can handle the evaluation in two ways: first as a self-evaluation of your performance and second as an evaluation by your team members. A self-evaluation may be easier on your self-esteem but it also may not help you learn enough about your successes and failures to improve significantly.

Whenever any of us completes a project, we are fully aware of many things we would like to do better. In most instances, we started out with fairly ambitious goals of everything going well. By the end, we may be happy to have survived the experience.

Once you have completed a project as project manager, you will no doubt have many plans for doing it better in the future. I recommend that you write these plans down as part of your self-evaluation.

To begin your self-evaluation, create a list of all your original goals for your project. They may include

- Creating a cohesive team of communicators who end up with a successful project and the incentive to work together again
- Maintaining good professional relationships with others in the organization, including your manager
- Completing the project on time and on budget
- Producing publications that the audience considers to be excellent
- Keeping track of all the time and activities so that you will know how to estimate better next time

Evaluate your own performance against your goals. You will most likely find that you have accomplished some of your goals and not others. Give yourself praise for the things you did well and analyze the areas where you felt you could have done better. You may feel that you produced excellent publications that are already receiving accolades from the audiences, but the publications project came in 6 months late. Of course, the development project was also late, but everyone complained about your project's lateness. In your self-evaluation, you need to decide how you can better educate your management about the publications process so that they understand the integral relationship between development schedule and the publications schedule.

You may, at the end of the project, feel that your team worked well but that you did not have nearly enough time to do all the team-building activities that you had planned. Consider how you could schedule your time and the team's activities better next time to ensure that you have a more cohesive and supportive team at the end.

Once you have finished your self-evaluation, review it with your manager. Ask for feedback from your manager that focuses on the areas you want to improve. Your manager may have some ideas that will point you in the right direction for improvement. By sharing the self-evaluation with your manager as soon as the project is complete, you will be communicating more effectively exactly what you have been doing to grow as a manager. In addition, the self-evaluation will provide immediate information to your manager that might otherwise be forgotten by the time your own performance appraisal comes around.

If you are feeling particularly brave and confident, you could share your self-evaluation with your team members and ask them to evaluate your performance. As a starting point, I recommend that you ask for individual evaluations. It is especially difficult to face the collective criticism of an entire group. There is also a tendency for a group to admit to negative feelings, if they exist. One individual's negative attitudes can easily influence everyone else's. With individual evaluations you may get a better representation of different points of view.

After your team members have written their evaluations, give them your self-evaluation to read. They may find that the problems they experienced are already well understood by you and that you are looking for ways to improve your performance. For example, the team may have felt a need for more communication. If you have already acknowledged the need for more communication in your self-evaluation, they will be pleased that you all perceive the same problem and understand the need for a team solution. In fact, team members may come up with good suggestions for solving some of the problems you perceived with your project management. They may be able to contribute something that will make your job go more smoothly.

 Guideline: Consider writing a self-evaluation and asking your team to evaluate your performance as a project manager.

Developing productivity measures

"Productivity measures" has a frightening sound to it—reminiscent of company goons watching worker progress through video cameras or recording the number of keystrokes per minute entered into the computer. Productivity measures have been tainted with the hint of "Big Brother" lurking somewhere behind the scene. However, productivity measures need not be viewed negatively. Only by measuring our productivity can we hope to improve it. If we have no way of knowing what might make us productive or unproductive, we will not know how to make changes in our progress.

Productivity is often defined as the amount of goods produced for the amount of effort. The government measures national productivity by dividing the cost of goods sold by the number of worker hours required to make those good. For years, such measures of productivity have meant that quantity was preferred over quality. Only recently have we begun to worry about the quality of our efforts.

In keeping quality concerns at the fore, we must redefine productivity as our ability to make the best quality required by our customers in the least amount of time. If we include quality in our productivity equation, we must call into question the productivity of a publications group that yearly produces thousands of pages of information that is difficult for the intended audiences to use.

We might increase the productivity of this group by increasing the number of pages they produce, or more likely in downsizing, by reducing the number of staff available to produce the same or more pages. But such an increase in productivity not only fails to improve usability, it might even decrease it.

If we add quality to our equation, then we increase productivity by producing more useful information with the same number of staff members. We can find the time to produce higher-quality work with the same staff by searching for opportunities to improve our internal productivity. By reducing errors early in the process, building strong communication links among team members, and being vigilant in keeping projects under control, we can reduce the amount of time we spend on rework. Instead, we can use the found time to do a better job.

In the previous chapters of Part Six, I discussed a number of ways to evaluate the successes and mistakes of a publications project. Many of the evaluation tools we have are qualitative ones, although certain measures of customer satisfaction can be quantified, as can the results from usability assessment. Most of our ways of assessing the team process are qualitative as well, associated with our standard techniques of performance appraisal. However, many of our organizations are demanding that we look at ways of measuring the success of the publications organization. If you have not already been asked to provide quantitative evidence of your organization's productivity or the productivity of your team members and yourself, you will be soon.

As you begin to design a method for measuring productivity, you have a number of possibilities to consider, some of which will be more effective than others. Do not consider using hours per page as a productivity measure. Instead, look at the more useful measures, such as

- Percentage of time devoted to editing
- Percentage of time needed for rework, either because of deficiencies found through editing or changes that occur because the product changes
- Ability to meet project deadlines and produce high-quality work
- Ability to evaluate your own progress toward a goal
- Ability to monitor, control, and accommodate change
- Ability to produce innovative work within existing constraints of time and budget

Each of these measures requires that you monitor your project carefully so that you know how much time is being spent on editing and rework. They also require that you communicate effectively among your team members so that they immediately inform you when they observe deviations from the original schedule or scope of work. They also mean that you are open to continually evaluating the quality of your work product and to finding the time for innovation in meeting your audiences' needs.

Hours per page as a dangerous productivity measuring tool

Many people in upper management, unfortunately, like simple, easy-to-understand measures of productivity. As soon as anyone in publications mentions that we estimate projects in terms of hours per page, there seems to be an immediate assumption that hours per page can be used to measure the productivity of teams and individual contributors.

I have mentioned elsewhere in this book that hours per page is a dangerous tool for measuring productivity, primarily because physical and conceptual pages are so different from each other. You may discover, for example, that one writer in your group produces a first draft in 2 hours per page, while another writer take 3 hours per page. Upon closer examination, however, you find that the faster writer is working with a well-understood technology and has the advantage of a cooperative and enthusiastic development team. The slower writer is in the midst of learning an entirely new technology and is working with an overstressed development team that is a year behind their own schedule. In using hours per page as a productivity measure, we quickly discover that we are "comparing apples and oranges."

The only way that hours per page can be used as a productivity measure occurs when all other variables are equal. To use the measure, you would need two identically skilled writers working on the same project with the same subject-matter experts. Then, if you found that one writer produced a first draft at 3 hours per page while another took 5 hours per page, you might have a valid point of comparison.

Another, even greater, danger in using hours per page as a productivity measure is that it will cause you to destroy the credibility of your tracking system. As soon as your team members find that you are assessing their productivity by the numbers of hours they report, they will begin to report fewer hours to make themselves look more productive. Hidden hours are the bane of a project estimating and tracking system. A project that you believe you completed at 5 hours per page, but which really took 6 hours per page, will result in a nightmare of problems as soon as you use the results to estimate the next project.

Guideline: Resist using hours per page as a productivity measure. Reserve it as your best tool for estimating projects and assessing progress toward completion.

Using editing percentages to measure writing productivity

Early in the book, I strongly recommended that you include editing as part of the standard list of activities performed by a publications team. If you do not have an independent editor, you may find that you either do all the editing yourself or you institute a system of peer editing. When you set up your original Project Plan in Part Two, you estimated editing as a percentage of writing time. If you estimated 1,000 hours of writing for a project, using a 15-percent rule of thumb, you also included 150 hours of editing.

The recommended 15 percent of writing time for editing is a very general figure. It takes into account the differences in experience and skill that are likely among members of a team. It also allows for developmental editing at the beginning of the project in addition to mechanical edits and copyedits throughout the project. Of course, the percentage you allocate to editing will depend upon the type of editing you want to occur through the publications-development life cycle.

Since 15-percent editing is a rule of thumb, you may want to set editing percentages for each team member. Then, once the project is complete, you can compare the estimated percentages with the actuals. Let us say, for example, that you have selected 15 percent as your editing percentage. However, your writers are at distinctly different skill levels, with senior writers and junior writers mixed on the team. At the end of the project, you may find that you or the editor has spent 25 percent of the writing time editing the work of the most junior team member but only 10 percent of writing time editing the most senior team member. As a result, you may conclude that the senior writer is more productive than the junior writer, requiring less of the editor's time and less time reworking problems with drafts. Fine. That is probably exactly what you expected. You hope, in fact, that the junior writer has, in the process, learned a lot about technical communication and will require less editing in the future.

But what if the figures were reversed? At the end of the project, you discover to your surprise that you have used 25 percent for editing the work of the senior writer and only 10 percent for the junior writer. You might conclude that you have a very fine junior writer on your hands. You might also conclude that your senior writer is having some serious productivity problems. Or the junior writer may be revising the error-message section, whereas the senior writer is designing a completely new style of user's guide.

The percentage spent editing a writer's work is a potentially effective way of measuring productivity. It allows you to take more difficult projects into account, as well as differences in experience and skill. As writers become more experienced with your product and your process, they should require less editing time—up to a point.

You must balance the need for editing time against the estimated hours per page. Certainly, writers might be able to spend extra time catching problems with a draft and could be encouraged to do so to increase their own skill level and decrease editing time. However, you do not want writers to become afraid of the editor, spending many extra hours per page to get the copy perfect. More editing may actually allow writers to be more productive.

Although editing as a percentage of writing time may decrease as a result, you will find that your per page estimates are quickly being exceeded. In balancing the relationship between writing hours and editing hours, look for a point of maximum efficiency. It is frequently more efficient for writers to turn over a draft to an editor quickly, rather than agonizing over difficult problems. Writers may spend hours perfecting the grammar and spelling on a draft, only to have the developmental editor inform them that it needs a major reorganization. It is far better if the problems are caught early.

You also know that few people are able to edit their own work effectively. After having worked hard to understand a subject and express it clearly, you have little objectivity left for unbiased editing. Writing time is spent more efficiently if a skilled editor gets involved early. You have a balance to achieve between writing and editing. You want writers to spend enough time rereading and editing their own work so that they do not waste the editor's time with errors they might have caught themselves. You also do not want writers to get sloppy in their work and expect the editor to clean up the mess. On the other hand, you do not want writers to be reluctant to submit their work to the editors.

Editing Hours as a Percent of Writing Hours

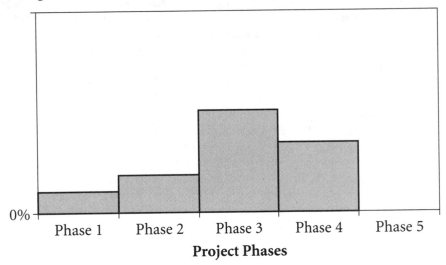

Figure 28.2 An example of editing as a percentage of writing through the phases of the publications-development life cycle

In using editing percentages as a productivity measurement, encourage the writers to work with the editors to decide when editing is best scheduled, how much time to spend on writing early drafts, and how much time is appropriate for editing. I recommend that you strive for editing percentages of 10 to 15 percent. If they go much lower than that, you either have writers who are very skilled or writers who are spending too much time on their drafts.

Recognize, as well, that editing percentages will shift from project to project, depending upon the complexity of the assignments. On a new project, for example, in which your team is completely redesigning the publications set, you may find that editing percentages, especially at the early stages of the project, increase over previous projects. If you have factored in the risk of more editing in your original estimate, the final productivity measures may be exactly as you had expected.

As you track editing during the course of the project, track the relationship to the project schedule. If you have instituted a system of developmental editing, you will likely have more editing hours at the beginning of the project than if you do only copyediting. If you have instituted format templates and project-specific style sheets, you should have fewer copyediting hours at the end of the project. Your editing hours as a percentage of total writing time might be graphed as illustrated in Figure 28.2.

Note that in this example project, some developmental editing occurs as early as Phase 1 when the Information Plan is being designed. Editing increases in Phase 2: Content Specification, in part because writing hours are low and because developmental editors are most effective if they can contribute early to organizational decisions. A better early organization of information means less reorganizing later.

Most editing occurs during Phase 3: Implementation. However, the percentage of editing in relationship to writing hours may actually decrease because of the large number of writing hours in Phase 3. At this point, editors are performing a literary edit on early drafts and a preliminary copyedit on the first-draft deliverable. At the end of the project (Phase 4), the amount of copyediting time is likely to be high once again. However, the percentage of editing to writing may be high because writing time has decreased. No editing takes place in Phase 5: Evaluation.

If you have predicted the flow of editing time in your original Project Plan, you can measure the productivity of individuals and the team by looking at the correspondence between actual editing percentages and your estimates. For example, if you find that the editing percentages during later phases of the project are higher than you had predicted, you may have a productivity problem with some writers. If there is more copyediting to do than you had predicted, your writers may not be catching as many copy errors as they should be or they may be making the same errors that the editor had marked earlier.

Whatever you find to be the reasons for the differences in the editing cycle from estimate to actual, use the information to work on productivity improvements. In our organization, we saw a substantial increase in productivity of both writers and editors when we instituted style templates several years ago. Because the writers were required to use the templates and the templates were designed to eliminate most formatting errors, we found that the amount of time we spent copyediting format and correcting errors decreased substantially. As a result, we were able to reduce the percentage of time we allocated to the production process.

Not only are the raw percentages useful in evaluating productivity. Most developmental editors form fairly accurate judgments about writer productivity during the course of a project. Editors are always enthusiastic about writers who are "easy to edit." They make global comments about style and organization that the writer is able to apply consistently. They mention a particular problem one time and never see it again. They help a writer with organizational problems, and the new organization looks very good.

Other writers are less easy to edit. They have difficulty following global recommendations for change. They continue to make the same errors over and over again. They resist the editor's recommendations and continue using writing styles and formats that are not in keeping with corporate standards. These writers require a lot of extra effort on the editor's part and may cause the project to proceed more slowly. They will, of course, eventually affect the overall hours per page, but the problem is better measured at the editing stage.

In one case I found that an experienced writer required a great deal of time from the editing staff. The percentage of time devoted to editing her work did not seem to improve much over several projects. The problem was noted in the writer's annual performance appraisal with an action plan for improvement. While there was an implicit comparison between this writer and others on the team, the writer was primarily evaluated for her own progress. You may generally expect that the percentage of editing time will be lower for senior writers than junior writers, taking into account differences in project assignments. If this expectation does not hold true, there may be a measurable productivity problem.

In another case, the manager retained before-and-after copies of her writers' edited materials. In that way she could measure improvement and evaluate the effectiveness of the editing process.

 Guideline: Establish guidelines for editing as a percentage of writing time and evaluate your team members on how well their work follows the guidelines.

Using the ability to meet deadlines as a productivity measure

The ability to meet scheduled deadlines is extremely important in a development project. Writers who consistently miss deadlines are usually considered to be less productive and reliable than writers who consistently make their deadlines. Meeting deadlines is especially important when the writer sets the schedule. If you have committed yourself to making a particular deadline, you are expected to do so unless some emergency intervenes.

As project manager, you may want to track the number of deadlines met successfully or exceeded by a team member. Certainly, extenuating circumstances present themselves. No one is likely to be able to meet all the deadlines that they have committed themselves to. They are less likely to meet deadlines that others have imposed with no feedback or room for adjustment. However, if you find a team member who consistently misses deadlines when everyone else on the team is meeting them, you may have a productivity problem.

As soon as a deadline problem appears, you need to investigate further. There may be circumstances beyond the writer's control that are affecting deadlines. However, you should expect to be told about schedule problems as soon as the writer recognizes them. A writer who waits until the last minute to inform the project manager of a schedule slip ensures that little can be done to bring the schedule back into control. If you find out about schedule problems early enough, you may be able to provide assistance in solving the problem.

In some cases, writers slip the schedule themselves because they do not have a firm idea of their goals. If a writer misses a deadline because he or she wants to write 200 pages on a topic rather than the 100 pages called for in the Content Specifications, you may have a productivity problem. Part of the challenge of meeting deadlines is to recognize that you cannot take on a bigger task without approval. If the writers recognize that the topic is growing, they should immediately report the increased scope to the project manager. Together, writers and manager can negotiate a change in the schedule.

If you use deadline adherence as a productivity measure, you should also include an assessment of the writer's ability to keep you informed. You may still have a writer who always misses deadlines, but at least you have established some communication about the schedule problems. You can let the writers know that you are available to help them, either by shifting responsibilities or changing the scope of the project.

 Guideline: Consider the importance of meeting deadlines to the success of your project. If you, your team members, or individuals on the team consistently miss deadlines you have agreed to meet, you may have a productivity problem.

Using the ability to evaluate progress as a productivity measure

Not only is the writer's ability to meet deadlines a measure of productivity, so is the ability of the writer to assess his or her own progress during the course of the project. We can use information about previous projects and the relationship between claims of percent complete and the real percent complete to help us monitor project changes. We can, in like manner, use a writer's estimates of progress and percent complete to evaluate productivity and effectiveness. Writers who consistently overestimate the degree of completeness of their projects may need training to evaluate the project signs and their own work habits effectively.

As a project manager, you will be frustrated with your inability to manage project change if you have team members who seem unable to assess their progress toward a goal. Most likely, you will receive overly optimistic completion estimates. However, you can work on this productivity problem by keeping good records and doing frequent reality checks with your team. You might point out, for example, that your team members gave you the same percent complete estimates last month as this month. Obviously something is wrong. Perhaps the project is going into hysterical rework mode. Or perhaps the writers have no idea where they are on a project from day to day and cannot estimate their percent complete accurately. I recommend that you ask writers to count something—pages, topics, headings—that will give them an idea of what has been done and what is left to do. A percent complete calculation should not be a guess or wishful thinking.

Good estimates of percent complete have an influence on overall project productivity. While an individual's inability to estimate his or her percent complete may not cause productivity to decrease, more than likely good estimates of percent complete will result in a more productive project. If, as project manager, you are able to assess accurately the progress of your team, you will be better able to make decisions about current and future courses of action. If you learn that the project is behind schedule, you may be able to make changes to bring it back on schedule. If you learn that one writer is getting far behind the schedule, you can find some help for the writer.

Better and more rapid decision making that leads to better project control will eventually translate into higher productivity. Conversely, poor estimates of percent complete will likely give you a false sense of security. It is better to know exactly where you stand so that you can do something about it, than to be lulled by inadequate information. In any event, never blame the manager, or you will not get "bad news" in the future.

Guideline: Use the ability of your team to estimate its own progress accurately as a way to evaluate productivity.

Using monitoring of change as a productivity measure

Not only is it important for team members to estimate their progress accurately, it is also important that they are aware of the necessity for keeping the overall project under control. Productivity is enhanced when everyone on the team takes responsibility for monitoring change. As project manager, you cannot be aware of every action taken by every team member. Nor can you know about all of the subtle changes taking place in the product that is affecting your team's productivity.

If you have carefully scheduled your project and laid out the scope of work in detail to your team, each team member should recognize the boundaries of his or her own effort. As a result, team members will be able to judge when they are exceeding their scope because of external changes to the project. For example, a writer notices that she is beginning to exceed the number of pages estimated for a chapter, in the manual she is writing. She is supposed to have 25 pages at first draft, but she has already written 21 and is only half done. The writer informs you of the change immediately. You can sit down together and review the reasons for the increase in scope. Perhaps the writer is including more details than are needed by the audience. Or perhaps the engineering team has added functions to the section of the project being written about. That means that the original 25-page chapter will likely turn out to be 35 pages (a 40-percent increase) if nothing is done.

The point is that the writer has notified the project manager of the change in enough time for a course of action to be planned and acted upon. If the project manager recommends that the writer cut back on the detail or negotiates a change to the schedule, the overall productivity level of the project will be maintained.

Guideline: Ensure that your team members keep you well informed about project changes either in their own work or in the work of members of the product-development team. By maintaining a strong communication link between team members and project manager, you will have an opportunity to keep productivity high on your project. By remaining calm and offering to help, you will encourage more teamwork than if you resort to blame.

Using the ability to produce innovative designs as a productivity measure

Because of challenging schedules and insufficient staff, you will often find yourself in the rut of continuously updating a library of publications that you fear are no longer meeting the needs of your customers. You spend so much time just adding new features and correcting problems that you have little time to take a fresh look at the project. Yet you know that a fresh look might result in fewer but more useful pages of information.

If you have instituted a program of evaluating your team's productivity and searching for areas of improvement, you may find the time for a redesign effort that could have a significant effect on the quality of your publications and the productivity of your team. A team that finds the time to produce innovations in the design of publications while maintaining accuracy and completeness is a very productive team. Such a team introduces online help systems and online documentation before marketing and development insist on it. An innovative team continually searches for new ways to produce better information more efficiently.

Guideline: Find ways to improve the quality of your team's publications while maintaining a high level of efficiency. Look for innovative solutions that will improve your customer's satisfaction with the information they receive.

Preparing for the Project's Future

Projects, like people, have futures as well as pasts. In Chapters 26 through 28, we concentrated on the project's past with wrap-up reports and evaluations. In this chapter, we turn to the future, both immediate and long term. If the publications your team has just completed will be immediately updated for a new version, you or another project manager will move quickly into maintenance mode. Decide if you want to retain the original design or to design a new look that will be more useful to your customers.

Even if you are immediately moving into maintenance mode or on to another new project, do not forget about the critical importance of establishing a record of your project and maintaining good archives. Too often, project managers move on, assuming that someone else will clean up after them. It doesn't work that way. You are responsible for leaving your project in good shape for the future. A warning—do not wait too long. The longer you are away from a completed project, the more you will forget and the less incentive you will have to perform archiving tasks.

Make sure that your Project Management Notebook is updated and properly filed. Include a project summary, with a brief description of the project and a calendar of major events, so that the next manager can use it to come up to speed quickly.

Finally, consider how you will handle records of a project that is at the end of its life.

Guideline: Don't neglect your final project tasks, even if they are not your favorite part of a project. The project will suffer permanent damage if you do not ensure that records are organized and material archived.

Preparing for maintenance

Most often, when a publications project ends, the next version of the project has already begun. The marketing and development teams have begun planning the next release of the product, the next edition of a report or bulletin is in the planning stages, or the scientific team is well into the next stages of its research. Consequently, the publications project manager has the responsibility for planning the next version of the publications.

I mentioned earlier that 1.0 versions of anything, including publications, are never as complete, accurate, well planned, or effective as we had hoped they would be at the beginning of the initial project. We run out of time to do all the things that would make the publications better, we run out of resources, and we often run out of energy after completing the race to get everything out the door. We did not know as much about the audience or their goals as we would have liked. In fact, the audience for a very new and innovative product may have gone largely undefined. After the first version is done, however, we earn a second chance.

In Chapter 5, I discussed one of the critical questions that we ask ourselves at the beginning of many publications projects:

Should we create a new design from scratch or simply update the existing publications?

Often, the answer to this question is dictated by the budget. Having spent huge sums of money on the initial development, senior management wants to assess the success of sales effort before committing new funds to the new versions. They view publications as an opportunity to save money. The books are written; now, they need only be revised by adding a few new items to the text.

Because the second version of a product is often very similar to the first version, with the original errors corrected and features and functions added that did not make the first-release date, the second version of the publications may not need much updating. Unfortunately, the realities of the second release of a product, when the expense of the initial development effort is still being recouped, often remain the reality during the life of the product. For years, the original publications are placed in maintenance mode. Corrections are made; bits and pieces of new features and functions are added on. After a few rounds of this process, the publications, like the product, start to resemble an old house—patches everywhere, rooms added on helter-skelter, until little of the original design remains.

The patchwork approach can be deadly for publications and for products:

- The first version may have been designed with too little information about the audience and their goals in the first place.
- The needs and character of the customers will likely have changed.
- New approaches to information design have emerged.
- New tools for formatting, graphics, electronic presentation, and multimedia have emerged.

The revised publications become increasingly outdated as they are patched. The original writers, who liked the challenge of creating something new, have moved on to companies where new publications are still being designed. The maintenance writers become bored because they rarely have the opportunity to try something new. They spend their days adding sentences here and there, occasionally having the opportunity to write an entirely new chapter. However, for the sake of a consistent style, they cannot change the original approach to the material.

I do not advocate that you throw the original work on a project to the winds, always starting anew. You will not have the resources you need to do so, and you often have new projects on your plates. However, you should not condemn older publications to a state of progressive deterioration.

If you have been tracking customer satisfaction and continuing to assess customer requirements for information, you will become aware of the shortcomings of your original design. With increased information about customers and their goals, you have an opportunity to do an excellent job redesigning an existing set of publications. You can apply some fresh thinking to the process and consider taking advantage of advances in technology to increase the quality of existing publications.

You have a balance to achieve in managing a mix of new and update projects in your publications organization. Consider setting a regular schedule to determine if a library of publications has become obsolete. If they have, assign a team to revamp them from scratch. One company I work with called this the Clean White Sheet committee. The heart of such an effort is customer information. Use the regular maintenance time as an opportunity for learning more about your customers—they will appreciate the effort.

Guideline: Prepare for the updating effort by considering the possibility of a complete or partial redesign of existing publications.

Archiving project records and materials

Begin your archiving and cleanup task as soon as possible after the end of the project and before your team members are dispersed. Collect everything from your team members, including all their own records and files. Don't let them throw anything away yet. Go through your own files, and make careful decisions about what you keep and what you throw away. Remember that you may regret tomorrow that one piece of paper you threw away without careful examination. In this section, I provide guidelines for what you need to keep and carefully archive for future use and reference.

I assume that your team has been keeping careful backups of all computer files associated with a publications set and all records associated with the development effort. At the end of a project, you will need to do a lot of housecleaning. Certain information will be important as a record of the project, including both computer and hardcopy files:

- An archive of computer files containing the final softcopy versions of all text and graphics. Be certain that you purge outdated drafts and multiple copies of files (which you should not have had in the first place). They could be disastrous in the future if someone mixes them up with the final copies.

- The project-management computer files containing planning documents, project correspondence, spreadsheets, meeting minutes, phone logs, and other communication artifacts. If your company is following ISO 9000 requirements, you may have to archive your development notes in a central file that can be audited.

- A paper "make copy" of all the printed text and graphics assembled. You may find yourself reprinting before the next version is ready.

- Paper copies of all original artwork so that they are not lost. Lost art is a very common problem on publications revisions.

- The printer's plates if you ordinarily keep these in your possession. If the printer keeps them, create a record of their exact location. It is best to retain all materials from the printers, including documentation of how the printing was done.

- The locations of all other work that is in the hands of outside organizations, such as a master copy of a CD-ROM. You should retain all materials created if you can.

- A record of all job correspondence with outside vendors, including photographers, artists, printers, and anyone else who assisted with the project.

- Copies of all review comments dated and organized by publication. You may be called upon to prove that your publication was reviewed for accuracy and completeness by technical experts and that you incorporated their comments into your drafts.

In addition to all the archives, make a list of everything that was archived, and keep the list in an accessible file.

When you create your archive, assume that you will be long gone and that someone new will have to figure out where everything is and exactly what you did to begin new versions of the publications.

You should archive the original computer files so that you have both an electronic and a paper record of exactly what the publications looked like on their date of completion. You should keep your project records as evidence that you followed good project-management procedures. In fact, standards such as ISO 9000 require that records of project management be maintained to prove that good practices were followed.

My recommendation that you keep copies of the review comments you received on drafts comes from experience in litigation. Your organization may have to produce earlier copies of publications and evidence that technical experts reviewed the drafts and took care that the written information was correct. In one case, a company had to demonstrate that the technical experts had approved the text of the documentation and were ultimately responsible for its accuracy. In another case, a company had to demonstrate that a user had been taught to perform a procedure correctly in a computer-based training (CBT) instruction ten years earlier. Unfortunately, because the CBT had been updated frequently, the company could not produce the exact version used in 1987 and lost the case.

Many organizations do not have well-established procedures for archiving projects. They throw everything out at the end of the project and start on the new version immediately. One company could not find the original computer files for earlier publications when they decided to convert them to CD-ROM. The files had to be

End-of-project checklist

1. All duplicate versions of computer files have been purged.
2. All remaining computer files of the entire publications set have been archived on disk or tape.
3. All computer files of project-management activities have been archived on disk or tape.
4. A "make copy" of all printed publications has been stored in the appropriate place and its location noted in your Project Management Notebook.
5. All original artwork has been stored and its location noted in your Project Management Notebook.
6. All materials have been returned from the printers and other outside vendors, properly stored, and their locations noted in your Project Management Notebook.
7. Printing plates and other master copying devices (such as CD-ROM, video masters) have been returned to you or their locations noted in your Project Management Notebook.
8. All vendor job correspondence has been placed in the Project Management Notebook.
9. All review comments on drafts of the publications have been organized and stored and their locations noted.

Figure 29.1   End-of-project checklist

recreated. Frequently, organizations have lost all the original illustrations on a project. The cost of recreating hundreds of technical illustrations is high.

Figure 29.1 provides a guideline for an end-of-project checklist.

Guideline: Establish a policy for archiving your projects, taking into account as many future needs as you can anticipate. Assume that you will not be there to remember what was done.

Completing the Project Management Notebook

If you have faithfully been keeping your Project Management Notebook up to date throughout the project, you will have little to do at the end of the project to pull together all the details. The last items to go into your Project Management Notebook are

- The project wrap-up report
- A report of the project wrap-up meeting
- The archive file for the project
- A complete history of the project, including a calendar of events

A brief history of the project should include a calendar of major project events with brief annotations for each event. The calendar will provide a good summary record of what occurred on the project and when it happened. A new manager taking over the project can use the summary to become acquainted with the project history quickly.

Once the Project Management Notebook is complete, either include it in the paper archives, or file it in a safe place that others will be able to access. I recommend that you keep either the originals or copies of the notebooks in your departmental library. They can be a useful tool for new project managers and for anyone who wants to review exactly what happened on a particular project.

 Guideline: Complete your Project Management Notebook, and file it for safekeeping.

Composing the project description

In addition to the Project Management Notebook, a brief description of each project, the project manager, a list of the team members, and a list of the books and other media produced may be added to a file of project descriptions. A project-description file is an easy way of keeping track of what you and others in your organization have produced each year and over several years. An assembled file of project descriptions for several years can represent an impressive array of work done by your publications organization.

 Guideline: Keep a file of project descriptions to remind everyone of the variety of work produced by your technical communicators.

Preparing for the project end-of-life

At some point, a library of publications, along with the product they support, may be slated for a project end-of-life. The end-of-life marks the point when your organization decides to stop selling a product and begins to phase out support for it. Usually, a phaseout schedule is planned that provides some support for the remaining owners of a product for a defined period of time. During this phaseout time, you may decide that technical manuals may still be purchased but that no further updates will be produced.

Once a publications product reaches the end of its life, you need to decide how to handle the archives. After a number of years of maintaining records of each revision cycle, your project archives will be extensive. You may decide to discard all the archives after support has been ended, or you may decide to keep representative copies of each revision of the publications. That way, they will still be available for someone who is interested in the history of the project and wants to know what was published. You may also choose to keep your Project Management Notebooks, although it may be simpler to keep the computer files rather than the hardcopy.

There is always a chance that someone will ask for copies of early manuals for a product and request records. Use your industry's practice as a guideline. In some industries, the technical publications last far longer than the products they once supported. For example, one can still find copies of the original operation and maintenance manuals for most of the automobiles manufactured in the United States, although perhaps not from the original manufacturers. In the software industry, where the half-life of application software is usually less than 10 years, products are phased out more quickly, and manuals become obsolete.

In deciding how to handle the end-of-life for your publications, consider the tradeoff between the cost of storage and the cost of having a problem that will require a history of the publications life cycle. The long-term tradeoff may favor discarding publications that are no longer being used.

Remember that the end of one project usually marks the beginning of another. At this final juncture, you have a wonderful opportunity to involve your team at the earlier stages of product development in the new project that begins tomorrow.

APPENDIX

A

Information-
Plan Template

This template provides you with the information you need to produce a complete Information Plan for a writing project. All the headings here are actual headings you will use to compose your own report.

Begin your Information Plan by providing the following information:

Client company/project:

Project manager:

Tentative start date:

Include review notes in your introduction to the Information Plan. Information Plans, like other deliverables, are usually delivered in first-draft form, reviewed by the involved parties, and submitted for second-draft review and sign-off. Refer to the following guidelines to include appropriate notes and other information at both draft stages.

First Draft—Your first draft of the project Information Plan explains the documentation strategy the project team plans to support.

Include a note with the first draft indicating a date and time when comments must be returned to the project manager.

Final Draft—Once all the client reviewers agree on the strategies outlined in the Information Plan, incorporate any remaining changes, and remove the date and time note included on the first draft. In its place, include a sign-off approval for the plan, which should be signed by the project manager and the client representative, as follows:

Please sign below to indicate approval of the Information Plan.

_____   _____
Approver's Signature (Client)   Date

_____   _____
Title of Approver (Client)

_____   _____
Approver's Signature (Project Team) Date

_____   _____
Title of Approver (Project Team)

572 · Appendix A

Also add a note indicating that readers should contact the project manager if they have any questions about the plan.

Purpose of the project

In this section, explain the purpose of the technical project. Provide some background explaining the client's motivation for producing the product and its documentation. For example, is it because they've introduced a new product that requires a new documentation approach? In this section, it's appropriate to include information about the client's marketing strategies for the product. What is this product's niche? What's special about it that the documentation should highlight from a sales angle?

Purpose of the documentation

In this section, include information about the needs that the documentation addresses. For example, is it supposed to supplement a training effort, or is it a stand-alone document set meant to be a user's sole information resource?

Usability goals for the documentation

In this section, describe the usability goals you have established for the documentation. How will you ensure that users will be successful in using the documentation to learn and use the product? For example, have you established the amount of time users should allow for performing particular tasks? Can you ensure that users are able to perform the tasks within the allotted time with as few errors or calls for help as possible?

Product description

In this section, include a brief description of the product and its basic functions. This information should be kept brief, since more detailed information about product functionality is included in the Content Specification for the individual deliverables.

Audience profile

Describe the background and experience of the audience(s) for the documentation. What are their expectations about the product? In what kind of environment do they work? Are there any special circumstances surrounding their use of the product?

Include a brief description of the individual audiences. In this description, include only information that will have an impact on the final design and organization of the documentation for these users. For example, if one audience contains people with very similar educational backgrounds, this fact may be less important to the documentation project than the fact that some have no typing experience and will be expected to use a keyboard.

Indicate how you gathered the audience information. For example, if you interviewed actual users, indicate as much. If there are no actual users and you must rely on marketing's perceptions about the audience, indicate this as well.

Task description

Identify all the essential tasks required to accomplish a meaningful outcome using this product. Correlate this list according to the audiences identified in the previous section. For example, you might indicate that an audience of pole installers will use the documentation to find information about selecting the proper poles, digging holes, and installing poles. Provide only basic task information at this point, since detailed information about tasks is included in the Content Specifications for the individual deliverable.

User/task matrix

Draw a user / task matrix to illustrate the information you have gathered about audience and tasks. In each box, indicate how likely it is that the audience subgroup will perform the high-level task. Use a scale of 1 to 10, with 1 least likely and 10 most likely.

	Users			
Tasks	*Customer Engineers*	*Experienced Technicians*	*Novice Technicians*	*Assembly Line Workers*
Installation	10	8	2	1
Operations	2	4	4	10
Diagnostics	10	9	5	0
Maintenance	8	10	10	0

Design implications

Discuss the ways in which the audience and task analyses influence the design of the documents.

For example, if you're designing one book for an audience of programmers, you may decide that flowcharts would be useful graphics to include. However, you might want to avoid flowcharts in another book designed for end users who may be put off by the highly technical look of a flowchart. Your task analysis also comes into play as you compose this section. For example, pole installers will probably not want to haul around a heavy 3-inch ring binder; for these users, you'd probably want to plan on a small-format book that perhaps contains only quick-reference information to use during an installation, with complete documentation kept back at the home site for detailed reference.

The detailed design implications address concerns at two levels: What's the proper information to include in individual volumes, and how should that information be presented within those volumes? Is there a need for reference manuals? Task-oriented user's guides? Quick-reference cards? Are some of the concepts so esoteric that some users will need a purely conceptual piece? Should one manual contain a combination of one or more of the aforementioned types?

At this point, it is important to identify how the documents in the set will work together. Does the library address all the audience and task needs identified in your analyses?

How will the information be provided: Hardcopy? Online? Your design implications help you select the right media for your deliverables, as discussed in "Media selection."

Documentation strategies and concerns

In this section, explain your usability research and testing strategy. Do you intend to test the product to assess its usability? Will this be a formal process? Will you use reader-comment forms to solicit responses after the book is in the field? Do you intend to question beta users about the documentation's usability, so that you can implement changes before the documentation is distributed to a larger audience?

Explain how the revision process, if any, affects the project. Will the documents need revision? How frequently? How do the information-design strategies outlined in the Information Plan accommodate the revision schedule and make the set easy to maintain?

Describe any production concerns that could potentially have an impact on the project, for example, lengthy lead times to accommodate a Government Printing Office printing schedule, typesetting, and so on.

Indicate how the Information Plan complements any training development taking place. You should include information about how the documentation will be used to support a training effort, or vice versa, since together training and documentation form a complete learning product.

Indicate whether the documentation is to be translated and localized. If so, what are the plans for translating screens, converting from English to metric units, and modifying the product and documentation in any other way to accommodate a foreign audience?

Describe the document-distribution plans. Indicate what package, if any, the various manuals ship with. Indicate whether any manuals make an existing manual obsolete, so that this information can be communicated to the proper distribution centers.

Media selection

Describe what media will be used to deliver the documentation. The design implications point to a delivery strategy for the documentation you produce. Keep in mind that some of your documentation may be delivered online. Indicate what information is to be moved online and its general format. Will some of the online material consist of help text? Or complete reference material? You might want to indicate whether demo disks will be part of the package, so that you can plan for getting the support needed to produce these. Indicate in your Information Plan what is most appropriate to your project, and provide production details for the products, including information about the page sizes and binding for the documents. Typical learning products include the following:

- Quick-start guide
- Task reference
- Dictionary reference
- Concept guide
- Installation guide
- Quick reference

Along with each of the learning products included in the plan, address any production issues affecting the documentation. Will any manuals be in color? Will they be typeset? Will they be offset printed or photocopied? You may want to include even more detailed information about the printing if it affects your plans for the project.

Indicate what format and tools will be used to implement the design. In addition to the text-processing tools used, what other graphics packages, editors, or other software will be used to complete the project?

Indicate how the manuals will be packaged. For paper documentation, describe the binding method. Include specifications for tabs and other special features that must be ordered in advance. For nonpaper documentation, describe the appropriate packaging methods.

Constraints

Describe some of the anticipated problems or limiting factors on the project. If you work on several projects, you might want to supply ratings for a number of the dependencies that typically affect progress on your projects.

Client project team

List the pivotal contributors on the client's team by title and name to record formally who has been pledged to support the project on the client's end. Here are some possible titles:

- R & D project engineer
- Product marketing
- Technical marketing
- Manufacturing representative

Client review team

List the principal reviewers on the project. This information is important because it ensures that reviewers have been assigned and that they have been limited to a manageable number.

Writing project team

List the project team members assigned to the project:

- Project manager
- Writers
- Editors
- Artists
- Production assistants

Roles and responsibilities

Include here a statement about the kind of information and support all the responsible parties have promised to give to the project. This may include information about the kind of source material to be provided, who is responsible for coordinating reviews and consolidating comments, who must write progress reports, who is responsible for ensuring that a prototype of the product is made available to the writing staff, and so on.

Client's schedule

Attach a copy of the milestone chart developed for your project, along with any spreadsheet information that addresses hours and costs associated with the project.

APPENDIX

B

Audience-Analysis Checklist

The questions listed here provide guidelines for conducting a user analysis. Some of the questions may not be relevant to your particular user groups.

Personal characteristics

- What is the user's gender?
- What is the user's age?
- What is the user's height and weight?
- Is the user handicapped in any way?
- Is the user color-blind?
- What is the user's preferred hand for the task?
- Is the user sufficiently dexterous to perform the task?

Subject-matter questions

- What is the user's level of schooling?
- What degrees, if any, has the user obtained, and in what fields?
- What is the user's experience in performing this or similar tasks?
- What is the user's prior knowledge of the product or system?
- How did the user learn about this product or similar products? On-the-job training? Formal education? Training programs?
- Has the user been trained in the use of this or similar products?
- How current is the schooling or training that the user has in this or similar products?
- Does the user have personal interests outside of the work environment that might support learning how to use this or similar products?
- If the user has prior experience using this product, what are the depth and frequency of that experience?

Attitude questions

- What is the user's attitude toward learning the new product or process? Enthusiastic? Curious? Worried? Hostile? Afraid?
- Is the user motivated to learn the new product or system?
- In general, is the user open to learning new behaviors and ideas?
- Does the user work alone on this product? Are there others in the user's environment using the same product?
- Is there much turnover in the user's job?
- What is the impact of the new product or system on the user's job?
- What are the consequences if the user makes a mistake or performs poorly with the new product?
- Is the user under pressure to perform quickly or especially accurately with the product?
- How much has the user been involved in the decision to purchase or develop the new product?

Language questions

- Does the user know the specialized terminology in the field associated with the product? To what extent?
- What is the user's general skill with language? A fluent speaker? A hesitant speaker?
- Is the user a native speaker of the language used in the documentation and product? If not, what degree of difficulty does the user have with the language?
- Does the user speak the language of the documentation and product in the work environment?

Tool-use questions

- What is the user's reading level?
- Does the user express a preference for text or graphics as a primary learning mode?
- What is the user's familiarity with using reference tools such as indexes, headers and footers, tables of contents, online-search systems?
- What is the user's keyboard experience and ability? Mouse and cursor experience? Experience with graphic-user interfaces?

Cultural and behavioral questions

- Are there differences in some users' workplace behaviors that will affect their use of the product or process?

- How have national and cultural differences among users affected their prior knowledge and prior experience?
- How do national and cultural differences affect the users' environment?
- Do the users fall into a particular socioeconomic class in the culture that may affect performance with the product?
- Is the users' workplace behavior prescribed by a trade union or professional association?

Environment-Analysis Checklist

The questions listed here provide guidelines for conducting an environment analysis. Some of the questions may not be relevant to your particular user situation.

- Where will the user perform the tasks with the product?
- Where will the documentation be used?
- For each possible environment, what is the light level? Heating? Noise? Altitude? Humidity? Available space?
- What is the user's physical workspace like?
- What time of day will users perform tasks? Which days of the week?
- What support will be available to the user when and where the tasks are being performed?
- Are the tasks performed regularly? Intermittently? Only as needed?
- Is the performance of tasks associated with other events? Times of year? Times of day? Product cycle?
- Will anyone oversee the use of the products or the documentation? If so, who and under what circumstances?
- Will the documentation be modified by the customer or user?
- Will the documentation be used for training?
- How much room is available for learning products in the area where the user will most likely perform the tasks?
- Where will the user keep the documentation in relation to the area where the user will perform the tasks with the product?
- Will the users have any difficulty obtaining sufficient copies of the documentation?

Content-Specifications Template

This template provides you with the information you need to produce the Content Specifications for one of the deliverables on a publications project. The Content Specifications ask for more detailed information about audience, product definition, and marketing strategy as a basis for identifying users and their tasks in using a product. While the Information Plan addresses strategies for compiling a complete library of publications, the Content Specifications present a plan for completing a single element of the library.

The Content Specifications template is very complete. You may not be able to fill in all the information asked for when you first begin the project; fill in information later as you learn more about it.

Begin your Content Specifications by providing the following information:

Date:
Client company/project:
Working title:
Project manager:

Include review notes in your introduction to the Content Specifications. Content Specifications are usually delivered in first-draft form, reviewed by the involved parties, and submitted for second-draft review and sign-off. Refer to the following guidelines to include appropriate notes and other information at both draft stages.

First Draft—Your first draft of the Content Specifications explains the documentation strategy for a single manual (or other publication element) and outlines the objectives and content for that manual in some detail.

Include a note with the first draft indicating a date and time when comments must be returned to the project manager.

Final Draft—Once all the client reviewers agree on the strategies outlined in the Content Specifications, incorporate any remaining changes, and remove the date and time note included on the first draft. In its place, include a sign-off approval for the specification, which should be signed by the project manager and the client representative, as follows:

Please sign below to indicate approval of the Content Specifications.

Approver's Signature (Client)	Date
Title of Approver (Client)	
Approver's Signature (Project Team)	Date
Title of Approver (Project Team)	

Also add a note indicating that reviewers should contact the writing project manager if they have any questions about the specifications.

Goals and objectives of the publication

In this section, explain the goals and objectives you plan to meet with your design of this publication. First, describe how your publication fits into the entire library of documents being prepared for the product. Then, concentrate on your goals. What unique needs does this publication meet? Stating this information explicitly makes the purpose of the publication clear to the reviewers.

State your usability objective for the publication. What usability criteria might be used to measure the success of your design.

Product/process description

In this section, include a brief description of the product or process and its basic functions. This information should provide more detail then the product or process description included in the Information Plan for the project. At the Content Specification stage, you probably know more about the product or process functionality than was known while the Information Plan was being developed, so this should be fairly easy to do. However, don't include *everything* you know about the product or process in the description. Include only enough information to communicate the product's basic purpose and applications to the reviewers.

Audience profile

Describe the background and experience of the audience(s) for the publication. What are their expectations about the product? In what kind of environment do they work? Are there any special circumstances surrounding their use of the product?

In this description, include only information that will have an impact on the final design and organization of the publication. For example, if one audience contains people with very similar educational backgrounds, this fact may be less important to the publications project than the fact that some have no typing experience and will be expected to use a keyboard.

Indicate how you gathered the audience information. For example, if you interviewed actual users, indicate as much. If there are no actual users and you must rely on marketing's perceptions about the audience, indicate that as well.

The audience profile for the Content Specifications differs from the one included in the Information Plan in two ways. Because the Content Specifications describe the audience for an individual library publication, it may describe only a subset of the audiences addressed in the Information Plan. Also, at this point in the project, you know more about the audience than was known at the Information Plan stage, so your description of the Content Specifications audience is likely to be more detailed and accurate.

Usability goal and testing

Describe your usability goal for the publication, and explain how you plan to test the usability. Describe the characteristics that your library publication will need if it is to meet the usability requirements of the audience. Briefly describe the type of tests you plan to conduct, when you plan to conduct them (the stages of product or publication development), and what you plan to do with the results of the tests.

Publication objectives

Describe the overall objectives for the publication. Briefly describe what the user will understand and be able to do while using this publication. Explain how the publication will be designed to support these objectives.

Publication organization

Provide a brief overview of the structure of the various sections, explaining why they're sequenced as listed. For user's guides and other task-oriented material, identify all the essential tasks that will be described in the book. For reference or concept books, describe what the user will be able to do or understand after using each major section of the publication. This section defines the logic governing your proposed organization. Do not simply list the chapter titles and contents; you do that in other sections. Think of the content of this section as an introduction to the detailed task information provided later.

Publication content

Provide a list of the sections to be included in the publication. This provides reviewers with a way to check on the terminology proposed for section titles and provides them with an impression of the overall organization as it will be presented to the user.

Overview by section

Using the section titles listed in the "Publication content" section, compose an outline of each section's contents as far down in the heading hierarchy as you are able to go at this point in the project (at least to second-level heads).

Avoid the temptation to provide a simple, unannotated outline of the section's contents. To get yourself in the proper frame of mind to compose this information, keep in mind your audience for the Content Specifications. You are addressing the client reviewers and members of your own project team, *not* the end users for the product. Your aim is to explain the publication's content to the reviewers, making very clear to them how you are structuring the publication to meet its objectives. When you list a section heading (which normally corresponds to a task), describe the contents and then answer the questions, "Why include this information, and why here?" For example, you may decide to include an installation section as an appendix. To justify this choice, you might write, "Appendix A includes installation instructions. While installation is logically the first task the user performs, it is performed only once. For this reason, we've included installation as an appendix, so that the body of the manual focuses on the task information that the user will reference most frequently."

Begin your section description with an objectives statement. Explain how the user will be transformed after using the information in this section. Explicitly stating what the user should be able to do after using each section helps keep you user- and task-focused, so that you exclude extraneous information.

Include your working titles for the headings within the section. Then, briefly describe the contents of the section, including any applicable information about any unique approach you are taking.

With the general structure and objectives laid out, follow these writing guidelines to ensure that your section contents are presented in a task-oriented, easily assimilable way:

- Write the headings in the style you plan to use (such as infinitive, gerund, imperative).
- Organize the publication into appropriate sections, chapters, and parts, according to what you know about your audience and tasks:
  - Organize the sections into modules by logical groups (aim for seven or fewer modules per section).
  - If a section includes subheadings, make sure that there are at least two.
  - If you are writing a combination manual, such as a combined user's and reference guide, consider grouping chapters within major parts so that users can find information more easily.

Make sure that your outline for a book includes descriptions (or placeholders) for all the applicable parts in the list that follows. This will be useful for planning production at the end of the project, and all pages (even title pages and legal notices pages) must be listed to obtain an accurate page count for the manual. Use this list as a template so that you're reminded to include all the information needed to compose a complete publication:

- Front cover
- Inside front cover (This is where the legal notices, or disclaimers, go.)
- Title page
- Preface
- Table of contents
- Part introductions (if parts are appropriate)
- Chapters or sections
- Appendixes
- Glossary
- Index
- Reader-response form/mailer
- Back cover

For other types of publications, include the standard required sections as well.

Estimated page and graphics counts

Include information about the page counts (or other metrics) you are estimating for the individual sections. Use the following table as a template.

Make sure that you track your page counts carefully as you continue with the writing phase. An increase to the page counts typically means that more time will be needed to complete the writing.

Chapter	Number of Graphics	Total Number of Pages
Front matter		
Title page and copyright notice		
Table of contents		
Chapter 1: Name		
Section name		
Section name		
Section name		
Chapter 2: Name		
Section name		
Section name		
Section name		
Total		

Project Wrap-Up Report

This template provides you with the information you need to produce a project documentation wrap-up report. The template is most appropriate for book projects. If you are handling a usability, research consulting, online, or other type of project, some of the sections will differ. All the headings here are actual headings you will use to compose your own report.

The project wrap-up report is a significant part of the project history that you have been maintaining through the publication-development life cycle. The data that you collect and discuss here will be very important in helping you improve future estimates.

The project wrap-up report summarizes the time spent performing project activities. It describes the unique challenges of the project and reports on how we might improve performance on future projects.

In addition, the wrap-up report gives you a final opportunity to assess the project in light of the original dependencies identified in the Information Plan.

Begin your wrap-up report by providing the following information:

Project name:
Document name:
Project manager:
Report date:

Brief project description

In this section, briefly describe the project so that future project-managers will be able to understand the type of work being discussed. In the description, stress aspects of the project that were especially noteworthy.

Be certain to include information on the following:

- the original objectives and goals of the project and whether these objectives were met
- technology
- list of the information products products (i.e., each book by type, online help, CBT, and others)

586

- areas of the client/company that contributed to the project (i.e., marketing, engineering, field service, customer support)
- duration of the product with start and end dates
- size of the staff used to complete the project by title

Projected, actual, and billed totals

Use the following table to summarize the project statistics. Begin with the hours, dollars, page count, and hours per page originally estimated for the project. Then, add up your actual hours and dollars expended, along with the final page count and the final hours per page achieved. If there is a difference between the actual hours and cost and the amounts billed to the client, note those in the final column.

If you have any discrepancy between estimated and actual numbers (and billed numbers), you will need to explain the discrepancies in the rest of the report.

Item	Estimated	Actual	Billed
Total project hours Total project cost Number of pages Hours per page	$	$	$

Project time by task summary

Separate project task summaries are required for each information product delivered.

In the task-summary tables, estimate the amount of time spent on project phases and activities. Since we base scheduling and estimating on standard percentages, we would like to know how closely your project resembled the standards. Please note the estimated and actual hours expended to reach each of the major project milestones. Then, calculate the percent of the total hours estimated and actually expended. For example, we frequently estimate the first draft will take approximately 60 percent of total project hours. If your project differed significantly from this percentage, you should explain why in the following report.

In addition to milestones, we are also interested in the amount of time used in certain activities that are tracked. Record the hours you used in project management, writing, editing, graphics, and production, and calculate the percentage of total hours for each activity. For example, if you used 12 percent of your total time for project management but had only budgeted for 7 percent, you need to explain the difference in the report.

Item	Hours		Percent of total hours	
	Estimate	Actual	Estimate	Actual
Milestones				
Information Plan				
Content Spec				
First draft				
Second draft				
Final draft	.		.	
Writing				
Editing				
Graphics				
Production				
Project management		.		.
Total hours		.		100.00
Total hours / page				

Dependency rating summary

In the next section, record the relationship between the dependencies you thought you would encounter at the beginning of the project and the dependencies as they actually occurred. If your project hours per page increased substantially, you will have experienced a change in the dependencies. For example, hours per page increase when information is not readily available or the product was less stable than we were led to believe.

If the final ratings differ substantially from the initial ratings, you will need to explain the differences in the report.

Dependency	Initial Rating	Final Rating
Stability of product		
Information availability		
Prototype availability		
Subject-matter experts		
Review process		
Writing experience of staff		
Technical experience of staff		
Team experience of staff		
Audience understanding		

Project activities and related issues

In each of the sections below, briefly describe the activities that you include for that category. Please emphasize any activity that was particularly unusual. For example, if all the graphics were created originally by hand and then had to be transferred to electronic media, describe what happened in this section.

Sometimes, you will find it difficult to decide exactly what to include in a category. For example, your writers may have been responsible for many of the graphics in the text or worked with the graphic artists to plan the graphics. If you have included some time for graphics in the writing category, please explain.

The purpose of the activities description is to ensure that future project managers understand what was included in a category so that they are able to make useful comparisons with their own projects and estimate more effectively.

Be certain to explain any discrepancy between the total and percentage of time for each category and the original estimates.

Writing
Editing
Graphics
Production
Project management

Project milestones and related issues

In this section, explain how you divided activities among the milestones. Emphasize any extraordinary events that should be noted by future project managers. For example, if you had budgeted 30% of total project time for the Information Plan and Content Specifications, but actually used 45% of the time, explain what happened here.

Information Plan
Content Specifications
First draft
Second draft
Final draft

Evaluating the project dependencies

In this section, explain briefly what happened for each dependency. Place special emphasis on the difference between the original factor predicted and what actually happened on the project.

Stability of product
Information availability
Prototype availability
Subject-matter experts
Review process
Writing experience of staff
Technical experience of staff
Team experience of staff
Audience understanding

Problems encountered

This section is one of the most important sections of the wrap-up report and the center of the discussions in the project wrap-up report and the center of the discussions in the project wrap-up meeting. Discuss anything that slowed your progress or affected your team's productivity. For example, if reviewers were slow in returning review copies, resulting in delays in the schedule, note that problem here. Remember, however, that this document will be read by the entire product-development team. Be as fair in your assessment as possible, and be generous in your critique of yourself and others.

Recommendations for process improvements

In this section, discuss how you and others involved in the publications-development process should be able to improve in future projects. For example, you might note that your team would have met the schedule and stayed within the budget if you had spent more time in Phase 1: Information Planning. Find ways that you can improve first; then, discuss how others might be able to work more effectively with your team.

Bibliography

Abshire, Gary M., and Dan Culberson. "A Team Approach to Producing Good Documentation." *IEEE Transactions on Professional Communication*, PC28, 4 (December 1985): 38–41.

Allen, Lori, and Mary Bryant. "The Postmortem Process: Learning to Negotiate Change." In *Proceedings of the Florida Technical Writing* Conference. Orlando, FL, 1991: 55–57.

Andriole, Stephen J. *Rapid Application Prototyping: The Storyboard Approach to User Requirements Analysis*. 2d ed. Boston: QED Technical Publishing Group. 1992.

Atkinson, Jennifer M. "Quality in the Trenches." In *Proceedings of the 37th International Technical Communication Conference*. Washington, DC: Society for Technical Communication, 1990: MG-26–28.

Badiru, A. B. "Recovering from a Crisis at Tinker Air Force Base." *pm network: the Professional Magazine of the Project Management Institute*, 7, 2 (February 1993): 10–23.

Barker, Thomas T., ed. *Perspectives on Software Documentation: Inquiries and Innovations*. Baywood's Technical Communications Series. Amityville, NY: Baywood Publishing Company, Inc., 1991.

Barr, John P., and Stephanie Rosenbaum. "Documentation and Training Productivity Benchmarks." *Technical Communication*, 37, 4 (1990): 399–408.

Barrett, Edward. *Text, ConText, and HyperText: Writing With and For the Computer*. Cambridge, MA: MIT Press, 1989.

Barrier, Michael. "Small Firms Put Quality First." *Nation's Business*, May 1992, 22–32.

Bartolome, Fernando, and Andre Laurent. "The Manager: Master and Servant of Power." *Harvard Business Review*, November–December 1986, 77–81.

Baxley, Deborah, "Management—The Missing Link." In *Proceedings of the 38th International Technical Communication Conference*. Arlington, VA: Society for Technical Communication, 1991: MG-59.

Bell, Lydia V. "Documentation Quality Assurance." In *Proceedings of the 37th International Technical Communication Conference*. Washington, DC: Society for Technical Communication, 1990: WE-111-112.

Berkeley, Dina, Robert De Hoog, and Patrick Humphreys. *Software Development Project Management: Process and Support*. West Sussex, England: Ellis Horwood Limited, 1990.

Berliner, D. C., et al. "Behaviors, Measures, and Instruments for Performance Evaluation in Simulated Environments," Paper presented at the Workshop on the Quantification of Human Performance, Albuquerque, NM, 1965.

Blue, Lee. "Communicate!" In *Proceedings of the 38th International Technical Communication Conference*. Arlington, VA: Society for Technical Communication, 1991: MG-30–32.

Bosley, Deborah S. "Designing Effective Technical Communication Teams." *Technical Communication*, 38, 4 (1991): 504–512.

Bresko, Laura L. "Software Development and the Technical Communicator." In *Proceedings of the 38th International Technical Communication Conference*. Arlington, VA: Society for Technical Communication, 1991: MG-61–63.

Brockmann, R. John. *Writing Better Computer User Documentation: From Paper to Hypertext: Version 2.0*. New York: John Wiley & Sons, Inc. 1990.

Brooks, Frederick P., Jr. *The Mythical Man-Month: Essays on Software Engineering*. Reading, MA: Addison-Wesley Publishing Company, 1975.

Brown, William N. "Harley Davidsons or BMWs? Managing Quality in Technical Documents and Presentations." In *Proceedings of the 37th International Technical Communication Conference*. Washington, DC: Society for Technical Communication, 1990: MG-29–32.

Buchanan, Carol. "Quality in the Publishing Process." In *Proceedings of the 37th International Technical Communication Conference*. Washington, DC: Society for Technical Communication, 1990: MG-93–95.

Buehler, Mary Fran. "Defining Quality: It Is Not the Same as Goodness." In *Proceedings of the 34th International Technical Communication Conference*. Washington, DC: Society for Technical Communication, 1987: MPD-37-39.

_____. "How Managers (Try to) Solve People Problems: What If." *Technical Communication*, 37, 4 (1990): 386–391.

Burke, Alanna C. "Managing Ourselves Through Quality Teams." In *Proceedings of the 39th International Technical Communication Conference*. Arlington, VA: Society for Technical Communication, 1992: 714–715.

Burnett, Rebecca E. "Substantive Conflict in a Cooperative Context: A Way to Improve the Collaborative Planning of Workplace Documents." *Technical Communication*, 38, 4 (1991): 532–539.

Burnette, Monica. "Managing English-to-Japanese Translation Projects," *Technical Communication*, 39, 3 (1992): 438–443.

Burton, Sarah K. "The Real Crisis of Documentation: Managerial Monkey Wrenches." In *Proceedings of the 36th International Technical Communication Conference*. Washington, DC: Society for Technical Communication, 1989: MG-135–138.

Caernarven-Smith, Patricia. "Communication Management." *Technical Communication*, 37, 3 (1990): 310–311.

Caird, Helen G., ed. *Publications Cost Management*. Anthology Series No. 3. Washington, DC: Society for Technical Communication, May 1975.

Camp, Robert C. *Benchmarking: The Search for Industry Best Practices that Lead to Superior Performance*. Milwaukee, WI: Quality Press, 1989.

Cantando, Mary. "Using Positive Language to Motivate Others." In *Proceedings of the 38th International Technical Communication Conference*. Arlington, VA: Society for Technical Communication, 1991: MG-37.

Carroll, John M. *The Nurnberg Funnel: Designing Minimalist Instruction for Practical Computer Skill*. Cambridge, MA: The MIT Press, 1990.

Coe, Marlana A. "Customer Satisfaction: New Expectations of the Technical Communicator." In *Proceedings of the 38th International Technical Communication Conference*. Arlington, VA: Society for Technical Communication, 1991: MG-55–58.

Cooper, Kenneth G. "The Rework Cycle: How It Really Works ... And Reworks ..." *pm network: the Professional Magazine of the Project Management Institute*, 7, 2 (February 1993): 25–28.

———. "The Rework Cycle: Benchmarks for the Project Manager." *Project Management Journal*, 24, 1 (March 1993): 17–21.

Coppola, Carolyn M. "Owning Chunks of Information Rather than Books: A Team Writing Approach." In *Proceedings of the 37th International Technical Communication Conference*. Washington, DC: Society for Technical Communication, 1990: MG-2–4.

Crosby, Philip B. *Quality Is Free*. New York: McGraw-Hill Book Company, 1979.

———. *Quality without Tears*. New York: New American Library, 1984.

Dalla Santa, T. M. "The Whys and Hows of Effective Performance Appraisals." *Technical Communication*, 37, 4 (1990): 392–395.

Daniels, Peter B. "Information Transfer in the New Culture, Part 1." In *Proceedings of the 39th International Technical Communication Conference*. Arlington, VA: Society for Technical Communication, 1992: 797–799.

Debs, Mary Beth. "Recent Research on Collaborative Writing Industry." *Technical Communication* 38, 4 (1991): 476–484.

DeMarco, Tom. *Controlling Software Projects: Management, Measurement, & Estimation*. Englewood Cliffs, NJ: Yourdon Press, 1982.

Diehl, Van. "Designing for Usability—The Learning Products Contribution." Presented at the 39th STC Annual Conference, Atlanta, GA, 1992.

Dillard, James D. "Maximizing Documentation Usability and Product Quality Through Structure Rapid Prototyping." In *Proceedings of the 39th International Technical Communication Conference*. Arlington, VA: Society for Technical Communication, 1992: 119–122.

Dintruff, Diane L., Edith E. Lueke, Kathleen R. Milhaven, and Brenda Neff. "Gathering Advance Customer Information: Enhancing Customers' Partnerships." In *IPCC Conference Record* (1988): 237–239.

Doheny-Farina, Stephen, ed. *Effective Documentation: What We Have Learned from Research*. Cambridge, MA: MIT Press, 1988.

Dreger, J. Brian. *Project Management: Effective Scheduling*. New York: Van Nostrand Reinhold, 1992.

Dumas, Joseph S. and Janice C. Redish. *A Practical Guide to Usability Testing*. Norwood, NJ: Ablex Publishing Corporation, 1993.

Dunlap, Johnny. "Customer Satisfaction—The Documentation Challenge." In *Proceedings of the 39th International Technical Communication Conference*. Arlington, VA: Society for Technical Communication, 1992: 700–703.

Edwards, Arthur W. "A Quality System for Technical Documentation." In *Proceedings of the 36th International Technical Communication Conference*. Washington, DC: Society for Technical Communication, 1989: MG-43–46.

Ellingwood, Jane. "Information Vending: Planning a Project." In *Proceedings of the 36th International Technical Communication Conference*. Washington, DC: Society for Technical Communication, 1989: MG-98–100.

Etz, Donald V. "Confucius for the Technical Communicator: Selections from The Analects." *Technical Communication*, 39, 4 (1992): 641–644.

Flynn, Laurie. "What If Software Worked the Way that People Do?" *San Jose Mercury News*, January 3, 1993.

_____. "In the Laboratory or Shopping Mall, Testers Are at Work," *San Jose Mercury News*, April 4, 1993.

Fredrickson, Lola. "Calculating an Estimate for a Technical Writing Project." In *Proceedings of the 35th International Technical Communication Conference*. Washington, DC: Society for Technical Communication, 1988: MPD-37–40.

_____. "Quality in Technical Communication: A Definition for the 1990s." *Technical Communication*, 39, 3 (1992): 394–398.

Frost, Toby. "Open Systems: The Next Step." In *Proceedings of the 39th International Technical Communication Conference*. Arlington, VA: Society for Technical Communication, 1992: 803–806.

_____. "Quality: Is Our Documentation World-Class?" In *Proceedings of the 39th International Technical Communication Conference*. Arlington, VA: Society for Technical Communication, 1992: 693–696.

Gagne, Robert M. "Task Analysis—Its Relation to Content Analysis." *Educational Psychologist*, 11 (1974): 11–18.

Galitz, W. O. *Humanizing Office Automation*. Wellesley, MA: QED Information Sciences, 1984.

Gambaro, Sharon A. "Technical Writers as Communicators, Collaborators, Catalysts." In *Proceedings of the 36th International Technical Communication Conference*. Washington, DC: Society for Technical Communication, 1989: MG-82–83.

Garvin, David A. "Competing on the Eight Dimensions of Quality." *Harvard Business Review*, (November–December 1987): 101–109.

Gatien, Gary. "Managing in the New Corporate Environment." *Technical Communication*, 37, 4 (1990): 415–419.

Gervickas, Vicki. "Prototyping: A Model Approach to Development." In *Proceedings of the 34th International Technical Communication Conference*. Washington, DC: Society for Technical Communication, 1987: WE-161–162.

Gilbert, Catherine, E. "Managing in the '90s: Vision for the Future." In *Proceedings of the 39th International Technical Communication Conference*. Arlington, VA: Society for Technical Communication, 1992: 730–732.

Grech, Christine. "Computer Documentation Doesn't Pass Muster." *PC Computing Magazine*, (April 1992): 212–214.

Greenleaf, Jenny. "Out of the Ivory Town and Into the Trenches: The Writer Joins the Development Team." In *IPCC Conference Record* (1988): 384–393.

Grove, Laurel K., Regina E. Lundgren, and Patricia C. Hays. "Winning Respect Throughout the Organization." *Technical Communication*, 39 (3), 1992: 384–393.

Guillemette, Ronald A. "Prototyping: An Alternate Method for Developing Documentation." *Technical Communication*, 34, 3 (1987): 35–141.

Gurak, Laura J. "Technical Communicators as Product Developers: Examining Our Values About Technology." In *Proceedings of the 39th International Technical Communication Conference*. Arlington, VA: Society for Technical Communication, 1992: 405–406.

Hacker, Julian F. "Rapid Prototyping: A Development Model for Technical Manuals." In *Proceedings of the 39th International Technical Communication Conference*. Arlington, VA: Society for Technical Communication, 1992: 123–126.

Hackos, JoAnn. T. "Documentation Management: Why Should We Manage?" In *Proceedings of the 36th International Technical Communication Conference*. Washington, DC: Society for Technical Communication, 1989: MG-12–14.

_____. "Establishing Quality Benchmarks for Technical Publications." In *Proceedings of the 39th International Technical Communication Conference*. Arlington, VA: Society for Technical Communication, 1992: 684–685.

_____. "Managing Creative People." *Technical Communication*, 37, 4 (1990): 375–380.

_____. "Managing the Document Review Process." In *Proceedings of the 32nd International Technical Communication Conference*. Washington, DC: Society for Technical Communication, 1985: 171–173.

_____. "Writers in a New Technical Environment: A Problem for Writing Managers." In *Proceedings of the 33rd International Technical Communication Conference*. Washington, DC: Society for Technical Communication, 1986: MPD-85–87.

Hackos, JoAnn T. and Stephen Tilden. "Personality Type in Technical Communication." In *Proceedings of the 35th International Technical Communication Conference*. Washington, DC: Society for Technical Communication, 1988: RET-16–18.

Haramundanis, Katherine. *The Art of Technical Documentation*. Cambridge, Massachusetts: Digital Press, 1992.

Hardaker, Maurice, and Bryan K. Ward. "How to Make a Team Work." *Harvard Business Review* (November–December 1987): 112–119.

Harvey, Dorian Flood. "Managing Technical and Marketing Communication Departments." In *Proceedings of the 39th International Technical Communication Conference*. Arlington, VA: Society for Technical Communication, 1992: 755–758.

Henke, Kristine A. "Measuring Editing Quality Contributions." In *Proceedings of the 35th International Technical Communication Conference*. Washington, DC: Society for Technical Communication, 1988: WE-34–36.

Herrstrom, David S. "An Approach to Estimating the Cost of Product Documentation, with Some Hypotheses." In *Proceedings of the 34th International Technical Communication Conference*. Washington, DC: Society for Technical Communication, 1987: MPD-24–27.

Hewlett-Packard. *The HP Editorial Design System: An Introduction*. Hewlett-Packard Company, 1989.

Hosier, William J. "An Approach to Documentation Quality Through Controlled Process." In *Proceedings of the 37th International Technical Communication Conference*. Washington, DC: Society for Technical Communication, 1990: WE-52–54.

Hubbard, Scott E. *Validating Information Products: A Step-By-Step Approach*. Dayton, OH: NCR Corporation, 1989.

Humphrey, Watts S. *Managing the Software Process*. Reading, MA: Addison-Wesley Publishing Company, 1989.

Jereb, Barry. "Plain English on the Plant Floor." *Visual Communication*, 20, 2 (Spring 1986): 219–225.

Jonassen, David H., Wallace H. Hannum, and Martin Tessmer. *The Handbook of Task Analysis Procedures*. New York: Praeger, 1989.

Jones, Daniel R. "Exploring Quality: What Robert Pirsig's Zen and the Art of Motorcycle Maintenance Can Teach Us About Technical Communication." *IEEE Transactions on Professional Communication*, 32, 3 (September 1989): 154–158.

Jones, Ralph J. "Information Vending: Finding the Right Vendors." In *Proceedings of the 36th International Technical Communication Conference*. Washington, DC: Society for Technical Communication, 1989: MG-95–97.

———. "Managing By the Numbers." *Technical Communication*, 37, 4 (1990): 409–414.

Kerzner, Harold. *Project Management: A Systems Approach to Planning, Scheduling, and Controlling*. 2nd ed. New York: Van Nostrand Reinhold Company, 1984.

Klein, Janice A., and Pamela A. Posey. "Good Supervisors Are Good Supervisors—Anywhere." *Harvard Business Review* (November–December 1986): 125–128.

Kleinmann, Susan D. "The Complexity of Workplace Review." *Technical Communication*, 38, 4 (1991): 520–526.

Knapp, Joan. "A New Role for the Technical Communicator: Member of a Design Team." In *Proceedings of the 31st International Technical Communication Conference*. Washington, DC: Society for Technical Communication, 1984: WE-30–33.

Kuntz, Richard W. "Taking the Mystery Out of Planning." In *Proceedings of the 33rd International Technical Communication Conference*. Washington, DC: Society for Technical Communication, 1986: 111–113.

Lamons, Bob. "Pacesetter or Passenger? Your Choice." *Marketing News*, 27, 7 (March 29 1993).

Lasecke, Joyce, and Lola Frederickson. "Needs Assessment: A First Step Toward Meeting Customer Expectations." In *Proceedings of the 38th International Technical Communication Conference*. Arlington, VA: Society for Technical Communication, 1991: MG-102–105.

Lenk, Donald S. "Managing Subcontracted Documentation Development." In *Proceedings of the 36th International Technical Communication Conference*. Washington, DC: Society for Technical Communication, 1989: MG-101–103.

———. "Quality Information: Measuring Your Product and Your Process." In *Proceedings of the 39th International Technical Communication Conference*. Arlington, VA: Society for Technical Communication, 1992: 356–359.

Leonard, David C. "For the Technical Communication Manager: Understanding and Managing Conflict." In *Proceedings of the 39th International Technical Communication Conference*. Arlington, VA: Society for Technical Communication, 1992: 780–783.

Lillies, Philip. "Formulas for Estimating Printing Costs." In *Proceedings of the 36th International Technical Communication Conference*. Washington, DC: Society for Technical Communication, 1989: MG-107–108.

Livingstone, Dick. "Living Happily with Publication Clients." In *Proceedings of the 36th International Technical Communication Conference*. Washington, DC: Society for Technical Communication, 1989: WE-46–48.

Los Alamos National Laboratories. *Levels of Edit*. Personal communication from Helen Sinoradzki, July 1990.

Maggiore, James G. "In Pursuit of THE Electronic Office." In *Proceedings of the 39th International Technical Communication Conference*. Arlington, VA: Society for Technical Communication, 1992: 776–779.

Magyar, Miki. "Communication Management." In *Proceedings of the 36th International Technical Communication Conference*. Washington, DC: Society for Technical Communication, 1989: MG-53–55.

Mahan, Virginia. "The Team Relationship: Give and Take." In *Proceedings of the 39th International Technical Communication Conference*. Arlington, VA: Society for Technical Communication, 1992: 711–713.

Manes, Robert A. "Assessing Relative Productivity Factors in Documentation Project Estimates." In *Proceedings of the 39th International Technical Communication Conference*. Arlington, VA: Society for Technical Communication, 1992: 719–725.

Mattingly, William A. "Documentation Management: Why Do We Need it? An Introduction to the Panel." In *Proceedings of the 36th International Technical Communication Conference*. Washington, DC: Society for Technical Communication, 1989, page MG-11.

McGeary, Patrick. "Documentation Management Techniques." In *Proceedings of the 38th International Technical Communication Conference*. Arlington, VA: Society for Technical Communication, 1991: MG-22–25.

McNally, Susan A., and Mary Jane F. Mueller. "Wake Me When It's Over." In *Proceedings of the 37th International Technical Communication Conference*. Washington, DC: Society for Technical Communication, 1990: MG-53–54.

Morison, Susan B. "Estimating Resources." In *Proceedings of the 34th International Technical Communication Conference*. Washington, DC: Society for Technical Communication, 1987: MPD-100–102.

Murphy, Stephen. "Researching Benchmarks for a Corporate Documentation Group." In *Proceedings of the 39th International Technical Communication Conference*. Arlington, VA: Society for Technical Communication, 1992: 723–725.

Nereson, Sally. "Learning and Working with the Client's Political Structure." In *Proceedings of the 37th International Technical Communication Conference*. Washington, DC: Society for Technical Communication, 1990: MG-46–48.

Nicholas, John M. *Managing Business and Engineering Projects: Concepts and Implementation*. Englewood Cliffs, NJ: Prentice-Hall, 1990.

Peters, Tom. *Liberation Management: Necessary Disorganization for the Nanosecond Nineties*. New York: Alfred A. Knopf, 1992.

Philpott, Dorothy, and Gail Atkins. "Standards & Guidelines—the 3Cs." In *Proceedings of the 37th International Technical Communication Conference*. Washington, DC: Society for Technical Communication, 1990: MG-82–84.

Prekeges, James G. "Accurate Estimating and Scheduling." In *Proceedings of the 35th International Technical Communication Conference*. Washington, DC: Society for Technical Communication, 1988: MPD-47–49.

Price, Jonathan and Henry Korman. *How to Communicate Technical Information*. Redwood City, CA: The Benjamin/Cummings Publishing Company, Inc., 1993.

Raymond, Judith, and Carole Yee. "The Collaborative Process and Professional Ethics." *IEEE Transactions on Professional Communication*, 33, 2 (June 1990): 77–81.

Redish, Janice C., Joseph S. Dumas, and JoAnn T. Hackos. "Finding the Real Problems: Making Sense of What You See and Hear in a Usability Test." In *Proceedings: Usability Concepts and Procedures, Third Conference on Quality in Documentation*. Waterloo, Ontario: The Centre for Professional Writing, 1992: 139–160.

Roberts, Beverly A. "Information Vending: Ensuring Quality." In *Proceedings of the 36th International Technical Communication Conference*. Washington, DC: Society for Technical Communication, 1989: MG-93–94.

Roman, Daniel D. *Managing Projects: A Systems Approach*. New York: Elsevier Science Publishing Co., Inc., 1986.

Sachs, Irwin M. "Estimating Publication Costs." In *Proceedings of the 34th International Technical Communication Conference*. Washington, DC: Society for Technical Communication, 1987: MPD-20–23.

Schultz, Susan I., Jennifer J. Darrow, Frank X. Kavanagh, and Marjorie J. Morse. *The Digital Technical Documentation Handbook*. Burlington, MA: Digital Press, 1993.

Schwartz, David M. "Developing and Managing Style Sheets for a Publication Department." In *Proceedings of the 38th International Technical Communication Conference*. Arlington, VA: Society for Technical Communication, 1991: MG-94–96.

Shirk, Henrietta Nickels. "Humanists Versus Technologists: New Challenges For Publications Managers." In *Proceedings of the 36th International Technical Communication Conference*. Washington, DC: Society for Technical Communication, 1989: MG-4–5.

Simpson, Henry, and Steven M. Casey. *Developing Effective User Documentation: A Human Factors Approach*. New York: McGraw-Hill Book Company, 1988.

Simpson, Mark. "The Practice of Collaboration in Usability Test Design." *Technical Communication*, 38, 4 (1991): 527–531.

Sloane, Bruce C. "Training Documentation Reviewers: How to Get Meaningful Reviews of Your Documentation." In *Proceedings of the 36th International Technical Communication Conference*. Washington, DC: Society for Technical Communication, 1989: MG-58–59.

Smith, Preston G., and Donald G. Reinertsen. *Developing Products in Half the Time*. New York: Van Nostrand Reinhold, 1991.

Smudde, Peter, "A Practical Model of the Document-Development Process." *Technical Communication*, 38, 3 (1991): 316–323.

Sole, Terrence D., and Gary Bist. "The Design Document: Key to Managing Documentation Development." *IEEE Transactions on Professional Communication*, PC28, 3 (September 1985): 70–74.

Souther, James W. "Identifying the Informational Needs of Readers; A Management Responsibility." *IEEE Transactions on Professional Communication*, 24, 2 (June 1991): 9–12.

Stalk, George, Jr., and Thomas M. Hout. *Competing Against Time: How Time-Based Competition Is Reshaping Global Markets*. New York: The Free Press, 1990.

Stevens, Dawn, M., and Tiffany Corgan. "Integrated Development Teams: Breaking Down the Barriers." In *Proceedings of the 39th International Technical Communication Conference*. Arlington, VA: Society for Technical Communication, 1992: 17–19.

Stratton, Charles R. "Collaborative Writing in the Workplace." *IEEE Transactions on Professional Communication*, 32, 3 (September 1989): 178–182.

Sullivan, Patricia. "Beyond a Narrow Conception of Usability Testing." *IEEE Transactions on Professional Communication*, 32, 4 (December 1989): 256–264.

_____. "Collaboration Between Organizations: Contributions Outsiders Can Make to Negotiation and Cooperation During Composition." *Technical Communication*, 38, 4 (1991): 485–492.

Tao, Cynthia M. "Information Vending: Coordinating a Project." In *Proceedings of the 36th International Technical Communication Conference*. Washington, DC: Society for Technical Communication, 1989: MG-90–92.

Tarutz, Judith A. *Technical Editing: The Practical Guide for Editors and Writers*, Reading, MA: Addison-Wesley Publishing Company, 1992.

Tillman, Jean. "Documentating a Prolific Product: A Unique Approach." In *Technical Communication*, 38, 4 (1991): 546–548.

Topf, Mel A. "A Course in Document Management." *IEEE Transactions on Professional Communication*, PC30, 4 (December 1987): 254–257.

Trivadi, Kalpana. "The Team Approach for Quality Documentation." In *Proceedings of the 39th International Technical Communication Conference*. Arlington, VA: Society for Technical Communication, 1992: 716–717.

Van Buren, Robert, and Mary Fran Buehler. *The Levels of Edit*. 2d ed. Arlington, Virginia: Society for Technical Communication, 1991.

Vanderlinden, Gay, Thomas G. Cocklin, and Martha McKita. "Testing and Developing Minimalist Tutorials: A Case History." In *Proceedings of the 35th International Technical Communication Conference*. Washington, DC: Society for Technical Communication, 1988: RET-196–199.

Washington, Durthy A. "Developing a Corporate Style Guide: Pitfalls and Panaceas." *Technical Communication*, 38, 4 (1991): 553–555.

Watson, Nancy E., and Michael Barnes. "Archiving: A Bedtime Story." In *Proceedings of the 39th International Technical Communication Conference*. Arlington, VA: Society for Technical Communication, 1992: 348–350.

Weinberg, Gerald M. *Quality Software Management: Vol. 1 Systems Thinking*. New York: Dorset House Publishing, 1992.

Wurman, Richard Saul. *Follow the Yellow Brick Road*. New York: Bantam Books, 1992.

Xerox Publishing Standards: A Manual of Style and Design. New York: Watson-Guptill Publications, 1988.

Yeo, Sarah C. "Project Management Skills for Team Members." In *Proceedings of the 39th International Technical Communication Conference*. Arlington, VA: Society for Technical Communication, 1992: 796.

Zeidenstein, Kathryn. "Collaboration as Innovation: Why Technical Communicators Should Be Members of the Software Development Team." In *IPCC Conference Record* (1988): 79–82.

Zells, Lois. *Managing Software Projects: Selecting and Using PC-Based Project Management Systems*. Wellesley, MA: QED Information Sciences, Inc., 1990.

Index